C000262342

CORE STATUTES ON COMMERCIAL & CONSUMER LAW 2021–22

Graham Stephenson

The *Macmillan Core Statutes* series

Macmillan Core Statutes

CORE STATUTES ON
Contract, Tort & Restitution
Graham Stephenson

CORE STATUTES ON
Criminal Law
Mark James

CORE STATUTES ON
Family Law
Frances Burton

CORE STATUTES ON
Property Law
Peter Luther & Alan Moran

CORE STATUTES ON
Company Law
Cowan Ervine

CORE STATUTES ON
Employment Law
Rachel Horton

CORE STATUTES ON
Commercial & Consumer Law
Graham Stephenson

CORE
EU Legislation
Paul Drury

CORE STATUTES ON
Conflict of Laws
Emmanuel Maganaris

CORE STATUTES ON
Criminal Justice & Sentencing
Martin Wasik

CORE STATUTES ON
Evidence
Jonathan McGahan

CORE DOCUMENTS ON
International Law
Karen Hulme

CORE DOCUMENTS ON
European & International Human Rights
Rhona Smith

CORE STATUTES ON
Intellectual Property
Margaret Dowie-Whybrow

The Macmillan Core Statutes series has been developed to meet the needs of today's law students. Compiled by experienced lecturers, each title contains the essential materials needed at LLB level and, where applicable, on GDL/CPE courses. They are specifically designed to be easy to use under exam conditions and in the lecture hall.

www.macmillanihe.com/corestatutes

macmillan
international
HIGHER EDUCATION

RED GLOBE
PRESS

This edition published 2021 by
RED GLOBE PRESS

Previous editions published under the imprint PALGRAVE

Red Globe Press in the UK is an imprint of Macmillan Education Limited,
registered in England, company number 01755588, of 4 Crinan Street,
London, N1 9XW.

Red Globe Press® is a registered trademark in the United States,
the United Kingdom, Europe and other countries.

ISBN 978-1-352-01262-0 paperback

This book is printed on paper suitable for recycling and made from fully
managed and sustained forest sources. Logging, pulping and manufacturing
processes are expected to conform to the environmental regulations of
the country of origin.

A catalogue record for this book is available from the British Library.

A catalog record for this book is available from the Library of Congress.

CONTENTS

ALPHABETICAL LIST OF CONTENTS

PREFACE

Dear Reader,

Thank you for buying *Core Statutes on Commercial and Consumer Law*. As you have acquired this particular book it is likely you are pursuing an optional course in either commercial law or consumer law. The former is concerned primarily with business-to-business legal relationships. Consumer law on the other hand is specifically concerned with the legal obligations of businesses towards the ultimate consumer in relation to goods and services provided by the former, in other words consumer rights. Parliament has for a long time attempted to regulate relationships between businesses by means of legislation such as the Bills of Exchange Act 1882, the Factors Act 1889 and the old Sale of Goods Act of 1893. Consumer law is likewise largely enshrined in statutory form, but this is, in the main, a more recent development over the last 40 years or so. Hence, there is a clear rationale for a book of updated core statutes covering the relevant ground.

The book has four parts to it. The first part of the book consists of primary legislation starting with the 1882 Bills of Exchange Act, including on its way the monolith that is the ground-breaking Consumer Credit Act 1974, the much amended Sale of Goods Act 1979, and culminating in the Consumer Rights Act of 2015, the first real attempt to provide a codification of consumer rights.

Secondly, there is a selection of secondary legislation covering, for example, product safety, misleading marketing, unfair trading, consumer contracts made off business premises, online and so on, timeshares and package travel. Thirdly, it has been decided to retain, at least for the time being, a small number of EU directives that underpin some of the legislation which has come about as a consequence of our membership and which still might be useful as guides to interpretation. Finally, there are included some important documents on rules relating to documentary credits and international sales contracts.

The book is designed to cover the central statutory provisions of consumer and commercial law in one easily accessible and updated volume and should provide a useful source in the study of these areas.

Good luck with your studies.

Graham Stephenson
June 2021

STATUTES

BILLS OF EXCHANGE ACT 1882
(45 & 46 Vict., c. 61)

PART I

PRELIMINARY

1. **Short title**

This Act may be cited as the Bills of Exchange Act, 1882.

2. **Interpretation of terms**

In this Act, unless the context otherwise requires, —

'Acceptance' means an acceptance completed by delivery or notification.

'Action' includes counter claim and set off.

'Banker' includes a body of persons whether incorporated or not who carry on the business of banking.

'Bankrupt' includes any person whose estate is vested in a trustee or assignee under the law for the time being in force relating to bankruptcy.

'Bearer' means the person in possession of a bill or note which is payable to bearer.

'Bill' means bill of exchange, and 'note' means promissory note.

'Delivery' means transfer of possession, actual or constructive, from one person to another.

'Holder' means the payee or indorsee of a bill or note who is in possession of it, or the bearer thereof.

'Indorsement' means an indorsement completed by delivery.

'Issue' means the first delivery of a bill or note, complete in form to a person who takes it as a holder.

'Person' includes a body of persons whether incorporated or not.

'postal operator' has the meaning given by section 125(1) of the Postal Services Act 2011.

'Value' means valuable consideration.

'Written' includes printed, and 'writing' includes print.

PART II

BILLS OF EXCHANGE

Form and interpretation

3. **Bill of exchange defined**

(1) A bill of exchange is an unconditional order in writing, addressed by one person to another, signed by the person giving it, requiring the person to whom it is addressed to pay on demand or at a fixed or determinable future time a sum certain in money to or to the order of a specified person, or to bearer.

(2) An instrument which does not comply with these conditions, or which orders any act to be done in addition to the payment of money, is not a bill of exchange.

(3) An order to pay out of a particular fund is not unconditional within the meaning of this section; but an unqualified order to pay, coupled with (a) an indication of a particular fund out of which the drawee is to re-imburse himself or a particular account to be debited with the amount, or (b) a statement of the transaction which gives rise to the bill, is unconditional.

(4) A bill is not invalid by reason—

    (a) That it is not dated;

    (b) That it does not specify the value given, or that any value has been given therefor;

    (c) That it does not specify the place where it is drawn or the place where it is payable.

4. **Inland and foreign bills**

(1) An inland bill is a bill which is or on the face of it purports to be (a) both drawn and payable within the British Islands, or (b) drawn within the British Islands upon some person resident therein. Any other bill is a foreign bill.

For the purposes of this Act 'British Islands' means any part of the United Kingdom of Great Britain and Ireland, the islands of Man, Guernsey, Jersey, Alderney, and Sark, and the islands adjacent to any of them being part of the dominions of Her Majesty.

(2) Unless the contrary appear on the face of the bill the holder may treat it as an inland bill.

5. Effect where different parties to bill are the same person

(1) A bill may be drawn payable to, or to the order of, the drawer; or it may be drawn payable to, or to the order of, the drawee.

(2) Where in a bill drawer and drawee are the same person, or where the drawee is a fictitious person or a person not having capacity to contract, the holder may treat the instrument, at his option, either as a bill of exchange or as a promissory note.

6. Address to drawee

(1) The drawee must be named or otherwise indicated in a bill with reasonable certainty.

(2) A bill may be addressed to two or more drawees whether they are partners or not, but an order addressed to two drawees in the alternative or to two or more drawees in succession is not a bill of exchange.

7. Certainty required as to payee

(1) Where a bill is not payable to bearer, the payee must be named or otherwise indicated therein with reasonable certainty.

(2) A bill may be made payable to two or more payees jointly, or it may be made payable in the alternative to one of two, or one or some of several payees. A bill may also be made payable to the holder of an office for the time being.

(3) Where the payee is a fictitious or non-existing person the bill may be treated as payable to bearer.

8. What bills are negotiable

(1) When a bill contains words prohibiting transfer, or indicating an intention that it should not be transferable, it is valid as between the parties thereto, but is not negotiable.

(2) A negotiable bill may be payable either to order or to bearer.

(3) A bill is payable to bearer which is expressed to be so payable, or on which the only or last indorsement is an indorsement in blank.

(4) A bill is payable to order which is expressed to be so payable, or which is expressed to be payable to a particular person, and does not contain words prohibiting transfer or indicating an intention that it should not be transferable.

(5) Where a bill, either originally or by indorsement, is expressed to be payable to the order of a specified person, and not to him or his order, it is nevertheless payable to him or his order at his option.

9. Sum payable

(1) The sum payable by a bill is a sum certain within the meaning of this Act, although it is required to be paid—

    (a) With interest.

    (b) By stated instalments.

    (c) By stated instalments, with a provision that upon default in payment of any instalment the whole shall become due.

    (d) According to an indicated rate of exchange or according to a rate of exchange to be ascertained as directed by the bill.

(2) Where the sum payable is expressed in words and also in figures, and there is a discrepancy between the two, the sum denoted by the words is the amount payable.

(3) Where a bill is expressed to be payable with interest, unless the instrument otherwise provides, interest runs from the date of the bill, and if the bill is undated from the issue thereof.

10. Bill payable on demand

(1) A bill is payable on demand—

    (a) Which is expressed to be payable on demand, or at sight, or on presentation; or

    (b) In which no time for payment is expressed.

(2) Where a bill is accepted or indorsed when it is overdue, it shall, as regards the acceptor who so accepts, or any indorser who so indorses it, be deemed a bill payable on demand.

11. Bill payable at a future time

A bill is payable at a determinable future time within the meaning of this Act which is expressed to be payable—

(1) At a fixed period after date or sight.

(2) On or at a fixed period after the occurrence of a specified event which is certain to happen, though the time of happening may be uncertain.

An instrument expressed to be payable on a contingency is not a bill, and the happening of the event does not cure the defect.

12. Omission of date in bill payable after date

Where a bill expressed to be payable at a fixed period after date is issued undated, or where the acceptance of a bill payable at a fixed period after sight is undated, any holder may insert therein the true date of issue or acceptance, and the bill shall be payable accordingly.

Provided that (1) where the holder in good faith and by mistake inserts a wrong date, and (2) in every case where a wrong date is inserted, if the bill subsequently comes into the hands of a holder in due course the bill shall not be avoided thereby, but shall operate and be payable as if the date so inserted had been the true date.

13. Ante-dating and post-dating

(1) Where a bill or an acceptance or any indorsement on a bill is dated, the date shall, unless the contrary be proved, be deemed to be the true date of the drawing, acceptance, or indorsement, as the case may be.

(2) A bill is not invalid by reason only that it is ante-dated or post-dated, or that it bears date on a Sunday.

14. Computation of time of payment

Where a bill is not payable on demand the day on which it falls due is determined as follows:

(1) The bill is due and payable in all cases on the last day of the time of payment as fixed by the bill or, if that is a non-business day, on the succeeding business day.

(2) Where a bill is payable at a fixed period after date, after sight, or after the happening of a specified event, the time of payment is determined by excluding the day from which the time is to begin to run and by including the day of payment.

(3) Where a bill is payable at a fixed period after sight, the time begins to run from the date of the acceptance if the bill be accepted, and from the date of noting or protest if the bill be noted or protested for non-acceptance, or for non-delivery.

15. Case of need

The drawer of a bill and any indorser may insert therein the name of a person to whom the holder may resort in case of need, that is to say, in case the bill is dishonoured by non-acceptance or non-payment. Such person is called the referee in case of need. It is in the option of the holder to resort to the referee in case of need or not as he may think fit.

16. Optional stipulations by drawer or indorser

The drawer of a bill, and any indorser may insert therein an express stipulation—

(1) Negativing or limiting his own liability to the holder:

(2) Waiving as regards himself some or all of the holder's duties.

17. Definition and requisites of acceptance

(1) The acceptance of a bill is the signification by the drawee of his assent to the order of the drawer.

(2) An acceptance is invalid unless it complies with the following conditions, namely:

    (a) It must be written on the bill and be signed by the drawee. The mere signature of the drawee without additional words is sufficient.

    (b) It must not express that the drawee will perform his promise by any other means than the payment of money.

18.   Time for acceptance

A bill may be accepted—

(1)   before it has been signed by the drawer, or while otherwise incomplete:

(2)   When it is overdue, or after it has been dishonoured by a previous refusal to accept, or by non-payment:

(3)   When a bill payable after sight is dishonoured by non-acceptance, and the drawee subsequently accepts it, the holder, in the absence of any different agreement, is entitled to have the bill accepted as of the date of first presentment to the drawee for acceptance.

19.   General and qualified acceptance

(1)   An acceptance is either (a) general or (b) qualified.

(2)   A general acceptance assents without qualification to the order of the drawer. A qualified acceptance in express terms varies the effect of the bill as drawn.

In particular an acceptance is qualified which is—

    (a)   conditional, that is to say, which makes payment by the acceptor dependent on the fulfilment of a condition therein stated:

    (b)   partial, that is to say, an acceptance to pay part only of the amount for which the bill is drawn:

    (c)   local, that is to say, an acceptance to pay only at a particular specified place:

An acceptance to pay at a particular place is a general acceptance, unless it expressly states that the bill is to be paid there only and not elsewhere:

    (d)   qualified as to time:

    (e)   the acceptance of some one or more of the drawees, but not of all.

20.   Inchoate instruments

(1)   Where a simple signature on a blank paper is delivered by the signer in order that it may be converted into a bill, it operates as a prima facie authority to fill it up as a complete bill for any amount using the signature for that of the drawer, or the acceptor, or an indorser; and, in like manner, when a bill is wanting in any material particular, the person in possession of it has a prima facie authority to fill up the omission in any way he thinks fit.

(2)   In order that any such instrument when completed may be enforceable against any person who became a party thereto prior to its completion, it must be filled up within a reasonable time, and strictly in accordance with the authority given. Reasonable time for this purpose is a question of fact.

Provided that if any such instrument after completion is negotiated to a holder in due course it shall be valid and effectual for all purposes in his hands and he may enforce it as if it had been filled up within a reasonable time and strictly in accordance with the authority given.

21.   Delivery

(1)   Every contract on a bill, whether it be the drawer's, the acceptor's, or an indorser's is incomplete and revocable, until delivery of the instrument in order to give effect thereto.

Provided that where an acceptance is written on a bill, and the drawee gives notice to or according to the directions of the person entitled to the bill that he has accepted it, the acceptance then becomes complete and irrevocable.

(2)   As between immediate parties, and as regards a remote party other than a holder in due course, the delivery—

    (a)   in order to be effectual must be made either by or under the authority of the party drawing, accepting, or indorsing, as the case may be:

    (b)   may be shown to have been conditional or for a special purpose only, and not for the purpose of transferring the property in the bill.

But if the bill be in the hands of a holder in due course a valid delivery of the bill by all parties prior to him so as to make them liable to him is conclusively presumed.

(3)   Where a bill is no longer in the possession of a party who has signed it as drawer, acceptor, or indorser, a valid and unconditional delivery by him is presumed until the contrary is proved.

Capacity and authority of parties

22.   **Capacity of parties**

(1)   Capacity to incur liability as a party to a bill is coextensive with capacity to contract.

Provided that nothing in this section shall enable a corporation to make itself liable as drawer, acceptor, or indorser of a bill unless it is competent to it so to do under the law for the time being in force relating to corporations.

(2)   Where a bill is drawn or indorsed by an infant, minor, or corporation having no capacity or power to incur liability on a bill, the drawing or indorsement entitles the holder to receive payment of the bill, and to enforce it against any other party thereto.

23.   **Signature essential to liability**

No person is liable as drawer, indorser, or acceptor of a bill who has not signed it as such: Provided that

(1)   Where a person signs a bill in a trade or assumed name, he is liable thereon as if he had signed it in his own name:

(2)   The signature of the name of a firm is equivalent to the signature by the person so signing of the names of all persons liable as partners in that firm.

24.   **Forged or unauthorised signature**

Subject to the provisions of this Act, where a signature on a bill is forged or placed thereon without the authority of the person whose signature it purports to be, the forged or unauthorised signature is wholly inoperative, and no right to retain the bill or to give a discharge therefor or to enforce payment thereof against any party thereto can be acquired through or under that signature, unless the party against whom it is sought to retain or enforce payment of the bill is precluded from setting up the forgery or want of authority.

Provided that nothing in this section shall affect the ratification of an unauthorised signature not amounting to a forgery.

25.   **Procuration signatures**

A signature by procuration operates as notice that the agent has but a limited authority to sign, and the principal is only bound by such signature if the agent in so signing was acting within the actual limits of his authority.

26.   **Person signing as agent or in representative capacity**

(1)   Where a person signs a bill as drawer, indorser, or acceptor, and adds words to his signature, indicating that he signs for or on behalf of a principal, or in a representative character, he is not personally liable thereon; but the mere addition to his signature of words describing him as an agent, or as filling a representative character, does not exempt him from personal liability.

(2)   In determining whether a signature on a bill is that of the principal or that of the agent by whose hand it is written, the construction most favourable to the validity of the instrument shall be adopted.

The consideration for a bill

27.   **Value and holder for value**

(1)   Valuable consideration for a bill may be constituted by,—

     (a)   Any consideration sufficient to support a simple contract;

     (b)   An antecedent debt or liability. Such a debt or liability is deemed valuable consideration whether the bill is payable on demand or at a future time.

(2)   Where value has at any time been given for a bill the holder is deemed to be a holder for value as regards the acceptor and all parties to the bill who became parties prior to such time.

(3)   Where the holder of a bill has a lien on it, arising either from contract or by implication of law, he is deemed to be a holder for value to the extent of the sum for which he has a lien.

28. Accommodation bill or party

(1) An accommodation party to a bill is a person who has signed a bill as drawer, acceptor, or indorser, without receiving value therefor, and for the purpose of lending his name to some other person.

(2) An accommodation party is liable on the bill to a holder for value; and it is immaterial whether, when such holder took the bill, he knew such party to be an accommodation party or not.

29. Holder in due course

(1) A holder in due course is a holder who has taken a bill, complete and regular on the face of it, under the following conditions, namely,

     (a) That he became the holder of it before it was overdue, and without notice that it had been previously dishonoured, if such was the fact:

     (b) That he took the bill in good faith and for value, and that at the time the bill was negotiated to him he had no notice of any defect in the title of the person who negotiated it.

(2) In particular the title of a person who negotiates a bill is defective within the meaning of this Act when he obtained the bill, or the acceptance thereof, by fraud, duress or force and fear, or other unlawful means, or for an illegal consideration, or when he negotiates it in breach of faith, or under such circumstances as amount to a fraud.

(3) A holder (whether for value or not), who derives his title to a bill through a holder in due course, and who is not himself a party to any fraud or illegality affecting it, has all the rights of that holder in due course as regards the acceptor and all parties to the bill prior to that holder.

30. Presumption of value and good faith

(1) Every party whose signature appears on a bill is prima facie deemed to have become a party thereto for value.

(2) Every holder of a bill is prima facie deemed to be a holder in due course; but if in an action on a bill it is admitted or proved that the acceptance, issue, or subsequent negotiation of the bill is affected with fraud, duress, or force and fear, or illegality, the burden of proof is shifted, unless and until the holder proves that, subsequent to the alleged fraud or illegality, value has in good faith been given for the bill.

Negotiation of bills

31. Negotiation of bill

(1) A bill is negotiated when it is transferred from one person to another in such a manner as to constitute the transferee the holder of the bill.

(2) A bill payable to bearer is negotiated by delivery.

(3) A bill payable to order is negotiated by the indorsement of the holder completed by delivery.

(4) Where, the holder of a bill payable to his order transfers it for value without indorsing it, the transfer gives the transferee such title as the transferor had in the bill, and the transferee in addition acquires the right to have the indorsement of the transferor.

(5) Where any person is under obligation to indorse a bill in a representative capacity, he may indorse a bill in such terms as to negative personal liability.

32. Requisites of a valid indorsement

An indorsement in order to operate as a negotiation must comply with the following conditions, namely: —

(1) It must be written on the bill itself and signed by the indorser. The simple signature of the indorser on the bill, without additional words, is sufficient.

An indorsement written on an allonge or a 'copy' of a bill issued or negotiated in a country where 'copies' are recognised, is deemed to have been written on the bill itself.

(2) It must be an indorsement of the entire bill. A partial indorsement, that is to say, an indorsement which purports to transfer to the indorsee a part only of the amount payable, or which purports to transfer the bill to two or more indorsees severally, does not operate as a negotiation of the bill.

(3) Where a bill is payable to the order of two or more payees or indorsees who are not partners all must indorse, unless the one indorsing has authority to indorse for the others.

(4) Where, in a bill payable to order, the payee or indorsee is wrongly designated, or his name is mis-spelt, he may indorse the bill as therein described, adding, if he think fit, his proper signature.

(5) Where there are two or more indorsements on a bill, each indorsement is deemed to have been made in the order in which it appears on the bill, until the contrary is proved.

(6) An indorsement may be made in blank or special. It may also contain terms making it restrictive.

33. Conditional indorsement

Where a bill purports to be indorsed conditionally the condition may be disregarded by the payer, and payment to the indorsee is valid whether the condition has been fulfilled or not.

34. Indorsement in blank and special indorsement

(1) An indorsement in blank specifies no indorsee, and a bill so indorsed becomes payable to bearer.

(2) A special indorsement specifies the person to whom, or to whose order, the bill is to be payable.

(3) The provisions of this Act relating to a payee apply with the necessary modifications to an indorsee under a special indorsement.

(4) When a bill has been indorsed in blank, any holder may convert the blank indorsement into a special indorsement by writing above the indorser's signature a direction to pay the bill to or to the order of himself or some other person.

35. Restrictive indorsement

(1) An indorsement is restrictive which prohibits the further negotiation of the bill or which expresses that it is a mere authority to deal with the bill as thereby directed and not a transfer of ownership thereof, as, for example, if a bill be indorsed 'Pay D. only', or 'Pay D. for the account of X.,' or 'Pay D. or order for collection.'

(2) A restrictive indorsement gives the indorsee the right to receive payment of the bill and to sue any party thereto that his indorser could have sued, but gives him no power to transfer his rights as indorsee unless it expressly authorises him to do so.

(3) Where a restrictive indorsement authorises further transfer, all subsequent indorsees take the bill with the same rights and subject to the same liabilities as the first indorsee under the restrictive indorsement.

36. Negotiation of overdue or dishonoured bills

(1) Where a bill is negotiable in its origin it continues to be negotiable until it has been (a) restrictively indorsed or (b) discharged by payment or otherwise.

(2) Where an overdue bill is negotiated, it can only be negotiated subject to any defect of title affecting it at its maturity, and thenceforward no person who takes it can acquire or give a better title than that which the person from whom he took it had.

(3) A bill payable on demand is deemed to be overdue within the meaning and for the purposes of this section, when it appears on the face of it to have been in circulation for an unreasonable length of time. What is an unreasonable length of time for this purpose is a question of fact.

(4) Except where an indorsement bears date after the maturity of the bill, every negotiation is prima facie deemed to have been effected before the bill was overdue.

(5) Where a bill which is not overdue has been dishonoured any person who takes it with notice of the dishonour takes it subject to any defect of title attaching thereto at the time of dishonour, but nothing in this subsection shall affect the rights of a holder in due course.

37. Negotiation of bill to party already liable thereon

Where a bill is negotiated back to the drawer, or to a prior indorser or to the acceptor, such party may, subject to the provisions of this Act, reissue and further negotiate the bill, but he is not entitled to enforce payment of the bill against any intervening party to whom he was previously liable.

38. Rights of the holder

The rights and powers of the holder of a bill are as follows:

(1) He may sue on the bill in his own name:

(2)   Where he is a holder in due course, he holds the bill free from any defect of title of prior parties, as well as from mere personal defences available to prior parties among themselves, and may enforce payment against all parties liable on the bill:

(3)   Where his title is defective (a) if he negotiates the bill to a holder in due course, that holder obtains a good and complete title to the bill, and (b) if he obtains payment of the bill the person who pays him in due course gets a valid discharge for the bill.

General duties of the holder

39.   When presentment for acceptance is necessary

(1)   Where a bill is payable after sight, presentment for acceptance is necessary in order to fix the maturity of the instrument.

(2)   Where a bill expressly stipulates that it shall be presented for acceptance, or where a bill is drawn payable elsewhere than at the residence or place of business of the drawee, it must be presented for acceptance before it can be presented for payment.

(3)   In no other case is presentment for acceptance necessary in order to render liable any party to the bill.

(4)   Where the holder of a bill, drawn payable elsewhere than at the place of business or residence of the drawee, has not time, with the exercise of reasonable diligence, to present the bill for acceptance before presenting it for payment on the day that it falls due, the delay caused by presenting the bill for acceptance before presenting it for payment is excused, and does not discharge the drawer and the indorsers.

40.   Time for presenting bill payable after sight

(1)   Subject to the provisions of this Act, when a bill payable after sight is negotiated, the holder must either present it for acceptance or negotiate it within a reasonable time.

(2)   If he do not do so, the drawer and all indorsers prior to that holder are discharged.

(3)   In determining what is a reasonable time within the meaning of this section, regard shall be had to the nature of the bill, the usage of trade with respect to similar bills, and the facts of the particular case.

41.   Rules as to presentment for acceptance and excuses for non-presentment

(1)   A bill is duly presented for acceptance which is presented in accordance with the following rules:

(a)   The presentment must be made by or on behalf of the holder to the drawee or to some person authorised to accept or refuse acceptance on his behalf at a reasonable hour on a business day and before the bill is overdue:

(b)   Where a bill is addressed to two or more drawees, who are not partners, presentment must be made to them all, unless one has authority to accept for them all, then presentment must be made to him only:

(c)   Where the drawee is dead presentment may be made to his personal representative:

(d)   Where the drawee is bankrupt, presentment may be made to him or to his trustee:

(e)   Where authorised by agreement or usage, a presentment through a postal operator is sufficient.

(2)   Presentment in accordance with these rules is excused, and a bill may be treated as dishonoured by non-acceptance—

(a)   Where the drawee is dead or bankrupt, or is a fictitious person or a person not having capacity to contract by bill:

(b)   Where, after the exercise of reasonable diligence, such presentment cannot be effected:

(c)   Where although the presentment has been irregular, acceptance has been refused on some other ground.

(3)   The fact that the holder has reason to believe that the bill, on presentment, will be dishonoured does not excuse presentment.

42.   Non-acceptance

(1)   When a bill is duly presented for acceptance and is not accepted within the customary time, the person presenting it must treat it as dishonoured by non-acceptance. If he do not, the holder shall lose his right of recourse against the drawer and indorsers.

43.   Dishonour by non-acceptance and its consequences

(1)   A bill is dishonoured by non-acceptance—
  (a)   when it is duly presented for acceptance, and such an acceptance as is prescribed by this Act is refused or cannot be obtained; or
  (b)   when presentment for acceptance is excused and the bill is not accepted.
(2)   Subject to the provisions of this Act when a bill is dishonoured by non-acceptance an immediate right of recourse against the drawer and indorsers accrues to the holder, and no presentment for payment is necessary.

44.   Duties as to qualified acceptances

(1)   The holder of a bill may refuse to take a qualified acceptance, and if he does not obtain an unqualified acceptance may treat the bill as dishonoured by non-acceptance.
(2)   Where a qualified acceptance is taken, and the drawer or an indorser has not expressly or impliedly authorised the holder to take a qualified acceptance, or does not subsequently assent thereto, such drawer or indorser is discharged from his liability on the bill.
        The provisions of this subsection do not apply to a partial acceptance, whereof due notice has been given. Where a foreign bill has been accepted as to part, it must be protested as to the balance.
(3)   When the drawer or indorser of a bill receives notice of a qualified acceptance, and does not within a reasonable time express his dissent to the holder he shall be deemed to have assented thereto.

45.   Rules as to presentment for payment

Subject to the provisions of this Act a bill must be duly presented for payment. If it be not so presented the drawer and indorsers shall be discharged.

A bill is duly presented for payment which is presented in accordance with the following rules:—

(1)   Where the bill is not payable on demand, presentment must be made on the day it falls due.
(2)   Where the bill is payable on demand then, subject to the provisions of this Act, presentment must be made within a reasonable time after its issue in order to render the drawer liable, and within a reasonable time after the indorsement, in order to render the indorser liable.
        In determining what is a reasonable time, regard shall be had to the nature of the bill, the usage of trade with regard to similar bills, and the facts of the particular case.
(3)   Presentment must be made by the holder or by some person authorised to receive payment on his behalf at a reasonable hour on a business day, at the proper place as hereinafter defined, either to the person designated by the bill as payer, or to some person authorised to pay or refuse payment on his behalf if with the exercise of reasonable diligence such person can there be found.
(4)   A bill is presented at the proper place:—
  (a)   Where a place of payment is specified in the bill and the bill is there presented.
  (b)   Where no place of payment is specified, but the address of the drawee or acceptor is given in the bill, and the bill is there presented.
  (c)   Where no place of payment is specified and no address given, and the bill is presented at the drawee's or acceptor's place of business if known, and if not, at his ordinary residence if known.
  (d)   In any other case if presented to the drawer or acceptor wherever he can be found, or if presented at his last known place of business or residence.
(5)   Where a bill is presented at the proper place, and after the exercise of reasonable diligence no person authorised to pay or refuse payment can be found there, no further presentment to the drawee or acceptor is required.
(6)   Where a bill is drawn upon, or accepted by two or more persons who are not partners, and no place of payment is specified, presentment must be made to them all.

(7)   Where the drawee or acceptor of a bill is dead, and no place of payment is specified, presentment must be made to a personal representative, if such there be, and with the exercise of reasonable diligence he can be found.

(8)   Where authorised by agreement or usage a presentment through a postal operator is sufficient.

46.   Excuses for delay or non-presentment for payment

(1)   Delay in making presentment for payment is excused when the delay is caused by circumstances beyond the control of the holder, and not imputable to his default, misconduct, or negligence. When the cause of delay ceases to operate presentment must be made with reasonable diligence.

(2)   Presentment for payment is dispensed with, —

(a)   Where, after the exercise of reasonable diligence presentment, as required by this Act, cannot be effected.

The fact that the holder has reason to believe that the bill will, on presentment, be dishonoured, does not dispense with the necessity for presentment.

(b)   Where the drawee is a fictitious person.

(c)   As regards the drawer where the drawee or acceptor is not bound, as between himself and the drawee, to accept or pay the bill, and the drawer has no reason to believe that the bill would be paid if presented.

(d)   As regards an indorser, where the bill was accepted or made for the accommodation of the indorser, and he has no reason to expect that the bill would be paid if presented.

(e)   By waiver of presentment, expressed or implied.

47.   Dishonour by non-payment

(1)   A bill is dishonoured by non-payment (a) when it is duly presented for payment and payment is refused or cannot be obtained, or (b) when presentment is excused and the bill is overdue and unpaid.

(2)   Subject to the provisions of this Act, when a bill is dishonoured by non-payment, an immediate right of recourse against the drawer and indorsers accrues to the holder.

48.   Notice of dishonour and effect of non-notice

Subject to the provisions of this Act, when a bill has been dishonoured by non-acceptance or by non-payment, notice of dishonour must be given to the drawer and each indorser, and any drawer or indorser to whom such notice is not given is discharged; provided that —

(1)   Where a bill is dishonoured by non-acceptance, and notice of dishonour is not given, the rights of the holder in due course subsequent to the omission, shall not be prejudiced by the omission.

(2)   Where a bill is dishonoured by non-acceptance and due notice of dishonour is given, it shall not be necessary to give notice of a subsequent dishonour by nonpayment unless the bill shall in the meantime have been accepted.

49.   Rules as of notice of dishonour

Notice of dishonour in order to be valid and effectual must be given in accordance with the following rules: —

(1)   The notice must be given by or on behalf of the holder, or by or on behalf of an indorser who, at the time of giving it, is himself liable on the bill.

(2)   Notice of dishonour may be given by an agent either in his own name, or in the name of any party entitled to give notice whether that party be his principal or not.

(3)   Where the notice is given by or on behalf of the holder, it enures for the benefit of all subsequent holders and all prior indorsers who have a right of recourse against the party to whom it is given.

(4)   Where notice is given by or on behalf of an indorser entitled to give notice as herein-before provided, it enures for the benefit of the holder and all indorsers subsequent to the party to whom notice is given.

(5)   The notice may be given in writing or by personal communication, and may be given in any terms which sufficiently identify the bill, and intimate that the bill has been dishonoured by non-acceptance or non-payment.

(6) The return of a dishonoured bill to the drawer or an indorser is, in point of form, deemed a sufficient notice of dishonour.

(7) A written notice need not be signed, and an insufficient written notice may be supplemented and validated by verbal communication. A misdescription of the bill shall not vitiate the notice unless the party to whom the notice is given is in fact misled thereby.

(8) Where notice of dishonour is required to be given to any person, it may be given either to the party himself, or to his agent in that behalf.

(9) Where the drawer or indorser is dead, and the party giving notice knows it, the notice must be given to a personal representative if such there be, and with the exercise of reasonable diligence he can be found.

(10) Where the drawer or indorser is bankrupt, notice may be given either to the party himself or to the trustee.

(11) Where there are two or more drawers or indorsers who are not partners, notice must be given to each of them, unless one of them has authority to receive such notice for the others.

(12) The notice may be given as soon as the bill is dishonoured and must be given within a reasonable time thereafter.

   In the absence of special circumstances notice is not deemed to have been given within a reasonable time, unless—

   (a) where the person giving and the person to receive notice reside in the same place, the notice is given or sent off in time to reach the latter on the day after the dishonour of the bill.

   (b) where the person giving and the person to receive notice reside in different places, the notice is sent off on the day after the dishonour of the bill, if there be a post at a convenient hour on that day, and if there be no such post on that day then by the next post thereafter.

(13) Where a bill when dishonoured is in the hands of an agent, he may either himself give notice to the parties liable on the bill, or he may give notice to his principal. If he gives notice to his principal, he must do so within the same time as if he were the holder, and the principal upon receipt of such notice has himself the same time for giving notice as if the agent had been an independent holder.

(14) Where a party to a bill receives due notice of dishonour, he has after the receipt of such notice the same period of time for giving notice to antecedent parties that the holder has after the dishonour.

(15) Where a notice of dishonour is duly addressed and posted, the sender is deemed to have given due notice of dishonour, notwithstanding any miscarriage by the postal operator concerned.

50. Excuses for non-notice and delay

(1) Delay in giving notice of dishonour is excused where the delay is caused by circumstances beyond the control of the party giving notice, and not imputable to his default, misconduct, or negligence. When the cause of delay ceases to operate the notice must be given with reasonable diligence.

(2) Notice of dishonour is dispensed with—

   (a) When, after the exercise of reasonable diligence, notice as required by this Act cannot be given to or does not reach the drawer or indorser sought to be charged:

   (b) By waiver express or implied. Notice of dishonour may be waived before the time of giving notice has arrived, or after the omission to give due notice:

   (c) As regards the drawer in the following cases, namely, (1) where drawer and drawee are the same person, (2) where the drawee is a fictitious person or a person not having capacity to contract, (3) where the drawer is the person to whom the bill is presented for payment, (4) where the drawee or acceptor is as between himself and the drawer under no obligation to accept or pay the bill, (5) where the drawer has countermanded payment:

   (d) As regards the indorser in the following cases, namely (1) where the drawee is a fictitious person or a person not having the capacity to contract and the indorser was aware of the fact at the time he indorsed the bill, (2) where the indorser is the person to whom the bill is presented for payment, (3) where the bill was accepted or made for his accommodation.

51. Noting or protest of bill

(1) Where an inland bill has been dishonoured it may, if the holder think fit, be noted for non-acceptance or non-payment, as the case may be; but it shall not be necessary to note or protest any such bill in order to preserve the recourse against the drawer or indorser.

(2) Where a foreign bill, appearing on the face of it to be such, has been dishonoured by non-acceptance it must be duly protested for non-acceptance and where such a bill, which has not been previously dishonoured by non-acceptance, is dishonoured by non-payment it must be duly protested for non-payment. If it be not so protested the drawer and indorsers are discharged. Where a bill does not appear on the face of it to be a foreign bill, protest thereof in the case of dishonour is unnecessary.

(3) A bill which has been protested for non-acceptance may be subsequently protested for non-payment.

(4) Subject to the provisions of this Act, when a bill is noted or protested, it may be noted on the day of its dishonour and must be noted not later than the next succeeding business day. When a bill has been duly noted, the protest may be subsequently extended as of the date of the noting.

(5) Where the acceptor of the bill becomes bankrupt or insolvent or suspends payment before it matures, the holder may cause the bill to be protested for better security against the drawer and indorsers.

(6) A bill must be protested at the place where it is dishonoured:
Provided that—
   (a) When a bill is presented through a postal operator, and returned by post dishonoured, it may be protested at the place to which it is returned and on the day of its return if received during business hours, and if not received during business hours, then not later than the next business day;
   (b) When a bill drawn payable at the place of business or residence of some person other than the drawee, has been dishonoured by non-acceptance, it must be protested for non-payment at the place where it is expressed to be payable, and no further presentment for payment to, or demand on, the drawee is necessary.

(7) A protest must contain a copy of the bill, and must be signed by the notary making it, and must specify—
   (a) The person at whose request the bill is protested:
   (b) The place and date of protest, the cause or reason for protesting the bill, the demand made, and the answer given, if any, or the fact that the drawee or acceptor could not be found.

(7A) In subsection (7) 'notary' includes a person who, for the purposes of the Legal Services Act 2007, is an authorised person in relation to any activity which constitutes a notarial activity (within the meaning of that Act).

(8) Where a bill is lost or destroyed, or is wrongly detained from the person entitled to hold it, protest may be made on a copy or written particulars thereof.

(9) Protest is dispensed with by any circumstance which would dispense with notice of dishonour. Delay in noting or protesting is excused when the delay is caused by circumstances beyond the control of the holder, and not imputable to his default, misconduct, or negligence. When the cause of delay ceases to operate the bill must be noted or protested with reasonable diligence.

52. Duties of holder as regards drawee or acceptor

(1) When a bill is accepted generally presentment for payment is not necessary in order to render the acceptor liable.

(2) When by the terms of a qualified acceptance presentment for payment is required, the acceptor, in the absence of an express stipulation to that effect, is not discharged by the omission to present the bill for payment on the day that it matures.

(3) In order to render the acceptor of a bill liable it is not necessary to protest it, or that notice of dishonour should be given to him.

(4)   Subject to Part 4A (presentment by electronic means), where the holder of a bill presents it for payment, he shall exhibit the bill to the person from whom he demands payment, and when a bill is paid the holder shall forthwith deliver it up to the party paying it.

Liabilities of parties

53.   Funds in hands of drawee

(1)   A bill, of itself, does not operate as an assignment of funds in the hands of the drawee available for the payment thereof, and the drawee of a bill who does not accept as required by this Act is not liable on the instrument. This subsection shall not extend to Scotland.

(2)   In Scotland, where the drawee of a bill other than a cheque has in his hands funds available for the payment thereof, the bill operates as an assignment of the sum, for which it is drawn in favour of the holder, from the time when the bill is presented to the drawee.

54.   Liability of acceptor

The acceptor of a bill, by accepting it—

(1)   Engages that he will pay it according to the tenor of his acceptance:

(2)   Is precluded from denying to a holder in due course:

    (a)   The existence of the drawer, the genuineness of his signature, and his capacity and authority to draw the bill;

    (b)   In the case of a bill payable to drawer's order, the then capacity of the drawer to indorse, but not the genuineness or validity of his indorsement;

    (c)   In the case of a bill payable to the order of a third person, the existence of the payee and his then capacity to indorse, but not the genuineness or validity of his indorsement.

55.   Liability of drawer or indorser

(1)   The drawer of a bill by drawing it—

    (a)   Engages that on due presentment it shall be accepted and paid according to its tenor, and that if it be dishonoured he will compensate the holder or any indorser who is compelled to pay it, provided that the requisite proceedings on dishonour be duly taken;

    (b)   Is precluded from denying to a holder in due course the existence of the payee and his then capacity to indorse.

(2)   The indorser of a bill by indorsing it—

    (a)   Engages that on due presentment it shall be accepted and paid according to its tenor, and that if it be dishonoured he will compensate the holder or a subsequent indorser who is compelled to pay it, provided that the requisite proceedings on dishonour be duly taken;

    (b)   Is precluded from denying to a holder in due course the genuineness and regularity in all respects of the drawer's signature and all previous indorsements;

    (c)   Is precluded from denying to his immediate or a subsequent indorsee that the bill was at the time of his indorsement a valid and subsisting bill, and that he had then a good title thereto.

56.   Stranger signing bill liable as indorser

Where a person signs a bill otherwise than as drawer or acceptor, he thereby incurs the liabilities of an indorser to a holder in due course.

57.   Measure of damages against parties to dishonoured bill

Where a bill is dishonoured, the measure of damages, which shall be deemed to be liquidated damages, shall be as follows:

(1)   The holder may recover from any party liable on the bill, and the drawer who has been compelled to pay the bill may recover from the acceptor, and an indorser who has been compelled to pay the bill may recover from the acceptor or from the drawer, or from a prior indorser—

(a)   The amount of the bill:

(b)   Interest thereon from the time of presentment for payment if the bill is payable on demand, and from the maturity of the bill in any other case:

(c)   The expenses of noting, or, when protest is necessary, and the protest has been extended, the expenses of protest.

...

(3)   Where by this Act interest may be recovered as damages, such interest may, if justice require it, be withheld wholly or in part, and where a bill is expressed to be payable with interest at a given rate, interest as damages may or may not be given at the same rate as interest proper.

58.   Transferor by delivery and transferee

(1)   Where the holder of a bill payable to bearer negotiates it by delivery without indorsing it, he is called a 'transferor by delivery.'

(2)   A transferor by delivery is not liable on the instrument.

(3)   A transferor by delivery who negotiates a bill thereby warrants to his immediate transferee being a holder for value that the bill is what it purports to be, that he has a right to transfer it, and that at the time of the transfer he is not aware of any fact which renders it valueless.

Discharge of bill

59.   Payment in due course

(1)   A bill is discharged by payment in due course by or on behalf of the drawee or acceptor.
      'Payment in due course' means payment made at or after the maturity of the bill to the holder thereof in good faith and without notice that his title to the bill is defective.

(2)   Subject to the provisions herein-after contained, when a bill is paid by the drawer or an indorser it is not discharged; but

(a)   Where a bill payable to, or to the order of, a third party is paid by the drawer, the drawer may enforce payment thereof against the acceptor, but may not re-issue the bill.

(b)   Where a bill is paid by an indorser, or where a bill payable to drawer's order is paid by the drawer, the party paying it is remitted to his former rights as regards the acceptor or antecedent parties, and he may, if he thinks fit, strike out his own and subsequent indorsements, and again negotiate the bill.

(3)   Where an accommodation bill is paid in due course by the party accommodated the bill is discharged.

60.   Banker paying demand draft whereon indorsement is forged

When a bill payable to order on demand is drawn on a banker, and the banker on whom it is drawn, pays the bill in good faith and in the ordinary course of business, it is not incumbent on the banker to show that the indorsement of the payee or any subsequent indorsement was made by or under the authority of the person whose indorsement it purports to be, and the banker is deemed to have paid the bill in due course, although such indorsement has been forged or made without authority.

61.   Acceptor the holder at maturity

When the acceptor of a bill is or becomes the holder of it at or after its maturity, in his own right, the bill is discharged.

62.   Express waiver

(1)   When the holder of a bill at or after its maturity absolutely and unconditionally renounces his rights against the acceptor the bill is discharged.
      The renunciation must be in writing, unless the bill is delivered up to the acceptor.

(2)   The liabilities of any party to a bill may in like manner be renounced by the holder before, at, or after its maturity; but nothing in this section shall affect the rights of a holder in due course without notice of the renunciation.

63.   Cancellation

(1)   Where a bill is intentionally cancelled by the holder or his agent, and the cancellation is apparent thereon, the bill is discharged.

(2)   In like manner any party liable on a bill may be discharged by the intentional cancellation of his signature by the holder or his agent. In such case any indorser who would have had a right of recourse against the party whose signature is cancelled, is also discharged.

(3)   A cancellation made unintentionally, or under a mistake, or without the authority of the holder is inoperative; but where a bill or any signature thereon appears to have been cancelled the burden of proof lies on the party who alleges that the cancellation was made unintentionally, or under a mistake, or without authority.

64.   Alteration of bill

(1)   Where a bill or acceptance is materially altered without the assent of all parties liable on the bill, the bill is avoided except as against a party who has himself made, authorised, or assented to the alteration, and subsequent indorsers.

Provided that,

Where a bill has been materially altered, but the alteration is not apparent, and the bill is in the hands of a holder in due course, such holder may avail himself of the bill as if it had not been altered, and may enforce payment of it according to its original tenor.

(2)   In particular the following alterations are material, namely, any alteration of the date, the sum payable, the time of payment, the place of payment, and where a bill has been accepted generally, the addition of a place of payment without the acceptor's assent.

Acceptance and payment for honour

65.   Acceptance for honour supra protest

(1)   Where a bill of exchange has been protested for dishonour by non-acceptance, or protested for better security, and is not overdue, any person, not being a party already liable thereon, may, with the consent of the holder, intervene and accept the bill *supra protest*, for the honour of any party liable thereon, or for the honour of the person for whose account the bill is drawn.

(2)   A bill may be accepted for honour for part only of the sum for which it is drawn.

(3)   An acceptance for honour supra protest in order to be valid must—

(a)   be written on the bill, and indicate that it is an acceptance for honour;

(b)   be signed by the acceptor for honour:

(4)   Where an acceptance for honour does not expressly state for whose honour it is made, it is deemed to be an acceptance for the honour of the drawer.

(5)   Where a bill payable after sight is accepted for honour, its maturity is calculated from the date of the noting for non-acceptance, and not from the date of the acceptance for honour.

66.   Liability of acceptor for honour

(1)   The acceptor for honour of a bill by accepting it engages that he will, on due presentment, pay the bill according to the tenor of his acceptance, if it is not paid by the drawee, provided it has been duly presented for payment, and protested for non-payment, and that he receives notice of these facts.

(2)   The acceptor for honour is liable to the holder and to all parties to the bill subsequent to the party for whose honour he has accepted.

67.   Presentment to acceptor for honour

(1)   Where a dishonoured bill has been accepted for honour supra protest, or contains a reference in case of need, it must be protested for non-payment before it is presented for payment to the acceptor for honour, or referee in case of need.

(2)   Where the address of the acceptor for honour is in the same place where the bill is protested for non-payment, the bill must be presented to him not later than the day following its maturity; and where the address of the acceptor for honour is in some

place other than the place where it was protested for non-payment, the bill must be forwarded not later than the day following its maturity for presentment to him.

(3) Delay in presentment or non-presentment is excused by any circumstances which would excuse delay in presentment for payment or non-presentment for payment.

(4) When a bill of exchange is dishonoured by the acceptor for honour it must be protested for non-payment by him.

68. Payment for honour supra protest

(1) Where a bill has been protested for non-payment any person may intervene and pay it *supra protest* for the honour of any party liable thereon, or for the honour of the person for whose account the bill is drawn.

(2) Where two or more persons offer to pay a bill for the honour of different parties, the person whose payment will discharge most parties to the bill shall have the preference.

(3) Payment for honour *supra protest*, in order to operate as such and not as a mere voluntary payment, must be attested by a notarial act of honour which may be appended to the protest or form an extension of it.

(4) The notarial act of honour must be founded on a declaration made by the payer for honour, or his agent in that behalf, declaring his intention to pay the bill for honour, and for whose honour he pays.

(5) Where a bill has been paid for honour, all parties subsequent to the party for whose honour it is paid are discharged, but the payer for honour is subrogated for, and succeeds to both the rights and duties of, the holder as regards the party for whose honour he pays, and all parties liable to that party.

(6) The payer for honour on paying to the holder the amount of the bill and the notarial expenses incidental to its dishonour is entitled to receive both the bill itself and the protest. If the holder do not on demand deliver them up he shall be liable to the payer for honour in damages.

(7) Where the holder of a bill refuses to receive payment *supra protest* he shall lose his right of recourse against any party who would have been discharged by such payment.

Lost instruments

69. Holder's right to duplicate of lost bill

Where a bill has been lost before it is overdue, the person who was the holder of it may apply to the drawer to give him another bill of the same tenor, giving security to the drawer if required to indemnify him against all persons whatever in case the bill alleged to have been lost shall be found again.

If the drawer on request as aforesaid refuses to give such duplicate bill, he may be compelled to do so.

70. Action on lost bill

In any action or proceeding upon a bill, the court or a judge may order that the loss of the instrument shall not be set up, provided an indemnity be given to the satisfaction of the court or judge against the claims of any other person upon the instrument in question.

Bill in a set

71. Rules as to sets

(1) Where a bill is drawn in a set, each part of the set being numbered and containing a reference to the other parts, the whole of the parts constitute one bill.

(2) Where the holder of a set indorses two or more parts to different persons, he is liable to every such part, and every indorser subsequent to him is liable on the part he has himself indorsed as if the said parts were separate bills.

(3) Where two or more parts of a set are negotiated to different holders in due course, the holder whose title first accrues is as between such holders deemed the true owner of the bill; but nothing in this subsection shall affect the rights of a person who in the course accepts or pays the part first presented to him.

(4) The acceptance may be written on any part, and it must be written on one part only.

If the drawee accepts more than one part, and such accepted parts get into the hands of different holders in due course, he is liable on every such part as if it were a separate bill.

(5) When the acceptor of a bill drawn in a set pays it without requiring the part bearing the acceptance to be delivered up to him, and that part at maturity is outstanding in the hands of a holder in due course, he is liable to the holder thereof.

(6) Subject to the preceding rules, where any one part of a bill drawn in a set is discharged by payment or otherwise, the whole bill is discharged.

Conflict of laws

72. Rules where laws conflict

Where a bill drawn in one country is negotiated, accepted, or payable in another, the rights, duties, and liabilities of the parties thereto are determined as follows:

(1) The validity of a bill as regards requisites in form is determined by the law of the place of issue, and the validity as regards requisites in form of the supervening contracts, such as acceptance, or indorsement, or acceptance supra protest, is determined by the law of the place where such contract was made.

Provided that—

    (a) Where a bill is issued out of the United Kingdom it is not invalid by reason only that it is not stamped in accordance with the law of the place of issue:

    (b) Where a bill, issued out of the United Kingdom, conforms, as regards requisites in form, to the law of the United Kingdom, it may, for the purpose of enforcing payment thereof, be treated as valid as between all persons who negotiate, hold, or become parties to it in the United Kingdom.

(2) Subject to the provisions of this Act, the interpretation of the drawing, indorsement, acceptance, or acceptance supra protest of a bill, is determined by the law of the place where such contract is made.

Provided that where an inland bill is indorsed in a foreign country the indorsement shall as regards the payer be interpreted according to the law of the United Kingdom.

(3) The duties of the holder with respect to presentment for acceptance or payment and the necessity for or sufficiency of a protest or notice of dishonour, or otherwise, are determined by the law of the place where the act is done or the bill is dishonoured.

...

(5) Where a bill is drawn in one country and is payable in another, the due date thereof is determined according to the law of the place where it is payable.

PART III
CHEQUES ON A BANKER

73. Cheque defined

A cheque is a bill of exchange drawn on a banker payable on demand. Except as otherwise provided in this Part, the provisions of this Act applicable to a bill of exchange payable on demand apply to a cheque.

74. Presentment of cheque for payment

Subject to the provisions of this Act—

(1) Where a cheque is not presented for payment within a reasonable time of its issue, and the drawer or the person on whose account it is drawn had the right at the time of such presentment as between him and the banker to have the cheque paid and suffers actual damage through the delay, he is discharged to the extent of such damage, that is to say, to the extent to which such drawer or person is a creditor of such banker to a larger amount than he would have been had such cheque been paid.

(2) In determining what is a reasonable time regard shall be had to the nature of the instrument, the usage of trade and of bankers, and the facts of the particular case.

(3) The holder of such cheque as to which such drawer or person is discharged shall be a creditor, in lieu of such drawer or person, of such banker to the extent of such discharge, and entitled to recover the amount from him.

74A.   Presentment of cheque for payment: alternative place of presentment

Where the banker on whom a cheque is drawn—

(a)   has by notice published in the London, Edinburgh and Belfast Gazettes specified an address at which cheques drawn on him may be presented, and

(b)   has not by notice so published cancelled the specification of that address, the cheque is also presented at the proper place if it is presented there.

75.   Revocation of banker's authority

The duty and authority of a banker to pay a cheque drawn on him by his customer are determined by—

(1)   Countermand of payment:

(2)   Notice of the customer's death.

Crossed cheques

76.   General and special crossings defined

(1)   Where a cheque bears across its face an addition of—

(a)   The words 'and company' or any abbreviation thereof between two parallel transverse lines either with or without the words 'not negotiable'; or

(b)   Two parallel transverse lines simply, either with or without the words 'not negotiable';

that addition constitutes a crossing, and the cheque is crossed generally.

(2)   Where a cheque bears across its face an addition of the name of a banker, either with or without the words 'not negotiable', that addition constitutes a crossing, and the cheque is crossed specially and to that banker.

77.   Crossing by drawer or after issue

(1)   A cheque may be crossed generally or specially by the drawer.

(2)   Where a cheque is uncrossed, the holder may cross it generally or specially.

(3)   Where a cheque is crossed generally the holder may cross it specially.

(4)   Where a cheque is crossed generally or specially, the holder may add the words 'not negotiable.'

(5)   Where a cheque is crossed specially, the banker to whom it is crossed may again cross it specially to another banker for collection.

(6)   Where an uncrossed cheque, or a cheque crossed generally is sent to a banker for collection, he may cross it specially to himself.

78.   Crossing a material part of cheque

A crossing authorised by this Act is a material part of the cheque; it shall not be lawful for any person to obliterate or except as authorised by this Act, to add to or alter the crossing.

79.   Duties of banker as to crossed cheques

(1)   Where a cheque is crossed specially to more than one banker except when crossed to an agent for collection being a banker, the banker on whom it is drawn shall refuse payment thereof.

(2)   Where the banker on whom a cheque is drawn which is so crossed nevertheless pays the same, or pays a cheque crossed generally otherwise than to a banker, or if crossed specially otherwise than to the banker to whom it is crossed, or his agent for collection being a banker, he is liable to the true owner of the cheque for any loss he may sustain owing to the cheque having been so paid.

Provided that where a cheque is presented for payment which does not at the time of presentment appear to be crossed, or to have had a crossing which had been obliterated, or to have been added to or altered otherwise than as authorised by this Act, the banker paying the cheque in good faith and without negligence shall not be responsible or incur any liability, nor shall the payment be questioned by reason of the cheque having been crossed, or of the crossing having been obliterated or having been added to or altered otherwise than as authorised by this Act, and of payment having been made otherwise than to a banker or to the banker to whom the cheque is or was crossed, or to his agent for collection being a banker as the case may be.

80. Protection to banker and drawer where cheque is crossed

Where the banker, on whom a crossed cheque (including a cheque which under section 81A below or otherwise is not transferable) is drawn in good faith and without negligence pays it, if crossed generally to a banker, and if crossed specially, to the banker to whom it is crossed, or his agent for collection being a banker, the banker paying the cheque, and, if the cheque has come into the hands of the payee, the drawer, shall respectively be entitled to the same rights and be placed in the same position as if payment of the cheque had been made to the true owner thereof.

81. Effect of crossing on holder

Where a person takes a crossed cheque which bears on it the words 'not negotiable,' he shall not have and shall not be capable of giving a better title to the cheque than that which the person from whom he took it had.

81A. Non-transferable cheques

(1) Where a cheque is crossed and bears across its face the words 'account payee' or 'a/c payee', either with or without the words 'only', the cheque shall not be transferable, but shall only be valid as between the parties thereto.

(2) A banker is not to be treated for the purposes of section 80 above as having been negligent by reason only of his failure to concern himself with any purported indorsement of a cheque which under subsection (1) above or otherwise is not transferable.

...

PART IV
PROMISSORY NOTES

83. Promissory note defined

(1) A promissory note is an unconditional promise in writing made by one person to another signed by the maker, engaging to pay, on demand or at a fixed or determinable future time, a sum certain in money, to, or to the order of, a specified person or to bearer.

(2) An instrument in the form of a note payable to maker's order is not a note within the meaning of this section unless and until it is indorsed by the maker.

(3) A note is not invalid by reason only that it contains also a pledge of collateral security with authority to sell or dispose thereof.

(4) A note which is, or on the face of it purports to be, both made and payable within the British Islands is an inland note. Any other note is a foreign note.

84. Delivery necessary

A promissory note is inchoate and incomplete until delivery thereof to the payee or bearer.

85. Joint and several notes

(1) A promissory note may be made by two or more makers, and they may be liable thereon jointly, or jointly and severally according to its tenor.

(2) Where a note runs 'I promise to pay' and is signed by two or more persons it is deemed to be their joint and several note.

86. Note payable on demand

(1) Where a note payable on demand has been indorsed, it must be presented for payment within a reasonable time of the indorsement. If it be not so presented the indorser is discharged.

(2) In determining what is a reasonable time, regard shall be had to the nature of the instrument, the usage of trade, and the facts of the particular case.

(3) Where a note payable on demand is negotiated, it is not deemed to be overdue for the purpose of affecting the holder with defects of title of which he had no notice, by reason that it appears that a reasonable time for presenting it for payment has elapsed since its issue.

87. Presentment of note for payment

(1) Where a promissory note is in the body of it made payable at a particular place, it must be presented for payment at that place in order to render the maker liable. In any other case, presentment for payment is not necessary to render the maker liable.

(2) Presentment for payment is necessary in order to render the indorser of a note liable.

(3) Where a note is in the body of it made payable at a particular place, presentment at that place is necessary in order to render an indorser liable; but when a place of payment is indicated by way of memorandum only, presentment at that place is sufficient to render the indorser liable, but a presentment to the maker elsewhere, if sufficient in other respects, shall also suffice.

(4) This section is subject to Part 4A (presentment by electronic means).

88. Liability of maker

The maker of a promissory note by making it—

(1) Engages that he will pay it according to its tenor;

(2) Is precluded from denying to a holder in due course the existence of the payee and his then capacity to indorse.

89. Application of Part II to notes

(1) Subject to the provisions in this part and, except as by this section provided, the provisions of this Act relating to bills of exchange apply, with the necessary modifications, to promissory notes.

(2) In applying those provisions the maker of a note shall be deemed to correspond with the acceptor of a bill, and the first indorser of a note shall be deemed to correspond with the drawer of an accepted bill payable to drawer's order.

(3) The following provisions as to bills do not apply to notes; namely, provisions relating to—

    (a) Presentment for acceptance;

    (b) Acceptance;

    (c) Acceptance supra protest;

    (d) Bills in a set.

(4) Where a foreign note is dishonoured, protest thereof is unnecessary.

PART 4A
PRESENTMENT OF CHEQUES AND OTHER INSTRUMENTS BY ELECTRONIC MEANS

89A. Presentment of instruments by electronic means

(1) Presentment for payment of an instrument to which this section applies may be effected by provision of an electronic image of both faces of the instrument, instead of by presenting the physical instrument, if the person to whom presentment is made accepts the presentment as effective.

This is subject to regulations under subsection (2) and to section 89C.

(2) The Treasury may by regulations prescribe circumstances in which subsection (1) does not apply.

(3) Regulations under subsection (2) may in particular prescribe circumstances by reference to—

    (a) descriptions of instrument;

    (b) arrangements under which presentment is made;

    (c) descriptions of persons by or to whom presentment is made;

    (d) descriptions of persons receiving payment or on whose behalf payment is received.

(4) Where presentment for payment is made under subsection (1)—

    (a) any requirement—

        (i) that the physical instrument must be exhibited, presented or delivered on or in connection with presentment or payment (including after presentment or payment or in connection with dishonour for non-payment), or

        (ii) as to the day, time or place on or at which presentment of the physical instrument may be or is to be made, and

      (b)   any other requirement which is inconsistent with subsection (1), does not apply.

(5)   Subsection (4) does not affect any requirement as to the latest time for presentment.

(6)   References in subsections (4) and (5) to a requirement are to a requirement or prohibition, whether imposed by or under any enactment, by a rule of law or by the instrument in question.

(7)   Where an instrument is presented for payment under this section—

      (a)   any banker providing the electronic image,

      (b)   any banker to whom it is provided, and

      (c)   any banker making payment of the instrument as a result of provision of the electronic image,

are subject to the same duties in relation to collection and payment of the instrument as if the physical instrument had been presented.

This is subject to any provision made by or under this Part.

89B. Instruments to which section 89A applies

(1)   Subject to subsection (2), section 89A applies to—

      (a)   a cheque, or

      (b)   any other bill of exchange or any promissory note or other instrument—

          (i)   which appears to be intended by the person creating it to enable a person to obtain payment from a banker indicated in it of the sum so mentioned,

          (ii)   payment of which requires the instrument to be presented, and

          (iii)   which, but for section 89A, could not be presented otherwise than by presenting the physical instrument.

(2)   Section 89A does not apply to any banknote (within the meaning given in section 208 of the Banking Act 2009).

(3)   The reference in subsection (1) to the person creating an instrument is—

      (a)   in the case of a bill of exchange, a reference to the drawer;

      (b)   in the case of a promissory note, a reference to the maker.

(4)   For the purposes of subsection (1)(b)(i) an indication may be by code or number and need not indicate that payment is intended to be obtained from the banker.

89C. Banker's obligation in relation to accepting physical instrument for presentment

Provision of an electronic image of an instrument does not constitute presentment of the instrument under section 89A if the arrangements between—

      (a)   the banker authorised to collect payment of the instrument on behalf of a customer, and

      (b)   that customer,

do not permit the customer to pay in the physical instrument but instead require an electronic image to be provided (whether to that banker or to any other person).

89D. Copies of instruments and evidence of payment

(1)   The Treasury may by regulations make provision for—

      (a)   requiring a copy of an instrument paid as a result of presentment under section 89A to be provided, on request, to the creator of the instrument by the banker who paid the instrument;

      (b)   a copy of an instrument provided in accordance with the regulations to be evidence of receipt by a person identified in accordance with the regulations of the sum payable by the instrument.

(2)   Regulations under subsection (1)(a) may in particular—

      (a)   prescribe the manner and form in which a copy is to be provided;

      (b)   require the copy to be certified to be a true copy of the electronic image provided to the banker making the payment on presentment under section 89A;

      (c)   provide for the copy to be accompanied by prescribed information;

      (d)   require any copy to be provided free of charge or permit charges to be made for the provision of copies in prescribed circumstances.

(3)   The reference in subsection (1)(a) to the creator of the instrument is—

      (a)   in the case of a bill of exchange, a reference to the drawer;

      (b)   in the case of a promissory note, a reference to the maker.

89E. Compensation in cases of presentment by electronic means

(1) The Treasury may by regulations make provision for the responsible banker to compensate any person for any loss of a kind specified by the regulations which that person incurs in connection with electronic presentment or purported electronic presentment of an instrument.

(2) In this section 'electronic presentment or purported electronic presentment of an instrument' includes—

    (a) presentment of an instrument to which section 89A applies under that section;

    (b) presentment of any other instrument by any means involving provision of an electronic image by which it may be presented for payment;

    (c) purported presentment for payment by any means involving provision of an electronic image of an instrument that may not be presented for payment in that way;

    (d) provision, in purported presentment for payment, of—

        (i) an electronic image that purports to be, but is not, an image of a physical instrument (including an image that has been altered electronically), or

        (ii) an electronic image of an instrument which has no legal effect; or

    (e) provision, in presentment or purported presentment for payment, of an electronic image which has been stolen.

(3) In this section, the 'responsible banker', in relation to electronic presentment or purported electronic presentment of an instrument, means—

    (a) the banker who is authorised to collect payment of the instrument on a customer's behalf, or

    (b) if the holder of the instrument is a banker, that banker.

(4) In this section—

    (a) references to an instrument include references to an instrument which has no legal effect (whether because it has been fraudulently altered or created, or because it has been discharged, or otherwise);

    (b) in relation to an electronic image which is not an image of a physical instrument, references to the instrument are to a purported instrument (of which it purports to be an image); and

    (c) in relation to an instrument which is not a bill of exchange or promissory note, references to the holder are to the payee or indorsee of the instrument who is in possession of it or, if it is payable to bearer, the person in possession of it.

(5) Regulations under this section may in particular make provision for—

    (a) the responsible banker to be required to pay compensation irrespective of fault;

    (b) the amount of compensation to be reduced by virtue of anything done, or any failure to act, by the person to whom compensation is payable.

(6) Nothing in this section or regulations under it is to be taken to—

    (a) prevent the responsible banker claiming a contribution from any other person, or

    (b) affect any remedy available to the responsible banker in contract or otherwise.

(7) Except so far as regulations under this section provide expressly, nothing in this section or regulations under it is to be taken to affect any liability of the responsible banker which exists apart from this section or any such regulations.

89F. Supplementary

(1) Regulations under this Part may—

    (a) include incidental, supplementary and consequential provision;

    (b) make transitory or transitional provision or savings;

    (c) make different provision for different cases or circumstances or for different purposes;

    (d) make provision subject to exceptions.

(2) The power to make regulations under this Part is exercisable by statutory instrument.

(3) An instrument containing—

    (a) regulations under section 89A or 89D, or

    (b) the first regulations to be made under section 89E,

may not be made unless a draft of the instrument has been laid before, and approved by resolution of, each House of Parliament.

(4)   An instrument containing any other regulations under section 89E is subject to annulment in pursuance of a resolution of either House of Parliament.

(5)   For the purposes of this Part, a banker collects payment of an instrument on behalf of a customer by—

(a)   receiving payment of the instrument for the customer, or

(b)   receiving payment of the instrument for the banker (but not as holder), having—

(i)   credited the customer's account with the amount of the instrument, or

(ii)   otherwise given value to the customer in respect of the instrument.

(6)   Section 89E(4) applies for the purposes of subsection (5) in its application to section 89E.

PART V
SUPPLEMENTARY

90.   Good faith

A thing is deemed to be done in good faith, within the meaning of this Act, where it is in fact done honestly, whether it is done negligently or not.

91.   Signature

(1)   Where, by this Act, any instrument or writing is required to be signed by any person, it is not necessary that he should sign it with his own hand, but it is sufficient if his signature is written thereon by some other person by or under his authority.

(2)   In the case of a corporation, where, by this Act, any instrument or writing is required to be signed, it is sufficient if the instrument or writing be sealed with the corporate seal.

But nothing in this section shall be construed as requiring the bill or note of a corporation to be under seal.

92.   Computation of time

Where by this Act, the time limited for doing any act or thing is less than three days, in reckoning time, non-business days are excluded.

'Non-business days' for the purposes of this Act mean—

(a)   Saturday, Sunday, Good Friday, Christmas Day:

(b)   A bank holiday under the Banking and Financial Dealings Act 1971:

(c)   A day appointed by Royal proclamation as a public fast or thanksgiving day:

(d)   A day declared by an order under section 2 of the Banking and Financial Dealings Act 1971 to be a non-business day.

Any other day is a business day.

93.   When noting equivalent to protest

For the purposes of this Act, where a bill or note is required to be protested within a specified time or before some further proceeding is taken, it is sufficient that the bill has been noted for protest before the expiration of the specified time or the taking of the proceeding; and the formal protest may be extended at any time thereafter as of the date of the noting.

94.   Protest when notary not accessible

(1)   Where a dishonoured bill or note is authorised or required to be protested, and the services of a notary cannot be obtained at the place where the bill is dishonoured, any householder, or substantial resident of the place may, in the presence of two witnesses, give a certificate, signed by them, attesting to the dishonour of the bill, and the certificate shall in all respects operate as if it were a formal protest of the bill.

The form given in Schedule I to this Act may be used with necessary modifications, and if used shall be sufficient.

(2)   In subsection (1) 'notary' includes a person who, for the purposes of the Legal Services Act 2007, is an authorised person in relation to any activity which constitutes a notarial activity (within the meaning of that Act).

95.   Dividend warrants may be crossed

The provisions of this Act as to crossed cheques shall apply to a warrant for payment of dividend.

...

97.   Savings

    (1)   The rules in bankruptcy relating to bills of exchange, promissory notes, and cheques, shall continue to apply thereto notwithstanding anything in this Act contained.

    (2)   The rules of common law including the law merchant, save in so far as they are inconsistent with the express provisions of this Act, shall continue to apply to bills of exchange, promissory notes, and cheques—

    (3)   Nothing in this Act or in any repeal effected thereby shall affect—

        (a)   Any law or enactment for the time being in force relating to the revenue:

        (b)   The provisions of the Companies Act, 1862, or Acts amending it, or any Act relating to joint stock banks or companies:

        (c)   The provisions of any Act relating to or confirming the privileges of the Bank of England or the Bank of Ireland respectively:

        (d)   The validity of any usage relating to dividend warrants, or the indorsements thereof.

98.   Saving of summary diligence in Scotland

Nothing in this Act or in any repeal effected thereby shall extend or restrict, or in any way alter the law and practice in Scotland in regard to summary diligence.

99.   Construction with other Acts, etc.

Where any Act or document refers to any enactment repealed by this Act, the Act or document shall be construed, and shall operate as if it referred to the corresponding provisions of this Act.

100.   Parole evidence allowed in certain judicial proceedings in Scotland

In any judicial proceeding in Scotland, any fact relating to a bill of exchange, bank cheque, or promissory note, which is relevant to any question of liability thereon, may be proved by parole evidence: Provided that this enactment shall not in any way affect the existing law and practice whereby the party who is, according to the tenor of any bill of exchange, bank cheque, or promissory note, debtor to the holder in the amount thereof, may be required, as a condition of obtaining a sist of diligence, or suspension of a charge, or threatened charge, to make such consignation, or to find such caution as the court or judge before whom the cause is depending may require.

SCHEDULES

Section 94

FIRST SCHEDULE

Form of protest which may be used when the services of a notary cannot be obtained.

Know all men that I, *A. B.* householder, of in the county of in the United Kingdom, at the request of *C. D.*, there being no notary public available, did on the day of 188 at _____ demand payment *or* acceptance of the bill of exchange hereunder written, from *E. F.*, to which demand he made answer [state answer, if any] wherefore I now, in the presence of *G. H.* and *J. K.* do protest the said bill of exchange.

                    (Signed) A. B.

                        G. H.⎱ *Witnesses*
                        J. K.⎰

N.B.—The bill itself should be annexed, or a copy of the bill and all that is written thereon should be underwritten.

FACTORS ACT 1889
(52 & 53 Vict., c. 45)

Preliminary

1.   **Definitions**

For the purposes of this Act—

(1)   The expression 'mercantile agent' shall mean a mercantile agent having in the customary course of his business as such agent authority either to sell goods or to consign goods for the purpose of sale, or to buy goods, or to raise money on the security of goods:

(2)   A person shall be deemed to be in possession of goods or of the documents of title to goods, where the goods or documents are in the actual custody or are held by any other person subject to his control or for him or on his behalf:

(3)   The expression 'goods' shall include wares and merchandise:

(4)   The expression 'document of title' shall include any bill of lading, dock warrant, warehouse-keeper's certificate, and warrant or order for the delivery of goods, and any other document used in the ordinary course of business as proof of the possession or control of goods, or authorising or purporting to authorise, either by endorsement or by delivery, the possessor of the document to transfer or receive goods thereby represented:

(5)   The expression 'pledge' shall include any contract pledging, or giving a lien or security on, goods, whether in consideration of an original advance or of any further or continuing advance or of any pecuniary liability:

(6)   The expression 'person' shall include any body of persons corporate or unincorporate.

Dispositions by mercantile agents

2.   **Powers of mercantile agent with respect to disposition of goods**

(1)   Where a mercantile agent is, with the consent of the owner, in possession of goods or of the documents of title to goods, any sale, pledge, or other disposition of the goods, made by him when acting in the ordinary course of business of a mercantile agent, shall, subject to the provisions of this Act, be as valid as if he were expressly authorised by the owner of the goods to make the same; provided that the person taking under the disposition acts in good faith, and has not at the time of the disposition notice that the person making the disposition has not authority to make the same.

(2)   Where a mercantile agent has, with the consent of the owner, been in possession of goods or of the documents of title to goods, any sale, pledge, or other disposition, which would have been valid if the consent had continued, shall be valid notwithstanding the determination of the consent; provided that the person taking under the disposition has not at the time thereof notice that the consent has been determined.

(3)   Where a mercantile agent has obtained possession of any documents of title to goods by reason of his being or having been, with the consent of the owner, in possession of the goods represented thereby, or of any other documents of title to the goods, his possession of the first-mentioned documents shall, for the purposes of this Act, be deemed to be with the consent of the owner.

(4)   For the purposes of this Act the consent of the owner shall be presumed in the absence of evidence to the contrary.

3.   **Effect of pledges of documents of title**

A pledge of the documents of title to goods shall be deemed to be a pledge of the goods.

4.   **Pledge for antecedent debt**

Where a mercantile agent pledges goods as security for a debt or liability due from the pledgor to the pledgee before the time of the pledge, the pledgee shall acquire no further right to the goods than could have been enforced by the pledgor at the time of the pledge.

5.   **Rights acquired by exchange of goods or documents**

The consideration necessary for the validity of a sale, pledge, or other disposition of goods, in pursuance of this Act, may be either a payment in cash, or the delivery or transfer of other goods, or of a document of title to goods, or of a negotiable security, or any other valuable consideration; but where goods are pledged by a mercantile agent in consideration of the delivery or transfer of other goods, or of a document of title to goods, or of a negotiable security, the pledgee shall acquire no right or interest in the goods so pledged in excess of the value of the goods, documents, or security when so delivered or transferred in exchange.

6.   Agreements through clerks, &c.

For the purposes of this Act an agreement made with a mercantile agent through a clerk or other person authorised in the ordinary course of business to make contracts of sale or pledge on his behalf shall be deemed to be an agreement with the agent.

7.   Provisions as to consignors and consignees

(1)   Where the owner of goods has given possession of the goods to another person for the purpose of consignment or sale, or has shipped the goods in the name of another person, and the consignee of the goods has not had notice that such person is not the owner of the goods, the consignee shall, in respect of advances made to or for the use of such person, have the same lien on the goods as if such person were the owner of the goods, and may transfer any such lien to another person.

(2)   Nothing in this section shall limit or affect the validity of any sale, pledge, or disposition, by a mercantile agent.

Dispositions by sellers and buyers of goods

8.   Disposition by seller remaining in possession

Where a person, having sold goods, continues, or is, in possession of the goods or of the documents of title to the goods, the delivery or transfer by that person, or by a mercantile agent acting for him, of the goods or documents of title under any sale, pledge, or other disposition thereof, or under any agreement for sale, pledge, or other disposition thereof, to any person receiving the same in good faith and without notice of the previous sale, shall have the same effect as if the person making the delivery or transfer were expressly authorised by the owner of the goods to make the same.

9.   Disposition by buyer obtaining possession

Where a person, having bought or agreed to buy goods, obtains with the consent of the seller possession of the goods or the documents of title to the goods, the delivery or transfer, by that person or by a mercantile agent acting for him, of the goods or documents of title under any sale, pledge, or other disposition thereof, or under any agreement for sale, pledge, or other disposition thereof, to any person receiving the same in good faith and without notice of any lien or other right of the original seller in respect of the goods, shall have the same effect as if the person making the delivery or transfer were a mercantile agent in possession of the goods or documents of title with the consent of the owner.

For the purposes of this section—

(i)   the buyer under a conditional sale agreement shall be deemed not to be a person who has bought or agreed to buy goods, and

(ii)   'conditional sale agreement' means an agreement for the sale of goods which is a consumer credit agreement within the meaning of the Consumer Credit Act 1974 under which the purchase price or part of it is payable in instalments, and the property in the goods is to remain in the seller (notwithstanding that the buyer is to be in possession of the goods) until such conditions as to the payment of instalments or otherwise as may be specified in the agreement are fulfilled.

10.   Effect of transfer of documents on vendor's lien or right of stoppage in transitu

Where a document of title to goods has been lawfully transferred to a person as a buyer or owner of the goods, and that person transfers the document to a person who takes the document in good faith and for valuable consideration, the last-mentioned transfer shall have the same effect for defeating any vendor's lien or right of stoppage in transitu as the transfer of a bill of lading has for defeating the right of stoppage in transitu.

Supplemental

11.   Mode of transferring documents

For the purposes of this Act, the transfer of a document may be by endorsement, or, where the document is by custom or by its express terms transferable by delivery or makes the goods deliverable to the bearer, then by delivery.

12.   Saving for rights of true owner

(1)   Nothing in this Act shall authorise an agent to exceed or depart from his authority as between himself and his principal, or exempt him from any liability, civil or criminal, for so doing.

(2)   Nothing in this Act shall prevent the owner of goods from recovering the goods from any agent or his trustee in bankruptcy at any time before the sale or pledge thereof, or shall prevent the owner of goods pledged by an agent from having the right to redeem the goods at any time before the sale thereof, on satisfying the claim for which the goods were pledged, and paying to the agent, if by him required, any money in respect of which the agent would by law be entitled to retain the goods or the documents of title thereto, or any of them, by way of lien as against the owner, or from recovering from any person with whom the goods have been pledged any balance of money remaining in his hands as the produce of the sale of the goods after deducting the amount of his lien.

(3)   Nothing in this Act shall prevent the owner of goods sold by an agent from recovering from the buyer the price agreed to be paid for the same, or any part of that price, subject to any right of set off on the part of the buyer against the agent.

13.   Saving for common law powers of agent

The provisions of this Act shall be construed in amplification and not in derogation of the powers exercisable by an agent independently of this Act.

16.   Extent of Act

This Act shall not extend to Scotland.

17.   Short title

This Act may be cited as the Factors Act, 1889.

CHEQUES ACT 1957
(5 & 6 Eliz. 2, c. 36)

1.   Protection of bankers paying unindorsed or irregularly indorsed cheques, etc.

(1)   Where a banker in good faith and in the ordinary course of business pays a cheque drawn on him which is not indorsed or is irregularly indorsed, he does not in doing so, incur any liability by reason only of the absence of, or irregularity in indorsement, and he is deemed to have paid it in due course.

(2)   Where a banker in good faith and in the ordinary course of business pays any such instrument as the following namely—

(a)   a document issued by a customer of his which, though not a bill of exchange, is intended to enable a person to obtain payment from him of the sum mentioned in the document;

(b)   a draft payable on demand drawn by him upon himself, whether payable at the head office or some other office of his bank; he does not, in so doing, incur any liability by reason only of the absence of, or irregularity in, indorsement, and the payment discharges the instrument.

2.   Rights of bankers collecting cheques not indorsed by holders

A banker who gives value for, or has a lien on, a cheque payable to order which the holder delivers to him for collection without indorsing it, has such (if any) rights as he would have had if, upon delivery, the holder had indorsed it in blank.

3.   Unindorsed cheques as evidence of payment

(1)   An unindorsed cheque which appears to have been paid by the banker on whom it is drawn is evidence of the receipt by the payee of the sum payable by the cheque.

(2)   For the purposes of subsection (1) above, a copy of a cheque to which that subsection applies is evidence of the cheque if—

(a)   the copy is made by the banker in whose possession the cheque is after presentment and,

(b)   it is certified by him to be a true copy of the original.

4.   Protection of bankers collecting payment of cheques, &c.

(1)   Where a banker, in good faith and without negligence—

(a)   receives payment for a customer of an instrument to which this section applies; or

(b)   having credited a customer's account with the amount of such an instrument, receives payment thereof for himself;

and the customer has no title, or a defective title, to the instrument, the banker does not incur any liability to the true owner of the instrument by reason only of having received payment thereof.

(2)   This section applies to the following instruments, namely:—

(a)   cheques (including cheques which under section 81A(1) of the Bills of Exchange Act 1882 or otherwise are not transferable);

(b)   any document issued by a customer of a banker which, though not a bill of exchange, is intended to enable a person to obtain payment from that banker of the sum mentioned in the document;

(c)   any document issued by a public officer is intended to enable a person to obtain payment from the Paymaster General or the Queen's and Lord Treasurer's Remembrancer of the sum mentioned in the document but is not a bill of exchange;

(d)   any draft payable on demand drawn by a banker upon himself whether payable at the head office or some other office of his bank.

(3)   A banker is not to be treated for the purposes of this section as having been negligent by reason only of his failure to concern himself with absence of, or irregularity in, indorsement of an instrument.

5.   Application of certain provisions of Bills of Exchange Act, 1882, to instruments not being bills of exchange

The provisions of the Bills of Exchange Act, 1882, relating to crossed cheques shall, so far as applicable, have effect in relation to instruments (other than cheques) to which the last foregoing section applies as they have effect in relation to cheques.

6.   Construction, saving and repeal

(1)   This Act shall be construed as one with the Bills of Exchange Act, 1882.

(2)   The foregoing provisions of this Act do not make negotiable any instrument which, apart from them, is not negotiable.

...

7.   Provisions as to Northern Ireland

This Act extends to Northern Ireland, ...

8.   Short title and commencement

(1)   This Act may be cited as the Cheques Act, 1957.

(2)   This Act shall come into operation at the expiration of a period of three months beginning with the day on which it is passed.

HIRE-PURCHASE ACT 1964
(1964, c. 53)

PART III
TITLE TO MOTOR VEHICLES ON HIRE-PURCHASE OR CONDITIONAL SALE

27. Protection of purchasers of motor vehicles

(1) This section applies where a motor vehicle has been bailed or (in Scotland) hired under a hire-purchase agreement, or has been agreed to be sold under a conditional sale agreement, and, before the property in the vehicle has become vested in the debtor, he disposes of the vehicle to another person.

(2) Where the disposition referred to in subsection (1) above is to a private purchaser, and he is a purchaser of the motor vehicle in good faith without notice of the hire-purchase or conditional sale agreement (the 'relevant agreement') that disposition shall have effect as if the creditor's title to the vehicle has been vested in the debtor immediately before that disposition.

(3) Where the person to whom the disposition referred to in subsection (1) above is made (the 'original purchaser') is a trade or finance purchaser, then if the person who is the first private purchaser of the motor vehicle after that disposition (the 'first private purchaser') is a purchaser of the vehicle in good faith without notice of the relevant agreement, the disposition of the vehicle to the first private purchaser shall have effect as if the title of the creditor to the vehicle had been vested in the debtor immediately before he disposed of it to the original purchaser.

(4) Where, in a case within subsection (3) above—

    (a) the disposition by which the first private purchaser becomes a purchaser of the motor vehicle in good faith without notice of the relevant agreement is itself a bailment or hiring under a hire-purchase agreement, and

    (b) the person who is the creditor in relation to that agreement disposes of the vehicle to the first private purchaser, or a person claiming under him, by transferring to him the property in the vehicle in pursuance of a provision in the agreement in that behalf, the disposition referred to in paragraph (b) above (whether or not the person to whom it is made is a purchaser in good faith without notice of the relevant agreement) shall as well as the disposition referred to in paragraph (a) above, have effect as mentioned in subsection (3) above.

(5) The preceding provisions of this section apply—

    (a) notwithstanding anything in section 21 of the Sale of Goods Act 1979 (sale of goods by a person not the owner), but

    (b) without prejudice to the provisions of the Factors Acts (as defined by section 61(1) of the said Act of 1979) or any other enactment enabling the apparent owner of goods to dispose of them as if he were the true owner.

(6) Nothing in this section shall exonerate the debtor from any liability (whether criminal or civil) to which he would be subject apart from this section; and, in a case where the debtor disposes of the motor vehicle to a trade or finance purchaser, nothing in this section shall exonerate—

    (a) that trade or finance purchaser, or

    (b) any other trade or finance purchaser who becomes a purchaser of the vehicle and is not a person claiming under the first private purchaser,

from any liability (whether criminal or civil) to which he would be subject apart from this section.

28. Presumptions relating to dealings with motor vehicles

(1) Where in any proceedings (whether criminal or civil) relating to a motor vehicle it is proved—

    (a) that the vehicle was bailed or (in Scotland) hired under a hire-purchase agreement, or was agreed to be sold under a conditional sale agreement and

    (b) that a person (whether a party to the proceedings or not) became a private purchaser of the vehicle in good faith without notice of the hire-purchase or conditional sale agreement (the 'relevant agreement'), this section shall have effect for the purposes of the operation of section 27 of this Act in relation to those proceedings.

(2) It shall be presumed for those purposes unless the contrary is proved, that the disposition of the vehicle to the person referred to in subsection (1)(b) above (the 'relevant purchaser') was made by the debtor.

(3) If it is proved that that disposition was not made by the debtor, then it shall be presumed for those purposes, unless the contrary is proved—

(a) that the debtor disposed of the vehicle to a private purchaser purchasing in good faith without notice of the relevant agreement, and

(b) that the relevant purchaser is or was a person claiming under the person to whom the debtor so disposed of the vehicle.

(4) If it is proved that the disposition of the vehicle to the relevant purchaser was not made by the debtor, and that the person to whom the debtor disposed of the vehicle (the 'original purchaser') was a trade or finance purchaser, then it shall be presumed for those purposes, unless the contrary is proved,

(a) that the person who, after the disposition of the vehicle to the original purchaser, first became a private purchaser of the vehicle was a purchaser in good faith without notice of the relevant agreement, and

(b) that the relevant purchaser is or was a person claiming under the original purchaser.

(5) Without prejudice to any other method of proof, where in any proceedings a party thereto admits a fact, that fact shall, for the purposes of this section, be taken as against him to be proved in relation to those proceedings.

29. Interpretation of Part III

(1) In this Part of this Act—

'conditional sale agreement' means an agreement for the sale of goods under which the purchase price or part of it is payable by instalments, and the property in the goods is to remain in the seller (notwithstanding that the buyer is to be in possession of the goods) until such conditions as to the payment of instalments or otherwise as may be specified in the agreement are fulfilled;

'creditor' means the person by whom goods are bailed or (in Scotland) hired under a hire-purchase agreement or as the case may be, the seller under a conditional sale agreement, or the person to whom his rights and duties have passed by assignment or operation of law;

'disposition' means any sale or contract of sale (including a conditional sale agreement), any bailment or (in Scotland) hiring under a hire-purchase agreement and any transfer of the property of goods in pursuance of a provision in that behalf contained in a hire-purchase agreement, and includes any transaction purporting to be a disposition (as so defined), and 'dispose of' shall be construed accordingly:

'hire-purchase agreement' means an agreement, other than a conditional sale agreement, under which—

(a) goods are bailed or (in Scotland) hired in return for periodical payments by the person to whom they are bailed or hired, and

(b) the property in the goods will pass to that person if the terms of the agreement are complied with and one or more of the following occurs—

(i) the exercise of an option to purchase by that person,

(ii) the doing of any other specified act by any party to the agreement,

(iii) the happening of any other specified events; and

'motor vehicle' means a mechanically propelled vehicle intended or adapted for use on roads to which the public has access.

(2) In this Part of this Act 'trade or finance purchaser' means a purchaser who, at the time of the disposition made to him, carries on a business which consists, wholly or partly—

(a) of purchasing motor vehicles for the purpose of offering or exposing them for sale, or

(b)   of providing finance by purchasing motor vehicles for the purpose of bailing or (in Scotland) hiring them under hire-purchase agreements or agreeing to sell them under conditional sale agreements,

and 'private purchaser' means a purchaser who, at the time of the disposition made to him, does not carry on any such business.

(3)   For the purposes of this Part of this Act a person becomes a purchaser of a motor vehicle if, and at the time when, a disposition of the vehicle is made to him; and a person shall be taken to be a purchaser of a motor vehicle without notice of a hire-purchase agreement or conditional sale agreement if, at the time of the disposition made to him, he has no actual notice that the vehicle is or was the subject of any such agreement.

(4)   In this Part of this Act the 'debtor' in relation to a motor vehicle which has been bailed or hired under a hire-purchase agreement, or, as the case may be, agreed to be sold under a conditional sale agreement, means the person who at the material time (whether the agreement has before that time been terminated or not) either—

(a)   is the person to whom the vehicle is bailed or hired under that agreement, or

(b)   is, in relation to the agreement, the buyer,

including a person who at that time is, by virtue of section 130(4) of the Consumer Credit Act 1974 treated as a bailee or (in Scotland) a custodier of the vehicle.

(5)   In this Part of this Act any reference to the title of the creditor to a motor vehicle which has been bailed or (in Scotland) hired under a hire-purchase agreement or agreed to be sold under a conditional sale agreement, and is disposed of by the debtor, is a reference to such title (if any) to the vehicle as, immediately before that disposition, was vested in the person who then was the creditor in relation to the agreement.

SUPPLY OF GOODS (IMPLIED TERMS) ACT 1973
(1973, c. 13)

8.   Implied terms as title

(1)   In every relevant hire-purchase agreement, other than one to which subsection (2) below applies, there is—

(a)   an implied term on the part of the creditor that he will have a right to sell the goods at the time when the property is to pass; and

(b)   an implied term that—

(i)   the goods are free, and will remain free until the time when the property is to pass, from any charge or encumbrance not disclosed or known to the person to whom the goods are bailed or (in Scotland) hired before the agreement is made, and

(ii)   that person will enjoy quiet possession of the goods except so far as it may be disturbed by any person entitled to the benefit of any charge or encumbrance so disclosed or known.

(2)   In a relevant hire-purchase agreement, in the case of which there appears from the agreement or is to be inferred from the circumstances of the agreement an intention that the creditor should transfer only such title as he or a third person may have, there is—

(a)   an implied term that all charges or encumbrances known to the creditor and not known to the person to whom the goods are bailed or hired have been disclosed to that person before the agreement is made; and

(b)   an implied term that neither—

(i)   the creditor; nor

(ii)   in a case where the parties to the agreement intend that any title which may be transferred shall be only such title as a third person may have, that person; nor

(iii) anyone claiming through or under the creditor or that third person not otherwise than under a charge or encumbrance disclosed or known to the person to whom the goods are bailed or hired, before the agreement is made; will disturb the quiet possession of the person to whom the goods are bailed or hired.

(3) As regards England and Wales and Northern Ireland, the term implied by subsection (1)(a) above is a condition and the terms implied by subsections (1)(b), (2)(a) and (2)(b) above are warranties.

9. Bailing or hiring by description

(1) Where under a relevant hire-purchase agreement goods are bailed or (in Scotland) hired by description, there is an implied term that the goods will correspond with the description, and if under the agreement the goods are bailed or hired by reference to a sample as well as a description, it is not sufficient that the bulk of the goods corresponds with the sample if the goods do not also correspond with the description.

(1A) As regards England and Wales and Northern Ireland, the term implied by subsection 1) above is a condition.

(2) Goods shall not be prevented from being bailed or hired by description by reason only that, being exposed for sale, bailment or hire, they are selected by the person to whom they are bailed or hired.

10. Implied undertakings as to quality or fitness

(1) Except as provided by this section and section 11 below and subject to the provisions of any other enactment, including any enactment of the Parliament of Northern Ireland or the Northern Ireland Assembly, there is no implied term as to the quality or fitness for any particular purpose of goods bailed or (in Scotland) hired under a relevant hire-purchase agreement.

(2) Where the creditor bails or hires goods under a relevant hire purchase agreement in the course of a business, there is an implied term that the goods supplied under the agreement are of satisfactory quality.

(2A) For the purposes of this Act, goods are of satisfactory quality if they meet the standard that a reasonable person would regard as satisfactory, taking account of any description of the goods, the price (if relevant) and all the other relevant circumstances.

(2B) For the purposes of this Act, the quality of goods includes their state and condition and the following (among others) are in appropriate cases aspects of the quality of goods—
(a) fitness for all the purposes for which goods of the kind in question are commonly supplied,
(b) appearance and finish,
(c) freedom from minor defects,
(d) safety, and
(e) durability.

(2C) The term implied by subsection (2) above does not extend to any matter making the quality of goods unsatisfactory—
(a) which is specifically drawn to the attention of the person to whom the goods are bailed or hired before the agreement is made,
(b) where that person examines the goods before the agreement is made, which that examination ought to reveal, or
(c) where the goods are bailed or hired by reference to a sample, which would have been apparent on a reasonable examination of the sample.

(3) Where the creditor bails or hires goods under a relevant hire-purchase agreement in the course of a business and the person to whom the goods are bailed or hired, expressly or by implication, makes known—
(a) to the creditor in the course of negotiations conducted by the creditor in relation to the making of the hire-purchase agreement, or
(b) to a credit-broker in the course of negotiations conducted by that broker in relation to goods sold by him to the creditor before forming the subject matter of the hire-purchase agreement,
any particular purpose for which the goods are being bailed or hired, there is an implied term that the goods supplied under the agreement are reasonably fit for that purpose, whether or not that is a purpose for which such goods are commonly supplied, except where the circumstances show that the person to whom the goods are bailed or hired does not rely, or that it is unreasonable for him to rely, on the skill or judgment of the creditor or credit-broker.

(4)   An implied term as to quality or fitness for a particular purpose may be annexed to a relevant hire-purchase agreement by usage.

(5)   The preceding provisions of this section apply to a relevant hire-purchase agreement made by a person who in the course of a business is acting as agent for the creditor as they apply to an agreement made by the creditor in the course of a business, except where the creditor is not bailing or hiring in the course of a business and either the person to whom the goods are bailed or hired knows that fact or reasonable steps are taken to bring it to the notice of that person before the agreement is made.

(6)   In subsection (3) above and this subsection—
    (a)   'credit-broker' means a person acting in the course of a business of credit brokerage;
    (b)   'credit brokerage' means the effecting of introductions of individuals desiring to obtain credit—
        (i)   to persons carrying on any business so far as it relates to the provision of credit, or
        (ii)   to other persons engaged in credit brokerage.

(7)   As regards England and Wales and Northern Ireland, the terms implied by subsections (2) and (3) above are conditions.

11.   Samples

(1)   Where under a relevant hire-purchase agreement goods are bailed or (in Scotland) hired by reference to a sample, there is an implied term—
    (a)   that the bulk will correspond with the sample in quality; and
    (b)   that the person to whom the goods are bailed or hired will have a reasonable opportunity of comparing the bulk with the sample; and
    (c)   that the goods will be free from any defect, making their quality unsatisfactory, which would not be apparent on reasonable examination of the sample.

(2)   As regards England and Wales and Northern Ireland, the term implied by subsection (1) above is a condition.

11A.   Modification of remedies for breach of statutory condition in non-consumer cases

(1)   Where in the case of a relevant hire purchase agreement—
    (a)   the person to whom goods are bailed would, apart from this subsection, have the right to reject them by reason of a breach on the part of the creditor of a term implied by section 9, 10 or 11(1)(a) or (c) above, but
    (b)   the breach is so slight that it would be unreasonable for him to reject them,
    the breach is not to be treated as a breach of condition but may be treated as a breach of warranty.

(2)   This section applies unless a contrary intention appears in, or is to be implied from, the agreement.

(3)   It is for the creditor to show—
    (a)   that a breach fell within subsection (1)(b) above, and
    (b)   that the agreement was a relevant hire-purchase agreement.

(5)   This section does not apply to Scotland.

12.   Exclusion of implied terms

An express term does not negative a term implied by this Act unless inconsistent with it.

15.   Supplementary

(1)   In sections 8 to 14 above and this section—
'business' includes a profession and the activities of any government department (including a Northern Ireland department), or local or public authority;
'buyer' and 'seller' includes a person to whom rights and duties under a conditional sale agreement have passed by assignment or operation of law;
'conditional sale agreement' means an agreement for the sale of goods under which the purchase price or part of it is payable by instalments, and the property in the goods is to remain in the seller (notwithstanding that the buyer is to be in possession of the goods) until such conditions as to the payment of instalments or otherwise as may be specified in the agreement are fulfilled;

'consumer sale' has the same meaning as in section 55 of the Sale of Goods Act 1979 (as set out in paragraph 11 of Schedule 1 to that Act);

'creditor' means the person by whom the goods are bailed or (in Scotland) hired under a relevant hire-purchase agreement or the person to whom his rights and duties under the agreement have passed by assignment or operation of law; and

'hire-purchase agreement' means an agreement, other than conditional sale agreement, under which—

    (a)   goods are bailed or (in Scotland) hired in return for periodical payments by the person to whom they are bailed or hired, and

    (b)   the property in the goods will pass to that person if the terms of the agreement are complied with and one or more of the following occurs—

        (i)   the exercise of an option to purchase by that person,

        (ii)   the doing of any other specified act by any party to the agreement,

        (iii)   the happening of any other specified event, and a hire–purchase agreement is relevant if it is not a contract to which Chapter 2 of Part 1 of the Consumer Rights Act 2015 applies.

(4)   Nothing in sections 8 to 13 above shall prejudice the operation of any other enactment including any enactment of the Parliament of Northern Ireland or the Northern Ireland Assembly or any rule of law whereby any term, other than one relating to quality or fitness, is to be implied in any relevant hire-purchase agreement.

CONSUMER CREDIT ACT 1974
(1974, c. 39)

PART II
CREDIT AGREEMENTS, HIRE AGREEMENTS AND LINKED TRANSACTIONS

8.   Consumer credit agreements

(1)   A consumer credit agreement is an agreement between an individual ('the debtor') and any other person ('the creditor') by which the creditor provides the debtor with credit of any amount.

(2)   ...

(3)   A consumer credit agreement is a regulated credit agreement for the purposes of this Act if it—

    (a)   is a regulated credit agreement for the purpose of Chapter 14A of Part 2 of the Regulated Activities Order; and

    (b)   if entered into on or after 21st March 2016, is not an agreement the purpose of which is the acquisition or retention, by an individual acting for purposes outside of any trade, business or profession carried on by the individual, of property rights in land or in an existing or projected building.

(3A)   A reference in paragraph (3)(b) to any land or building—

    (a)   in relation to an agreement entered into before exit day, is a reference to any land or building in the United Kingdom or within the territory of an EEA State;

    (b)   in relation to an agreement entered into on or after exit day, is a reference to any land or building in the United Kingdom.

(4)   Subsection (1) does not apply in relation to an agreement that is a green deal plan (see instead section 189B).

9.   Meaning of credit

(1)   In this Act 'credit' includes a cash loan, and any other form of financial accommodation.

(2)   Where credit is provided otherwise than in sterling it shall be treated for the purposes of this Act as provided in sterling of an equivalent amount.

(3)   Without prejudice to the generality of subsection (1), the person by whom goods are bailed or (in Scotland) hired to an individual under a hire-purchase agreement shall be taken to provide him with fixed-sum credit to finance the transaction of an amount equal to the total price of the goods less the aggregate of the deposit (if any) and the total charge for credit.

(4)   For the purposes of this Act, an item entering into the total charge for credit shall not be treated as credit even though time is allowed for its payment.

10.   Running-account credit and fixed-sum credit

(1)   For the purposes of this Act—

(a)   running-account credit is a facility under a consumer credit agreement whereby the debtor is enabled to receive from time to time (whether in his own person, or by another person) from the creditor or a third party cash, goods and services (or any of them) to an amount or value such that, taking into account payments made by or to the credit of the debtor, the credit limit (if any) is not at any time exceeded; and

(b)   fixed-sum credit is any other facility under a consumer credit agreement whereby the debtor is enabled to receive credit (whether in one amount or by instalments).

(2)   In relation to running-account credit, 'credit limit' means, as respects any period, the maximum debit balance which, under the credit agreement, is allowed to stand on the account during that period, disregarding any term of the agreement allowing that maximum to be exceeded merely temporarily.

(3)   For the purposes of any provision of this Act that specifies an amount of credit (except section 17(1)(a)), running-account credit shall be taken not to exceed the amount specified in that provision ('the specified amount') if—

(a)   the credit limit does not exceed the specified amount; or

(b)   whether or not there is a credit limit, and if there is, notwithstanding that it exceeds the specified amount,—

(i)   the debtor is not enabled to draw at any one time an amount which, so far as (having regard to section 9(4)) it represents credit, exceeds the specified amount, or

(ii)   the agreement provides that, if the debit balance rises above a given amount (not exceeding the specified amount), the rate of the total charge for credit increases or any other condition favouring the creditor or his associate comes into operation, or

(iii) at the time the agreement is made it is probable, having regard to the terms of the agreement and any other relevant considerations, that the debit balance will not at any time rise above the specified amount.

11.   Restricted-use credit and unrestricted-use credit

(1)   A restricted-use credit agreement is a regulated consumer credit agreement—

(a)   to finance a transaction between the debtor and the creditor, whether forming part of that agreement or not, or

(b)   to finance a transaction between the debtor and a person (the 'supplier') other than the creditor, or

(c)   to refinance any existing indebtedness of the debtor's, whether to the creditor or another person, and 'restricted-use credit' shall be construed accordingly.

(2)   An unrestricted-use credit agreement is a regulated consumer credit agreement not falling within subsection (1), and 'unrestricted-use credit' shall be construed accordingly.

(3)   An agreement does not fall within subsection (1) if the credit is in fact provided in such a way as to leave the debtor free to use it as he chooses, even though certain uses would contravene that or any other agreement.

(4)   An agreement may fall within subsection (1)(b) although the identity of the supplier is unknown at the time the agreement is made.

12.   Debtor-creditor-supplier agreements

A debtor-creditor-supplier agreement is a regulated consumer credit agreement being—

(a)   a restricted-use credit agreement which falls within section 11(1)(a), or

(b)   a restricted-use credit agreement which falls within section 11(1)(b) and is made by the creditor under pre-existing arrangements, or in contemplation of future arrangements, between himself and the supplier, or

(c)   an unrestricted-use credit agreement which is made by the creditor under pre-existing arrangements between himself and a person (the 'supplier') other than the debtor in the knowledge that the credit is to be used to finance a transaction between the debtor and the supplier.

13.   Debtor-creditor agreements

A debtor-creditor agreement is a regulated consumer credit agreement being—

(a)   a restricted-use credit agreement which falls within section 11(1)(b) but is not made by the creditor under pre-existing arrangements, or in contemplation of future arrangements, between himself and the supplier, or

(b)   a restricted-use credit agreement which falls within section 11(1)(c), or

(c)   an unrestricted-use credit agreement which is not made by the creditor under pre-existing arrangements between himself and a person (the 'supplier') other than the debtor in the knowledge that the credit is to be used to finance a transaction between the debtor and the supplier.

14.   Credit-token agreements

(1)   A credit-token is a card, check, voucher, coupon, stamp, form, booklet or other document or thing given to an individual by a person carrying on a consumer credit business, who undertakes—

(a)   that on the production of it (whether or not some other action is also required) he will supply cash, goods and services (or any of them) on credit, or

(b)   that where, on the production of it to a third party (whether or not any other action is also required), the third party supplies cash, goods and services (or any of them), he will pay the third party for them (whether or not deducting any discount or commission), in return for payment to him by the individual.

(2)   A credit-token agreement is a regulated agreement for the provision of credit in connection with the use of a credit-token.

(3)   Without prejudice to the generality of section 9(1), the person who gives to an individual an undertaking falling within subsection (1)(b) shall be taken to provide him with credit drawn on whenever a third party supplies him with cash, goods or services.

(4)   For the purposes of subsection (1), use of an object to operate a machine provided by the person giving the object or a third party shall be treated as the production of the object to him.

15.   Consumer hire agreements

(1)   A consumer hire agreement is an agreement made by a person with an individual (the 'hirer') for the bailment or (in Scotland) the hiring of goods to the hirer, being an agreement which—

(a)   is not a hire-purchase agreement, and

(b)   is capable of subsisting for more than three months,

(c)   ...

(2)   A consumer hire agreement is a regulated agreement within the meaning of this Act if it is a regulated consumer hire agreement for the purposes of Chapter 14B of Part 2 of the Regulated Activities Order.

17.   Small agreements

(1)   A small agreement is—

(a)   a regulated consumer credit agreement for credit not exceeding £50, other than a hire-purchase or conditional sale agreement; or

(b)   a regulated consumer hire agreement which does not require the hirer to make payments exceeding £50,

being an agreement which is either unsecured or secured by a guarantee or indemnity only (whether or not the guarantee or indemnity is itself secured).

(2)   For the purposes of paragraph (a) of subsection (1), running-account credit shall be taken not to exceed the amount specified in that paragraph if the credit limit does not exceed that amount.

(3)   Where—

(a)   two or more small agreements are made at or about the same time between the same parties, and

(b)   it appears probable that they would instead have been made as a single agreement but for the desire to avoid the operation of provisions of this Act which would have applied to that single agreement but, apart from this subsection, are not applicable to the small agreements,

this Act applies to the small agreements as if they were regulated agreements other than small agreements.

(4) If, apart from this subsection, subsection (3) does not apply to any agreements but would apply if, for any party or parties to any of the agreements, there were substituted an associate of that party, or associates of each of those parties, as the case may be, then subsection (3) shall apply to the agreements.

18. Multiple agreements

(1) This section applies to an agreement (a 'multiple agreement') if its terms are such as—

    (a) to place a part of it within one category of agreement mentioned in this Act, and another part of it within a different category of agreement so mentioned, or within a category of agreement not so mentioned, or

    (b) to place it, or a part of it, within two or more categories of agreement so mentioned.

(2) Where a part of an agreement falls within subsection (1), that part shall be treated for the purposes of this Act as a separate agreement.

(3) Where an agreement falls within subsection (1)(b), it shall be treated as an agreement in each of the categories in question, and this Act shall apply to it accordingly.

(4) Where under subsection (2) a part of a multiple agreement is to be treated as a separate agreement, the multiple agreement shall (with any necessary modifications) be construed accordingly; and any sum payable under the multiple agreement, if not apportioned by the parties, shall for the purposes of proceedings in any court relating to the multiple agreement be apportioned by the court as may be requisite.

(5) In the case of an agreement for running-account credit, a term of the agreement allowing the credit limit to be exceeded merely temporarily shall not be treated as a separate agreement or as providing fixed-sum credit in respect of the excess.

(6) This Act does not apply to a multiple agreement so far as the agreement relates to goods if under the agreement payments are to be made in respect of the goods in the form of rent (other than a rentcharge) issuing out of land.

19. Linked transactions

(1) A transaction entered into by the debtor or hirer, or a relative of his, with any other person ('the other party'), except one for the provision of security, is a linked transaction in relation to an actual or prospective regulated agreement (the 'principal agreement') of which it does not form part if—

    (a) the transaction is entered into in compliance with a term of the principal agreement; or

    (b) the principal agreement is a debtor-creditor-supplier agreement and the transaction is financed, or to be financed, by the principal agreement; or

    (c) the other party is a person mentioned in subsection (2), and a person so mentioned initiated the transaction by suggesting it to the debtor or hirer, or his relative, who enters into it—

       (i) to induce the creditor or owner to enter into the principal agreement, or

       (ii) for another purpose related to the principal agreement, or

       (iii) where the principal agreement is a restricted-use credit agreement, for a purpose related to a transaction financed, or to be financed, by the principal agreement.

(2) The persons referred to in subsection (1)(c) are—

    (a) the creditor or owner, or his associate;

    (b) a person who, in the negotiation of the transaction, is represented by a credit-broker who is also a negotiator in antecedent negotiations for the principal agreement;

    (c) a person who, at the time the transaction is initiated, knows that the principal agreement has been made or contemplates that it might be made.

(3) A linked transaction entered into before the making of the principal agreement has no effect until such time (if any) as that agreement is made.

(4) Regulations may exclude linked transactions of the prescribed description from the operation of subsection (3).

20. Total charge for credit

In this Act, the 'total charge for credit' has the meaning given by the Regulated Activities Order for the purposes of Chapter 14A of Part 2 of that Order.

PART IV
SEEKING BUSINESS

Canvassing, etc.

48. Definition of canvassing off trade premises (regulated agreements)

(1) An individual (the 'canvasser') canvasses a regulated agreement off trade premises if he solicits the entry (as debtor or hirer) of another individual (the 'consumer') into the agreement by making oral representations to the consumer, or any other individual, during a visit by the canvasser to any place (not excluded by subsection (2)) where the consumer, or that other individual, as the case may be, is, being a visit—

    (a) carried out for the purpose of making such oral representations to individuals who are at that place, but

    (b) not carried out in response to a request made on a previous occasion.

(2) A place is excluded from subsection (1) if it is a place where a business is carried on (whether on a permanent or temporary basis) by—

    (a) the creditor or owner, or

    (b) a supplier, or

    (c) the canvasser, or the person whose employee or agent the canvasser is, or

    (d) the consumer.

49. Prohibition of canvassing debtor-creditor agreements off trade premises

(1) It is an offence to canvas debtor-creditor agreements off trade premises.

(2) It is also an offence to solicit the entry of an individual (as debtor) into a debtor-creditor agreement during a visit carried out in response to a request made on a previous occasion, where—

    (a) the request was not in writing signed by or on behalf of the person making it, and

    (b) if no request for the visit had been made, the soliciting would have constituted the canvassing of a debtor-creditor agreement off trade premises.

(3) Subsections (1) and (2) do not apply to any soliciting for an agreement enabling the debtor to overdraw on a current account of any description kept with the creditor, where—

    (a) the FCA has determined that current accounts of that description kept with the creditor are excluded from subsections (1) and (2), and

    (b) the debtor already keeps an account with the creditor (whether a current account or not).

(4) A determination under subsection (3)(a)—

    (a) may be made subject to such conditions as the FCA thinks fit, and

    (b) shall be made only where the FCA is of opinion that it is not against the interests of debtors.

(5) If soliciting is done in breach of a condition imposed under subsection (4)(a), the determination under subsection (3)(a) does not apply to it.

50. Circulars to minors

(1) A person commits an offence who, with a view to financial gain, sends to a minor any document inviting him to—

    (a) borrow money, or

    (b) obtain goods on credit or hire, or

    (c) obtain services on credit, or

    (d) apply for information or advice on borrowing money or otherwise obtaining credit, or hiring goods.

(2) In proceedings under subsection (1) in respect of the sending of a document to a minor, it is a defence for the person charged to prove that he did not know, and had no reasonable cause to suspect, that he was a minor.

(3)   Where a document is received by a minor at any school or other educational establishment for minors, a person sending it to him at that establishment knowing or suspecting it to be such an establishment shall be taken to have reasonable cause to suspect that he is a minor.

PART V
ENTRY INTO CREDIT OR HIRE AGREEMENTS

Preliminary matters

55.   Disclosure of information

(1)   Regulations may require specified information to be disclosed in the prescribed manner to the debtor or hirer before a regulated agreement is made.

(2)   If regulations under subsection (1) are not complied with, the agreement is enforceable against the debtor or hirer on an order of the court only (and for these purposes a retaking of goods or land to which the agreement relates is an enforcement of the agreement).

55C. Copy of draft consumer credit agreement

(1)   Before a regulated consumer credit agreement, other than an excluded agreement, is made, the creditor must, if requested, give to the debtor without delay a copy of the prospective agreement (or such of its terms as have at that time been reduced to writing).

(2)   Subsection (1) does not apply if at the time the request is made, the creditor is unwilling to proceed with the agreement.

(3)   A breach of the duty imposed by subsection (1) is actionable as a breach of statutory duty.

(4)   For the purposes of this section an agreement is an excluded agreement if it is—

    (a)   an agreement secured on land,

    (b)   an agreement under which a person takes an article in pawn,

    (c)   an agreement under which the creditor provides the debtor with credit which exceeds £60,260 and which is not a residential renovation agreement, or

    (d)   an agreement entered into by the debtor wholly or predominantly for the purposes of a business carried on, or intended to be carried on, by him.

(5)   Article 60C (5) and (6) of the Regulated Activities Order applies for the purposes of subsection (4)(d).

56.   Antecedent negotiations

(1)   In this Act 'antecedent negotiations' means any negotiations with the debtor or hirer—

    (a)   conducted by the creditor or owner in relation to the making of any regulated agreement, or

    (b)   conducted by a credit-broker in relation to goods sold or proposed to be sold by the credit-broker to the creditor before forming the subject matter of a debtor-creditor-supplier agreement within section 12(a), or

    (c)   conducted by the supplier in relation to a transaction financed or proposed to be financed by a debtor-creditor-supplier agreement within section 12(b) or (c), and 'negotiator' means the person by whom negotiations are so conducted with the debtor or hirer.

(2)   Negotiations with the debtor in a case falling within subsection (1)(b) or (c) shall be deemed to be conducted by the negotiator in the capacity of agent of the creditor as well as in his actual capacity.

(3)   An agreement is void if, and to the extent that, it purports in relation to an actual or prospective regulated agreement—

    (a)   to provide that a person acting as, or on behalf of, a negotiator is to be treated as the agent of the debtor or hirer, or

    (b)   to relieve a person from liability for acts or omissions of any person acting as, or on behalf of, a negotiator.

(4)   For the purposes of this Act, antecedent negotiations shall be taken to begin when the negotiator and the debtor or hirer first enter into communication (including communication by advertisement), and to include any representations made by the negotiator to the debtor or hirer and any other dealings between them.

57. Withdrawal from prospective agreement

(1) The withdrawal of a party from a prospective regulated agreement shall operate to apply this Part to the agreement, any linked transaction and any other thing done in anticipation of the making of the agreement as it would apply if the agreement were made and then cancelled under section 69.

(2) The giving to a party of a written or oral notice which, however expressed, indicates the intention of the other party to withdraw from a prospective regulated agreement operates as a withdrawal from it.

(3) Each of the following shall be deemed to be the agent of the creditor or owner for the purpose of receiving a notice under subsection (2)—

(a) a credit-broker or supplier who is the negotiator in antecedent negotiations, and

(b) any person who, in the course of a business carried on by him, acts on behalf of the debtor or hirer in any negotiations for the agreement.

(4) Where the agreement, if made, would not be a cancellable agreement, subsection (1) shall nevertheless apply as if the contrary were the case.

58. Opportunity for withdrawal from prospective land mortgage

(1) Before sending to the debtor or hirer, for his signature, an unexecuted agreement in a case where the prospective regulated agreement is to be secured on land (the 'mortgaged land'), the creditor or owner shall give the debtor or hirer a copy of the unexecuted agreement which contains a notice in the prescribed form indicating the right of the debtor or hirer to withdraw from the prospective agreement, and how and when the right is exercisable, together with a copy of any other document referred to in the unexecuted agreement.

(2) Subsection (1) does not apply to—

(a) a restricted-use credit agreement to finance the purchase of the mortgaged land, or

(b) an agreement for a bridging loan in connection with the purchase of the mortgaged land or other land.

59. Agreement to enter future agreement void

(1) An agreement is void if, and to the extent that, it purports to bind a person to enter as debtor or hirer into a prospective regulated agreement.

(2) Regulations may exclude from the operation of subsection (1) agreements such as are described in the regulations.

Making the agreement

60. Form and content of agreements

(1) The Treasury shall make regulations as to the form and content of documents embodying regulated agreements, and the regulations shall contain such provisions as appear to them appropriate with a view to ensuring that the debtor or hirer is made aware of—

(a) the rights and duties conferred or imposed on him by the agreement,

(b) the amount and rate of the total charge for credit (in the case of a consumer credit agreement),

(c) the protection and remedies available to him under this Act, and

(d) any other matters which, in the opinion of the Treasury, it is desirable for him to know about in connection with the agreement.

(2) Regulations under subsection (1) may in particular—

(a) require specified information to be included in the prescribed manner in documents, and other specified material to be excluded;

(b) contain requirements to ensure that specified information is clearly brought to the attention of the debtor or hirer, and that one part of a document is not given insufficient or excessive prominence compared with another.

(3) If, on an application made to the FCA by a person carrying on a consumer credit business or a consumer hire business, it appears to the FCA impracticable for the applicant to comply with any requirement of regulations under subsection (1) in a particular case, it may, by notice to the applicant direct that the requirement be waived

or varied in relation to such agreements, and subject to such conditions (if any), as it may specify, and this Act and the regulations shall have effect accordingly.

(4)　The FCA shall give a notice under subsection (3) only if it is satisfied that to do so would not prejudice the interests of debtors or hirers.

(5)　An application may be made under subsection (3) only if it relates to—

    (a)　a consumer credit agreement secured on land,

    (b)　a consumer credit agreement under which a person takes an article in pawn,

    (c)　a consumer credit agreement under which the creditor provides the debtor with credit which exceeds £60,260 and which is not a residential renovation agreement,

    (d)　a consumer credit agreement entered into by the debtor wholly or predominantly for the purposes of a business carried on, or intended to be carried on, by him, or

    (e)　a consumer hire agreement.

(6)　Article 60C(5) and (6) of the Regulated Activities Order applies for the purposes of subsection (5)(d).

61.　Signing of agreement

(1)　A regulated agreement is not properly executed unless—

    (a)　a document in the prescribed form itself containing all the prescribed terms and conforming to regulations under section 60(1) is signed in the prescribed manner both by the debtor or hirer and by or on behalf of the creditor or owner, and

    (b)　the document embodies all the terms of the agreement, other than implied terms, and

    (c)　the document is, when presented or sent to the debtor or hirer for signature, in such a state that all its terms are readily legible.

(2)　In addition, where the agreement is one to which section 58(1) applies, it is not properly executed unless—

    (a)　the requirements of section 58(1) were complied with, and

    (b)　the unexecuted agreement was sent, for his signature, to the debtor or hirer by an appropriate method not less than seven days after a copy of it was given to him under section 58(1), and

    (c)　during the consideration period, the creditor or owner refrained from approaching the debtor or hirer (whether in person, by telephone or letter, or in any other way) except in response to a specific request made by the debtor or hirer after the beginning of the consideration period, and

    (d)　no notice of withdrawal by the debtor or hirer was received by the creditor or owner before the sending of the unexecuted agreement.

(3)　In subsection (2)(c), 'the consideration period' means the period beginning with the giving of the copy under section 58(1) and ending—

    (a)　at the expiry of seven days after the day on which the unexecuted agreement is sent, for his signature, to the debtor or hirer, or

    (b)　on its return by the debtor or hirer after signature by him, whichever first occurs.

(4)　Where the debtor or hirer is a partnership or an unincorporated body of persons, subsection (1)(a) shall apply with the substitution for 'by the debtor or hirer' of 'by or on behalf of the debtor or hirer's'.

61A.　Duty to supply copy of executed consumer credit agreement

(1)　Where a regulated consumer credit agreement, other than an excluded agreement, has been made, the creditor must give a copy of the executed agreement, and any other document referred to in it, to the debtor.

(2)　Subsection (1) does not apply if—

    (a)　a copy of the unexecuted agreement (and of any other document referred to in it) has already been given to the debtor, and

    (b)　the unexecuted agreement is in identical terms to the executed agreement.

(3)　In a case referred to in subsection (2), the creditor must inform the debtor in writing—

    (a)　that the agreement has been executed,

    (b)　that the executed agreement is in identical terms to the unexecuted agreement a copy of which has already been given to the debtor, and

    (c)   that the debtor has the right to receive a copy of the executed agreement if the debtor makes a request for it at any time before the end of the period referred to in section 66A(2).

(4)   Where a request is made under subsection (3)(c) the creditor must give a copy of the executed agreement to the debtor without delay.

(5)   If the requirements of this section are not observed, the agreement is not properly executed.

(6)   For the purposes of this section, an agreement is an excluded agreement if it is—
    (a)   a cancellable agreement, or
    (b)   an agreement—
        (i)   secured on land,
        (ii)   under which the creditor provides the debtor with credit which exceeds £60,260, or
        (iii)   entered into by the debtor wholly or predominantly for the purposes of a business carried on, or intended to be carried on, by him,
        unless the creditor or a credit intermediary has complied with or purported to comply with regulation 3(2) of the Consumer Credit (Disclosure of Information) Regulations 2010.

(6A)   An agreement is not an excluded agreement by virtue of subsection (6)(b)(ii) if it is a residential renovation agreement.

(7)   Article 60C(5) and (6) of the Regulated Activities order applies for the purposes of subsection (6)(b)(iii).

(8)   In this section, 'credit intermediary' means a person who in the course of business—
    (a)   carries on any of the activities specified in article 36A(1)(d) to (f) of the Regulated Activities Order for a consideration that is or includes a financial consideration, and
    (b)   does not do so as a creditor.

61B.   Duty to supply copy of overdraft agreement

(1)   Where an authorised business overdraft agreement or an authorised non-business overdraft agreement has been made, a document containing the terms of the agreement must be given to the debtor.

(2)   The creditor must provide the document referred to in subsection (1) to the debtor before or at the time the agreement is made unless—
    (a)   the creditor has provided the debtor with the information referred to in regulation 10(3) of the Consumer Credit (Disclosure of Information) Regulations 2010, in which case it must be provided after the agreement is made,
    (b)   the creditor has provided the debtor with the information referred to in regulation 10(3)(c), (e), (f), (h) and (k) of those Regulations, in which case it must be provided immediately after the agreement is made, or
    (c)   the agreement is an agreement of a description referred to in regulation 10(4)(b) of those Regulations, in which case it must be provided immediately after the agreement is made.

(3)   If the requirements of this section are not observed, the agreement is enforceable against the debtor on an order of the court only (and for these purposes a retaking of goods or land to which the agreement relates is an enforcement of the agreement).

62.   Duty to supply copy of unexecuted agreement: excluded agreements

(1)   If in the case of a regulated agreement which is an excluded agreement the unexecuted agreement is presented personally to the debtor or hirer for his signature, but on the occasion when he signs it the document does not become an executed agreement, a copy of it, and of any other document referred to in it, must be there and then delivered to him.

(2)   If the unexecuted agreement is sent to the debtor or hirer for his signature, a copy of it, and of any other document referred to in it, must be sent to him at the same time.

(3)   A regulated agreement which is an excluded agreement is not properly executed if the requirements of this section are not observed.

(4)   In this section, 'excluded agreement' has the same meaning as in section 61A.

63.   Duty to supply copy of executed agreement: excluded agreements

(1)   If in the case of a regulated agreement which is an excluded agreement the unexecuted agreement is presented personally to the debtor or hirer for his signature, and on the occasion when he signs it the document becomes an executed agreement, a copy of the executed agreement, and of any other document referred to in it, must be there and then delivered to him.

(2)   A copy of the executed agreement, and of any other document referred to in it, must be given to the debtor or hirer within the seven days following the making of the agreement unless—

(a)   subsection (1) applies, or

(b)   the unexecuted agreement was sent to the debtor or hirer for his signature and, on the occasion of his signing it, the document became an executed agreement.

(3)   In the case of a cancellable agreement, a copy under subsection (2) must be sent by an appropriate method.

(4)   In the case of a credit-token agreement, a copy under subsection (2) need not be given within the seven days following the making of the agreement if it is given before or at the time when the credit-token is given to the debtor.

(5)   A regulated agreement which is an excluded agreement is not properly executed if the requirements of this section are not observed.

(6)   In this section, 'excluded agreement' has the same meaning as in section 61A.

64.   Duty to give notice of cancellation rights

(1)   In the case of a cancellable agreement, a notice in the prescribed form indicating the right of the debtor or hirer to cancel the agreement, how and when that right is exercisable, and the name and address of a person to whom notice of cancellation may be given,—

(a)   must be included in every copy given to the debtor or hirer under section 62 or 63, and

(b)   except where section 63(2) applied, must also be sent by an appropriate method to the debtor or hirer within the seven days following the making of the agreement.

(2)   In the case of a credit-token agreement, a notice under subsection (1)(b) need not be sent by an appropriate method within the seven days following the making of the agreement if either—

(a)   it is sent by an appropriate method to the debtor or hirer before the credit-token is given to him, or

(b)   it is sent by an appropriate method to him together with the credit-token.

(3)   Regulations may provide that except where section 63(2) applied a notice sent under subsection (1)(b) shall be accompanied by a further copy of the executed agreement, and of any other document referred to in it.

(4)   Regulations may provide that subsection (1)(b) is not to apply in the case of agreements such as are described in the regulations, being agreements made by a particular person, if—

(a)   on an application by that person to the FCA, the FCA has determined that, having regard to—

(i)   the manner in which antecedent negotiations for agreements with the applicant of that description are conducted, and

(ii)   the information provided to debtors or hirers before such agreements are made, the requirement imposed by subsection (1)(b) can be dispensed with without prejudicing the interests of debtors or hirers, and

(b)   any conditions imposed by the FCA in making the determination are complied with.

(5)   A cancellable agreement is not properly executed if the requirements of this section are not observed.

65.   Consequences of improper execution

(1)   An improperly-executed regulated agreement is enforceable against the debtor or hirer on an order of the court only.

(2)   A retaking of goods or land to which a regulated agreement relates is an enforcement of the agreement.

66.   Acceptance of credit-tokens

(1)   The debtor shall not be liable under a credit-token agreement for use made of the credit-token by any person unless the debtor had previously accepted the credit-token, or the use constituted an acceptance of it by him.

(2)   The debtor accepts a credit-token when—

    (a)   it is signed, or

    (b)   a receipt for it is signed, or

    (c)   it is first used,

either by the debtor himself or by a person who, pursuant to the agreement, is authorised by him to use it.

Withdrawal from certain agreements

66A.   Withdrawal from consumer credit agreement

(1)   The debtor under a regulated consumer credit agreement, other than an excluded agreement, may withdraw from the agreement, without giving any reason, in accordance with this section.

(2)   To withdraw from an agreement under this section the debtor must give oral or written notice of the withdrawal to the creditor before the end of the period of 14 days beginning with the relevant day.

(3)   For the purposes of subsection (2) the relevant day is whichever is the latest of the following—

    (a)   the day on which the agreement is made;

    (b)   where the creditor is required to inform the debtor of the credit limit under the agreement, the day on which the creditor first does so;

    (c)   in the case of an agreement to which section 61A (duty to supply copy of executed consumer credit agreement) applies, the day on which the debtor receives a copy of the agreement under that section or on which the debtor is informed as specified in subsection (3) of that section;

    (d)   in the case of an agreement to which section 63 (duty to supply copy of executed agreement: excluded agreements) applies, the day on which the debtor receives a copy of the agreement under that section.

(4)   Where oral notice under this section is given to the creditor it must be given in a manner specified in the agreement.

(5)   Where written notice under this section is given by facsimile transmission or electronically—

    (a)   it must be sent to the number or electronic address specified for the purpose in the agreement, and

    (b)   where it is so sent, it is to be regarded as having been received by the creditor at the time it is sent (and section 176A does not apply).

(6)   Where written notice under this section is given in any other form—

    (a)   it must be sent by post to, or left at, the postal address specified for the purpose in the agreement, and

    (b)   where it is sent by post to that address, it is to be regarded as having been received by the creditor at the time of posting (and section 176 does not apply).

(7)   Subject as follows, where the debtor withdraws from a regulated consumer credit agreement under this section—

    (a)   the agreement shall be treated as if it had never been entered into, and

    (b)   where an ancillary service relating to the agreement is or is to be provided by the creditor, or by a third party on the basis of an agreement between the third party and the creditor, the ancillary service contract shall be treated as if it had never been entered into.

(8)   In the case referred to in subsection (7)(b) the creditor must without delay notify any third party of the fact that the debtor has withdrawn from the agreement.

(9)   Where the debtor withdraws from an agreement under this section—

(a) the debtor must repay to the creditor any credit provided and the interest accrued on it (at the rate provided for under the agreement), but

(b) the debtor is not liable to pay to the creditor any compensation, fees or charges except any non-returnable charges paid by the creditor to a public administrative body.

(10) An amount payable under subsection (9) must be paid without undue delay and no later than the end of the period of 30 days beginning with the day after the day on which the notice of withdrawal was given (and if not paid by the end of that period may be recovered by the creditor as a debt).

(11) Where a regulated consumer credit agreement is a conditional sale, hire-purchase or credit-sale agreement and—

(a) the debtor withdraws from the agreement under this section after the credit has been provided, and

(b) the sum payable under subsection (9)(a) is paid in full by the debtor,

title to the goods purchased or supplied under the agreement is to pass to the debtor on the same terms as would have applied had the debtor not withdrawn from the agreement.

(12) In subsections (2), (4), (5), (6) and (9)(a) references to the creditor include a person specified by the creditor in the agreement.

(13) In subsection (7)(b) the reference to an ancillary service means a service that relates to the provision of credit under the agreement and includes in particular an insurance or payment protection policy.

(14) For the purposes of this section, an agreement is an excluded agreement if it is—

(a) an agreement for credit exceeding £60,260, other than a residential renovation agreement.

(b) an agreement secured on land,

(c) a restricted-use credit agreement to finance the purchase of land, or

(d) an agreement for a bridging loan in connection with the purchase of land.

Cancellation of certain agreements within cooling-off period

67. Cancellable agreements

(1) Subject to subsection (2) a regulated agreement may be cancelled by the debtor or hirer in accordance with this Part if the antecedent negotiations included oral representations made when in the presence of the debtor or hirer by an individual acting as, or on behalf of, the negotiator, unless—

(a) the agreement is secured on land, or is a restricted-use credit agreement to finance the purchase of land or is an agreement for a bridging loan in connection with the purchase of land, or

(b) the unexecuted agreement is signed by the debtor or hirer at premises at which any of the following is carrying on any business (whether on a permanent or temporary basis)—

(i) the creditor or owner;

(ii) any party to a linked transaction (other than the debtor or hirer or a relative of his);

(iii) the negotiator in any antecedent negotiations.

(2) This section does not apply where section 66A applies.

68. Cooling-off period

The debtor or hirer may serve notice of cancellation of a cancellable agreement between his signing of the unexecuted agreement and—

(a) the end of the fifth day following the day on which he received a copy under section 63(2) or a notice under section 64(1)(b), or

(b) if (by virtue of regulations made under section 64(4)) section 64(1)(b) does not apply, the end of the fourteenth day following the day on which he signed the unexecuted agreement.

69. Notice of cancellation

(1) If within the period specified in section 68 the debtor or hirer under a cancellable agreement serves on—

(a)   the creditor or owner, or

(b)   the person specified in the notice under section 64(1), or

(c)   a person who (whether by virtue of subsection (6) or otherwise) is the agent of the creditor or owner, a notice (a 'notice of cancellation') which, however expressed and whether or not conforming to the notice given under section 64(1), indicates the intention of the debtor or hirer to withdraw from the agreement, the notice shall operate—

    (i)   to cancel the agreement, and any linked transaction, and

    (ii)   to withdraw any offer by the debtor or hirer, or his relative, to enter into a linked transaction.

(2)   In the case of a debtor-creditor-supplier agreement for restricted-use credit financing—

    (a)   the doing of work or supply of goods to meet an emergency, or

    (b)   the supply of goods which, before service of the notice of cancellation, had by the act of the debtor or his relative become incorporated in any land or thing not comprised in the agreement or any linked transaction,

subsection (1) shall apply with the substitution of the following for paragraph (i)—

    '(i)   to cancel only such provisions of the agreement and any linked transaction as—

        (aa) relate to the provision of credit, or

        (bb) require the debtor to pay an item in the total charge for credit, or

        (cc) subject the debtor to any obligation other than to pay for the doing of the said work, or the supply of the said goods'.

(3)   Except so far as is otherwise provided, references in this Act to the cancellation of an agreement or transaction do not include a case within subsection (2).

(4)   Except as otherwise provided by or under this Act, an agreement or transaction cancelled under subsection (1) shall be treated as if it had never been entered into.

(5)   Regulations may exclude linked transactions of the prescribed description from subsection (1)(i) or (ii).

(6)   Each of the following shall be deemed to be the agent of the creditor or owner for the purpose of receiving a notice of cancellation—

    (a)   a credit-broker or supplier who is the negotiator in antecedent negotiations, and

    (b)   any person who, in the course of a business carried on by him, acts on behalf of the debtor or hirer in any negotiations for the agreement.

(7)   Whether or not it is actually received by him, a notice of cancellation sent to a person shall be deemed to be served on him—

    (a)   in the case of a notice sent by post, at the time of posting, and

    (b)   in the case of a notice transmitted in the form of an electronic communication in accordance with section 176A(i), at the time of transmission.

70.   Cancellation: recovery of money paid by debtor or hirer

(1)   On the cancellation of a regulated agreement, and of any linked transaction,—

    (a)   any sum paid by the debtor or hirer, or his relative, under or in contemplation of the agreement or transaction, including any item in the total charge for credit, shall become repayable, and

    (b)   any sum, including any item in the total charge for credit, which but for the cancellation is, or would or might become, payable by the debtor or hirer, or his relative, under the agreement or transaction shall cease to be, or shall not become, so payable, and

    (c)   in the case of a debtor-creditor-supplier agreement falling within section 12(b), any sum paid on the debtor's behalf by the creditor to the supplier shall become repayable to the creditor.

(2)   If, under the terms of a cancelled agreement or transaction, the debtor or hirer, or his relative, is in possession of any goods, he shall have a lien on them for any sum repayable to him under subsection (1) in respect of that agreement or transaction, or any other linked transaction.

(3)   A sum repayable under subsection (1) is repayable by the person to whom it was originally paid, but in the case of a debtor-creditor-supplier agreement falling within

section 12(b) the creditor and the supplier shall be under a joint and several liability to repay sums paid by the debtor, or his relative, under the agreement or under a linked transaction falling within section 19(1)(b) and accordingly, in such a case, the creditor shall be entitled, in accordance with rules of court, to have the supplier made a party to any proceedings brought against the creditor to recover any such sums.

(4) Subject to any agreement between them, the creditor shall be entitled to be indemnified by the supplier for loss suffered by the creditor in satisfying his liability under subsection (3), including costs reasonably incurred by him in defending proceedings instituted by the debtor.

(5) Subsection (1) does not apply to any sum which, if not paid by a debtor, would be payable by virtue of section 71, and applies to a sum paid or payable by a debtor for the issue of a credit-token only where the credit-token has been returned to the creditor or surrendered to a supplier.

(6) If the total charge for credit includes an item in respect of a fee or commission charged by a credit-broker, the amount repayable under subsection (1) in respect of that item shall be the excess over £5 of the fee or commission.

(7) If the total charge for credit includes any sum payable or paid by the debtor to a credit-broker otherwise than in respect of a fee or commission charged by him, that sum shall for the purposes of subsection (6) be treated as if it were such a fee or commission.

(8) So far only as is necessary to give effect to section 69(2), this section applies to an agreement or transaction within that subsection as it applies to a cancelled agreement or transaction.

71.　Cancellation: repayment of credit

(1) Notwithstanding the cancellation of a regulated consumer credit agreement, other than a debtor-creditor-supplier agreement for restricted-use credit, the agreement shall continue in force so far as it relates to repayment of credit and payment of interest.

(2) If, following the cancellation of a regulated consumer credit agreement, the debtor repays the whole or a portion of the credit—
(a) before the expiry of one month following service of the notice of cancellation, or
(b) in the case of a credit repayable by instalments, before the date on which the first instalment is due,
no interest shall be payable on the amount repaid.

(3) If the whole of a credit repayable by instalments is not repaid on or before the date specified in subsection (2)(b), the debtor shall not be liable to repay any of the credit except on receipt of a request in writing in the prescribed form, signed by or on behalf of the creditor, stating the amounts of the remaining instalments (recalculated by the creditor as nearly as may be in accordance with the agreement and without extending the repayment period), but excluding any sum other than principal and interest.

(4) Repayment of a credit, or payment of interest, under a cancelled agreement shall be treated as duly made if it is made to any person on whom, under section 69, a notice of cancellation could have been served, other than a person referred to in section 69(6)(b).

72.　Cancellation: return of goods

(1) This section applies where any agreement or transaction relating to goods, being—
(a) a restricted-use debtor-creditor-supplier agreement, a consumer hire agreement, or a linked transaction to which the debtor or hirer under any regulated agreement is a party, or
(b) a linked transaction to which a relative of the debtor or hirer under any regulated agreement is a party,
is cancelled after the debtor or hirer (in a case within paragraph (a)) or the relative (in a case within paragraph (b)) has acquired possession of the goods by virtue of the agreement or transaction.

(2) In this section—
(a) 'the possessor' means the person who has acquired possession of the goods as mentioned in subsection (1),
(b) 'the other party' means the person from whom the possessor acquired possession, and

(c)   'the pre-cancellation period' means the period beginning when the possessor acquired possession and ending with the cancellation.

(3)   The possessor shall be treated as having been under a duty throughout the pre-cancellation period—

    (a)   to retain possession of the goods, and

    (b)   to take reasonable care of them.

(4)   On the cancellation, the possessor shall be under a duty, subject to any lien, to restore the goods to the other party in accordance with this section, and meanwhile to retain possession of the goods and take reasonable care of them.

(5)   The possessor shall not be under any duty to deliver the goods except at his own premises and in pursuance of a request in writing signed by or on behalf of the other party and served on the possessor either before, or at the time when, the goods are collected from those premises.

(6)   If the possessor—

    (a)   delivers the goods (whether at his own premises or elsewhere) to any person on whom, under section 69, a notice of cancellation could have been served (other than a person referred to in section 69(6)(b)), or

    (b)   sends the goods at his own expense to such a person, he shall be discharged from any duty to retain the goods or deliver them to any person.

(7)   Where the possessor delivers the goods as mentioned in subsection (6)(a), his obligation to take care of the goods shall cease: and if he sends the goods as mentioned in subsection (6)(b), he shall be under a duty to take reasonable care to see that they are received by the other party and not damaged in transit, but in other respects his duty to take care of the goods shall cease.

(8)   Where, at any time during the period of 21 days following the cancellation, the possessor receives such a request as is mentioned in subsection (5), and unreasonably refuses or unreasonably fails to comply with it, his duty to take reasonable care of the goods shall continue until he delivers or sends the goods as mentioned in subsection (6), but if within that period he does not receive such a request his duty to take reasonable care of the goods shall cease at the end of that period.

(9)   The preceding provisions of this section do not apply to—

    (a)   perishable goods, or

    (b)   goods which by their nature are consumed by use and which, before the cancellation, were so consumed, or

    (c)   goods supplied to meet an emergency, or

    (d)   goods which, before the cancellation, had become incorporated in any land or thing not comprised in the cancelled agreement or a linked transaction.

(10)   Where the address of the possessor is specified in the executed agreement, references in this section to his own premises are to that address and no other.

(11)   Breach of a duty imposed by this section is actionable as a breach of statutory duty.

73.   Cancellation: goods given in part-exchange

(1)   This section applies on the cancellation of a regulated agreement where, in antecedent negotiations, the negotiator agreed to take goods in part-exchange (the 'part-exchange goods') and those goods have been delivered to him.

(2)   Unless, before the end of the period of ten days beginning with the date of cancellation, the part-exchange goods are returned to the debtor or hirer in a condition substantially as good as when they were delivered to the negotiator, the debtor or hirer shall be entitled to recover from the negotiator a sum equal to the part-exchange allowance (as defined in subsection (7)(b)).

(3)   In the case of a debtor-creditor-supplier agreement within section 12(b), the negotiator and the creditor shall be under a joint and several liability to pay to the debtor a sum recoverable under subsection (2).

(4)   Subject to any agreement between them, the creditor shall be entitled to be indemnified by the negotiator for loss suffered by the creditor in satisfying his liability under subsection (3), including costs reasonably incurred by him in defending proceedings instituted by the debtor.

(5) During the period of ten days beginning with the date of cancellation, the debtor or hirer, if he is in possession of goods to which the cancelled agreement relates, shall have a lien on them for—
  (a) delivery of the part-exchange goods, in a condition substantially as good as when they were delivered to the negotiator, or
  (b) a sum equal to the part-exchange allowance;
  and if the lien continues to the end of that period it shall thereafter subsist only as a lien for a sum equal to the part-exchange allowance.
(6) Where the debtor or hirer recovers from the negotiator or creditor, or both of them jointly, a sum equal to the part-exchange allowance, then, if the title of the debtor or hirer to the part-exchange goods has not vested in the negotiator, it shall so vest on the recovery of that sum.
(7) For the purposes of this section—
  (a) the negotiator shall be treated as having agreed to take goods in part-exchange if, in pursuance of the antecedent negotiations, he either purchased or agreed to purchase those goods or accepted or agreed to accept them as part of the consideration for the cancelled agreement, and
  (b) the part-exchange allowance shall be the sum agreed as such in the antecedent negotiations or, if no such agreement was arrived at, such sum as it would have been reasonable to allow in respect of the part-exchange goods if no notice of cancellation had been served.
(8) In an action brought against the creditor for a sum recoverable under subsection (2), he shall be entitled, in accordance with rules of court, to have the negotiator made a party to the proceedings.

Exclusion of certain agreements from Part V

74. Exclusion of certain agreements from Part V

(1) Except as provided in subsections (1A) to (2), this Part does not apply to—
  (a) a non-commercial agreement,
  (b) a debtor-creditor agreement enabling the debtor to overdraw on a current account,
  (c) a debtor-creditor agreement to finance the making of such payments arising on, or connected with, the death of a person as may be prescribed, or
  (d) a small debtor-creditor-supplier agreement for restricted-use credit.
(1A) Section 56 (antecedent negotiations) applies to a non-commercial agreement.
(1B) Where an agreement that falls within subsection (1)(b) is an authorised business overdraft agreement the following provisions apply—
  (b) section 56 (antecedent negotiations);
  (c) section 60 (regulations on form and content of agreements);
  (d) section 61B (duty to supply copy of overdraft agreement).
(1C) Where an agreement that falls within subsection (1)(b) is an authorised non-business overdraft agreement the following provisions apply—
  (a) section 55 (regulations on disclosure of information;
  (c) section 55C (copy of draft consumer credit agreement);
  (d) section 56 (antecedent negotiations);
  (e) section 60 (regulations on form and content of agreements);
  (f) section 61B (duty to supply copy of overdraft agreement).
(1D) Where an agreement that falls within subsection (1)(b) would be an authorised non-business overdraft agreement but for the fact that the credit is not repayable on demand or within three months the following provisions apply—
  (a) section 55 (regulations on disclosure of information);
  (d) section 55C (copy of draft consumer credit agreement);
  (e) section 56 (antecedent negotiations);
  (f) section 60 (regulations on form and content of agreements);
  (g) section 61 (signing of agreement);
  (h) section 61A (duty to supply copy of executed agreement);
  (i) section 66A (withdrawal from consumer credit agreement).

(1E) In the case of an agreement that falls within subsection (1)(b) but does not fall within subsection (1B), (1C) or (1D), section 56 (antecedent negotiations) applies.

(1F) The following provisions apply to a debtor-creditor agreement to finance the making of such payments arising on, or connected with, the death of a person as may be prescribed—

    (a)   section 55 (regulations on disclosure of information);

    (d)   section 55C (copy of draft consumer credit agreement);

    (e)   section 56 (antecedent negotiations);

    (f)   section 60 (regulations on form and content of agreements);

    (g)   section 61 (signing of agreement);

    (h)   section 61A (duty to supply copy of executed agreement);

    (i)   section 66A (withdrawal from consumer credit agreement).

(2) The following provisions apply to a small debtor-creditor-supplier agreement for restricted-use credit—

    (a)   section 55 (regulations on disclosure of information);

    (b)   section 56 (antecedent negotiations);

    (c)   section 66A (withdrawal from consumer credit agreement).

(2A) In the case of an agreement to which the Cancellation of Contracts made in a Consumer's Home or Place of Work etc. Regulations 2008 apply the reference in subsection (2) to a small agreement shall be construed as if in section 17(1)(a) and (b) '£42' were substituted for '£50'.

(3) Subsection (1)(c) applies only where the FCA so determines, and such a determination—

    (a)   may be made subject to such conditions as the FCA thinks fit, and

    (b)   shall be made only if the FCA is of the opinion that it is not against the interests of debtors.

(3A) ...

(4) If any term of an agreement falling within subsection (1)(d) is expressed in writing, regulations under section 60(1) shall apply to that term (subject to section 60(3)) as if the agreement were a regulated agreement not falling within subsection (1)(d).

PART VI
MATTERS ARISING DURING CURRENCY OF CREDIT OR HIRE AGREEMENTS

75.   Liability of creditor for breaches by supplier

(1) If the debtor under a debtor-creditor-supplier agreement falling within section 12(b) or (c) has, in relation to a transaction financed by the agreement, any claim against the supplier in respect of a misrepresentation or breach of contract, he shall have a like claim against the creditor, who, with the supplier, shall accordingly be jointly and severally liable to the debtor.

(2) Subject to any agreement between them, the creditor shall be entitled to be indemnified by the supplier for loss suffered by the creditor in satisfying his liability under subsection(1), including costs reasonably incurred by him in defending proceedings instituted by the debtor.

(3) Subsection (1) does not apply to a claim—

    (a)   under a non-commercial agreement,

    (b)   so far as the claim relates to any single item to which the supplier has attached a cash price not exceeding £100 or more than £30,000, or

    (c)   under a debtor-creditor-supplier agreement for running-account credit—

        (i)   which provides for the making of payments by the debtor in relation to specified periods which, in the case of an agreement which is not secured on land, do not exceed three months, and

        (ii)   which requires that the number of payments to be made by the debtor in repayments of the whole amount of the credit provided in each such period shall not exceed one.

(4) This section applies notwithstanding that the debtor, in entering into the transaction, exceeded the credit limit or otherwise contravened any term of the agreement.

(5) In an action brought against the creditor under subsection (1) he shall be entitled, in accordance with rules of court, to have the supplier made a party to the proceedings.

75A. Further provision for liability of creditor for breaches by supplier

(1) If the debtor under a linked credit agreement has a claim against the supplier in respect of a breach of contract the debtor may pursue that claim against the creditor where any of the conditions in subsection (2) are met.

(2) The conditions in subsection (1) are—
  (a) that the supplier cannot be traced,
  (b) that the debtor has contacted the supplier but the supplier has not responded,
  (c) that the supplier is insolvent, or
  (d) that the debtor has taken reasonable steps to pursue his claim against the supplier but has not obtained satisfaction for his claim.

(3) The steps referred to in subsection (2)(d) need not include litigation.

(4) For the purposes of subsection (2)(d) a debtor is to be deemed to have obtained satisfaction where he has accepted a replacement product or service or other compensation from the supplier in settlement of his claim.

(5) In this section 'linked credit agreement' means a regulated consumer credit agreement' which serves exclusively to finance an agreement for the supply of specific goods or the provision of a specific service and where—
  (a) the creditor uses the services of the supplier in connection with the preparation or making of the credit agreement, or
  (b) the specific goods or provision of a specific service are explicitly specified in the credit agreement.

(6) This section does not apply where—
  (a) the cash value of the goods or service is £30,000 or less,
  (b) the linked credit agreement is for credit which exceeds £60,260 and is not a residential renovation agreement, or
  (c) the linked credit agreement is entered into by the debtor wholly or predominantly for the purposes of a business carried on, or intended to be carried on, by him.

(7) Article 60C(5) and (6) of the Regulated Activities Order applies for the purposes of subsection (6)(c).

(8) This section does not apply to an agreement secured on land.

76. Duty to give notice before taking certain action

(1) The creditor or owner is not entitled to enforce a term of a regulated agreement by—
  (a) demanding earlier payment of any sum, or
  (b) recovering possession of any goods or land, or
  (c) treating any right conferred on the debtor or hirer by the agreement as terminated, restricted or deferred,
except by or after giving the debtor or hirer not less than seven days' notice of his intention to do so.

(2) Subsection (1) applies only where—
  (a) a period for the duration of the agreement is specified in the agreement, and
  (b) that period has not ended when the creditor or owner does an act mentioned in subsection (1),
but so applies notwithstanding that, under the agreement, any party is entitled to terminate it before the end of the period so specified.

(3) A notice under subsection (1) is ineffective if not in the prescribed form.

(4) Subsection (1) does not prevent a creditor from treating the right to draw on any credit as restricted or deferred and taking such steps as may be necessary to make the restriction or deferment effective.

(5) Regulations may provide that subsection (1) is not to apply to agreements described by the regulations.

(6) Subsection (1) does not apply to a right of enforcement arising by reason of any breach by the debtor or hirer of the regulated agreement.

77. Duty to give information to debtor under fixed-sum credit agreement

(1) The creditor under a regulated agreement for fixed-sum credit, within the prescribed period after receiving a request in writing to that effect from the debtor and payment of a fee of £1, shall give the debtor a copy of the executed agreement (if any) and of any

other document referred to in it, together with a statement signed by or on behalf of the creditor showing, according to the information to which it is practicable for him to refer,—

    (a)   the total sum paid under the agreement by the debtor;

    (b)   the total sum which has become payable under the agreement by the debtor but remains unpaid, and the various amounts comprised in that total sum, with the date when each became due; and

    (c)   the total sum which is to become payable under the agreement by the debtor, and the various amounts comprised in that total sum, with the date, or mode of determining the date, when each becomes due.

(2)   If the creditor possesses insufficient information to enable him to ascertain the amounts and dates mentioned in subsection (1)(c), he shall be taken to comply with that paragraph if his statement under subsection (1) gives the basis on which, under the regulated agreement, they would fall to be ascertained.

(2A) Subsection (2B) applies if the regulated agreement is a green deal plan.

(2B) The duty imposed on the creditor by subsection (1) may be discharged by another person acting on the creditor's behalf.

(3)   Subsection (1) does not apply to—

    (a)   an agreement under which no sum is, or will or may become, payable by the debtor, or

    (b)   a request made less than one month after a previous request under that subsection relating to the same agreement was complied with.

(4)   If the creditor under an agreement fails to comply with subsection (1)—

    (a)   he is not entitled, while the default continues, to enforce the agreement; and

    (b)   …

(5)   This section does not apply to a non-commercial agreement.

77A. Statements to be provided in relation to fixed-sum credit agreements

(1)   The creditor under a regulated agreement for fixed-sum credit must give the debtor statements under this section.

(1A) The statements must relate to consecutive periods.

(1B) The first such period must begin with either—

    (a)   the day on which the agreement is made, or

    (b)   the day the first movement occurs on the debtor's account with the creditor relating to the agreement.

(1C) No such period may exceed a year.

(1D) For the purposes of subsection (1C), a period of a year which expires on a non-working day may be regarded as expiring on the next working day.

(1E) Each statement under this section must be given to the debtor before the end of the period of thirty days beginning with the day after the end of the period to which the statement relates.

(2)   Regulations may make provision about the form and content of statements under this section.

(2A) Subsection (2B) applies if the regulated agreement is a green deal plan.

(2B) Any duty imposed on the creditor by this section may be discharged by another person acting on the creditor's behalf.

(3)   The debtor shall have no liability to pay any sum in connection with the preparation or the giving to him of a statement under this section.

(4)   The creditor is not required to give the debtor any statement under this section once the following conditions are satisfied—

    (a)   that there is no sum payable under the agreement by the debtor; and

    (b)   that there is no sum which will or may become so payable.

(5)   Subsection (6) applies if at a time before the conditions mentioned in subsection (4) are satisfied the creditor fails to give the debtor—

    (a)   a statement under this section within the period mentioned in subsection (1)(a); or

    (b)   …

(6)   Where this subsection applies in relation to a failure to give a statement under this section to the debtor—

    (a)   the creditor shall not be entitled to enforce the agreement during the period of non-compliance;

(b)   the debtor shall have no liability to pay any sum of interest to the extent calculated by reference to the period of non-compliance or to any part of it; and

(c)   the debtor shall have no liability to pay any default sum which (apart from this paragraph)—

    (i)   would have become payable during the period of non-compliance; or

    (ii)   would have become payable after the end of that period in connection with a breach of the agreement which occurs during that period (whether or not the breach continues after the end of that period).

(7)   In this section 'the period of non-compliance' means, in relation to a failure to give a statement under this section to the debtor, the period which—

(a)   begins immediately after the end of the period mentioned in paragraph (a) or (as the case may be) paragraph (b) of subsection (5); and

(b)   ends at the end of the day on which the statement is given to the debtor or on which the conditions mentioned in subsection (4) are satisfied, whichever is earlier.

(8)   This section does not apply in relation to a non-commercial agreement or to a small agreement.

(9)   This section does not apply where the holder of a current account overdraws on the account without a pre-arranged overdraft or exceeds a pre-arranged overdraft limit.

77B. Fixed-sum credit agreement: statement of account to be provided on request

(1)   This section applies to a regulated consumer credit agreement—

(a)   which is for fixed-sum credit,

(b)   which is of fixed duration,

(c)   where the credit is repayable in instalments by the debtor, and

(d)   which is not an excluded agreement.

(2)   Upon a request from the debtor, the creditor must as soon as reasonably practicable give to the debtor a statement in writing which complies with subsections (3) to (5).

(3)   The statement must include a table showing the details of each instalment owing under the agreement as at the date of the request.

(4)   Details to be provided under subsection (3) must include—

(a)   the date on which the instalment is due,

(b)   the amount of the instalment,

(c)   any conditions relating to payment of the instalment, and

(d)   a breakdown of the instalment showing how much of it is made up of capital repayment, interest payment and other charges.

(5)   Where the rate of interest is variable or the charges under the agreement may be varied, the statement must also indicate clearly and concisely that the information in the table is valid only until the rate of interest or charges are varied.

(6)   The debtor may make a request under subsection (2) at any time that the agreement is in force unless a previous request has been made less than a month before and has been complied with.

(7)   The debtor shall have no liability to pay any sum in connection with the preparation or the giving of a statement under this section.

(7A) Subsection (7B) applies if the regulated agreement is a green deal plan.

(7B) The duty imposed on the creditor by this section may be discharged by another person acting on the creditor's behalf.

(8)   A breach of the duty imposed by this section is actionable as a breach of statutory duty.

(9)   For the purposes of this section, an agreement is an excluded agreement if it is—

(a)   an agreement secured on land,

(b)   an agreement under which a person takes an article in pawn,

(c)   an agreement under which the creditor provides the debtor with credit which exceeds £60,260 and which is not a residential renovation agreement, or

(d)   an agreement entered into by the debtor wholly or predominantly for the purpose of a business carried on, or intended to be carried on, by him.

(10) Article 60C(5) and (6) of the Regulated Activities Order applies for the purposes of subsection (9)(d).

78. Duty to give information to debtor under running-account credit agreement

(1) The creditor under a regulated agreement for running-account credit, within the prescribed period after receiving a request in writing to that effect from the debtor and payment of a fee of £1, shall give the debtor a copy of the executed agreement (if any) and of any other document referred to in it, together with a statement signed by or on behalf of the creditor showing, according to the information to which it is practicable for him to refer,—

    (a) the state of the account, and

    (b) the amount, if any, currently payable under the agreement by the debtor to the creditor, and

    (c) the amounts and due dates of any payments which, if the debtor does not draw further on the account, will later become payable under the agreement by the debtor to the creditor.

(1A) Where a request under subsection (1) also amounts to a request under Regulation 49 of the Payments Services Regulations 2017 (information during period of contract), subsection (1) applies as if the words "and payment of a fee of £1" were omitted.

(2) If the creditor possesses insufficient information to enable him to ascertain the amounts and dates mentioned in subsection (1)(c), he shall be taken to comply with that paragraph if his statement under subsection (1) gives the basis on which, under the regulated agreement, they would fall to be ascertained.

(3) Subsection (1) does not apply to—

    (a) an agreement under which no sum is, or will or may become, payable by the debtor, or

    (b) a request made less than one month after a previous request under that subsection relating to the same agreement was complied with.

(4) Where running-account credit is provided under a regulated agreement, the creditor shall give the debtor statements in the prescribed form, and with the prescribed contents—

    (a) showing according to the information to which it is practicable for him to refer, the state of the account at regular intervals of not more than twelve months, and

    (b) where the agreement provides, in relation to specified periods, for the making of payments by the debtor, or the charging against him of interest or any other sum, showing according to the information to which it is practicable for him to refer the state of the account at the end of each of those periods during which there is any movement in the account.

(4A) Regulations may require a statement under subsection (4) to contain also information in the prescribed terms about the consequences of the debtor—

    (a) failing to make payments as required by the agreement; or

    (b) only making payments of a prescribed description in prescribed circumstances.

(5) A statement under subsection (4) shall be given within the prescribed period after the end of the period to which the statement relates.

(6) If the creditor under an agreement fails to comply with subsection (1)—

    (a) he is not entitled, while the default continues, to enforce the agreement; and

    (b) ...

(7) This section does not apply to a non-commercial agreement, and subsections (4) to (5) do not apply to a small agreement.

78A. Duty to give information to debtor on change of rate of interest

(1) Where the rate of interest charged under a regulated consumer credit agreement, other than an excluded agreement, is to be varied, the creditor must inform the debtor in writing of the matters mentioned in subsection (3) before the variation can take effect.

(2) But subsection (1) does not apply where—

    (a) the agreement provides that the creditor is to inform the debtor in writing periodically of the matters mentioned in subsection (3) in relation to any variation, at such times as may be provided for in the agreement,

    (b) the agreement provides that the rate of interest is to vary according to a reference rate,

    (c) the reference rate is publicly available,

     (d)   information about the reference rate is available on the premises of the creditor, and

     (e)   the variation of the rate of interest results from a change to the reference rate.

(3)   The matters referred to in subsections (1) and (2)(a) are—

     (a)   the variation in the rate of interest,

     (b)   the amount of any payments that are to be made after the variation has effect, if different, expressed as a sum of money where practicable, and

     (c)   if the number or frequency of payments changes as a result of the variation, the new number or frequency.

(4)   In the case of an agreement mentioned in subsection (5) this section applies as follows—

     (a)   the obligation in subsection (1) only applies if the rate of interest increases, and

     (b)   subsection (3) is to be read as if paragraphs (b) and (c) were omitted.

(5)   The agreements referred to in subsection (4) are—

     (a)   an authorised business overdraft agreement,

     (b)   an authorised non-business overdraft agreement, or

     (c)   an agreement which would be an authorised non-business overdraft agreement but for the fact that the credit is not repayable on demand or within three months.

(6)   For the purposes of this section an agreement is an excluded agreement if it is—

     (a)   a debtor-creditor agreement arising where the holder of a current account overdraws on the account without a pre-arranged overdraft or exceeds a prearranged overdraft limit, or

     (b)   an agreement secured on land.

79.   Duty to give hirer information

(1)   The owner under a regulated consumer hire agreement, within the prescribed period after receiving a request in writing to that effect from the hirer and payment of a fee of £1, shall give to the hirer a copy of the executed agreement and of any other document referred to in it, together with a statement signed by or on behalf of the owner showing, according to the information to which it is practicable for him to refer, the total sum which has become payable under the agreement by the hirer but remains unpaid and the various amounts comprised in that total sum, with the date when each became due.

(2)   Subsection (1) does not apply to—

     (a)   an agreement under which no sum is, or will or may become, payable by the hirer, or

     (b)   a request made less than one month after a previous request under that subsection relating to the same agreement was complied with.

(3)   If the owner under an agreement fails to comply with subsection (1)—

     (a)   he is not entitled, while the default continues, to enforce the agreement; and

     (b)   ...

(4)   This section does not apply to a non-commercial agreement.

80.   Debtor or hirer to give information about goods

(1)   Where a regulated agreement, other than a non-commercial agreement, requires the debtor or hirer to keep goods to which the agreement relates in his possession or control, he shall, within seven working days after he has received a request in writing to that effect from the creditor or owner, tell the creditor or owner where the goods are.

(2)   If the debtor or hirer fails to comply with subsection (1), and the default continues for 14 days, he commits an offence.

82.   Variation of agreements

(1)   Where, under a power contained in a regulated agreement, the creditor or owner varies the agreement, the variation shall not take effect before notice of it is given to the debtor or hirer in the prescribed manner.

(1A) Subsection (1) does not apply to a variation in the rate of interest charged under an agreement not secured on land (see section 78A).

(1B) Subsection (1) does not apply to a variation in the rate of interest charged under an agreement secured on land if—

  (a) the agreement falls within subsection (1D), and

  (b) the variation is a reduction in the rate.

(1C) Subsection (1) does not apply to a variation in any other charge under an agreement if—

  (a) the agreement falls within subsection (1D), and

  (b) the variation is a reduction in the charge.

(1D) The agreements referred to in subsections (1B) and (1C) are—

  (a) an authorised business overdraft agreement,

  (b) an authorised non-business overdraft agreement, or

  (c) an agreement which would be an authorised non-business overdraft agreement but for the fact that the credit is not repayable on demand or within three months.

(1E) Subsection (1) does not apply to a debtor-creditor agreement arising where the holder of a current account overdraws on the account without a pre-arranged overdraft or exceeds a pre-arranged overdraft limit.

(2) Where an agreement (a 'modifying agreement') varies or supplements an earlier agreement, the modifying agreement shall for the purposes of this Act be treated as—

  (a) revoking the earlier agreement, and

  (b) containing provisions reproducing the combined effect of the two agreements, and obligations outstanding in relation to the earlier agreement shall accordingly be treated as outstanding instead in relation to the modifying agreement.

(2A) Subsection (2) does not apply if the earlier agreement or the modifying agreement is an exempt agreement … .

(2B) Subsection (2) does not apply if the modifying agreement varies—

  (a) the amount of the repayment to be made under the earlier agreement, or

  (b) the duration of the agreement,

as a result of the discharge of part of the debtor's indebtedness under the earlier agreement by virtue of section 94(3).

(3) If the earlier agreement is a regulated agreement but (apart from this subsection) the modifying agreement is not then, unless the modifying agreement is—

  (a) for running account credit; or

  (b) an exempt agreement …,

it shall be treated as a regulated agreement.

(4) If the earlier agreement is a regulated agreement for running-account credit, and by the modifying agreement the creditor allows the credit limit to be exceeded but intends the excess to be merely temporary, Part V (except section 56) shall not apply to the modifying agreement.

(5) If—

  (a) the earlier agreement is a cancellable agreement, and

  (b) the modifying agreement is made within the period applicable under section 68 to the earlier agreement,

then, whether or not the modifying agreement would, apart from this subsection, be a cancellable agreement, it shall be treated as a cancellable agreement in respect of which a notice may be served under section 68 not later than the end of the period applicable under that section to the earlier agreement.

(5A) Subsection (5) does not apply where the modifying agreement is an exempt agreement …

(6) Except under subsection (5), a modifying agreement shall not be treated as a cancellable agreement.

(6A) If—

  (a) the earlier agreement is an agreement to which section 66A (right of withdrawal) applies, and

  (b) the modifying agreement is made within the period during which the debtor may give notice of withdrawal from the earlier agreement (see section 66A(2)),

then, whether or not the modifying agreement would, apart from this subsection, be an agreement to which section 66A applies, it shall be treated as such an agreement in respect of which notice may be given under subsection (2) of that section within the period referred to in paragraph (b) above.

(6B) Except as provided for under subsection (6A) section 66A does not apply to a modifying agreement.

(7) This section does not apply to a non-commercial agreement.

(8)   In this section, an 'exempt agreement' means an agreement which is an exempt agreement for the purposes of Chapter 14A of Part 2 of the Regulated Activities Order by virtue of Article 60C(2) (regulated mortgage contracts and regulated home purchase plans) or article 60D (exemption relating to purchase of land for non-residential purposes) of that order.

83.   Liability for misuse of credit facilities

(1)   The debtor under a regulated consumer credit agreement shall not be liable to the creditor for any loss arising from use of the credit facility by another person not acting, or to be treated as acting, as the debtor's agent.

(2)   This section does not apply to a non-commercial agreement, or to any loss in so far as it arises from misuse of an instrument to which section 4 of the Cheques Act 1957 applies.

84.   Misuse of credit-tokens

(1)   Section 83 does not prevent the debtor under a credit-token agreement from being made liable to the extent of £35 (or the credit limit if lower) for loss to the creditor arising from use of the credit-token by other persons during a period beginning when the credit-token ceases to be in the possession of any authorised person and ending when the credit-token is once more in the possession of an authorised person.

(2)   Section 83 does not prevent the debtor under a credit-token agreement from being made liable to any extent for loss to the creditor from use of the credit-token by a person who acquired possession of it with the debtor's consent.

(3)   Subsection (1) and (2) shall not apply to any use of the credit-token after the creditor has been given oral or written notice that it is lost or stolen, or is for any other reason liable to misuse.

(3A) Subsections (1) and (2) shall not apply to any use, in connection with a distance contract (other than an excepted contract), of a card which is a credit-token.

(3B) In subsection (3A), 'distance contract' and 'excepted contract' have the meanings given in the Consumer Protection (Distance Selling) Regulations 2000.

(3C) Subsections (1) and (2) shall not apply to any use, in connection with a distance selling contract within the meaning of the Financial Services (Distance Marketing) Regulations 2004, of a card which is a credit-token.

(4)   Subsections (1) and (2) shall not apply unless there are contained in the credit-token agreement in the prescribed manner particulars of the name, address and telephone number of a person stated to be the person to whom notice is to be given under subsection (3).

(5)   Notice under subsection (3) takes effect when received, but where it is given orally, and the agreement so requires, it shall be treated as not taking effect if not confirmed in writing within seven days.

(6)   Any sum paid by the debtor for the issue of the credit-token to the extent (if any) that it has not been previously offset by use made of the credit-token, shall be treated as paid towards satisfaction of any liability under subsection (1) or (2).

(7)   The debtor, the creditor, and any person authorised by the debtor to use the credit-token, shall be authorised persons for the purposes of subsection (1).

(8)   Where two or more credit-tokens are given under one credit-token agreement, the preceding provisions of this section apply to each credit-token separately.

85.   Duty on issue of new credit-tokens

(1)   Whenever, in connection with a credit-token agreement, a credit-token (other than the first) is given by the creditor to the debtor, the creditor shall give the debtor a copy of the executed agreement (if any) and of any other document referred to in it.

(2)   If the creditor fails to comply with this section—
(a)   he is not entitled, while the default continues, to enforce the agreement, and
(b)   ...

(3)   This section does not apply to a small agreement.

86.   Death of debtor or hirer

(1)   The creditor or owner under a regulated agreement is not entitled, by reason of the death of the debtor or hirer, to do an act specified in paragraphs (a) to (e) of section 87(1) if at the death the agreement is fully secured.

(2)   If at the death of the debtor or hirer a regulated agreement is only partly secured or is unsecured, the creditor or owner is entitled, by reason of the death of the debtor or hirer, to do an act specified in paragraphs (a) to (e) of section 87(1) on an order of the court only.

(3)   This section applies in relation to the termination of an agreement only where—
    (a)   a period for its duration is specified in the agreement, and
    (b)   that period has not ended when the creditor or owner purports to terminate the agreement,
but so applies notwithstanding that, under the agreement, any party is entitled to terminate it before the end of the period so specified.

(4)   This section does not prevent the creditor from treating the right to draw on any credit as restricted or deferred, and taking such steps as may be necessary to make the restriction or deferment effective.

(5)   This section does not affect the operation of any agreement providing for payment of sums—
    (a)   due under the regulated agreement, or
    (b)   becoming due under it on the death of the debtor or hirer,
    out of the proceeds of a policy of assurance on his life.

(6)   For the purposes of this section an act is done by reason of the death of the debtor or hirer if it is done under a power conferred by the agreement which is—
    (a)   exercisable on his death, or
    (b)   exercisable at will and exercised at any time after his death.

PART VII
DEFAULT AND TERMINATION

Information sheets

86A.   FCA to prepare information sheets on arrears and default

(1)   The FCA shall prepare and issue an arrears information sheet and a default information sheet.

(2)   The arrears information sheet shall include information to help debtors and hirers who receive notices under section 86B or 86C.

(3)   The default information sheet shall include information to help debtors and hirers who receive default notices.

(4)   Regulations may make provision about the information to be included in an information sheet.

(5)   An information sheet takes effect for the purposes of this Part at the end of the period of three months beginning with the day on which it is issued or on such later date as the FCA may specify in relation to the information sheet.

(6)   If the FCA revises an information sheet after it has been issued, it shall issue the revised information sheet.

(7)   A revised information sheet takes effect for the purposes of this Part at the end of the period of three months beginning with the day on which it is issued or on such later date as the FCA may specify in relation to the information sheet.

Sums in arrears and default sums

86B.   Notice of sums in arrears under fixed-sum credit agreements etc.

(1)   This section applies where at any time the following conditions are satisfied—
    (a)   that the debtor or hirer under an applicable agreement is required to have made at least two payments under the agreement before that time;
    (b)   that the total sum paid under the agreement by him is less than the total sum which he is required to have paid before that time;

(c)   that the amount of the shortfall is no less than the sum of the last two payments which he is required to have made before that time;

(d)   that the creditor or owner is not already under a duty to give him notices under this section in relation to the agreement; and

(e)   if a judgment has been given in relation to the agreement before that time, that there is no sum still to be paid under the judgment by the debtor or hirer.

(2)   The creditor or owner—

(a)   shall, within the period of 14 days beginning with the day on which the conditions mentioned in subsection (1) are satisfied, give the debtor or hirer a notice under this section; and

(b)   after the giving of that notice, shall give him further notices under this section at intervals of not more than six months.

(3)   The duty of the creditor or owner to give the debtor or hirer notices under this section shall cease when either of the conditions mentioned in subsection (4) is satisfied; but if either of those conditions is satisfied before the notice required by subsection (2)(a) is given, the duty shall not cease until that notice is given.

(4)   The conditions referred to in subsection (3) are—

(a)   that the debtor or hirer ceases to be in arrears;

(b)   that a judgment is given in relation to the agreement under which a sum is required to be paid by the debtor or hirer.

(5)   For the purposes of subsection (4)(a) the debtor or hirer ceases to be in arrears when—

(a)   no payments, which he has ever failed to make under the agreement when required, are still owing;

(b)   no default sum, which has ever become payable under the agreement in connection with his failure to pay any sum under the agreement when required, is still owing;

(c)   no sum of interest, which has ever become payable under the agreement in connection with such a default sum, is still owing; and

(d)   no other sum of interest, which has ever become payable under the agreement in connection with his failure to pay any sum under the agreement when required, is still owing.

(6)   A notice under this section shall include a copy of the current arrears information sheet under section 86A.

(7)   The debtor or hirer shall have no liability to pay any sum in connection with the preparation or the giving to him of a notice under this section.

(8)   Regulations may make provision about the form and content of notices under this section.

(9)   In the case of an applicable agreement under which the debtor or hirer must make all payments he is required to make at intervals of one week or less, this section shall have effect as if in subsection (1)(a) and (c) for 'two' there were substituted 'four'.

(10)   If an agreement mentioned in subsection (9) was made before the beginning of the relevant period, only amounts resulting from failures by the debtor or hirer to make payments he is required to have made during that period shall be taken into account in determining any shortfall for the purposes of subsection (1)(c).

(11)   In subsection (10) 'relevant period' means the period of 20 weeks ending with the day on which the debtor or hirer is required to have made the most recent payment under the agreement.

(12)   In this section 'applicable agreement' means an agreement which falls within subsection (12A) or (12B).

(12A)   An agreement falls within this subsection if—

(a)   it is a regulated agreement for fixed-sum credit; and

(b)   it is not—

(i)   a non-commercial agreement;

(ii)   a small agreement; or

(iii)   a green deal plan.

(12B)   An agreement falls within this subsection if—

(a)   it is a regulated consumer hire agreement; and

   (b) it is neither a non-commercial agreement nor a small agreement.
  (13) In this section—
   (a) 'payments' in relation to an applicable agreement which is a regulated agreement for fixed-sum credit means payments to be made at predetermined intervals provided for under the terms of the agreement; and
   (b) 'payments' in relation to an applicable agreement which is a regulated consumer hire agreement means any payments to be made by the hirer in relation to any period in consideration of the bailment or hiring to him of goods under the agreement.

86C. Notice of sums in arrears under running-account credit agreements

  (1) This section applies where at any time the following conditions are satisfied—
   (a) that the debtor under an applicable agreement is required to have made at least two payments under the agreement before that time;
   (b) that the last two payments which he is required to have made before that time have not been made;
   (c) that the creditor has not already been required to give a notice under this section in relation to either of those payments; and
   (d) if a judgment has been given in relation to the agreement before that time, that there is no sum still to be paid under the judgment by the debtor.
  (2) The creditor shall, no later than the end of the period within which he is next required to give a statement under section 78(4) in relation to the agreement, give the debtor a notice under this section.
  (3) The notice shall include a copy of the current arrears information sheet under section 86A.
  (4) The notice may be incorporated in a statement or other notice which the creditor gives the debtor in relation to the agreement by virtue of another provision of this Act.
  (5) The debtor shall have no liability to pay any sum in connection with the preparation or the giving to him of the notice.
  (6) Regulations may make provision about the form and content of notices under this section.
  (7) In this section 'applicable agreement' means an agreement which—
   (a) is a regulated agreement for running-account credit; and
   (b) is neither a non-commercial agreement nor a small agreement.
  (8) In this section 'payments' means payments to be made at predetermined intervals provided for under the terms of the agreement.

86D. Failure to give notice of sums in arrears

  (1) This section applies where the creditor or owner under an agreement is under a duty to give the debtor or hirer notices under section 86B but fails to give him such a notice—
   (a) within the period mentioned in subsection (2)(a) of that section; or
   (b) within the period of six months beginning with the day after the day on which such a notice was last given to him.
  (2) This section also applies where the creditor under an agreement is under a duty to give the debtor a notice under section 86C but fails to do so before the end of the period mentioned in subsection (2) of that section.
  (3) The creditor or owner shall not be entitled to enforce the agreement during the period of non-compliance.
  (4) The debtor or hirer shall have no liability to pay—
   (a) any sum of interest to the extent calculated by reference to the period of non-compliance or to any part of it; or
   (b) any default sum which (apart from this paragraph)—
    (i) would have become payable during the period of non-compliance; or
    (ii) would have become payable after the end of that period in connection with a breach of the agreement which occurs during that period (whether or not the breach continues after the end of that period).
  (5) In this section 'the period of non-compliance' means, in relation to a failure to give a notice under section 86B or 86C to the debtor or hirer, the period which—
   (a) begins immediately after the end of the period mentioned in (as the case may be) subsection (1)(a) or (b) or (2); and

    (b)   ends at the end of the day mentioned in subsection (6).

(6)   That day is—

    (a)   in the case of a failure to give a notice under section 86B as mentioned in subsection (1)(a) of this section, the day on which the notice is given to the debtor or hirer;

    (b)   in the case of a failure to give a notice under that section as mentioned in subsection (1)(b) of this section, the earlier of the following—

        (i)   the day on which the notice is given to the debtor or hirer;

        (ii)   the day on which the condition mentioned in subsection (4)(a) of that section is satisfied;

    (c)   in the case of a failure to give a notice under section 86C, the day on which the notice is given to the debtor.

86E. Notice of default sums

(1)   This section applies where a default sum becomes payable under a regulated agreement by the debtor or hirer.

(2)   The creditor or owner shall, within the prescribed period after the default sum becomes payable, give the debtor or hirer a notice under this section.

(3)   The notice under this section may be incorporated in a statement or other notice which the creditor or owner gives the debtor or hirer in relation to the agreement by virtue of another provision of this Act.

(4)   The debtor or hirer shall have no liability to pay interest in connection with the default sum to the extent that the interest is calculated by reference to a period occurring before the 29th day after the day on which the debtor or hirer is given the notice under this section.

(5)   If the creditor or owner fails to give the debtor or hirer the notice under this section within the period mentioned in subsection (2), he shall not be entitled to enforce the agreement until the notice is given to the debtor or hirer.

(6)   The debtor or hirer shall have no liability to pay any sum in connection with the preparation or the giving to him of the notice under this section.

(7)   Regulations may—

    (a)   provide that this section does not apply in relation to a default sum which is less than a prescribed amount;

    (b)   make provision about the form and content of notices under this section.

(8)   This section does not apply in relation to a non-commercial agreement or to a small agreement.

86F. Interest on default sums

(1)   This section applies where a default sum becomes payable under a regulated agreement by the debtor or hirer.

(2)   The debtor or hirer shall only be liable to pay interest in connection with the default sum if the interest is simple interest.

Default notices

87. Need for default notice

(1)   Service of a notice on the debtor or hirer in accordance with section 88 (a 'default notice') is necessary before the creditor or owner can become entitled, by reason of any breach by the debtor or hirer of a regulated agreement,—

    (a)   to terminate the agreement, or

    (b)   to demand earlier payment of any sum, or

    (c)   to recover possession of any goods or land, or

    (d)   to treat any right conferred on the debtor or hirer by the agreement as terminated, restricted or deferred, or

    (e)   to enforce any security.

(2)   Subsection (1) does not prevent the creditor from treating the right to draw upon any credit as restricted or deferred, and taking such steps as may be necessary to make the restriction or deferment effective.

(3)   The doing of an act by which a floating charge becomes fixed is not enforcement of a security.

(4)   Regulations may provide that section (1) is not to apply to agreements described by the regulations.

(5)   Subsection (1)(d) does not apply in a case referred to in section 98A(4) (termination or suspension of debtor's right to draw on credit under open-end agreement).

88.   Contents and effect of default notice

(1)   The default notice must be in the prescribed form and specify—

     (a)   the nature of the alleged breach;

     (b)   if the breach is capable of remedy, what action is required to remedy it and the date before which that action is to be taken;

     (c)   if the breach is not capable of remedy, the sum (if any) required to be paid as compensation for the breach, and the date before which it is to be paid.

(2)   A date specified under subsection (1) must not be less than 14 days after the date of service of the default notice, and the creditor or owner shall not take action such as is mentioned in section 87(1) before the date so specified or (if no requirement is made under subsection (1)) before those 14 days have elapsed.

(3)   The default notice must not treat as a breach failure to comply with a provision of the agreement which becomes operative only on breach of some other provision, but if the breach of that other provision is not duly remedied or compensation demanded under subsection (1) is not duly paid, or (where no requirement is made under subsection (1)) if the 14 days mentioned in subsection (2) have elapsed, the creditor or owner may treat the failure as a breach and section 87(1) shall not apply to it.

(4)   The default notice must contain information in the prescribed terms about the consequences of failure to comply with it and any other prescribed matters relating to the agreement.

(4A) The default notice must also include a copy of the current default information sheet under section 86A.

(5)   A default notice making a requirement under subsection (1) may include a provision for the taking of action such as is mentioned in section 87(1) at any time after the restriction imposed by subsection (2) will cease, together with a statement that the provision will be ineffective if the breach is duly remedied or the compensation duly paid.

89.   Compliance with default notice

If before the date specified for that purpose in the default notice the debtor or hirer takes the action specified under section 88(1)(b) or (c) the breach shall be treated as not having occurred.

Further restriction of remedies for default

90.   Retaking of protected hire-purchase etc. goods

(1)   At any time when—

     (a)   the debtor is in breach of a regulated hire-purchase or a regulated conditional sale agreement relating to goods, and

     (b)   the debtor has paid to the creditor one-third or more of the total price of the goods and

     (c)   the property in the goods remains in the creditor,

the creditor is not entitled to recover possession of the goods from the debtor except on an order of the court.

(2)   Where under a hire-purchase or conditional sale agreement the creditor is required to carry out any installation and the agreement specifies, as part of the total price, the amount to be paid in respect of the installation (the 'installation charge') the reference in subsection (1)(b) to one-third of the total price shall be construed as a reference to the aggregate of the installation charge and one-third of the remainder of the total price.

(3)   In a case where—

     (a)   subsection (1)(a) is satisfied, but not subsection (1)(b), and

     (b)   subsection (1)(b) was satisfied on a previous occasion in relation to an earlier agreement, being a regulated hire-purchase or regulated conditional sale agreement, between the same parties, and relating to any of the goods comprised in the later agreement (whether or not other goods were also included), subsection (1) shall apply to the later agreement with the omission of paragraph (b).

(4)   If the later agreement is a modifying agreement, subsection (3) shall apply with the substitution, for the second reference to the later agreement, of a reference to the modifying agreement.

(5)   Subsection (1) shall not apply, or shall cease to apply, to an agreement if the debtor has terminated, or terminates, the agreement.

(6)   Where subsection (1) applies to an agreement at the death of the debtor, it shall continue to apply (in relation to the possessor of the goods) until the grant of probate or administration, or (in Scotland) confirmation (on which the personal representative would fall to be treated as the debtor).

(7)   Goods falling within this section are in this Act referred to as 'protected goods'.

91.   Consequences of breach of s. 90

If goods are recovered by the creditor in contravention of section 90—

(a)   the regulated agreement, if not previously terminated, shall terminate, and

(b)   the debtor shall be released from all liability under the agreement, and shall be entitled to recover from the creditor all sums paid by the debtor under the agreement.

92.   Recovery of possession of goods or land

(1)   Except under an order of the court, the creditor or owner shall not be entitled to enter any premises to take possession of goods subject to a regulated hire-purchase agreement, regulated conditional sale agreement or regulated consumer hire agreement.

(2)   At any time when the debtor is in breach of a regulated conditional sale agreement relating to land, the creditor is entitled to recover possession of the land from the debtor, or any person claiming under him, on an order of the court only.

(3)   An entry in contravention of section (1) or (2) is actionable as a breach of statutory duty.

93.   Interest not to be increased on default

The debtor under a regulated consumer credit agreement shall not be obliged to pay interest on sums which, in breach of the agreement, are unpaid by him at a rate—

(a)   where the total charge for credit includes an item in respect of interest, exceeding the rate of that interest, or

(b)   in any other case, exceeding what would be the rate of the total charge for credit if any items included in the total charge for credit by virtue of rules made by the FCA under paragraph (2)(d) of article 60M of the Regulated Activities Order were disregarded.

Early payment by debtor

94.   Right to complete payments ahead of time

(1)   The debtor under a regulated consumer credit agreement is entitled at any time, by notice to the creditor and the payment to the creditor of all amounts payable by the debtor to him under the agreement and any amount which the creditor claims under section 95A(2) or section 95B(2) (less any rebate allowable under section 95), to discharge the debtor's indebtedness under the agreement.

(2)   A notice under subsection (1) may embody the exercise by the debtor of any option to purchase goods conferred on him by the agreement, and deal with any other matter arising on, or in relation to, the termination of the agreement.

(3)   The debtor under a regulated consumer credit agreement, other than an agreement secured on land, is entitled at any time to discharge part of his indebtedness by taking the steps in subsection (4).

(4)   The steps referred to in subsection (3) are as follows—

(a)   he provides notice to the creditor,

(b)   he pays to the creditor some of the amount payable by him to the creditor under the agreement before the time fixed by the agreement, and

(c)   he makes the payment—
     (i)   before the end of the period of 28 days beginning with the day following that on which notice under paragraph (a) was received by the creditor, or
     (ii)   on or before any later date specified in the notice.
(5)   Where a debtor takes the steps in subsection (4) his indebtedness shall be discharged by an amount equal to the sum of the amount paid and any rebate allowable under section 95 less any amount which the creditor claims under section 95A(2) or section 95B(2).
(6)   A notice—
     (a)   under subsection (1), other than a notice relating to a regulated consumer credit agreement secured on land, or
     (b)   under subsection (4)(a), need not be in writing.

95.   Rebate on early settlement

(1)   Regulations may provide for the allowance of a rebate of charges for credit to the debtor under a regulated consumer credit agreement where, under section 94, on refinancing, on breach of the agreement, or for any other reason, his indebtedness is discharged or is discharged in part or becomes payable before the time fixed by the agreement, or any sum becomes payable by him before the time so fixed.
(2)   Regulations under subsection (1) may provide for calculation of the rebate by reference to any sums paid or payable by the debtor or his relative under or in connection with the agreement (whether to the creditor or some other person), including sums under linked transactions and other items in the total charge for credit.

95A.   Compensatory amount

(1)   This section applies where—
     (a)   a regulated consumer credit agreement, other than an agreement secured on land, provides for the rate of interest on the credit to be fixed for a period of time, and
     (b)   under section 94 the debtor discharges all or part of his indebtedness during that period.
(2)   The creditor may claim an amount equal to the cost which the creditor has incurred as a result only of the debtor's indebtedness being discharged during that period if—
     (a)   the amount of the payment under section 94 exceeds £8,000 or, where more than one such payment is made in any 12 month period, the total of those payments exceeds £8,000,
     (b)   the agreement is not a debtor-creditor agreement enabling the debtor to overdraw on a current account, and
     (c)   the amount of the payment under section 94 is not paid from the proceeds of a contract of payment protection insurance.
(3)   The amount in subsection (2)—
     (a)   must be fair,
     (b)   must be objectively justified, and
     (c)   must not exceed whichever is the higher of—
          (i)   the relevant percentage of the amount of the payment under section 94, and
          (ii)   the total amount of interest that would have been paid by the debtor under the agreement in the period from the date on which the debtor makes the payment under section 94 to the date fixed by the agreement for the discharge of the indebtedness of the debtor.
(4)   In subsection (3)(c)(i) 'relevant percentage' means—
     (a)   1%, where the period from the date on which the debtor makes the payment under section 94 to the date fixed by the agreement for the discharge of the indebtedness of the debtor is more than one year, or
     (b)   0.5%, where that period is equal to or less than one year.

95B. Compensatory amount: green deal finance

(1) This section applies where—

   (a) a regulated consumer credit agreement provides for the rate of interest on the credit to be fixed for a period of time ('the fixed rate period'),

   (b) the agreement is a green deal plan which is of a duration specified for the purposes of this section in regulations, and

   (c) under section 94 the debtor discharges all or part of his indebtedness during the fixed rate period.

(2) The creditor may claim an amount equal to the cost which the creditor has incurred as a result only of the debtor's indebtedness being discharged during the fixed rate period if—

   (a) the amount of the payment under section 94 is not paid from the proceeds of a contract of payment protection insurance, and

   (b) such other conditions as may be specified for the purposes of this section in regulations are satisfied.

(3) The amount in subsection (2)—

   (a) must be fair,

   (b) must be objectively justified,

   (c) must be calculated by the creditor in accordance with provision made for the purposes of this section in regulations, and

   (d) must not exceed the total amount of interest that would have been paid by the debtor under the agreement in the period from the date on which the debtor makes the payment under section 94 to the date fixed by the agreement for the discharge of the indebtedness of the debtor.

(4) If a creditor could claim under either section 95A or this section, the creditor may choose under which section to claim.

96. Effect on linked transactions

(1) Where for any reason the indebtedness of the debtor under a regulated consumer credit agreement is discharged before the time fixed by the agreement, he, and any relative of his, shall at the same time be discharged from any liability under a linked transaction, other than a debt which has already become payable.

(2) Subsection (1) does not apply to a linked transaction which is itself an agreement providing the debtor or his relative with credit.

(3) Regulations may exclude linked transactions of the prescribed description from the operation of subsection (1).

97. Duty to give information

(1) The creditor under a regulated consumer credit agreement, within the prescribed period after he has received a request to that effect from the debtor, shall give the debtor a statement in the prescribed form indicating, according to the information to which it is practicable for him to refer, the amount of the payment required to discharge the debtor's indebtedness under the agreement, together with the prescribed particulars showing how the amount is arrived at.

(2) Subsection (1) does not apply to a request made less than one month after a previous request under that subsection relating to the same agreement was complied with.

(2A) A request under subsection (1) need not be in writing unless the agreement is secured on land.

(3) If the creditor fails to comply with subsection (1)—

   (a) he is not entitled, while the default continues, to enforce the agreement; and

   (b) …

97A. Duty to give information on partial repayment

(1) Where a debtor under a regulated consumer credit agreement—

   (a) makes a payment by virtue of which part of his indebtedness is discharged under section 94, and

   (b) at the same time or subsequently requests the creditor to give him a statement concerning the effect of the payment on the debtor's indebtedness, the creditor must give the statement to the debtor before the end of the period of seven working days beginning with the day following that on which the creditor receives the request.

(2) The statement shall be in writing and shall contain the following particulars —

    (a) a description of the agreement sufficient to identify it,

    (b) the name, postal address and, where appropriate, any other address of the creditor and the debtor,

    (c) where the creditor is claiming an amount under section 95A(2) or section 95B(2), that amount and the method used to determine it,

    (d) the amount of any rebate to which the debtor is entitled —

        (i) under the agreement, or

        (ii) by virtue of section 95 where that is higher,

    (e) where the amount of the rebate mentioned in paragraph (d)(ii) is given, a statement indicating that this amount has been calculated having regard to the Consumer Credit (Early Settlement) Regulations 2004,

    (f) where the debtor is not entitled to any rebate, a statement to this effect,

    (g) any change to —

        (i) the number, timing or amount of repayments to be made under the agreement, or

        (ii) the duration of the agreement,

    which results from the partial discharge of the indebtedness of the debtor, and

    (h) the amount of the debtor's indebtedness remaining under the agreement at the date the creditor gives the statement.

Termination of agreements

98. Duty to give notice of termination (non-default cases)

(1) The creditor or owner is not entitled to terminate a regulated agreement except by or after giving the debtor or hirer not less than seven days' notice of the termination.

(2) Subsection (1) applies only where —

    (a) a period for the duration of the agreement is specified in the agreement, and

    (b) that period has not ended when the creditor or owner does an act mentioned in subsection (1),

but so applies notwithstanding that, under the agreement, any party is entitled to terminate it before the end of the period so specified.

(3) A notice under subsection (1) is ineffective if not in the prescribed form.

(4) Subsection (1) does not prevent a creditor from treating the right to draw on any credit as restricted or deferred and taking such steps as may be necessary to make the restriction or deferment effective.

(5) Regulations may provide that subsection (1) is not to apply to agreements described by the regulations.

(6) Subsection (1) does not apply to the termination of a regulated agreement by reason of any breach by the debtor or hirer of the agreement.

98A. Termination etc. of open-end consumer credit agreements

(1) The debtor under a regulated open-end consumer credit agreement, other than an excluded agreement, may by notice terminate the agreement, free of charge, at any time, subject to any period of notice not exceeding one month provided for by the agreement.

(2) Notice under subsection (1) need not be in writing unless the creditor so requires.

(3) Where a regulated open-end consumer credit agreement, other than an excluded agreement, provides for termination of the agreement by the creditor —

    (a) the termination must be by notice served on the debtor, and

    (b) the termination may not take effect until after the end of the period of two months, or such longer period as the agreement may provide, beginning with the day after the day on which notice is served.

(4) Where a regulated open-end consumer credit agreement, other than an excluded agreement, provides for termination or suspension by the creditor of the debtor's right to draw on credit —

      (a)   to terminate or suspend the right to draw on credit the creditor must serve a notice on the debtor before the termination or suspension or, if that is not practicable, immediately afterwards,

      (b)   the notice must give reasons for the termination or suspension, and

      (c)   the reasons must be objectively justified.

(5)   Subsection (4)(a) and (b) does not apply where giving the notice—

      (a)   is prohibited by an EU obligation, or

      (b)   would, or would be likely to, prejudice—

          (i)   the prevention or detection of crime,

          (ii)   the apprehension or prosecution of offenders, or

          (iii)   the administration of justice.

(6)   An objectively justified reason under subsection (4)(c) may, for example, relate to—

      (a)   the unauthorised or fraudulent use of credit, or

      (b)   a significantly increased risk of the debtor being unable to fulfil his obligation to repay the credit.

(7)   Subsections (1) and (3) do not affect any right to terminate an agreement for breach of contract.

(8)   For the purposes of this section an agreement is an excluded agreement if it is—

      (a)   an authorised non-business overdraft agreement,

      (b)   an authorised business overdraft agreement,

      (c)   a debtor-creditor agreement arising where the holder of a current account overdraws on the account without a pre-arranged overdraft or exceeds a prearranged overdraft limit, or

      (d)   an agreement secured on land.

99.   Right to terminate hire-purchase etc. agreements

(1)   At any time before the final payment by the debtor under a regulated hire-purchase or regulated conditional sale agreement falls due, the debtor shall be entitled to terminate the agreement by giving notice to any person entitled or authorised to receive the sums payable under the agreement.

(2)   Termination of an agreement under subsection (1) does not affect any liability under the agreement which has accrued before the termination.

(3)   Subsection (1) does not apply to a conditional sale agreement relating to land after the title to the land has passed to the debtor.

(4)   In the case of a conditional sale agreement relating to goods, where the property in the goods, having become vested in the debtor, is transferred to a person who does not become the debtor under the agreement, the debtor shall not thereafter be entitled to terminate the agreement under subsection (1).

(5)   Subject to subsection (4), where a debtor under a conditional sale agreement relating to goods terminates the agreement under this section after the property in the goods has become vested in him, the property in the goods shall thereupon vest in the person (the 'previous owner') in whom it was vested immediately before it became vested in the debtor:

    Provided that if the previous owner has died, or any other event has occurred whereby that property, if vested in him immediately before that event, would thereupon have vested in some other person, the property shall be treated as having devolved as if it had been vested in the previous owner immediately before his death or immediately before that event, as the case may be.

100.   Liability of debtor on termination of hire-purchase etc. agreement

(1)   Where a regulated hire-purchase or regulated conditional sale agreement is terminated under section 99 the debtor shall be liable, unless the agreement provides for a smaller payment, or does not provide for any payment, to pay to the creditor the amount (if any) by which one-half of the total price exceeds the aggregate of the sums paid and the sums due in respect of the total price immediately before the termination.

(2)   Where under a hire-purchase or conditional sale agreement the creditor is required to carry out any installation and the agreement specifies, as part of the total price, the amount to be paid in respect of the installation (the 'installation charge') the reference

in subsection (1) to one-half of the total price shall be construed as a reference to the aggregate of the installation charge and one-half of the remainder of the total price.

(3)   If in any action the court is satisfied that a sum less than the amount specified in subsection (1) would be equal to the loss sustained by the creditor in consequence of the termination of the agreement by the debtor, the court may make an order for the payment of that sum in lieu of the amount specified in subsection (1).

(4)   If the debtor has contravened an obligation to take reasonable care of the goods or land, the amount arrived at under subsection (1) shall be increased by the sum required to recompense the creditor for that contravention, and subsection (2) shall have effect accordingly.

(5)   Where the debtor, on the termination of the agreement, wrongfully retains possession of goods to which the agreement relates, then, in any action brought by the creditor to recover possession of the goods from the debtor, the court, unless it is satisfied that having regard to the circumstances it would not be just to do so, shall order the goods to be delivered to the creditor without giving the debtor an option to pay the value of the goods.

101. Right to terminate hire agreement

(1)   The hirer under a regulated consumer hire agreement is entitled to terminate the agreement by giving notice to any person entitled or authorised to receive the sums payable under the agreement.

(2)   Termination of an agreement under subsection (1) does not affect any liability under the agreement which has accrued before the termination.

(3)   A notice under subsection (1) shall not expire earlier than eighteen months after the making of the agreement, but apart from that the minimum period of notice to be given under subsection (1), unless the agreement provides for a shorter period, is as follows.

(4)   If the agreement provides for the making of payments by the hirer to the owner at equal intervals, the minimum period of notice is the length of one interval or three months, whichever is less.

(5)   If the agreement provides for the making of such payments at differing intervals, the minimum period of notice is the length of the shortest interval or three months, whichever is less.

(6)   In any other case, the minimum period of notice is three months.

(7)   This section does not apply to—

    (a)   any agreement which provides for the making by the hirer of payments which in total (and without breach of the agreement) exceed £1,500 in any year, or

    (b)   any agreement where—

        (i)   goods are bailed or (in Scotland) hired to the hirer for the purposes of a business carried on by him, or the hirer holds himself out as requiring the goods for those purposes, and

        (ii)   the goods are selected by the hirer, and acquired by the owner for the purposes of the agreement at the request of the hirer from any person other than the owner's associate, or

    (c)   any agreement where the hirer requires, or holds himself out as requiring, the goods for the purpose of bailing or hiring them to other persons in the course of a business carried on by him.

(8)   If, on an application made to the FCA by a person carrying on a consumer hire business, it appears to the FCA that it would be in the interest of hirers to do so, it may direct that, subject to such conditions (if any) as it may specify, this section shall not apply to consumer hire agreements made by the applicant, and this Act shall have effect accordingly.

(8A) If it appears to the FCA that it would be in the interests of hirers to do so, it may direct that, subject to such conditions (if any) as it may specify, this section shall not apply to a consumer hire agreement if the agreement falls within a specified description; and this Act shall have effect accordingly.

(9)   In the case of a modifying agreement, subsection (3) shall apply with the substitution for 'the making of the agreement' of 'the making of the original agreement'.

102. Agency for receiving notice of rescission

(1) Where the debtor or hirer under a regulated agreement claims to have a right to rescind the agreement, each of the following shall be deemed to be the agent of the creditor or owner for the purpose of receiving any notice rescinding the agreement which is served by the debtor or hirer—
   (a) a credit-broker or supplier who was the negotiator in antecedent negotiations, and
   (b) any person who, in the course of a business carried on by him, acted on behalf of the debtor or hirer in any negotiations for the agreement.

(2) In subsection (1) 'rescind' does not include—
   (a) service of a notice of cancellation, or
   (b) termination of an agreement under section 99 or 101 or by the exercise of a right or power in that behalf expressly conferred by the agreement.

103. Termination statements

(1) If an individual (the 'customer') serves on any person (the 'trader') a notice—
   (a) stating that—
      (i) the customer was the debtor or hirer under a regulated agreement described in the notice, and the trader was the creditor or owner under the agreement, and
      (ii) the customer has discharged his indebtedness to the trader under the agreement, and
      (iii) the agreement has ceased to have any operation; and
   (b) requiring the trader to give the customer a notice, signed by or on behalf of the trader, confirming that those statements are correct,
   the trader shall, within the prescribed period after receiving the notice, either comply with it or serve on the customer a counter-notice stating that, as the case may be, he disputes the correctness of the notice or asserts that the customer is not indebted to him under the agreement.

(2) Where the trader disputes the correctness of the notice he shall give particulars of the way in which he alleges it to be wrong.

(3) Subsection (1) does not apply in relation to any agreement if the trader has previously complied with that subsection on the service of a notice under it with respect to that agreement.

(4) Subsection (1) does not apply to a non-commercial agreement

(5) ...

(6) A breach of the duty imposed by subsection (1) is actionable as a breach of statutory duty.

104. Goods not to be treated as subject to landlord's hypothec in Scotland

Goods comprised in a hire-purchase agreement or goods comprised in a conditional sale agreement which have not become vested in the debtor shall not be treated in Scotland as subject to the landlord's hypothec—
   (a) during the period between the service of a default notice in respect of the goods and the date on which the notice expires or is earlier complied with; or
   (b) if the agreement is enforceable on an order of the court only, during the period between the commencement and termination of an action by the creditor to enforce the agreement.

PART VIII
SECURITY

General

105. Form and content of securities

(1) Any security provided in relation to a regulated agreement shall be expressed in writing.

(2) Regulations may prescribe the form and content of documents ('security instruments') to be made in compliance with subsection (1).

(3) Regulations under subsection (2) may in particular—

      (a)   require specified information to be included in the prescribed manner in documents, and other specified material to be excluded;

      (b)   contain requirements to ensure that specified information is clearly brought to the attention of the surety, and that one part of a document is not given insufficient or excessive prominence compared with another.

(4)   A security instrument is not properly executed unless—

      (a)   a document in the prescribed form, itself containing all the prescribed terms and conforming to regulations under subsection (2), is signed in the prescribed manner by or on behalf of the surety, and

      (b)   the document embodies all the terms of the security, other than implied terms, and

      (c)   the document, when presented or sent for the purpose of being signed by or on behalf of the surety, is in such state that its terms are readily legible, and (d) when the document is presented or sent for the purpose of being signed by or on behalf of the surety there is also presented or sent a copy of the document.

(5)   A security instrument is not properly executed unless—

      (a)   where the security is provided after, or at the time when, the regulated agreement is made, a copy of the executed agreement, together with a copy of any other document referred to in it, is given to the surety at the time the security is provided, or

      (b)   where the security is provided before the regulated agreement is made, a copy of the executed agreement, together with a copy of any other document referred to in it, is given to the surety within seven days after the regulated agreement is made.

(6)   Subsection (1) does not apply to a security provided by the debtor or hirer.

(7)   If—

      (a)   in contravention of subsection (1) a security is not expressed in writing, or

      (b)   a security instrument is improperly executed,

the security, so far as provided in relation to a regulated agreement, is enforceable against the surety on an order of the court only.

(8)   If an application for an order under subsection (7) is dismissed (except on technical grounds only) section 106 (ineffective securities) shall apply to the security.

(9)   Regulations under section 60(1) shall include provision requiring documents embodying regulated agreements also to embody any security provided in relation to a regulated agreement by the debtor or hirer.

106. Ineffective securities

Where, under any provision of this Act, this section is applied to any security provided in relation to a regulated agreement, then, subject to section 177 (saving for registered charges)—

      (a)   the security, so far as it is so provided, shall be treated as never having effect;

      (b)   any property lodged with the creditor or owner solely for the purposes of the security as so provided shall be returned by him forthwith;

      (c)   the creditor or owner shall take any necessary action to remove or cancel an entry in any register, so far as the entry relates to the security as so provided; and

      (d)   any amount received by the creditor or owner on realisation of the security shall, so far as it is referable to the agreement, be repaid to the surety.

107. Duty to give information to surety under fixed-sum credit agreement

(1)   The creditor under a regulated agreement for fixed-sum credit in relation to which security is provided, within the prescribed period after receiving a request in writing to that effect from the surety and payment of a fee of £1, shall give to the surety (if a different person from the debtor)—

      (a)   a copy of the executed agreement (if any) and of any other document referred to in it;

      (b)   a copy of the security instrument (if any); and

    (c)   a statement signed by or on behalf of the creditor showing, according to the information to which it is practicable for him to refer, —
- (i) the total sum paid under the agreement by the debtor,
- (ii) the total sum which has become payable under the agreement by the debtor but remains unpaid, and the various amounts comprised in that total sum, with the date when each became due, and
- (iii) the total sum which is to become payable under the agreement by the debtor, and the various amounts comprised in that total sum, with the date, or mode of determining the date, when each becomes due.

(2) If the creditor possesses insufficient information to enable him to ascertain the amounts and dates mentioned in subsection (1)(c)(iii), he shall be taken to comply with that sub-paragraph if his statement under subsection (1)(c) gives the basis on which, under the regulated agreement, they would fall to be ascertained.

(3) Subsection (1) does not apply to —
- (a) an agreement under which no sum is, or will or may become, payable by the debtor, or
- (b) a request made less than one month after a previous request under that subsection relating to the same agreement was complied with.

(4) If the creditor under an agreement fails to comply with subsection (1)—
- (a) he is not entitled, while the default continues, to enforce the security, so far as provided in relation to the agreement; and
- (b) ...

(5) This section does not apply to a non-commercial agreement.

108. Duty to give information to surety under running-account credit agreement

(1) The creditor under a regulated agreement for running-account credit in relation to which security is provided, within the prescribed period after receiving a request in writing to that effect from the surety and payment of a fee of £1, shall give to the surety (if a different person from the debtor)—
- (a) a copy of the executed agreement (if any) and of any other document referred to in it;
- (b) a copy of the security instrument (if any); and
- (c) a statement signed by or on behalf of the creditor showing, according to the information to which it is practicable for him to refer, —
  - (i) the state of the account, and
  - (ii) the amount, if any, currently payable under the agreement by the debtor to the creditor, and
  - (iii) the amounts and due dates of any payments which, if the debtor does not draw further on the account, will later become payable under the agreement by the debtor to the creditor.

(2) If the creditor possesses insufficient information to enable him to ascertain the amounts and dates mentioned in subsection (1)(c)(iii), he shall be taken to comply with that sub-paragraph if his statement under subsection (1)(c) gives the basis on which, under the regulated agreement, they would fall to be ascertained.

(3) Subsection (1) does not apply to —
- (a) an agreement under which no sum is, or will or may become, payable by the debtor, or
- (b) a request made less than one month after a previous request under that subsection relating to the same agreement was complied with.

(4) If the creditor under an agreement fails to comply with subsection (1)—
- (a) he is not entitled, while the default continues, to enforce the security, so far as provided in relation to the agreement; and
- (b) ...

(5) This section does not apply to a non-commercial agreement.

109. Duty to give information to surety under consumer hire agreement

(1) The owner under a regulated consumer hire agreement in relation to which security is provided, within the prescribed period after receiving a request in writing to that effect

from the surety and payment of a fee of £1, shall give to the surety (if a different person from the hirer)—

(a)   a copy of the executed agreement and of any other document referred to in it;

(b)   a copy of the security instrument (if any); and

(c)   a statement signed by or on behalf of the owner showing, according to the information to which it is practicable for him to refer, the total sum which has become payable under the agreement by the hirer but remains unpaid and the various amounts comprised in that total sum, with the date when each became due.

(2)   Subsection (1) does not apply to—

(a)   an agreement under which no sum is, or will or may become, payable by the hirer, or

(b)   a request made less than one month after a previous request under that subsection relating to the same agreement was complied with.

(3)   If the owner under an agreement fails to comply with subsection (1)—

(a)   he is not entitled, while the default continues, to enforce the security, so far as provided in relation to the agreement; and

(b)   ...

(4)   This section does not apply to a non-commercial agreement.

110. Duty to give information to debtor or hirer

(1)   The creditor or owner under a regulated agreement, within the prescribed period after receiving a request in writing to that effect from the debtor or hirer and payment of a fee of £1, shall give the debtor or hirer a copy of any security instrument executed in relation to the agreement after the making of the agreement.

(2)   Subsection (1) does not apply to—

(a)   a non-commercial agreement, or

(b)   an agreement under which no sum is, or will or may become, payable by the debtor or hirer, or

(c)   a request made less than one month after a previous request under subsection (1) relating to the same agreement was complied with.

(3)   If the creditor or owner under an agreement fails to comply with subsection (1)—

(a)   he is not entitled, while the default continues, to enforce the security (so far as provided in relation to the agreement); and

(b)   ...

111. Duty to give surety copy of default etc. notice

(1)   When a default notice or a notice under section 76(1) or 98(1) is served on a debtor or hirer, a copy of the notice shall be served by the creditor or owner on any surety (if a different person from the debtor or hirer).

(2)   If the creditor or owner fails to comply with subsection (1) in the case of any surety, the security is enforceable against the surety (in respect of the breach or other matter to which the notice relates) on an order of the court only.

113. Act not to be evaded by use of security

(1)   Where a security is provided in relation to an actual or prospective regulated agreement, the security shall not be enforced so as to benefit the creditor or owner, directly or indirectly, to an extent greater (whether as respects the amount of any payment or the time or manner of its being made) than would be the case if the security were not provided and any obligations of the debtor or hirer, or his relative, under or in relation to the agreement were carried out to the extent (if any) to which they would be enforced under this Act.

(2)   In accordance with subsection (1), where a regulated agreement is enforceable on an order of the court or the FCA only, any security provided in relation to the agreement is enforceable (so far as provided in relation to the agreement) where such an order has been made in relation to the agreement, but not otherwise.

(3) Where—
    (a) a regulated agreement is cancelled under section 69(1) or becomes subject to section 69(2), or
    (b) a regulated agreement is terminated under section 91, or
    (c) in relation to any agreement an application for an order under section 65(1) or 124(1) or a notice under section 28A of the Financial Services and Markets Act 2000 is dismissed (except on technical grounds only), or
    (d) a declaration is made by the court under section 142(1) (refusal of enforcement order) as respects any regulated agreement,
    section 106 shall apply to any security provided in relation to the agreement.

(4) Where subsection (3)(d) applies and the declaration relates to a part only of the regulated agreement, section 106 shall apply to the security only so far as it concerns that part.

(5) In the case of a cancelled agreement, the duty imposed on the debtor or hirer by section 71 or 72 shall not be enforceable before the creditor or owner has discharged any duty imposed on him by section 106 (as applied by subsection (3)(a)).

(6) If the security is provided in relation to a prospective agreement or transaction, the security shall be enforceable in relation to the agreement or transaction only after the time (if any) when the agreement is made; and until that time the person providing the security shall be entitled, by notice to the creditor or owner, to require that section 106 shall thereupon apply to the security.

(7) Where an indemnity or guarantee is given in a case where the debtor or hirer is a minor, or an indemnity is given in a case where he is otherwise not of full capacity, the reference in subsection (1) to the extent to which his obligations would be enforced shall be read in relation to the indemnity or guarantee as a reference to the extent to which those obligations would be enforced if he were of full capacity.

(8) Subsections (1) and (3) also apply where a security is provided in relation to an actual or prospective linked transaction, and in that case—
    (a) references to the agreement shall be read as references to the linked transaction, and
    (b) references to the creditor or owner shall be read as references to any person (other than the debtor or hirer, or his relative) who is a party, or prospective party, to the linked transaction.

Pledges

114. Pawn-receipts

(1) At the time he receives the article, a person who takes any article in pawn under a regulated agreement shall give to the person from whom he receives it a receipt in the prescribed form (a 'pawn-receipt').

(2) A person who takes any article in pawn from an individual whom he knows to be, or who appears to be and is, a minor commits an offence.

(3) This section and sections 117 to 122 do not apply to—
    (a) a pledge of documents of title or of bearer bonds, or
    (b) a non-commercial agreement.

116. Redemption period

(1) A pawn is redeemable at any time within six months after it was taken.

(2) Subject to subsection (1), the period within which a pawn is redeemable shall be the same as the period fixed by the parties for the duration of the credit secured by the pledge, or such longer period as they may agree.

(3) If the pawn is not redeemed by the end of the period laid down by subsections (1) and (2) (the 'redemption period'), it nevertheless remains redeemable until it is realised by the pawnee under section 121 except where under section 120(1)(a) the property in it passes to the pawnee.

(4) No special charge shall be made for redemption of a pawn after the end of the redemption period, and charges in respect of the safe keeping of the pawn shall not be at a higher rate after the end of the redemption period than before.

117. Redemption procedure

(1)   On surrender of the pawn-receipt, and payment of the amount owing, at any time when the pawn is redeemable, the pawnee shall deliver the pawn to the bearer of the pawn-receipt.

(2)   Subsection (1) does not apply if the pawnee knows or has reasonable cause to suspect that the bearer of the pawn-receipt is neither the owner of the pawn nor authorised by the owner to redeem it.

(3)   The pawnee is not liable to any person in tort or delict for delivering the pawn where subsection (1) applies, or refusing to deliver it where the person demanding delivery does not comply with subsection (1) or, by reason of subsection (2), subsection (1) does not apply.

118. Loss etc. of pawn-receipt

(1)   A person (the 'claimant') who is not in possession of the pawn-receipt but claims to be the owner of the pawn, or to be otherwise entitled or authorised to redeem it, may do so at any time when it is redeemable by tendering to the pawnee in place of the pawn-receipt—

    (a)   a statutory declaration made by the claimant in the prescribed form, and with the prescribed contents, or

    (b)   where the pawn is security for fixed-sum credit not exceeding £75 or running-account credit on which the credit limit does not exceed £75, and the pawnee agrees, a statement in writing in the prescribed form, and with the prescribed contents, signed by the claimant.

(2)   On compliance by the claimant with subsection (1), section 117 shall apply as if the declaration or statement were the pawn-receipt, and the pawn-receipt itself shall become inoperative for the purposes of section 117.

119. Unreasonable refusal to deliver pawn

(1)   If a person who has taken a pawn under a regulated agreement refuses without reasonable cause to allow the pawn to be redeemed, he commits an offence.

(2)   On the conviction in England and Wales of a pawnee under subsection (1) where the offence does not amount to theft, Chapter 3 of Part 7 of the Sentencing Code shall apply as if the pawnee had been convicted of stealing the pawn.

(3)   On the conviction in Northern Ireland of a pawnee under subsection (1) where the offence does not amount to theft, section 27 (orders for restitution) of the Theft Act (Northern Ireland) 1969, and any provision of the Theft Act (Northern Ireland) 1969 relating to that section, shall apply as if the pawnee had been convicted of stealing the pawn.

120. Consequence of failure to redeem

(1)   If at the end of the redemption period the pawn has not been redeemed—

    (a)   notwithstanding anything in section 113, the property in the pawn passes to the pawnee where—

        (i)   the redemption period is six months,

        (ii)   the pawn is security for fixed-sum credit not exceeding £75 or running-account credit on which the credit limit does not exceed £75, and

        (iii)   the pawn was not immediately before the making of the regulated consumer credit agreement a pawn under another regulated consumer credit agreement in respect of which the debtor has discharged his indebtedness in part under section 94(3); or

    (b)   in any other case the pawn becomes realisable by the pawnee.

(2)   Where the debtor or hirer is entitled to apply to the court for a time order under section 129, subsection (1) shall apply with the substitution, for 'at the end of the redemption period' of 'after the expiry of five days following the end of the redemption period'.

121. Realisation of pawn

(1)   When a pawn has become realisable by him, the pawnee may sell it, after giving to the pawnor (except in such cases as may be prescribed) not less than the prescribed period of notice of the intention to sell, indicating in the notice the asking price and such other particulars as may be prescribed.

(2) Within the prescribed period after the sale takes place, the pawnee shall give the pawnor the prescribed information in writing as to the sale, its proceeds and expenses.

(3) Where the net proceeds of sale are not less than the sum which, if the pawn had been redeemed on the date of the sale, would have been payable for its redemption, the debt secured by the pawn is discharged and any surplus shall be paid by the pawnee to the pawnor.

(4) Where subsection (3) does not apply, the debt shall be treated as from the date of sale as equal to the amount by which the net proceeds of sale fall short of the sum which would have been payable for the redemption of the pawn on that date.

(5) In this section the 'net proceeds of sale' is the amount realised (the 'gross amount') less the expenses (if any) of the sale.

(6) If the pawnor alleges that the gross amount is less than the true market value of the pawn on the date of sale, it is for the pawnee to prove that he and any agents employed by him in the sale used reasonable care to ensure that the true market value was obtained, and if he fails to do so subsections (3) and (4) shall have effect as if the reference in subsection (5) to the gross amount were a reference to the true market value.

(7) If the pawnor alleges that the expenses of the sale were unreasonably high, it is for the pawnee to prove that they were reasonable, and if he fails to do so subsections (3) and (4) shall have effect as if the reference in subsection (5) to expenses were a reference to reasonable expenses.

Negotiable instruments

123. Restrictions on taking and negotiating instruments

(1) A creditor or owner shall not take a negotiable instrument, other than a bank note or cheque, in discharge of any sum payable—
   (a) by the debtor or hirer under a regulated agreement, or
   (b) by any person as surety in relation to the agreement.

(2) The creditor or owner shall not negotiate a cheque taken by him in discharge of a sum payable as mentioned in subsection (1) except to a banker (within the meaning of the Bills of Exchange Act 1882).

(3) The creditor or owner shall not take a negotiable instrument as security for the discharge of any sum payable as mentioned in subsection (1).

(4) A person takes a negotiable instrument as security for the discharge of a sum if the sum is intended to be paid in some other way, and the negotiable instrument is to be presented for payment only if the sum is not paid in that way.

(5) This section does not apply where the regulated agreement is a non-commercial agreement.

(6) The Treasury may by order provide that this section shall not apply where the regulated agreement has a connection with a country outside the United Kingdom.

124. Consequences of breach of s. 123

(1) After any contravention of section 123 has occurred in relation to a sum payable as mentioned in section 123(1)(a), the agreement under which the sum is payable is enforceable against the debtor or hirer on an order of the court only.

(2) After any contravention of section 123 has occurred in relation to a sum payable by any surety, the security is enforceable on an order of the court only.

(3) Where an application for an order under subsection (2) is dismissed (except on technical grounds only) section 106 shall apply to the security.

125. Holders in due course

(1) A person who takes a negotiable instrument in contravention of section 123(1) or (3) is not a holder in due course, and is not entitled to enforce the instrument.

(2) Where a person negotiates a cheque in contravention of section 123(2), his doing so constitutes a defect in his title within the meaning of the Bills of Exchange Act 1882.

(3) If a person mentioned in section 123(1)(a) and (b) ('the protected person') is liable to a holder in due course of an instrument taken from the protected person in contravention of section 123(1) or (3), or taken from the protected person and negotiated in contravention of section 123(2), the creditor or owner shall indemnify the protected person in respect of that liability.

(4)   Nothing in this Act affects the rights of the holder in due course of any negotiable instrument.

Land mortgages

126. Enforcement of land mortgages

(1)   A land mortgage securing a regulated agreement or a regulated mortgage contract (within the meaning of the Regulated Activities Order), is enforceable (so far as provided in relation to the agreement) on an order of the court only.

(2)   Subject to section 140A(5) (unfair relationships between creditors and debtors) for the purposes of subsection (1) and Part 9 (judicial control), a regulated mortgage contract which would, but for article 60C(2) of the Financial Services and Markets Act 2000 (Regulated Activities) Order 2001 be a regulated agreement is to be treated as if it were a regulated agreement.

(3)   In this section, "regulated mortgage contract" has the meaning given by article 61(3) of the Regulated Activities Order (regulated mortgage contracts).

PART IX
JUDICIAL CONTROL

Enforcement of certain regulated agreements and securities

127. Enforcement orders in cases of infringement

(1)   In the case of an application for an enforcement order under—
   (za)   section 55(2) (disclosure of information), or
   (zb)   section 61B(3) (duty to supply copy of overdraft agreement), or
   (a)   section 65(1) (improperly executed agreements), or
   (b)   section 105(7)(a) or (b) (improperly executed security instruments), or
   (c)   section 111(2) (failure to serve copy of notice on surety), or
   (d)   section 124(1) or (2) (taking of negotiable instrument in contravention of section 123),
   the court shall dismiss the application if, but … only if, it considers it just to do so having regard to—
      (i)   prejudice caused to any person by the contravention in question, and the degree of culpability for it; and
      (ii)   powers conferred on the court by subsection (2) and sections 135 and 136.

(2)   If it appears to the court just to do so, it may in an enforcement order reduce or discharge any sum payable by the debtor or hirer, or any surety, so as to compensate him for prejudice suffered as a result of the contravention in question.

(3), (4), (5) …

128. Enforcement orders on death of debtor or hirer

The court shall make an order under section 86(2) if, but only if, the creditor or owner proves that he has been unable to satisfy himself that the present and future obligations of the debtor or hirer under the agreement are likely to be discharged.

Extension of time

129. Time orders

(1)   Subject to subsection (3) below, if it appears to the court just to do so—
   (a)   on an application for an enforcement order; or
   (b)   on an application made by a debtor or hirer under this paragraph after service on him of—
      (i)   a default notice, or
      (ii)   a notice under section 76(1) or 98(1); or
   (ba)   on an application made by a debtor or hirer under this paragraph after he has been given a notice under section 86B or 86C; or

     (c)   in an action brought by a creditor or owner to enforce a regulated agreement or any security, or recover possession of any goods or land to which a regulated agreement relates,

the court may make an order under this section (a 'time order').

(2)   A time order shall provide for one or both of the following, as the court considers just—

    (a)   the payment by the debtor or hirer or any surety of any sum owed under a regulated agreement or a security by such instalments, payable at such times, as the court having regard to the means of the debtor or hirer and any surety, considers reasonable;

    (b)   the remedying by the debtor or hirer of any breach of a regulated agreement (other than non-payment of money) within such period as the court may specify.

(3)   Where in Scotland a time to pay direction or a time order has been made in relation to a debt, it shall not thereafter be competent to make a time order in relation to the same debt.

129A. Debtor or hirer to give notice of intent etc. to creditor or owner

(1)   A debtor or hirer may make an application under section 129(1)(ba) in relation to a regulated agreement only if—

    (a)   following his being given the notice under section 86B or 86C, he gave a notice within subsection (2) to the creditor or owner; and

    (b)   a period of at least 14 days has elapsed after the day on which he gave that notice to the creditor or owner.

(2)   A notice is within this subsection if it—

    (a)   indicates that the debtor or hirer intends to make the application;

    (b)   indicates that he wants to make a proposal to the creditor or owner in relation to his making of payments under the agreement; and

    (c)   gives details of that proposal.

130. Supplemental provisions about time orders

(1)   Where in accordance with rules of court an offer to pay any sum by instalments is made by the debtor or hirer and accepted by the creditor or owner, the court may in accordance with rules of court make a time order under section 129(2)(a) giving effect to the offer without hearing evidence of means.

(2)   In the case of a hire-purchase or conditional sale agreement only, a time order under section 129(2)(a) may deal with sums which, although not payable by the debtor at the time the order is made, would if the agreement continued in force become payable under it subsequently.

(3)   A time order under section 129(2)(a) shall not be made where the regulated agreement is secured by a pledge if, by virtue of regulations made under section 76(5), 87(4) or 98(5), service of a notice is not necessary for enforcement of the pledge.

(4)   Where, following the making of a time order in relation to a regulated hire-purchase or conditional sale agreement or a regulated consumer hire agreement, the debtor or hirer is in possession of the goods, he shall be treated (except in the case of a debtor to whom the creditor's title has passed) as a bailee or (in Scotland) a custodier of the goods under the terms of the agreement, notwithstanding that the agreement has been terminated.

(5)   Without prejudice to anything done by the creditor or owner before the commencement of the period specified in a time order made under section 129(2)(b) ('the relevant period'),—

    (a)   he shall not while the relevant period subsists take in relation to the agreement any action such as is mentioned in section 87(1);

    (b)   where—

        (i)   a provision of the agreement ('the secondary provision') becomes operative only on breach of another provision of the agreement ('the primary provision'), and

        (ii)   the time order provides for the remedying of such a breach of the primary provision within the relevant period,

he shall not treat the secondary provision as operative before the end of that period;

(c) if while the relevant period subsists the breach to which the order relates is remedied it shall be treated as not having occurred.

(6) On the application of any person affected by a time order, the court may vary or revoke the order.

Interest

130A. Interest payable on judgment debts etc.

(1) If the creditor or owner under a regulated agreement wants to be able to recover from the debtor or hirer post-judgment interest in connection with a sum that is required to be paid under a judgment given in relation to the agreement (the 'judgment sum'), he—

(a) after the giving of that judgment, shall give the debtor or hirer a notice under this section (the 'first required notice'); and

(b) after the giving of the first required notice, shall give the debtor or hirer further notices under this section at intervals of not more than six months.

(2) The debtor or hirer shall have no liability to pay post-judgment interest in connection with the judgment sum to the extent that the interest is calculated by reference to a period occurring before the day on which he is given the first required notice.

(3) If the creditor or owner fails to give the debtor or hirer a notice under this section within the period of six months beginning with the day after the day on which such a notice was last given to the debtor or hirer, the debtor or hirer shall have no liability to pay post-judgment interest in connection with the judgment sum to the extent that the interest is calculated by reference to the whole or to a part of the period which—

(a) begins immediately after the end of that period of six months; and

(b) ends at the end of the day on which the notice is given to the debtor or hirer.

(4) The debtor or hirer shall have no liability to pay any sum in connection with the preparation or the giving to him of a notice under this section.

(5) A notice under this section may be incorporated in a statement or other notice which the creditor or owner gives the debtor or hirer in relation to the agreement by virtue of another provision of this Act.

(6) Regulations may make provision about the form and content of notices under this section.

(7) This section does not apply in relation to post-judgment interest which is required to be paid by virtue of any of the following—

(a) section 4 of the Administration of Justice (Scotland) Act 1972;

(b) Article 127 of the Judgments Enforcement (Northern Ireland) Order 1981;

(c) section 74 of the County Courts Act 1984.

(8) This section does not apply in relation to a non-commercial agreement or to a small agreement.

(9) In this section 'post-judgment interest' means interest to the extent calculated by reference to a period occurring after the giving of the judgment under which the judgment sum is required to be paid.

Protection of property pending proceedings

131. Protection orders

The court, on application of the creditor or owner under a regulated agreement, may make such orders as it thinks just for protecting any property of the creditor or owner, or property subject to any security, from damage or depreciation pending the determination of any proceedings under this Act, including orders restricting or prohibiting use of the property or giving directions as to its custody.

Hire and hire-purchase etc. agreements

132. Financial relief for hirer

(1) Where the owner under a regulated consumer hire agreement recovers possession of goods to which the agreement relates otherwise than by action, the hirer may apply to the court for an order that—

    (a)   the whole or part of any sum paid by the hirer to the owner in respect of the goods shall be repaid, and

    (b)   the obligation to pay the whole or part of any sum owed by the hirer to the owner in respect of the goods shall cease,

and if it appears to the court just to do so, having regard to the extent of the enjoyment of the goods by the hirer, the court shall grant the application in full or in part.

(2)   Where in proceedings relating to a regulated consumer hire agreement the court makes an order for the delivery to the owner of goods to which the agreement relates the court may include in the order the like provision as may be made in an order under subsection (1).

133. Hire-purchase etc. agreements: special powers of court

(1)   If, in relation to a regulated hire-purchase or conditional sale agreement, it appears to the court just to do so—

    (a)   on an application for an enforcement order or time order; or

    (b)   in an action brought by the creditor to recover possession of goods to which the agreement relates,

       the court may—

       (i)   make an order (a 'return order') for the return to the creditor of goods to which the agreement relates;

       (ii)   make an order (a 'transfer order') for the transfer to the debtor of the creditor's title to certain goods to which the agreement relates ('the transferred goods'), and the return to the creditor of the remainder of the goods.

(2)   In determining for the purposes of this section how much of the total price has been paid ('the paid-up sum'), the court may—

    (a)   treat any sum paid by the debtor, or owed by the creditor, in relation to the goods as part of the paid-up sum;

    (b)   deduct any sum owed by the debtor in relation to the goods (otherwise than as part of the total price) from the paid-up sum,

and make corresponding reductions in amounts so owed.

(3)   Where a transfer order is made, the transferred goods shall be such of the goods to which the agreement relates as the court thinks just; but a transfer order shall be made only where the paid-up sum exceeds the part of the total price referable to the transferred goods by an amount equal to at least one-third of the unpaid balance of the total price.

(4)   Notwithstanding the making of a return order or transfer order, the debtor may at any time before the goods enter the possession of the creditor, on payment of the balance of the total price and the fulfilment of any other necessary conditions, claim the goods ordered to be returned to the creditor.

(5)   When, in pursuance of a time order or under this section, the total price of goods under a regulated hire-purchase agreement or regulated conditional sale agreement is paid and any other necessary conditions are fulfilled, the creditor's title to the goods vests in the debtor.

(6)   If, in contravention of a return order or transfer order, any goods to which the order relates are not returned to the creditor, the court, on the application of the creditor, may—

    (a)   revoke so much of the order as relates to those goods, and

    (b)   order the debtor to pay the creditor the unpaid portion of so much of the total price as is referable to those goods.

(7)   For the purposes of this section, the part of the total price referable to any goods is the part assigned to those goods by the agreement or (if no such assignment is made) the part determined by the court to be reasonable.

134. Evidence of adverse detention in hire-purchase etc. cases

(1)   Where goods are comprised in a regulated hire-purchase agreement, regulated conditional sale agreement or regulated consumer hire agreement, and the creditor or owner—

(a)   brings an action or makes an application to enforce a right to recover possession of the goods from the debtor or hirer and

(b)   proves that a demand for the delivery of the goods was included in the default notice under section 88(5), or that, after the right to recover possession of the goods accrued but before the action was begun or the application was made, he made a request in writing to the debtor or hirer to surrender the goods,

then, for the purposes of the claim of the creditor or owner to recover possession of the goods, the possession of them by the debtor or hirer shall be deemed to be adverse to the creditor or owner.

(2)   In subsection (1) 'the debtor or hirer' includes a person in possession of the goods at any time between the debtor's or hirer's death and the grant of probate or administration, or (in Scotland) confirmation.

(3)   Nothing in this section affects a claim for damages for conversion or (in Scotland) for delict.

Supplemental provisions as to orders

135. Power to impose conditions, or suspend operation of order

(1)   If it considers it just to do so, the court may in an order made by it in relation to a regulated agreement include provisions—

(a)   making the operation of any term of the order conditional on the doing of specified acts by any party to the proceedings;

(b)   suspending the operation of any term of the order either—

(i)   until such time as the court subsequently directs, or

(ii)   until the occurrence of a specified act or omission.

(2)   The court shall not suspend the operation of a term requiring the delivery up of goods by any person unless satisfied that the goods are in his possession or control.

(3)   In the case of a consumer hire agreement, the court shall not so use its powers under subsection (1)(b) as to extend the period for which, under the terms of the agreement, the hirer is entitled to possession of the goods to which the agreement relates.

(4)   On the application of any person affected by a provision included under subsection (1), the court may vary the provision.

136. Power to vary agreements and securities

The court may in an order made by it under this Act include such provision as it considers just for amending any agreement or security in consequence of a term of the order.

Unfair relationships

140A. Unfair relationships between creditors and debtors

(1)   The court may make an order under section 140B in connection with a credit agreement if it determines that the relationship between the creditor and the debtor arising out of the agreement (or the agreement taken with any related agreement) is unfair to the debtor because of one or more of the following—

(a)   any of the terms of the agreement or of any related agreement;

(b)   the way in which the creditor has exercised or enforced any of his rights under the agreement or any related agreement;

(c)   any other thing done (or not done) by, or on behalf of, the creditor (either before or after the making of the agreement or any related agreement).

(2)   In deciding whether to make a determination under this section the court shall have regard to all matters it thinks relevant (including matters relating to the creditor and matters relating to the debtor).

(3)   For the purposes of this section the court shall (except to the extent that it is not appropriate to do so) treat anything done (or not done) by, or on behalf of, or in relation to, an associate or a former associate of the creditor as if done (or not done) by, or on behalf of, or in relation to, the creditor.

(4)   A determination may be made under this section in relation to a relationship notwithstanding that the relationship may have ended.

(5)   An order under section 140B shall not be made in connection with a credit agreement which is an exempt agreement for the purposes of Chapter 14A of Part 2 of the

Regulated Activities Order by virtue of article 60C(2) of that Order (regulated mortgage contracts and regulated home purchase plans).

140B. Powers of court in relation to unfair relationships

(1) An order under this section in connection with a credit agreement may do one or more of the following—

    (a) require the creditor, or any associate or former associate of his, to repay (in whole or in part) any sum paid by the debtor or by a surety by virtue of the agreement or any related agreement (whether paid to the creditor, the associate or the former associate or to any other person);

    (b) require the creditor, or any associate or former associate of his, to do or not to do (or to cease doing) anything specified in the order in connection with the agreement or any related agreement;

    (c) reduce or discharge any sum payable by the debtor or by a surety by virtue of the agreement or any related agreement;

    (d) direct the return to a surety of any property provided by him for the purposes of a security;

    (e) otherwise set aside (in whole or in part) any duty imposed on the debtor or on a surety by virtue of the agreement or any related agreement;

    (f) alter the terms of the agreement or of any related agreement;

    (g) direct accounts to be taken, or (in Scotland) an accounting to be made, between any persons.

(2) An order under this section may be made in connection with a credit agreement only—

    (a) on an application made by the debtor or by a surety;

    (b) at the instance of the debtor or a surety in any proceedings in any court to which the debtor and the creditor are parties, being proceedings to enforce the agreement or any related agreement; or

    (c) at the instance of the debtor or a surety in any other proceedings in any court where the amount paid or payable under the agreement or any related agreement is relevant.

(3) An order under this section may be made notwithstanding that its effect is to place on the creditor, or any associate or former associate of his, a burden in respect of an advantage enjoyed by another person.

(4) An application under subsection (2)(a) may only be made—

    (a) in England and Wales, to the county court;

    (b) in Scotland, to the sheriff court;

    (c) in Northern Ireland, to the High Court (subject to subsection (6)).

(5) In Scotland such an application may be made in the sheriff court for the district in which the debtor or surety resides or carries on business.

(6) In Northern Ireland such an application may be made to the county court if the credit agreement is an agreement under which the creditor provides the debtor with—

    (a) fixed-sum credit not exceeding £15,000; or

    (b) running-account credit on which the credit limit does not exceed £15,000.

(7) …

(8) A party to any proceedings mentioned in subsection (2) shall be entitled, in accordance with rules of court, to have any person who might be the subject of an order under this section made a party to the proceedings.

(9) If, in any such proceedings, the debtor or a surety alleges that the relationship between the creditor and the debtor is unfair to the debtor, it is for the creditor to prove to the contrary.

140C. Interpretation of ss. 140A and 140B

(1) In this section and in sections 140A and 140B 'credit agreement' means any agreement between an individual (the 'debtor') and any other person (the 'creditor') by which the creditor provides the debtor with credit of any amount.

(2) References in this section and in sections 140A and 140B to the creditor or to the debtor under a credit agreement include—

     (a)   references to the person to whom his rights and duties under the agreement have passed by assignment or operation of law;

     (b)   where two or more persons are the creditor or the debtor, references to any one or more of those persons.

(3)   The definition of 'court' in section 189(1) does not apply for the purposes of sections 140A and 140B.

(4)   References in sections 140A and 140B to an agreement related to a credit agreement (the 'main agreement') are references to—

     (a)   a credit agreement consolidated by the main agreement;

     (b)   a linked transaction in relation to the main agreement or to a credit agreement within paragraph (a);

     (c)   a security provided in relation to the main agreement, to a credit agreement within paragraph (a) or to a linked transaction within paragraph (b).

(5)   In the case of a credit agreement which is not a regulated consumer credit agreement, for the purposes of subsection (4) a transaction shall be treated as being a linked transaction in relation to that agreement if it would have been such a transaction had that agreement been a regulated consumer credit agreement.

(6)   For the purposes of this section and section 140B the definitions of 'security' and 'surety' in section 189(1) apply (with any appropriate changes) in relation to—

     (a)   a credit agreement which is not a consumer credit agreement as if it were a consumer credit agreement; and

     (b)   a transaction which is a linked transaction by virtue of subsection (5).

(7)   For the purposes of this section a credit agreement (the 'earlier agreement') is consolidated by another credit agreement (the 'later agreement') if—

     (a)   the later agreement is entered into by the debtor (in whole or in part) for purposes connected with debts owed by virtue of the earlier agreement; and

     (b)   at any time prior to the later agreement being entered into the parties to the earlier agreement included—

        (i)   the debtor under the later agreement; and

        (ii)   the creditor under the later agreement or an associate or a former associate of his.

(8)   Further, if the later agreement is itself consolidated by another credit agreement (whether by virtue of this subsection or subsection (7)), then the earlier agreement is consolidated by that other agreement as well.

Miscellaneous

141. Jurisdiction and parties

(1)   In England and Wales the county court shall have jurisdiction to hear and determine—

     (a)   any action by the creditor or owner to enforce a regulated agreement or any security relating to it;

     (b)   any action to enforce any linked transaction against the debtor or hirer or his relative,

and such an action shall not be brought in any other court.

(2)   Where an action or application is brought in the High Court which, by virtue of this Act, ought to have been brought in the county court it shall not be treated as improperly brought, but shall be transferred to the county court.

(3)   In Scotland the sheriff court shall have jurisdiction to hear and determine any action falling within subsection (1) and such an action shall not be brought in any other court.

(3A) Subject to subsection (3B) an action which is brought in the sheriff court by virtue of subsection (3) shall be brought only in one of the following courts, namely—

     (a)   the court for the place where the debtor or hirer is domiciled (within the meaning of section 41 or 42 of the Civil Jurisdiction and Judgments Act 1982);

     (b)   the court for the place where the debtor or hirer carries on business; and

     (c)   where the purpose of the action is to assert, declare or determine proprietary or possessory rights, or rights of security, in or over movable property, or to obtain authority to dispose of movable property, the court for the place where the property is situated.

(3B) Subsection (3A) shall not apply—

    (a)   where Rule 3 of Schedule 8 to the said Act of 1982 applies; or

    (b)   where the jurisdiction of another court has been prorogated by an agreement entered into after the dispute has arisen.

(4)   In Northern Ireland the county court shall have jurisdiction to hear and determine any action or application falling within subsection (1).

(5)   Except as may be provided by rules of court, all the parties to a regulated agreement, and any surety, shall be made parties to any proceedings relating to the agreement.

142.　Power to declare rights of parties

(1)   Where under any provision of this Act a thing can be done by a creditor or owner on an enforcement order only, and either—

    (a)   the court dismisses (except on technical grounds only) an application for an enforcement order, or

    (b)   where no such application has been made or such an application has been dismissed on technical grounds only an interested party applies to the court for a declaration under this subsection,

the court may if it thinks just make a declaration that the creditor or owner is not entitled to do that thing, and thereafter no application for an enforcement order in respect of it shall be entertained.

(2)   Where—

    (a)   a regulated agreement or linked transaction is cancelled under section 69(1), or becomes subject to section 69(2), or

    (b)   a regulated agreement is terminated under section 91, and an interested party applies to the court for a declaration under this subsection, the court may make a declaration to that effect.

PART X

ANCILLARY CREDIT BUSINESSES

Definitions

145.　Types of ancillary credit business

(1)   An ancillary credit business is any business so far as it comprises or relates to—

    (a)   credit brokerage,

    (b)   debt-adjusting,

    (c)   debt-counselling,

    (d)   debt-collecting,

    (da) debt administration,

    (db) the provision of credit information services, or

    (e)   the operation of a credit reference agency.

(2)   'Credit brokerage' means the carrying on of an activity of the kind specified by article 36A(1)(a) to(c) of the Regulated Activities Order (credit broking), disregarding the effect of paragraph (2) of that article;

(5)   'Debt adjusting' means the carrying on of an activity of the kind specified by article 39D of that Order (debt adusting);

(6)   'Debt counselling' means carrying on the activity of the kind specified by article 39E of that Order (debt counselling);

(7)   'Debt collecting' means the carrying on of an activity of the kind specified by article 39F of that Order (debt collecting);

(7A) 'Debt administration' means the carrying on of an activity of the kind specified by article 39G of that Order (debt administration), disregarding the effect of paragraph (3) of that article;

(7B) A person ('P') provides credit information services if P carries on, by way of business, an activity of the kind specified by article 89A(1) of that Order (providing credit information services);

(8)   A person ('P') operates a credit reference agency if P carries on, by way of business, an activity specified by article 89B of that Order (providing credit references).

153. Definition of canvassing off trade premises (agreements for ancillary credit services)

(1)   An individual (the 'canvasser') canvasses off trade premises the services of a person carrying on an ancillary credit business if he solicits the entry of another individual (the 'consumer') into an agreement for the provision to the consumer of those services by making oral representations to the consumer, or any other individual, during a visit by the canvasser to any place (not excluded by subsection (2)) where the consumer, or that other individual as the case may be, is, being a visit—

     (a)   carried out for the purpose of making such oral representations to individuals who are at that place, but

     (b)   not carried out in response to a request made on a previous occasion.

(2)   A place is excluded from subsection (1) if it is a place where (whether on a permanent or temporary basis)—

     (a)   the ancillary credit business is carried on, or

     (b)   any business is carried on by the canvasser or the person whose employee or agent the canvasser is, or by the consumer.

154. Prohibition of canvassing certain ancillary credit services off trade premises

It is an offence to canvass off trade premises the services of a person carrying on a business of credit-brokerage, debt-adjusting, debt-counselling or the provision of credit information services.

155. Right to recover brokerage fees

(1)   Subject to subsection (2A), the excess over £5 of a fee or commission for his services charged by a credit-broker to an individual to whom this subsection applies shall cease to be payable or, as the case may be, shall be recoverable by the individual if the introduction does not result in his entering into a relevant agreement within the six months following the introduction (disregarding any agreement which is cancelled under section 69(1) or becomes subject to section 69(2)).

(2)   Subsection (1) applies to an individual who sought an introduction for a purpose which would have been fulfilled by his entry into—

     (a)   a regulated agreement, or

     (b)   in the case of an individual desiring to obtain credit to finance the acquisition or provision of a dwelling occupied or to be occupied by that individual or a relative of that individual, an agreement for credit secured on land,

     (c)   a credit agreement which is an exempt agreement for the purposes of Chapter 14A of Part 2 of the Regulated Activities Order, or

     (d)   an agreement which is not a regulated credit agreement or a regulated consumer hire agreement but which would be such an agreement if the law applicable to the agreement were the law of a part of the United Kingdom.

(2A) But subsection (1) does not apply where—

     (a)   the fee or commission relates to the effecting of an introduction of a kind mentioned in article 36E of the Regulated Activities Order (activities in relation to certain agreements relating to land); and

     (b)   the person charging the fee or commission is an authorised person or an approved representative, within the meaning of the Financial Services and Markets Act 2000.

(3)   An agreement is a relevant agreement for the purposes of subsection (1) in relation to an individual if it is an agreement such as is referred to in subsection (2) in relation to that individual.

(4)   In the case of an individual desiring to obtain credit under a consumer credit agreement, any sum payable or paid by him to a credit-broker otherwise than as a fee or commission for the credit-broker's services shall for the purposes of subsection (1) be treated as such a fee or commission if it enters, or would enter, into the total charge for credit.

Credit reference agencies

157. Duty to disclose name etc. of agency

(A1) Where a creditor under a prospective regulated agreement, other than an excluded agreement, decides not to proceed with it on the basis of information obtained by the creditor from a credit reference agency, the creditor must, when informing the debtor of the decision—

    (a) inform the debtor that this decision has been reached on the basis of information from a credit reference agency, and

    (b) provide the debtor with the particulars of the agency including its name, address and telephone number.

(1) In any other case, a creditor, owner or negotiator, within the prescribed period after receiving a request in writing to that effect from the debtor or hirer, shall give him notice of the name and address of any credit reference agency from which the creditor, owner or negotiator has, during the antecedent negotiations, applied for information about his financial standing.

(2) Subsection (1) does not apply to a request received more than 28 days after the termination of the antecedent negotiations, whether on the making of the regulated agreement or otherwise.

(2A) A creditor is not required to disclose information under this section if such disclosure—

    (a) contravenes the GDPR,

    (b) is prohibited by any other EU obligation,

    (c) would create or be likely to create a serious risk that any person would be subject to violence or intimidation, or

    (d) would, or would be likely to, prejudice—

        (i) the prevention or detection of crime,

        (ii) the apprehension or prosecution of offenders, or

        (iii) the administration of justice.

(3) If the creditor, owner or negotiator fails to comply with subsection (A1) or (1) he commits an offence.

(4) For the purposes of subsection (A1) an agreement is an excluded agreement if it is—

    (a) a consumer hire agreement, or

    (b) an agreement secured on land.

158. Duty of agency to disclose filed information

(1) A credit reference agency, within the prescribed period after receiving,—

    (a) a request in writing to that effect from a consumer, and

    (b) such particulars as the agency may reasonably require to enable them to identify the file, and

    (c) a fee of £2,

shall give the consumer a copy of the file relating to it kept by the agency.

(2) When giving a copy of the file under subsection (1), the agency shall also give the consumer a statement in the prescribed form of the consumer's rights under section 159.

(3) If the agency does not keep a file relating to the consumer it shall give the consumer notice of that fact, but need not return any money paid.

(4) If the agency contravenes any provision of this section it commits an offence.

(4A) In this section 'consumer' means—

    (a) a partnership consisting of two or three persons not all of whom are bodies corporate; or

    (b) an unincorporated body of persons which does not consist entirely of bodies corporate and is not a partnership.

(5) In this Act 'file', in relation to an individual, means all the information about him kept by a credit reference agency, regardless of how the information is stored, and 'copy of the file', as respects information not in plain English, means a transcript reduced into plain English.

159. Correction of wrong information

  (1) Any individual (the 'objector') given—

      (a) information under Article 15(1) to (3) of the GDPR (confirmation of processing, access to data and safeguards for third country transfers) by a credit reference agency, or

      (b) information under section 158,

    who considers that an entry in his file is incorrect, and that if it is not corrected he is likely to be prejudiced, may give notice to the agency requiring it either to remove the entry from the file or amend it.

  (2) Within 28 days after receiving a notice under subsection (1), the agency shall by notice inform the objector that it has—

      (a) removed the entry from the file, or

      (b) amended the entry, or

      (c) taken no action,

    and if the notice states that the agency has amended the entry it shall include a copy of the file so far as it comprises the amended entry.

  (3) Within 28 days after receiving a notice under subsection (2), or where no such notice was given, within 28 days after the expiry of the period mentioned in subsection (2), the objector may, unless he has been informed by the agency that it has removed the entry from his file, serve a further notice on the agency requiring it to add to the file an accompanying notice of correction (not exceeding 200 words) drawn up by the objector, and include a copy of it when furnishing information included in or based on that entry.

  (4) Within 28 days after receiving a notice under subsection (3), the agency, unless it intends to apply to the relevant authority under subsection (5), shall by notice inform the objector that it has received the notice under subsection (3) and intends to comply with it.

  (5) If—

      (a) the objector has not received a notice under subsection (4) within the time required, or

      (b) it appears to the agency that it would be improper for it to publish a notice of correction because it is incorrect, or unjustly defames any person, or is frivolous or scandalous, or is for any other reason unsuitable, the objector or, as the case may be, the agency may, in the prescribed manner and on payment of the prescribed fee, apply to the the relevant authority, who may make such order on the application as he thinks fit.

  (6) If a person to whom an order under this section is directed fails to comply with it within the period specified in the order he commits an offence.

  (7) The Information Commissioner may vary or revoke any order made by him under this section.

  (8) In this section 'the relevant authority' means

      (a) where the objector is a partnership or other unincorporated body of persons, the FCA, and

      (b) in any other case, the Information Commissioner.

160. Alternative procedure for business consumers

  (1) The FCA, on an application made by a credit reference agency, may direct that this section shall apply to the agency if it is satisfied—

      (a) that compliance with section 158 in the case of consumers who carry on a business would adversely affect the service provided to its customers by the agency, and

      (b) that, having regard to the methods employed by the agency and to any other relevant facts, it is probable that consumers carrying on a business would not be prejudiced by the making of the direction.

  (2) Where an agency to which this section applies receives a request, particulars and a fee under section 158(1) from a consumer who carries on a business and section 158(3) does not apply, the agency, instead of complying with section 158, may elect to deal with the matter under the following subsections.

  (3) Instead of giving the consumer a copy of the file, the agency shall within the prescribed period give notice to the consumer that it is proceeding under this section, and by

notice give the consumer such information included in or based on entries in the file as the FCA may direct, together with a statement in the prescribed form of the consumer's rights under subsections (4) and (5).

(4) If within 28 days after receiving the information given to the consumer under subsection (3), or such longer period as the FCA may allow, the consumer—

    (a) gives notice to the FCA that the consumer is dissatisfied with the information, and

    (b) satisfies the FCA that the consumer has taken such steps in relation to the agency as may be reasonable with a view to removing the cause of the consumer's dissatisfaction, and

    (c) pays the FCA the prescribed fee,

the FCA may direct the agency to give the FCA a copy of the file, and the FCA may disclose to the consumer such of the information on the file as the FCA thinks fit.

(5) Section 159 applies with any necessary modifications to information given to the consumer under this section as it applies to information given under section 158.

(6) If an agency making an election under subsection (2) fails to comply with subsection (3) or (4) it commits an offence.

(7) In this section 'consumer' has the same meaning as in section 158.

PART XI
ENFORCEMENT OF ACT

161. Enforcement authorities

(1) The following authorities ('enforcement authorities') have a duty to enforce this Act and regulations made under it—

    (a) ...

    (b) in Great Britain, the local weights and measures authority,

    (c) in Northern Ireland, the Department of Commerce for Northern Ireland.

(1A) Subsection (1) does not limit any function of the FCA in relation to the enforcement of this Act or regulations made under it.

(1B) For the investigatory powers available to a local weights and measures authority or the Department of Enterprise, Trade and Investment in Northern Ireland for the purposes of the duty in subsection (1), see Schedule 5 to the Consumer Rights Act 2015.

...

(3) Every local weights and measures authority shall, whenever the FCA requires, report to it in such form and with such particulars as he requires on the exercise of their functions under this Act.

...

166. Notification of convictions and judgments to FCA

Where a person is convicted of an offence or has a judgment given against him by or before any court in the United Kingdom and it appears to the court—

    (a) having regard to the functions of the FCA under the Financial Services and Markets Act 2000, that the conviction or judgment should be brought to the FCA's attention, and

    (b) that it may not be brought to its attention unless arrangements for that purpose are made by the court,

the court may make such arrangements notwithstanding that the proceedings have been finally disposed of.

167. Penalties

(1) An offence under a provision of this Act specified in column 1 of Schedule 1 is triable in the mode or modes indicated in column 3, and on conviction is punishable as indicated in column 4 (where a period of time indicates the maximum term of imprisonment, and a monetary amount indicates the maximum fine, for the offence in question).

168. Defences

(1) In any proceedings for an offence under this Act it is a defence for the person charged to prove—

(a)   that his act or omission was due to a mistake, or to reliance on information supplied to him, or to an act or omission by another person, or to an accident or some other cause beyond his control, and

(b)   that he took all reasonable precautions and exercised all due diligence to avoid such an act or omission by himself or any person under his control.

(2)   If in any case the defence provided by subsection (1) involves the allegation that the act or omission was due to an act or omission by another person or to reliance on information supplied by another person, the person charged shall not, without leave of the court, be entitled to rely on that defence unless, within a period ending seven clear days before the hearing, he has served on the prosecutor a notice giving such information identifying or assisting in the identification of that other person as was then in his possession.

169. Offences by bodies corporate

Where at any time a body corporate commits an offence under this Act with the consent or connivance of, or because of neglect by, any individual, the individual commits the like offence if at that time—

(a)   he is a director, manager, secretary or similar officer of the body corporate, or

(b)   he is purporting to act as such an officer, or

(c)   the body corporate is managed by its members of whom he is one.

170. No further sanctions for breach of Act

(1)   A breach of any requirement made (otherwise than by any court) by or under this Act or by or under the Financial Services Act 2000 by virtue of an order under section 107 of the Financial Services Act 2012 shall incur no civil or criminal sanction as being such a breach, except to the extent (if any) expressly provided by or under this Act.

(2)   In exercising its functions under this Act the FCA may take account of any matter appearing to it to constitute a breach of a requirement made by or under this Act, whether or not any sanction for that breach is provided by or under this Act and, if it is so provided, whether or not proceedings have been brought in respect of the breach.

(3)   Subsection (1) does not prevent the grant of an injunction, or the making of an order of certiorari, mandamus or prohibition or as respects Scotland the grant of an interdict or of an order under section 91 of the Court of Session Act 1868 (order for specific performance of statutory duty).

171. Onus of proof in various proceedings

(1)   If an agreement contains a term signifying that in the opinion of the parties section 10(3)(b)(iii) does not apply to the agreement, it shall be taken not to apply unless the contrary is proved.

(2)   It shall be assumed in any proceedings, unless the contrary is proved, that when a person initiated a transaction as mentioned in section 19(1)(c) he knew the principal agreement had been made, or contemplated that it might be made.

(4)   In proceedings brought by the creditor under a credit-token agreement—

(a)   it is for the creditor to prove that the credit-token was lawfully supplied to the debtor, and was accepted by him, and

(b)   if the debtor alleges that any use made of the credit-token was not authorised by him, it is for the creditor to prove either—

(i)   that the use was so authorised, or

(ii)   that the use occurred before the creditor had been given notice under section 84(3).

(5)   In proceedings under section 50(1) in respect of a document received by a minor at any school or other educational establishment for minors, it is for the person sending it to him at that establishment to prove that he did not know or suspect it to be such an establishment.

(6)   In proceedings under section 119(1) it is for the pawnee to prove that he had reasonable cause to refuse to allow the pawn to be redeemed.

(7)   ...

172. Statements by creditor or owner to be binding

(1) A statement by a creditor or owner is binding on him if given under—
section 77(1),
section 78(1),
section 79(1),
section 97(1),
section 107(1)(c),
section 108(1)(c),
or section 109(1)(c).

(2) Where a trader—
  (a) gives a customer a notice in compliance with section 103(1)(b), or
  (b) gives a customer a notice under section 103(1) asserting that the customer is not indebted to him under an agreement,
  the notice is binding on the trader.

(3) Where in proceedings before any court—
  (a) it is sought to reply on a statement or notice given as mentioned in subsection (1) or (2), and
  (b) the statement or notice is shown to be incorrect, the court may direct such relief (if any) to be given to the creditor or owner from the operation of subsection (1) or (2) as appears to the court to be just.

173. Contracting-out forbidden

(1) A term contained in a regulated agreement or linked transaction, or in any other agreement relating to an actual or prospective regulated agreement or linked transaction, is void if, and to the extent that, it is inconsistent with a provision for the protection of the debtor or hirer or his relative or any surety contained in this Act or in any regulation made under this Act.

(2) Where a provision specifies the duty or liability of the debtor or hirer or his relative or any surety in certain circumstances, a term is inconsistent with that provision if it purports to impose, directly or indirectly, an additional duty or liability on him in those circumstances.

(3) Notwithstanding subsection (1), a provision of this Act under which a thing may be done in relation to any person on an order of the court or the FCA only shall not be taken to prevent its being done at any time with that person's consent given at that time, but the refusal of such consent shall not give rise to any liability.

174A. Powers to require provision of information or documents etc.

(1) Every power conferred on a relevant authority by or under this Act (however expressed) to require the provision or production of information or documents includes the power—
  (a) to require information to be provided or produced in such form as the authority may specify, including, in relation to information recorded otherwise than in a legible form, in a legible form;
  (b) to take copies of, or extracts from, any documents provided or produced by virtue of the exercise of the power;
  (c) to require the person who is required to provide or produce any information or document by virtue of the exercise of the power—
    (i) to state, to the best of his knowledge and belief, where the information or document is;
    (ii) to give an explanation of the information or document;
    (iii) to secure that any information provided or produced, whether in a document or otherwise, is verified in such manner as may be specified by the authority;
    (iv) to secure that any document provided or produced is authenticated in such manner as may be so specified;
  (d) to specify a time at or by which a requirement imposed by virtue of paragraph (c) must be complied with.

(2) Every power conferred on a relevant authority by or under this Act (however expressed) to inspect or to seize documents at any premises includes the power to take copies of, or extracts from, any documents inspected or seized by virtue of the exercise of the power.

(3) But a relevant authority has no power under this Act—
    (a) to require another person to provide or to produce,
    (b) to seize from another person, or
    (c) to require another person to give access to premises for the purposes of the inspection of,
any information or document which the other person would be entitled to refuse to provide or produce in proceedings in the High Court on the grounds of legal professional privilege or (in Scotland) in proceedings in the Court of Session on the grounds of confidentiality of communications.

(4) In subsection (3) 'communications' means—
    (a) communications between a professional legal adviser and his client;
    (b) communications made in connection with or in contemplation of legal proceedings and for the purposes of those proceedings.

(5) In this section, 'relevant authority' means an enforcement authority or an officer of an enforcement authority.

PART XII
SUPPLEMENTAL

175. Duty of persons deemed to be agents

Where under this Act a person is deemed to receive a notice or payment as agent of the creditor or owner under a regulated agreement, he shall be deemed to be under a contractual duty to the creditor or owner to transmit the notice, or remit the payment, to him forthwith.

176. Service of documents

(1) A document to be served under this Act by one person ('the server') on another person ('the subject') is to be treated as properly served on the subject if dealt with as mentioned in the following subsections.

(2) The document may be delivered or sent by an appropriate method to the subject, or addressed to him by name and left at his proper address.

(3) For the purposes of this Act, a document sent by post to, or left at, the address last known to the server as the address of a person shall be treated as sent by post to, or left at, his proper address.

(4) Where the document is to be served on the subject as being the person having any interest in land, and it is not practicable after reasonable inquiry to ascertain the subject's name or address, the document may be served by—
    (a) addressing it to the subject by the description of the person having that interest in the land (naming it), and
    (b) delivering the document to some responsible person on the land or affixing it, or a copy of it, in a conspicuous position on the land.

(5) Where a document to be served on the subject as being a debtor, hirer or surety, or as having any other capacity relevant for the purposes of this Act, is served at any time on another person who—
    (a) is the person last known to the server as having that capacity, but
    (b) before that time had ceased to have it, the document shall be treated as having been served at that time on the subject.

(6) Anything done to a document in relation to a person who (whether to the knowledge of the server or not) has died shall be treated for the purposes of subsection (5) as service of the document on that person if it would have been so treated had he not died.

(7) The following enactments shall not be construed as authorising service on the Public Trustee (in England and Wales) or the Probate Judge (in Northern Ireland) of any document which is to be served under this Act—
section 9 of the Administration of Estates Act 1925;
section 3 of the Administration of Estates Act (Northern Ireland) 1955.

(8) References in the preceding subsections to the serving of a document on a person include the giving of the document to that person.

176A. Electronic transmission of documents

(1) A document is transmitted in accordance with this subsection if—

    (a) the person to whom it is transmitted agrees that it may be delivered to him by being transmitted to a particular electronic address in a particular electronic form,

    (b) it is transmitted to that address in that form, and

    (c) the form in which the document is transmitted is such that any information in the document which is addressed to the person to whom the document is transmitted is capable of being stored for future reference for an appropriate period in a way which allows the information to be reproduced without charge.

(2) A document transmitted in accordance with subsection (1) shall, unless the contrary is proved, be treated for the purposes of this Act, except section 69, as having been delivered on the working day immediately following the day on which it is transmitted.

(3) In this section, 'electronic address' includes any number or address used for the purposes of receiving electronic communications.

177. Saving for registered charges

(1) Nothing in this Act affects the rights of a proprietor of a registered charge (within the meaning of the Land Registration Act 2002), who—

    (a) became the proprietor under a transfer for valuable consideration without notice of any defect in the title arising (apart from this section) by virtue of this Act, or

    (b) derives title from such a proprietor.

(2) Nothing in this Act affects the operation of section 104 of the Law of Property Act 1925 (protection of purchaser where mortgagee exercises power of sale).

(3) Subsection (1) does not apply to a proprietor carrying on a consumer credit business, a consumer hire business or a business of debt-collecting or debt administration.

(4) Where, by virtue of subsection (1), a land mortgage is enforced which apart from this section would be treated as never having effect, the original creditor or owner shall be liable to indemnify the debtor or hirer against any loss thereby suffered by him.

(5) In the application of this section to Scotland for subsections (1) to (3) there shall be substituted the following subsections—

    (1) 'Nothing in this Act affects the rights of a creditor in a heritable security who—

        (a) became the creditor under a transfer for value without notice of any defect in the title arising (apart from this section) by virtue of this Act; or

        (b) derives title from such a creditor.

    (2) Nothing in this Act affects the operation of section 41 of the Conveyancing (Scotland) Act 1924 (protection of purchasers), or of that section as applied to standard securities by section 32 of the Conveyancing and Feudal Reform (Scotland) Act 1970.

    (3) Subsection (1) does not apply to a creditor carrying on a consumer credit business, a consumer hire business or a business of debt-collecting or debt administration.'

(6) In the application of this section to Northern Ireland—

    (a) any reference to the proprietor of a registered charge (within the meaning of the Land Registration Act 2002) shall be construed as a reference to the registered owner of a charge under the Local Registration of Title (Ireland) Act 1891 or Part IV of the Land Registration Act (Northern Ireland) 1970, and

    (b) for the reference to section 104 of the Law Property Act 1925 there shall be substituted a reference to section 21 of the Conveyancing and Law Property Act 1881 and section 5 of the Conveyancing Act 1911.

178. Local Acts

The Treasury or the Department of Commerce for Northern Ireland may by order make such amendments or repeals of any provision of any local Act as appears to the Treasury or, as the case may be, the Department, necessary or expedient in consequence of the replacement by this Act of the enactments relating to pawnbrokers and moneylenders.

Regulations, orders, etc.

179. Power to prescribe form etc. of secondary documents

(1) Regulations may be made as to the form and content of credit-cards, trading-checks, receipts, vouchers and other documents or things issued by creditors, owners or suppliers under or in connection with regulated agreements or by other persons in connection with linked transactions, and may in particular—

    (a) require specified information to be included in the prescribed manner in documents, and other specified material to be excluded;

    (b) contain requirements to ensure that specified information is clearly brought to the attention of the debtor or hirer, or his relative, and that one part of a document is not given insufficient or excessive prominence compared with another.

(2) If a person issues any document or thing in contravention of regulations under subsection (1) then, as from the time of the contravention but without prejudice to anything done before it, this Act shall apply as if the regulated agreement had been improperly executed by reason of a contravention of regulations under section 60(1).

180. Power to prescribe form etc. of copies

(1) Regulations may be made as to the form and content of documents to be issued as copies of any executed agreement, security instrument or other document referred to in this Act, and may in particular—

    (a) require specified information to be included in the prescribed manner in any copy, and contain requirements to ensure that such information is clearly brought to the attention of a reader of the copy;

    (b) authorise the omission from a copy of certain material contained in the original, or the inclusion of such material in condensed form.

(2) A duty imposed by any provision of this Act to supply a copy of any document—

    (a) is not safisfied unless the copy supplied is in the prescribed form and conforms to the prescribed requirements;

    (b) is not infringed by the omission of any material, or its inclusion in condensed form, if that is authorised by regulations;

and references in this Act to copies shall be construed accordingly.

(3) Regulations may provide that a duty imposed by this Act to supply a copy of a document referred to in an unexecuted agreement or an executed agreement shall not apply to documents of a kind specified in the regulations.

181. Power to alter monetary limits etc.

(1) The Treasury may by order made by statutory instrument amend, or further amend, any of the following provisions of this Act so as to reduce or increase a sum mentioned in that provision, namely, sections, 17(1), ... 70(6), 75(3)(b), 77(1), 78(1), 79(1), 84(1), 101(7)(a), 107(1), 108(1), 109(1), 110(1), ... 140B(6), 155(1) and 158(1).

(2) An order under subsection (1) amending section, 17(1), ... 75(3)(b) or 139(5) or (7) or 140B(6) shall be of no effect unless a draft of the order has been laid before and approved by each House of Parliament.

182. Regulations and orders

(1) Any power of the Treasury to make regulations or orders under this Act, except the power conferred by sections 181 and 192 shall be exercisable by statutory instrument subject to annulment in pursuance of a resolution of either House of Parliament.

(2) Where a power to make regulations or orders is exercisable by the Treasury by virtue of this Act, regulations or orders made in the exercise of that power may—

    (a) make different provision in relation to different cases or classes of case, and

    (b) exclude certain cases or classes of case, and

    (c) contain such transitional provision as the Treasury thinks fit.

(3) Regulations may provide that specified expressions, when used as described by the regulations, are to be given the prescribed meaning, notwithstanding that another meaning is intended by the person using them.

(4) Any power conferred on the Treasury by this Act to make orders includes power to vary or revoke an order so made.

183. Determinations etc. by FCA

(1) The FCA may vary or revoke any determination made, or direction given, by it under this Act.

Interpretation

184. Associates

(1) A person is an associate of an individual if that person is—
    (a) the individual's husband or wife or civil partner,
    (b) a relative of—
        (i) the individual, or
        (ii) the individual's husband or wife or civil partner, or
    (c) the husband or wife or civil partner of a relative of—
        (i) the individual, or
        (ii) the individual's husband or wife or civil partner.

(2) A person is an associate of any person with whom he is in partnership, and of the husband or wife or civil partner or a relative of any individual with whom he is in partnership.

(3) A body corporate is an associate of another body corporate—
    (a) if the same person is a controller of both, or a person is a controller of one and persons who are his associates, or he and persons who are his associates, are controllers of the other; or
    (b) if a group of two or more persons is controller of each company, and the groups either consist of the same persons or could be regarded as consisting of the same persons by treating (in one or more cases) a member of either group as replaced by a person of whom he is an associate.

(4) A body corporate is an associate of another person if that person is a controller of it or if that person and persons who are his associates together are controllers of it.

(5) In this section 'relative' means brother, sister, uncle, aunt, nephew, niece, lineal ancestor or lineal descendant, references to a husband or wife include a former husband or wife and a reputed husband or wife, and references to a civil partner include a former civil partner and a reputed civil partner; and for the purposes of this subsection a relationship shall be established as if any illegitimate child, step-child or adopted child of a person were the legitimate child of the relationship in question.

185. Agreement with more than one debtor or hirer

(1) Where an actual or prospective regulated agreement has two or more debtors or hirers (not being a partnership or an unincorporated body of persons)—
    (a) anything required by or under this Act to be done to or in relation to the debtor or hirer shall be done to or in relation to each of them; and
    (b) anything done under this Act by or on behalf of one of them shall have effect as if done by or on behalf of all of them.

(2) Notwithstanding subsection (1)(a), where credit is provided under an agreement to two or more debtors jointly, in performing his duties—
    (a) in the case of fixed-sum credit, under section 77A, or
    (b) in the case of running-account credit, under section 78(4),
the creditor need not give statements to any debtor who has signed and given to him a notice (a 'dispensing notice') authorising him not to comply in the debtor's case with section 77A or (as the case may be) 78(4).

(2A) A dispensing notice given by a debtor is operative from when it is given to the creditor until it is revoked by a further notice given to the creditor by the debtor.

(2B) But subsection (2) does not apply if (apart from this subsection) dispensing notices would be operative in relation to all of the debtors to whom the credit is provided.

(2C) Any dispensing notices operative in relation to an agreement shall cease to have effect if any of the debtors dies.

(2D) A dispensing notice which is operative in relation to an agreement shall be operative also in relation to any subsequent agreement which, in relation to the earlier agreement, is a modifying agreement.

(3) Subsection (1)(b) does not apply for the purposes of section 61(1)(a) …

(4)   Where a regulated agreement has two or more debtors or hirers (not being a partnership or an unincorporated body of persons), section 86 applies to the death of any of them.

(5)   An agreement for the provision of credit, or the bailment or (in Scotland) the hiring of goods, to two or more persons jointly where—

    (a)   one or more of those persons is an individual, and

    (b)   one or more of them is not an individual,

    is a consumer credit agreement or consumer hire agreement if it would have been one had they all been individuals; and each person within paragraph (b) shall accordingly be included among the debtors or hirers under the agreement.

(6)   Where subsection (5) applies, references in this Act to the signing of any document by the debtor or hirer shall be construed in relation to a body corporate within paragraph (b) of that subsection as referring to a signing on behalf of the body corporate.

186. Agreement with more than one creditor or owner

Where an actual or prospective regulated agreement has two or more creditors or owners, anything required by or under this Act to be done to, or in relation to, or by, the creditor or owner shall be effective if done to, or in relation to, or by, any one of them.

187. Arrangements between creditor and supplier

(1)   A consumer credit agreement shall be treated as entered into under pre-existing arrangements between a creditor and a supplier if it is entered into in accordance with, or in furtherance of, arrangements previously made between persons mentioned in subsection (4)(a), (b) or (c).

(2)   A consumer credit agreement shall be treated as entered into in contemplation of future arrangements between a creditor and a supplier if it is entered into in the expectation that arrangements will subsequently be made between persons mentioned in subsection (4)(a), (b) or (c) for the supply of cash, goods and services (or any of them) to be financed by the consumer credit agreement.

(3)   Arrangements shall be disregarded for the purposes of subsection (1) or (2) if—

    (a)   they are arrangements for the making, in specified circumstances, of payments to the supplier by the creditor, and

    (b)   the creditor holds himself out as willing to make, in such circumstances, payments of the kind to suppliers generally.

(3A) Arrangements shall also be disregarded for the purposes of subsections (1) and (2) if they are arrangements for the electronic transfer of funds from a current account at a bank within the meaning of the Bankers' Book Evidence Act 1879.

(4)   The persons referred to in subsections (1) and (2) are—

    (a)   the creditor and the supplier;

    (b)   one of them and an associate of the other's;

    (c)   an associate of one and an associate of the other's.

(5)   Where the creditor is an associate of the supplier's, the consumer credit agreement shall be treated, unless the contrary is proved, as entered into under pre-existing arrangements between the creditor and the supplier.

187A. Definition of 'default sum'

(1)   In this Act 'default sum' means, in relation to the debtor or hirer under a regulated agreement, a sum (other than a sum of interest) which is payable by him under the agreement in connection with a breach of the agreement by him.

(2)   But a sum is not a default sum in relation to the debtor or hirer simply because, as a consequence of his breach of the agreement, he is required to pay it earlier than he would otherwise have had to.

188. Examples of use of new terminology

(1)   Schedule 2 shall have effect for illustrating the use of terminology employed in this Act.

(2)   The examples given in Schedule 2 are not exhaustive.

(3)   In the case of conflict between Schedule 2 and any other provision of this Act, that other provision shall prevail.

(4)   The Treasury may by order amend Schedule 2 by adding further examples or in any other way.

189. Definitions

(1) In this Act, unless the context otherwise requires—

'advertisement' includes every form of advertising, whether in a publication, by television or radio, by display of notices, signs, labels, showcards or goods, by distribution of samples, circulars, catalogues, price lists or other material, by exhibition of pictures, models or films, or in any other way, and references to the publishing of advertisements shall be construed accordingly;

'ancillary credit business' has the meaning given in section 145(1);

'antecedent negotiations' has the meaning given by section 56;

'appropriate method' means—

(a)   post, or

(b)   transmission in the form of an electronic communication in accordance with section 176A(1);

'assignment', in relation to Scotland, means assignation;

'associate' shall be construed in accordance with section 184;

'authorised business overdraft agreement' means a debtor-creditor agreement which provides authorisation in advance for the debtor to overdraw on a current account, where the agreement is entered into by the debtor wholly or predominantly for the purposes of the debtor's business (see subsection (2A));

'authorised non-business overdraft agreement' means a debtor-creditor agreement which provides authorisation in advance for the debtor to overdraw on a current account where—

(a)   the credit must be repaid on demand or within three months, and

(b)   the agreement is not entered into by the debtor wholly or predominantly for the purposes of the debtor's business (see subsection (2A));

…

'bill of sale' has the meaning given by section 4 of the Bills of Sale Act 1878 or, for Northern Ireland, by section 4 of the Bills of Sale (Ireland) Act 1879;

'building society' means a building society within the meaning of the Building Societies Act 1986;

'business' includes profession or trade, and references to a business apply subject to subsection (2);

'cancellable agreement' means a regulated agreement which, by virtue of section 67, may be cancelled by the debtor or hirer;

'canvass' shall be construed in accordance with sections 48 and 153;

'cash' includes money in any form;

'charity' means as respects England and Wales a charity registered under the Charities Act 2011 or an exempt charity (within the meaning of that Act), and as respects Northern Ireland an institution or other organisation established for charitable purposes only ('organisation' including any persons administering a trust and 'charitable' being construed in the same way as if it were contained in the Income Tax Acts), and as respects Scotland a body entered in the Scottish Charity Register;

'conditional sale agreement' means an agreement for the sale of goods or land under which the purchase price or part of it is payable by instalments, and the property in the goods or land is to remain in the seller (notwithstanding that the buyer is to be in possession of the goods or land) until such conditions as to the payment of instalments or otherwise as may be specified in the agreement are fulfilled;

'consumer credit agreement' has the meaning given by section 8, and includes a consumer credit agreement which is cancelled under section 69(1), or becomes subject to section 69(2), so far as the agreement remains in force;

'consumer credit business' means any business being carried on by a person so far as it comprises or relates to—

(a)   the provision of credit by him, or

(b)   otherwise his being a creditor,

under regulated consumer credit agreements;

'consumer hire agreement' has the meaning given by section 15;

'consumer hire business' means any business being carried on by a person so far as it comprises or relates to—

    (a)   the bailment or (in Scotland) the hiring of goods by him, or

    (b)   otherwise his being an owner,

under regulated consumer hire agreements;

'controller', in relation to a body corporate, means a person—

    (a)   in accordance with whose directions or instructions the directors of the body corporate or of another body corporate which is its controller (or any of them) are accustomed to act, or

    (b)   who, either alone or with any associate or associates, is entitled to exercise, or control the exercise of, one third or more of the voting power at any general meeting of the body corporate or of another body corporate which is its controller;

'copy' shall be construed in accordance with section 180;

...

'court' means in relation to England and Wales the county court, in relation to Scotland the sheriff court and in relation to Northern Ireland the High Court or the county court;

'credit' shall be construed in accordance with section 9;

'credit-broker' means a person carrying on a business of credit-brokerage;

'credit-brokerage' has the meaning given by section 145(2);

'credit information services' is to be read in accordance with section 145(7B);

'credit intermediary' has the meaning given by section 160A;

'credit limit' has the meaning given by section 10(2);

'creditor' means the person providing credit under a consumer credit agreement or the person to whom his rights and duties under the agreement have passed by assignment or operation of law, and in relation to a prospective consumer agreement, includes the prospective creditor;

'credit reference agency' is to be read in accordance with section 145(8);

'credit-sale agreement' means an agreement for the sale of goods, under which the purchase price or part of it is payable by instalments, but which is not a conditional sale agreement;

'credit-token' has the meaning given by section 14(1);

'credit-token agreement' means a regulated agreement for the provision of credit in connection with the use of a credit-token;

'debt-adjusting' has the meaning given by section 145(5);

'debt administration' has the meaning given by section 145(7A);

'debt-collecting' has the meaning given by section 145(7);

'debt-counselling' has the meaning given by section 145(6);

'debtor' means the individual receiving credit under a consumer credit agreement or the person to whom his rights and duties under the agreement have passed by assignment or operation of law, and in relation to a prospective consumer credit agreement includes the prospective debtor;

'debtor-creditor agreement' has the meaning given by section 13;

'debtor-creditor-supplier agreement' has the meaning given by section 12;

'default notice' has the meaning given by section 87(1);

'default sum' has the meaning given by section 187A;

'deposit' means any sum payable by a debtor or hirer by way of deposit or downpayment, or credited or to be credited to him on account of any deposit or downpayment, whether the sum is to be or has been paid to the creditor or owner or any other person, or is to be or has been discharged by a payment of money or a transfer or delivery of goods or by any other means;

'documents' includes information recorded in any form;

...

'electric line' has the meaning given by the Electricity Act 1989 or, for Northern Ireland the Electricity Supply (Northern Ireland) Order 1972;

'electronic communication' means an electronic communication within the meaning of the Electronic Communications Act 2000;

'embodies' and related words shall be construed in accordance with subsection (4);

'enforcement authority' has the meaning given by section 161(1);

'enforcement order' means an order under section 65(1), 105(7)(a) or (b), 111(2) or 124(1) or (2);

'executed agreement' means a document, signed by or on behalf of the parties, embodying the terms of a regulated agreement, or such of them as have been reduced to writing;

'FCA' means the Financial Conduct Authority;

'finance' means to finance wholly or partly, and 'financed' and 'refinanced' shall be construed accordingly;

'file' and 'copy of the file' have the meanings given by section 158(5);

'fixed-sum credit' has the meaning given by section 10(1)(b);

'friendly society' means a society registered under the Friendly Societies Acts 1896 to 1971;

'future arrangements' shall be construed in accordance with section 187;

'the UK GPDR' has the same meaning as in Parts 5 to 7 of the Data Protection Act 2018 (see section 3(10), (11) and (14) of that Act);

'give' means deliver or send by post to;

'goods' has the meaning given by section 61(1) of the Sale of Goods Act 1979;

'High Court' means Her Majesty's High Court of Justice, or the Court of Session in Scotland or the High Court of Justice in Northern Ireland;

'hire-purchase agreement' means an agreement, other than a conditional sale agreement, under which—

(a)   goods are bailed or (in Scotland) hired in return for periodical payments by the person to whom they are bailed or hired, and

(b)   the property in the goods will pass to that person if the terms of the agreement are complied with and one or more of the following occurs—

(i)   the exercise of an option to purchase by that person,

(ii)   the doing of any other specified act by any party to the agreement,

(iii)   the happening of any other specified event;

'hirer' means the individual to whom goods are bailed or (in Scotland) hired under a consumer hire agreement, or the person to whom his rights and duties under the agreement have passed by assignment or operation of law, and in relation to a prospective consumer hire agreement includes the prospective hirer;

'individual' includes—

(a)   a partnership consisting of two or three persons not all of whom are bodies corporate; and

(b)   an incorporated body of persons which does not consist entirely of bodies corporate and is not a partnership;

'installation' means—

(a)   the installing of any electric line or any gas or water pipe,

(b)   the fixing of goods to the premises where they are to be used, and the alteration of premises to enable goods to be used on them,

(c)   where it is reasonably necessary that goods should be constructed or erected on the premises where they are to be used, any work carried out for the purpose of constructing or erecting them on those premises;

...

'judgment' includes an order or decree made by any court;

'land' includes an interest in land, and in relation to Scotland includes heritable subjects of whatever description;

'land improvement company' means an improvement company as defined by section 7 of the Improvement of Land Act 1899;

'land mortgage' includes any security charged on land;

'linked transaction' has the meaning given by section 19(1);

'local authority', in relation to England and Wales, means the Greater London Council, a county council, a London borough council, a district council, the Common Council of the City of London, or the Council of the Isles of Scilly, and in relation to Scotland, means a council constituted under section 2 of the Local Government etc. (Scotland) Act 1994, and, in relation to Northern Ireland, means a district council;

'modifying agreement' has the meaning given by section 82(2);

'mortgage', in relation to Scotland, includes any heritable security;

'multiple agreement' has the meaning given by section 18(1);

'negotiator' has the meaning given by section 56(1);

'non-commercial agreement' means a consumer credit agreement or a consumer hire agreement not made by the creditor or owner in the course of a business carried on by him;

'notice' means notice in writing;

'notice of cancellation' has the meaning given by section 69(1);

'open-end' in relation to a consumer credit agreement, means of no fixed duration;

'owner' means a person who bails or (in Scotland) hires out goods under a consumer hire agreement or the person to whom his rights and duties under the agreement have passed by assignment or operation of law, and in relation to a prospective consumer hire agreement, includes the prospective bailor or person from whom the goods are to be hired;

'pawn' means any article subject to a pledge;

'pawn-receipt' has the meaning given by section 114;

'pawnee' and 'pawnor' include any person to whom the rights and duties of the original pawnee or the original pawnor, as the case may be, have passed by assignment or operation of law;

'payment' includes tender;

...

'pledge' means the pawnee's rights over an article taken in pawn;

'prescribed' means prescribed by regulations made by the Treasury;

'pre-existing arrangements' shall be construed in accordance with section 187;

'principal agreement' has the meaning given by section 19(1);

'protected goods' has the meaning given by section 90(7);

'redemption period' has the meaning given by section 116(3);

'Regulated Activities Order' means the Financial Services and Markets Act 2000 (Regulated Activities) Order 2001;

'regulated agreement' means a consumer credit agreement which is a regulated agreement (within the meaning of section 8(3)) or a consumer hire agreement which is a regulated agreement (within the meaning in section 15(2));

'regulations' means regulations made by the Treasury;

'relative', except in section 184, means a person who is an associate by virtue of section 184(1);

'representation' includes any condition or warranty, and any other statement or undertaking, whether oral or in writing;

'residential renovation agreement' means a consumer credit agreement—

(a)   which is secured on land; and

(b)   the purpose of which is the renovation of residential property, as described in Article 2(2)(a) of Directive 2008/48/EC of the European Parliament and of the Council of 23rd April 2008 on credit agreements for consumers.

'restricted-use credit agreement' and 'restricted-use credit' have the meanings given by section 11(1);

'rules of court', in relation to Northern Ireland means, in relation to the High Court, rules made under section 7 of the Northern Ireland Act 1962, and, in relation to any other court, rules made by the authority having for the time being power to make rules regulating the practice and procedure in that court;

'running-account credit' shall be construed in accordance with section 10;

'security', in relation to an actual or prospective consumer credit agreement or consumer hire agreement, or any linked transaction, means a mortgage, charge, pledge, bond, debenture, indemnity, guarantee, bill, note or other right provided by the debtor or hirer, or at his request (express or implied), to secure the carrying out of the obligations of the debtor or hirer under the agreement;

'security instrument' has the meaning given by section 105(2);

'serve on' means deliver or send by an appropriate method to;

'signed' shall be construed in accordance with subsection (3);

'small agreement' has the meaning given by section 17(1), and 'small' in relation to an agreement within any category shall be construed accordingly;

'supplier' has the meaning given by section 11(1)(b) or 12(c) or 13(c) or, in relation to an agreement failing within section 11(1)(a), means the creditor, and includes a person to whom the rights and duties of a supplier (as so defined) have passed by assignment or operation of law, or (in relation to a prospective agreement) the prospective supplier;

'surety' means the person by whom any security is provided, or the person to whom his rights and duties in relation to the security have passed by assignment or operation of law;

'technical grounds' shall be construed in accordance with subsection (5);

'time order' has the meaning given by section 129(1);

'total charge for credit' has the meaning given by section 20;

'total price' means the total sum payable by the debtor under a hire-purchase agreement or a conditional sale agreement, including any sum payable on the exercise of an option to purchase, but excluding any sum payable as a penalty or as compensation or damages for a breach of the agreement;

'unexecuted agreement' means a document embodying the terms of a prospective regulated agreement, or such of them as it is intended to reduce to writing;

'unrestricted-use credit agreement' and 'unrestricted-use credit' have the meanings given by section 11(2);

'working day' means any day other than—

(a)   Saturday or Sunday,

(b)   Christmas Day or Good Friday,

(c)   a bank holiday within the meaning given by section 1 of the Banking and Financial Dealings Act 1971.

(1A) In section 70(4), 73(4) and 75(2) and paragraphs 14 and 15 of Schedule A1 'costs', in relation to proceedings in Scotland, means expenses.

(2)   A person is not to be treated as carrying on a particular type of business merely because occasionally he enters into transactions belonging to a business of that type.

(2A) For the purpose of the definitions of 'authorised business overdraft agreement' and 'authorised non-business overdraft agreement' article 60C(5) and (6) of the Regulated Activities Order applies.

(3)   Any provision of this Act requiring a document to be signed is complied with by a body corporate if the document is sealed by that body.

This subsection does not apply to Scotland.

(4)   A document embodies a provision if the provision is set out either in the document itself or in another document referred to in it.

(5)   An application dismissed by the court or the FCA shall, if the court or the FCA (as the case may be) so certifies, be taken to be dismissed on technical grounds only.

(6)   Except in so far as the context otherwise requires, any reference in this Act to an enactment shall be construed as a reference to that enactment as amended by or under any other enactment, including this Act.

(7)   In this Act, except where otherwise indicated—

(a)   a reference to a numbered Part, section or Schedule is a reference to the Part or section of, or the Schedule to, this Act so numbered, and

(b)   a reference in a section to a numbered subsection is a reference to the subsection of that section so numbered, and

(c)   a reference in a section, subsection or Schedule to a numbered paragraph is a reference to the paragraph of that section, subsection or Schedule so numbered.

190. Financial provisions

(1)   There shall be defrayed out of money provided by Parliament—

(a)   all expenses incurred by the Treasury in consequence of the provisions of this Act;

(b)   any expenses incurred in consequence of those provisions by any other Minister of the Crown or Government department;

(c)   any increase attributable to this Act in the sums payable out of money so provided under the Superannuation Act 1972 or the Fair Trading Act 1973.

193. Short title and extent

(1)   This Act may be cited as the Consumer Credit Act 1974.

(2)   This Act extends to Northern Ireland.

Section 167

SCHEDULE 1
PROSECUTION AND PUNISHMENT OF OFFENCES

1 Section	2 Offence	3 Mode of prosecution	4 Imprisonment or fine
49(1)	Canvassing debtor-creditor agreements off trade premises.	Summarily. (b) On indictment.	The prescribed sum. 2 years or a fine or both.
49(2)	Soliciting debtor-creditor agreements during visits made in response to previous oral requests.	Summarily. (b) On indictment.	The prescribed sum. 2 years or a fine or both.
50(1) ...	Sending circulars to minors.	(a) Summarily. (b) On indictment.	The prescribed sum. 2 years or a fine or both.
79(3)	Failure of owner under consumer hire agreement to supply copies of documents etc.	Summarily.	Level 4 on the standard scale.
80(2) ...	Failure to tell creditor or owner whereabouts of goods.	Summarily.	Level 3 on the standard scale.
114(2)	Taking pledges from minors.	(a) Summarily.	The prescribed sum.
119(1)	Unreasonable refusal to allow pawn to be redeemed.	Summarily.	Level 4 on the standard scale.
154	Canvassing ancillary credit services off trade premises.	(a) Summarily. (b) On indictment.	The prescribed sum. 1 year or a fine or both.
157(3)	Refusal to give name etc. of credit reference agency.	Summarily.	Level 4 on the standard scale.
158(4)	Failure of credit reference agency to disclose filed information.	Summarily.	Level 4 on the standard scale.
159(6)	Failure of credit reference agency to correct information.	Summarily.	Level 4 on the standard scale.

Section 188(1)

SCHEDULE 2
EXAMPLES OF USE OF NEW TERMINOLOGY

PART I
LIST OF TERMS

Term	Defined in section	Illustrated by examples(s)
Advertisement	189(1)	2
Antecedent negotiations	56	1, 2, 3, 4
Cancellable agreement	67	4
Consumer credit agreement	8	5, 6, 7, 15, 19, 21
Consumer hire agreement	15	20, 24
Credit	9	16, 19, 21
Credit-broker	189(1)	2
Credit limit	10(2)	6, 7, 19, 22, 23
Creditor	189(1)	1, 2, 3, 4
Credit-sale agreement	189(1)	5
Credit-token	14	3, 14, 16
Credit-token agreement	14	3, 14, 16, 22
Debtor-creditor agreement	13	8, 16, 17, 18
Debtor-creditor-supplier agreement	12	8, 16
Fixed-sum credit	10	9, 10, 17, 23
Hire-purchase agreement	189(1)	10
Individual	189(1)	19, 24
Linked transaction	19	11

Modifying agreement	82(2)	24
Multiple agreement	18	16, 18
Negotiator	56(1)	1, 2, 3, 4
...		
Pre-existing arrangements	187	8, 21
Restricted-use credit	11	10, 12, 13, 14, 16
Running-account credit	10	15, 16, 18, 23
Small agreement	17	16, 17, 22
Supplier	189(1)	3, 14
Total charge for credit	20	5, 10
Total price	189(1)	10
Unrestricted-use credit	11	8, 12, 16, 17, 18

PART II
EXAMPLES

Example 1

Facts   Correspondence passes between an employee of a money-lending company (writing on behalf of the company) and an individual about the terms on which the company would grant him a loan under a regulated agreement.

Analysis   The correspondence constitutes antecedent negotiations falling within section 56(1)(a), the moneylending company being both creditor and negotiator.

Example 2

Facts   Representations are made about goods in a poster displayed by a shopkeeper near the goods, the goods being selected by a customer who has read the poster and then sold by the shopkeeper to a finance company introduced by him (with whom he has a business relationship). The goods are disposed of by the finance company to the customer under a regulated hire-purchase agreement.

Analysis   The representations in the poster constitute antecedent negotiations falling within section 56(1)(b), the shopkeeper being the credit-broker and negotiator and the finance company being the creditor. The poster is an advertisement and the shopkeeper is the advertiser.

Example 3

Facts   Discussions take place between a shopkeeper and a customer about goods the customer wishes to buy using a credit-card issued by the D Bank under a regulated agreement.

Analysis   The discussions constitute antecedent negotiations falling within section 56(1)(c), the shopkeeper being the supplier and negotiator and the D Bank the creditor. The credit-card is a credit-token as defined in section 14(1), and the regulated agreement under which it was issued is a credit-token agreement as defined in section 14(2).

Example 4

Facts   Discussions take place and correspondence passes between a secondhand car dealer and a customer about a car, which is then sold by the dealer to the customer under a regulated conditional sale agreement. Subsequently, on a revocation of that agreement by consent, the car is resold by the dealer to a finance company introduced by him (with whom he has a business relationship), who in turn dispose of it to the same customer under a regulated hire-purchase agreement.

Analysis   The discussions and correspondence constitute antecedent negotiations in relation both to the conditional sale agreement and the hire-purchase agreement. They fall under section 56(1) in relation to the conditional sale agreement, the dealer being the creditor and the negotiator. In relation to the hire-purchase agreement they fall within section 56(1)(b), the dealer continuing to be treated as the negotiator but the finance company now being the creditor. Both agreements are cancellable if the discussions took place when the individual conducting the negotiations (whether the 'negotiator' or his employee or agent) was in the presence of the debtor, unless the unexecuted agreement was signed by the debtor at trade premises (as defined in section 67(b)). If the discussions all took place by telephone however, or the unexecuted agreement was signed by the debtor on trade premises (as so defined) the agreements are not cancellable.

Example 5

Facts   E agrees to sell to F (an individual) an item of furniture in return for 24 monthly instalments of £10 payable in arrear. The property in the goods passes to F immediately.
Analysis   This is a credit-sale agreement (see definition of 'credit-sale agreement' in section 189(1)). The credit provided amounts to £240 less the amount which constitutes the total charge for credit (within the meaning given by section 20). (This amount is required to be deducted by section 9(4).) Accordingly the agreement falls within section 8(2) and is a consumer credit agreement.

Example 6

Facts   The G Bank grants H (an individual) an unlimited overdraft, with an increased rate of interest on so much of any debit balance as exceeds £2,000.
Analysis   Although the overdraft purports to be unlimited, the stipulation for increased interest above £2,000 brings the agreement within section 10(3)(b)(ii) and it is a consumer credit agreement.

Example 7

Facts   J is an individual who owns a small shop which usually carries a stock worth about £1,000. K makes a stocking agreement under which he undertakes to provide on short-term credit the stock needed from time to time by J without any specified limit.
Analysis   Although the agreement appears to provide unlimited credit, it is probable, having regard to the stock usually carried by J, that his indebtedness to K will not at any time rise above £5,000. Accordingly the agreement falls within section 10(3)(b)(iii) and is a consumer credit agreement.

Example 8

Facts   U, a moneylender, lends £500 to V (an individual) knowing he intends to use it to buy office equipment from W. W introduced V to U, it being his practice to introduce customers needing finance to him. Sometimes U gives W a commission for this and sometimes not. U pays the £500 direct to V.
Analysis   Although this appears to fall under section 11(1)(b), it is excluded by section 11(3) and is therefore (by section 11(2)) an unrestricted-use credit agreement. Whether it is a debtor-creditor agreement (by section 13(c)) or a debtor-creditor-supplier agreement (by section 12(c)) depends on whether the previous dealings between U and W amount to 'pre-existing arrangements', that is whether the agreement can be taken to have been entered into 'in accordance with, or in furtherance of' arrangements previously made between U and W, as laid down in section 187(1).

Example 9

Facts   A agrees to lend B (an individual) £4,500 in nine monthly instalments of £500.
Analysis   This is a cash loan and is a form of credit (see section 9 and definition of 'cash' in section 189(1)). Accordingly it falls within section 10(1)(b) and is fixed-sum credit amounting to £4,500.

Example 10

Facts   C (in England) agrees to bail goods to D (an individual) in return for periodical payments. The agreement provides for the property in the goods to pass to D on payment of a total of £7,500 and the exercise by D of an option to purchase. The sum of £7,500 includes a down-payment of £1,000. It also includes an amount which, according to regulations made under section 20(1), constitutes a total charge for credit of £1,500.
Analysis   This is a hire-purchase agreement with a deposit of £1,000 and a total price of £7,500 (see definitions of 'hire-purchase agreement', 'deposit' and 'total price' in section 189(1)). By section 9(3), it is taken to provide credit amounting to £7,500 - (£1,500 + £1,000), which equals £5,000. Under section 8(2), the agreement is therefore a consumer credit agreement, and under sections 9(3) and 11(l) it is a restricted-use credit agreement for fixed-sum credit. A similar result would follow if the agreement by C had been a hiring agreement in Scotland.

Example 11

Facts   X (an individual) borrows £500 from Y (Finance). As a condition of the granting of the loan X is required—
(a)   to execute a second mortgage on his house in favour of Y (Finance), and
(b)   to take out a policy of insurance on his life with Y (Insurances).

In accordance with the loan agreement, the policy is charged to Y (Finance) as collateral security for the loan. The two companies are associates within the meaning of section 184(3).

Analysis   The second mortgage is a transaction for the provision of security and accordingly does not fall within section 19(1), but the taking out of the insurance policy is a linked transaction falling within section 19(1)(a). The charging of the policy is a separate transaction (made between different parties) for the provision of security and again is excluded from section 19(1). The only linked transaction is therefore the taking out of the insurance policy. If X had not been required by the loan agreement to take out the policy, but it had been done at the suggestion of Y (Finance) to induce them to enter into the loan agreement, it would have been a linked transaction under section 19(1) (c)(i) by virtue of section 19(2)(a).

Example 12

Facts   The N Bank agrees to lend O (an individual) £2,000 to buy a car from P. To make sure the loan is used as intended, the N Bank stipulates that the money must be paid by it direct to P.

Analysis   The agreement is a consumer credit agreement by virtue of section 8(2). Since it falls within section 11(1)(b), it is a restricted-use credit agreement, P being the supplier. If the N Bank had not stipulated for direct payment to the supplier, section 11(3) would have operated and made the agreement into one for unrestricted-use credit.

Example 13

Facts   Q, a debt-adjuster, agrees to pay off debts owed by R (an individual) to various moneylenders. For this purpose the agreement provides for the making of a loan by Q to R in return for R's agreeing to repay the loan by instalments with interest. The loan money is not paid over to R but retained by Q and used to pay off the money lenders.

Analysis   This is an agreement to refinance existing indebtedness of the debtor's, and if the loan by Q does not exceed £5,000 is a restricted-use credit agreement falling within section 11(1)(c).

Example 14

Facts   On payment of £1, S issues to T (an individual) a trading check under which T can spend up to £20 at any shop which has agreed, or in future agrees, to accept S's trading checks.

Analysis   The trading check is a credit-token falling within section 14(1)(b). The credit-token agreement is a restricted-use credit agreement within section 11(1)(b), any shop in which the credit-token is used being the 'supplier'. The fact that further shops may be added after the issue of the credit-token is irrelevant in view of section 11(4).

Example 15

Facts   A retailer L agrees with M (an individual) to open an account in M's name and, in return for M's promise to pay a specified minimum sum into the account each month and to pay a monthly charge for credit, agrees to allow to be debited to the account, in respect of purchases made by M from L, such sums as will not increase the debit balance at any time beyond the credit limit, defined in the agreement as a given multiple of the specified minimum sum.

Analysis   This agreement provides credit falling within the definition of running-account credit in section 10(1)(a). Provided the credit limit is not over £5,000, the agreement falls within section 8(2) and is a consumer credit agreement for running-account credit.

Example 16

Facts   Under an unsecured agreement, A (Credit), an associate of the A Bank, issues to B (an individual) a credit-card for use in obtaining cash on credit from A (Credit), to be paid by branches of the A Bank (acting as agent of A (Credit)), or goods or cash from suppliers or banks who have agreed to honour credit-cards issued by A (Credit). The credit limit is £30.

Analysis   This is a credit-token agreement falling within section 14(1)(a) and (b). It is a regulated consumer credit agreement for running-account credit. Since the credit limit does not exceed £30, the agreement is a small agreement. So far as the agreement relates to goods it is a debtor-creditor-supplier agreement within section 12(b), since it provides restricted-use credit under section 11(1) (b). So far as it relates to cash it is a debtor-creditor agreement within section 13(c) and the credit it provides is unrestricted-use credit. This is therefore a multiple agreement. In that the whole agreement falls within several of the categories of agreement mentioned in this Act, it is, by section 18(3), to be treated as an agreement in each of those categories. So far as it is a debtor-creditor-supplier agreement providing restricted-use credit it is, by section 18(2), to be treated as a separate agreement; and similarly so far as it is a debtor-creditor agreement providing unrestricted-use credit. (See also Example 22.)

Example 17

Facts   The manager of the C Bank agrees orally with D (an individual) to open a current account in D's name. Nothing is said about overdraft facilities. After maintaining the account in credit for some weeks, D draws a cheque in favour of E for an amount exceeding D's credit balance by £20. E presents the cheque and the Bank pay it.

Analysis   In drawing the cheque D, by implication, requests the Bank to grant him an overdraft of £20 on its usual terms as to interest and other charges. In deciding to honour the cheque, the Bank by implication accept the offer. This constitutes a regulated small consumer credit agreement for unrestricted-use, fixed sum credit. It is a debtor-creditor agreement, and falls within section 74(1)(b). (Compare Example 18.)

Example 18

Facts   F (an individual) has had a current account with the G Bank for many years. Although usually in credit, the account has been allowed by the Bank to become overdrawn from time to time. The maximum such overdraft has been is about £1,000. No explicit agreement has ever been made about overdraft facilities. Now, with a credit balance of £500, F draws a cheque for £1,300.

Analysis   It might well be held that the agreement with F (express or implied) under which the Bank operate his account includes an implied term giving him the right to overdraft facilities up to say £1,000. If so, the agreement is a regulated consumer credit agreement for unrestricted-use, running-account credit. It is a debtor-creditor agreement, and falls within section 74(1)(b). It is also a multiple agreement, part of which (i.e. the part not dealing with the overdraft), as referred to in section 18(1)(a), falls within a category of agreement not mentioned in this Act. (Compare Example 17.)

Example 19

Facts   H (a finance house) agrees with J (a partnership of individuals) to open an unsecured loan account in J's name on which the debit balance is not to exceed £7,500 (having regard to payments into the account made from time to time by J). Interest is to be payable in advance on this sum, with provision for yearly adjustments. H is entitled to debit the account with interest, a 'setting-up' charge, and other charges. Before J has an opportunity to draw on the account it is initially debited with £2,250 for advance interest and other charges.

Analysis   This is a personal running-account credit agreement (see sections 8(1) and 10(1)(a), and definition of 'individual' in section 189(1)). By section 10(2) the credit limit is £7,000. By section 9(4) however the initial debit of £2,250, and any other charges later debited to the account by H, are not to be treated as credit even though time is allowed for their payment. Effect is given to this by section 10(3). Although the credit limit of £7,000 exceeds the amount (£5,000) specified in section 8(2) as the maximum for a consumer credit agreement, so that the agreement is not within section 10(3)(a), it is caught by section 10(3)(b)(i). At the beginning J can effectively draw (as credit) no more than £4,750, so the agreement is a consumer credit agreement.

Example 20

Facts   K (in England) agrees with L (an individual) to bail goods to L for a period of three years certain at £2,200 a year, payable quarterly. The agreement contains no provision for the passing of the property in the goods to L.

Analysis   This is not a hire-purchase agreement (see paragraph (b) of the definition of that term in section 189(1)), and is capable of subsisting for more than three months. Paragraphs (a) and (b) of section 15(1) are therefore satisfied, but paragraph (c) is not. The payments by L must exceed £5,000 if he conforms to the agreement. It is true that under section 101 L has a right to terminate the agreement on giving K three months' notice expiring not earlier than eighteen months after the making of the agreement, but that section applies only where the agreement is a regulated consumer hire agreement apart from the section (see subsection (1)). So the agreement is not a consumer hire agreement, though it would be if the hire charge were say £1,500 a year, or there were a 'break' clause in it operable by either party before the hire charges exceeded £5,000. A similar result would follow if the agreement by K had been a hiring agreement in Scotland.

Example 21

Facts The P Bank decides to issue cheque cards to its customers under a scheme whereby the bank undertakes to honour cheques of up to £30 in every case where the payee has taken the cheque in reliance on the cheque card, whether the customer has funds in his account or not. The P Bank writes to the major retailers advising them of this scheme and also publicises it by advertising. The Bank issues a cheque card to Q (an individual), who uses it to pay by cheque for goods costing £20 bought by Q from R, a major retailer. At the time, Q has £500 in his account at the P Bank.

Analysis The agreement under which the cheque card is issued to Q is a consumer credit agreement even though at all relevant times Q has more than £30 in his account. This is because Q is free to draw out his whole balance and then use the cheque card, in which case the Bank has bound itself to honour the cheque. In other words the cheque card agreement provides Q with credit, whether he avails himself of it or not. Since the amount of the credit is not subject to any express limit, the cheque card can be used any number of times. It may be presumed however that section 10(3)(b)(iii) will apply. The agreement is an unrestricted-use debtor-creditor agreement (by section 13(c)). Although the P Bank wrote to R informing R of the P Bank's willingness to honour any cheque taken by R in reliance on a cheque card, this does not constitute pre-existing arrangements as mentioned in section 13(c) because section 187(3) operates to prevent it. The agreement is not a credit-token agreement within section 14(1)(b) because payment by the P Bank to R, would be a payment of the cheque and not a payment for the goods.

Example 22

Facts The facts are as in Example 16. On one occasion B uses the credit-card in a way which increases his debit balance with A (Credit) to £40. A (Credit) writes to B agreeing to allow the excess on that occasion only, but stating that it must be paid off within one month.

Analysis In exceeding his credit limit B, by implication, requests A (Credit) to allow him a temporary excess (compare Example 17). A (Credit) is thus faced by B's action with the choice of treating it as a breach of contract or granting his implied request. He does the latter. If he had done the former, B would be treated as taking credit to which he was not entitled (see section 14(3)) and, subject to the terms of his contract with A (Credit), would be liable to damages for breach of contract. As it is, the agreement to allow the excess varies the original credit-token agreement by adding a new term. Under section 10(2), the new term is to be disregarded in arriving at the credit limit, so that the credit-token agreement at no time ceases to be a small agreement. By section 82(2) the later agreement is deemed to revoke the original agreement and contain provisions reproducing the combined effect of the two agreements. By section 82(4), this later agreement is exempted from Part V (except section 56).

Example 23

Facts Under an oral agreement made on 10th January, X (an individual) has an overdraft on his current account at the Y bank with a credit limit of £100. On 15th February, when his overdraft stands at £90, X draws a cheque for £25. It is the first time that X has exceeded his credit limit, and on 16th February the bank honours the cheque.

Analysis The agreement of 10th January is a consumer credit agreement for running-account credit. The agreement of 15th–16th February varies the earlier agreement by adding a term allowing the credit limit to be exceeded merely temporarily. By section 82(2) the later agreement is deemed to revoke the earlier agreement and reproduce the combined effect of the two agreements. By section 82(4), Part V of this Act (except section 56) does not apply to the later agreement. By section 18(5), a term allowing a merely temporary excess over the credit limit is not to be treated as a separate agreement, or as providing fixed-sum credit. The whole of the £115 owed to the bank by X on 16th February is therefore running-account credit.

Example 24

Facts   On 1st March 1975 Z (in England) enters into an agreement with A (an unincorporated body of persons) to bail to A equipment consisting of two components (component P and component Q). The agreement is not a hire-purchase agreement and is for a fixed term of 3 years, so paragraphs (a) and (b) of section 15(1) are both satisfied. The rental is payable monthly at a rate of £2,400 a year, but the agreement provides that this is to be reduced to £1,200 a year for the remainder of the agreement if at any time during its currency A returns component Q to the owner Z. On 5th May 1976 A is incorporated as A Ltd., taking over A's assets and liabilities. On 1st March 1977, A Ltd. returns component Q. On 1st January 1978, Z and A Ltd. agree to extend the earlier agreement by one year, increasing the rental for the final year by £250 to £1,450.

Analysis   When entered into on 1st March 1975, the agreement is a consumer hire agreement. A falls within the definition of 'individual' in section 189(1) and if A returns component Q before 1st May 1976 the total rental will not exceed £5,000 (see section 15(1)(c)). When this date is passed without component Q having been returned it is obvious that the total rental must now exceed £5,000. Does this mean that the agreement then ceases to be a consumer hire agreement? The answer is no, because there has been no change in the terms of the agreement, and without such a change the agreement cannot move from one category to the other. Similarly, the fact that A's rights and duties under the agreement pass to a body corporate on 5th May 1976 does not cause the agreement to cease to be a consumer hire agreement (see definition of 'hirer' in section 189(1)). The effect of the modifying agreement of 1st January 1978 is governed by section 82(2), which requires it to be treated as containing provisions reproducing the combined effect of the two actual agreements, that is to say as providing that—

(a)   obligations outstanding on 1st January 1978 are to be treated as outstanding under the modifying agreement;

(b)   the modifying agreement applies at the old rate of hire for the months of January and February 1978; and

(c)   for the year beginning 1st March 1978 A Ltd. will be the bailee of component P at a rental of £1,450.

The total rental under the modifying agreement is £1,850. Accordingly the modifying agreement is a regulated agreement. Even if the total rental under the modifying agreement exceeded £5,000 it would still be regulated because of the provisions of section 82(3).

UNFAIR CONTRACT TERMS ACT 1977
(1977, c. 50)

PART I

1.   Scope of Part I

(1)   For the purposes of this Part of this Act, 'negligence' means the breach—

    (a)   of any obligation, arising from the express or implied terms of a contract, to take reasonable care or exercise reasonable skill in the performance of the contract;

    (b)   of any common law duty to take reasonable care or exercise reasonable skill (but not any stricter duty);

    (c)   of the common duty of care imposed by the Occupiers' Liability Act 1957 or the Occupier's Liability Act (Northern Ireland) 1957.

(2)   This Part of the Act is subject to Part III; and in relation to contracts, the operation of sections 2, 3 and 7 is subject to the exceptions made by Schedule I.

(3)   In the case of both contract and tort, sections 2 to 7 apply (except where the contrary is stated in section 6(4)) only to business liability, that is liability to breach of obligations or duties arising—

    (a)   from things done or to be done by a person in the course of a business (whether his own business or another's); or

    (b)   from the occupation of premises used for business purposes of the occupier;

and references to liability are to be read accordingly but liability of an occupier of premises for breach of an obligation or duty towards a person obtaining access to the premises for recreational or educational purposes, being liability for loss or damage suffered by reason of the dangerous state of the premises, is not a business liability of the occupier unless granting that person such access for the purposes concerned falls within the business purposes of the occupier.

(4) In relation to any breach of duty or obligation, it is immaterial for any purpose of this Part of this Act whether the breach was inadvertent or intentional, or whether liability for it arises directly or vicariously.

2. Negligence liability

(1) A person cannot by reference to any contract term or to a notice given to persons generally or to particular persons exclude or restrict his liability for death or personal injury resulting from negligence.

(2) In the case of other loss or damage, a person cannot so exclude or restrict his liability for negligence except in so far as the term or notice satisfies the requirement of reasonableness.

(3) Where a contract term or notice purports to exclude or restrict liability for negligence a person's agreement to or awareness of it is not of itself to be taken as indicating his voluntary acceptance of any risk.

(4) This section does not apply to—
    (a) a term in a consumer contract, or
    (b) a notice to the extent it is a consumer notice,
(but see the provision made about such contracts and notices in sections 62 and 65 of the Consumer Rights Act 2015).

3. Liability arising in contract

(1) This section applies as between contracting parties where one of them deals on the other's written standard terms of business.

(2) As against that party, the other cannot by reference to any contract term—
    (a) when himself in breach of contract, exclude or restrict any liability of his in respect of the breach; or
    (b) claim to be entitled—
        (i) to render a contractual performance substantially different from that which was reasonably expected of him, or
        (ii) in respect of the whole or any part of his contractual obligation, to render no performance at all,
except in so far as (in any of the cases mentioned above in this subsection) the contract term satisfies the requirement of reasonableness.

(3) This section does not apply to a term in a consumer contract (but see the provision made about such contracts in section 62 of the Consumer Rights Act 2015).

6. Sale and hire-purchase

(1) Liability for breach of the obligations arising from—
    (a) section 12 of the Sale of Goods Act 1979 (seller's implied undertakings as to title, etc.);
    (b) section 8 of the Supply of Goods (Implied Terms) Act 1973 (the corresponding thing in relation to hire-purchase),
cannot be excluded or restricted by reference to any contract term.

(1A) Liability for breach of the obligations arising from—
    (a) section 13,14 or 15 of the 1979 Act (seller's implied undertakings as to conformity of goods with description or sample, or as to their quality or fitness for purpose),
    (b) sections 9, 10 or 11 of the 1973 Act (the corresponding provisions in relation to hire-purchase),
cannot be excluded or restricted by reference to a contract term except in so far as the term satisfies the requirement of reasonableness.

(4) The liabilities referred to in this section are not only the business liabilities defined by section 1(3), but include those arising under any contract of sale of goods or hire-purchase agreement.

(5) This section does not apply to a consumer contract (but see the provision made about such contracts in section 31 of the Consumer Rights Act 2015).

7.   Miscellaneous contracts under which goods pass

(1)   Where the possession or ownership of goods passes under or in pursuance of a contract not governed by the law of sale of goods or hire-purchase, subsections (2) to (4) below apply as regards the effect (if any) to be given to contract terms excluding or restricting liability for breach of obligation arising by implication of law from the nature of the contract.

(1A) Liability in respect of the goods' correspondence with description or sample, or their quality or fitness for particular purpose, cannot be excluded or restricted by reference to such a term except in so far as the term satisfies the requirement of reasonableness.

(3A) Liability for breach of the obligations arising under section 2 of the Supply of Goods and Services Act 1982 (implied terms about title etc. in certain contracts for the transfer of the property in goods) cannot be excluded or restricted by reference to any such term.

(4)   Liability in respect of—
       (a)   the right to transfer ownership of the goods, or give possession; or
       (b)   the assurance of quiet possession to a person taking goods in pursuance of the contract,
       cannot (in a case to which subsection (3A) above does not apply) be excluded or restricted by reference to any such term except in so far as the term satisfies the requirement of reasonableness.

(4A) This section does not apply to a consumer contract (but see the provision made about such contracts in section 31 of the Consumer Rights Act 2015).

(5)   …

10.   Evasion by means of secondary contract

A person is not bound by any contract term prejudicing or taking away rights of his which arise under, or in connection with the performance of, another contract, so far as those rights extend to the enforcement of another's liability which this Part of this Act prevents that other from excluding or restricting.

11.   The 'reasonableness' test

(1)   In relation to a contract term, the requirement of reasonableness for the purposes of this Part of this Act, section 3 of the Misrepresentation Act 1967 and section 3 of the Misrepresentation Act (Northern Ireland) 1967 is that the term shall have been a fair and reasonable one to be included having regard to the circumstances which were, or ought reasonably to have been, known to or in the contemplation of the parties when the contract was made.

(2)   In determining for the purposes of section 6 or 7 above whether a contract term satisfies the requirement of reasonableness, regard shall be had in particular to the matters specified in Schedule 2 to this Act; but this subsection does not prevent the court or arbitrator from holding, in accordance with any rule of law, that a term which purports to exclude or restrict any relevant liability is not a term of the contract.

(3)   In relation to a notice (not being a notice having contractual effect), the requirement of reasonableness under this Act is that it should be fair and reasonable to allow reliance on it, having regard to all the circumstances obtaining when the liability arose or (but for the notice) would have arisen.

(4)   Where by reference to a contract term or notice a person seeks to restrict liability to a specified sum of money, and the question arises (under this or any other Act) whether the term or notice satisfies the requirement of reasonableness, regard shall be had in particular (but without prejudice to subsection (2) above in the case of contract terms) to—
       (a)   the resources which he could expect to be available to him for the purpose of meeting the liability should it arise; and
       (b)   how far it was open to him to cover himself by insurance.

(5)   It is for those claiming that a contract term or notice satisfies the requirement of reasonableness to show that it does.

13. Varieties of exemption clause

(1) To the extent that this Part of this Act prevents the exclusion or restriction of any liability it also prevents—

(a) making the liability or its enforcement subject to restrictive or onerous conditions;

(b) excluding or restricting any right or remedy in respect of the liability, or subjecting a person to any prejudice in consequence of his pursuing any such right or remedy;

(c) excluding or restricting rules of evidence or procedure;

and (to that extent) sections 2, 6 and 7 also prevent excluding or restricting liability by reference to terms and notices which exclude or restrict the relevant obligation or duty.

(2) But an agreement in writing to submit present or future differences to arbitration is not to be treated under this Part of this Act as excluding or restricting any liability.

14. Interpretation of Part I

In this Part of the Act—

'business' includes a profession and the activities of any government department or local or public authority;

'consumer contract' has the same meaning as in the Consumer Rights Act 2015 (see section 61;

'consumer notice' has the same meaning as in the Consumer Rights Act 2015 (see section 61);

'goods' has the same meaning as in the Sale of Goods Act 1979;

'hire-purchase agreement' has the same meaning as in the Consumer Credit Act 1974;

'negligence' has the meaning given by section 1(1);

'notice' includes an announcement, whether or not in writing, and any other communication or pretended communication; and

'personal injury' includes any disease and any impairment of physical or mental condition.

PART II

15. Scope of Part II

(1) This Part of this Act is subject to Part III of this Act and does not affect the validity of any discharge or indemnity given by a person in consideration of the receipt by him of compensation in settlement of any claim which he has.

(2) Subject to subsection (3) below, sections 16 and 17 of this Act apply to any contract only to the extent that the contract—

(a) relates to the transfer of the ownership or possession of goods from one person to another (with or without work having been done on them);

(b) constitutes a contract of service or apprenticeship;

(c) relates to services of whatever kind, including (without prejudice to the foregoing generality) carriage, deposit and pledge, care and custody, mandate, agency, loan and services relating to the use of land;

(d) relates to the liability of an occupier of land to persons entering upon or using that land;

(e) relates to a grant of any right or permission to enter upon or use land not amounting to an estate or interest in the land.

(3) Notwithstanding anything in subsection (2) above, sections 16 and 17—

(a) do not apply to any contract to the extent that the contract—

(i) is a contract of insurance (including a contract to pay an annuity on human life);

(ii) relates to the formation, constitution or dissolution of any body corporate or unincorporated association or partnership;

(b) apply to—

a contract of marine salvage or towage;

a charter party of a ship or hovercraft;

a contract for the carriage of goods by ship or hovercraft; or

a contract to which subsection (4) below relates,
only to the extent that—
  (i)   both parties deal or hold themselves out as dealing in the course of a
         business (and then only in so far as the contract purports to exclude or
         restrict liability for breach of duty in respect of death or personal injury);
(4)   This subsection relates to a contract in pursuance of which goods are carried by ship
      or hovercraft and which either—
  (a)   specifies ship or hovercraft as the means of carriage over part of the journey to
         be covered; or
  (b)   makes no provision as to the means of carriage and does not exclude ship or
         hovercraft as that means,
      in so far as the contract operates for and in relation to the carriage of the goods by
      that means.

16.   Liability for breach of duty

(1)   Subject to subsection (1A) below, where a term of a contract, or a provision of a notice
      given to persons generally or to particular persons, purports to exclude or restrict
      liability for breach of duty arising in the course of any business or from the occupation
      of any premises used for business purposes of the occupier, that term or provision—
  (a)   shall be void in any case where such exclusion or restriction is in respect of
         death or personal injury;
  (b)   shall, in any other case, have no effect if it was not fair and reasonable to
         incorporate the term in the contract or, as the case may be, if it is not fair and
         reasonable to allow reliance on the provision.
(1A) Nothing in paragraph (b) of subsection (1) above shall be taken as implying that a
      provision of a notice has effect in circumstances where, apart from that paragraph, it
      would not have effect.
(2)   Subsection (1)(a) above does not affect the validity of any discharge and indemnity
      given by a person, on or in connection with an award to him of compensation for
      pneumoconiosis attributable to employment in the coal industry, in respect of any
      further claim arising from his contracting that disease.
(3)   Where under subsection (1) above a term of a contract or a provision of a notice is
      void or has no effect, the fact that a person agreed to, or was aware of, the term or
      provision shall not of itself be sufficient evidence that he knowingly and voluntarily
      assumed any risk.
(4)   This section does not apply to—
  (a)   a term in a consumer contract,
  (b)   a notice to the extent it is a consumer notice,
      (but see the provision made about such contracts and notices in sections 62 and 65
      of the Consumer Rights Act 2015).

17.   Control of unreasonable exemptions in … standard form contracts

(1)   Any term of a contract which is a … standard form contract shall have no effect for the
      purpose of enabling a party to the contract—
  (a)   who is in breach of a contractual obligation, to exclude or restrict any liability of
         his to the … customer in respect of the breach;
  (b)   in respect of a contractual obligation, to render no performance, or to render a
         performance substantially different from that which the … customer reasonably
         expected from the contract;
      if it was not fair and reasonable to incorporate the term in the contract.
(2)   In this section 'customer' means a party to a standard form contract who deals on
      the basis of written standard terms of business of the other party to the contract who
      himself deals in the course of a business.
(3)   This section does not apply to a term in a consumer contract (but see the provision
      made about such contracts in section 62 of the Consumer Rights Act 2015).

20.   **Obligations implied by law in sale and hire-purchase contracts**

(1)   Any term of a contract which purports to exclude or restrict liability for breach of the obligations arising from—

    (a)   section 12 of the Sale of Goods Act 1979 (seller's implied undertakings as to title etc.);

    (b)   section 8 of the Supply of Goods (Implied Terms) Act 1973 (implied terms as to title in hire-purchase agreements),

    shall be void.

(1A)   Any term of a contract which purports to exclude or restrict liability for breach of the obligations arising from—

    (a)   section 13, 14 or 15 of the 1979 Act (seller's implied undertakings as to conformity of goods with description or sample, or as to their quality or fitness for a particular purpose);

    (b)   section 9, 10 or 11 of the said Act of 1973 (the corresponding things in relation to hire-purchase),

    shall have effect only if it was fair and reasonable to incorporate the term in the contract.

(1B)   This section does not apply to a consumer contract (but see the provision made about such contracts in section 31 of the Consumer Rights Act 2015).

21.   **Obligations implied by law in other contracts for the supply of goods**

(1)   Any term of a contract to which this section applies purporting to exclude or restrict liability for breach of an obligation such as is referred to in subsection (3) below shall have no effect if it was not fair and reasonable to incorporate the term in the contract;

(2)   This section applies to any contract to the extent that it relates to any such matter as is referred to in section 15(2)(a) of this Act, but does not apply to—

    (a)   a contract of sale of goods or a hire-purchase agreement; or

    (b)   a charterparty of a ship or hovercraft.

(3)   An obligation referred to in this subsection is an obligation incurred under a contract in the course of a business and arising by implication of law from the nature of the contract which relates—

    (a)   to the correspondence of goods with description or sample, or to the quality or fitness of goods for any particular purpose; or

    (b)   to any right to transfer ownership or possession of goods, or to the enjoyment of quiet possession of goods.

(3A)   Notwithstanding anything in the foregoing provisions of this section, any term of a contract which purports to exclude or restrict liability for breach of the obligations arising under section 11B of the Supply of Goods and Services Act 1982 (implied terms about title, freedom from encumbrances and quiet possession in certain contracts for the transfer of property in goods) shall be void.

(3B)   This section does not apply to a consumer contract (but see the provision made about such contracts in section 31 of the Consumer Rights Act 2015).

23.   **Evasion by means of secondary contract**

Any term of any contract shall be void which purports to exclude or restrict, or has the effect of excluding or restricting—

(a)   the exercise, by a party to any other contract, of any right or remedy which arises in respect of that other contract in consequence of breach of duty, or of obligation, liability for which could not by virtue of the provisions of this Part of this Act be excluded or restricted by a term of that other contract;

(b)   the application of the provisions of this Part of this Act in respect of that or any other contract.

24.   **The 'reasonableness' test**

(1)   In determining for the purposes of this Part of this Act whether it was fair and reasonable to incorporate a term in a contract, regard shall be had only to the circumstances which were, or ought reasonably to have been, known to or in the contemplation of the parties to the contract at the time the contract was made.

(2)   In determining for the purposes of section 20 or 21 of this Act whether it was fair and reasonable to incorporate a term in a contract, regard shall be had in particular to the matters specified in Schedule 2 to this Act; but this subsection shall not prevent a court or arbiter from holding in accordance with any rule of law, that a term which purports to exclude or restrict any relevant liability is not a term of the contract.

(2A) In determining for the purposes of this Part of this Act whether it is fair and reasonable to allow reliance on a provision of a notice (not being a notice having contractual effect), regard shall be had to all the circumstances obtaining when the liability arose or (but for the provision) would have arisen.

(3)   Where a term in a contract or a provision of a notice purports to restrict liability to a specified sum of money, and the question arises for the purposes of this Part of this Act whether it was fair and reasonable to incorporate the term in the contract or whether it is fair and reasonable to allow reliance on the provision, then, without prejudice to subsection (2) above in the case of a term in a contract, regard shall be had in particular to—
   (a)   the resources which the party seeking to rely on that term or provision could expect to be available to him for the purpose of meeting the liability should it arise;
   (b)   how far it was open to that party to cover himself by insurance.

(4)   The onus of proving that it was fair and reasonable to incorporate a term in a contract or that it is fair and reasonable to allow reliance on a provision of a notice shall lie on the party so contending.

25.   Interpretation of Part II

(1)   In this Part of this Act—
   'breach of duty' means the breach—
   (a)   of any obligation, arising from the express or implied terms of a contract, to take reasonable care or exercise reasonable skill in the performance of the contract;
   (b)   of any common law duty to take reasonable care or exercise reasonable skill;
   (c)   of the duty of reasonable care imposed by section 2(1) of the Occupiers' Liability (Scotland) Act 1960;
   'business' includes a profession and the activities of any government department or local or public authority;
   'consumer contract' has the same meaning as in the Consumer Rights Act 2015 (see section 61);
   'consumer notice' has the same meaning as in the Consumer Rights Act 2015 (see section 61);
   'goods' has the same meaning as in the Sale of Goods Act 1979;
   'hire-purchase agreement' has the same meaning as in section 189(1) of the Consumer Credit Act 1974;
   'notice' includes an announcement, whether or not in writing, and any other communication or pretended communication;
   'personal injury' includes any disease and any impairment of physical or mental condition.

(2)   In relation to any breach of duty or obligation, it is immaterial for any purpose of this Part of this Act whether the act or omission giving rise to that breach was inadvertent or intentional or whether liability for it arises directly or vicariously.

(3)   In this Part of this Act, any reference to excluding or restricting any liability includes—
   (a)   making the liability or its enforcement subject to any restrictive or onerous conditions;
   (b)   excluding or restricting any right or remedy in respect of the liability, or subjecting a person to any prejudice in consequence of his pursuing any such right or remedy;
   (c)   excluding or restricting any rule of evidence or procedure;
   ...

(5)   In sections 15, 16, 20 and 21 of this Act, any reference to excluding or restricting liability for breach of any obligation or duty shall include a reference to excluding or restricting the obligation or duty itself.

PART III

26. International supply contracts

(1) The limits imposed by this Act on the extent to which a person may exclude or restrict liability by reference to a contract term do not apply to liability arising under such a contract as is described in subsection (3) below.

(2) The terms of such a contract are not subject to any requirement of reasonableness under section 3: and nothing in Part II of this Act should require the incorporation of the terms of such a contract to be fair and reasonable for them to have effect.

(3) Subject to subsection (4), that description of contract is one whose characteristics are the following—

    (a) either it is a contract of sale of goods or it is one under or in pursuance of which the possession of ownership of goods passes, and

    (b) it is made by parties whose places of business (or, if they have none, habitual residences) are in the territories of different States (the Channel Islands and the Isle of Man being treated for this purpose as different States from the United Kingdom).

(4) A contract falls within subsection (3) above only if either—

    (a) the goods in question are, at the time of the conclusion of the contract, in the course of carriage, or will be carried, from the territory of one State to the territory of another; or

    (b) the acts constituting the offer and acceptance have been done in the territories of different States; or

    (c) the contract provides for the goods to be delivered to the territory of a state other than that within whose territory those acts were done.

27. Choice of law clauses

(1) Where the law applicable to a contract is the law of any part of the United Kingdom only by choice of the parties (and apart from that choice would be the law of some country outside the United Kingdom) sections 2 to 7 and 16 to 21 of this Act do not operate as part of the law applicable to the contract.

(2) This Act has effect notwithstanding any contract term which applies or purports to apply the law of some country outside the United Kingdom, where—

    (a) the term appears to the court, or arbitrator or arbiter to have been imposed wholly or mainly for the purpose of enabling the party imposing it to evade the operation of this Act;

29. Saving for other relevant legislation

(1) Nothing in this Act removes or restricts the effect of, or prevents reliance upon, any contractual provision which—

    (a) is authorised or required by the express terms or necessary implication of an enactment; or

    (b) being made with a view to compliance with an international agreement to which the United Kingdom is a party, does not operate more restrictively than is contemplated by the agreement.

(2) A contract term is to be taken—

    (a) for the purposes of Part I of this Act, as satisfying the requirement of reasonableness ...

if it is incorporated or approved by, or incorporated pursuant to a decision or ruling of, a competent authority acting in the exercise of any statutory jurisdiction or function and is not a term in a contract to which the competent authority is itself a party.

(3) In this section—

'competent authority' means any court, arbitrator or arbiter, government department or public authority;

'enactment' means any legislation (including subordinate legislation) of the United Kingdom or Northern Ireland and any instrument having effect by virtue of such legislation; and

'statutory' means conferred by an enactment.

SCHEDULES

SCHEDULE 1
SCOPE OF SECTIONS 2, 3 AND 7

1.   Sections 2 and 3 of this Act do not extend to—
         (a)   any contract of insurance (including a contract to pay an annuity on human life);
         (b)   any contract so far as it relates to the creation or transfer of an interest in land, or to
               the termination of such an interest, whether by extinction, merger, surrender, forfeiture
               or otherwise;
         (c)   any contract so far as it relates to the creation or transfer of a right or interest in
               any patent, trade mark, copyright or design right, registered design, technical or
               commercial information or other intellectual property, or relates to the termination of
               any such right or interest;
         (d)   any contract so far as it relates—
               (i)   to the formation or dissolution of a company (which means any body corporate
                      or unincorporated association and includes a partnership), or
               (ii)   to its constitution or the rights or obligations of its corporators or members;
         (e)   any contract so far as it relates to the creation or transfer of securities or of any right
               or interest in securities.
         (f)   anything that is governed by Article 6 of Regulation (EU) no 181/2011 of the European
               Parliament and of the Council of the 16th of February 2011 concerning the rights of
               passengers in bus and coach transport amending Regulation (EC) no 2006/2004.
2.   Section 2(1) extends to—
         (a)   any contract of marine salvage or towage;
         (b)   any charterparty of a ship or hovercraft; and
         (c)   any contract for the carriage of goods by ship or hovercraft;
         but subject to this sections 2, 3 and 7 do not extend to any such contract.
3.   Where goods are carried by ship or hovercraft in pursuance of a contract which either—
         (a)   specifies that as the means of carriage over part of the journey to be covered, or
         (b)   makes no provision as to the means of carriage and does not exclude that means,
         then sections 2(2) and 3 do not extend to the contract as it operates for and in relation to
         the carriage of the goods by that means.
4.   Section 2(1) and (2) do not extend to a contract of employment, except in favour of the
         employee.
5.   Section 2(1) does not affect the validity of any discharge and indemnity given by a
         person, on or in connection with an award to him of compensation for pneumoconiosis
         attributable to employment in the coal industry, in respect of any further claim arising from
         his contracting the disease.

Sections 11(2) and 24(2)   SCHEDULE 2
              'GUIDELINES' FOR APPLICATION OF REASONABLENESS TEST

The matters to which regard is to be had in particular for the purposes of sections 6(1A), 7(1A) and
(4), 20 and 21 are any of the following which appear to be relevant—
(a)   the strength of the bargaining positions of the parties relative to each other, taking into
         account (among other things) alternative means by which the customer's requirements
         could have been met;
(b)   whether the customer received an inducement to agree to the term, or in accepting it had
         an opportunity of entering into a similar contract with other persons, but without having to
         accept a similar term;
(c)   whether the customer knew or ought reasonably to have known of the existence and extent
         of the term (having regard, among other things, to any custom of the trade and any previous
         course of dealing between the parties);
(d)   where the term excludes or restricts any relevant liability if some condition is not complied
         with, whether it was reasonable at the time of the contract to expect that compliance with
         that condition would be practicable
(e)   whether the goods were manufactured, processed or adapted to the special order of the
         customer.

SALE OF GOODS ACT 1979
(1979, c. 54)

PART I
CONTRACTS TO WHICH ACT APPLIES

1.   Contracts to which Act applies

(1)   This Act applies to contracts of sale of goods made on or after (but not to those made before) 1 January 1894.

(2)   In relation to contracts made on certain dates, this Act applies subject to the modification of certain of its sections as mentioned in Schedule 1 below.

(3)   Any such modification is indicated in the section concerned by a reference to Schedule 1 below.

(4)   Accordingly, where a section does not contain such a reference, this Act applies in relation to the contract concerned without such modification of the section.

(5)   Certain sections or subsections of this Act do not apply to a contract to which Chapter 2 of Part 1 of the Consumer Rights Act 2015 applies.

(6)   Where that is the case it is indicated in the section concerned.

PART II
FORMATION OF THE CONTRACT

Contract of Sale

2.   Contract of sale

(1)   A contract of sale of goods is a contract by which the seller transfers or agrees to transfer the property in goods to the buyer for a money consideration, called the price.

(2)   There may be a contract of sale between one part owner and another.

(3)   A contract of sale may be absolute or conditional.

(4)   Where under a contract of sale the property in the goods is transferred from the seller to the buyer the contract is called a sale.

(5)   Where under a contract of sale the transfer of the property in the goods is to take place at a future time or subject to some condition later to be fulfilled the contract is called an agreement to sell.

(6)   An agreement to sell becomes a sale when the time elapses or the conditions are fulfilled subject to which the property in the goods is to be transferred.

3.   Capacity to buy and sell

(1)   Capacity to buy and sell is regulated by the general law concerning capacity to contract and to transfer and acquire property.

(2)   Where necessaries are sold and delivered to a minor or to a person who by reason of … drunkenness is incompetent to contract, he must pay a reasonable price for them.

(3)   In subsection (2) above 'necessaries' means goods suitable to the condition in life of the minor or other person concerned and to his actual requirements at the time of the sale and delivery.

4.   How contract of sale is made

(1)   Subject to this and any other Act, a contract of sale may be made in writing (either with or without seal), or by word of mouth, or partly in writing and partly by word of mouth, or may be implied from the conduct of the parties.

(2)   Nothing in this section affects the law relating to corporations.

5.   Existing or future goods

(1)   The goods which form the subject of a contract of sale may be either existing goods, owned or possessed by the seller, or goods to be manufactured or acquired by him after the making of the contract of sale, in this Act called future goods.

(2)   There may be a contract for the sale of goods the acquisition of which by the seller depends on a contingency which may or may not happen.

(3)   Where by a contract of sale the seller purports to effect a present sale of future goods, the contract operates as an agreement to sell the goods.

6.   Goods which have perished

Where there is a contract for the sale of specific goods, and the goods without the knowledge of the seller have perished at the time when the contract is made, the contract is void.

7.   Goods perishing before sale but after agreement to sell

Where there is an agreement to sell specific goods and subsequently the goods, without any fault on the part of the seller or buyer, perish before the risk passes to the buyer, the agreement is avoided.

8.   Ascertainment of price

(1)   The price in a contract of sale may be fixed by the contract, or may be left to be fixed in a manner agreed by the contract, or may be determined by the course of dealing between the parties.

(2)   Where the price is not determined as mentioned in subsection (1) above the buyer must pay a reasonable price.

(3)   What is a reasonable price is a question of fact dependent on the circumstances of each particular case.

9.   Agreement to sell at valuation

(1)   Where there is an agreement to sell goods on the terms that the price is to be fixed by the valuation of a third party, and he cannot or does not make the valuation, the agreement is avoided; but if the goods or any part of them have been delivered to and appropriated by the buyer he must pay a reasonable price for them.

(2)   Where the third party is prevented from making the valuation by the fault of the seller or buyer, the party not at fault may maintain an action for damages against the party at fault.

Implied terms etc.

10.   Stipulations about time

(1)   Unless a different intention appears from the terms of the contract, stipulations as to time of payment are not of the essence of a contract of sale.

(2)   Whether any other stipulation as to time is or is not of the essence of the contract depends on the terms of the contract.

(3)   In a contract of sale 'month' prima facie means calendar month.

11.   When condition to be treated as warranty

(1)   This section does not apply to Scotland.

(2)   Where a contract of sale is subject to a condition to be fulfilled by the seller, the buyer may waive the condition, or may elect to treat the breach of the condition as a breach of warranty and not as a ground for treating the contract as repudiated.

(3)   Whether a stipulation in a contract of sale is a condition, the breach of which may give rise to a right to treat the contract as repudiated, or a warranty, the breach of which may give rise to a claim for damages but not to a right to reject the goods and treat the contract as repudiated, depends in each case on the construction of the contract; and a stipulation may be a condition, though called a warranty in the contract.

(4)   Subject to section 35A below where a contract of sale is not severable and the buyer has accepted the goods or part of them, the breach of a condition to be fulfilled by the seller can only be treated as a breach of warranty, and not as a ground for rejecting the goods and treating the contract as repudiated, unless there is an express or implied term of the contract to that effect.

(4A) Subsection (4) does not apply to a contract to which Chapter 2 of Part 1 of the Consumer Rights Act 2015 applies (but see the provision made about such contracts in sections 19 to 22 of that Act).

(6)   Nothing in this section affects a condition or warranty whose fulfilment is excused by law by reason of impossibility or otherwise.

(7)   Paragraph 2 of Schedule 1 below applies in relation to a contract made before 22 April 1967 or (in the application of this Act to Northern Ireland) 28 July 1967.

12. Implied terms about title, etc.

(1) In a contract of sale, other than one to which subsection (3) below applies, there is an implied term on the part of the seller that in the case of a sale he has a right to sell the goods, and in the case of an agreement to sell he will have such a right at the time when the property is to pass.

(2) In a contract of sale, other than one to which subsection (3) below applies, there is also an implied term that—

    (a) the goods are free, and will remain free until the time when the property is to pass, from any charge or encumbrance not disclosed or known to the buyer before the contract is made, and

    (b) the buyer will enjoy quiet possession of the goods except so far as it may be disturbed by the owner or other person entitled to the benefit of any charge or encumbrance so disclosed or known.

(3) This subsection applies to a contract of sale in the case of which there appears from the contract or is to be inferred from its circumstances an intention that the seller should transfer only such title as he or a third person may have.

(4) In a contract to which subsection (3) above applies there is an implied term that all charges or encumbrances known to the seller and not known to the buyer have been disclosed to the buyer before the contract is made.

(5) In a contract to which subsection (3) above applies there is also an implied term that none of the following will disturb the buyer's quiet possession of the goods, namely—

    (a) the seller;

    (b) in a case where the parties to the contract intend that the seller should transfer only such title as a third person may have, that person;

    (c) anyone claiming through or under the seller or that third person otherwise than under a charge or encumbrance disclosed or known to the buyer before the contract is made.

(5A) As regards England and Wales and Northern Ireland, the term implied by subsection (1) above is a condition and the terms implied by subsections (2), (4) and (5) above are warranties.

(6) Paragraph 3 of Schedule 1 below applies in relation to a contract made before 18 May 1973.

(7) This section does not apply to a contract to which Chapter 2 of Part 1 of the Consumer Rights Act 2015 applies (but see the provision made about such contracts in section 17 of that Act).

13. Sale by description

(1) Where there is a contract for the sale of goods by description, there is an implied term that the goods will correspond with the description.

(1A) As regards England and Wales and Northern Ireland, the term implied by subsection (1) above is a condition.

(2) If the sale is by sample as well as by description it is not sufficient that the bulk of the goods corresponds with the sample if the goods do not also correspond with the description.

(3) A sale of goods is not prevented from being a sale by description by reason only that, being exposed for sale or hire, they are selected by the buyer.

(4) Paragraph 4 of Schedule 1 below applies in relation to a contract made before 18 May 1973.

(5) This section does not apply to a contract to which Chapter 2 of Part 1 of the Consumer Rights Act 2015 applies (but see the provision made about such contracts in section 11 of that Act).

14. Implied terms about quality or fitness

(1) Except as provided by this section and section 15 below and subject to any other enactment, there is no implied term about the quality or fitness for any particular purpose of goods supplied under a contract of sale.

(2) Where the seller sells goods in the course of a business, there is an implied term that the goods supplied under the contract are of satisfactory quality.

(2A) For the purposes of this Act, goods are of satisfactory quality if they meet the standard that a reasonable person would regard as satisfactory, taking account of any description of the goods, the price (if relevant) and all the other relevant circumstances.

(2B) For the purposes of this Act, the quality of goods includes their state and condition and the following (among others) are in appropriate cases aspects of the quality of goods—
    (a)   fitness for all the purposes for which goods of the kind in question are commonly supplied,
    (b)   appearance and finish,
    (c)   freedom from minor defects,
    (d)   safety, and
    (e)   durability.

(2C) The term implied by subsection (2) above does not extend to any matter making the quality of goods unsatisfactory—
    (a)   which is specifically drawn to the buyer's attention before the contract is made,
    (b)   where the buyer examines the goods before the contract is made, which that examination ought to reveal, or
    (c)   in the case of a contract for sale by sample, which would have been apparent on a reasonable examination of the sample.

(3)   Where the seller sells goods in the course of a business and the buyer, expressly or by implication, makes known—
    (a)   to the seller, or
    (b)   where the purchase price or part of it is payable by instalments and the goods were previously sold by a credit-broker to the seller, to that credit-broker,
    any particular purpose for which the goods are being bought, there is an implied term that the goods supplied under the contract are reasonably fit for that purpose, whether or not that is a purpose for which such goods are commonly supplied, except where the circumstances show that the buyer does not rely, or that it is unreasonable for him to rely, on the skill or judgment of the seller or credit-broker.

(4)   An implied term about quality or fitness for a particular purpose may be annexed to a relevant contract of sale by usage.

(5)   The preceding provisions of this section apply to a sale by a person who in the course of a business is acting as agent for another as they apply to a sale by a principal in the course of a business, except where that other is not selling in the course of a business and either the buyer knows that fact or reasonable steps are taken to bring it to the notice of the buyer before the contract is made.

(6)   As regards England and Wales and Northern Ireland, the terms implied by subsections (2) and (3) above are conditions.

(7)   Paragraph 5 of Schedule 1 below applies in relation to a contract made on or after 18 May 1973 and before the appointed day, and paragraph 6 in relation to one made before 18 May 1973.

(8)   In subsection (7) above and paragraph 5 of Schedule 1 below references to the appointed day are to the day appointed for the purposes of those provisions by an order of the Secretary of State made by statutory instrument.

(9)   This section does not apply to a contract to which Chapter 2 of Part 1 of the Consumer Rights Act 2015 applies (but see the provision made about such contracts in sections 9, 10 and 18 of that Act).

Sale by sample

15.   Sale by sample

(1)   A contract of sale is a contract for sale by sample where there is an express or implied term to that effect in the contract.

(2)   In the case of a contract for sale by sample there is an implied term—
    (a)   that the bulk will correspond with the sample in quality;
    (b)   ...
    (c)   that the goods will be free from any defect, making their quality unsatisfactory which would not be apparent on reasonable examination of the sample.

(3)   As regards England and Wales and Northern Ireland, the term implied by subsection (2) above is a condition.

(4)   Paragraph 7 of Schedule 1 below applies in relation to a contract made before 18 May 1973.

(5) This section does not apply to a contract to which Chapter 2 of Part 1 of the Consumer Rights Act applies (but see the provision made about such contracts in sections 13 and 18 of that Act).

Miscellaneous

15A. Modification of remedies for breach of condition in non-consumer cases

(1) Where in the case of a contract of sale—

    (a) the buyer would, apart from this subsection, have the right to reject goods by reason of a breach on the part of the seller of a term implied by section 13, 14 or 15 above, but

    (b) the breach is so slight that it would be unreasonable for him to reject them,

the breach is not to be treated as a breach of condition but may be treated as a breach of warranty.

(2) This section applies unless a contrary intention appears in, or is to be implied from, the contract.

(3) It is for the seller to show that a breach fell within subsection (1)(b) above.

(4) This section does not apply to Scotland.

15B. Remedies for breach of contract as respects Scotland

(1) Where in a contract of sale the seller is in breach of any term of the contract (express or implied), the buyer shall be entitled—

    (a) to claim damages, and

    (b) if the breach is material, to reject any goods delivered under the contract and treat it as repudiated.

(1A) Subsection (1) does not apply to a contract to which Chapter 2 of Part 1 of the Consumer Rights Act 2015 applies (but see the provision made about such contracts in sections 19 to 22 of that Act).

(3) This section applies to Scotland only.

PART III
EFFECTS OF THE CONTRACT

Transfer of property as between seller and buyer

16. Goods must be ascertained

Subject to section (20A) below where there is a contract for the sale of unascertained goods no property in the goods is transferred to the buyer unless and until the goods are ascertained.

17. Property passes when intended to pass

(1) Where there is a contract for the sale of specific or ascertained goods the property in them is transferred to the buyer at such time as the parties to the contract intend it to be transferred.

(2) For the purpose of ascertaining the intention of the parties regard shall be had to the terms of the contract, the conduct of the parties and the circumstances of the case.

18. Rules for ascertaining intention

Unless a different intention appears, the following are rules for ascertaining the intention of the parties as to the time at which the property in the goods is to pass to the buyer.

Rule 1.—Where there is an unconditional contract for the sale of specific goods in a deliverable state the property in the goods passes to the buyer when the contract is made, and it is immaterial whether the time of payment or the time of delivery, or both, be postponed.

Rule 2.—Where there is a contract for the sale of specific goods and the seller is bound to do something to the goods for the purpose of putting them into a deliverable state, the property does not pass until the thing is done and the buyer has notice that it has been done.

Rule 3. — Where there is a contract for the sale of specific goods in a deliverable state but the seller is bound to weigh, measure, test, or do some other act or thing with reference to the goods for the purpose of ascertaining the price, the property does not pass until the act or thing is done and the buyer has notice that it has been done.

Rule 4. — When goods are delivered to the buyer on approval or on sale or return or other similar terms the property in the goods passes to the buyer —

(a) when he signifies his approval or acceptance to the seller or does any other act adopting the transaction;

(b) if he does not signify his approval or acceptance to the seller but retains the goods without giving notice of rejection, then, if a time has been fixed for the return of the goods, on the expiration of that time, and, if no time has been fixed, on the expiration of a reasonable time.

Rule 5. — (1) Where there is a contract for the sale of unascertained or future goods by description, and goods of that description and in a deliverable state are unconditionally appropriated to the contract, either by the seller with the assent of the buyer or by the buyer with the assent of the seller, the property in the goods then passes to the buyer; and the assent may be express or implied, and may be given either before or after the appropriation is made.

(2) Where, in pursuance of the contract, the seller delivers the goods to the buyer or to a carrier or other bailee or custodier (whether named by the buyer or not) for the purpose of transmission to the buyer, and does not reserve the right of disposal, he is to be taken to have unconditionally appropriated the goods to the contract.

(3) Where there is a contract for the sale of a specified quantity of unascertained goods in a deliverable state forming part of a bulk which is identified either in the contract or by subsequent agreement between the parties and the bulk is reduced to (or to less than) that quantity, then, if the buyer under that contract is the only buyer to whom goods are then due out of the bulk —

(a) the remaining goods are to be taken as appropriated to that contract at the time when the bulk is so reduced; and

(b) the property in those goods then passes to that buyer.

(4) Paragraph (3) above applies also (with the necessary modifications) where a bulk is reduced to (or to less than) the aggregate of the quantities due to a single buyer under separate contracts relating to that bulk and he is the only buyer to whom goods are then due out of that bulk.

19. Reservation of right of disposal

(1) Where there is a contract for the sale of specific goods or where goods are subsequently appropriated to the contract, the seller may, by the terms of the contract or appropriation, reserve the right of disposal of the goods until certain conditions are fulfilled; and in such a case, notwithstanding the delivery of the goods to the buyer, or to a carrier or other bailee or custodier for the purpose of transmission to the buyer, the property in the goods does not pass to the buyer until the conditions imposed by the seller are fulfilled.

(2) Where goods are shipped, and by the bill of lading the goods are deliverable to the order of the seller or his agent, the seller is prima facie to be taken to reserve the right of disposal.

(3) Where the seller of goods draws on the buyer for the price, and transmits the bill of exchange and bill of lading to the buyer together to secure acceptance or payment of the bill of exchange, the buyer is bound to return the bill of lading if he does not honour the bill of exchange, and if he wrongfully retains the bill of lading the property in the goods does not pass to him.

20. Passing of risk

(1) Unless otherwise agreed, the goods remain at the seller's risk until the property in them is transferred to the buyer, but when the property in them is transferred to the buyer the goods are at the buyer's risk whether delivery has been made or not.

(2) But where delivery has been delayed through the fault of either buyer or seller the goods are at the risk of the party at fault as regards any loss which might not have occurred but for such fault.

(3)   Nothing in this section affects the duties or liabilities of either seller or buyer as a bailee or custodier of the goods of the other party.

(4)   This section does not apply to a contract to which Chapter 2 of Part 1 of the Consumer Rights Act 2015 applies (but see the provision made about such contracts in section 29 of that Act).

20A.   Undivided shares in goods forming part of a bulk

(1)   This section applies to a contract for the sale of a specified quantity of unascertained goods if the following conditions are met—

    (a)   the goods or some of them form part of a bulk which is identified either in the contract or by subsequent agreement between the parties; and

    (b)   the buyer has paid the price for some or all of the goods which are the subject of the contract and which form part of the bulk.

(2)   Where this section applies, then (unless the parties agree otherwise), as soon as the conditions specified in paragraphs (a) and (b) of subsection (1) above are met or at such later time as the parties may agree—

    (a)   property in an undivided share in the bulk is transferred to the buyer; and

    (b)   the buyer becomes an owner in common of the bulk.

(3)   Subject to subsection (4) below, for the purposes of this section, the undivided share of a buyer in a bulk at any time shall be such share as the quantity of goods paid for and due to the buyer out of the bulk bears to the quantity of goods in the bulk at that time.

(4)   Where the aggregate of the undivided shares of buyers in a bulk determined under subsection (3) above would at any time exceed the whole of the bulk at that time, the undivided share in the bulk of each buyer shall be reduced proportionately so that the aggregate of the undivided shares is equal to the whole bulk.

(5)   Where a buyer has paid the price for only some of the goods due to him out of a bulk, any delivery to the buyer out of the bulk shall, for the purposes of this section, be ascribed in the first place to the goods in respect of which payment has been made.

(6)   For the purpose of this section payment of part of the price for any goods shall be treated as payment for a corresponding part of the goods.

20B.   Deemed consent by co-owner to dealings in bulk goods

(1)   A person who has become an owner in common of a bulk by virtue of section 20A above shall be deemed to have consented to—

    (a)   any delivery of goods out of the bulk to any other owner in common of the bulk, being goods which are due to him under his contract;

    (b)   any removal, dealing with, delivery or disposal of goods in the bulk by any other person who is an owner in common of the bulk in so far as the goods fall within that co-owner's undivided share in the bulk at the time of the removal, dealing, delivery or disposal.

(2)   No cause of action shall accrue to anyone against a person by reason of that person having acted in accordance with paragraph (a) or (b) of subsection (1) above in reliance on any consent deemed to have been given under that subsection.

(3)   Nothing in this section or section 20A above shall—

    (a)   impose an obligation on a buyer of goods out of a bulk to compensate any other buyer of goods out of that bulk for any shortfall in the goods received by that other buyer;

    (b)   affect any contractual arrangement between buyers of goods out of a bulk for adjustments between themselves; or

    (c)   affect the rights of any buyer under his contract.

Transfer of title

21.   Sale by person not the owner

(1)   Subject to this Act, where goods are sold by a person who is not their owner, and who does not sell them under the authority or with the consent of the owner, the buyer acquires no better title to the goods than the seller had, unless the owner of the goods is by his conduct precluded from denying the seller's authority to sell.

(2)   Nothing in this Act affects—
    (a)   the provisions of the Factors Acts or any enactment enabling the apparent owner of goods to dispose of them as if he were their true owner;
    (b)   the validity of any contract of sale under any special common law or statutory power of sale or under the order of a court of competent jurisdiction.

22.   Market overt

(1)   ...
(2)   This section does not apply to Scotland.
(3)   Paragraph 8 of Schedule 1 below applies in relation to a contract under which goods were sold before 1 January 1968 or (in the application of this Act to Northern Ireland) 29 August 1967.

23.   Sale under voidable title

When the seller of goods has a voidable title to them, but his title has not been avoided at the time of the sale, the buyer acquires a good title to the goods, provided he buys them in good faith and without notice of the seller's defect of title.

24.   Seller in possession after sale

Where a person having sold goods continues or is in possession of the goods, or of the documents of title to the goods, the delivery or transfer by that person, or by a mercantile agent acting for him, of the goods or documents of title under any sale, pledge, or other disposition thereof, to any person receiving the same in good faith and without notice of the previous sale, has the same effect as if the person making the delivery or transfer were expressly authorised by the owner of the goods to make the same.

25.   Buyer in possession after sale

(1)   Where a person having bought or agreed to buy goods obtains, with the consent of the seller, possession of the goods or the documents of title to the goods, the delivery or transfer by that person, or by a mercantile agent acting for him, of the goods or documents of title, under any sale, pledge, or other disposition thereof, to any person receiving the same in good faith and without notice of any lien or other right of the original seller in respect of the goods, has the same effect as if the person making the delivery or transfer were a mercantile agent in possession of the goods or documents of title with the consent of the owner.
(2)   For the purposes of subsection (1) above—
    (a)   the buyer under a conditional sale agreement is to be taken not to be a person who has bought or agreed to buy goods, and
    (b)   'conditional sale agreement' means an agreement for the sale of goods which is a consumer credit agreement within the meaning of the Consumer Credit Act 1974 under which the purchase price or part of it is payable by instalments, and the property in the goods is to remain in the seller (notwithstanding that the buyer is to be in possession of the goods) until such conditions as to the payment of instalments or otherwise as may be specified in the agreement are fulfilled.
(3)   Paragraph 9 of Schedule 1 below applies in relation to a contract under which a person buys or agrees to buy goods and which is made before the appointed day.
(4)   In subsection (3) above and paragraph 9 of Schedule 1 below references to the appointed day are to the day appointed for the purposes of those provisions by an order of the Secretary of State made by statutory instrument.

26.   Supplementary to sections 24 and 25

In sections 24 and 25 above 'mercantile agent' means a mercantile agent having in the customary course of his business as such agent authority either—
    (a)   to sell goods, or
    (b)   to consign goods for the purpose of sale, or
    (c)   to buy goods, or
    (d)   to raise money on the security of goods.

PART IV
PERFORMANCE OF THE CONTRACT

27. Duties of seller and buyer

It is the duty of the seller to deliver the goods, and of the buyer to accept and pay for them, in accordance with the terms of the contract of sale.

28. Payment and delivery are concurrent conditions

Unless otherwise agreed, delivery of the goods and payment of the price are concurrent conditions, that is to say, the seller must be ready and willing to give possession of the goods to the buyer in exchange for the price and the buyer must be ready and willing to pay the price in exchange for possession of the goods.

29. Rules about delivery

(1) Whether it is for the buyer to take possession of the goods or for the seller to send them to the buyer is a question depending in each case on the contract, express or implied, between the parties.

(2) Apart from any such contract, express or implied, the place of delivery is the seller's place of business if he has one, and if not, his residence; except that, if the contract is for the sale of specific goods, which to the knowledge of the parties when the contract is made are in some other place, then that place is the place of delivery.

(3) Where under the contract of sale the seller is bound to send the goods to the buyer, but no time for sending them is fixed, the seller is bound to send them within a reasonable time.

(3A) Subsection (3) does not apply to a contract to which Chapter 2 of Part 1 of the Consumer Rights Act 2015 applies (but see the provision about such contracts made in section 28 of that Act).

(4) Where the goods at the time of sale are in the possession of a third person, there is no delivery by seller to buyer unless and until the third person acknowledges to the buyer that he holds the goods on his behalf; but nothing in this section affects the operation of the issue or transfer of any document of title to goods.

(5) Demand or tender of delivery may be treated as ineffectual unless made at a reasonable hour; and what is a reasonable hour is a question of fact.

(6) Unless otherwise agreed, the expenses of and incidental to putting the goods into a deliverable state must be borne by the seller.

30. Delivery of wrong quantity

(1) Where the seller delivers to the buyer a quantity of goods less than he contracted to sell, the buyer may reject them, but if the buyer accepts the goods so delivered he must pay for them at the contract rate.

(2) Where the seller delivers to the buyer a quantity of goods larger than he contracted to sell, the buyer may accept the goods included in the contract and reject the rest, or he may reject the whole.

(2A) A buyer may not—

(a) where the seller delivers a quantity of goods less than he contracted to sell, reject the goods under subsection (1) above, or

(b) where the seller delivers a quantity of goods larger than he contracted to sell, reject the whole under subsection (2) above,

if the shortfall or, as the case may be, excess is so slight that it would be unreasonable for him to do so.

(2B) It is for the seller to show that a shortfall or excess fell within subsection (2A) above.

(2C) Subsections (2A) and (2B) above do not apply to Scotland.

(3) Where the seller delivers to the buyer a quantity of goods larger than he contracted to sell and the buyer accepts the whole of the goods so delivered he must pay for them at the contract rate.

(5) This section is subject to any usage of trade, special agreement, or course of dealing between the parties.

(6) This section does not apply to a contract to which Chapter 2 of Part 1 of the Consumer Rights Act 2015 applies (but see the provision made about such contracts in section 25 of that Act).

31. Instalment deliveries

(1) Unless otherwise agreed, the buyer of goods is not bound to accept delivery of them by instalments.

(2) Where there is a contract for the sale of goods to be delivered by stated instalments, which are to be separately paid for, and the seller makes defective deliveries in respect of one or more instalments, or the buyer neglects or refuses to take delivery of or pay for one or more instalments, it is a question in each case depending on the terms of the contract and the circumstances of the case whether the breach of contract is a repudiation of the whole contract or whether it is a severable breach giving rise to a claim for compensation but not to a right to treat the whole contract as repudiated.

(3) This section does not apply to a contract to which Chapter 2 of Part 1 of the Consumer Rights Act 2015 applies (but see the provision made about such contracts in section 26 of that Act).

32. Delivery to carrier

(1) Where, in pursuance of a contract of sale, the seller is authorised or required to send the goods to the buyer, delivery of the goods to a carrier (whether named by the buyer or not) for the purpose of transmission to the buyer is prima facie deemed to be delivery of the goods to the buyer.

(2) Unless otherwise authorised by the buyer, the seller must make such contract with the carrier on behalf of the buyer as may be reasonable having regard to the nature of the goods and the other circumstances of the case; and if the seller omits to do so, and the goods are lost or damaged in course of transit, the buyer may decline to treat the delivery to the carrier as a delivery to himself or may hold the seller responsible in damages.

(3) Unless otherwise agreed, where goods are sent by the seller to the buyer by a route involving sea transit, under circumstances in which it is usual to insure, the seller must give such notice to the buyer as may enable him to insure them during their sea transit, and if the seller fails to do so, the goods are at his risk during such sea transit.

(4) This section does not apply to a contract to which Chapter 2 of Part 1 of the Consumer Rights Act 2015 applies (but see the provision made about such contracts in section 29 of that Act).

33. Risk where goods are delivered at distant place

(1) Where the seller of goods agrees to deliver them at his own risk at a place other than that where they are when sold, the buyer must nevertheless (unless otherwise agreed) take any risk of deterioration in the goods necessarily incident to the course of transit.

(2) This section does not apply to a contract to which Chapter 2 of Part 1 of the Consumer Rights Act 2015 applies (but see the provision made about such contracts in section 29 of that Act).

34. Buyer's right of examining the goods

(1) Unless otherwise agreed, when the seller tenders delivery of goods to the buyer, he is bound on request to afford the buyer a reasonable opportunity of examining the goods for the purpose of ascertaining whether they are in conformity with the contract and, in the case of a contract for sale by sample, of comparing the bulk with the sample.

(2) Nothing in this section affects the operation of section 22 (time limit for short-term right to reject) of the Consumer Rights Act 2015.

35. Acceptance

(1) The buyer is deemed to have accepted the goods subject to subsection (2) below—

    (a) when he intimates to the seller that he has accepted them, or

    (b) when the goods have been delivered to him and he does any act in relation to them which is inconsistent with the ownership of the seller.

(2) Where goods are delivered to the buyer, and he has not previously examined them, he is not deemed to have accepted them under subsection (1) above until he has had a reasonable opportunity of examining them for the purpose—

    (a) of ascertaining whether they are in conformity with the contract, and

    (b) in the case of a contract for sale by sample, of comparing the bulk with the sample.

(4) The buyer is also deemed to have accepted the goods when after the lapse of a reasonable time he retains the goods without intimating to the seller that he has rejected them.

(5) The questions that are material in determining for the purposes of subsection (4) above whether a reasonable time has elapsed include whether the buyer has had a reasonable opportunity of examining the goods for the purpose mentioned in subsection (1) above.

(6) The buyer is not by virtue of this section deemed to have accepted the goods merely because—

    (a) he asks for, or agrees to, their repair by or under an arrangement with the seller, or

    (b) the goods are delivered to another under a sub-sale or other disposition.

(7) Where the contract is for the sale of goods making one or more commercial units, a buyer accepting any goods included in a unit is deemed to have accepted all the goods making the unit; and in this subsection 'commercial unit' means a unit division of which would materially impair the value of the goods or the character of the unit.

(8) Paragraph 10 of Schedule 1 below applies in relation to a contract made before 22 April 1967 or (in the application of this Act to Northern Ireland) 28 July 1967.

(9) This section does not apply to a contract to which Chapter 2 of Part 1 of the Consumer Rights Act 2015 applies (but see the provision made about such contracts in section 21 of that Act).

35A. Right of partial rejection

(1) If the buyer—

    (a) has the right to reject the goods by reason of a breach on the part of the seller that affects some or all of them, but

    (b) accepts some of the goods, including, where there are any goods unaffected by the breach, all such goods,

he does not by accepting them lose his right to reject the rest.

(2) In the case of a buyer having the right to reject an instalment of goods, subsection (1) above applies as if references to the goods were references to the goods comprised in the instalment.

(3) For the purposes of subsection (1) above, goods are affected by a breach if by reason of the breach they are not in conformity with the contract.

(4) This section applies unless a contrary intention appears in, or is to be implied from, the contract.

(5) This section does not apply to a contract to which Chapter 2 of Part 1 of the Consumer Rights Act 2015 applies (but see the provision made about such contracts in section 21 of that Act).

36. Buyer not bound to return rejected goods

(1) Unless otherwise agreed, where goods are delivered to the buyer, and he refuses to accept them, having the right to do so, he is not bound to return them to the seller, but it is sufficient if he intimates to the seller that he refuses to accept them.

(2) This section does not apply to a contract to which Chapter 2 of Part 1 of the Consumer Rights Act 2015 applies (but see the provision made about such contracts in section 20 of that Act).

37. Buyer's liability for not taking delivery of goods

(1) When the seller is ready and willing to deliver the goods, and requests the buyer to take delivery, and the buyer does not within a reasonable time after such request take delivery of the goods, he is liable to the seller for any loss occasioned by his neglect or refusal to take delivery, and also for a reasonable charge for the care and custody of the goods.

(2) Nothing in this section affects the rights of the seller where the neglect or refusal of the buyer to take delivery amounts to a repudiation of the contract.

PART V
RIGHTS OF UNPAID SELLER AGAINST THE GOODS

Preliminary

38.   Unpaid seller defined

(1)   The seller of goods is an unpaid seller within the meaning of this Act—

 (a)   when the whole of the price has not been paid or tendered;

 (b)   when a bill of exchange or other negotiable instrument has been received as conditional payment, and the condition on which it was received has not been fulfilled by reason of the dishonour of the instrument or otherwise.

(2)   In this Part of this Act 'seller' includes any person who is in the position of a seller, as, for instance, an agent of the seller to whom the bill of lading has been indorsed, or a consignor or agent who has himself paid (or is directly responsible for) the price.

39.   Unpaid seller's rights

(1)   Subject to this and any other Act, notwithstanding that the property in the goods may have passed to the buyer, the unpaid seller of goods, as such, has by implication of law—

 (a)   a lien on the goods or right to retain them for the price while he is in possession of them;

 (b)   in the case of the insolvency of the buyer, a right of stopping the goods in transit after he has parted with the possession of them;

 (c)   a right of re-sale as limited by this Act.

(2)   Where the property in goods has not passed to the buyer, the unpaid seller has (in addition to his other remedies) a right of withholding delivery similar to and coextensive with his rights of lien or retention and stoppage in transit where the property has passed to the buyer.

Unpaid seller's lien

41.   Seller's lien

(1)   Subject to this Act, the unpaid seller of goods who is in possession of them is entitled to retain possession of them until payment or tender of the price in the following cases:—

 (a)   where the goods have been sold without any stipulation as to credit;

 (b)   where the goods have been sold on credit but the term of credit has expired;

 (c)   where the buyer becomes insolvent.

(2)   The seller may exercise his lien or right of retention notwithstanding that he is in possession of the goods as agent or bailee or custodier for the buyer.

42.   Part delivery

Where an unpaid seller has made part delivery of the goods, he may exercise his lien or right of retention on the remainder, unless such part delivery has been made under such circumstances as to show an agreement to waive the lien or right of retention.

43.   Termination of lien

(1)   The unpaid seller of goods loses his lien or right of retention in respect of them—

 (a)   when he delivers the goods to a carrier or other bailee or custodier for the purpose of transmission to the buyer without reserving the right of disposal of the goods;

 (b)   when the buyer or his agent lawfully obtains possession of the goods;

 (c)   by waiver of the lien or right of retention.

(2)   An unpaid seller of goods who has a lien or right of retention in respect of them does not lose his lien or right of retention by reason only that he has obtained judgment or decree for the price of the goods.

Stoppage in transit

44.   Right of stoppage in transit

Subject to this Act, when the buyer of goods becomes insolvent the unpaid seller who has parted with the possession of the goods has the right of stopping them in transit, that is to say, he may resume possession of the goods as long as they are in course of transit, and may retain them until payment or tender of the price.

45.   Duration of transit

(1)   Goods are deemed to be in course of transit from the time when they are delivered to a carrier or other bailee or custodier for the purpose of transmission to the buyer, until the buyer or his agent in that behalf takes delivery of them from the carrier or other bailee or custodier.

(2)   If the buyer or his agent in that behalf obtains delivery of the goods before their arrival at the appointed destination, the transit is at an end.

(3)   If, after the arrival of the goods at the appointed destination, the carrier or other bailee or custodier acknowledges to the buyer or his agent that he holds the goods on his behalf and continues in possession of them as bailee or custodier for the buyer or his agent, the transit is at an end, and it is immaterial that a further destination for the goods may have been indicated by the buyer.

(4)   If the goods are rejected by the buyer, and the carrier or other bailee or custodier continues in possession of them, the transit is not deemed to be at an end, even if the seller has refused to receive them back.

(5)   When goods are delivered to a ship chartered by the buyer it is a question depending on the circumstances of the particular case whether they are in the possession of the master as a carrier or as agent to the buyer.

(6)   Where the carrier or other bailee or custodier wrongfully refuses to deliver the goods to the buyer or his agent in that behalf, the transit is deemed to be at an end.

(7)   Where part delivery of the goods has been made to the buyer or his agent in that behalf, the remainder of the goods may be stopped in transit, unless such part delivery has been made under such circumstances as to show an agreement to give up possession of the whole of the goods.

46.   How stoppage in transit is effected

(1)   The unpaid seller may exercise his right of stoppage in transit either by taking actual possession of the goods or by giving notice of his claim to the carrier or other bailee or custodier in whose possession the goods are.

(2)   The notice may be given either to the person in actual possession of the goods or to his principal.

(3)   If given to the principal, the notice is ineffective unless given at such time and under such circumstances that the principal, by the exercise of reasonable diligence, may communicate it to his servant or agent in time to prevent a delivery to the buyer.

(4)   When notice of stoppage in transit is given by the seller to the carrier or other bailee or custodier in possession of the goods, he must re-deliver the goods to, or according to the directions of, the seller; and the expenses of the re-delivery must be borne by the seller.

Resale etc. by buyer

47.   Effect of sub-sale etc. by buyer

(1)   Subject to this Act, the unpaid seller's right of lien or retention or stoppage in transit is not affected by any sale or other disposition of the goods which the buyer may have made, unless the seller has assented to it.

(2)   Where a document of title to goods has been lawfully transferred to any person as buyer or owner of the goods, and that person transfers the document to a person who takes it in good faith and for valuable consideration, then—

(a)   if the last-mentioned transfer was by way of sale the unpaid seller's right of lien or retention or stoppage in transit is defeated; and

(b)   if the last-mentioned transfer was made by way of pledge or other disposition for value, the unpaid seller's right of lien or retention of stoppage in transit can only be exercised subject to the rights of the transferee.

Rescission: and re-sale by seller

48.   Rescission: and re-sale by seller

(1)   Subject to this section, a contract of sale is not rescinded by the mere exercise by an unpaid seller of his right of lien or retention or stoppage in transit.

(2)   Where an unpaid seller who has exercised his right of lien or retention or stoppage in transit re-sells the goods, the buyer acquires a good title to them as against the original buyer.

(3)   Where the goods are of a perishable nature, or where the unpaid seller gives notice to the buyer of his intention to re-sell, and the buyer does not within a reasonable time pay or tender the price, the unpaid seller may re-sell the goods and recover from the original buyer damages for any loss occasioned by his breach of contract.

(4)   Where the seller expressly reserves the right of re-sale in case the buyer should make default, and on the buyer making default re-sells the goods, the original contract of sale is rescinded but without prejudice to any claim the seller may have for damages.

PART VI
ACTIONS FOR BREACH OF THE CONTRACT

Seller's remedies

49.   Action for price

(1)   Where, under a contract of sale, the property in the goods has passed to the buyer and he wrongfully neglects or refuses to pay for the goods according to the terms of the contract, the seller may maintain an action against him for the price of the goods.

50.   Damages for non-acceptance

(1)   Where the buyer wrongfully neglects or refuses to accept and pay for the goods, the seller may maintain an action against him for damages for non-acceptance.

(2)   The measure of damages is the estimated loss directly and naturally resulting, in the ordinary course of events, from the buyer's breach of contract.

(3)   Where there is an available market for the goods in question the measure of damages is prima facie to be ascertained by the difference between the contract price and the market or current price at the time or times when the goods ought to have been accepted or (if no time was fixed for acceptance) at the time of the refusal to accept.

51.   Damages for non-delivery

(1)   Where the seller wrongfully neglects or refuses to deliver the goods to the buyer, the buyer may maintain an action against the seller for damages for non-delivery.

(2)   The measure of damages is the estimated loss directly and naturally resulting, in the ordinary course of events, from the seller's breach of contract.

(3)   Where there is an available market for the goods in question the measure of damages is prima facie to be ascertained by the difference between the contract price and the market or current price of the goods at the time or times when they ought to have been delivered or (if no time was fixed) at the time of the refusal to deliver.

(4)   This section does not apply to a contract to which Chapter 2 of Part 1 of the Consumer Rights Act 2015 applies (but see the provision made about such contracts in section 19 of that Act).

52.   Specific performance

(1)   In any action for breach of contract to deliver specific or ascertained goods the court may, if it thinks fit, on the plaintiff's application, by its judgment or decree direct that the contract shall be performed specifically, without giving the defendant the option of retaining the goods on payment of damages.

(3) The judgment or decree may be unconditional, or on such terms and conditions as to damages, payment of the price and otherwise as seem just to the court.

(5) This section does not apply to a contract to which Chapter 2 of Part 1 of the Consumer Rights Act 2015 applies (but see the provision made about such contracts in section 19 of that Act).

53. Remedy for breach of warranty

(1) Where there is a breach of warranty by the seller, or where the buyer elects (or is compelled) to treat any breach of a condition on the part of the seller as a breach of warranty, the buyer is not by reason only of such breach of warranty entitled to reject the goods; but he may—

(a) set up against the seller the breach of warranty in diminution or extinction of the price, or

(b) maintain an action against the seller for damages for the breach of warranty.

(2) The measure of damages for breach of warranty is the estimated loss directly and naturally resulting, in the ordinary course of events, from the breach of warranty.

(3) In the case of breach of warranty of quality such loss is prima facie the difference between the value of the goods at the time of delivery to the buyer and the value they would have had if they had fulfilled the warranty.

(4) The fact that the buyer has set up the breach of warranty in diminution or extinction of the price does not prevent him from maintaining an action for the same breach of warranty if he has suffered further damage.

(4A) This section does not apply to a contract to which Chapter 2 of Part 1 of the Consumer Rights Act 2015 applies (but see the provision made about such contracts in section 19 of that Act).

(5) This section does not apply to Scotland.

53A. Measure of damages as respects Scotland

(1) The measure of damages for the seller's breach of contract is the estimated loss directly and naturally resulting, in the ordinary course of events, from the breach.

(2) Where the seller's breach consists of the delivery of goods which are not of the quality required by the contract and the buyer retains the goods, such loss as aforesaid is prima facie the difference between the value of the goods at the time of delivery to the buyer and the value they would have had if they had fulfilled the contract.

(2A) This section does not apply to a contract to which Chapter 2 of Part 1 of the Consumer Rights Act 2015 applies (but see the provision made about such contracts in section 19 of that Act).

(3) This section applies to Scotland only.

54. Interest, etc.

(1) Nothing in this Act affects the right of the buyer or the seller to recover interest or special damages in any case where by law interest or special damages may be recoverable, or to recover money paid where the consideration for the payment of it has failed.

(2) This section does not apply to a contract to which Chapter 2 of Part 1 of the Consumer Rights Act 2015 applies (but see the provision made about such contracts in section 19 of that Act).

PART VII
SUPPLEMENTARY

55. Exclusion of implied terms

(1) Where a right, duty or liability would arise under a contract of sale of goods by implication of law, it may (subject to the Unfair Contract Terms Act 1977) be negatived or varied by express agreement, or by the course of dealing between the parties, or by such usage as binds both parties to the contract.

(1A) Subsection (1) does not apply to a contract to which Chapter 2 of Part 1 of the Consumer Rights Act 2015 applies (but see the provision made about such contracts in section 31 of that Act).

(2)   An express term does not negative a term implied by this Act unless inconsistent with it.

(3)   Paragraph 11 of Schedule 1 below applies in relation to a contract made on or after 18 May 1973 and before 1 February 1978, and paragraph 12 in relation to one made before 18 May 1973.

56.   Conflict of laws

Paragraph 13 of Schedule 1 below applies in relation to a contract made on or after 18 May 1973 and before 1 February 1978, so as to make provision about conflict of laws in relation to such a contract.

57.   Auction sales

(1)   Where goods are put up for sale by auction in lots, each lot is prima facie deemed to be the subject of a separate contract of sale.

(2)   A sale by auction is complete when the auctioneer announces its completion by the fall of the hammer, or in other customary manner; and until the announcement is made any bidder may retract his bid.

(3)   A sale by auction may be notified to be subject to a reserve or upset price, and a right to bid may also be reserved expressly by or on behalf of the seller.

(4)   Where a sale by auction is not notified to be subject to a right to bid by or on behalf of the seller, it is not lawful for the seller to bid himself or to employ any person to bid at the sale, or for the auctioneer knowingly to take any bid from the seller or any such person.

(5)   A sale contravening subsection (4) above may be treated as fraudulent by the buyer.

(6)   Where, in respect of a sale by auction, a right to bid is expressly reserved (but not otherwise) the seller or any one person on his behalf may bid at the auction.

58.   Payment into court in Scotland

(1)   In Scotland where a buyer has elected to accept goods which he might have rejected, and to treat a breach of contract as only giving rise to a claim for damages, he may, in an action by the seller for the price, be required, in the discretion of the court before which the action depends, to consign or pay into court the price of the goods, or part of the price, or to give other reasonable security for its due payment.

(2)   This section does not apply to a contract to which Chapter 2 of Part 1 of the Consumer Rights Act 2015 applies (but see the provision made about such contracts in section 27 of that Act).

59.   Reasonable time a question of fact

Where a reference is made in this Act to a reasonable time the question what is a reasonable time is a question of fact.

60.   Rights etc. enforceable by action

Where a right, duty or liability is declared by this Act, it may (unless otherwise provided by this Act) be enforced by action.

61.   Interpretation

(1)   In this Act, unless the context or subject matter otherwise requires,—

'action' includes counterclaim and set-off, and in Scotland condescendence and claim and compensation;

'bulk' means a mass or collection of goods of the same kind which—

(a)   is contained in a defined space or area; and

(b)   is such that any goods in the bulk are interchangeable with any other goods therein of the same number or quantity;

'business' includes a profession and the activities of any government department (including a Northern Ireland department) or local or public authority;

'buyer' means a person who buys or agrees to buy goods;

'contract of sale' includes an agreement to sell as well as a sale;

'credit-broker' means a person acting in the course of a business of credit brokerage carried on by him, that is a business of effecting introductions of individuals desiring to obtain credit—

(a)   to persons carrying on any business so far as it relates to the provision of credit, or

(b)   to other persons engaged in credit brokerage;

'defendant' includes in Scotland defender, respondent, and claimant in a multiplepoinding;

'delivery' means voluntary transfer of possession from one person to another; except that in relation to sections 20A and 20B above it includes such appropriation of goods to the contract as results in property in the goods being transferred to the buyer;

'document of title to goods' has the same meaning as it has in the Factors Acts;

'Factors Acts' means the Factors Act 1889, the Factors (Scotland) Act 1890, and any enactment amending or substituted for the same;

'fault' means wrongful act or default;

'future goods' means goods to be manufactured or acquired by the seller after the making of the contract of sale;

'goods' includes all personal chattels other than things in action and money, and in Scotland all corporeal moveables except money; and in particular 'goods' includes emblements, industrial growing crops, and things attached to or forming part of the land which are agreed to be severed before sale or under the contract of sale; and includes an undivided share in goods;

'plaintiff' includes pursuer, complainer, claimant in a multiplepoinding and defendant or defender counter-claiming;

'property' means the general property in goods, and not merely a special property;

'sale' includes a bargain and sale as well as a sale and delivery;

'seller' means a person who sells or agrees to sell goods;

'specific goods' means goods identified and agreed on at the time a contract of sale is made; and includes an undivided share, specified as a fraction or percentage, of goods identified and agreed on as aforesaid;

'warranty' (as regards England and Wales and Northern Ireland) means an agreement with reference to goods which are the subject of a contract of sale, but collateral to the main purpose of such contract, the breach of which gives rise to a claim for damages, but not to a right to reject the goods and treat the contract as repudiated.

(3)   A thing is deemed to be done in good faith within the meaning of this Act when it is in fact done honestly, whether it is done negligently or not.

(4)   A person is deemed to be insolvent within the meaning of this Act if he has either ceased to pay his debts in the ordinary course of business or he cannot pay his debts as they become due, ...

(5)   Goods are in a deliverable state within the meaning of this Act when they are in such a state that the buyer would under the contract be bound to take delivery of them.

(6)   As regards the definition of 'business' in subsection (1) above, paragraph 14 of Schedule 1 below applies in relation to a contract made on or after 18 May 1973 and before 1 February 1978, and paragraph 15 in relation to one made before 18 May 1973.

62.   Savings: rule of law etc.

(1)   The rules in bankruptcy relating to contracts of sale apply to those contracts, anything in this Act.

(2)   The rules of the common law, including the law merchant, except in so far as they are inconsistent with the provisions of legislation including this Act and the Consumer Rights Act 2015, and in particular the rules relating to the law of principal and agent and the effect of fraud, misrepresentation, duress or coercion, mistake, or other invalidating cause, apply to contracts for the sale of goods.

(3)   Nothing in this Act or the Sale of Goods Act 1893 affects the enactments relating to bills of sale, or any enactment relating to the sale of goods which is not expressly repealed or amended by this Act or that.

(4)   The provisions of this Act about contracts of sale do not apply to a transaction in the form of a contract of sale which is intended to operate by way of mortgage, pledge, charge, or other security.

(5)   Nothing in this Act prejudices or affects the landlord's right of hypothec.

64.   Short title and commencement

(1)   This Act may be cited as the Sale of Goods Act 1979.

(2)   This Act comes into force on 1 January 1980.

SUPPLY OF GOODS AND SERVICES ACT 1982
(1982, c. 29)

PART I
SUPPLY OF GOODS

Contracts for the transfer of property in goods

1.   The contracts concerned

(1)   In this Act in its application to England and Wales and Northern Ireland a 'relevant contract for the transfer of goods' means a contract under which one person transfers or agrees to transfer to another the property in goods, other than an excepted contract, and other than a contract to which Chapter 2 of Part 1 of the Consumer Rights Act 2015 applies.

(2)   For the purposes of this section an excepted contract means any of the following—

     (a)   a contract of sale of goods;

     (b)   a hire-purchase agreement;

     (c)   ...

     (d)   a transfer or agreement to transfer which is made by deed and for which there is no consideration other than the presumed consideration imported by the deed;

     (e)   a contract intended to operate by way of mortgage, pledge, charge or other security.

(3)   For the purposes of this Act in its application to England and Wales and Northern Ireland a contract is a contract for the transfer of goods whether or not services are also provided or to be provided under the contract, and (subject to subsection (2) above) whatever is the nature of the consideration for the transfer or agreement to transfer.

2.   Implied terms about title, etc.

(1)   In a relevant contract for the transfer of goods, other than one to which subsection (3) below applies, there is an implied condition on the part of the transferor that in the case of a transfer of the property in the goods he has a right to transfer the property and in the case of an agreement to transfer the property in the goods he will have such a right at the time when the property is to be transferred.

(2)   In a relevant contract for the transfer of goods, other than one to which subsection (3) below applies, there is also an implied warranty that—

     (a)   the goods are free, and will remain free until the time when the property is to be transferred, from any charge or encumbrance not disclosed or known to the transferee before the contract is made, and

     (b)   the transferee will enjoy quiet possession of the goods except so far as it may be disturbed by the owner or other person entitled to the benefit of any charge or encumbrance so disclosed or known.

(3)   This subsection applies to a relevant contract for the transfer of goods in the case of which there appears from the contract or is to be inferred from its circumstances an intention that the transferor should transfer only such title as he or a third person may have.

(4)   In a contract to which subsection (3) above applies there is an implied warranty that all charges or encumbrances known to the transferor and not known to the transferee have been disclosed to the transferee before the contract is made.

(5)   In a contract to which subsection (3) above applies, there is also an implied warranty that none of the following will disturb the transferee's quiet possession of the goods, namely—
    (a)   the transferor;
    (b)   in a case where the parties to the contract intend that the transferor should transfer only such title as a third person may have, that person;
    (c)   anyone claiming through or under the transferor or that third person otherwise than under a charge or encumbrance disclosed or known to the transferee before the contract is made.

3. Implied terms where transfer is by description

(1)   This section applies where, under a relevant contract for the transfer of goods, the transferor transfers or agrees to transfer the property in the goods by description.

(2)   In such case there is an implied condition that the goods will correspond with the description.

(3)   If the transferor transfers or agrees to transfer the property in the goods by sample as well as by description it is not sufficient that the bulk of the goods corresponds with the sample if the goods do not also correspond with the description.

(4)   A contract is not prevented from falling within subsection (1) above by reason only that, being exposed for supply, the goods are selected by the transferee.

4. Implied terms about quality or fitness

(1)   Except as provided by this section and section 5 below and subject to the provision of any other enactment, there is no implied condition or warranty about the quality or fitness for any particular purpose of goods supplied under a relevant contract for the transfer of goods.

(2)   Where, under such a contract, the transferor transfers the property in goods in the course of a business, there is an implied condition that the goods supplied under the contract are of satisfactory quality.

(2A)   For the purposes of this section and section 5 below, goods are of satisfactory quality if they meet the standard that a reasonable person would regard as satisfactory, taking account of any description of the goods, the price (if relevant) and all the other relevant circumstances.

(3)   The condition implied by subsection (2) above does not extend to any matter making the quality of goods unsatisfactory—
    (a)   which is specifically drawn to the transferee's attention before the contract is made,
    (b)   where the transferee examines the goods before the contract is made, which that examination ought to reveal, or
    (c)   where the property in the goods is transferred by reference to a sample, which would have been apparent on a reasonable examination of the sample.

(4)   Subsection (5) below applies where, under a relevant contract for the transfer of goods, the transferor transfers the property in goods in the course of a business and the transferee, expressly or by implication, makes known—
    (a)   to the transferor, or
    (b)   where the consideration or part of the consideration for the transfer is a sum payable by instalments and the goods were previously sold by a credit-broker to the transferor, to that credit-broker,
any particular purpose for which the goods are being acquired.

(5)   In that case there is (subject to subsection (6) below) an implied condition that the goods supplied under the contract are reasonably fit for that purpose, whether or not that is a purpose for which such goods are commonly supplied.

(6)   Subsection (5) above does not apply where the circumstances show that the transferee does not rely, or that it is unreasonable for him to rely, on the skill or judgment of the transferor or credit-broker.

(7)   An implied condition or warranty about quality or fitness for a particular purpose may be annexed by usage to a relevant contract for the transfer of goods.

(8)   The preceding provisions of this section apply to a transfer by a person who in the course of a business is acting as agent for another as they apply to a transfer by a principal in the course of a business, except where that other is not transferring in the course of a business and either the transferee knows that fact or reasonable steps are taken to bring it to the transferee's notice before the contract concerned is made.

5.   Implied terms where transfer is by sample

(1)   This section applies where, under a relevant contract for the transfer of goods, the transferor transfers or agrees to transfer the property in the goods by reference to a sample.

(2)   In such a case there is an implied condition—

     (a)   that the bulk will correspond with the sample in quality; and

     (b)   that the transferee will have a reasonable opportunity of comparing the bulk with the sample; and

     (c)   that the goods will be free from any defect, making their quality unsatisfactory, which would not be apparent on reasonable examination of the sample.

(4)   For the purposes of this section a transferor transfers or agrees to transfer the property in goods by reference to a sample where there is an express or implied term to that effect in the contract concerned.

5A.   Modification of remedies for breach of statutory condition in non-consumer cases

(1)   Where in the case of a relevant contract for the transfer of goods—

     (a)   the transferee would, apart from this subsection, have the right to treat the contract as repudiated by reason of a breach on the part of the transferor of a term implied by section 3, 4 or 5(2)(a) or (c) above, but

     (b)   the breach is so slight that it would be unreasonable for him to do so,

     the breach is not to be treated as a breach of condition but may be treated as a breach of warranty.

(2)   This section applies unless a contrary intention appears in, or is to be implied from, the contract.

(3)   It is for the transferor to show that a breach fell within subsection (1)(b) above.

Contracts for the hire of goods

6.   The contracts concerned

(1)   In this Act in its application to England and Wales and Northern Ireland a relevant contract for the hire of goods means a contract under which one person bails or agrees to bail goods to another by way of hire, other than a hire-purchase contract, and other than a contract to which Chapter 2 of Part 1 of the Consumer Rights Act 2015 applies.

(2)   ...

(3)   For the purposes of this Act in its application to England and Wales and Northern Ireland a relevant contract is a contract for the hire of goods whether or not services are also provided or to be provided under the contract, and ... whatever is the nature of the consideration for the bailment or agreement to bail by way of hire.

7.   Implied terms about right to transfer possession, etc.

(1)   In a relevant contract for the hire of goods there is an implied condition on the part of the bailor that in the case of a bailment he has a right to transfer possession of the goods by way of hire for the period of the bailment and in the case of an agreement to bail he will have such a right at the time of the bailment.

(2)   In a relevant contract for the hire of goods there is also an implied warranty that the bailee will enjoy quiet possession of the goods for the period of the bailment except so far as the possession may be disturbed by the owner or other person entitled to the benefit of any charge or encumbrance disclosed or known to the bailee before the contract is made.

(3)   The preceding provisions of this section do not affect the right of the bailor to repossess the goods under an express or implied term of contract.

8.   Implied terms where hire is by description

(1)   This section applies where, under a relevant contract for the hire of goods, the bailor bails or agrees to bail the goods by description.

(2)   In such a case there is an implied condition that the goods will correspond with the description.

(3)   If under the contract the bailor bails or agrees to bail the goods by reference to a sample as well as a description it is not sufficient that the bulk of the goods corresponds with the sample if the goods do not also correspond with the description.

(4)   A contract is not prevented from falling within subsection (1) above by reason only that, being exposed for supply, the goods are selected by the bailee.

9.   Implied terms about quality or fitness

(1)   Except as provided by this section and section 10 below and subject to the provisions of any other enactment, there is no implied condition or warranty about the quality or fitness for any particular purpose of goods bailed under a relevant contract for the hire of goods.

(2)   Where, under such a contract, the bailor bails goods in the course of a business, there is an implied condition that the goods supplied under the contract are of satisfactory quality.

(2A) For the purposes of this section and section 10 below, goods are of satisfactory quality if they meet the standard that a reasonable person would regard as satisfactory, taking account of any description of the goods, the consideration for the bailment (if relevant) and all the other relevant circumstances.

(3)   The condition implied by subsection (2) above does not extend to any matter making the quality of goods unsatisfactory—

(a)   which is specifically drawn to the bailee's attention before the contract is made,

(b)   where the bailee examines the goods before the contract is made, which that examination ought to reveal, or

(c)   where the goods are bailed by reference to a sample, which would have been apparent on a reasonable examination of the sample.

(4)   Subsection (5) below applies where, under a relevant contract for the hire of goods, the bailor bails goods in the course of a business and the bailee, expressly or by implication, makes known—

(a)   to the bailor in the course of negotiations conducted by him in relation to the making of the contract, or

(b)   to a credit-broker in the course of negotiations conducted by that broker in relation to goods sold by him to the bailor before forming the subject matter of the contract,

any particular purpose for which the goods are being bailed.

(5)   In that case there is (subject to subsection (6) below) an implied condition that the goods supplied under the contract are reasonably fit for that purpose, whether or not that is a purpose for which such goods are commonly supplied.

(6)   Subsection (5) above does not apply where the circumstances show that the bailee does not rely, or that it is unreasonable for him to rely, on the skill or judgment of the bailor or credit-broker.

(7)   An implied condition or warranty about quality or fitness for a particular purpose may be annexed by usage to a relevant contract for the hire of goods.

(8)   The preceding provisions of this section apply to a bailment by a person who in the course of a business is acting as agent for another as they apply to a bailment by a principal in the course of a business, except where that other is not bailing in the course of a business and either the bailee knows that fact or reasonable steps are taken to bring it to the bailee's notice before the contract concerned is made.

10.   Implied terms where hire is by sample

(1)   This section applies where, under a relevant contract for the hire of goods, the bailor bails or agrees to bail the goods by reference to a sample.

(2)   In such a case there is an implied condition—

(a)   that the bulk will correspond with the sample in quality; and

    (b)   that the bailee will have a reasonable opportunity of comparing the bulk with the sample; and

    (c)   that the goods will be free from any defect, making their quality unsatisfactory, which would not be apparent on reasonable examination of the sample.

(4)   For the purposes of this section a bailor bails or agrees to bail goods by reference to a sample where there is an express or implied term to that effect in the contract concerned.

10A. Modification of remedies for breach of statutory condition in non-consumer cases

(1)   Where in the case of a relevant contract for the hire of goods—

    (a)   the bailee would, apart from this subsection, have the right to treat the contract as repudiated by reason of a breach on the part of the bailor of a term implied by section 8, 9 or 10(2)(a) or (c) above, but

    (b)   the breach is so slight that it would be unreasonable for him to do so,

the breach is not to be treated as a breach of condition but may be treated as a breach of warranty.

(2)   This section applies unless a contrary intention appears in, or is to be implied from, the contract.

(3)   It is for the bailor to show that a breach fell within subsection (1)(b) above.

Exclusion of implied terms, etc.

11. Exclusion of implied terms, etc.

(1)   Where a right, duty or liability would arise under a relevant contract for the transfer of goods or a relevant contract for the hire of goods by implication of law, it may (subject to subsection (2) below and the 1977 Act) be negatived or varied by express agreement, or by the course of dealing between the parties, or by such usage as binds both parties to the contract.

(2)   An express condition or warranty does not negative a condition or warranty implied by the preceding provisions of this Act unless inconsistent with it.

(3)   Nothing in the preceding provisions of this Act prejudices the operation of any other enactment or any rule of law whereby any condition or warranty (other than one relating to quality or fitness) is to be implied in a relevant contract for the transfer of goods or a relevant contract for hire of goods.

PART IA
SUPPLY OF GOODS AS RESPECTS SCOTLAND

Contracts for the transfer of property in goods

11A. The contracts concerned

(1)   In this Act in its application to Scotland a 'relevant contract for the transfer of goods' means a contract under which one person transfers or agrees to transfer to another the property in goods, other than an excepted contract, and other than a contract to which Chapter 2 of Part 1 of the Consumer Rights Act applies.

(2)   For the purposes of this section an excepted contract means any of the following—

    (a)   a contract of sale of goods;

    (b)   a hire-purchase agreement;

    (c)   ...

    (d)   a transfer or agreement to transfer for which there is no consideration;

    (e)   a contract intended to operate by way of mortgage, pledge, charge or other security.

(3)   For the purposes of this Act in its application to Scotland a relevant contract is a contract for the transfer of goods whether or not services are also provided or to be provided under the contract, and (subject to subsection (2) above) whatever is the nature of the consideration for the transfer or agreement to transfer.

11B. Implied terms about title, etc.

(1)   In a relevant contract for the transfer of goods, other than one to which subsection (3) below applies, there is an implied term on the part of the transferor that in the case of a transfer of the property in the goods he has a right to transfer the property and in the case of an agreement to transfer the property in the goods he will have such a right at the time when the property is to be transferred.

(2)   In a relevant contract for the transfer of goods, other than one to which subsection (3) below applies, there is also an implied term that—

(a)   the goods are free, and will remain free until the time when the property is to be transferred, from any charge or encumbrance not disclosed or known to the transferee before the contract is made, and

(b)   the transferee will enjoy quiet possession of the goods except so far as it may be disturbed by the owner or other person entitled to the benefit of any charge or encumbrance so disclosed or known.

(3)   This subsection applies to a relevant contract for the transfer of goods in the case of which there appears from the contract or is to be inferred from its circumstances an intention that the transferor should transfer only such title as he or a third person may have.

(4)   In a contract to which subsection (3) above applies there is an implied term that all charges or encumbrances known to the transferor and not known to the transferee have been disclosed to the transferee before the contract is made.

(5)   In a contract to which subsection (3) above applies there is also an implied term that none of the following will disturb the transferee's quiet possession of the goods, namely—

(a)   the transferor;

(b)   in a case where the parties to the contract intend that the transferor should transfer only such title as a third person may have, that person;

(c)   anyone claiming through or under the transferor or that third person otherwise than under a charge or encumbrance disclosed or known to the transferee before the contract is made.

11C. Implied terms where transfer is by description

(1)   This section applies where, under a relevant contract for the transfer of goods, the transferor transfers or agrees to transfer the property in the goods by description.

(2)   In such a case there is an implied term that the goods will correspond with the description.

(3)   If the transferor transfers or agrees to transfer the property in the goods by reference to a sample as well as by description it is not sufficient that the bulk of the goods corresponds with the sample if the goods do not also correspond with the description.

(4)   A contract is not prevented from falling within subsection (1) above by reason only that, being exposed for supply, the goods are selected by the transferee.

11D. Implied terms about quality or fitness

(1)   Except as provided by this section and section 11E below and subject to the provisions of any other enactment, there is no implied term about the quality or fitness for any particular purpose of goods supplied under a relevant contract for the transfer of goods.

(2)   Where, under such a contract, the transferor transfers the property in goods in the course of a business, there is an implied term that the goods supplied under the contract are of satisfactory quality.

(3)   For the purposes of this section and section 11E below, goods are of satisfactory quality if they meet the standard that a reasonable person would regard as satisfactory, taking account of any description of the goods, the price (if relevant) and all the other relevant circumstances.

(4)   The term implied by subsection (2) above does not extend to any matter making the quality of goods unsatisfactory—

(a)   which is specifically drawn to the transferee's attention before the contract is made,

    (b)   where the transferee examines the goods before the contract is made, which that examination ought to reveal, or

    (c)   where the property in the goods is, or is to be, transferred by reference to a sample, which would have been apparent on a reasonable examination of the sample.

  (5)   Subsection (6) below applies where, under a relevant contract for the transfer of goods, the transferor transfers the property in goods in the course of a business and the transferee, expressly or by implication, makes known—

    (a)   to the transferor, or

    (b)   where the consideration or part of the consideration for the transfer is a sum payable by instalments and the goods were previously sold by a credit-broker to the transferor, to that credit-broker,

    any particular purpose for which the goods are being acquired.

  (6)   In that case there is (subject to subsection (7) below) an implied term that the goods supplied under the contract are reasonably fit for the purpose, whether or not that is a purpose for which such goods are commonly supplied.

  (7)   Subsection (6) above does not apply where the circumstances show that the transferee does not rely or that it is unreasonable for him to rely, on the skill or judgment of the transferor or credit-broker.

  (8)   An implied term about quality or fitness for a particular purpose may be annexed by usage to a relevant contract for the transfer of goods.

  (9)   The preceding provisions of this section apply to a transfer by a person who in the course of a business is acting as agent for another as they apply to a transfer by a principal in the course of a business, except where that other is not transferring in the course of a business and either the transferee knows that fact or reasonable steps are taken to bring it to the transferee's notice before the contract concerned is made.

11E.   Implied terms where transfer is by sample

  (1)   This section applies where, under a relevant contract for the transfer of goods, the transferor transfers or agrees to transfer the property in the goods by reference to a sample.

  (2)   In such a case there is an implied term—

    (a)   that the bulk will correspond with the sample in quality;

    (b)   that the transferee will have a reasonable opportunity of comparing the bulk with the sample; and

    (c)   that the goods will be free from any defect, making their quality unsatisfactory, which would not be apparent on reasonable examination of the sample.

  (3)   For the purposes of this section a transferor transfers or agrees to transfer the property in goods by reference to a sample where there is an express or implied term to that effect in the contract concerned.

11F.   Remedies for breach of contract

  (1)   Where in a relevant contract for the transfer of goods a transferor is in breach of any term of the contract (express or implied), the other party to the contract (in this section referred to as 'the transferee') shall be entitled—

    (a)   to claim damages; and

    (b)   if the breach is material, to reject any goods delivered under the contract and treat it as repudiated.

Contracts for the hire of goods

11G.   The contracts concerned

  (1)   In this Act in its application to Scotland a 'relevant contract for the hire of goods' means a contract under which one person ('the supplier') hires or agrees to hire goods to another, other than a hire-purchase agreement.

  (2)   ...

(3)   For the purposes of this Act in its application to Scotland a relevant contract is a contract for the hire of goods whether or not services are also provided or to be provided under the contract, and ... whatever is the nature of the consideration for the hire or agreement to hire.

11H.   Implied terms about right to transfer possession etc.

(1)   In a relevant contract for the hire of goods there is an implied term on the part of the supplier that—

     (a)   in the case of a hire, he has a right to transfer possession of the goods by way of hire for the period of the hire; and

     (b)   in the case of an agreement to hire, he will have such a right at the time of commencement of the period of the hire.

(2)   In a relevant contract for the hire of goods there is also an implied term that the person to whom the goods are hired will enjoy quiet possession of the goods for the period of the hire except so far as the possession may be disturbed by the owner or other person entitled to the benefit of any charge or encumbrance disclosed or known to the person to whom the goods are hired before the contract is made.

(3)   The preceding provisions of this section do not affect the right of the supplier to repossess the goods under an express or implied term of the contract.

11I.   Implied terms where hire is by description

(1)   This section applies where, under a relevant contract for the hire of goods, the supplier hires or agrees to hire the goods by description.

(2)   In such a case there is an implied term that the goods will correspond with the description.

(3)   If under the contract the supplier hires or agrees to hire the goods by reference to a sample as well as by description it is not sufficient that the bulk of the goods corresponds with the sample if the goods do not also correspond with the description.

(4)   A contract is not prevented from falling within subsection (1) above by reason only that, being exposed for supply, the goods are selected by the person to whom the goods are hired.

11J.   Implied terms about quality or fitness

(1)   Except as provided by this section and section 11K below and subject to the provisions of any other enactment, there is no implied term about the quality or fitness for any particular purpose of goods hired under a relevant contract for the hire of goods.

(2)   Where, under such a contract, the supplier hires goods in the course of a business, there is an implied term that the goods supplied under the contract are of satisfactory quality.

(3)   For the purposes of this section and section 11K below, goods are of satisfactory quality if they meet the standard that a reasonable person would regard as satisfactory, taking account of any description of the goods, the consideration for the hire (if relevant) and all the other relevant circumstances.

(4)   The term implied by subsection (2) above does not extend to any matter making the quality of goods unsatisfactory—

     (a)   which is specifically drawn to the attention of the person to whom the goods are hired before the contract is made, or

     (b)   where that person examines the goods before the contract is made, which that examination ought to reveal; or

     (c)   where the goods are hired by reference to a sample, which would have been apparent on reasonable examination of the sample.

(5)   Subsection (6) below applies where, under a relevant contract for the hire of goods, the supplier hires goods in the course of a business and the person to whom the goods are hired, expressly or by implication, makes known—

     (a)   to the supplier in the course of negotiations conducted by him in relation to the making of the contract; or

     (b)   to a credit-broker in the course of negotiations conducted by that broker in relation to goods sold by him to the supplier before forming the subject matter of the contract, any particular purpose for which the goods are being hired.

(6)   In that case there is (subject to subsection (7) below) an implied term that the goods supplied under the contract are reasonably fit for that purpose, whether or not that is a purpose for which such goods are commonly supplied.

(7)   Subsection (6) above does not apply where the circumstances show that the person to whom the goods are hired does not rely, or that it is unreasonable for him to rely, on the skill or judgment of the hirer or credit-broker.

(8)   An implied term about quality or fitness for a particular purpose may be annexed by usage to a relevant contract for the hire of goods.

(9)   The preceding provisions of this section apply to a hire by a person who in the course of a business is acting as agent for another as they apply to a hire by a principal in the course of a business, except where that other is not hiring in the course of a business and either the person to whom the goods are hired knows that fact or reasonable steps are taken to bring it to that person's notice before the contract concerned is made.

11K.   Implied terms where hire is by sample

(1)   This section applies where, under a relevant contract for the hire of goods, the supplier hires or agrees to hire the goods by reference to a sample.

(2)   In such a case there is an implied term—
    (a)   that the bulk will correspond with the sample in quality; and
    (b)   that the person to whom the goods are hired will have a reasonable opportunity of comparing the bulk with the sample; and
    (c)   that the goods will be free from any defect, making their quality unsatisfactory, which would not be apparent on reasonable examination of the sample.

(3)   For the purposes of this section a supplier hires or agrees to hire goods by reference to a sample where there is an express or implied term to that effect in the contract concerned.

Exclusion of implied terms, etc.

11L.   Exclusion of implied terms etc.

(1)   Where a right, duty or liability would arise under a relevant contract for the transfer of goods or a relevant contract for the hire of goods by implication of law, it may (subject to subsection (2) below and the 1977 Act) be negatived or varied by express agreement, or by the course of dealing between the parties, or by such usage as binds both parties to the contract.

(2)   An express term does not negative a term implied by the preceding provisions of this Part of this Act unless inconsistent with it.

(3)   Nothing in the preceding provisions of this Part of this Act prejudices the operation of any other enactment or any rule of law whereby any term (other than one relating to quality or fitness) is to be implied in a relevant contract for the transfer of goods or a relevant contract for the hire of goods.

PART II
SUPPLY OF SERVICES

12.   The contracts concerned

(1)   In this Act a 'relevant contract for the supply of a service' means, subject to subsection (2) below a contract under which a person ('the supplier') agrees to carry out a service, other than a contract to which Chapter 4 of Part 1 of the Consumer Rights Act applies.

(2)   For the purposes of this Act, a contract of service or apprenticeship is not a contract for the supply of a service.

(3)   Subject to subsection (2) above, a relevant contract is a contract for the supply of a service for the purposes of this Act whether or not goods are also—
    (a)   transferred or to be transferred, or
    (b)   bailed or to be bailed by way of hire,

under the contract, and whatever is the nature of the consideration for which the service is to be carried out.

(4)   The Secretary of State may by order provide that one or more of sections 13 to 15 below shall not apply to services of a description specified in the order, and such an order may make different provision for different circumstances.

(5)   The power to make an order under subsection (4) above shall be exercisable by statutory instrument subject to annulment in pursuance of a resolution of either House of Parliament.

13.   Implied term about care and skill

In a relevant contract for the supply of a service where the supplier is acting in the course of a business, there is an implied term that the supplier will carry out the service with reasonable care and skill.

14.   Implied term about time of performance

(1)   Where, under a relevant contract for the supply of a service by a supplier acting in the course of a business, the time for the service to be carried out is not fixed by the contract, left to be fixed in a manner agreed by the contract or determined by the course of dealing between the parties, there is an implied term that the supplier will carry out the service within a reasonable time.

(2)   What is a reasonable time is a question of fact.

15.   Implied term about consideration

(1)   Where, under a relevant contract for the supply of a service, the consideration for the service is not determined by the contract, left to be determined in a manner agreed by the contract or determined by the course of dealing between the parties, there is an implied term that the party contracting with the supplier will pay a reasonable charge.

(2)   What is a reasonable charge is a question of fact.

16.   Exclusion of implied terms, etc.

(1)   Where a right, duty or liability would arise under a relevant contract for the supply of a service by virtue of this Part of this Act, it may (subject to subsection (2) below and the 1977 Act) be negatived or varied by express agreement, or by the course of dealing between the parties, or by such usage as binds both parties to the contract.

(2)   An express term does not negative a term implied by this Part of this Act unless inconsistent with it.

(3)   Nothing in this Part of this Act prejudices—

    (a)   any rule of law which imposes on the supplier a duty stricter than that imposed by section 13 or 14 above; or

    (b)   subject to paragraph (a) above, any rule of law whereby any term not inconsistent with this Part of this Act is to be implied in a relevant contract for the supply of a service.

(4)   This Part of this Act has effect to any other enactment which defines or restricts the rights, duties or liabilities arising in connection with a service of any description.

PART III
SUPPLEMENTARY

18.   Interpretation: general

(1)   In the preceding provisions of this Act and this section—

'bailee', in relation to a relevant contract for the hire of goods means (depending on the context) a person to whom the goods are bailed under a contract, or a person to whom they are to be so bailed, or a person to whom the rights under the contract of either of those persons have passed;

'bailor', in relation to a relevant contract for the hire of goods, means (depending on the context) a person who bails the goods under the contract, or a person who agrees to do so, or a person to whom the duties under the contract of either of those persons have passed;

'business' includes a profession and the activities of any government department or local or public authority;

'credit-broker' means a person acting in the course of a business of credit brokerage carried on by him;

'credit brokerage' means the effecting of introductions—

    (a)   of individuals desiring to obtain credit to persons carrying on any business so far as it relates to the provision of credit; or

    (b)   of individuals desiring to obtain goods on hire to persons carrying on a business which comprises or relates to the bailment or as regards Scotland the hire of goods under a relevant contract for the hire of goods; or

    (c)   of individuals desiring to obtain credit, or to obtain goods on hire, to other credit-brokers;

'enactment' means any legislation (including subordinate legislation) of the United Kingdom or Northern Ireland;

'goods' includes all personal chattels, other than things in action and money, and as regards Scotland all corporeal moveables; and in particular 'goods' includes emblements, industrial growing crops, and things attached to or forming part of the land which are agreed to be severed before the transfer bailment or hire concerned or under the contract concerned;

'hire-purchase agreement' has the same meaning as in the 1974 Act;

'property', in relation to goods, means the general property in them and not merely a special property;

    ...

'transferee', in relation to a relevant contract for the transfer of goods, means (depending on the context) a person to whom the property in the goods is transferred under the contract, or a person to whom the property is to be so transferred, or a person to whom the rights under the contract of either of those persons have passed;

'transferor', in relation to a relevant contract for the transfer of goods, means (depending on the context) a person who transfers the property in the goods under the contract, or a person who agrees to do so, or a person to whom the duties under the contract of either of those persons have passed.

(2)   In subsection (1) above, in the definitions of bailee, bailor, transferee and transferor, a reference to rights or duties passing is to their passing by assignment, assignation operation of law or otherwise.

(3)   For the purposes of this Act, the quality of goods includes their state and condition and the following (among others) are in appropriate cases aspects of the quality of goods—

    (a)   fitness for all the purposes for which goods of the kind in question are commonly supplied,

    (b)   appearance and finish,

    (c)   freedom from minor defects,

    (d)   safety, and

    (e)   durability.

19.   Interpretation: references to Acts

In this Act—

'the 1973 Act' means the Supply of Goods (Implied Terms) Act 1973;

'the 1974 Act' means the Consumer Credit Act 1974;

'the 1977 Act' means the Unfair Contract Terms Act 1977; and

'the 1979 Act' means the Sale of Goods Act 1979.

20.   Citation, transitional provisions, commencement and extent

(1)   This Act may be cited as the Supply of Goods and Services Act 1982.

    ...

CONSUMER PROTECTION ACT 1987
(1987, c. 43)

PART I
PRODUCT LIABILITY

1.   Purpose and construction of Part I

(1)   This Part was enacted for the purpose of making such provision as was necessary in order to comply with the product liability Directive and shall be construed accordingly.

(2)   In this Part, except in so far as the context otherwise requires—

...

'dependant' and 'relative' have the same meaning as they have in, respectively, the Fatal Accidents Act 1976 and the Damages (Scotland) Act 1976;

'producer', in relation to a product, means—

(a)   the person who manufactured it;

(b)   in the case of a substance which has not been manufactured but has been won or abstracted, the person who won or abstracted it;

(c)   in the case of a product which has not been manufactured, won or abstracted but essential characteristics of which are attributable to an industrial or other process having been carried out (for example, in relation to agricultural produce), the person who carried out that process;

'product' means any goods or electricity and (subject to subsection (3) below) includes a product which is comprised in another product, whether by virtue of being a component part or raw material or otherwise; and

'the product liability Directive' means the Directive of the Council of the European Union, dated 25th July 1985, (No. 85/374/EEC) on the approximation of the laws, regulations and administrative provisions of the member States concerning liability for defective products.

(3)   For the purposes of this Part a person who supplies any product in which products are comprised, whether by virtue of being component parts or raw materials or otherwise, shall not be treated by reason only of his supply of that product as supplying any of the products so comprised.

2.   Liability for defective products

(1)   Subject to the following provisions of this Part, where any damage is caused wholly or partly by a defect in a product, every person to whom subsection (2) below applies shall be liable for the damage.

(2)   This subsection applies to—

(a)   the producer of the product;

(b)   any person who, by putting his name on the product or using a trade mark or other distinguishing mark in relation to the product, has held himself out to be the producer of the product;

(c)   any person who has imported the product into the United Kingdom in order, in the course of any business of his, to supply it to another.

(3)   Subject as aforesaid, where any damage is caused wholly or partly by a defect in a product, any person who supplied the product (whether to the person who suffered the damage, to the producer of any product in which the product in question is comprised or to any other person) shall be liable for the damage if—

(a)   the person who suffered the damage requests the supplier to identify one or more of the persons (whether still in existence or not) to whom subsection (2) above applies in relation to the product;

(b)   that request is made within a reasonable period after the damage occurs and at a time when it is not reasonably practicable for the person making the request to identify all those persons; and

(c)   the supplier fails, within a reasonable period after receiving the request, either to comply with the request or to identify the person who supplied the product to him.

(5)   Where two or more persons are liable by virtue of this Part for the same damage, their liability shall be joint and several.

(6)   This section shall be without prejudice to any liability arising otherwise than by virtue of this Part.

3.   Meaning of 'defect'

(1)   Subject to the following provisions of the section, there is a defect in a product for the purposes of this Part if the safety of the product is not such as persons generally are entitled to expect; and for those purposes 'safety', in relation to a product, shall include safety with respect to products comprised in that product and safety in the context of risks of damage to property, as well as in the context of risks of death or personal injury.

(2)   In determining for the purposes of subsection (1) above what persons generally are entitled to expect in relation to a product all the circumstances shall be taken into account, including—

     (a)   the manner in which, and purposes for which, the product has been marketed, its get-up, the use of any mark in relation to the product and any instructions for, or warnings with respect to, doing or refraining from doing anything with or in relation to the product;

     (b)   what might reasonably be expected to be done with or in relation to the product; and

     (c)   the time when the product was supplied by its producer to another;

and nothing in this section shall require a defect to be inferred from the fact alone that the safety of a product which is supplied after that time is greater than the safety of the product in question.

4.   Defences

(1)   In any civil proceedings by virtue of this Part against any person ('the person proceeded against') in respect of a defect in a product it shall be a defence for him to show—

     (a)   that the defect is attributable to compliance with any requirement imposed by or under any enactment or with any retained EU obligation; or

     (b)   that the person proceeded against did not at any time supply the product to another; or

     (c)   that the following conditions are satisfied, that is to say—

         (i)   that the only supply of the product to another by the person proceeded against was otherwise than in the course of a business of that person's; and

         (ii)   that section 2(2) above does not apply to that person or applies to him by virtue only of things done otherwise than with a view to profit; or

     (d)   that the defect did not exist in the product at the relevant time; or

     (e)   that the state of scientific and technical knowledge at the relevant time was not such that a producer of products of the same description as the product in question might be expected to have discovered the defect if it had existed in his products while they were under his control; or

     (f)   that the defect—

         (i)   constituted a defect in a product ('the subsequent product') in which the product in question had been comprised; and

         (ii)   was wholly attributable to the design of the subsequent product or to compliance by the producer of the product in question with instructions given by the producer of the subsequent product.

(2)   In this section 'the relevant time', in relation to electricity, means the time at which it was generated, being a time before it was transmitted or distributed, and in relation to any other product, means—

     (a)   if the person proceeded against is a person to whom subsection (2) of section 2 above applies in relation to the product, the time when he supplied the product to another;

     (b)   if that subsection does not apply to that person in relation to the product, the time when the product was last supplied by a person to whom that subsection does apply in relation to the product.

5.   Damage giving rise to liability

(1)   Subject to the following provisions of this section, in this Part 'damages' means death or personal injury or any loss of or damage to any property (including land).

(2)   A person shall not be liable under section 2 above in respect of any defect in a product for the loss of or any damage to the product itself or for the loss of or any damage to the whole or any part of any product which has been supplied with the product in question comprised in it.

(3)   A person shall not be liable under section 2 above for any loss of or damage to any property which, at the time it is lost or damaged, is not—

    (a)   of a description of property ordinarily intended for private use, occupation or consumption; and

    (b)   intended by the person suffering the loss or damage mainly for his own private use, occupation or consumption.

(4)   No damages shall be awarded to any person by virtue of this Part in respect of any loss of or damage to any property if the amount which would fall to be so awarded to that person, apart from this subsection and any liability for interest, does not exceed £275.

(5)   In determining for the purposes of this Part who has suffered any loss of or damage to property and when any such loss or damage occurred, the loss or damage shall be regarded as having occurred at the earliest time at which a person with an interest in the property had knowledge of the material facts about the loss or damage.

(6)   For the purposes of subsection (5) above the material facts about any loss of or damage to any property are such facts about the loss or damage as would lead a reasonable person with an interest in the property to consider the loss or damage sufficiently serious to justify his instituting proceedings for damages against a defendant who did not dispute liability and was able to satisfy a judgment.

(7)   For the purposes of subsection (5) above a person's knowledge includes knowledge which he might reasonably have been expected to acquire—

    (a)   from facts observable or ascertainable by him; or

    (b)   from facts ascertainable by him with help of appropriate expert advice which it is reasonable for him to seek;

but a person shall not be taken by virtue of this subsection to have knowledge of a fact ascertainable by him only with the help of expert advice unless he has failed to take all reasonable steps to obtain (and, where appropriate, to act on) that advice.

(8)   Subsections (5) to (7) above shall not extend to Scotland.

6.   Application of certain enactments etc.

(1)   Any damage for which a person is liable under section 2 above shall be deemed to have been caused—

    (a)   for the purposes of the Fatal Accidents Act 1976, by that person's wrongful act, neglect or default;

    (b)   for the purposes of section 3 of the Law Reform (Miscellaneous Provisions) (Scotland) Act 1940 (contribution among joint wrongdoers), by that person's wrongful act or negligent act or omission;

    (c)   for the purposes of sections 3 to 6 of the Damages (Scotland) Act 2011 (rights of relatives of a deceased), by that person's act or omission, and

    (d)   for the purposes of Part II of the Administration of Justice Act 1982 (damages for personal injuries, etc. — Scotland), by an act or omission giving rise to liability in that person to pay damages.

(2)   Where—

    (a)   a person's death is caused wholly or partly by a defect in a product, or a person dies after suffering damage which has been so caused;

    (b)   a request such as mentioned in paragraph (a) of subsection (3) of section 2 above is made to a supplier of the product by that person's personal representatives or, in the case of a person whose death is caused wholly or partly by the defect, by any dependant or relative of that person; and

    (c)   the conditions specified in paragraphs (b) and (c) of that subsection are satisfied in relation to that request, this Part shall have effect for the purposes of the Law Reform (Miscellaneous Provisions) Act 1934, the Fatal Accidents Acts 1976 and the Damages (Scotland) Act 2011 as if liability of the supplier to that person under that subsection did not depend on that person having requested the supplier to identify certain persons or on the said conditions having been satisfied in relation to a request made by that person.

(3) Section 1 of the Congenital Disabilities (Civil Liability) Act 1976 shall have effect for the purposes of this Part as if—

    (a) a person were answerable to a child in respect of an occurrence caused wholly or partly by a defect in a product if he is or has been liable under section 2 above in respect of any effect of the occurrence on a parent of the child, or would be so liable if the occurrence caused a parent of the child to suffer damage;

    (b) the provisions of this Part relating to liability under section 2 above applied in relation to liability by virtue of paragraph (a) above under the said section 1; and

    (c) subsection (6) of the said section 1 (exclusion of liability) were omitted.

(4) Where any damage is caused partly by a defect in a product and partly by the fault of the person suffering the damage, the Law Reform (Contributory Negligence) Act 1945 and section 5 of the Fatal Accidents Act 1976 (contributory negligence) shall have effect as if the defect were the fault of every person liable by virtue of this Part for the damage caused by the defect.

(5) In subsection (4) above 'fault' has the same meaning as in the said Act of 1945.

(6) Schedule 1 to this Act shall have effect for the purpose of amending the Limitation Act 1980 and the Prescription and Limitation (Scotland) Act 1973 in their application in relation to the bringing of actions by virtue of this Part.

(7) It is hereby declared that liability by virtue of this Part is to be treated as liability in tort for the purposes of any enactment conferring jurisdiction on any court with respect to any matter.

(8) Nothing in this Part shall prejudice the operation of section 12 of the Nuclear Installations Act 1965 (rights to compensation for certain breaches of duties confined to rights under that Act).

7.   Prohibition on exclusions from liability

The liability of a person by virtue of this Part to a person who has suffered damage caused wholly or partly by a defect in a product, or to a dependant or relative of such a person, shall not be limited or excluded by any contract term, by any notice or by any other provision.

8.   ....

9.   Application of Part I to Crown

(1) Subject to subsection (2) below, this Part shall bind the Crown.

(2) The Crown shall not, as regards the Crown's liability by virtue of this Part, be bound by this Part further than the Crown is made liable in tort or in reparation under the Crown Proceedings Act 1947, as that Act has effect from time to time.

PART II
CONSUMER SAFETY

11.   Safety regulations

(1) The Secretary of State may by regulations under this section ('safety regulations') make such provision as he considers appropriate for the purpose of securing—

    (a) that goods to which this section applies are safe;

    (b) that goods to which this section applies which are unsafe, or would be unsafe in the hands of persons of a particular description, are not made available to persons generally or, as the case may be, to persons of that description, and

    (c) that appropriate information is, and inappropriate information is not, provided in relation to goods to which this section applies.

(2) Without prejudice to the generality of subsection (1) above, safety regulations may contain provision—

(a) with respect to the composition or contents, design, construction, finish or packing of goods to which this section applies, with respect to standards for such goods and with respect to other matters relating to such goods;

(b) with respect to the giving, refusal, alteration or cancellation of approvals of such goods, of descriptions of such goods or of standards for such goods;

(c) with respect to the conditions that may be attached to any approval given under the regulations;

(d) for requiring such fees as may be determined by or under the regulations to be paid on the giving or alteration of any approval under the regulations and on the making of an application for such an approval or alteration;

(e) with respect to appeals against refusals, alterations and cancellations of approvals given under the regulations and against the conditions contained in such approvals;

(f) for requiring goods to which this section applies to be approved under the regulations or to conform to the requirements of the regulations or to descriptions or standards specified in or approved by or under the regulations;

(g) with respect to the testing or inspection of goods to which this section applies (including provision for determining the standards to be applied in carrying out any test or inspection);

(h) with respect to the way of dealing with goods of which some or all do not satisfy a test required by or under the regulations or a standard connected with a procedure so required;

(i) for requiring a mark, warning or instruction or any other information relating to goods to be put on or to accompany the goods or to be used or provided in some other manner in relation to the goods, and for securing that inappropriate information is not given in relation to goods either by means of misleading marks or otherwise;

(j) for prohibiting persons from supplying, or from offering to supply, agreeing to supply, exposing for supply or possessing for supply, goods to which this section applies and component parts and raw materials for such goods;

(k) for requiring information to be given to any such person as may be determined by or under the regulations for the purpose of enabling that person to exercise any function conferred on him by the regulations.

(3) Without prejudice as aforesaid, safety regulations may contain provision—

(a) for requiring persons on whom functions are conferred by or under section 27 below to have regard, in exercising their functions so far as relating to any provision of safety regulations, to matters specified in a direction issued by the Secretary of State with respect to that provision;

(b) for securing that a person shall not be guilty of an offence under section 12 below unless it is shown that the goods in question do not conform to a particular standard;

(c) for securing that proceedings for such an offence are not brought in England and Wales except by or with the consent of the Secretary of State or the Director of Public Prosecutions;

(d) for securing that proceedings for such an offence are not brought in Northern Ireland except by or with consent of the Secretary of State or the Director of Public Prosecutions for Northern Ireland;

(e) for enabling a magistrate's court in England and Wales or Northern Ireland to try an information or, in Northern Ireland, a complaint in respect of such an offence if the information was laid or the complaint made within twelve months from the time when the offence was committed;

(f) for enabling summary proceedings for such an offence to be brought in Scotland at any time within twelve months from the time when the offence was committed; and

       (g)   for determining the persons by whom, and the manner in which, anything required to be done by or under the regulations is to be done.

(4)   Safety regulations shall not provide for any contravention of the regulations to be an offence.

(5)   Where the Secretary of State proposes to make safety regulations it shall be his duty before he makes them—

       (a)   to consult such organisations as appear to him to be representative of interests substantially affected by the proposal;

       (b)   to consult such other persons as he considers appropriate; and

       (c)   in the case of proposed regulations relating to goods suitable for use at work to consult the Health and Safety Executive in relation to the application of the proposed regulations to Great Britain;

but the preceding provisions of this subsection shall not apply in the case of regulations which provide for the regulations to cease to have effect at the end of a period of not more than twelve months beginning with the day on which they come into force and which contain a statement that it appears to the Secretary of State that the need to protect the public requires that the regulations should be made without delay.

(6)   The power to make safety regulations shall be exercisable by statutory instrument subject to annulment in pursuance of a resolution of either House of Parliament and shall include power—

       (a)   to make different provision for different cases; and

       (b)   to make such supplemental, consequential and transitional provision as the Secretary of State considers appropriate.

(7)   This section applies to any goods other than—

       (a)   growing crops and things comprised in land by virtue of being attached to it;

       (b)   water, food, feeding stuff and fertiliser;

       (c)   ...

       (d)   controlled drugs and licensed medicinal products.

12.   Offences against the safety regulations

(1)   Where safety regulations prohibit a person from supplying or offering or agreeing to supply any goods or from exposing or possessing any goods for supply that person shall be guilty of an offence if he contravenes the prohibition.

(2)   Where safety regulations require a person who makes or processes any goods in the course of carrying on a business—

       (a)   to carry out a particular test or use a particular procedure in connection with the making or processing of the goods with a view to ascertaining whether the goods satisfy any requirements of such regulations; or

       (b)   to deal or not to deal in a particular way with a quantity of the goods of which the whole or part does not satisfy such a test or does not satisfy standards connected with such a procedure,

that person shall be guilty of an offence if he does not comply with the requirement.

(3)   If a person contravenes a provision of safety regulations which prohibits or requires the provision, by means of a mark or otherwise, of information of a particular kind in relation to goods, he shall be guilty of an offence.

(4)   Where safety regulations require any person to give information to another for the purpose of enabling that other to exercise any function, that person shall be guilty of an offence if—

       (a)   he fails without reasonable cause to comply with the requirement; or

       (b)   in giving the information which is required of him—

          (i)   he makes any statement which he knows is false in a material particular; or

          (ii)   he recklessly makes any statement which is false in a material particular.

(5)   A person guilty of an offence under this section shall be liable on summary conviction to imprisonment for a term not exceeding six months or to a fine not exceeding level 5 on the standard scale or to both.

13. Prohibition notices and notices to warn

(1) The Secretary of State may—

   (a) serve on any person a notice ('a prohibition notice') prohibiting that person, except with the consent of the Secretary of State, from supplying, or from offering to supply, agreeing to supply or possessing for supply, any relevant goods which the Secretary of State considers are unsafe and which are described in the notice;

   (b) serve on any person a notice ('a notice to warn') requiring that person at his own expense to publish, in a form and manner and on occasions specified in the notice, a warning about any relevant goods which the Secretary of State considers are unsafe, which that person supplies or has supplied and which are described in the notice.

(2) Schedule 2 to this Act shall have effect with respect to prohibition notices and notices to warn, and the Secretary of State may by regulations make provision specifying the manner in which information is to be given to any person under that Schedule.

(3) A consent given by the Secretary of State for the purposes of a prohibition notice may impose such conditions on the doing of anything for which the consent is required as the Secretary of State considers appropriate.

(4) A person who contravenes a prohibition notice or a notice to warn shall be guilty of an offence and liable on summary conviction to imprisonment for a term not exceeding six months or to a fine not exceeding level 5 on the standard scale or to both.

(5) The power to make regulations under subsection (2) above shall be exercisable by statutory instrument subject to annulment in pursuance of a resolution of either House of Parliament and shall include power—

   (a) to make different provision for different cases; and (b) to make such supplemental, consequential and transitional provision as the Secretary of State considers appropriate.

(6) In this section 'relevant goods' means—

   (a) in relation to a prohibition notice, any goods to which section 11 above applies; and

   (b) in relation to a notice to warn, any goods to which that section applies or any growing crops or things comprised in land by virtue of being attached to it.

(7) A notice may not be given under this section in respect of any aspect of the safety of goods or any risk or category of risk associated with goods concerning which provision is contained in the General Product Safety Regulations 2005.

14. Suspension notices

(1) Where an enforcement authority has reasonable grounds for suspecting that any safety provision has been contravened in relation to any goods, the authority may serve a notice ('suspension notice') prohibiting the person on whom it is served, for such period ending not more than six months after the date of the notice as is specified therein, from doing any of the following things without the consent of the authority, that is to say, supplying the goods, offering to supply them, agreeing to supply them or exposing them for supply.

(2) A suspension notice served by an enforcement authority in respect of any goods shall—

   (a) describe the goods in a manner sufficient to identify them;

   (b) set out the grounds on which the authority suspects that a safety provision has been contravened in relation to the goods, and

   (c) state that, and the manner in which, the person on whom the notice is served may appeal against the notice under section 15 below.

(3) A suspension notice served by an enforcement authority for the purpose of prohibiting a person for any period from doing the things mentioned in subsection (1) above in relation to any goods may also require that person to keep the authority informed of the whereabouts throughout that period of any of those goods in which he has an interest.

(4) Where a suspension notice has been served on any person in respect of any goods, no further such notice shall be served on that person in respect of the same goods unless—

   (a) proceedings against that person for an offence in respect of a contravention in relation to the goods of a safety provision (not being an offence under this section); or

   (b) proceedings for the forfeiture of the goods under section 16 or 17 below, are pending at the end of the period specified in the first-mentioned notice.

(5)   A consent given by an enforcement authority for the purposes of subsection (1) above may impose such conditions on the doing of anything for which the consent is required as the authority considers appropriate.

(6)   Any person who contravenes a suspension notice shall be guilty of an offence and liable on summary conviction to imprisonment for a term not exceeding six months or to a fine not exceeding level 5 on the standard scale or to both.

(7)   Where an enforcement authority serves a suspension notice in respect of any goods, the authority shall be liable to pay compensation to any person having an interest in the goods in respect of any loss or damage caused by reason of the service of the notice if—

    (a)   there has been no contravention in relation to the goods of any safety provision; and

    (b)   the exercise of the power is not attributable to any neglect or default by that person.

(8)   Any disputed question as to the right to or the amount of any compensation payable under this section shall be determined by arbitration or, in Scotland, by a single arbiter appointed, failing agreement between the parties, by the sheriff.

15.   Appeals against suspension notices

(1)   Any person having an interest in any goods in respect of which a suspension notice is for the time being in force may apply for an order setting aside the notice.

(2)   An application under this section may be made—

    (a)   to any magistrates' court in which proceedings have been brought in England and Wales or Northern Ireland—

        (i)   for an offence in respect of a contravention in relation to the goods of any safety provision; or

        (ii)   for the forfeiture of the goods under section 16 below;

    (b)   where no such proceedings have been so brought, by way of complaint to a magistrates' court; or

    (c)   in Scotland, by summary application to the sheriff.

(3)   On an application under this section to a magistrates' court in England and Wales or Northern Ireland the court shall make an order setting aside the suspension notice only if the court is satisfied that there has been no contravention in relation to the goods of any safety provision.

(4)   On an application under this section to the sheriff he shall make an order setting aside the suspension notice only if he is satisfied that at the date of making the order—

    (a)   proceedings for an offence in respect of a contravention in relation to the goods of any safety provision; or

    (b)   proceedings for the forfeiture of the goods under section 17 below, have not been brought or, having been brought, have been concluded.

(5)   Any person aggrieved by an order made under this section by a magistrates' court in England and Wales or Northern Ireland, or by a decision of such a court not to make such an order, may appeal against that order or decision—

    (a)   in England and Wales, to the Crown Court;

    (b)   in Northern Ireland, to the county court;

and an order so made may contain such provision as appears to the court to be appropriate for delaying the coming into force of the order pending the making and determination of any appeal (including any application under section III of the Magistrates' Courts Act 1980 or Article 146 of the Magistrates' Courts (Northern Ireland) Order 1981 (statement of case)).

16.   Forfeiture: England and Wales and Northern Ireland

(1)   An enforcement authority in England and Wales or Northern Ireland may apply under this section for an order for the forfeiture of any goods on the grounds that there has been a contravention in relation to the goods of a safety provision.

(2)   An application under this section may be made—

    (a)   where proceedings have been brought in a magistrates' court for an offence in respect of a contravention in relation to some or all of the goods of any safety provision, to that court;

    (b)   where an application with respect to some or all of the goods has been made to a magistrates' court under section 15 above or section 33 below, to that court; and

(c)   where no application for the forfeiture of the goods has been made under paragraph (a) or (b) above, by way of complaint to a magistrates' court.

(3)   On an application under this section the court shall make an order for the forfeiture of any goods only if it is satisfied that there has been a contravention in relation to the goods of a safety provision.

(4)   For the avoidance of doubt it is declared that a court may infer for the purposes of this section that there has been a contravention in relation to any goods of a safety provision if it is satisfied that any such provision has been contravened in relation to goods which are representative of those goods (whether by reason of being of the same design or part of the same consignment or batch or otherwise).

(5)   Any person aggrieved by an order made under this section by a magistrates' court, or by a decision of such a court not to make such an order, may appeal against that order or decision—

(a)   in England and Wales, to the Crown Court;

(b)   in Northern Ireland, to the county court;

and an order so made may contain such provision as appears to the court to be appropriate for delaying the coming into force of the order pending the making and determination of any appeal (including any application under section III of the Magistrates' Courts Act 1980 or Article 146 of the Magistrates' Courts (Northern Ireland) Order 1981 (statement of case)).

(6)   Subject to subsection (7) below, where any goods are forfeited under this section they shall be destroyed in accordance with such directions as the court may give.

(7)   On making an order under this section a magistrates' court may, if it considers it appropriate to do so, direct that the goods to which the order relates shall (instead of being destroyed) be released, to such person as the court may specify, on condition that that person—

(a)   does not supply those goods to any person otherwise than as mentioned in section 46(7)(a) or (b) below, and

(b)   complies with any order to pay costs or expenses (including any order under section 35 below) which has been made against that person in the proceedings for the order for forfeiture.

17.   Forfeiture: Scotland

(1)   In Scotland a sheriff may make an order for forfeiture of any goods in relation to which there has been a contravention of a safety provision—

(a)   on an application by the procurator-fiscal made in the manner specified in section 310 of the Criminal Procedure (Scotland) Act 1975; or

(b)   where a person is convicted of any offence in respect of any such contravention, in addition to any other penalty which the sheriff may impose.

(2)   The procurator-fiscal making an application under subsection (1)(a) above shall serve on any person appearing to him to be the owner of, or otherwise to have an interest in, the goods to which the application relates a copy of the application, together with a notice giving him the opportunity to appear at the hearing of the application to show cause why the goods should not be forfeited.

(3)   Service under subsection (2) above shall be carried out, and such service may be proved, in the manner specified for citation of an accused in summary proceedings under the Criminal Procedure (Scotland) Act 1975.

(4)   Any person upon whom notice is served under subsection (2) above and any other person claiming to be the owner of, or otherwise to have an interest in, goods to which an application under this section relates shall be entitled to appear at the hearing of the application to show cause why the goods should not be forfeited.

(5)   The sheriff shall not make an order following an application under subsection (1)(a) above—

(a)   if any person on whom notice is served under subsection (2) above does not appear, unless service of the notice on that person is proved; or

(b)   if no notice under subsection (2) above has been served, unless the court is satisfied that in the circumstances it was reasonable not to serve notice on any person.

(6)   The sheriff shall make an order under this section only if he is satisfied that there has been a contravention in relation to those goods of a safety provision.

(7)   For the avoidance of doubt it is declared that the sheriff may infer for the purposes of this section that there has been a contravention in relation to any goods of a safety provision if he is satisfied that any such provision has been contravened in relation to any goods which are representative of those goods (whether by reason of being of the same design or part of the same consignment or batch or otherwise).

(8)   Where an order for the forfeiture of any goods is made following an application by the procurator-fiscal under subsection (1)(a) above, any person who appeared, or was entitled to appear, to show cause why goods should not be forfeited may, within twenty-one days of the making of the order, appeal to the High Court by Bill of Suspension on the ground of an alleged miscarriage of justice; and section 182(5)(a) to (e) of the Criminal Procedure (Scotland) Act 1995 shall apply to an appeal under this subsection as it applies to a stated case under Part X of that Act.

(9)   An order following an application under subsection (1)(a) above shall not take effect—
   (a)   until the end of the period of twenty-one days beginning with the day after the day on which the order is made; or
   (b)   if an appeal is made under subsection (8) above within that period, until the appeal is determined or abandoned.

(10) An order under subsection (1)(b) above shall not take effect—
   (a)   until the end of the period within which an appeal against the order could be brought under the Criminal Procedure (Scotland) Act 1975; or
   (b)   if an appeal is made within that period, until the appeal is determined or abandoned.

(11) Subject to subsection (12) below, goods forfeited under this section shall be destroyed in accordance with such directions as the sheriff may give.

(12) If he thinks fit the sheriff may direct that the goods be released, to such person as he may specify, on condition that that person does not supply those goods to any other person otherwise than as mentioned in section 46(7)(a) or (b) below.

18.   Power to obtain information

(1)   If the Secretary of State considers that, for the purpose of deciding whether—
   (a)   to make, vary or revoke any safety regulations; or
   (b)   to serve, vary or revoke a prohibition notice; or
   (c)   to serve or revoke a notice to warn,
   he requires information which another person is likely to be able to furnish, the Secretary of State may serve on the other person a notice under this section.

(2)   A notice served on any person under this section may require that person—
   (a)   to furnish to the Secretary of State, within a period specified in the notice, such information as is so specified;
   (b)   to produce such records as are specified in the notice at a time and place so specified and to permit a person appointed by the Secretary of State for the purpose to take copies of the records at that time and place.

(3)   A person shall be guilty of an offence if he—
   (a)   fails, without reasonable cause, to comply with a notice served on him under this section; or
   (b)   in purporting to comply with a requirement which by virtue of paragraph (a) of subsection (2) above is contained in such a notice—
      (i)   furnishes information which he knows is false in a material particular; or
      (ii)   recklessly furnishes information which is false in a material particular.

(4)   A person guilty of an offence under subsection (3) above shall—
   (a)   in the case of an offence under paragraph (a) of that subsection, be liable on summary conviction to a fine not exceeding level 5 on the standard scale; and
   (b)   in the case of an offence under paragraph (b) of that subsection be liable—
      (i)   on conviction on indictment, to a fine,
      (ii)   on summary conviction, to a fine not exceeding the statutory maximum.

19. Interpretation of Part II

(1) In this Part—

'controlled drug' means a controlled drug within the meaning of the Misuse of Drugs Act 1971;

'feeding stuff' and 'fertiliser' have the same meaning as in Part IV of the Agriculture Act 1970;

'food' does not include anything containing tobacco but, subject to that, has the same meaning as in the Food Safety Act 1990 or, in relation to Northern Ireland, the same meaning as in the Food and Drugs Act (Northern Ireland) 1958;

'licensed medicinal product' means—

    (a) any medicinal product within the meaning of the Medicines Act 1968 in respect of which a product licence within the meaning of that Act is for the time being in force; or

    (b) any other article or substance in respect of which any such licence is for the time being in force in pursuance of an order under section 104 or 105 of that Act (application of Act to other articles and substances); or

    (c) a veterinary medicinal product that has a marketing authorisation under the Veterinary Medicines Regulations 2006;

'safe', in relation to any goods, means such that there is no risk, or no risk apart from one reduced to a minimum, that any of the following will (whether immediately or after a definite or indefinite period) cause the death of, or any personal injury to, any person whatsoever, that is to say—

    (a) the goods;

    (b) the keeping, use or consumption of the goods;

    (c) the assembly of any of the goods which are, or are to be supplied unassembled;

    (d) any emission or leakage from the goods or, as a result of the keeping, use or consumption of the goods, from anything else; or

    (e) reliance on the accuracy of any measurement, calculation or other reading made by or by means of the goods,

and 'unsafe' shall be construed accordingly;

'tobacco' includes any tobacco product within the meaning of the Tobacco Products Duty Act 1979 and any article or substance containing tobacco and intended for oral or nasal use.

(2) In the definition of 'safe' in subsection (1) above, references to the keeping, use or consumption of any goods are references to—

    (a) the keeping, use or consumption of the goods by the persons by whom, and in all or any of the ways or circumstances in which, they might reasonably be expected to be kept, used or consumed; and

    (b) the keeping, use or consumption of the goods either alone or in conjunction with other goods in conjunction with which they might reasonably be expected to be kept, used or consumed.

PART IV
ENFORCEMENT OF PARTS II AND III

27. Enforcement

(1) Subject to the following provisions of this section—

    (a) it shall be the duty of every weights and measures authority in Great Britain to enforce within their area the safety provisions …; and

    (b) it shall be the duty of every district council in Northern Ireland to enforce within their area the safety provisions.

(2) The Secretary of State may by regulations—

    (a) wholly or partly transfer any duty imposed by subsection (1) above on a weights and measures authority or a district council in Northern Ireland to such other person who has agreed to the transfer as is specified in the regulations;

    (b) relieve such an authority or council of any such duty so far as it is exercisable in relation to such goods as may be described in the regulations.

(3)   The power to make regulations under subsection (2) above shall be exercisable by
statutory instrument subject to annulment in pursuance of a resolution of either House
of Parliament and shall include power—
(a)   to make different provision for different cases; and
(b)   to make such supplemental, consequential and transitional provision as the
Secretary of State considers appropriate.

(3A) For the investigatory powers available to a person for the purposes of the duty imposed by
subsection (1), see Schedule 5 to the Consumer Rights Act 2015 (as well as section 29).

(4)   Nothing in this section shall authorise any weights and measures authority, or any
person whom functions are conferred by regulations under subsection (2) above, to
bring proceedings in Scotland for an offence.

(5)   Nothing in this section shall authorise the acquisition by or on behalf of an enforcement
authority of any interest in land.

29.   Powers of search etc.

(1)   Subject to the following provisions of this Part, a duly authorised officer of an
enforcement authority may at any reasonable hour and on production, if required, of
his credentials exercise the powers conferred by subsection(4).

(4)   If the officer has reasonable grounds for suspecting that any goods are manufactured
or imported goods which have not been supplied in the United Kingdom since they
were manufactured or imported he may—
(a)   for the purpose of ascertaining whether there has been any contravention of
any safety provision in relation to the goods, require any person carrying on a
business, or employed in connection with a business, to produce any records
relating to the business;
(b)   for the purpose of ascertaining (by testing or otherwise) whether there has been
any such contravention, seize and detain the goods;
(c)   take copies of, or of any entry in, any records produced by virtue of paragraph
(a) above.

(7)   If and to the extent that it is reasonably necessary to do so to prevent a contravention
of any safety provision ..., the officer may, for the purpose of exercising his power
under subsection (4) above to seize any goods—
(a)   require any person having authority to do so to open any container or to open
any vending machine; and
(b)   himself open or break open any such container or machine where a requirement
made under paragraph (a) above in relation to the container or machine has not
been complied with.

(8)   The officer may not exercise a power under this section to secure disclosure by a
telecommunications operator or postal operator of communications data without the
consent of the operator.

(9)   In subsection (8) 'communications data', 'postal operator' and 'telecommunications
operator' have the same meaning as in the Investigatory Powers Act 2016 (see
sections 261 and 262 of that Act).

30.   Provisions supplemental to s. 29

(1)   An officer seizing any goods under section 29(4) above shall inform the following
persons that the goods have been so seized, that is to say—
(a)   the person from whom they are seized; and
(b)   in the case of imported goods seized on any premises under the control of the
Commissioners of Customs and Excise, the importer of those goods (within the
meaning of the Customs and Excise Management Act 1979).

(2)   If a justice of the peace—
(a)   is satisfied by any written information on oath that there are reasonable grounds
for believing either—
(i)   that any records which any officer has power to inspect under section 29(4)
above are on any premises and that their inspection is likely to disclose
evidence that there has been a contravention of any safety provision ...; or
(ii)   that such a contravention has taken place, is taking place or is about to
take place on any premises; and

(b)   is also satisfied by any such information either—

    (i)   that admission to the premises has been or is likely to be refused and that notice of intention to apply for a warrant under this section has been given to the occupier; or

    (ii)   that an application for admission, or the giving of such a notice, would defeat the object of entry or that the premises are unoccupied or that the occupier is temporarily absent and it might defeat the object of the entry to await his return,

the justice may by warrant under his hand, which shall continue in force for a period of one month, authorise any officer of an enforcement authority to enter the premises, if need be by force.

(3)   An officer entering any premises by virtue of a warrant under subsection (2) above may take with him such other persons and such equipment as may appear to him necessary.

(4)   On leaving any premises which a person is authorised to enter by a warrant under subsection (2) above, that person shall, if the premises are unoccupied or the occupier is temporarily absent, leave the premises as effectively secured against trespassers as he found them.

(5)   If any person who is not an officer of an enforcement authority purports to act as such under section 29(4) above of this section he shall be guilty of an offence and liable on summary conviction to a fine not exceeding level 5 on the standard scale.

(6)   Where any goods seized by an officer under section 29(4) above are submitted to a test, the officer shall inform the persons mentioned in subsection (1) above of the result of the test and, if—

(a)   proceedings are brought for an offence in respect of a contravention in relation to the goods of any safety provision or for the forfeiture of the goods under section 16 or 17 above, or a suspension notice is served in respect of any goods; and

(b)   the officer is requested to do so and it is practicable to comply with the request,

the officer shall allow any person who is a party to the proceedings or, as the case may be, has an interest in the goods to which the notice relates to have the goods tested.

(7)   The Secretary of State may by regulations provide that any test of goods seized under section 29(4) above by an officer of an enforcement authority shall—

(a)   be carried out at the expense of the authority in a manner and by a person prescribed by or determined under the regulations; or

(b)   be carried out either as mentioned in paragraph (a) above or by the authority in a manner prescribed by the regulations.

(8)   The power to make regulations under subsection (7) above shall be exercisable by statutory instrument subject to annulment in pursuance of a resolution of either House of Parliament and shall include power—

(a)   to make different provision for different cases; and

(b)   to make such supplemental, consequential and transitional provisions as the Secretary of State considers appropriate.

(9)   In the application of this section to Scotland, the reference in subsection (2) above to a justice of the peace shall include a reference to a sheriff and the references to written information on oath shall be construed as references to evidence on oath.

(10)   In the application of this section to Northern Ireland, the references in subsection (2) above to any information on oath shall be construed as references to any complaint on oath.

31.   Power of customs officer to detain goods

(1)   A customs officer may, for the purpose of facilitating the exercise by an enforcement authority or officer of such an authority of any functions conferred on the authority or officer by or under Part II of this Act, or by or section 29(4) of this Act or Schedule 5 to the Consumer Rights Act 2015 in its application for the purposes of the safety provisions, seize any imported goods and detain them for not more than two working days.

(2)   Anything seized and detained under this section shall be dealt with during the period of its detention in such manner as the Commissioners of Customs and Excise may direct.

(3)   In subsection (1) above the reference to two working days is a reference to a period of forty-eight hours calculated from the time when the goods in question are seized but disregarding so much of any period as falls on a Saturday or Sunday or on Christmas Day, Good Friday or a day which is a bank holiday under the Banking and Financial Dealings Act 1971 in the part of the United Kingdom where the goods are seized.

(4)   In this section and section 32 below 'customs officer' means any officer within the meaning of the Customs and Excise Management Act 1979.

32.   Obstruction of authorised officer

(1)   Any person who—

     (a)   intentionally obstructs any officer of an enforcement authority who is acting in pursuance of any provision of section 29(4) or any customs officer who is acting in pursuance of section 31; or

     (b)   intentionally fails to comply with any requirements made of him by any officer of an enforcement authority under any provision of section 29(4), or

     (c)   without reasonable cause fails to give any officer of an enforcement authority who is so acting any other assistance or information which the officer may reasonably require of him for the purposes of the exercise of the officer's functions under section 29(4),

shall be guilty of an offence and liable on summary conviction to a fine not exceeding level 5 on the standard scale.

(2)   A person shall be guilty of an offence if, in giving any information which is required of him by virtue of subsection (1)(c) above—

     (a)   he makes any statement which he knows is false in a material particular, or

     (b)   he recklessly makes a statement which is false in a material particular.

(3)   A person guilty of an offence under subsection (2) above shall be liable—

     (a)   on conviction on indictment to a fine;

     (b)   on summary conviction, to a fine not exceeding the statutory maximum.

PART V
MISCELLANEOUS AND SUPPLEMENTAL

37.   Power of Commissioners of Revenue and Customs to disclose information

(1)   If they think it appropriate to do so for the purpose of facilitating the exercise by any person to whom subsection (2) below applies of any function conferred on that person by or under Part II of this Act, or by or under Part IV of this Act in its application for the purposes of the safety provisions, the Commissioners for Her Majesty's Revenue and Customs may authorise the disclosure to that person of any information obtained or held for the purposes of the exercise by Her Majesty's Revenue and Customs of their functions in relation to imported goods.

(2)   This subsection applies to an enforcement authority and to any officer of an enforcement authority.

(3)   A disclosure of information made to any person under subsection (1) above shall be made in such manner as may be directed by the Commissioners for Her Majesty's Revenue and Customs and may be through such persons acting on behalf of that person as may be so directed.

(4)   Information may be disclosed to a person under subsection (1) above whether or not the disclosure of the information has been requested by or on behalf of that person.

39.   Defence of due diligence

(1)   Subject to the following provisions of this section, in proceedings against any person for an offence to which this section applies it shall be a defence for that person to show that he took all reasonable steps and exercised all due diligence to avoid committing the offence.

(2)   Where in any proceedings against any person for such an offence the defence provided by subsection (1) above involves an allegation that the commission of the offence was due—

(a)   to the act or default of another; or

(b)   to reliance on information given by another,

that person shall not, without the leave of the court, be entitled to rely on the defence unless, not less than seven clear days before the hearing of the proceedings, he has served a notice under subsection (3) below on the person bringing the proceedings.

(3)   A notice under this subsection shall give such information identifying or assisting in the identification of the person who committed the act or default or gave the information as is in the possession of the person serving the notice at the time he serves it.

(4)   It is hereby declared that a person shall not be entitled to rely on the defence provided by subsection (1) above by reason of his reliance on information supplied by another, unless he shows that it was reasonable in all the circumstances for him to have relied on the information, having regard in particular—

(a)   to the steps which he took, and those which might reasonably have been taken, for the purpose of verifying the information, and

(b)   to whether he had any reason to disbelieve the information.

(5)   This section shall apply to an offence under section 12(1), (2) or (3), 13(4) or 14(6) above.

40.   Liability of persons other than principal offender

(1)   Where the commission by any person of an offence to which section 39 above applies is due to an act or default committed by some other person in the course of any business of his, the other person shall be guilty of the offence and may be proceeded against and punished by virtue of this subsection whether or not proceedings are taken against the first-mentioned person.

(2)   Where a body corporate is guilty of an offence under this Act (including where it is so guilty by virtue of subsection (1) above) in respect of any act or default which is shown to have been committed with the consent or connivance of, or to be attributable to any neglect on the part of, any director, manager, secretary or other similar officer of the body corporate or any person who was purporting to act in any such capacity he, as well as the body corporate, shall be guilty of that offence and shall be liable to be proceeded against and punished accordingly.

(3)   Where the affairs of a body corporate are managed by its members, subsection (2) above shall apply in relation to the acts and defaults of a member in connection with his functions of management as if he were a director of the body corporate.

41.   Civil proceedings

(1)   An obligation imposed by safety regulations shall be a duty owed to any person who may be affected by a contravention of the obligation and, subject to any provisions to the contrary in the regulations and to the defences and other incidents applying to actions for breach of statutory duty, a contravention of any such obligation shall be actionable accordingly.

(2)   This Act shall not be construed as conferring any other right of action in civil proceedings, apart from the right conferred by virtue of Part I of this Act, in respect of any loss or damage suffered in consequence of a contravention of a safety provision …

(3)   Subject to any provision to the contrary in the agreement itself, an agreement shall not be void or unenforceable by reason only of a contravention of a safety provision …

(4)   Liability by virtue of subsection (1) above shall not be limited or excluded by any contract term, by any notice or (subject to the power contained in subsection (1) above to limit or exclude it in safety regulations) by any other provision.

(5)   Nothing in subsection (1) above shall prejudice the operation of section 12 of the Nuclear Installations Act 1965 (rights to compensation for certain breaches of duties confined to rights under that Act).

(6)   In this section 'damage' includes personal injury and death.

42.   Reports etc.

(1)   It shall be the duty of the Secretary of State at least once in every five years to lay before each House of Parliament a report on the exercise during the period to which the report relates of the functions which under Part II of this Act, or under Part IV of this Act in its application for the purposes of the safety provisions, are exercisable by the Secretary of State, weights and measures authorities, district councils in Northern

Ireland and persons on whom functions are conferred by regulations made under section 27(2) above.

(2) The Secretary of State may from time to time prepare and lay before each House of Parliament such other reports on the exercise of those functions as he considers appropriate.

(3) Every weights and measures authority, every district council in Northern Ireland and every person on whom functions are conferred by regulations under subsection (2) of section 27 above shall, whenever the Secretary of State so directs, make a report to the Secretary of State on the exercise of the functions exercisable by that authority or council under that section or by that person by virtue of any such regulations.

(4) A report under subsection (3) above shall be in such form and shall contain such particulars as are specified in the direction of the Secretary of State.

(5) The first report under subsection (1) above shall be laid before each House of Parliament not more than five years after the laying of the last report under section 8(2) of the Consumer Safety Act 1978.

43. Financial provisions

(1) There shall be paid out of money provided by Parliament—

   (a) any expenses incurred or compensation payable by a Minister of the Crown or Government department in consequence of any provision of this Act; and

   (b) any increase attributable to this Act in the sums payable out of money so provided under any other Act.

(2) Any sums received by a Minister of the Crown or Government department by virtue of this Act shall be paid into the Consolidated Fund.

44. Service of documents etc.

(1) Any documents required or authorised by virtue of this Act to be served on a person may be so served—

   (a) by delivering it to him or by leaving it at his proper address or by sending it by post to him at that address; or

   (b) if the person is a body corporate, by serving it in accordance with paragraph (a) above on the secretary or clerk of that body; or

   (c) if the person is a partnership, by serving it in accordance with that paragraph on a partner or on a person having control or management of the partnership business.

(2) For the purposes of subsection (1) above, and for the purposes of section 7 of the Interpretation Act 1978 (which relates to the service of documents by post) in its application to that subsection, the proper address of any person on whom a document is to be served by virtue of this Act shall be his last known address except that—

   (a) in the case of service on a body corporate or its secretary or clerk, it shall be the address of the registered or principal office of the body corporate;

   (b) in the case of service on a partnership or a partner or a person having the control or management of a partnership business, it shall be the principal office of the partnership; and for the purposes of this subsection the principal office of a company registered outside the United Kingdom or of a partnership carrying on business outside the United Kingdom is its principal office within the United Kingdom.

(3) The Secretary of State may by regulations make provision for the manner in which any information is to be given to any person under any provision of Part IV of this Act.

(4) Without prejudice to the generality of subsection (3) above regulations made by the Secretary of State may prescribe the person, or manner of determining the person, who is to be treated for the purposes of section 30 above as the person from whom goods were seized where the goods were seized from a vending machine.

(5) The power to make regulations under subsection (3) or (4) above shall be exercisable by statutory instrument subject to annulment in pursuance of a resolution of either House of Parliament and shall include power—

   (a) to make different provision for different cases; and

   (b) to make such supplemental, consequential and transitional provision as the Secretary of State considers appropriate.

45.   Interpretation

(1)   In this Act, expect in so far as the context otherwise requires —

'aircraft' includes gliders, balloons and hovercraft;

'business' includes a trade or profession and the activities of a professional or trade association or of a local authority or other public authority;

'conditional sale agreement', 'credit-sale agreement' and 'hire-purchase agreement' have the same meanings as in the Consumer Credit Act 1974 but as if in the definitions in that Act 'goods' had the same meaning as in this Act;

'contravention' includes a failure to comply and cognate expressions shall be construed accordingly;

'enforcement authority' means the Secretary of State, any other Minister of the Crown in charge of a Government department, any such department and any authority, council or other person on whom functions under this Act are conferred by or under section 27 above;

'gas' has the same meaning as in Part I of the Gas Act 1986;

'goods' includes substances, growing crops and things comprised in land by virtue of being attached to it and any ship, aircraft or vehicle;

'information' includes accounts, estimates and returns;

'magistrates' court', in relation to Northern Ireland, means a court of summary jurisdiction;

'modifications' includes additions, alterations and omissions, and cognate expressions shall be construed accordingly;

'motor vehicle' has the same meaning as in the Road Traffic Act 1988;

'notice' means a notice in writing;

'notice to warn' means a notice under section 13(1)(b) above;

'officer', in relation to an enforcement authority, means a person authorised in writing to assist the authority in carrying out its functions under or for the purposes of the enforcement of any of the safety provisions or of any of the provisions made by or under Part III of this Act;

'personal injury' includes any disease and any other impairment of a person's physical or mental condition;

'premises' includes any place and any ship, aircraft or vehicle;

'prohibition notice' means a notice under section 13(1)(a) above;

'records' includes any books or documents and any records in non-documentary form;

'safety provision' means any provision of safety regulations, a prohibition notice or a suspension notice;

'safety regulations' means regulations under section 11 above;

'ship' includes any boat and any other description of vessel used in navigation;

'subordinate legislation' has the same meaning as in the Interpretation Act 1978;

'substance' means any natural or artificial substance, whether in solid, liquid or gaseous form or in the form of a vapour, and includes substances that are comprised in or mixed with other goods;

'supply' and cognate expressions shall be construed in accordance with section 46 below;

'suspension notice' means a notice under section 14 above.

(2)   Except in so far as the context otherwise requires, references in this Act to a contravention of a safety provision shall, in relation to any goods, include references to anything which would constitute such a contravention if the goods were supplied to any person.

(3)   References in this Act to any goods in relation to which any safety provision has been or may have been contravened shall include references to any goods which it is not reasonably practicable to separate from any such goods.

(5)   In Scotland, any reference in this Act to things comprised in land by virtue of being attached to it is a reference to moveables which have become heritable by accession to heritable property.

46.   Meaning of 'supply'

(1)   Subject to the following provisions of this section, references in this Act to supplying goods shall be construed as references to doing any of the following, whether as principal or agent, that is to say—

(a)   selling, hiring out or lending the goods;

(b)   entering into a hire-purchase agreement to furnish the goods;

(c)   the performance of any contract for work and materials to furnish the goods;

(d)   providing the goods in exchange for any consideration ... other than money;

(e)   providing the goods in or in connection with the performance of any statutory function; or

(f)   giving the goods as a prize or otherwise making a gift of the goods;

and, in relation to gas or water, those references shall be construed as including references to providing the service by which the gas or water is made available for use.

(2)   For the purposes of any reference in this Act to supplying goods, where a person ('the ostensible supplier') supplies goods to another person ('the customer') under a hire-purchase agreement, conditional sale agreement or credit-sale agreement or under an agreement for the hiring of goods (other than a hire-purchase agreement) and the ostensible supplier—

(a)   carries on the business of financing the provision of goods for others by means of such agreements; and

(b)   in the course of that business acquired his interest in the goods supplied to the customer as a means of financing the provision of them for the customer by a further person ('the effective supplier'),

the effective supplier and not the ostensible supplier shall be treated as supplying the goods to the customer.

(3)   Subject to subsection (4) below, the performance of any contract by the erection of any building or structure on any land or by the carrying out of any other building works shall be treated for the purposes of this Act as a supply of goods in so far as, but only in so far as, it involves the provision of any goods to any person by means of their incorporation into the building, structure or works.

(4)   Except for the purposes of, and in relation to, notices to warn ..., references in this Act to supplying goods shall not include references to supplying goods comprised in land where the supply is effected by the creation or disposal of an interest in the land.

(5)   Except in Part I of this Act references in this Act to a person's supplying goods shall be confined to references to that person's supplying goods in the course of a business of his, but for the purposes of this subsection it shall be immaterial whether the business is a business of dealing in the goods.

(6)   For the purposes of subsection (5) above goods shall not be treated as supplied in the course of a business if they are supplied, in pursuance of an obligation arising under or in connection with the insurance of the goods, to the person with whom they were insured.

(7)   Except for the purposes of, and in relation to, prohibition notices or suspension notices, references in Parts 2 or 4 of this Act to supplying goods shall not include—

(a)   references to supplying goods where the person supplied carries on a business of buying goods of the same description as those goods and repairing or reconditioning them,

(b)   references to supplying goods by a sale of articles as scrap (that is to say, for the value of materials included in the articles rather than for the value of the articles themselves).

(8)   Where any goods have at any time been supplied by being hired out or lent to any person, neither a continuation or renewal of the hire or loan (whether on the same or different terms) nor any transaction for the transfer after that time of any interest in the goods to the person to whom they were hired or lent shall be treated for the purposes of this Act as a further supply of the goods to that person.

(9)   A ship, aircraft or motor vehicle shall not be treated for the purposes of this Act as supplied to any person by reason only that services consisting in the carriage of goods or passengers in that ship, aircraft or vehicle, or in its use for any other purpose, are

provided to that person in pursuance of an agreement relating to the use of the ship, aircraft or vehicle for a particular period or for particular voyages, flights or journeys.

47. Savings for certain privileges

(1) Nothing in this Act shall be taken as requiring any person to produce any records if he would be entitled to refuse to produce those records in any proceedings in any court on the ground that they are the subject of legal professional privilege or, in Scotland, that they contain a confidential communication made by or to an advocate or solicitor in that capacity, or as authorising any person to take possession of any records which are in the possession of a person who would be so entitled.

(2) Nothing in this Act shall be construed as requiring a person to answer any question or give any information if to do so would incriminate that person or that person's spouse or civil partner.

49. Northern Ireland

(1) This Act shall extend to Northern Ireland with the exception of—
   (a) the provisions of Part I ...;
   (b) any provision amending or repealing an enactment which does not so extend; and
   (c) any other provision so far as it has effect for the purposes of, or in relation to, a provision falling within paragraph (a) or (b) above.

   ...

50. Short title, commencement and transitional provision

(1) This Act may be cited as the Consumer Protection Act 1987.

(2) This Act shall come into force on such day as the Secretary of State may by order made by statutory instrument appoint, and different days may be so appointed for different provisions or for different purposes.

(3) The Secretary of State shall not make an order under subsection (2) above bringing into force the repeal of the Trade Descriptions Act 1972, a repeal of any provision of that Act or a repeal of that Act or of any provision of it for any purposes, unless a draft of the order has been laid before, and approved by a resolution of, each House of Parliament.

(4) An order under subsection (2) above bringing a provision into force may contain such transitional provision in connection with the coming into force of that provision as the Secretary of State considers appropriate.

(5) Without prejudice to the generality of the power conferred by subsection (4) above, the Secretary of State may by order provide for any regulations made under the Consumer Protection Act 1961 or the Consumer Protection Act (Northern Ireland) 1965 to have effect as if made under section 11 above and for any regulations to have effect with such modifications as he considers appropriate for that purpose.

(6) The power of the Secretary of State by order to make such provision as is mentioned in subsection (5) above, shall, in so far as it is not exercised by an order under subsection (2) above, be exercisable by statutory instrument subject to annulment in pursuance of a resolution of either House of Parliament.

(7) Nothing in this Act or in any order under subsection (2) above shall make any person liable by virtue of Part I of this Act for any damage caused wholly or partly by a defect in a product which was supplied to any person by its producer before the coming into force of Part I of this Act.

(8) Expressions used in subsection (7) above and in Part I of this Act have the same meaning in that subsection as in that Part.

SCHEDULES

SCHEDULE 2

PROHIBITION NOTICES AND NOTICES TO WARN

PART I
PROHIBITION NOTICES

1.   A prohibition notice in respect of any goods shall—
        (a)   state that the Secretary of State considers that the goods are unsafe;
        (b)   set out the reasons why the Secretary of State considers that the goods are unsafe;
        (c)   specify the day on which the notice is to come into force; and
        (d)   state that the trader may at any time make representations in writing to the Secretary of State for the purpose of establishing that the goods are safe.

2.   (1)   If representations in writing about a prohibition notice are made by the trader to the Secretary of State, it shall be the duty of the Secretary of State to consider whether to revoke the notice and—
              (a)   if he decides to revoke it, to do so;
              (b)   in any other case, to appoint a person to consider those representations, any further representations made (whether in writing or orally) by the trader about the notice and the statements of any witnesses examined under this Part of this Schedule.
        (2)   Where the Secretary of State has appointed a person to consider representations about a prohibition notice, he shall serve a notification on the trader which—
              (a)   states that the trader may make oral representations to the appointed person for the purpose of establishing that the goods to which the notice relates are safe; and
              (b)   specifies the place and time at which the oral representations may be made.
        (3)   The time specified in a notification served under sub-paragraph (2) above shall not be before the end of the period of twenty-one days beginning with the day on which the notification is served, unless the trader otherwise agrees.
        (4)   A person on whom a notification has been served under sub-paragraph (2) above or his representative may, at the place and time specified in the notification—
              (a)   make oral representations to the appointed person for the purpose of establishing that the goods in question are safe; and
              (b)   call and examine witnesses in connection with representations.

3.   (1)   Where representations in writing about a prohibition notice are made by the trader to the Secretary of State at any time after a person has been appointed to consider representations about that notice, then, whether or not the appointed person has made a report to the Secretary of State, the following provisions of this paragraph shall apply instead of paragraph 2 above.
        (2)   The Secretary of State shall, before the end of the period of one month beginning with the day on which he receives the representations, serve a notification on the trader which states—
              (a)   that the Secretary of State has decided to revoke the notice, has decided to vary it or, as the case may be, has decided neither to revoke nor to vary it; or
              (b)   that, a person having been appointed to consider representations about the notice, the trader may, at a place and time specified in the notification, make oral representations to the appointed person for the purpose of establishing that the goods to which the notice relates are safe.
        (3)   The time specified in a notification served for the purposes of sub-paragraph (2)(b) above shall not be before the end of the period of twenty-one days beginning with the day on which the notification is served, unless the trader otherwise agrees or the time is the time already specified for the purposes of paragraph 2(2)(b) above.
        (4)   A person on whom a notification has been served for the purposes of sub-paragraph (2)(b) above or his representative may, at the place and time specified in the notification—
              (a)   make oral representations to the appointed person for the purpose of establishing that the goods in question are safe; and

(b)   call and examine witnesses in connection with the representations.

4.   (1)   Where a person is appointed to consider representations about a prohibition notice, it shall be his duty to consider—

    (a)   any written representations made by the trader about the notice, other than those in respect of which a notification is served under paragraph 3(2)(a) above;

    (b)   any oral representations made under paragraph 2(4) or 3(4) above; and

    (c)   any statements made by witnesses in connection with the oral representations, and after considering any matters under this paragraph, to make a report (including recommendations) to the Secretary of State about the matters considered by him and the notice.

    (2)   It shall be the duty of the Secretary of State to consider any report made to him under sub-paragraph (1) above and, after considering the report, to inform the trader of his decision with respect to the prohibition notice to which the report relates.

5.   (1)   The Secretary of State may revoke or vary a prohibition notice by serving on the trader a notification stating that the notice is revoked or, as the case may be, is varied as specified in the notification.

    (2)   The Secretary of State shall not vary a prohibition notice so as to make the effect of the notice more restrictive for the trader.

    (3)   Without prejudice to the power conferred by section 13(2) of this Act, the service of a notification under sub-paragraph (1) above shall be sufficient to satisfy the requirement of paragraph 4(2) above that the trader shall be informed of the Secretary of State's decision.

PART II
NOTICES TO WARN

6.   (1)   If the Secretary of State proposes to serve a notice to warn on any person in respect of any goods, the Secretary of State, before he serves the notice shall serve on that person a notification which—

    (a)   contains a draft of the proposed notice;

    (b)   states that the Secretary of State proposes to serve a notice in the form of the draft on that person;

    (c)   states that the Secretary of State considers that the goods described in the draft are unsafe;

    (d)   sets out the reasons why the Secretary of State considers that those goods are unsafe; and

    (e)   states that that person may make representations to the Secretary of State for the purpose of establishing that the goods are safe if, before the end of the period of fourteen days beginning with the day on which the notification is served, he informs the Secretary of State—

    (i)   of his intention to make representations; and

    (ii)   whether the representations will be made only in writing or both in writing and orally.

    (2)   Where the Secretary of State has served a notification containing a draft of a proposed notice to warn on any person, he shall not serve a notice to warn on that person in respect of the goods to which the proposed notice relates unless—

    (a)   the period of fourteen days beginning with the day on which the notification was served expires without the Secretary of State being informed as mentioned in sub-paragraph (1)(e) above;

    (b)   the period of twenty-eight days beginning with that day expires without any written representations being made by that person to the Secretary of State about the proposed notice; or

    (c)   the Secretary of State has considered a report about the proposed notice by a person appointed under paragraph 7(1) below.

7.   (1)   Where a person on whom a notification containing a draft of a proposed notice to warn has been served—

    (a)   informs the Secretary of State as mentioned in paragraph 6(1)(e) above before the end of the period of fourteen days beginning with the day on which the notification was served; and

(b)   makes written representations to the Secretary of State about the proposed notice before the end of the period of twenty-eight days beginning with that day, the Secretary of State shall appoint a person to consider those representations, any further representations made by that person about the draft notice and the statements of any witnesses examined under this Part of this Schedule.

(2)   Where—

(a)   the Secretary of State has appointed a person to consider representations about a proposed notice to warn; and

(b)   the person whose representations are to be considered has informed the Secretary of State for the purposes of paragraph 6(1)(e) above that the representations he intends to make will include oral representations,

the Secretary of State shall inform the person intending to make the representations of the place and time at which oral representations may be made to the appointed person.

(3)   Where a person on whom a notification containing a draft of a proposed notice to warn has been served is informed of a time for the purposes of sub-paragraph (2) above, that time shall not be—

(a)   before the end of the period of twenty-eight days beginning with the day on which the notification was served; or

(b)   before the end of the period of seven days beginning with the day on which that person is informed of the time.

(4)   A person who has been informed of a place and time for the purposes of sub-paragraph (2) above or his representative may, at that place and time—

(a)   make oral representations to the appointed person for the purpose of establishing that the goods to which the proposed notice relates are safe; and

(b)   call and examine witnesses in connection with the representations.

8.   (1)   Where a person is appointed to consider representations about a proposed notice to warn, it shall be his duty to consider—

(a)   any written representations made by the person on whom it is proposed to serve the notice; and

(b)   in a case where a place and time has been appointed under paragraph 7(2) above for oral representations to be made by that person or his representative, any representations so made and any statements made by witnesses in connection with those representations,

and, after considering those matters to make a report (including recommendations) to the Secretary of State about the matters considered by him and the proposal to serve the notice.

(2)   It shall be the duty of the Secretary of State to consider any report made to him under sub-paragraph (1) above, and after considering the report, to inform the person on whom it was proposed that a notice to warn should be served of his decision with respect to the proposal.

(3)   If at any time after serving a notification on a person under paragraph 6 above the Secretary of State decides not to serve on that person either the proposed notice to warn or that notice with modifications, the Secretary of State shall inform that person of the decision, and nothing done for the purposes of any of the preceding provisions of this Part of this Schedule before that person was so informed shall—

(a)   entitle the Secretary of State subsequently to serve the proposed notice or the notice with modifications; or

(b)   require the Secretary of State, or any person appointed to consider representations about the proposed notice, subsequently to do anything in respect of, or in consequence of, any such representations.

(4)   Where a notification containing a draft of a proposed notice to warn is served on a person in respect of any goods, a notice to warn served on him in consequence of a decision made under sub-paragraph (2) above shall either be in the form of the draft or shall be less onerous than the draft.

(9)   The Secretary of State may revoke a notice to warn by serving on the person on whom the notice was served a notification stating that the notice is revoked.

PART III
GENERAL

10. (1) Where in a notification served on any person under this Schedule the Secretary of State has appointed a time for the making of oral representations or the examination of witnesses, he may, by giving that person such notification as the Secretary of State considers appropriate, change that time to a later time or appoint further times at which further representations may be made or the examination of witnesses may be continued; and paragraphs 2(4), 3(4) and 7(4) above shall have effect accordingly.

(2) For the purposes of this Schedule the Secretary of State may appoint a person (instead of the appointed person) to consider any representations or statements, if the person originally appointed, or last appointed under this sub-paragraph, to consider those representations or statements has died or appears to the Secretary of State to be otherwise unable to act.

11. In this Schedule—

'the appointed person' in relation to a prohibition notice or a proposal to serve a notice to warn, means the person for the time being appointed under this Schedule to consider representations about the notice or, as the case may be, about the proposed notice;

'notification' means a notification in writing;

'trader', in relation to a prohibition notice, means the person on whom the notice is or was served.

FOOD SAFETY ACT 1990
(1990, c. 16)

PART I
PRELIMINARY

2.　Extended meaning of 'sale' etc.

(1) For the purposes of this Act—
   (a) the supply of food, otherwise than on sale, in the course of a business; and
   (b) any other thing which is done with respect to food and is specified in an order made by the Secretary of State,

shall be deemed to be a sale of the food, and references to purchasers and purchasing shall be construed accordingly.

(2) This Act shall apply—
   (a) in relation to any food which is offered as a prize or reward or given away in connection with any entertainment to which the public are admitted, whether on payment of money or not, as if the food were, or had been, exposed for sale by each person concerned in the organisation of the entertainment;
   (b) in relation to any food which, for the purpose of advertisement or in furtherance of any trade or business, is offered as a prize or reward or given away, as if the food were, or had been, exposed for sale by the person offering or giving away the food; and
   (c) in relation to any food which is exposed or deposited in any premises for the purpose of being so offered or given away as mentioned in paragraph (a) or (b) above, as if the food were, or had been, exposed for sale by the occupier of the premises;

and in this subsection "entertainment" includes any social gathering, amusement, exhibition, performance, game, sport or trial of skill.

PART II
MAIN PROVISIONS

8.　Selling food not complying with food safety requirements

(1) ...

(2) For the purposes of this Part food fails to comply with food safety requirements if it is unsafe within the meaning of Article 14 of Regulation (EC) No 178/2002 and references

to food safety requirements as to food complying with such requirements shall be construed accordingly.

Consumer protection

14.   Selling food not of the nature or substance or quality demanded

(1)   Any person who sells to the purchaser's prejudice any food which is not of the nature or substance or quality demanded by the purchaser shall be guilty of an offence.

(2)   In subsection (1) above the reference to sale shall be construed as a reference to sale for human consumption; and in proceedings under that subsection it shall not be a defence that the purchaser was not prejudiced because he bought for analysis or examination.

15.   Falsely describing or presenting food

(1)   Any person who gives with any food sold by him, or displays with any food offered or exposed by him for sale or in his possession for the purpose of sale, a label, whether or not attached to or printed on the wrapper or container, which—

(a)   falsely describes the food; or

(b)   is likely to mislead as to the nature or substance or quality of the food,

shall be guilty of an offence.

(2)   Any person who publishes, or is a party to the publication of, an advertisement (not being such a label given or displayed by him as mentioned in subsection (1) above) which—

(a)   falsely describes any food; or

(b)   is likely to mislead as to the nature or substance or quality of any food,

shall be guilty of an offence.

(3)   Any person who sells, or offers or exposes for sale, or has in his possession for the purpose of sale, any food the presentation of which is likely to mislead as to the nature or substance or quality of the food shall be guilty of an offence.

(4)   In proceedings for an offence under subsection (1) or (2) above, the fact that a label or advertisement in respect of which the offence is alleged to have been committed contained an accurate statement of the composition of the food shall not preclude the court from finding that the offence was committed.

(5)   In this section references to sale shall be construed as references to sale for human consumption.

ARBITRATION ACT 1996
(1996, c. 23)

PART I
ARBITRATION PURSUANT TO AN ARBITRATION AGREEMENT

Introductory

1.   General principles

The provisions of this Part are founded on the following principles, and shall be construed accordingly—

(a)   the object of arbitration is to obtain the fair resolution of disputes by an impartial tribunal without unnecessary delay or expense;

(b)   the parties should be free to agree how their disputes are resolved, subject only to such safeguards as are necessary in the public interest;

(c)   in matters governed by this Part the court should not intervene except as provided by this Part.

2.   Scope of application of provisions

(1)   The provisions of this Part apply where the seat of the arbitration is in England and Wales or Northern Ireland.

(2)   The following sections apply even if the seat of the arbitration is outside England and Wales or Northern Ireland or no seat has been designated or determined—

(a)   sections 9 to 11 (stay of legal proceedings, &c.), and

(b)   section 66 (enforcement of arbitral awards).

(3)   The powers conferred by the following sections apply even if the seat of the arbitration is outside England and Wales or Northern Ireland or no seat has been designated or determined—

(a)   section 43 (securing the attendance of witnesses), and

(b)   section 44 (court powers exercisable in support of arbitral proceedings);

but the court may refuse to exercise any such power if, in the opinion of the court, the fact that the seat of the arbitration is outside England and Wales or Northern Ireland, or that when designated or determined the seat is likely to be outside England and Wales or Northern Ireland, makes it inappropriate to do so.

(4)   The court may exercise a power conferred by any provision of this Part not mentioned in subsection (2) or (3) for the purpose of supporting the arbitral process where—

(a)   no seat of the arbitration has been designated or determined, and

(b)   by reason of a connection with England and Wales or Northern Ireland the court is satisfied that it is appropriate to do so.

(5)   Section 7 (separability of arbitration agreement) and section 8 (death of a party) apply where the law applicable to the arbitration agreement is the law of England and Wales or Northern Ireland even if the seat of the arbitration is outside England and Wales or Northern Ireland or has not been designated or determined.

3.   The seat of the arbitration

In this Part 'the seat of the arbitration' means the juridical seat of the arbitration designated—

(a)   by the parties to the arbitration agreement, or

(b)   by any arbitral or other institution or person vested by the parties with powers in that regard, or

(c)   by the arbitral tribunal if so authorised by the parties,

or determined, in the absence of any such designation, having regard to the parties' agreement and all the relevant circumstances.

4.   Mandatory and non-mandatory provisions

(1)   The mandatory provisions of this Part are listed in Schedule 1 and have effect notwithstanding any agreement to the contrary.

(2)   The other provisions of this Part (the 'non-mandatory provisions') allow the parties to make their own arrangements by agreement but provide rules which apply in the absence of such agreement.

(3)   The parties may make such arrangements by agreeing to the application of institutional rules or providing any other means by which a matter may be decided.

(4)   It is immaterial whether or not the law applicable to the parties' agreement is the law of England and Wales or, as the case may be, Northern Ireland.

(5)   The choice of a law other than the law of England and Wales or Northern Ireland as the applicable law in respect of a matter provided for by a non-mandatory provision of this Part is equivalent to an agreement making provision about that matter.

For this purpose an applicable law determined in accordance with the parties' agreement, or which is objectively determined in the absence of any express or implied choice, shall be treated as chosen by the parties.

5.   Agreements to be in writing

(1)   The provisions of this Part apply only where the arbitration agreement is in writing, and any other agreement between the parties as to any matter is effective for the purposes of this Part only if in writing.

The expressions 'agreement', 'agree' and 'agreed' shall be construed accordingly.

(2)   There is an agreement in writing—

    (a)   if the agreement is made in writing (whether or not it is signed by the parties),

    (b)   if the agreement is made by exchange of communications in writing, or

    (c)   if the agreement is evidenced in writing.

(3)   Where parties agree otherwise than in writing by reference to terms which are in writing, they make an agreement in writing.

(4)   An agreement is evidenced in writing if an agreement made otherwise than in writing is recorded by one of the parties, or by a third party, with the authority of the parties to the agreement.

(5)   An exchange of written submissions in arbitral or legal proceedings in which the existence of an agreement otherwise than in writing is alleged by one party against another party and not denied by the other party in his response constitutes as between those parties an agreement in writing to the effect alleged.

(6)   References in this Part to anything being written or in writing include its being recorded by any means.

The arbitration agreement

6.   Definition of arbitration agreement

(1)   In this Part an 'arbitration agreement' means an agreement to submit to arbitration present or future disputes (whether they are contractual or not).

(2)   The reference in an agreement to a written form of arbitration clause or to a document containing an arbitration clause constitutes an arbitration agreement if the reference is such as to make that clause part of the agreement.

7.   Separability of arbitration agreement

Unless otherwise agreed by the parties, an arbitration agreement which forms or was intended to form part of another agreement (whether or not in writing) shall not be regarded as invalid, non-existent or ineffective because that other agreement is invalid, or did not come into existence or has become ineffective, and it shall for that purpose be treated as a distinct agreement.

8.   Whether agreement discharged by death of a party

(1)   Unless otherwise agreed by the parties, an arbitration agreement is not discharged by the death of a party and may be enforced by or against the personal representatives of that party.

(2)   Subsection (1) does not affect the operation of any enactment or rule of law by virtue of which a substantive right or obligation is extinguished by death.

Stay of legal proceedings

9.   Stay of legal proceedings

(1)   A party to an arbitration agreement against whom legal proceedings are brought (whether by way of claim or counterclaim) in respect of a matter which under the agreement is to be referred to arbitration may (upon notice to the other parties to the proceedings) apply to the court in which the proceedings have been brought to stay the proceedings so far as they concern that matter.

(2)   An application may be made notwithstanding that the matter is to be referred to arbitration only after the exhaustion of other dispute resolution procedures.

(3)   An application may not be made by a person before taking the appropriate procedural step (if any) to acknowledge the legal proceedings against him or after he has taken any step in those proceedings to answer the substantive claim.

(4)   On an application under this section the court shall grant a stay unless satisfied that the arbitration agreement is null and void, inoperative, or incapable of being performed.

(5)   If the court refuses to stay the legal proceedings, any provision that an award is a condition precedent to the bringing of legal proceedings in respect of any matter is of no effect in relation to those proceedings.

10. Reference of interpleader issue to arbitration

(1) Where in legal proceedings relief by way of interpleader is granted and any issue between the claimants is one in respect of which there is an arbitration agreement between them, the court granting the relief shall direct that the issue be determined in accordance with the agreement unless the circumstances are such that proceedings brought by a claimant in respect of the matter would not be stayed.

(2) Where subsection (1) applies but the court does not direct that the issue be determined in accordance with the arbitration agreement, any provision that an award is a condition precedent to the bringing of legal proceedings in respect of any matter shall not affect the determination of that issue by the court.

11. Retention of security where Admiralty proceedings stayed

(1) Where Admiralty proceedings are stayed on the ground that the dispute in question should be submitted to arbitration, the court granting the stay may, if in those proceedings property has been arrested or bail or other security has been given to prevent or obtain release from arrest—

(a) order that the property arrested be retained as security for the satisfaction of any award given in the arbitration in respect of that dispute, or

(b) order that the stay of those proceedings be conditional on the provision of equivalent security for the satisfaction of any such award.

(2) Subject to any provision made by rules of court and to any necessary modifications, the same law and practice shall apply in relation to property retained in pursuance of an order as would apply if it were held for the purposes of proceedings in the court making the order.

Commencement of arbitral proceedings

12. Power of court to extend time for beginning arbitral proceedings, &c.

(1) Where an arbitration agreement to refer future disputes to arbitration provides that a claim shall be barred, or the claimant's right extinguished, unless the claimant takes within a time fixed by the agreement some step—

(a) to begin arbitral proceedings, or

(b) to begin other dispute resolution procedures which must be exhausted before arbitral proceedings can be begun,

the court may by order extend the time for taking that step.

(2) Any party to the arbitration agreement may apply for such an order (upon notice to the other parties), but only after a claim has arisen and after exhausting any available arbitral process for obtaining an extension of time.

(3) The court shall make an order only if satisfied—

(a) that the circumstances are such as were outside the reasonable contemplation of the parties when they agreed the provision in question, and that it would be just to extend the time, or

(b) that the conduct of one party makes it unjust to hold the other party to the strict terms of the provision in question.

(4) The court may extend the time for such period and on such terms as it thinks fit, and may do so whether or not the time previously fixed (by agreement or by a previous order) has expired.

(5) An order under this section does not affect the operation of the Limitation Acts (see section 13).

(6) The leave of the court is required for any appeal from a decision of the court under this section.

13. Application of Limitation Acts

(1) The Limitation Acts apply to arbitral proceedings as they apply to legal proceedings.

(2) The court may order that in computing the time prescribed by the Limitation Acts for the commencement of proceedings (including arbitral proceedings) in respect of a dispute which was the subject matter—

(a) of an award which the court orders to be set aside or declares to be of no effect, or

(b) of the affected part of an award which the court orders to be set aside in part, or declares to be in part of no effect, the period between the commencement of the arbitration and the date of the order referred to in paragraph (a) or (b) shall be excluded.

(3) In determining for the purposes of the Limitation Acts when a cause of action accrued, any provision that an award is a condition precedent to the bringing of legal proceedings in respect of a matter to which an arbitration agreement applies shall be disregarded.

(4) In this Part 'the Limitation Acts' means—

    (a) in England and Wales, the Limitation Act 1980, the Foreign Limitation Periods Act 1984 and any other enactment (whenever passed) relating to the limitation of actions;

    (b) in Northern Ireland, the Limitation (Northern Ireland) Order 1989, the Foreign Limitation Periods (Northern Ireland) Order 1985 and any other enactment (whenever passed) relating to the limitation of actions.

14.   Commencement of arbitral proceedings

(1) The parties are free to agree when arbitral proceedings are to be regarded as commenced for the purposes of this Part and for the purposes of the Limitation Acts.

(2) If there is no such agreement the following provisions apply.

(3) Where the arbitrator is named or designated in the arbitration agreement, arbitral proceedings are commenced in respect of a matter when one party serves on the other party or parties a notice in writing requiring him or them to submit that matter to the person so named or designated.

(4) Where the arbitrator or arbitrators are to be appointed by the parties, arbitral proceedings are commenced in respect of a matter when one party serves on the other party or parties notice in writing requiring him or them to appoint an arbitrator or to agree to the appointment of an arbitrator in respect of that matter.

(5) Where the arbitrator or arbitrators are to be appointed by a person other than a party to the proceedings, arbitral proceedings are commenced in respect of a matter when one party gives notice in writing to that person requesting him to make the appointment in respect of that matter.

The arbitral tribunal

15.   The arbitral tribunal

(1) The parties are free to agree on the number of arbitrators to form the tribunal and whether there is to be a chairman or umpire.

(2) Unless otherwise agreed by the parties, an agreement that the number of arbitrators shall be two or any other even number shall be understood as requiring the appointment of an additional arbitrator as chairman of the tribunal.

(3) If there is no agreement as to the number of arbitrators, the tribunal shall consist of a sole arbitrator.

16.   Procedure for appointment of arbitrators

(1) The parties are free to agree on the procedure for appointing the arbitrator or arbitrators, including the procedure for appointing any chairman or umpire.

(2) If or to the extent that there is no such agreement, the following provisions apply.

(3) If the tribunal is to consist of a sole arbitrator, the parties shall jointly appoint the arbitrator not later than 28 days after service of a request in writing by either party to do so.

(4) If the tribunal is to consist of two arbitrators, each party shall appoint one arbitrator not later than 14 days after service of a request in writing by either party to do so.

(5) If the tribunal is to consist of three arbitrators—

    (a) each party shall appoint one arbitrator not later than 14 days after service of a request in writing by either party to do so, and

    (b) the two so appointed shall forthwith appoint a third arbitrator as the chairman of the tribunal.

(6) If the tribunal is to consist of two arbitrators and an umpire—

    (a) each party shall appoint one arbitrator not later than 14 days after service of a request in writing by either party to do so, and

   (b) the two so appointed may appoint an umpire at any time after they themselves are appointed and shall do so before any substantive hearing or forthwith if they cannot agree on a matter relating to the arbitration.

 (7) In any other case (in particular, if there are more than two parties) section 18 applies as in the case of a failure of the agreed appointment procedure.

17. Power in case of default to appoint sole arbitrator

 (1) Unless the parties otherwise agree, where each of two parties to an arbitration agreement is to appoint an arbitrator and one party ('the party in default') refuses to do so, or fails to do so within the time specified, the other party, having duly appointed his arbitrator, may give notice in writing to the party in default that he proposes to appoint his arbitrator to act as sole arbitrator.

 (2) If the party in default does not within 7 clear days of that notice being given —

   (a) make the required appointment, and

   (b) notify the other party that he has done so,

  the other party may appoint his arbitrator as sole arbitrator whose award shall be binding on both parties as if he had been so appointed by agreement.

 (3) Where a sole arbitrator has been appointed under subsection (2), the party in default may (upon notice to the appointing party) apply to the court which may set aside the appointment.

 (4) The leave of the court is required for any appeal from a decision of the court under this section.

18. Failure of appointment procedure

 (1) The parties are free to agree what is to happen in the event of a failure of the procedure for the appointment of the arbitral tribunal.

  There is no failure if an appointment is duly made under section 17 (power in case of default to appoint sole arbitrator), unless that appointment is set aside.

 (2) If or to the extent that there is no such agreement any party to the arbitration agreement may (upon notice to the other parties) apply to the court to exercise its powers under this section.

 (3) Those powers are —

   (a) to give directions as to the making of any necessary appointments;

   (b) to direct that the tribunal shall be constituted by such appointments (or any one or more of them) as have been made;

   (c) to revoke any appointments already made;

   (d) to make any necessary appointments itself.

 (4) An appointment made by the court under this section has effect as if made with the agreement of the parties.

 (5) The leave of the court is required for any appeal from a decision of the court under this section.

19. Court to have regard to agreed qualifications

In deciding whether to exercise, and in considering how to exercise, any of its powers under section 16 (procedure for appointment of arbitrators) or section 18 (failure of appointment procedure), the court shall have due regard to any agreement of the parties as to the qualifications required of the arbitrators.

20. Chairman

 (1) Where the parties have agreed that there is to be a chairman, they are free to agree what the functions of the chairman are to be in relation to the making of decisions, orders and awards.

 (2) If or to the extent that there is no such agreement, the following provisions apply.

 (3) Decisions, orders and awards shall be made by all or a majority of the arbitrators (including the chairman).

 (4) The view of the chairman shall prevail in relation to a decision, order or award in respect of which there is neither unanimity nor a majority under subsection (3).

21.   Umpire

(1)   Where the parties have agreed that there is to be an umpire, they are free to agree what the functions of the umpire are to be, and in particular —

(a)   whether he is to attend the proceedings, and

(b)   when he is to replace the other arbitrators as the tribunal with power to make decisions, orders and awards.

(2)   If or to the extent that there is no such agreement, the following provisions apply.

(3)   The umpire shall attend the proceedings and be supplied with the same documents and other materials as are supplied to the other arbitrators.

(4)   Decisions, orders and awards shall be made by the other arbitrators unless and until they cannot agree on a matter relating to the arbitration.

In that event they shall forthwith give notice in writing to the parties and the umpire, whereupon the umpire shall replace them as the tribunal with power to make decisions, orders and awards as if he were sole arbitrator.

(5)   If the arbitrators cannot agree but fail to give notice of that fact, or if any of them fails to join in the giving of notice, any party to the arbitral proceedings may (upon notice to the other parties and to the tribunal) apply to the court which may order that the umpire shall replace the other arbitrators as the tribunal with power to make decisions, orders and awards as if he were sole arbitrator.

(6)   The leave of the court is required for any appeal from a decision of the court under this section.

22.   Decision-making where no chairman or umpire

(1)   Where the parties agree that there shall be two or more arbitrators with no chairman or umpire, the parties are free to agree how the tribunal is to make decisions, orders and awards.

(2)   If there is no such agreement, decisions, orders and awards shall be made by all or a majority of the arbitrators.

23.   Revocation of arbitrator's authority

(1)   The parties are free to agree in what circumstances the authority of an arbitrator may be revoked.

(2)   If or to the extent that there is no such agreement the following provisions apply.

(3)   The authority of an arbitrator may not be revoked except —

(a)   by the parties acting jointly, or

(b)   by an arbitral or other institution or person vested by the parties with powers in that regard.

(4)   Revocation of the authority of an arbitrator by the parties acting jointly must be agreed in writing unless the parties also agree (whether or not in writing) to terminate the arbitration agreement.

(5)   Nothing in this section affects the power of the court —

(a)   to revoke an appointment under section 18 (powers exercisable in case of failure of appointment procedure), or

(b)   to remove an arbitrator on the grounds specified in section 24.

24.   Power of court to remove arbitrator

(1)   A party to arbitral proceedings may (upon notice to the other parties, to the arbitrator concerned and to any other arbitrator) apply to the court to remove an arbitrator on any of the following grounds —

(a)   that circumstances exist that give rise to justifiable doubts as to his impartiality;

(b)   that he does not possess the qualifications required by the arbitration agreement;

(c)   that he is physically or mentally incapable of conducting the proceedings or there are justifiable doubts as to his capacity to do so;

(d)   that he has refused or failed —

(i)   properly to conduct the proceedings, or

(ii)   to use all reasonable despatch in conducting the proceedings or making an award,

and that substantial injustice has been or will be caused to the applicant.

(2)   If there is an arbitral or other institution or person vested by the parties with power to remove an arbitrator, the court shall not exercise its power of removal unless satisfied that the applicant has first exhausted any available recourse to that institution or person.

(3)   The arbitral tribunal may continue the arbitral proceedings and make an award while an application to the court under this section is pending.

(4)   Where the court removes an arbitrator, it may make such order as it thinks fit with respect to his entitlement (if any) to fees or expenses, or the repayment of any fees or expenses already paid.

(5)   The arbitrator concerned is entitled to appear and be heard by the court before it makes any order under this section.

(6)   The leave of the court is required for any appeal from a decision of the court under this section.

25.   Resignation of arbitrator

(1)   The parties are free to agree with an arbitrator as to the consequences of his resignation as regards —

    (a)   his entitlement (if any) to fees or expenses, and

    (b)   any liability thereby incurred by him.

(2)   If or to the extent that there is no such agreement the following provisions apply.

(3)   An arbitrator who resigns his appointment may (upon notice to the parties) apply to the court —

    (a)   to grant him relief from any liability thereby incurred by him, and

    (b)   to make such order as it thinks fit with respect to his entitlement (if any) to fees or expenses or the repayment of any fees or expenses already paid.

(4)   If the court is satisfied that in all the circumstances it was reasonable for the arbitrator to resign, it may grant such relief as is mentioned in subsection (3)(a) on such terms as it thinks fit.

(5)   The leave of the court is required for any appeal from a decision of the court under this section.

26.   Death of arbitrator or person appointing him

(1)   The authority of an arbitrator is personal and ceases on his death.

(2)   Unless otherwise agreed by the parties, the death of the person by whom an arbitrator was appointed does not revoke the arbitrator's authority.

27.   Filling of vacancy, &c.

(1)   Where an arbitrator ceases to hold office, the parties are free to agree —

    (a)   whether and if so how the vacancy is to be filled,

    (b)   whether and if so to what extent the previous proceedings should stand, and

    (c)   what effect (if any) his ceasing to hold office has on any appointment made by him (alone or jointly).

(2)   If or to the extent that there is no such agreement, the following provisions apply.

(3)   The provisions of sections 16 (procedure for appointment of arbitrators) and 18 (failure of appointment procedure) apply in relation to the filling of the vacancy as in relation to an original appointment.

(4)   The tribunal (when reconstituted) shall determine whether and if so to what extent the previous proceedings should stand.

    This does not affect any right of a party to challenge those proceedings on any ground which had arisen before the arbitrator ceased to hold office.

(5)   His ceasing to hold office does not affect any appointment by him (alone or jointly) of another arbitrator, in particular any appointment of a chairman or umpire.

28.   Joint and several liability of parties to arbitrators for fees and expenses

(1)   The parties are jointly and severally liable to pay to the arbitrators such reasonable fees and expenses (if any) as are appropriate in the circumstances.

(2)   Any party may apply to the court (upon notice to the other parties and to the arbitrators) which may order that the amount of the arbitrators' fees and expenses shall be considered and adjusted by such means and upon such terms as it may direct.

(3)   If the application is made after any amount has been paid to the arbitrators by way of fees or expenses, the court may order the repayment of such amount (if any) as is shown to be excessive, but shall not do so unless it is shown that it is reasonable in the circumstances to order repayment.

(4)   The above provisions have effect subject to any order of the court under section 24(4) or 25(3)(b) (order as to entitlement to fees or expenses in case of removal or resignation of arbitrator).

(5)   Nothing in this section affects any liability of a party to any other party to pay all or any of the costs of the arbitration (see sections 59 to 65) or any contractual right of an arbitrator to payment of his fees and expenses.

(6)   In this section references to arbitrators include an arbitrator who has ceased to act and an umpire who has not replaced the other arbitrators.

29.   Immunity of arbitrator

(1)   An arbitrator is not liable for anything done or omitted in the discharge or purported discharge of his functions as arbitrator unless the act or omission is shown to have been in bad faith.

(2)   Subsection (1) applies to an employee or agent of an arbitrator as it applies to the arbitrator himself.

(3)   This section does not affect any liability incurred by an arbitrator by reason of his resigning (but see section 25).

Jurisdiction of the arbitral tribunal

30.   Competence of tribunal to rule on its own jurisdiction

(1)   Unless otherwise agreed by the parties, the arbitral tribunal may rule on its own substantive jurisdiction, that is, as to—
   (a)   whether there is a valid arbitration agreement,
   (b)   whether the tribunal is properly constituted, and
   (c)   what matters have been submitted to arbitration in accordance with the arbitration agreement.

(2)   Any such ruling may be challenged by any available arbitral process of appeal or review or in accordance with the provisions of this Part.

31.   Objection to substantive jurisdiction of tribunal

(1)   An objection that the arbitral tribunal lacks substantive jurisdiction at the outset of the proceedings must be raised by a party not later than the time he takes the first step in the proceedings to contest the merits of any matter in relation to which he challenges the tribunal's jurisdiction.
       A party is not precluded from raising such an objection by the fact that he has appointed or participated in the appointment of an arbitrator.

(2)   Any objection during the course of the arbitral proceedings that the arbitral tribunal is exceeding its substantive jurisdiction must be made as soon as possible after the matter alleged to be beyond its jurisdiction is raised.

(3)   The arbitral tribunal may admit an objection later than the time specified in subsection (1) or (2) if it considers the delay justified.

(4)   Where an objection is duly taken to the tribunal's substantive jurisdiction and the tribunal has power to rule on its own jurisdiction, it may—
   (a)   rule on the matter in an award as to jurisdiction, or
   (b)   deal with the objection in its award on the merits.
   If the parties agree which of these courses the tribunal should take, the tribunal shall proceed accordingly.

(5)   The tribunal may in any case, and shall if the parties so agree, stay proceedings whilst an application is made to the court under section 32 (determination of preliminary point of jurisdiction).

32.   Determination of preliminary point of jurisdiction

(1)   The court may, on the application of a party to arbitral proceedings (upon notice to the other parties), determine any question as to the substantive jurisdiction of the tribunal.

A party may lose the right to object (see section 73).

(2) An application under this section shall not be considered unless—

    (a)   it is made with the agreement in writing of all the other parties to the proceedings, or

    (b)   it is made with the permission of the tribunal and the court is satisfied—

        (i)   that the determination of the question is likely to produce substantial savings in costs,

        (ii)   that the application was made without delay, and

        (iii)   that there is good reason why the matter should be decided by the court.

(3) An application under this section, unless made with the agreement of all the other parties to the proceedings, shall state the grounds on which it is said that the matter should be decided by the court.

(4) Unless otherwise agreed by the parties, the arbitral tribunal may continue the arbitral proceedings and make an award while an application to the court under this section is pending.

(5) Unless the court gives leave, no appeal lies from a decision of the court whether the conditions specified in subsection (2) are met.

(6) The decision of the court on the question of jurisdiction shall be treated as a judgment of the court for the purposes of an appeal.

But no appeal lies without the leave of the court which shall not be given unless the court considers that the question involves a point of law which is one of general importance or is one which for some other special reason should be considered by the Court of Appeal.

The arbitral proceedings

33. General duty of the tribunal

(1) The tribunal shall—

    (a)   act fairly and impartially as between the parties, giving each party a reasonable opportunity of putting his case and dealing with that of his opponent, and

    (b)   adopt procedures suitable to the circumstances of the particular case, avoiding unnecessary delay or expense, so as to provide a fair means for the resolution of the matters falling to be determined.

(2) The tribunal shall comply with that general duty in conducting the arbitral proceedings, in its decisions on matters of procedure and evidence and in the exercise of all other powers conferred on it.

34. Procedural and evidential matters

(1) It shall be for the tribunal to decide all procedural and evidential matters, subject to the right of the parties to agree any matter.

(2) Procedural and evidential matters include—

    (a)   when and where any part of the proceedings is to be held;

    (b)   the language or languages to be used in the proceedings and whether translations of any relevant documents are to be supplied;

    (c)   whether any and if so what form of written statements of claim and defence are to be used, when these should be supplied and the extent to which such statements can be later amended;

    (d)   whether any and if so which documents or classes of documents should be disclosed between and produced by the parties and at what stage;

    (e)   whether any and if so what questions should be put to and answered by the respective parties and when and in what form this should be done;

    (f)   whether to apply strict rules of evidence (or any other rules) as to the admissibility, relevance or weight of any material (oral, written or other) sought to be tendered on any matters of fact or opinion, and the time, manner and form in which such material should be exchanged and presented;

    (g)   whether and to what extent the tribunal should itself take the initiative in ascertaining the facts and the law;

    (h)   whether and to what extent there should be oral or written evidence or submissions.

(3)   The tribunal may fix the time within which any directions given by it are to be complied with, and may if it thinks fit extend the time so fixed (whether or not it has expired).

35.   Consolidation of proceedings and concurrent hearings
(1)   The parties are free to agree—
  (a)   that the arbitral proceedings shall be consolidated with other arbitral proceedings, or
  (b)   that concurrent hearings shall be held, on such terms as may be agreed.
(2)   Unless the parties agree to confer such power on the tribunal, the tribunal has no power to order consolidation of proceedings or concurrent hearings.

36.   Legal or other representation
Unless otherwise agreed by the parties, a party to arbitral proceedings may be represented in the proceedings by a lawyer or other person chosen by him.

37.   Power to appoint experts, legal advisers or assessors
(1)   Unless otherwise agreed by the parties—
  (a)   the tribunal may—
    (i)   appoint experts or legal advisers to report to it and the parties, or
    (ii)   appoint assessors to assist it on technical matters,
    and may allow any such expert, legal adviser or assessor to attend the proceedings; and
  (b)   the parties shall be given a reasonable opportunity to comment on any information, opinion or advice offered by any such person.
(2)   The fees and expenses of an expert, legal adviser or assessor appointed by the tribunal for which the arbitrators are liable are expenses of the arbitrators for the purposes of this Part.

38.   General powers exercisable by the tribunal
(1)   The parties are free to agree on the powers exercisable by the arbitral tribunal for the purposes of and in relation to the proceedings.
(2)   Unless otherwise agreed by the parties the tribunal has the following powers.
(3)   The tribunal may order a claimant to provide security for the costs of the arbitration. This power shall not be exercised on the ground that the claimant is—
  (a)   an individual ordinarily resident outside the United Kingdom, or
  (b)   a corporation or association incorporated or formed under the law of a country outside the United Kingdom, or whose central management and control is exercised outside the United Kingdom.
(4)   The tribunal may give directions in relation to any property which is the subject of the proceedings or as to which any question arises in the proceedings, and which is owned by or is in the possession of a party to the proceedings—
  (a)   for the inspection, photographing, preservation, custody or detention of the property by the tribunal, an expert or a party, or
  (b)   ordering that samples be taken from, or any observation be made of or experiment conducted upon, the property.
(5)   The tribunal may direct that a party or witness shall be examined on oath or affirmation, and may for that purpose administer any necessary oath or take any necessary affirmation.
(6)   The tribunal may give directions to a party for the preservation for the purposes of the proceedings of any evidence in his custody or control.

39.   Power to make provisional awards
(1)   The parties are free to agree that the tribunal shall have power to order on a provisional basis any relief which it would have power to grant in a final award.
(2)   This includes, for instance, making—
  (a)   a provisional order for the payment of money or the disposition of property as between the parties, or
  (b)   an order to make an interim payment on account of the costs of the arbitration.

(3)   Any such order shall be subject to the tribunal's final adjudication; and the tribunal's final award, on the merits or as to costs, shall take account of any such order.

(4)   Unless the parties agree to confer such power on the tribunal, the tribunal has no such power.

This does not affect its powers under section 47 (awards on different issues, &c.).

40.   General duty of parties

(1)   The parties shall do all things necessary for the proper and expeditious conduct of the arbitral proceedings.

(2)   This includes—

   (a)   complying without delay with any determination of the tribunal as to procedural or evidential matters, or with any order or directions of the tribunal, and

   (b)   where appropriate, taking without delay any necessary steps to obtain a decision of the court on a preliminary question of jurisdiction or law (see sections 32 and 45).

41.   Powers of tribunal in case of party's default

(1)   The parties are free to agree on the powers of the tribunal in case of a party's failure to do something necessary for the proper and expeditious conduct of the arbitration.

(2)   Unless otherwise agreed by the parties, the following provisions apply.

(3)   If the tribunal is satisfied that there has been inordinate and inexcusable delay on the part of the claimant in pursuing his claim and that the delay—

   (a)   gives rise, or is likely to give rise, to a substantial risk that it is not possible to have a fair resolution of the issues in that claim, or

   (b)   has caused, or is likely to cause, serious prejudice to the respondent,

   the tribunal may make an award dismissing the claim.

(4)   If without showing sufficient cause a party—

   (a)   fails to attend or be represented at an oral hearing of which due notice was given, or

   (b)   where matters are to be dealt with in writing, fails after due notice to submit written evidence or make written submissions,

   the tribunal may continue the proceedings in the absence of that party or, as the case may be, without any written evidence or submissions on his behalf, and may make an award on the basis of the evidence before it.

(5)   If without showing sufficient cause a party fails to comply with any order or directions of the tribunal, the tribunal may make a peremptory order to the same effect, prescribing such time for compliance with it as the tribunal considers appropriate.

(6)   If a claimant fails to comply with a peremptory order of the tribunal to provide security for costs, the tribunal may make an award dismissing his claim.

(7)   If a party fails to comply with any other kind of peremptory order, then, without prejudice to section 42 (enforcement by court of tribunal's peremptory orders), the tribunal may do any of the following—

   (a)   direct that the party in default shall not be entitled to rely upon any allegation or material which was the subject matter of the order;

   (b)   draw such adverse inferences from the act of non-compliance as the circumstances justify;

   (c)   proceed to an award on the basis of such materials as have been properly provided to it;

   (d)   make such order as it thinks fit as to the payment of costs of the arbitration incurred in consequence of the non-compliance.

Powers of court in relation to arbitral proceedings

42.   Enforcement of peremptory orders of tribunal

(1)   Unless otherwise agreed by the parties, the court may make an order requiring a party to comply with a peremptory order made by the tribunal.

(2)   An application for an order under this section may be made—

   (a)   by the tribunal (upon notice to the parties),

   (b)   by a party to the arbitral proceedings with the permission of the tribunal (and upon notice to the other parties), or

(c)   where the parties have agreed that the powers of the court under this section shall be available.

(3)   The court shall not act unless it is satisfied that the applicant has exhausted any available arbitral process in respect of failure to comply with the tribunal's order.

(4)   No order shall be made under this section unless the court is satisfied that the person to whom the tribunal's order was directed has failed to comply with it within the time prescribed in the order or, if no time was prescribed, within a reasonable time.

(5)   The leave of the court is required for any appeal from a decision of the court under this section.

43.   Securing the attendance of witnesses

(1)   A party to arbitral proceedings may use the same court procedures as are available in relation to legal proceedings to secure the attendance before the tribunal of a witness in order to give oral testimony or to produce documents or other material evidence.

(2)   This may only be done with the permission of the tribunal or the agreement of the other parties.

(3)   The court procedures may only be used if—
(a)   the witness is in the United Kingdom, and
(b)   the arbitral proceedings are being conducted in England and Wales or, as the case may be, Northern Ireland.

(4)   A person shall not be compelled by virtue of this section to produce any document or other material evidence which he could not be compelled to produce in legal proceedings.

44.   Court powers exercisable in support of arbitral proceedings

(1)   Unless otherwise agreed by the parties, the court has for the purposes of and in relation to arbitral proceedings the same power of making orders about the matters listed below as it has for the purposes of and in relation to legal proceedings.

(2)   Those matters are—
(a)   the taking of the evidence of witnesses;
(b)   the preservation of evidence;
(c)   making orders relating to property which is the subject of the proceedings or as to which any question arises in the proceedings—
(i)   for the inspection, photographing, preservation, custody or detention of the property, or
(ii)   ordering that samples be taken from, or any observation be made of or experiment conducted upon, the property;
and for that purpose authorising any person to enter any premises in the possession or control of a party to the arbitration;
(d)   the sale of any goods the subject of the proceedings;
(e)   the granting of an interim injunction or the appointment of a receiver.

(3)   If the case is one of urgency, the court may, on the application of a party or proposed party to the arbitral proceedings, make such orders as it thinks necessary for the purpose of preserving evidence or assets.

(4)   If the case is not one of urgency, the court shall act only on the application of a party to the arbitral proceedings (upon notice to the other parties and to the tribunal) made with the permission of the tribunal or the agreement in writing of the other parties.

(5)   In any case the court shall act only if or to the extent that the arbitral tribunal, and any arbitral or other institution or person vested by the parties with power in that regard, has no power or is unable for the time being to act effectively.

(6)   If the court so orders, an order made by it under this section shall cease to have effect in whole or in part on the order of the tribunal or of any such arbitral or other institution or person having power to act in relation to the subject matter of the order.

(7)   The leave of the court is required for any appeal from a decision of the court under this section.

45.   Determination of preliminary point of law

(1)   Unless otherwise agreed by the parties, the court may on the application of a party to arbitral proceedings (upon notice to the other parties) determine any question of

law arising in the course of the proceedings which the court is satisfied substantially affects the rights of one or more of the parties.

An agreement to dispense with reasons for the tribunal's award shall be considered an agreement to exclude the court's jurisdiction under this section.

(2) An application under this section shall not be considered unless—
    (a) it is made with the agreement of all the other parties to the proceedings, or
    (b) it is made with the permission of the tribunal and the court is satisfied—
        (i) that the determination of the question is likely to produce substantial savings in costs, and
        (ii) that the application was made without delay.

(3) The application shall identify the question of law to be determined and, unless made with the agreement of all the other parties to the proceedings, shall state the grounds on which it is said that the question should be decided by the court.

(4) Unless otherwise agreed by the parties, the arbitral tribunal may continue the arbitral proceedings and make an award while an application to the court under this section is pending.

(5) Unless the court gives leave, no appeal lies from a decision of the court whether the conditions specified in subsection (2) are met.

(6) The decision of the court on the question of law shall be treated as a judgment of the court for the purposes of an appeal.

But no appeal lies without the leave of the court which shall not be given unless the court considers that the question is one of general importance, or is one which for some other special reason should be considered by the Court of Appeal.

The award

46. Rules applicable to substance of dispute

(1) The arbitral tribunal shall decide the dispute—
    (a) in accordance with the law chosen by the parties as applicable to the substance of the dispute, or
    (b) if the parties so agree, in accordance with such other considerations as are agreed by them or determined by the tribunal.

(2) For this purpose the choice of the laws of a country shall be understood to refer to the substantive laws of that country and not its conflict of laws rules.

(3) If or to the extent that there is no such choice or agreement, the tribunal shall apply the law determined by the conflict of laws rules which it considers applicable.

47. Awards on different issues, &c.

(1) Unless otherwise agreed by the parties, the tribunal may make more than one award at different times on different aspects of the matters to be determined.

(2) The tribunal may, in particular, make an award relating—
    (a) to an issue affecting the whole claim, or
    (b) to a part only of the claims or cross-claims submitted to it for decision.

(3) If the tribunal does so, it shall specify in its award the issue, or the claim or part of a claim, which is the subject matter of the award.

48. Remedies

(1) The parties are free to agree on the powers exercisable by the arbitral tribunal as regards remedies.

(2) Unless otherwise agreed by the parties, the tribunal has the following powers.

(3) The tribunal may make a declaration as to any matter to be determined in the proceedings.

(4) The tribunal may order the payment of a sum of money, in any currency.

(5) The tribunal has the same powers as the court—
    (a) to order a party to do or refrain from doing anything;
    (b) to order specific performance of a contract (other than a contract relating to land);
    (c) to order the rectification, setting aside or cancellation of a deed or other document.

49.   Interest

(1)   The parties are free to agree on the powers of the tribunal as regards the award of interest.

(2)   Unless otherwise agreed by the parties the following provisions apply.

(3)   The tribunal may award simple or compound interest from such dates, at such rates and with such rests as it considers meets the justice of the case—

(a)   on the whole or part of any amount awarded by the tribunal, in respect of any period up to the date of the award;

(b)   on the whole or part of any amount claimed in the arbitration and outstanding at the commencement of the arbitral proceedings but paid before the award was made, in respect of any period up to the date of payment.

(4)   The tribunal may award simple or compound interest from the date of the award (or any later date) until payment, at such rates and with such rests as it considers meets the justice of the case, on the outstanding amount of any award (including any award of interest under subsection (3) and any award as to costs).

(5)   References in this section to an amount awarded by the tribunal include an amount payable in consequence of a declaratory award by the tribunal.

(6)   The above provisions do not affect any other power of the tribunal to award interest.

50.   Extension of time for making award

(1)   Where the time for making an award is limited by or in pursuance of the arbitration agreement, then, unless otherwise agreed by the parties, the court may in accordance with the following provisions by order extend that time.

(2)   An application for an order under this section may be made—

(a)   by the tribunal (upon notice to the parties), or

(b)   by any party to the proceedings (upon notice to the tribunal and the other parties), but only after exhausting any available arbitral process for obtaining an extension of time.

(3)   The court shall only make an order if satisfied that a substantial injustice would otherwise be done.

(4)   The court may extend the time for such period and on such terms as it thinks fit, and may do so whether or not the time previously fixed (by or under the agreement or by a previous order) has expired.

(5)   The leave of the court is required for any appeal from a decision of the court under this section.

51.   Settlement

(1)   If during arbitral proceedings the parties settle the dispute, the following provisions apply unless otherwise agreed by the parties.

(2)   The tribunal shall terminate the substantive proceedings and, if so requested by the parties and not objected to by the tribunal, shall record the settlement in the form of an agreed award.

(3)   An agreed award shall state that it is an award of the tribunal and shall have the same status and effect as any other award on the merits of the case.

(4)   The following provisions of this Part relating to awards (sections 52 to 58) apply to an agreed award.

(5)   Unless the parties have also settled the matter of the payment of the costs of the arbitration, the provisions of this Part relating to costs (sections 59 to 65) continue to apply.

52.   Form of award

(1)   The parties are free to agree on the form of an award.

(2)   If or to the extent that there is no such agreement, the following provisions apply.

(3)   The award shall be in writing signed by all the arbitrators or all those assenting to the award.

(4)   The award shall contain the reasons for the award unless it is an agreed award or the parties have agreed to dispense with reasons.

(5)   The award shall state the seat of the arbitration and the date when the award is made.

53. Place where award treated as made

Unless otherwise agreed by the parties, where the seat of the arbitration is in England and Wales or Northern Ireland, any award in the proceedings shall be treated as made there, regardless of where it was signed, despatched or delivered to any of the parties.

54. Date of award

(1) Unless otherwise agreed by the parties, the tribunal may decide what is to be taken to be the date on which the award was made.

(2) In the absence of any such decision, the date of the award shall be taken to be the date on which it is signed by the arbitrator or, where more than one arbitrator signs the award, by the last of them.

55. Notification of award

(1) The parties are free to agree on the requirements as to notification of the award to the parties.

(2) If there is no such agreement, the award shall be notified to the parties by service on them of copies of the award, which shall be done without delay after the award is made.

(3) Nothing in this section affects section 56 (power to withhold award in case of non-payment).

56. Power to withhold award in case of non-payment

(1) The tribunal may refuse to deliver an award to the parties except upon full payment of the fees and expenses of the arbitrators.

(2) If the tribunal refuses on that ground to deliver an award, a party to the arbitral proceedings may (upon notice to the other parties and the tribunal) apply to the court, which may order that—

    (a) the tribunal shall deliver the award on the payment into court by the applicant of the fees and expenses demanded, or such lesser amount as the court may specify,

    (b) the amount of the fees and expenses properly payable shall be determined by such means and upon such terms as the court may direct, and

    (c) that out of the money paid into court there shall be paid out such fees and expenses as may be found to be properly payable and the balance of the money (if any) shall be paid out to the applicant.

(3) For this purpose the amount of fees and expenses properly payable is the amount the applicant is liable to pay under section 28 or any agreement relating to the payment of the arbitrators.

(4) No application to the court may be made where there is any available arbitral process for appeal or review of the amount of the fees or expenses demanded.

(5) References in this section to arbitrators include an arbitrator who has ceased to act and an umpire who has not replaced the other arbitrators.

(6) The above provisions of this section also apply in relation to any arbitral or other institution or person vested by the parties with powers in relation to the delivery of the tribunal's award.

    As they so apply, the references to the fees and expenses of the arbitrators shall be construed as including the fees and expenses of that institution or person.

(7) The leave of the court is required for any appeal from a decision of the court under this section.

(8) Nothing in this section shall be construed as excluding an application under section 28 where payment has been made to the arbitrators in order to obtain the award.

57. Correction of award or additional award

(1) The parties are free to agree on the powers of the tribunal to correct an award or make an additional award.

(2) If or to the extent there is no such agreement, the following provisions apply.

(3) The tribunal may on its own initiative or on the application of a party—

    (a) correct an award so as to remove any clerical mistake or error arising from an accidental slip or omission or clarify or remove any ambiguity in the award, or

(b)   make an additional award in respect of any claim (including a claim for interest or costs) which was presented to the tribunal but was not dealt with in the award.

These powers shall not be exercised without first affording the other parties a reasonable opportunity to make representations to the tribunal.

(4)   Any application for the exercise of those powers must be made within 28 days of the date of the award or such longer period as the parties may agree.

(5)   Any correction of an award shall be made within 28 days of the date the application was received by the tribunal or, where the correction is made by the tribunal on its own initiative, within 28 days of the date of the award or, in either case, such longer period as the parties may agree.

(6)   Any additional award shall be made within 56 days of the date of the original award or such longer period as the parties may agree.

(7)   Any correction of an award shall form part of the award.

58.   Effect of award

(1)   Unless otherwise agreed by the parties, an award made by the tribunal pursuant to an arbitration agreement is final and binding both on the parties and on any persons claiming through or under them.

(2)   This does not affect the right of a person to challenge the award by any available arbitral process of appeal or review or in accordance with the provisions of this Part.

Costs of the arbitration

59.   Costs of the arbitration

(1)   References in this Part to the costs of the arbitration are to—
(a)   the arbitrators' fees and expenses,
(b)   the fees and expenses of any arbitral institution concerned, and
(c)   the legal or other costs of the parties.

(2)   Any such reference includes the costs of or incidental to any proceedings to determine the amount of the recoverable costs of the arbitration (see section 63).

60.   Agreement to pay costs in any event

An agreement which has the effect that a party is to pay the whole or part of the costs of the arbitration in any event is only valid if made after the dispute in question has arisen.

61.   Award of costs

(1)   The tribunal may make an award allocating the costs of the arbitration as between the parties, subject to any agreement of the parties.

(2)   Unless the parties otherwise agree, the tribunal shall award costs on the general principle that costs should follow the event except where it appears to the tribunal that in the circumstances this is not appropriate in relation to the whole or part of the costs.

62.   Effect of agreement or award about costs

Unless the parties otherwise agree, any obligation under an agreement between them as to how the costs of the arbitration are to be borne, or under an award allocating the costs of the arbitration, extends only to such costs as are recoverable.

63.   The recoverable costs of the arbitration

(1)   The parties are free to agree what costs of the arbitration are recoverable.

(2)   If or to the extent there is no such agreement, the following provisions apply.

(3)   The tribunal may determine by award the recoverable costs of the arbitration on such basis as it thinks fit.

If it does so, it shall specify—
(a)   the basis on which it has acted, and
(b)   the items of recoverable costs and the amount referable to each.

(4)   If the tribunal does not determine the recoverable costs of the arbitration, any party to the arbitral proceedings may apply to the court (upon notice to the other parties) which may—

(a) determine the recoverable costs of the arbitration on such basis as it thinks fit, or

(b) order that they shall be determined by such means and upon such terms as it may specify.

(5) Unless the tribunal or the court determines otherwise—

(a) the recoverable costs of the arbitration shall be determined on the basis that there shall be allowed a reasonable amount in respect of all costs reasonably incurred, and

(b) any doubt as to whether costs were reasonably incurred or were reasonable in amount shall be resolved in favour of the paying party.

(6) The above provisions have effect subject to section 64 (recoverable fees and expenses of arbitrators).

(7) Nothing in this section affects any right of the arbitrators, any expert, legal adviser or assessor appointed by the tribunal, or any arbitral institution, to payment of their fees and expenses.

64. Recoverable fees and expenses of arbitrators

(1) Unless otherwise agreed by the parties, the recoverable costs of the arbitration shall include in respect of the fees and expenses of the arbitrators only such reasonable fees and expenses as are appropriate in the circumstances.

(2) If there is any question as to what reasonable fees and expenses are appropriate in the circumstances, and the matter is not already before the court on an application under section 63(4), the court may on the application of any party (upon notice to the other parties)—

(a) determine the matter, or

(b) order that it be determined by such means and upon such terms as the court may specify.

(3) Subsection (1) has effect subject to any order of the court under section 24(4) or 25(3)(b) (order as to entitlement to fees or expenses in case of removal or resignation of arbitrator).

(4) Nothing in this section affects any right of the arbitrator to payment of his fees and expenses.

65. Power to limit recoverable costs

(1) Unless otherwise agreed by the parties, the tribunal may direct that the recoverable costs of the arbitration, or of any part of the arbitral proceedings, shall be limited to a specified amount.

(2) Any direction may be made or varied at any stage, but this must be done sufficiently in advance of the incurring of costs to which it relates, or the taking of any steps in the proceedings which may be affected by it, for the limit to be taken into account.

Powers of the court in relation to award

66. Enforcement of the award

(1) An award made by the tribunal pursuant to an arbitration agreement may, by leave of the court, be enforced in the same manner as a judgment or order of the court to the same effect.

(2) Where leave is so given, judgment may be entered in terms of the award.

(3) Leave to enforce an award shall not be given where, or to the extent that, the person against whom it is sought to be enforced shows that the tribunal lacked substantive jurisdiction to make the award.

The right to raise such an objection may have been lost (see section 73).

(4) Nothing in this section affects the recognition or enforcement of an award under any other enactment or rule of law, in particular under Part II of the Arbitration Act 1950 (enforcement of awards under Geneva Convention) or the provisions of Part III of this Act relating to the recognition and enforcement of awards under the New York Convention or by an action on the award.

67.   Challenging the award: substantive jurisdiction

(1)   A party to arbitral proceedings may (upon notice to the other parties and to the tribunal) apply to the court—

    (a)   challenging any award of the arbitral tribunal as to its substantive jurisdiction; or

    (b)   for an order declaring an award made by the tribunal on the merits to be of no effect, in whole or in part, because the tribunal did not have substantive jurisdiction.

A party may lose the right to object (see section 73) and the right to apply is subject to the restrictions in section 70(2) and (3).

(2)   The arbitral tribunal may continue the arbitral proceedings and make a further award while an application to the court under this section is pending in relation to an award as to jurisdiction.

(3)   On an application under this section challenging an award of the arbitral tribunal as to its substantive jurisdiction, the court may by order—

    (a)   confirm the award,

    (b)   vary the award, or

    (c)   set aside the award in whole or in part.

(4)   The leave of the court is required for any appeal from a decision of the court under this section.

68.   Challenging the award: serious irregularity

(1)   A party to arbitral proceedings may (upon notice to the other parties and to the tribunal) apply to the court challenging an award in the proceedings on the ground of serious irregularity affecting the tribunal, the proceedings or the award.

A party may lose the right to object (see section 73) and the right to apply is subject to the restrictions in section 70(2) and (3).

(2)   Serious irregularity means an irregularity of one or more of the following kinds which the court considers has caused or will cause substantial injustice to the applicant—

    (a)   failure by the tribunal to comply with section 33 (general duty of tribunal);

    (b)   the tribunal exceeding its powers (otherwise than by exceeding its substantive jurisdiction: see section 67);

    (c)   failure by the tribunal to conduct the proceedings in accordance with the procedure agreed by the parties;

    (d)   failure by the tribunal to deal with all the issues that were put to it;

    (e)   any arbitral or other institution or person vested by the parties with powers in relation to the proceedings or the award exceeding its powers;

    (f)   uncertainty or ambiguity as to the effect of the award;

    (g)   the award being obtained by fraud or the award or the way in which it was procured being contrary to public policy;

    (h)   failure to comply with the requirements as to the form of the award; or

    (i)   any irregularity in the conduct of the proceedings or in the award which is admitted by the tribunal or by any arbitral or other institution or person vested by the parties with powers in relation to the proceedings or the award.

(3)   If there is shown to be serious irregularity affecting the tribunal, the proceedings or the award, the court may—

    (a)   remit the award to the tribunal, in whole or in part, for reconsideration,

    (b)   set the award aside in whole or in part, or

    (c)   declare the award to be of no effect, in whole or in part.

The court shall not exercise its power to set aside or to declare an award to be of no effect, in whole or in part, unless it is satisfied that it would be inappropriate to remit the matters in question to the tribunal for reconsideration.

(4)   The leave of the court is required for any appeal from a decision of the court under this section.

69.   Appeal on point of law

(1)   Unless otherwise agreed by the parties, a party to arbitral proceedings may (upon notice to the other parties and to the tribunal) appeal to the court on a question of law arising out of an award made in the proceedings.

An agreement to dispense with reasons for the tribunal's award shall be considered an agreement to exclude the court's jurisdiction under this section.

(2) An appeal shall not be brought under this section except—

(a) with the agreement of all the other parties to the proceedings, or

(b) with the leave of the court.

The right to appeal is also subject to the restrictions in section 70(2) and (3).

(3) Leave to appeal shall be given only if the court is satisfied—

(a) that the determination of the question will substantially affect the rights of one or more of the parties,

(b) that the question is one which the tribunal was asked to determine,

(c) that, on the basis of the findings of fact in the award—

(i) the decision of the tribunal on the question is obviously wrong, or

(ii) the question is one of general public importance and the decision of the tribunal is at least open to serious doubt, and

(d) that, despite the agreement of the parties to resolve the matter by arbitration, it is just and proper in all the circumstances for the court to determine the question.

(4) An application for leave to appeal under this section shall identify the question of law to be determined and state the grounds on which it is alleged that leave to appeal should be granted.

(5) The court shall determine an application for leave to appeal under this section without a hearing unless it appears to the court that a hearing is required.

(6) The leave of the court is required for any appeal from a decision of the court under this section to grant or refuse leave to appeal.

(7) On an appeal under this section the court may by order—

(a) confirm the award,

(b) vary the award,

(c) remit the award to the tribunal, in whole or in part, for reconsideration in the light of the court's determination, or

(d) set aside the award in whole or in part.

The court shall not exercise its power to set aside an award, in whole or in part, unless it is satisfied that it would be inappropriate to remit the matters in question to the tribunal for reconsideration.

(8) The decision of the court on an appeal under this section shall be treated as a judgment of the court for the purposes of a further appeal.

But no such appeal lies without the leave of the court which shall not be given unless the court considers that the question is one of general importance or is one which for some other special reason should be considered by the Court of Appeal.

70. Challenge or appeal: supplementary provisions

(1) The following provisions apply to an application or appeal under section 67, 68 or 69.

(2) An application or appeal may not be brought if the applicant or appellant has not first exhausted—

(a) any available arbitral process of appeal or review, and

(b) any available recourse under section 57 (correction of award or additional award).

(3) Any application or appeal must be brought within 28 days of the date of the award or, if there has been any arbitral process of appeal or review, of the date when the applicant or appellant was notified of the result of that process.

(4) If on an application or appeal it appears to the court that the award—

(a) does not contain the tribunal's reasons, or

(b) does not set out the tribunal's reasons in sufficient detail to enable the court properly to consider the application or appeal,

the court may order the tribunal to state the reasons for its award in sufficient detail for that purpose.

(5) Where the court makes an order under subsection (4), it may make such further order as it thinks fit with respect to any additional costs of the arbitration resulting from its order.

(6)   The court may order the applicant or appellant to provide security for the costs of the application or appeal, and may direct that the application or appeal be dismissed if the order is not complied with.

        The power to order security for costs shall not be exercised on the ground that the applicant or appellant is—

(a)   an individual ordinarily resident outside the United Kingdom, or

(b)   a corporation or association incorporated or formed under the law of a country outside the United Kingdom, or whose central management and control is exercised outside the United Kingdom.

(7)   The court may order that any money payable under the award shall be brought into court or otherwise secured pending the determination of the application or appeal, and may direct that the application or appeal be dismissed if the order is not complied with.

(8)   The court may grant leave to appeal subject to conditions to the same or similar effect as an order under subsection (6) or (7).

        This does not affect the general discretion of the court to grant leave subject to conditions.

71.   Challenge or appeal: effect of order of court

(1)   The following provisions have effect where the court makes an order under section 67, 68 or 69 with respect to an award.

(2)   Where the award is varied, the variation has effect as part of the tribunal's award.

(3)   Where the award is remitted to the tribunal, in whole or in part, for reconsideration, the tribunal shall make a fresh award in respect of the matters remitted within three months of the date of the order for remission or such longer or shorter period as the court may direct.

(4)   Where the award is set aside or declared to be of no effect, in whole or in part, the court may also order that any provision that an award is a condition precedent to the bringing of legal proceedings in respect of a matter to which the arbitration agreement applies, is of no effect as regards the subject matter of the award or, as the case may be, the relevant part of the award.

Miscellaneous

72.   Saving for rights of person who takes no part in proceedings

(1)   A person alleged to be a party to arbitral proceedings but who takes no part in the proceedings may question—

(a)   whether there is a valid arbitration agreement,

(b)   whether the tribunal is properly constituted, or

(c)   what matters have been submitted to arbitration in accordance with the arbitration agreement,

by proceedings in the court for a declaration or injunction or other appropriate relief.

(2)   He also has the same right as a party to the arbitral proceedings to challenge an award—

(a)   by an application under section 67 on the ground of lack of substantive jurisdiction in relation to him, or

(b)   by an application under section 68 on the ground of serious irregularity (within the meaning of that section) affecting him;

and section 70(2) (duty to exhaust arbitral procedures) does not apply in his case.

73.   Loss of right to object

(1)   If a party to arbitral proceedings takes part, or continues to take part, in the proceedings without making, either forthwith or within such time as is allowed by the arbitration agreement or the tribunal or by any provision of this Part, any objection—

(a)   that the tribunal lacks substantive jurisdiction,

(b)   that the proceedings have been improperly conducted,

(c)   that there has been a failure to comply with the arbitration agreement or with any provision of this Part, or

(d)   that there has been any other irregularity affecting the tribunal or the proceedings,

he may not raise that objection later, before the tribunal or the court, unless he shows that, at the time he took part or continued to take part in the proceedings, he did not know and could not with reasonable diligence have discovered the grounds for the objection.

(2) Where the arbitral tribunal rules that it has substantive jurisdiction and a party to arbitral proceedings who could have questioned that ruling—

(a) by any available arbitral process of appeal or review, or

(b) by challenging the award,

does not do so, or does not do so within the time allowed by the arbitration agreement or any provision of this Part, he may not object later to the tribunal's substantive jurisdiction on any ground which was the subject of that ruling.

74. Immunity of arbitral institutions, &c.

(1) An arbitral or other institution or person designated or requested by the parties to appoint or nominate an arbitrator is not liable for anything done or omitted in the discharge or purported discharge of that function unless the act or omission is shown to have been in bad faith.

(2) An arbitral or other institution or person by whom an arbitrator is appointed or nominated is not liable, by reason of having appointed or nominated him, for anything done or omitted by the arbitrator (or his employees or agents) in the discharge or purported discharge of his functions as arbitrator.

(3) The above provisions apply to an employee or agent of an arbitral or other institution or person as they apply to the institution or the person himself.

75. Charge to secure payment of solicitors' costs

The powers of the court to make declarations and orders under section 73 of the Solicitors Act 1974 or Article 71H of the Solicitors (Northern Ireland) Order 1976 (power to charge property recovered in the proceedings with the payment of solicitors' costs) may be exercised in relation to arbitral proceedings as if those proceedings were proceedings in the court.

Supplementary

76. Service of notices, &c.

(1) The parties are free to agree on the manner of service of any notice or other document required or authorised to be given or served in pursuance of the arbitration agreement or for the purposes of the arbitral proceedings.

(2) If or to the extent that there is no such agreement the following provisions apply.

(3) A notice or other document may be served on a person by any effective means.

(4) If a notice or other document is addressed, pre-paid and delivered by post—

(a) to the addressee's last known principal residence or, if he is or has been carrying on a trade, profession or business, his last known principal business address, or

(b) where the addressee is a body corporate, to the body's registered or principal office,

it shall be treated as effectively served.

(5) This section does not apply to the service of documents for the purposes of legal proceedings, for which provision is made by rules of court.

(6) References in this Part to a notice or other document include any form of communication in writing and references to giving or serving a notice or other document shall be construed accordingly.

77. Powers of court in relation to service of documents

(1) This section applies where service of a document on a person in the manner agreed by the parties, or in accordance with provisions of section 76 having effect in default of agreement, is not reasonably practicable.

(2) Unless otherwise agreed by the parties, the court may make such order as it thinks fit—

(a) for service in such manner as the court may direct, or

(b) dispensing with service of the document.

(3)   Any party to the arbitration agreement may apply for an order, but only after exhausting any available arbitral process for resolving the matter.

(4)   The leave of the court is required for any appeal from a decision of the court under this section.

78.   Reckoning periods of time

(1)   The parties are free to agree on the method of reckoning periods of time for the purposes of any provision agreed by them or any provision of this Part having effect in default of such agreement.

(2)   If or to the extent there is no such agreement, periods of time shall be reckoned in accordance with the following provisions.

(3)   Where the act is required to be done within a specified period after or from a specified date, the period begins immediately after that date.

(4)   Where the act is required to be done a specified number of clear days after a specified date, at least that number of days must intervene between the day on which the act is done and that date.

(5)   Where the period is a period of seven days or less which would include a Saturday, Sunday or a public holiday in the place where anything which has to be done within the period falls to be done, that day shall be excluded.

In relation to England and Wales or Northern Ireland, a 'public holiday' means Christmas Day, Good Friday or a day which under the Banking and Financial Dealings Act 1971 is a bank holiday.

79.   Power of court to extend time limits relating to arbitral proceedings

(1)   Unless the parties otherwise agree, the court may by order extend any time limit agreed by them in relation to any matter relating to the arbitral proceedings or specified in any provision of this Part having effect in default of such agreement.

This section does not apply to a time limit to which section 12 applies (power of court to extend time for beginning arbitral proceedings, &c.).

(2)   An application for an order may be made—

(a)   by any party to the arbitral proceedings (upon notice to the other parties and to the tribunal), or

(b)   by the arbitral tribunal (upon notice to the parties).

(3)   The court shall not exercise its power to extend a time limit unless it is satisfied—

(a)   that any available recourse to the tribunal, or to any arbitral or other institution or person vested by the parties with power in that regard, has first been exhausted, and

(b)   that a substantial injustice would otherwise be done.

(4)   The court's power under this section may be exercised whether or not the time has already expired.

(5)   An order under this section may be made on such terms as the court thinks fit.

(6)   The leave of the court is required for any appeal from a decision of the court under this section.

80.   Notice and other requirements in connection with legal proceedings

(1)   References in this Part to an application, appeal or other step in relation to legal proceedings being taken 'upon notice' to the other parties to the arbitral proceedings, or to the tribunal, are to such notice of the originating process as is required by rules of court and do not impose any separate requirement.

(2)   Rules of court shall be made—

(a)   requiring such notice to be given as indicated by any provision of this Part, and

(b)   as to the manner, form and content of any such notice.

(3)   Subject to any provision made by rules of court, a requirement to give notice to the tribunal of legal proceedings shall be construed—

(a)   if there is more than one arbitrator, as a requirement to give notice to each of them; and

(b)   if the tribunal is not fully constituted, as a requirement to give notice to any arbitrator who has been appointed.

(4)   References in this Part to making an application or appeal to the court within a specified period are to the issue within that period of the appropriate originating process in accordance with rules of court.

(5)   Where any provision of this Part requires an application or appeal to be made to the court within a specified time, the rules of court relating to the reckoning of periods, the extending or abridging of periods, and the consequences of not taking a step within the period prescribed by the rules, apply in relation to that requirement.

(6)   Provision may be made by rules of court amending the provisions of this Part—
(a)   with respect to the time within which any application or appeal to the court must be made, or
(b)   so as to keep any provision made by this Part in relation to legal proceedings in step with the corresponding provision of rules of court applying generally in relation to proceedings in the court.

(7)   Nothing in this section affects the generality of the power to make rules of court.

81.   Saving for certain matters governed by common law

(1)   Nothing in this Part shall be construed as excluding the operation of any rule of law consistent with the provisions of this Part, in particular, any rule of law as to—
(a)   matters which are not capable of settlement by arbitration;
(b)   the effect of an oral arbitration agreement; or
(c)   the refusal of recognition or enforcement of an arbitral award on grounds of public policy.

(2)   Nothing in this Act shall be construed as reviving any jurisdiction of the court to set aside or remit an award on the ground of errors of fact or law on the face of the award.

82.   Minor definitions

(1)   In this Part—
'arbitrator', unless the context otherwise requires, includes an umpire;
'available arbitral process', in relation to any matter, includes any process of appeal to or review by an arbitral or other institution or person vested by the parties with powers in relation to that matter;
'claimant', unless the context otherwise requires, includes a counterclaimant, and related expressions shall be construed accordingly;
'dispute' includes any difference;
'enactment' includes an enactment contained in Northern Ireland legislation;
'legal proceedings' means civil proceedings in England and Wales the High Court or the county court and Northern Ireland the High Court or a county court;
'peremptory order' means an order made under section 41(5) or made in exercise of any corresponding power conferred by the parties;
'premises' includes land, buildings, moveable structures, vehicles, vessels, aircraft and hovercraft;
'question of law' means—
(a)   for a court in England and Wales, a question of the law of England and Wales, and
(b)   for a court in Northern Ireland, a question of the law of Northern Ireland;
'substantive jurisdiction', in relation to an arbitral tribunal, refers to the matters specified in section 30(1)(a) to (c), and references to the tribunal exceeding its substantive jurisdiction shall be construed accordingly.

(2)   References in this Part to a party to an arbitration agreement include any person claiming under or through a party to the agreement.

83.   Index of defined expressions: Part I

In this Part the expressions listed below are defined or otherwise explained by the provisions indicated—

agreement, agree and agreed section 5(1)

agreement in writing	section 5(2) to (5)
arbitration agreement	sections 6 and 5(1)
arbitrator	section 82(1)
available arbitral process	section 82(1)

claimant	section 82(1)
commencement (in relation to arbitral proceedings)	section 14
costs of the arbitration	section 59
the court	section 105
dispute	section 82(1)
enactment	section 82(1)
legal proceedings	section 82(1)
Limitation Acts	section 13(4)
notice (or other document)	section 76(6)
party—	
-in relation to an arbitration agreement	section 82(2)
-where section 106(2) or (3) applies	section 106(4)
peremptory order	section 82(1) (and see section 41(5))
premises	section 82(1)
question of law	section 82(1)
recoverable costs	sections 63 and 64
seat of the arbitration	section 3
serve and service (of notice or other document)	section 76(6)
substantive jurisdiction (in relation to an arbitral tribunal)	section 82(1) (and see section 30(1) (a) to (c))
upon notice (to the parties or the tribunal)	section 80
written and in writing	section 5(6)

84. Transitional provisions

(1) The provisions of this Part do not apply to arbitral proceedings commenced before the date on which this Part comes into force.

(2) They apply to arbitral proceedings commenced on or after that date under an arbitration agreement whenever made.

(3) The above provisions have effect subject to any transitional provision made by an order under section 109(2) (power to include transitional provisions in commencement order).

PART II
OTHER PROVISIONS RELATING TO ARBITRATION

Domestic arbitration agreements

85. Modification of Part I in relation to domestic arbitration agreement

(1) In the case of a domestic arbitration agreement the provisions of Part I are modified in accordance with the following sections.

(2) For this purpose a 'domestic arbitration agreement' means an arbitration agreement to which none of the parties is—

(a) an individual who is a national of, or habitually resident in, a state other than the United Kingdom, or

(b) a body corporate which is incorporated in, or whose central control and management is exercised in, a state other than the United Kingdom,

and under which the seat of the arbitration (if the seat has been designated or determined) is in the United Kingdom.

(3) In subsection (2) 'arbitration agreement' and 'seat of the arbitration' have the same meaning as in Part I (see sections 3, 5(1) and 6).

86. Staying of legal proceedings

(1) In section 9 (stay of legal proceedings), subsection (4) (stay unless the arbitration agreement is null and void, inoperative, or incapable of being performed) does not apply to a domestic arbitration agreement.

(2) On an application under that section in relation to a domestic arbitration agreement the court shall grant a stay unless satisfied—

(a) that the arbitration agreement is null and void, inoperative, or incapable of being performed, or

(b)   that there are other sufficient grounds for not requiring the parties to abide by the arbitration agreement.

(3)   The court may treat as a sufficient ground under subsection (2)(b) the fact that the applicant is or was at any material time not ready and willing to do all things necessary for the proper conduct of the arbitration or of any other dispute resolution procedures required to be exhausted before resorting to arbitration.

(4)   For the purposes of this section the question whether an arbitration agreement is a domestic arbitration agreement shall be determined by reference to the facts at the time the legal proceedings are commenced.

87.   Effectiveness of agreement to exclude court's jurisdiction

(1)   In the case of a domestic arbitration agreement any agreement to exclude the jurisdiction of the court under—
(a)   section 45 (determination of preliminary point of law), or
(b)   section 69 (challenging the award: appeal on point of law),
is not effective unless entered into after the commencement of the arbitral proceedings in which the question arises or the award is made.

(2)   For this purpose the commencement of the arbitral proceedings has the same meaning as in Part I (see section 14).

(3)   For the purposes of this section the question whether an arbitration agreement is a domestic arbitration agreement shall be determined by reference to the facts at the time the agreement is entered into.

88.   Power to repeal or amend sections 85 to 87

(1)   The Secretary of State may by order repeal or amend the provisions of sections 85 to 87.

(2)   An order under this section may contain such supplementary, incidental and transitional provisions as appear to the Secretary of State to be appropriate.

(3)   An order under this section shall be made by statutory instrument and no such order shall be made unless a draft of it has been laid before and approved by a resolution of each House of Parliament.

Consumer arbitration agreements

89.   Application of unfair terms regulations to consumer arbitration agreements

(1)   The following sections extend the application of Part 2 (unfair terms) of the Consumer Rights Act 2015 in relation to a term which constitutes an arbitration agreement.
         For this purpose 'arbitration agreement' means an agreement to submit to arbitration present or future disputes or differences (whether or not contractual).

(2)   In those sections 'the Part' means Part 2 (unfair terms) of the Consumer Rights Act 2015.

(3)   Those sections apply whatever the law applicable to the arbitration agreement.

90.   Regulations apply where consumer is a legal person

The Part applies where the consumer is a legal person as they apply where the consumer is an individual.

91.   Arbitration agreement unfair where modest amount sought

(1)   A term which constitutes an arbitration agreement is unfair for the purposes of the Part so far as it relates to a claim for a pecuniary remedy which does not exceed the amount specified by order for the purposes of this section.

(2)   Orders under this section may make different provision for different cases and for different purposes.

(3)   The power to make orders under this section is exercisable—
(a)   for England and Wales, by the Secretary of State with the concurrence of the Lord Chancellor,
(b)   for Scotland, by the Secretary of State ... , and
(c)   for Northern Ireland, by the Department of Economic Development for Northern Ireland with the concurrence of the Lord Chancellor.

(4)   Any such order for England and Wales or Scotland shall be made by statutory instrument which shall be subject to annulment in pursuance of a resolution of either House of Parliament.

(5)   Any such order for Northern Ireland shall be a statutory rule for the purposes of the Statutory Rules (Northern Ireland) Order 1979 and shall be subject to negative resolution, within the meaning of section 41(6) of the Interpretation Act (Northern Ireland) 1954.

Small claims arbitration in the county court

92.   Exclusion of Part I in relation to small claims arbitration in the county court

Nothing in Part I of this Act applies to arbitration under section 64 of the County Courts Act 1984.

Appointment of judges as arbitrators

93.   Appointment of judges as arbitrators

(1)   An eligible High Court judge or an official referee may, if in all the circumstances he thinks fit, accept appointment as a sole arbitrator or as umpire by or by virtue of an arbitration agreement.

(2)   An eligible High Court shall not do so unless the Lord Chief Justice has informed him that, having regard to the state of business in the High Court and the Crown Court, he can be made available.

(3)   An official referee shall not do so unless the Lord Chief Justice has informed him that, having regard to the state of official referees' business, he can be made available.

(4)   The fees payable for the services of an eligible High Court judge or official referee as arbitrator or umpire shall be taken in the High Court.

(4A)   The Lord Chief Justice may nominate a senior judge (as defined in section 109(5) of the Constitutional Reform Act 2005) to exercise the functions of the Lord Chief Justice under this section.

(5)   In this section—
'arbitration agreement' has the same meaning as in Part I; and
'eligible High Court judge' means—
(a)   a puisne judge of the High Court, or
(b)   a person acting as High Court judge under or by virtue of section 9(1) of the Senior Courts Act 1981 to deal with official referees' business.
'official referee' means a person nominated under section 68(1)(a) of the Senior Courts Act 1981 to deal with official referees' business.

(6)   The provisions of Part I of this Act apply to arbitration before a person appointed under this section with the modifications specified in Schedule 2.

Statutory arbitrations

94.   Application of Part I to statutory arbitrations

(1)   The provisions of Part I apply to every arbitration under an enactment (a 'statutory arbitration'), whether the enactment was passed or made before or after the commencement of this Act, subject to the adaptations and exclusions specified in sections 95 to 98.

(2)   The provisions of Part I do not apply to a statutory arbitration if or to the extent that their application—
(a)   is inconsistent with the provisions of the enactment concerned, with any rules or procedure authorised or recognised by it, or
(b)   is excluded by any other enactment.

(3)   In this section and the following provisions of this Part 'enactment'—
(a)   in England and Wales, includes an enactment contained in subordinate legislation within the meaning of the Interpretation Act 1978;

(b)   in Northern Ireland, means a statutory provision within the meaning of section 1(f) of the Interpretation Act (Northern Ireland) 1954.

95.   General adaptation of provisions in relation to statutory arbitrations

(1)   The provisions of Part I apply to a statutory arbitration—
  (a)   as if the arbitration were pursuant to an arbitration agreement and as if the enactment were that agreement, and
  (b)   as if the persons by and against whom a claim subject to arbitration in pursuance of the enactment may be or has been made were parties to that agreement.

(2)   Every statutory arbitration shall be taken to have its seat in England and Wales, or, as the case may be, in Northern Ireland.

96.   Specific adaptations of provisions in relation to statutory arbitrations

(1)   The following provisions of Part I apply to a statutory arbitration with the following adaptations.

(2)   In section 30(1) (competence of tribunal to rule on its own jurisdiction), the reference in paragraph (a) to whether there is a valid arbitration agreement shall be construed as a reference to whether the enactment applies to the dispute or difference in question.

(3)   Section 35 (consolidation of proceedings and concurrent hearings) applies only so as to authorise the consolidation of proceedings, or concurrent hearings in proceedings, under the same enactment.

(4)   Section 46 (rules applicable to substance of dispute) applies with the omission of subsection (1)(b) (determination in accordance with considerations agreed by parties).

97.   Provisions excluded from applying to statutory arbitrations

The following provisions of Part I do not apply in relation to a statutory arbitration—
(a)   section 8 (whether agreement discharged by death of a party);
(b)   section 12 (power of court to extend agreed time limits);
(c)   sections 9(5), 10(2) and 71(4) (restrictions on effect of provision that award condition precedent to right to bring legal proceedings).

98.   Power to make further provision by regulations

(1)   The Secretary of State may make provision by regulations for adapting or excluding any provision of Part I in relation to statutory arbitrations in general or statutory arbitrations of any particular description.

(2)   The power is exercisable whether the enactment concerned is passed or made before or after the commencement of this Act.

(3)   Regulations under this section shall be made by statutory instrument which shall be subject to annulment in pursuance of a resolution of either House of Parliament.

PART III

RECOGNITION AND ENFORCEMENT OF CERTAIN FOREIGN AWARDS

Enforcement of Geneva Convention awards

99.   Continuation of Part II of the Arbitration Act 1950

Part II of the Arbitration Act 1950 (enforcement of certain foreign awards) continues to apply in relation to foreign awards within the meaning of that Part which are not also New York Convention awards.

Recognition and enforcement of New York Convention awards

100.   New York Convention awards

(1)   In this Part a 'New York Convention award' means an award made, in pursuance of an arbitration agreement, in the territory of a state (other than the United Kingdom) which is a party to the New York Convention.

(2)   For the purposes of subsection (1) and of the provisions of this Part relating to such awards—

(a)   'arbitration agreement' means an arbitration agreement in writing, and

(b)   an award shall be treated as made at the seat of the arbitration, regardless of where it was signed, despatched or delivered to any of the parties.

In this subsection 'agreement in writing' and 'seat of the arbitration' have the same meaning as in Part I.

(3)   If Her Majesty by Order in Council declares that a state specified in the Order is a party to the New York Convention, or is a party in respect of any territory so specified, the Order shall, while in force, be conclusive evidence of that fact.

(4)   In this section 'the New York Convention' means the Convention on the Recognition and Enforcement of Foreign Arbitral Awards adopted by the United Nations Conference on International Commercial Arbitration on 10th June 1958.

101. Recognition and enforcement of awards

(1)   A New York Convention award shall be recognised as binding on the persons as between whom it was made, and may accordingly be relied on by those persons by way of defence, set-off or otherwise in any legal proceedings in England and Wales or Northern Ireland.

(2)   A New York Convention award may, by leave of the court, be enforced in the same manner as a judgment or order of the court to the same effect.

As to the meaning of 'the court' see section 105.

(3)   Where leave is so given, judgment may be entered in terms of the award.

102. Evidence to be produced by party seeking recognition or enforcement

(1)   A party seeking the recognition or enforcement of a New York Convention award must produce—

(a)   the duly authenticated original award or a duly certified copy of it, and

(b)   the original arbitration agreement or a duly certified copy of it.

(2)   If the award or agreement is in a foreign language, the party must also produce a translation of it certified by an official or sworn translator or by a diplomatic or consular agent.

103. Refusal of recognition or enforcement

(1)   Recognition or enforcement of a New York Convention award shall not be refused except in the following cases.

(2)   Recognition or enforcement of the award may be refused if the person against whom it is invoked proves—

(a)   that a party to the arbitration agreement was (under the law applicable to him) under some incapacity;

(b)   that the arbitration agreement was not valid under the law to which the parties subjected it or, failing any indication thereon, under the law of the country where the award was made;

(c)   that he was not given proper notice of the appointment of the arbitrator or of the arbitration proceedings or was otherwise unable to present his case;

(d)   that the award deals with a difference not contemplated by or not falling within the terms of the submission to arbitration or contains decisions on matters beyond the scope of the submission to arbitration (but see subsection (4));

(e)   that the composition of the arbitral tribunal or the arbitral procedure was not in accordance with the agreement of the parties or, failing such agreement, with the law of the country in which the arbitration took place;

(f)   that the award has not yet become binding on the parties, or has been set aside or suspended by a competent authority of the country in which, or under the law of which, it was made.

(3)   Recognition or enforcement of the award may also be refused if the award is in respect of a matter which is not capable of settlement by arbitration, or if it would be contrary to public policy to recognise or enforce the award.

(4)   An award which contains decisions on matters not submitted to arbitration may be recognised or enforced to the extent that it contains decisions on matters submitted to arbitration which can be separated from those on matters not so submitted.

(5)   Where an application for the setting aside or suspension of the award has been made to such a competent authority as is mentioned in subsection (2)(f), the court before which the award is sought to be relied upon may, if it considers it proper, adjourn the decision on the recognition or enforcement of the award.

It may also on the application of the party claiming recognition or enforcement of the award order the other party to give suitable security.

104. Saving for other bases of recognition or enforcement

Nothing in the preceding provisions of this Part affects any right to rely upon or enforce a New York Convention award at common law or under section 66.

PART IV
GENERAL PROVISIONS

105. Meaning of 'the court': jurisdiction of High Court and county court

(1)   In this Act 'the court' means in England and Wales the High Court or the county court and in relation to Northern Ireland the High Court or a county court, subject to the following provisions.

(2)   The Lord Chancellor may by order make provision—
  (za)   allocating proceedings in England and Wales to the High Court or the county court;
  (a)   allocating proceedings under this Act to the High Court or to county courts; or
  (b)   specifying proceedings under this Act which may be commenced or taken only in the High Court or in the county court.

(3)   The Lord Chancellor may by order make provision requiring proceedings of any specified description under this Act in Northern Ireland in relation to which a county court has jurisdiction to be commenced or taken in one or more specified county courts.

Any jurisdiction so exercisable by a specified county court is exercisable through-out Northern Ireland.

(3A) The Lord Chancellor must consult the Lord Chief Justice of England and Wales or the Lord Chief Justice of Northern Ireland (as the case may be) before making an order under this section.

(3B) The Lord Chief Justice of England and Wales may nominate a judicial office holder (as defined in section 109(4) of the Constitutional Reform Act 2005) to exercise his functions under this section.

(3C) The Lord Chief Justice of Northern Ireland may nominate any of the following to exercise his functions under this section—
  (a)   the holder of one of the offices listed in Schedule 1 to the Justice (Northern Ireland) Act 2002;
  (b)   a Lord Justice of Appeal (as defined in section 88 of that Act).

(4)   An order under this section—
  (a)   may differentiate between categories of proceedings by reference to such criteria as the Lord Chancellor sees fit to specify, and
  (b)   may make such incidental or transitional provision as the Lord Chancellor considers necessary or expedient.

(5)   An order under this section for England and Wales shall be made by statutory instrument which shall be subject to annulment in pursuance of a resolution of either House of Parliament.

(6)   An order under this section for Northern Ireland shall be a statutory rule for the purposes of the Statutory Rules (Northern Ireland) Order 1979 which shall be subject to negative resolution (within the meaning of section 41(6) of the Interpretation Act (Northern Ireland) 1954).

106. Crown application

(1)   Part I of this Act applies to any arbitration agreement to which Her Majesty, either in right of the Crown or of the Duchy of Lancaster or otherwise, or the Duke of Cornwall, is a party.

(2) Where Her Majesty is party to an arbitration agreement otherwise than in right of the Crown, Her Majesty shall be represented for the purposes of any arbitral proceedings—

(a) where the agreement was entered into by Her Majesty in right of the Duchy of Lancaster, by the Chancellor of the Duchy or such person as he may appoint, and

(b) in any other case, by such person as Her Majesty may appoint in writing under the Royal Sign Manual.

(3) Where the Duke of Cornwall is party to an arbitration agreement, he shall be represented for the purposes of any arbitral proceedings by such person as he may appoint.

(4) References in Part I to a party or the parties to the arbitration agreement or to arbitral proceedings shall be construed, where subsection (2) or (3) applies, as references to the person representing Her Majesty or the Duke of Cornwall.

108. Extent

(1) The provisions of this Act extend to England and Wales and, except as mentioned below, to Northern Ireland.

(2) The following provisions of Part II do not extend to Northern Ireland—

section 92 (exclusion of Part I in relation to small claims arbitration in the county court), and

section 93 and Schedule 2 (appointment of judges as arbitrators).

(3) Sections 89, 90 and 91 (consumer arbitration agreements) extend to Scotland and the provisions of Schedules 3 and 4 (consequential amendments and repeals) extend to Scotland so far as they relate to enactments which so extend, subject as follows.

(4) The repeal of the Arbitration Act 1975 extends only to England and Wales and Northern Ireland.

109. Commencement

(1) The provisions of this Act come into force on such day as the Secretary of State may appoint by order made by statutory instrument, and different days may be appointed for different purposes.

(2) An order under subsection (1) may contain such transitional provisions as appear to the Secretary of State to be appropriate.

110. Short title

This Act may be cited as the Arbitration Act 1996.

SCHEDULES

Section 4(1)   SCHEDULE 1

MANDATORY PROVISIONS OF PART I

sections 9 to 11 (stay of legal proceedings);
section 12 (power of court to extend agreed time limits);
section 13 (application of Limitation Acts);
section 24 (power of court to remove arbitrator);
section 26(1) (effect of death of arbitrator);
section 28 (liability of parties for fees and expenses of arbitrators);
section 29 (immunity of arbitrator);
section 31 (objection to substantive jurisdiction of tribunal);
section 32 (determination of preliminary point of jurisdiction);
section 33 (general duty of tribunal);
section 37(2) (items to be treated as expenses of arbitrators);
section 40 (general duty of parties);
section 43 (securing the attendance of witnesses);
section 56 (power to withhold award in case of non-payment);
section 60 (effectiveness of agreement for payment of costs in any event);
section 66 (enforcement of award);
sections 67 and 68 (challenging the award: substantive jurisdiction and serious irregularity), and

sections 70 and 71 (supplementary provisions; effect of order of court) so far as relating to those sections;

section 72 (saving for rights of person who takes no part in proceedings);

section 73 (loss of right to object);

section 74 (immunity of arbitral institutions, &c.);

section 75 (charge to secure payment of solicitors' costs).

Section 93(6)

SCHEDULE 2
MODIFICATIONS OF PART I IN RELATION TO JUDGE-ARBITRATORS

Introductory

1. In this Schedule 'judge-arbitrator' means an eligible High Court judge or official referee appointed as arbitrator or umpire under section 93.

General

2. (1) Subject to the following provisions of this Schedule, references in Part I to the court shall be construed in relation to a judge-arbitrator, or in relation to the appointment of a judge-arbitrator, as references to the Court of Appeal.

    (2) The references in sections 32(6), 45(6) and 69(8) to the Court of Appeal shall in such a case be construed as references to the Supreme Court.

Arbitrator's fees

3. (1) The power of the court in section 28(2) to order consideration and adjustment of the liability of a party for the fees of an arbitrator may be exercised by a judge-arbitrator.

    (2) Any such exercise of the power is subject to the powers of the Court of Appeal under sections 24(4) and 25(3)(b) (directions as to entitlement to fees or expenses in case of removal or resignation).

Exercise of court powers in support of arbitration

4. (1) Where the arbitral tribunal consists of or includes a judge-arbitrator the powers of the court under sections 42 to 44 (enforcement of peremptory orders, summoning witnesses, and other court powers) are exercisable by the High Court and also by the judge-arbitrator himself.

    (2) Anything done by a judge-arbitrator in the exercise of those powers shall be regarded as done by him in his capacity as judge of the High Court and have effect as if done by that court.

    Nothing in this sub-paragraph prejudices any power vested in him as arbitrator or umpire.

Extension of time for making award

5. (1) The power conferred by section 50 (extension of time for making award) is exercisable by the judge-arbitrator himself.

    (2) Any appeal from a decision of a judge-arbitrator under that section lies to the Court of Appeal with the leave of that court.

Withholding award in case of non-payment

6. (1) The provisions of paragraph 7 apply in place of the provisions of section 56 (power to withhold award in the case of non-payment) in relation to the withholding of an award for non-payment of the fees and expenses of a judge-arbitrator.

    (2) This does not affect the application of section 56 in relation to the delivery of such an award by an arbitral or other institution or person vested by the parties with powers in relation to the delivery of the award.

7. (1) A judge-arbitrator may refuse to deliver an award except upon payment of the fees and expenses mentioned in section 56(1).

    (2) The judge-arbitrator may, on an application by a party to the arbitral proceedings, order that if he pays into the High Court the fees and expenses demanded, or such

lesser amount as the judge-arbitrator may specify—

    (a)   the award shall be delivered,

    (b)   the amount of the fees and expenses properly payable shall be determined by such means and upon such terms as he may direct, and

    (c)   out of the money paid into court there shall be paid out such fees and expenses as may be found to be properly payable and the balance of the money (if any) shall be paid out to the applicant.

(3)   For this purpose the amount of fees and expenses properly payable is the amount the applicant is liable to pay under section 28 or any agreement relating to the payment of the arbitrator.

(4)   No application to the judge-arbitrator under this paragraph may be made where there is any available arbitral process for appeal or review of the amount of the fees or expenses demanded.

(5)   Any appeal from a decision of a judge-arbitrator under this paragraph lies to the Court of Appeal with the leave of that court.

(6)   Where a party to arbitral proceedings appeals under sub-paragraph (5), an arbitrator is entitled to appear and be heard.

Correction of award or additional award

8.   Subsections (4) to (6) of section 57 (correction of award or additional award: time limit for application or exercise of power) do not apply to a judge-arbitrator.

Costs

9.   Where the arbitral tribunal consists of or includes a judge-arbitrator the powers of the court under section 63(4) (determination of recoverable costs) shall be exercised by the High Court.

10.   (1)   The power of the court under section 64 to determine an arbitrator's reasonable fees and expenses may be exercised by a judge-arbitrator.

      (2)   Any such exercise of the power is subject to the powers of the Court of Appeal under sections 24(4) and 25(3)(b) (directions as to entitlement to fees or expenses in case of removal or resignation).

Enforcement of award

11.   The leave of the court required by section 66 (enforcement of award) may in the case of an award of a judge-arbitrator be given by the judge-arbitrator himself.

Solicitors' costs

12.   The powers of the court to make declarations and orders under the provisions applied by section 75 (power to charge property recovered in arbitral proceedings with the payment of solicitors' costs) may be exercised by the judge-arbitrator.

Powers of court in relation to service of documents

13.   (1)   The power of the court under section 77(2) (powers of court in relation to service of documents) is exercisable by the judge-arbitrator.

      (2)   Any appeal from a decision of a judge-arbitrator under that section lies to the Court of Appeal with the leave of that court.

Powers of court to extend time limits relating to arbitral proceedings

14.   (1)   The power conferred by section 79 (power of court to extend time limits relating to arbitral proceedings) is exercisable by the judge-arbitrator himself.

      (2)   Any appeal from a decision of a judge-arbitrator under that section lies to the Court of Appeal with the leave of that court.

LATE PAYMENT OF COMMERCIAL DEBTS (INTEREST) ACT 1998
(1998, c. 20)

PART I
STATUTORY INTEREST ON QUALIFYING DEBTS

1. Statutory interest

(1) It is an implied term in a contract to which this Act applies that any qualifying debt created by the contract carries simple interest subject to and in accordance with this Part.

(2) Interest carried under that implied term (in this Act referred to as 'statutory interest') shall be treated, for the purposes of any rule of law or enactment (other than this Act) relating to interest on debts, in the same way as interest carried under an express contract term.

(3) This Part has effect subject to Part II (which in certain circumstances permits contract terms to oust or vary the right to statutory interest that would otherwise be conferred by virtue of the term implied by subsection (1)).

2. Contracts to which Act applies

(1) This Act applies to a contract for the supply of goods or services where the purchaser and the supplier are each acting in the course of a business, other than an excepted contract.

(2) In this Act 'contract for the supply of goods or services' means—
    (a) a contract of sale of goods; or
    (b) a contract (other than a contract of sale of goods) by which a person does any, or any combination, of the things mentioned in subsection (3) for a consideration that is (or includes) a money consideration.

(3) Those things are—
    (a) transferring or agreeing to transfer to another the property in goods;
    (b) bailing or agreeing to bail goods to another by way of hire or, in Scotland, hiring or agreeing to hire goods to another; and
    (c) agreeing to carry out a service.

(4) For the avoidance of doubt a contract of service or apprenticeship is not a contract for the supply of goods or services.

(5) The following are excepted contracts—
    (a) a consumer credit agreement;
    (b) a contract intended to operate by way of mortgage, pledge, charge or other security; and
    ...

(6) In this section—
    'business' includes a profession and the activities of any government department or local or public authority;
    'consumer credit agreement' has the same meaning as in the Consumer Credit Act 1974;
    'contract of sale of goods' and 'goods' have the same meaning as in the Sale of Goods Act 1979;
    'government department' includes any part of the Scottish Administration;
    'property in goods' means the general property in them and not merely a special property.

3. Qualifying debts

(1) A debt created by virtue of an obligation under a contract to which this Act applies to pay the whole or any part of the contract price is a 'qualifying debt' for the purposes of this Act, unless (when created) the whole of the debt is prevented from carrying statutory interest by this section.

(2) A debt does not carry statutory interest if or to the extent that it consists of a sum to which a right to interest or to charge interest applies by virtue of any enactment (other than section 1 of this Act).

This subsection does not prevent a sum from carrying statutory interest by reason of the fact that a court, arbitrator or arbiter would, apart from this Act, have power to award interest on it.

(3)   A debt does not carry (and shall be treated as never having carried) statutory interest if or to the extent that a right to demand interest on it, which exists by virtue of any rule of law, is exercised.

4.   Period for which statutory interest runs

(1)   Statutory interest runs in relation to a qualifying debt in accordance with this section (unless section 5 applies).

(2)   Statutory interest starts to run on the day after the relevant day for the debt, at the rate prevailing under section 6 at the end of the relevant day.

(2A) The relevant day for a debt is—

(a)   where there is an agreed payment day, that day, unless a different day is given by subsection (2D), (2E) or (2G);

(b)   where there is not an agreed payment day, the last day of the relevant 30-day period.

(2B) An 'agreed payment day' is a date agreed between the supplier and purchaser for the payment of the debt (that is, the day on which the debt is to be created by the contract).

(2C) A date agreed for payment of a debt may be a fixed date or may depend on the happening of an event or the failure of an event to happen.

(2D) Where—

(a)   the purchaser is a public authority, and

(b)   the last day of the relevant 30-day period falls earlier than the agreed payment day,

the relevant day is the last day of the relevant 30-day period, unless subsection (2G) applies.

(2E) Where—

(a)   the purchaser is not a public authority, and

(b)   the last day of the relevant 60-day period falls earlier than the agreed payment day,

the relevant day is the last day of the relevant 60-day period, unless subsection (2G) applies.

(2F) But subsection (2E) does not apply (and so the relevant day is the agreed payment day, unless subsection (2G) applies) if the agreed payment day is not grossly unfair to the supplier (see subsection (7A)).

(2G) Where the debt relates to an obligation to make an advance payment, the relevant day is the day on which the debt is treated by section 11 as having been created (instead of the agreed payment day or the day given by subsection (2D) or (2E)).

(2H) 'The relevant 30-day period' is the period of 30 days beginning with the later or latest of—

(a)   the day on which the obligation of the supplier to which the debt relates is performed;

(b)   the day on which the purchaser has notice of the amount of the debt or (where that amount is unascertained) the sum which the supplier claims is the amount of the debt;

(c)   where subsection (5A) applies, the day determined under subsection (5B).

(2I)   'The relevant 60-day period' is the period of 60 days beginning with the later or latest of—

(a)   the day on which the obligation of the supplier to which the debt relates is performed;

(b)   the day on which the purchaser has notice of the amount of the debt or (where the amount is unascertained) the sum which the supplier claims is the amount of the debt;

(c)   where subsection (5A) applies, the day determined under subsection (5B).

(3)   ...

(4)   ...

(5)   ...

(5A) This subsection applies where—
    (a)   there is a procedure of acceptance or verification (whether provided for by an enactment or by contract), under which the conforming of goods or services with the contract is to be ascertained, and
    (b)   the purchaser has notice of the amount of the debt on or before the day on which the procedure is completed.

(5B) For the purposes of subsections (2H)(c) and (2I)(c), the day in question is the day which is 30 days after the day on which the procedure is completed.

(5C) Where, in a case where subsection (5A) applies, the procedure in question is completed after the end of the period of 30 days beginning with the day on which the obligation of the supplier to which the debt relates is performed, the procedure is to be treated for the purposes of subsection (5B) as being completed immediately after the end of that period.

(5D) Subsection (5C) does not apply if—
    (a)   the supplier and the purchaser expressly agree in the contract a period for completing the procedure in question that is longer than the period mentioned in that subsection, and
    (b)   that longer period is not grossly unfair to the supplier (see subsection (7A)).

(6)   Where the debt is created by virtue of an obligation to pay a sum due in respect of a period of hire of goods, subsections (2H)(a) and (2I)(a) have effect as if they referred to the last day of that period.

(7)   Statutory interest ceases to run when the interest would cease to run if it were carried under an express contract term.

(7A) In determining for the purposes of subsection (2F) or (5D) whether something is grossly unfair, all circumstances of the case shall be considered; and, for that purpose, the circumstances of the case include in particular—
    (a)   anything that is a gross deviation from good commercial practice and contrary to good faith and fair dealing,
    (b)   the nature of the goods or services in question,
    (c)   whether the purchaser has any objective reason to deviate from the result which is provided for by subsection (2E) or (5C).

(8)   In this section—
'advance payment' has the same meaning as in section 11;
'enactment' included an enactment contained in subordinate legislation (within the meaning of the Interpretation Act 1978);
'public authority' means a contracting authority (within the meaning of regulation 2(1) of the Public Contracts Regulations 2015).

5.   Remission of statutory interest

(1)   This section applies where, by reason of any conduct of the supplier, the interests of justice require that statutory interest should be remitted in whole or part in respect of a period for which it would otherwise run in relation to a qualifying debt.

(2)   If the interests of justice require that the supplier should receive no statutory interest for a period, statutory interest shall not run for that period.

(3)   If the interests of justice require that the supplier should receive statutory interest at a reduced rate for a period, statutory interest shall run at such rate as meets the justice of the case for that period.

(4)   Remission of statutory interest under this section may be required—
    (a)   by reason of conduct at any time (whether before or after the time at which the debt is created); and
    (b)   for the whole period for which statutory interest would otherwise run or for one or more parts of that period.

(5)   In this section 'conduct' includes any act or omission.

5A.   Compensation arising out of late payment

(1)   Once statutory interest begins to run in relation to a qualifying debt, the supplier shall be entitled to a fixed sum (in addition to the statutory interest on the debt).

(2)   That sum shall be—
    (a)   for a debt less than £1,000, the sum of £40;
    (b)   for a debt of £1,000 or more, but less than £10,000, the sum of £70;

    (c)   for a debt of £10,000 or more, the sum of £100.

(2A) If the reasonable costs of the supplier in recovering the debt are not met by the fixed sum, the supplier shall also be entitled to a sum equivalent to the difference between the fixed sum and those costs.

(3)   The obligation to pay a sum under this section in respect of a qualifying debt shall be treated as part of the term implied by section 1(1) in the contract creating the debt.

(4)   Section 3(2)(b) of the Unfair Contract Terms Act 1977 (no reliance to be placed on certain contract terms) shall apply in cases where a contract term is not contained in written standard terms of the purchaser as well as in cases where the term is contained in such standard terms.

(5)   In this section 'contract term' means a term of the contract relating to a sum due to the supplier under this section.

6.   Rate of statutory interest

(1)   The Secretary of State shall by order made with the consent of the Treasury set the rate of statutory interest by prescribing—

    (a)   a formula for calculating the rate of statutory interest; or

    (b)   the rate of statutory interest.

(2)   Before making such an order the Secretary of State shall, among other things, consider the extent to which it may be desirable to set the rate so as to—

    (a)   protect suppliers whose financial position makes them particularly vulnerable if their qualifying debts are paid late; and

    (b)   deter generally the late payment of qualifying debts.

PART II

CONTRACT TERMS RELATING TO LATE PAYMENT OFQUALIFYING DEBTS

7.   Purpose of Part II

(1)   This Part deals with the extent to which the parties to a contract to which this Act applies may by reference to contract terms oust or vary the right to statutory interest that would otherwise apply when a qualifying debt created by the contract (in this Part referred to as 'the debt') is not paid.

(2)   This Part applies to contract terms agreed before the debt is created; after that time the parties are free to agree terms dealing with the debt.

(3)   This Part has effect without prejudice to any other ground which may affect the validity of a contract term.

8.   Circumstances where statutory interest may be ousted or varied

(1)   Any contract terms are void to the extent that they purport to exclude the right to statutory interest in relation to the debt, unless there is a substantial contractual remedy for late payment of the debt.

(2)   Where the parties agree a contractual remedy for late payment of the debt that is a substantial remedy, statutory interest is not carried by the debt (unless they agree otherwise).

(3)   The parties may not agree to vary the right to statutory interest in relation to the debt unless either the right to statutory interest as varied or the overall remedy for late payment of the debt is a substantial remedy.

(4)   Any contract terms are void to the extent that they purport to—

    (a)   confer a contractual right to interest that is not a substantial remedy for late payment of the debt, or

    (b)   vary the right to statutory interest so as to provide for a right to statutory interest that is not a substantial remedy for late payment of the debt,

unless the overall remedy for late payment of the debt is a substantial remedy.

(5)   Subject to this section, the parties are free to agree contract terms which deal with the consequences of late payment of the debt.

9.   Meaning of 'substantial remedy'

(1)   A remedy for the late payment of the debt shall be regarded as a substantial remedy unless—

(a)   the remedy is insufficient either for the purpose of compensating the supplier for late payment or for deterring late payment; and

(b)   it would not be fair or reasonable to allow the remedy to be relied on to oust or (as the case may be) to vary the right to statutory interest that would otherwise apply in relation to the debt.

(2)   In determining whether a remedy is not a substantial remedy, regard shall be had to all the relevant circumstances at the time the terms in question are agreed.

(3)   In determining whether subsection (1)(b) applies, regard shall be had (without prejudice to the generality of subsection (2)) to the following matters—

(a)   the benefits of commercial certainty;

(b)   the strength of the bargaining positions of the parties relative to each other;

(c)   whether the term was imposed by one party to the detriment of the other (whether by the use of standard terms or otherwise); and

(d)   whether the supplier received an inducement to agree to the term.

10.   Interpretation of Part II

(1)   In this Part—

'contract term' means a term of the contract creating the debt or any other contract term binding the parties (or either of them);

'contractual remedy' means a contractual right to interest or any contractual remedy other than interest;

'contractual right to interest' includes a reference to a contractual right to charge interest;

'overall remedy', in relation to the late payment of the debt, means any combination of a contractual right to interest, a varied right to statutory interest or a contractual remedy other than interest;

'substantial remedy' shall be construed in accordance with section 9.

(2)   In this Part a reference (however worded) to contract terms which vary the right to statutory interest is a reference to terms altering in any way the effect of Part I in relation to the debt (for example by postponing the time at which interest starts to run or by imposing conditions on the right to interest).

(3)   In this Part a reference to late payment of the debt is a reference to late payment of the sum due when the debt is created (excluding any part of that sum which is prevented from carrying statutory interest by section 3).

PART III
GENERAL AND SUPPLEMENTARY

11.   Treatment of advance payments of the contract price

(1)   A qualifying debt created by virtue of an obligation to make an advance payment shall be treated for the purposes of this Act as if it was created on the day mentioned in subsection (3), (4) or (5) (as the case may be).

(2)   In this section 'advance payment' means a payment falling due before the obligation of the supplier to which the whole contract price relates ('the supplier's obligation') is performed, other than a payment of a part of the contract price that is due in respect of any part performance of that obligation and payable on or after the day on which that part performance is completed.

(3)   Where the advance payment is the whole contract price, the debt shall be treated as created on the day on which the supplier's obligation is performed.

(4)   Where the advance payment is a part of the contract price, but the sum is not due in respect of any part performance of the supplier's obligation, the debt shall be treated as created on the day on which the supplier's obligation is performed.

(5)   Where the advance payment is a part of the contract price due in respect of any part performance of the supplier's obligation, but is payable before that part performance is completed, the debt shall be treated as created on the day on which the relevant part performance is completed.

(6)   Where the debt is created by virtue of an obligation to pay a sum due in respect of a period of hire of goods, this section has effect as if—
  (a)   references to the day on which the supplier's obligation is performed were references to the last day of that period; and
  (b)   references to part performance of that obligation were references to part of that period.

(7)   For the purposes of this section an obligation to pay the whole outstanding balance of the contract price shall be regarded as an obligation to pay the whole contract price and not as an obligation to pay a part of the contract price.

13.   Assignments, etc.

(1)   The operation of this Act in relation to a qualifying debt is not affected by—
  (a)   any change in the identity of the parties to the contract creating the debt; or
  (b)   the passing of the right to be paid the debt, or the duty to pay it (in whole or in part) to a person other than the person who is the original creditor or the original debtor when the debt is created.

(2)   Any reference in this Act to the supplier or the purchaser is a reference to the person who is for the time being the supplier or the purchaser or, in relation to a time after the debt in question has been created, the person who is for the time being the creditor or the debtor, as the case may be.

(3)   Where the right to be paid part of a debt passes to a person other than the person who is the original creditor when the debt is created, any reference in this Act to a debt shall be construed as (or, if the context so requires, as including) a reference to part of a debt.

(4)   A reference in this section to the identity of the parties to a contract changing, or to a right or duty passing, is a reference to it changing or passing by assignment or assignation, by operation of law or otherwise.

14.   Contract terms relating to the date for payment of the contract price

(1)   This section applies to any contract term which purports to have the effect of postponing the time at which a qualifying debt would otherwise be created by a contract to which this Act applies.

(2)   Sections 3(2)(b) and 17(1)(b) of the Unfair Contract Terms Act 1977 (no reliance to be placed on certain contract terms) shall apply in cases where such a contract term is not contained in written standard terms of the purchaser as well as in cases where the term is contained in such standard terms.

(3)   In this section 'contract term' has the same meaning as in section 10(1).

15.   Orders and regulations

(1)   Any power to make an order or regulations under this Act is exercisable by statutory instrument.

(2)   Any statutory instrument containing an order or regulations under this Act, other than an order under section 17(2), shall be subject to annulment in pursuance of a resolution of either House of Parliament.

16.   Interpretation

(1)   In this Act—
'contract for the supply of goods or services' has the meaning given in section 2(2); 'contract price' means the price in a contract of sale of goods or the money consideration referred to in section 2(2)(b) in any other contract for the supply of goods or services;
'purchaser' means (subject to section 13(2)) the buyer in a contract of sale or the person who contracts with the supplier in any other contract for the supply of goods or services;
'qualifying debt' means a debt falling within section 3(1);
'statutory interest' means interest carried by virtue of the term implied by sections 1(1); and 'supplier' means (subject to section 13(2)) the seller in a contract of sale of goods or the person who does one or more of the things mentioned in section 2(3) in any other contract for the supply of goods or services.

(2) In this Act any reference (however worded) to an agreement or to contract terms includes a reference to both express and implied terms (including terms established by a course of dealing or by such usage as binds the parties).

17. Short title, commencement and extent

(1) ...

(2) This Act (apart from this section) shall come into force on such day as the Secretary of State may by order appoint; and different days may be appointed for different descriptions of contract or for other different purposes.

An order under this subsection may specify a description of contract by reference to any feature of the contract (including the parties).

(3) The Secretary of State may by regulations make such transitional, supplemental or incidental provision (including provision modifying any provision of this Act) as the Secretary of State may consider necessary or expedient in connection with the operation of this Act while it is not fully in force.

(4) ...

(5) This Act extends to Northern Ireland.

FINANCIAL SERVICES AND MARKETS ACT 2000
(2000, c. 8)

PART XVI
THE OMBUDSMAN SCHEME

The scheme

225. The scheme and the scheme operator

(1) This Part provides for a scheme under which certain disputes may be resolved quickly and with minimum formality by an independent person.

(2) The scheme is to be administered by a body corporate ('the scheme operator').

(3) The scheme is to be operated under a name chosen by the scheme operator but is referred to in this Act as 'the ombudsman scheme'.

(4) Schedule 17 makes provision in connection with the ombudsman scheme and the scheme operator.

226. Compulsory jurisdiction

(1) A complaint which relates to an act or omission of a person ('the respondent') in carrying on an activity to which compulsory jurisdiction rules apply is to be dealt with under the ombudsman scheme if the conditions mentioned in subsection (2) are satisfied.

(2) The conditions are that—

(a) the complainant is eligible and wishes to have the complaint dealt with under the scheme;

(b) the respondent was an authorised person, or an electronic money issuer within the meaning of the Electronic Money Regulations 2011 or a payment service provider within the meaning of the Payment Services Regulations 2017, at the time of the act or omission to which the complaint relates; and

(c) the act or omission to which the complaint relates occurred at a time when compulsory jurisdiction rules were in force in relation to the activity in question.

(3) 'Compulsory jurisdiction rules' means rules—

(a) made by the FCA for the purposes of this section; and

(b) specifying the activities to which they apply.

(4) Only activities which are regulated activities, or which could be made regulated activities by an order under section 22, may be specified.

(5) Activities may be specified by reference to specified categories (however described).

(5A) If the FCA specifies activities which are account information services provided by authorised payment institutions or EEA authorised payment institutions, the FCA must specify to the same extent account information services provided by the registered account information service providers, or as the case may be, EEA registered account information providers.

(5B) Expressions used in subsection (5A) and in the Payment Services Regulations 2017 have the same meaning in that subsection as they do in those Regulations.

(6) A complainant is eligible, in relation to the compulsory jurisdiction of the ombudsman scheme, if he falls within a class of person specified in the rules as eligible.

(7) The rules—
    (a)   may include provision for persons other than individuals to be eligible; but
    (b)   may not provide for authorised persons to be eligible except in specified circumstances or in relation to complaints of a specified kind.

(7A) The rules must provide that a person within subsection (7B) is eligible in relation to a complaint to which subsection (7C) applies.

(7B) A person is within this subsection if he or she has been identified by a respondent, in carrying on an activity to which the rules apply, as—
    (a)   a politically exposed person;
    (b)   a family member of a politically exposed person; or
    (c)   a known or close associate of a politically exposed person.

(7C) This subsection applies to a complaint—
    (a)   that the complainant has been incorrectly identified as a person within subsection (7B); or
    (b)   relating to an act or omission of the respondent in consequence of the identification of the complainant as a person within subsection (7B).

(7D) In subsection (7B), "politically exposed person", "family member" and "known close associate" have the meanings given in regulation 35(12) of the Money Laundering, Terrorist Financing and Transfer of Funds (Information on the Payer) Regulations 2017.

(8) The jurisdiction of the scheme which results from this section is referred to in this Act as the 'compulsory jurisdiction'.

227. Voluntary jurisdiction

(1) A complaint which relates to an act or omission of a person ('the respondent') in carrying on an activity to which voluntary jurisdiction rules apply is to be dealt with under the ombudsman scheme if the conditions mentioned in subsection (2) are satisfied.

(2) The conditions are that—
    (a)   the complainant is eligible and wishes to have the complaint dealt with under the scheme;
    (b)   at the time of the act or omission to which the complaint relates, the respondent was participating in the scheme;
    (c)   at the time when the complaint is referred under the scheme, the respondent has not withdrawn from the scheme in accordance with its provisions;
    (d)   the act or omission to which the complaint relates occurred at a time when voluntary jurisdiction rules were in force in relation to the activity in question; and
    (e)   the complaint cannot be dealt with under the compulsory jurisdiction.

(3) 'Voluntary jurisdiction rules' means rules—
    (a)   made by the scheme operator for the purposes of this section; and
    (b)   specifying the activities to which they apply.

(4) The only activities which may be specified in the rules are activities which are, or could be, specified in compulsory jurisdiction rules.

(5) Activities may be specified by reference to specified categories (however described).

(6) The rules require the FCA's approval.

(7) A complainant is eligible, in relation to the voluntary jurisdiction of the ombudsman scheme, if he falls within a class of person specified in the rules as eligible.

(8) The rules may include provision for persons other than individuals to be eligible.

(9) A person qualifies for participation in the ombudsman scheme if he falls within a class of person specified in the rules in relation to the activity in question.

(10) Provision may be made in the rules for persons other than authorised persons to participate in the ombudsman scheme.

(11) The rules may make different provision in relation to complaints arising from different activities.

(12) The jurisdiction of the scheme which results from this section is referred to in this Act as the 'voluntary jurisdiction'.

(13) In such circumstances as may be specified in voluntary jurisdiction rules, a complaint—

    (a)   which relates to an act or omission occurring at a time before the rules came into force, and

    (b)   which could have been dealt with under a scheme which has to any extent been replaced by the voluntary jurisdiction, is to be dealt with under the ombudsman scheme even though paragraph (b) or (d) of subsection (2) would otherwise prevent that.

(14) In such circumstances as may be specified in voluntary jurisdiction rules, a complaint is to be dealt with under the ombudsman scheme even though—

    (a)   paragraph (b) or (d) of subsection (2) would otherwise prevent that, and

    (b)   the complaint is not brought within the scheme as a result of subsection (13), but only if the respondent has agreed that complaints of that kind were to be dealt with under the scheme.

Determination of complaints

228. Determination under the compulsory jurisdiction

(1) This section applies only in relation to the compulsory jurisdiction.

(2) A complaint is to be determined by reference to what is, in the opinion of the ombudsman, fair and reasonable in all the circumstances of the case.

(3) When the ombudsman has determined a complaint he must give a written statement of his determination to the respondent and to the complainant.

(4) The statement must—

    (a)   give the ombudsman's reasons for his determination;

    (b)   be signed by him; and

    (c)   require the complainant to notify him …, before a date specified in the statement, whether he accepts or rejects the determination.

(5) If the complainant notifies the ombudsman that he accepts the determination, it is binding on the respondent and the complainant and final.

(6) If, by the specified date, the complainant has not notified the ombudsman of his acceptance or rejection of the determination he is to be treated as having rejected it.

(6A) But the complainant is not to be treated as having rejected the determination by virtue of subsection (6) if—

    (a)   the complainant notifies the ombudsman after the specified date of the complainant's acceptance of the determination,

    (b)   the complainant has not previously notified the ombudsman of the complainant's rejection of the determination, and

    (c)   the ombudsman is satisfied that such conditions as may be prescribed by rules made by the scheme operator for the purposes of this section are satisfied.

(7) The ombudsman must notify the respondent of the outcome.

(7A) Where a determination is rejected by virtue of subsection (6), the notification under subsection (7) must contain a general description of the effect of subsection (6A).

(8) A copy of the determination on which appears a certificate signed by an ombudsman is evidence (or in Scotland sufficient evidence) that the determination was made under the scheme.

(9) Such a certificate purporting to be signed by an ombudsman is to be taken to have been duly signed unless the contrary is shown.

229. Awards

(1) This section applies only in relation to the compulsory jurisdiction.

(2) If a complaint which has been dealt with under the scheme is determined in favour of the complainant, the determination may include—

    (a)   an award against the respondent of such amount as the ombudsman considers fair compensation for loss or damage (of a kind falling within subsection (3)) suffered by the complainant ('a money award');

      (b)   a direction that the respondent take such steps in relation to the complainant as the ombudsman considers just and appropriate (whether or not a court could order those steps to be taken).

(3)   A money award may compensate for—
    (a)   financial loss; or
    (b)   any other loss, or any damage, of a specified kind.

(4)   The FCA may specify … the maximum amount which may be regarded as fair compensation for a particular kind of loss or damage specified under subsection (3)(b).

(5)   A money award may not exceed the monetary limit; but the ombudsman may, if he considers that fair compensation requires payment of a larger amount, recommend that the respondent pay the complainant the balance.

(6)   The monetary limit is such amount as may be specified.

(7)   Different amounts may be specified in relation to different kinds of complaint.

(8)   A money award—
    (a)   may provide for the amount payable under the award to bear interest at a rate and as from a date specified in the award; and
    (b)   is enforceable by the complainant in accordance with Part III of Schedule 17, or as the case may be, Part 3A of that Schedule.

(9)   Compliance with a direction under subsection (2)(b)—
    (a)   is enforceable by an injunction; or
    (b)   in Scotland, is enforceable by an order under section 45 of the Court of Session Act 1988.

(10)   Only the complainant may bring proceedings for an injunction or proceedings for an order.

(11)   'Specified' means specified in compulsory jurisdiction rules.

230. Costs

(1)   The scheme operator may by rules ('costs rules') provide for an ombudsman to have power, on determining a complaint under the compulsory jurisdiction, to award costs in accordance with the provisions of the rules.

(2)   Costs rules require the approval of the FCA.

(3)   Costs rules may not provide for the making of an award against the complainant in respect of the respondent's costs.

(4)   But they may provide for the making of an award against the complainant in favour of the scheme operator, for the purpose of providing a contribution to resources deployed in dealing with the complaint, if in the opinion of the ombudsman—
    (a)   the complainant's conduct was improper or unreasonable; or
    (b)   the complainant was responsible for an unreasonable delay.

(5)   Costs rules may authorise an ombudsman making an award in accordance with the rules to order that the amount payable under the award bears interest at a rate and as from a date specified in the order.

(6)   An amount due under an award made in favour of the scheme operator is recoverable as a debt due to the scheme operator.

(7)   Any other award made against the respondent is to be treated as a money award for the purposes of paragraph 16 of Schedule 17, or as the case may be, paragraph 16D of that Schedule.

230A. Reports of determinations

(1)   The scheme operator must publish a report of any determination made under this Part.

(2)   But if the ombudsman who makes the determination informs the scheme operator that, in the ombudsman's opinion, it is inappropriate to publish a report of that determination (or any part of it) the scheme operator must not publish a report of that determination (or that part).

(3)   Unless the complainant agrees, a report of a determination published by the scheme operator may not include the name of the complainant, or particulars which, in the opinion of the scheme operator, are likely to identify the complainant.

(4)   The scheme operator may charge a reasonable fee for providing a person with a copy of a report.

Information

231. Ombudsman's power to require information

(1) An ombudsman may, by notice in writing given to a party to a complaint, require that party—

    (a)   to provide specified information or information of a specified description; or

    (b)   to produce specified documents or documents of a specified description.

(2) The information or documents must be provided or produced—

    (a)   before the end of such reasonable period as may be specified; and

    (b)   in the case of information, in such manner or form as may be specified.

(3) This section applies only to information and documents the production of which the ombudsman considers necessary for the determination of the complaint.

(4) If a document is produced in response to a requirement imposed under this section, the ombudsman may—

    (a)   take copies or extracts from the document; or

    (b)   require the person producing the document to provide an explanation of the document.

(5) If a person who is required under this section to produce a document fails to do so, the ombudsman may require him to state, to the best of his knowledge and belief, where the document is.

(6) If a person claims a lien on a document, its production under this Part does not affect the lien.

(7) 'Specified' means specified in the notice given under subsection (1).

232. Powers of court where information required

(1) If a person ('the defaulter') fails to comply with a requirement imposed under section 231, the ombudsman may certify that fact in writing to the court and the court may enquire into the case.

(2) If the court is satisfied that the defaulter failed without reasonable excuse to comply with the requirement, it may deal with the defaulter (and, in the case of a body corporate, any director or other officer) as if he were in contempt; and officer in relation to a limited liability partnership means a member of the limited liability partnership.

(3) 'Court' means—

    (a)   the High Court;

    (b)   in Scotland, the Court of Session.

232A. Scheme operator's duty to provide information to FCA

If the scheme operator considers that it has information that, in its opinion, would or might be of assistance to the FCA in advancing one or more of the FCA's operational objectives, it must disclose that information to the FCA.

Funding

234. Industry funding

(1) For the purpose of funding—

    (a)   the establishment of the ombudsman scheme (whenever any relevant expense is incurred), and

    (b)   its operation in relation to the compulsory jurisdiction,

the FCA may make rules requiring the payment to it or to the scheme operator, by authorised persons or any class of authorised person, any electronic money issuer within the meaning of the Electronic Money Regulations 2011 or any payment service provider within the meaning of the Payment Services Regulations 2017 of specified amounts (or amounts calculated in a specified way).

(2) 'Specified' means specified in the rules.

Successors to businesses

234B. Transfers of liability

(1)   This section applies where a person (the 'successor') has assumed a liability (including a contingent one) of a person (the 'predecessor') who was, or (apart from this section) would have been, the respondent in respect of a complaint falling to be dealt with under the ombudsman scheme.

(2)   The complaint may (but need not) be dealt with under this Part as if the successor were the respondent.

ENTERPRISE ACT 2002
(2002, c. 40)

PART 1

General functions of CMA

5.   Acquisition of information etc

(1)   The CMA has the function of obtaining, compiling and keeping under review information about matters relating to the carrying out of its functions.

(2)   That function is to be carried out with a view to (among other things) ensuring that the CMA has sufficient information to take informed decisions and to carry out its other functions effectively.

(3)   In carrying out that function the CMA may carry out, commission or support (financially or otherwise) research.

6.   Provision of information etc. to the public

(1)   The CMA has the function of—

(a)   making the public aware of the ways in which competition may benefit consumers in, and the economy of, the United Kingdom; and

(b)   giving information or advice in respect of matters relating to any of its functions to the public.

(2)   In carrying out those functions the CMA may—

(a)   publish educational materials or carry out other educational activities; or

(b)   support (financially or otherwise) the carrying out by others of such activities or the provision by others of information or advice.

7.   Provision of information and advice to Ministers etc.

(1)   The CMA has the function of—

(a)   making proposals, or

(b)   giving other information or advice,

on matters relating to any of its functions to any Minister of the Crown or other public authority (including proposals, information or advice as to any aspect of the law or a proposed change in the law).

(1A) The CMA may, in particular, carry out the function under subsection (1)(a) by making a proposal in the form of a recommendation to a Minister of the Crown about the potential effect of a proposal for Westminster legislation on competition within any market or markets in the United Kingdom for goods or services.

(1B) The CMA must publish such a recommendation in such manner as the CMA considers appropriate for bringing the subject matter of the recommendation to the attention of those likely to be affected by it.

(2)   A Minister of the Crown may request the CMA to make proposals or give other information or advice on any matter relating to any of its functions; and the CMA shall, so far as is reasonably practicable and consistent with its other functions, comply with the request.

(3) In this section—
'market in the United Kingdom' includes—
(a) so far as it operates in the United Kingdom or a part of the United Kingdom, any market which operates there and in another country or territory or in part of another country or territory; and
(b) any market which operates only in a part of the United Kingdom;
and the reference to a market for goods or services includes a reference to a market for goods or services; and
'Westminster legislation' means—
(a) an Act of Parliament, or
(b) subordinate legislation (within the meaning given by section 21 of the Interpretation Act 1978).

8A. Exclusion of public consumer advice scheme

The CMA may not under this Part support a public consumer advice scheme, where the support of that scheme consists of providing, or securing the provision of, an arrangement for giving advice without charge to individual consumers on matters personal to them.

11. Super-complaints to CMA

(1) This section applies where a designated consumer body makes a complaint to the CMA that any feature, or combination of features, of a market in the United Kingdom for goods or services is or appears to be significantly harming the interests of consumers.
(2) The CMA must, within 90 days after the day on which it receives the complaint, publish a response stating how it proposes to deal with the complaint, and in particular—
(a) whether it has decided to take any action, or to take no action, in response to the complaint, and
(b) if it has decided to take action, what action it proposes to take.
(3) The response must state the CMA's reasons for its proposals.
(4) The Secretary of State may by order amend subsection (2) by substituting any period for the period for the time being specified there.
(5) 'Designated consumer body' means a body designated by the Secretary of State by order.
(6) The Secretary of State—
(a) may designate a body only if it appears to him to represent the interests of consumers of any description, and
(b) must publish (and may from time to time vary) other criteria to be applied by him in determining whether to make or revoke a designation.
(7) The CMA—
(a) must issue guidance as to the presentation by the complainant of a reasoned case for the complaint, and
(b) may issue such other guidance as appears to it to be appropriate for the purposes of this section.
(8) An order under this section—
(a) shall be made by statutory instrument, and
(b) shall be subject to annulment in pursuance of a resolution of either House of Parliament.
(9) In this section—
(a) references to a feature of a market in the United Kingdom for goods or services have the same meaning as if contained in Part 4, and
(b) 'consumer' means an individual who is a consumer within the meaning of that Part.

PART 8
ENFORCEMENT OF CERTAIN CONSUMER LEGISLATION

Introduction

210. Consumers

(1) In this Part references to consumers must be construed in accordance with this section.

(2) In relation to a domestic infringement a consumer is an individual in respect of whom the first and second conditions are satisfied.

(3) The first condition is that—

  (a) goods are or are sought to be supplied to the individual (whether by way of sale or otherwise) in the course of a business carried on by the person supplying or seeking to supply them, or

  (b) services are or are sought to be supplied to the individual in the course of a business carried on by the person supplying or seeking to supply them.

(4) The second condition is that—

  (a) the individual receives or seeks to receive the goods or services otherwise than in the course of a business carried on by him, or

  (b) the individual receives or seeks to receive the goods or services with a view to carrying on a business but not in the course of a business carried on by him.

(6) In relation to a Schedule 13 infringement a consumer is a person who is a consumer for the purposes of the listed enactment concerned.

(6A) An enactment is a listed enactment if it is specified in Schedule 13 or to the extent that it is so specified.

(6B) References to an enactment include—

  (a) references to subordinate legislation (within the meaning of the Interpretation Act 1978);

  (b) for the purposes of paragraph 6 of Schedule 13, references to the rule of law in Scotland;

  (c) for the purposes of paragraph 16 of Schedule 13, references to rules forming part of the law of any part of the United Kingdom made other than under an Act.

(7) ....

(8) A business includes—

  (a) a professional practice;

  (b) any other undertaking carried on for gain or reward;

  (c) any undertaking in the course of which goods or services are supplied otherwise than free of charge.

(9) The Secretary of State may by order modify Schedule 13.

(10) An order under this section must be made by statutory instrument subject to annulment in pursuance of a resolution of either House of Parliament.

211. Domestic infringements

(1) In this Part a domestic infringement is an act or omission which—

  (a) is done or made by a person in the course of a business,

  (b) falls within subsection (2), and

  (c) harms the collective interests of consumers...

(1A) But an act or omission which satisfies the condition in subsection (1) is a domestic infringement only if at least one of the following is satisfied—

  (a) the person supplying (or seeking to supply) goods or services has a place of business in the United Kingdom, or

  (b) the goods or services supplied (or sought to be supplied) to or for a person in the United Kingdom (see section 232).

(2) An act or omission falls within this subsection if it is of a description specified by the Secretary of State by order and consists of any of the following—

  (a) a contravention of an enactment which imposes a duty, prohibition or restriction enforceable by criminal proceedings;

  (b) an act done or omission made in breach of contract;

(c) an act done or omission made in breach of a non-contractual duty owed to a person by virtue of an enactment or rule of law and enforceable by civil proceedings;

(d) an act or omission in respect of which an enactment provides for a remedy or sanction enforceable by civil proceedings;

(e) an act done or omission made by a person supplying or seeking to supply goods or services as a result of which an agreement or security relating to the supply is void or unenforceable to any extent;

(f) an act or omission by which a person supplying or seeking to supply goods or services purports or attempts to exercise a right or remedy relating to the supply in circumstances where the exercise of the right or remedy is restricted or excluded under or by virtue of an enactment;

(g) an act or omission by which a person supplying or seeking to supply goods or services purports or attempts to avoid (to any extent) liability relating to the supply in circumstances where such avoidance is restricted or prevented under an enactment.

(3) But an order under this section may provide that any description of act or omission falling within subsection (2) is not a domestic infringement.

(4) For the purposes of subsection (2) it is immaterial—

(a) whether or not any duty, prohibition or restriction exists in relation to consumers as such;

(b) whether or not any remedy or sanction is provided for the benefit of consumers as such;

(c) whether or not any proceedings have been brought in relation to the act or omission;

(d) whether or not any person has been convicted of an offence in respect of the contravention mentioned in subsection (2)(a);

(e) whether or not there is a waiver in respect of the breach of contract mentioned in subsection (2)(b).

(5) References to an enactment include references to subordinate legislation (within the meaning of the Interpretation Act 1978 (c. 30)).

(6) The power to make an order under this section must be exercised by statutory instrument.

(7) But no such order may be made unless a draft of it has been laid before Parliament and approved by a resolution of each House.

212. Schedule 13 infringements

(1) In this Part a Schedule 13 infringement is an act or omission which contravenes a listed enactment and which harms the collective interests of consumers.

(2) References to a listed enactment must be construed in accordance with section 210.

213. Enforcers

(1) Each of the following is a general enforcer—

(a) the CMA;

(b) every local weights and measures authority in Great Britain;

(c) the Department of Enterprise, Trade and Investment in Northern Ireland.

(2) A designated enforcer is any person or body (whether or not incorporated) which the Secretary of State—

(a) thinks has as one of its purposes the protection of the collective interests of consumers, and

(b) designates by order.

(3) The Secretary of State may designate a public body only if he is satisfied that it is independent.

(4) The Secretary of State may designate a person or body which is not a public body only if the person or body (as the case may be) satisfies such criteria as the Secretary of State specifies by order.

(a) which is not a general enforcer, a designated enforcer or a CPC enforcer.

(5) ...

(5A) Each of the following (being bodies or persons designated by the Secretary of State under Article 5(1) of the CPC Regulation) is a CPC enforcer—

(a)   the CMA;

(b)   the Civil Aviation Authority;

(c)   the Financial Conduct Authority;

(d)   the Secretary of State for Health;

(e)   the Department of Health, Social Services and Public Safety in Northern Ireland;

(f)   the Office of Communications;

(g)   the Department of Enterprise, Trade and Investment in Northern Ireland;

(h)   every local weights and measures authority in Great Britain;

(i)   an enforcement authority within the meaning of section 120(15) of the Communications Act 2003 (regulation of premium rate services);

(j)   the Information Commissioner;

(k)   the Department for Infrastructure;

(l)   the Maritime and Coastguard Agency;

(m)   the Office of Rail and Road;

(n)   the Office of the Traffic Commissioner.

(6)   An order under this section may make different provision for different purposes.

(7)   The designation of a body by virtue of subsection (3) is conclusive evidence for the purposes of any question arising under this Part that the body is a public body.

(8)   An order under this section must be made by statutory instrument subject to annulment in pursuance of a resolution of either House of Parliament.

(9)   If requested to do so by a designated enforcer which is designated in respect of one or more Community infringements the Secretary of State must notify the Commission of the European Union—

(a)   of its name and purpose;

(b)   of the Community infringements in respect of which it is designated.

Enforcement orders and interim enforcement orders

214. Consultation

(1)   An enforcer must not make an application for an enforcement order unless—

(a)   the enforcer has engaged in appropriate consultation with the person against whom the enforcement order would be made, and

(b)   if the enforcer is not the CMA, the enforcer has given notice to the CMA of the enforcer's intention to apply for the enforcement order, and the minimum period has elapsed.

(1A) The appropriate minimum period is—

(a)   in the case of an enforcement order, 14 days beginning with the day on which notice under subsection (1)(b) is given;

(b)   in the case of an interim enforcement order, seven days beginning with the day on which notice under subsection (1)(b) is given.

(2)   Appropriate consultation is consultation for the purpose of—

(a)   achieving the cessation of the infringement in a case where an infringement is occurring;

(b)   ensuring that there will be no repetition of the infringement in a case where the infringement has occurred;

(c)   ensuring that there will be no repetition of the infringement in a case where the cessation of the infringement is achieved under paragraph (a);

(d)   ensuring that the infringement does not take place in the case of a Schedule 13 infringement which the enforcer believes is likely to take place.

(3)   Subsection (1) does not apply if the CMA thinks that an application for an enforcement order should be made without delay.

(4)   Subsection (1)(a) ceases to apply—

(a)   for the purposes of an application for an enforcement order at the end of the period of 14 days or, where subsection (4A) applies, 28 days beginning with the day after the person against whom the enforcement order would be made receives a request for consultation from the enforcer;

(b) for the purposes of an application for an interim enforcement order at the end of the period of seven days beginning with the day after the person against whom the interim enforcement order would be made receives a request for consultation from the enforcer.

(4A) This subsection applies where the person against whom the enforcement order would be made is a member of, or is represented by, a representative body, and that body operates a consumer code which has been approved by—

(a) an enforcer, other than a designated enforcer which is not a public body,

(b) a body which represents an enforcer mentioned in paragraph (a), or

(c) a group of enforcers mentioned in paragraph (a), or

(d) a community interest company whose objects include the approval of consumer codes.

(4B) In subsection (4A)—

'consumer code' means a code of practice or other document (however described) intended, with a view to safeguarding or promoting the interests of consumers, to regulate by any means the conduct of persons engaged in the supply of goods or services to consumers (or the conduct of their employees or representatives), and 'representative body' means an organization established to represent the interests of two or more businesses in a particular sector or area, and for this purpose 'business' has the meaning it bears in section 210.

(5) The Secretary of State may by order make rules in relation to consultation under this section.

(6) Such an order must be made by statutory instrument subject to annulment in pursuance of a resolution of either House of Parliament.

(7) In this section (except subsections (1A) and (4)) and in sections 215 and 216 references to an enforcement order include references to an interim enforcement order.

215. Applications

(1) An application for an enforcement order must name the person the enforcer thinks—

(a) has engaged or is engaging in conduct which constitutes a domestic or a Schedule 13 infringement, or

(b) is likely to engage in conduct which constitutes a Schedule 13 infringement.

(2) A general enforcer may make an application for an enforcement order in respect of any infringement.

(3) A designated enforcer may make an application for an enforcement order in respect of an infringement to which his designation relates.

(4) ...

(4A) A Schedule 13 enforcer may make an application for an enforcement order in respect of a Schedule 13 infringement.

(5) The following courts have jurisdiction to make an enforcement order—

(za) The High Court or the County Court if the person against whom the order is sought carries on a business or has a place of business in England and Wales;

(a) the High Court or a county court if the person against whom the order is sought carries on business or has a place of business in Northern Ireland;

(b) the Court of Session or the sheriff if the person against whom the order is sought carries on business or has a place of business in Scotland.

(6) ...

(7) ...

(8) ...

(9) An enforcer which is not the CMA must notify the CMA of the result of an application under this section.

216. Applications: directions by CMA

(1) This section applies if the CMA believes that an enforcer other than the CMA intends to apply for an enforcement order.

(2) In such a case the CMA may direct that if an application in respect of a particular infringement is to be made it must be made—

(a) only by the CMA, or

(b) only by such other enforcer as the CMA directs.

(3)   If the CMA directs that only it may make an application that does not prevent—
    (a)   the CMA or any enforcer from accepting an undertaking under section 219, or (b) the CMA from taking such other steps it thinks appropriate (apart from making an application) for the purpose of securing that the infringement is not committed, continued or repeated.

(4)   The CMA may vary or withdraw a direction given under this section.

(5)   The CMA must take such steps as it thinks appropriate to bring a direction (or a variation or withdrawal of a direction) to the attention of enforcers it thinks may be affected by it.

(6)   ...

217. Enforcement orders

(1)   This section applies if an application for an enforcement order is made under section 215 and the court finds that the person named in the application has engaged in conduct which constitutes the infringement.

(2)   This section also applies if such an application is made in relation to a Schedule 13 infringement and the court finds that the person named in the application is likely to engage in conduct which constitutes the infringement.

(3)   If this section applies the court may make an enforcement order against the person.

(4)   In considering whether to make an enforcement order the court must have regard to whether the person named in the application—
    (a)   has given an undertaking under section 219 in respect of conduct such as is mentioned in subsection (3) of that section;
    (b)   has failed to comply with the undertaking.

(5)   An enforcement order must—
    (a)   indicate the nature of the conduct to which the finding under subsection (1) or (2) relates, and
    (b)   direct the person to comply with subsection (6).

(6)   A person complies with this subsection if he—
    (a)   does not continue or repeat the conduct;
    (b)   does not engage in such conduct in the course of his business or another business;
    (c)   does not consent to or connive in the carrying out of such conduct by a body corporate with which he has a special relationship (within the meaning of section 222(3)).

(7)   But subsection (6)(a) does not apply in the case of a finding under subsection (2).

(8)   An enforcement order may require a person against whom the order is made to publish in such form and manner and to such extent as the court thinks appropriate for the purpose of eliminating any continuing effects of the infringement—
    (a)   the order;
    (b)   a corrective statement.

(9)   If the court makes a finding under subsection (1) or (2) it may accept an undertaking by the person—
    (a)   to comply with subsection (6), or
    (b)   to take steps which the court believes will secure that he complies with subsection (6).

(10)   An undertaking under subsection (9) may include a further undertaking by the person to publish in such form and manner and to such extent as the court thinks appropriate for the purpose of eliminating any continuing effects of the infringement—
    (a)   the terms of the undertaking;
    (b)   a corrective statement.

(10A) An enforcement order may require a person against whom the order is made to take enhanced consumer measures (defined in section 219A) within a period specified by the court.

(10B) An undertaking under subsection (9) may include a further undertaking by the person to take enhanced consumer measures within a period specified in the undertaking.

(10C) Subsections (10A) and (10B) are subject to section 219C in a case where the application for the enforcement order was made by a designated enforcer which is not a public body.

(10D)Where a person is required by an enforcement order or an undertaking under this section to take enhanced consumer measures, the order or undertaking may include requirements as to the provision of information or documents to the court by the person in order that the court may determine if the person is taking those measures.

(11) If the court—

    (a)   makes a finding under subsection (1) or (2), and

    (b)   accepts an undertaking under subsection (9),

it must not make an enforcement order in respect of the infringement to which the undertaking relates.

(12) An enforcement order made in a part of the United Kingdom by a court specified in relation to that part in the second or third column of the table has effect in another part of the United Kingdom as if made by a court specified in relation to that other part in the same column of the table—

England and Wales	The High Court	The county court
Scotland	The Court of Session	The sheriff
Northern Ireland	The High Court	A county court

218. Interim enforcement order

(1) The court may make an interim enforcement order against a person named in the application for the order if it appears to the court—

    (a)   that it is alleged that the person is engaged in conduct which constitutes a domestic or Schedule 13 infringement or is likely to engage in conduct which constitutes a Schedule 13 infringement,

    (b)   that if the application had been an application for an enforcement order it would be likely to be granted,

    (c)   that it is expedient that the conduct is prohibited or prevented (as the case may be) immediately, and

    (d)   if no notice of the application has been given to the person named in the application that it is appropriate to make an interim enforcement order without notice.

(2) An interim enforcement order must—

    (a)   indicate the nature of the alleged conduct, and

    (b)   direct the person to comply with subsection (3).

(3) A person complies with this subsection if he—

    (a)   does not continue or repeat the conduct;

    (b)   does not engage in such conduct in the course of his business or another business;

    (c)   does not consent to or connive in the carrying out of such conduct by a body corporate with which he has a special relationship (within the meaning of section 222(3)).

(4) But subsection (3)(a) does not apply in so far as the application is made in respect of an allegation that the person is likely to engage in conduct which constitutes a Schedule 13 infringement.

(5) An application for an interim enforcement order against a person may be made at any time before an application for an enforcement order against the person in respect of the same conduct is determined.

(6) An application for an interim enforcement order must refer to all matters—

    (a)   which are known to the applicant, and

    (b)   which are material to the question whether or not the application is granted.

(7) If an application for an interim enforcement order is made without notice the application must state why no notice has been given.

(8) The court may vary or discharge an interim enforcement order on the application of—

    (a)   the enforcer who applied for the order;

    (b)   the person against whom it is made.

(9) An interim enforcement order against a person is discharged on the determination of an application for an enforcement order made against the person in respect of the same conduct.

(10) If it appears to the court as mentioned in subsection (1)(a) to (c) the court may instead of making an interim enforcement order accept an undertaking from the person named in the application—

(a)   to comply with subsection (3), or

(b)   to take steps which the court believes will secure that he complies with subsection (3).

(11) An interim enforcement order made in a part of the United Kingdom by a court specified in relation to that part in the second or third column of the table has effect in another part of the United Kingdom as if made by a court specified in relation to that other part in the same column of the table—

England and Wales	The High Court	The county court
Scotland	The Court of Session	The sheriff
Northern Ireland	The High Court	A county court

Online interface orders and interim enforcement orders

218ZA Applications

(1)   The CMA may apply for an online interface order or an interim online interface order if the CMA thinks that there has been or is likely to be a Schedule 13 infringement.

(2)   An online interface order or an interim online interface order may be sought against the person the CMA thinks has engaged, is engaging or is likely to engage in conduct which constitutes the Schedule 13 infringement or against another person.

(3)   The following courts have jurisdiction to make an online interface order or an interim online interface order—

(a)   the High Court or the county court if the person against whom the order is sought carries on business or has a place of business in England and Wales;

(b)   the High Court or a county court if the person against whom the order is sought carries on business or has a place of business in Northern Ireland;

(c)   the Court of Session or the sheriff if the person against whom the order is sought carries on business or has a place of business in Scotland.

218ZB Online interface orders

(1)   The court may make an online interface order on an application under section 218ZA if it finds that—

(a)   there has been or is likely to be a Schedule 13 infringement,

(b)   there are no other available means of bringing about the cessation or prohibition of the infringement which, by themselves, would be wholly effective, and

(c)   it is necessary to make the order to avoid the risk of serious harm to the collective interests of consumers.

(2)   An online interface order must direct the person against whom it is made to do, or to co-operate with another person so that other person may do, one or more of the following—

(a)   remove content from or modify content on an online interface;

(b)   disable or restrict access to an online interface;

(c)   display a warning to consumers accessing an online interface;

(d)   delete a fully qualified domain name and take any steps necessary to facilitate the registration of that domain name by the CMA.

(3)   Where an online interface order is made, the CMA may publish in such form and manner as it thinks appropriate for the purpose of eliminating any continuing effects of the Schedule 13 infringement to which the order relates—

(a)   the online interface order, and

(b)   where known, the identity of the person who has engaged, is engaging or is likely to engage in conduct which constitutes the infringement.

(4)   An online interface order made in a part of the United Kingdom by a court specified in relation to that part in the second or third column of the table has effect in another part of the United Kingdom as if made by a court specified in relation to that other part in the same column of the table—

England and Wales	The High Court	The county court
Scotland	The Court of Session	The sheriff
Northern Ireland	The High Court	A county court

218ZC Interim online interface orders

(1) The court may make an interim online interface order on an application under section 218ZA if it appears to the court—
   (a) that it is alleged that there has been or is likely to be a Schedule 13 infringement,
   (b) that if the application had been an application for an online interface order it would be likely to be granted,
   (c) that it is expedient to bring about the cessation or prohibition of the Schedule 13 infringement immediately, and
   (d) if no notice of the application has been given to the person against whom the order is sought that it is appropriate to make an interim online interface order without notice.

(2) An interim online interface order must direct the person against whom it is made to do, or to co-operate with another person so that person may do, one or more of the following—
   (a) remove content from or modify content on an online interface;
   (b) disable or restrict access to an online interface;
   (c) display a warning to consumers accessing an online interface;
   (d) delete a fully qualified domain name and take any steps necessary to facilitate the registration of that domain name by the CMA.

(3) An application for an interim online interface order against a person may be made at any time before an application for an online interface order against the person in respect of the same infringement is determined.

(4) An application for an interim online interface order must refer to all matters—
   (a) which are known to the CMA, and
   (b) which are material to the question whether or not the application is granted.

(5) If an application for an interim online interface order is made without notice the application must state why no notice has been given.

(6) The court may vary or discharge an interim online interface order on the application of—
   (a) the CMA;
   (b) the person against whom it is made.

(7) An interim online interface order against a person is discharged on the determination of an application for an online interface order made against the person in respect of the same infringement.

(8) An interim online interface order made in a part of the United Kingdom by a court specified in relation to that part in the second or third column of the table has effect in another part of the United Kingdom as if made by a court specified in relation to that other part in the same column of the table—

England and Wales	The High Court	The county court
Scotland	The Court of Session	The sheriff
Northern Ireland	The High Court	A county court

218ZD Online interface orders: supplementary

(1) In sections 218ZA to 218ZC, 'online interface' means any software, including a website, part of a website or an application, that is operated by or on behalf of a trader, and which serves to give consumers access to the trader's goods and services.

(2) In subsection (1), 'trader' means a person acting for purposes relating to that person's trade, business, craft or profession, whether acting personally or through another person acting in the trader's name or on the trader's behalf.

(3) Nothing in sections 218ZA to 218ZC limits the operation of any provisions of this Part relating to—
   (a) enforcement orders,

      (b)   interim enforcement orders, or
      (c)   undertakings,
         in respect of Community infringements.

Enforcement procedure: supplementary

218A. Unfair commercial practices: substantiation of claims

(1)   This section applies where an application for an enforcement order, an interim enforcement order, an online interface order or an interim online interface order is made in respect of a Schedule 13 infringement involving a contravention of the Consumer Protection from Unfair Trading Regulations 2008.

(2)   For the purposes of considering the application the court may require the relevant person to provide evidence as to the accuracy of any factual claim made as part of a commercial practice of that person if, taking into account the legitimate interests of that person and any other party to the proceedings, it appears appropriate in the circumstances.

(2A) In subsection (2), 'the relevant person', in relation to an application, means—
     (a)   where the application is for an enforcement order or an interim enforcement order, the person named in the application under section 215(1);
     (b)   where the application is for an online interface order or an interim online interface order, the person alleged by the CMA to have engaged, be engaging or be likely to engage in conduct which constitutes the Community infringement, provided that person is either the person against whom the order is sought or otherwise a party to the proceedings.

(3)   If, having been required under subsection (2) to provide evidence as to the accuracy of a factual claim, a person—
     (a)   fails to provide such evidence, or
     (b)   provides evidence as to the accuracy of the factual claim that the court considers inadequate,
the court may consider that the factual claim is inaccurate.

(4)   In this section 'commercial practice' has the meaning given by regulation 2 of the Consumer Protection from Unfair Trading Regulations 2008.

219. Undertakings

(1)   This section applies if an enforcer has power to make an application for an enforcement order or an interim enforcement order under section 215 or for an online interface order or an interim online interface order under section 218ZA.

(2)   In such a case the enforcer may accept from a person to whom subsection (3) applies an undertaking that the person will comply with subsection (4).

(3)   This subsection applies to a person who the enforcer believes—
     (a)   has engaged in conduct which constitutes an infringement;
     (b)   is engaging in such conduct;
     (c)   is likely to engage in conduct which constitutes a Schedule 13 infringement.

(4)   A person complies with this subsection if he—
     (a)   does not continue or repeat the conduct;
     (b)   does not engage in such conduct in the course of his business or another business;
     (c)   does not consent to or connive in the carrying out of such conduct by a body corporate with which he has a special relationship (within the meaning of section 222(3)).

(5)   But subsection (4)(a) does not apply in the case of an undertaking given by a person in so far as subsection (3) applies to him by virtue of paragraph (c).

(5ZA)An undertaking under this section may include a further undertaking by a person—
     (a)   to take advanced consumer measures (defined in section 219C) within a period specified in the undertaking, and
     (b)   where such measures are included, to provide information or documents to the enforcer in order that the enforcer may determine if the person is taking those measures.

(5ZB) Subsection (5ZA) is subject to section 219C in a case where the enforcer is a designated enforcer which is not a public body.

(5A) A Schedule 13 enforcer who has accepted an undertaking under this section may—

   (a)   accept a further undertaking from the person concerned to publish the terms of the undertaking; or

   (b)   take steps itself to publish the undertaking.

(5B) In each case the undertaking shall be published in such form and manner and to such extent as the Schedule 13 enforcer thinks appropriate for the purpose of eliminating any continuing effects of the Schedule 13 infringement.

(6)   If an enforcer accepts an undertaking under this section it must notify the CMA—

   (a)   of the terms of the undertaking;

   (b)   of the identity of the person who gave it.

219A. Definition of enhanced consumer measures

(1)   In this Part, enhanced consumer measures are measures (not excluded by subsection (5)) falling within—

   (a)   the redress category described in subsection (2),

   (b)   the compliance category described in subsection (3), or

   (c)   the choice category described in subsection (4).

(2)   The measures in the redress category are—

   (a)   measures offering compensation or other redress to consumers—

      (i)   who have suffered loss as a result of the conduct which has given rise to the enforcement order or undertaking, or

      (ii)   where that conduct constitutes a Schedule 13 infringement, who have been affected by that conduct;

   (b)   where the conduct which has given rise to the enforcement order or undertaking relates to a contract, measures offering consumers falling within (a)(i) or (ii) the option to terminate (but not vary) that contract,

   (c)   where consumers falling within paragraph (a)(i) or (ii) cannot be identified, or cannot be identified without disproportionate cost to the subject of the enforcement order or undertaking, measures intended to be in the collective interests of consumers.

(3)   The measures in the compliance category are measures intended to prevent or reduce the risk of the occurrence or repetition of the conduct to which the enforcement order or undertaking relates (including measures with that purpose which may have the effect of improving compliance with consumer law more generally).

(4)   The measures in the choice category are measures intended to enable consumers to choose more effectively between persons supplying or seeking to supply goods or services.

(5)   The following are not enhanced consumer measures—

   (a)   a publication requirement included in an enforcement order as described in section 217(8),

   (b)   a publication requirement included in an undertaking accepted by the court as described in section 217(10), or

   (c)   a publication requirement included in an undertaking accepted by a Schedule 13 enforcer as described in section 219(5A)(a).

219B. Inclusion of enhanced consumer measures etc.

(1)   An enforcement order or undertaking may include only such enhanced consumer measures as the court or enforcer (as the case may be) considers to be just and reasonable.

(2)   For the purposes of subsection (1) the court or enforcer must in particular consider whether any proposed enhanced consumer measures are proportionate, taking into account—

   (a)   the likely benefit of the measures to consumers,

   (b)   the costs likely to be incurred by the subject of the enforcement order or undertaking, and

   (c)   the likely cost to consumers of obtaining the benefit of the measures.

(3)   The costs referred to in subsection (2)(b) are—
      (a)   the cost of the measures, and
      (b)   the reasonable administrative costs associated with taking the measures.
(4)   Where the conduct which has given rise to an enforcement order or undertaking constitutes a domestic infringement, the enforcement order or undertaking may include enhanced consumer measures in the redress category—
      (a)   only in a loss case, and
      (b)   only if the court or enforcer (as the case may be) is satisfied that the cost of such measures to the subject of the enforcement order or undertaking is unlikely to be more than the sum of the losses suffered by consumers as a result of the conduct which has given rise to the enforcement order or undertaking.
(4A) Where the conduct which has given rise to an enforcement order or undertaking constitutes a Community infringement, the enforcement order or undertaking may include enhanced consumer measures in the redress category for the benefit of consumers who have been affected by that conduct
(5)   The cost referred to in subsection (4)(b) does not include the administrative costs associated with taking the measures.
(6)   Subsection (7) applies if an enforcement order or undertaking includes enhanced consumer measures offering compensation and a settlement agreement is entered into in connection with the payment of compensation.
(7)   A waiver of a person's rights in the settlement agreement is not valid if it is a waiver of the right to bring civil proceedings in respect of conduct other than the conduct which has given rise to the enforcement order or undertaking.
(8)   The following definitions apply for the purposes of subsection (4)(a).
(9)   In the case of an enforcement order or undertaking under section 217, 'a loss case' means a case in which—
      (a)   subsection (1) of that section applies (a finding that a person has engaged in conduct which constitutes an infringement), and
      (b)   consumers have suffered loss as a result of that conduct.
(10) In the case of an undertaking under section 219, 'a loss case' means a case in which—
      (a)   subsection (3)(a) or (b) of that section applies (a belief that a person has engaged or is engaging in conduct which constitutes an infringement), and
      (b)   consumers have suffered loss as a result of that conduct.

219C. Availability of enhanced consumer measures to private enforcers

(1)   An enforcement order made on the application of a designated enforcer which is not a public body may require a person to take enhanced consumer measures only if the following conditions are satisfied.
(2)   An undertaking given under section 217(9) following an application for an enforcement order made by a designated enforcer which is not a public body, or an undertaking given to such an enforcer under section 219, may include a further undertaking by a person to take enhanced consumer measures only if the following conditions are satisfied.
(3)   The first condition is that the enforcer is specified for the purposes of this section by order made by the Secretary of State.
(4)   The second condition is that the enhanced consumer measures do not directly benefit the enforcer or an associated undertaking.
(5)   Enhanced consumer measures which directly benefit an enforcer or an associated undertaking include, in particular, measures which—
      (a)   require a person to pay money to the enforcer or associated undertaking,
      (b)   require a person to participate in a scheme which is designed to recommend persons supplying or seeking to supply goods or services to consumers and which is administered by the enforcer or associated undertaking, or
      (c)   would give the enforcer or associated undertaking a commercial advantage over any of its competitors.
(6)   The Secretary of State may make an order under subsection (3) specifying an enforcer only if the Secretary of State is satisfied that to do so is likely to—

(a)   improve the availability to consumers of redress for infringements to which the enforcer's designation relates,

(b)   improve the availability to consumers of information which enables them to choose more effectively between persons supplying or seeking to supply goods or services, or

(c)   improve compliance with consumer law.

(7)   The Secretary of State may make an order under subsection (3) specifying an enforcer only if the functions of the enforcer under this Part have been specified under section 24 of the Legislative and Regulatory Reform Act 2006 (functions to which principles under section 21 and code of practice under section 22 apply), to the extent that they are capable of being so specified.

(8)   The power to make an order under subsection (3)—

(a)   is exercisable by statutory instrument subject to annulment in pursuance of a resolution of either House of Parliament;

(b)   includes power to make incidental, supplementary, consequential, transitional, transitory or saving provision.

(9)   Subsection (10) applies if—

(a)   an enforcer exercises a function in relation to a person by virtue of subsection (1) or (2),

(b)   that function is a relevant function for the purposes of Part 2 (co-ordination of regulatory enforcement) of the Regulatory Enforcement and Sanctions Act 2008, and

(c)   a primary authority (within the meaning of that Part) has given advice or guidance under section 27(1) of that Act—

(i)   to that person in relation to that function, or

(ii)   to other local authorities (within the meaning of that Part) with that function as to how they should exercise it in relation to that person.

(10)   The enforcer must, in exercising the function in relation to that person, act consistently with that advice or guidance.

(11)   In this section 'associated undertaking', in relation to a designated enforcer, means—

(a)   a parent undertaking or subsidiary undertaking of the enforcer, or

(b)   a subsidiary undertaking of a parent undertaking of the enforcer,

and for this purpose 'parent undertaking' and 'subsidiary undertaking' have the meanings given by section 1162 of the Companies Act 2006.

220.   Further proceedings

(1)   This section applies if the court—

(a)   makes an enforcement order under section 217,

(b)   makes an interim enforcement order under section 218,

(c)   accepts an undertaking under either of those sections, or

(d)   makes an online interface order under section 218ZB or an interim online interface order under section 218ZC.

(1A)   This section does not apply in the case of a failure to comply with an order or undertaking which consists only of a failure to provide information or documents received by the order or undertaking as described in section 217(10D).

(2)   Any Schedule 13 enforcer has the same right to apply to the court in respect of a failure to comply with an order (apart from an online interface order or an interim online interface order) or undertaking as the enforcer who made the application for the order.

(3)   An application to the court in respect of a failure to comply with an undertaking may include an application for an enforcement order, an interim enforcement order, an online interface order or an interim online interface order.

(4)   If the court finds that an undertaking is not being complied with it may make an enforcement order, an interim enforcement order, an online interface order or an interim online interface order (instead of making any other order it has power to make).

(5)   In the case of an application for an enforcement order or for an interim enforcement order as mentioned in subsection (3) sections 214 and 216 must be ignored and sections 215, 217 or 218 (as the case may be) and 219A, 219B and 219C apply subject to the following modifications—

      (a)   section 215(1)(b) must be ignored;

      (b)   section 215(5) must be ignored and the application must be made to the court which accepted the undertaking;

      (c)   section 217(9), (10), (10B) and (11) must be ignored, and section 217(10C) and (10D) must be ignored to the extent that they relate to an undertaking under section 217(9);

      (d)   section 218(10) must be ignored.

      (e)   sections 219A, 219B and 219C must be ignored to the extent that they relate to an undertaking under section 217(9) or 219.

(5A) In the case of an application for an online interface order or an interim online interface order as mentioned in subsection (3), section 218ZA applies subject to the following modifications—

      (a)   in section 218ZA(1), the words 'or is likely to be' must be ignored;

      (b)   in section 218ZA(2), the reference to the person the CMA thinks has engaged, is engaging or is likely to engage in conduct which constitutes the Schedule 13 infringement is to be read as a reference to the person the CMA thinks has engaged or is engaging in such conduct;

      (c)   section 218ZA(3) must be ignored and the application must be made to the court which accepted the undertaking.

(6)   If an enforcer which is not the CMA makes an application in respect of the failure of a person to comply with an enforcement order, an interim enforcement order or an undertaking given under section 217 or 218 the enforcer must notify the CMA—

      (a)   of the application;

      (b)   of any order made by the court on the application.

221. ...

222. **Bodies corporate: accessories**

(1)   This section applies if the person whose conduct constitutes a domestic infringement or Schedule 13 infringement is a body corporate.

(2)   If the conduct takes place with the consent or connivance of a person (an accessory) who has a special relationship with the body corporate, the consent or connivance is also conduct which constitutes the infringement.

(3)   A person has a special relationship with a body corporate if he is—

      (a)   a controller of the body corporate, or

      (b)   a director, manager, secretary or other similar officer of the body corporate or a person purporting to act in such a capacity.

(4)   A person is a controller of a body corporate if—

      (a)   the directors of the body corporate or of another body corporate which is its controller are accustomed to act in accordance with the person's directions or instructions, or

      (b)   either alone or with an associate or associates he is entitled to exercise or control the exercise of one third or more of the voting power at any general meeting of the body corporate or of another body corporate which is its controller.

(5)   An enforcement order, an interim enforcement order, an online interface order or an interim online interface order may be made against an accessory in respect of an infringement whether or not such an order is made against the body corporate.

(6)   The court may accept an undertaking under section 217(9) or 218(10) from an accessory in respect of an infringement whether or not it accepts such an undertaking from the body corporate.

(7)   An enforcer may accept an undertaking under section 219 from an accessory in respect of an infringement whether or not it accepts such an undertaking from the body corporate.

(8)   Subsection (9) applies if—

      (a)   an enforcement order or an interim enforcement order is made as mentioned in subsection (5), or

      (b)   an undertaking is accepted as mentioned in subsection (6) or (7).

(9)   In such a case for subsection (6) of section 217, subsection (3) of section 218 or subsection (4) of section 219 (as the case may be) there is substituted the following subsection—

'( ) A person complies with this subsection if he—
- (a)   does not continue or repeat the conduct;
- (b)   does not in the course of any business carried on by him engage in conduct such as that which constitutes the infringement committed by the body corporate mentioned in section 222(1);
- (c)   does not consent to or connive in the carrying out of such conduct by another body corporate with which he has a special relationship (within the meaning of section 222(3)).'

(10) A person is an associate of an individual if—
- (a)   he is the spouse or civil partner of the individual;
- (b)   he is a relative of the individual;
- (c)   he is a relative of the individual's spouse or civil partner;
- (d)   he is the spouse or civil partner of a relative of the individual;
- (e)   he is the spouse or civil partner of a relative of the individual's spouse;
- (f)   he lives in the same household as the individual otherwise than merely because he or the individual is the other's employer, tenant, lodger or boarder;
- (g)   he is a relative of a person who is an associate of the individual by virtue of paragraph (f);
- (h)   he has at some time in the past fallen within any of paragraphs (a) to (g).

(11) A person is also an associate of—
- (a)   an individual with whom he is in partnership;
- (b)   an individual who is an associate of the individual mentioned in paragraph (a);
- (c)   a body corporate if he is a controller of it or he is an associate of a person who is a controller of the body corporate.

(12) A body corporate is an associate of another body corporate if—
- (a)   the same person is a controller of both;
- (b)   a person is a controller of one and persons who are his associates are controllers of the other;
- (c)   a person is a controller of one and he and persons who are his associates are controllers of the other;
- (d)   a group of two or more persons is a controller of each company and the groups consist of the same persons;
- (e)   a group of two or more persons is a controller of each company and the groups may be regarded as consisting of the same persons by treating (in one or more cases) a member of either group as replaced by a person of whom he is an associate.

(13) A relative is a brother, sister, uncle, aunt, nephew, niece, lineal ancestor or lineal descendant.

223. Bodies corporate: orders

(1)   This section applies if a court makes an enforcement order, an interim enforcement order, an online interface order or an interim online interface order against a body corporate and—
- (a)   at the time the order is made the body corporate is a member of a group of interconnected bodies corporate,
- (b)   at any time when the order is in force the body corporate becomes a member of a group of interconnected bodies corporate, or
- (c)   at any time when the order is in force a group of interconnected bodies corporate of which the body corporate is a member is increased by the addition of one or more further members.

(2)   The court may direct that the order is binding upon all of the members of the group as if each of them were the body corporate against which the order is made.

(3)   A group of interconnected bodies corporate is a group consisting of two or more bodies corporate all of whom are interconnected with each other.

(4)   Any two bodies corporate are interconnected—
- (a)   if one of them is a subsidiary of the other, or
- (b)   if both of them are subsidiaries of the same body corporate.

(5)   In this section 'subsidiary' has the meaning given by section 1159 of the Companies Act 2006.

223A. Investigatory powers

For the investigatory powers available for enforcers for the purposes of enforcers' functions under this Part, see Schedule 5 to the Consumer Rights Act 2015.

Miscellaneous

228. Evidence

(1) Proceedings under this Part are civil proceedings for the purposes of—

    (a) section 11 of the Civil Evidence Act 1968 (convictions admissible as evidence in civil proceedings);

    (b) section 10 of the Law Reform (Miscellaneous Provisions) (Scotland) Act 1968 (corresponding provision in Scotland);

    (c) section 7 of the Civil Evidence Act (Northern Ireland) 1971 (corresponding provision in Northern Ireland).

(2) In proceedings under this Part any finding by a court in civil proceedings that an act or omission mentioned in section 211(2)(b), (c) or (d) or 212(1) has occurred—

    (a) is admissible as evidence that the act or omission occurred;

    (b) unless the contrary is proved, is sufficient evidence that the act or omission occurred.

(3) But subsection (2) does not apply to any finding—

    (a) which has been reversed on appeal;

    (b) which has been varied on appeal so as to negative it.

229. Advice and information

(1) As soon as is reasonably practicable after the passing of this Act the CMA must prepare and publish advice and information with a view to—

    (a) explaining the provisions of this Part to persons who are likely to be affected by them, and

    (b) indicating how the CMA expects such provisions to operate.

(1A) As soon as is reasonably practicable after the commencement of Schedule 5 to the Consumer Rights Act 2015 (investigatory powers etc.) the CMA must prepare and publish advice and information with a view to—

    (a) explaining the provisions to that Schedule, so far as they relate to investigatory powers set out in paragraphs 13(2) and (3) and 19 of that Schedule, to persons who are likely to be affected by them, and

    (b) indicating how the CMA expects such provisions to operate.

(2) The CMA may at any time publish revised or new advice or information.

(3) Advice or information published in pursuance of subsection (1)(b) may include advice or information about the factors which the CMA may take into account in considering how to exercise the functions conferred on it by this Part.

(4) Advice or information published by the CMA under this section is to be published in such form and in such manner as it considers appropriate.

(5) In preparing advice or information under this section the CMA must consult such persons as it thinks are representative of persons affected by this Part.

(6) If any proposed advice or information relates to a matter in respect of which another enforcer may act the persons to be consulted must include that enforcer.

230. Notice to CMA of intended prosecution

(1) This section applies if a local weights and measures authority in England and Wales intends to start proceedings for an offence under an enactment or subordinate legislation specified by the Secretary of State by order for the purposes of this section.

(2) The authority must give the CMA—

    (a) notice of its intention to start the proceedings;

(3) The authority must not start the proceedings until whichever is the earlier of the following—

    (a) the end of the period of 14 days starting with the day on which the authority gives the notice;

    (b) the day on which it is notified by the CMA that the CMA has received the notice given under subsection (2).

(4) The authority must also notify the CMA of the outcome of the proceedings after they are finally determined.

(5) But such proceedings are not invalid by reason only of the failure of the authority to comply with this section.

(6) Subordinate legislation has the same meaning as in section 21(1) of the Interpretation Act 1978.

(7) An order under this section must be made by statutory instrument subject to annulment in pursuance of a resolution of either House of Parliament.

231. Notice of convictions and judgments to CMA

(1) This section applies if—

(a) a person is convicted of an offence by or before a court in the United Kingdom, or

(b) a judgment is given against a person by a court in civil proceedings in the United Kingdom.

(2) The court may make arrangements to bring the conviction or judgment to the attention of the CMA if it appears to the court—

(a) having regard to the functions of the CMA under this Part that it is expedient for the conviction or judgment to be brought to the attention of the CMA, and

(b) without such arrangements the conviction or judgment may not be brought to the attention of the CMA.

(3) For the purposes of subsection (2) it is immaterial that the proceedings have been finally disposed of by the court.

(4) Judgment includes an order or decree and references to the giving of the judgment must be construed accordingly.

Interpretation

232. Goods and services

(1) References in this Part to goods and services must be construed in accordance with this section.

(2) Goods include—

(a) buildings and other structures;

(b) ships, aircraft and hovercraft.

(3) The supply of goods includes—

(a) supply by way of sale, lease, hire or hire purchase;

(b) in relation to buildings and other structures, construction of them by one person for another.

(4) Goods or services which are supplied wholly or partly outside the United Kingdom must be taken to be supplied to or for a person in the United Kingdom if they are supplied in accordance with arrangements falling within subsection (5).

(5) Arrangements fall within this subsection if they are made by any means and—

(a) at the time the arrangements are made the person seeking the supply is in the United Kingdom, or

(b) at the time the goods or services are supplied (or ought to be supplied in accordance with the arrangements) the person responsible under the arrangements for effecting the supply is in or has a place of business in the United Kingdom.

233. Person supplying goods

(1) This section has effect for the purpose of references in this Part to a person supplying or seeking to supply goods under—

(a) a hire-purchase agreement;

(b) a credit-sale agreement;

(c) a conditional sale agreement.

(2) The references include references to a person who conducts any antecedent negotiations relating to the agreement.

(3) The following expressions must be construed in accordance with section 189 of the Consumer Credit Act 1974—

    (a)   hire-purchase agreement;
    (b)   credit-sale agreement;
    (c)   conditional sale agreement;
    (d)   antecedent negotiations.

234.   Supply of services

(1)   References in this Part to the supply of services must be construed in accordance with this section.

(2)   The supply of services does not include the provision of services under a contract of service or of apprenticeship whether it is express or implied and (if it is express) whether it is oral or in writing.

(3)   The supply of services includes—
    (a)   performing for gain or reward any activity other than the supply of goods;
    (b)   rendering services to order;
    (c)   the provision of services by making them available to potential users.

(4)   The supply of services includes making arrangements for the use of computer software or for granting access to data stored in any form which is not readily accessible.

(5)   The supply of services includes making arrangements by means of a relevant agreement (within the meaning of paragraph 17 of Schedule 3A to the Communications Act 2003 (the electronic communications code)) for sharing the use of electronic communications apparatus.

(6)   The supply of services includes permitting or making arrangements to permit the use of land in such circumstances as the Secretary of State specifies by order.

(7)   The power to make an order under subsection (6) must be exercised by statutory instrument.

(8)   But no such order may be made unless a draft of it has been laid before Parliament and approved by a resolution of each House.

235A. CPC Regulation

In this Part, the CPC Regulation is Regulation (EU) 2017/2394 of the European Parliament and the Council of 12 December 2017 on cooperation between national authorities responsible for the enforcement of consumer protection laws and repealing Regulation (EC) No 2006/2004.

235B. Dual enforcers

References in this Part to a general enforcer, a designated enforcer or a Schedule 13 enforcer are to be read, in the case of a person or body which is more than one kind of enforcer, as references to that person or body acting in its capacity as a general enforcer, designated enforcer or (as the case may be) Schedule 13 enforcer.

Crown

236.   Crown

(1)   This Part binds the Crown.

CONSUMERS, ESTATE AGENTS AND REDRESS ACT 2007
(2007, c. 17)

PART 4
MISCELLANEOUS AND GENERAL

Contracts concluded away from business premises

59.   Contracts concluded away from business premises

(1)   The Secretary of State may make regulations entitling a consumer who is a party to a protected contract to cancel the contract.

(2)   A protected contract is a contract between a consumer and a trader which is for the supply of goods or services to the consumer by a trader and is made—
   (a)   during a solicited visit by a trader to the consumer's home or place of work, or to the home of another individual, or
   (b)   after an offer made by the consumer during such a visit.
(3)   A visit is solicited if it is made at the express request of the consumer.
(4)   Regulations made under this section may make any provision which may be made by regulations under section 2(2) of the European Communities Act 1972 (by virtue of section 2(4) of that Act).
(5)   The regulations may in particular make provision—
   (a)   as to the circumstances in which the consumer may cancel the contract and the effect of such a cancellation;
   (b)   requiring the trader to inform the consumer of the matters within paragraph (a);
   (c)   for the enforcement of any requirement imposed by virtue of paragraph (b).
(6)   For the purposes of this section, 'consumer' and 'trader' in relation to a contract have the same meaning as they have for the purposes of the relevant Directive in relation to transactions within that Directive.
(7)   'The relevant Directive' means—
   (a)   Council Directive 85/577/EEC to protect the consumer in respect of contracts negotiated away from business premises, as it has effect from time to time, or
   (b)   if that Directive is repealed and re-enacted (with or without modification), that Directive as re-enacted.

CONSUMER RIGHTS ACT 2015
(2015, c. 15)

PART 1
CONSUMER CONTRACTS FOR GOODS, DIGITAL CONTENT AND SERVICES

CHAPTER 1
INTRODUCTION

1.   Where Part 1 applies
(1)   This Part applies where there is an agreement between a trader and a consumer for the trader to supply goods, digital content or services, if the agreement is a contract.
(2)   It applies whether the contract is written or oral or implied from the parties' conduct, or more than one of these combined.
(3)   Any of Chapters 2, 3 and 4 may apply to a contract—
   (a)   if it is a contract for the trader to supply goods, see Chapter 2;
   (b)   if it is a contract for the trader to supply digital content, see Chapter 3 (also, subsection (6));
   (c)   if it is a contract for the trader to supply a service, see Chapter 4 (also, subsection (6)).
(4)   In each case the Chapter applies even if the contract also covers something covered by another Chapter (a mixed contract).
(5)   Two or all three of those Chapters may apply to a mixed contract.
(6)   For provisions about particular mixed contracts, see—
   (a)   section 15 (goods and installation);
   (b)   section 16 (goods and digital content).
(7)   For other provision applying to contracts to which this Part applies, see Part 2 (unfair terms).

2.   Key definitions
(1)   These definitions apply in this Part (as well as the definitions in section 59).
(2)   'Trader' means a person acting for purposes relating to that person's trade, business, craft or profession, whether acting personally or through another person acting in the trader's name or on the trader's behalf.
(3)   'Consumer' means an individual acting for purposes that are wholly or mainly outside that individual's trade, business, craft or profession.

(4)   A trader claiming that an individual was not acting for purposes wholly or mainly outside the individual's trade, business, craft or profession must prove it.

(5)   For the purposes of Chapter 2, except to the extent mentioned in subsection (6), a person is not a consumer in relation to a sales contract if—
    (a)   the goods are second hand goods sold at public auction, and
    (b)   individuals have the opportunity of attending the sale in person.

(6)   A person is a consumer in relation to such a contract for the purposes of—
    (a)   sections 11(4) and (5), 12, 28 and 29, and
    (b)   the other provisions of Chapter 2 as they apply in relation to those sections.

(7)   'Business' includes the activities of any government department or local or public authority.

(8)   'Goods' means any tangible moveable items, but that includes water, gas and electricity if and only if they are put up for supply in a limited volume or set quantity.

(9)   'Digital content' means data which are produced and supplied in digital form.

CHAPTER 2
GOODS

What goods contracts are covered?

3.   **Contracts covered by this Chapter**
(1)   This Chapter applies to a contract for a trader to supply goods to a consumer.
(2)   It applies only if the contract is one of these (defined for the purposes of this Part in sections 5 to 8)—
    (a)   a sales contract;
    (b)   a contract for the hire of goods;
    (c)   a hire-purchase agreement;
    (d)   a contract for transfer of goods.
(3)   It does not apply—
    (a)   to a contract for a trader to supply coins or notes to a consumer for use as currency;
    (b)   to a contract for goods to be sold by way of execution or otherwise by authority of law;
    (c)   to a contract intended to operate as a mortgage, pledge, charge or other security;
    (d)   in relation to England and Wales or Northern Ireland, to a contract made by deed and for which the only consideration is the presumed consideration imported by the deed;
    (e)   in relation to Scotland, to a gratuitous contract.
(4)   A contract to which this Chapter applies is referred to in this Part as a 'contract to supply goods'.
(5)   Contracts to supply goods include—
    (a)   contracts entered into between one part owner and another;
    (b)   contracts for the transfer of an undivided share in goods;
    (c)   contracts that are absolute and contracts that are conditional.
(6)   Subsection (1) is subject to any provision of this Chapter that applies a section or part of a section to only some of the kinds of contracts listed in subsection (2).
(7)   A mixed contract (see section 1(4)) may be a contract of any of those kinds.

4.   **Ownership of goods**
(1)   In this Chapter ownership of goods means the general property in goods, not merely a special property.
(2)   For the time when ownership of goods is transferred, see in particular the following provisions of the Sale of Goods Act 1979 (which relate to contracts of sale)—

section 16:   goods must be ascertained
section 17:   property passes when intended to pass
section 18:   rules for ascertaining intention
section 19:   reservation of right of disposal
section 20A: undivided shares in goods forming part of a bulk
section 20B: deemed consent by co-owner to dealings in bulk goods

5.   Sales contracts

(1)   A contract is a sales contract if under it—

    (a)   the trader transfers or agrees to transfer ownership of goods to the consumer, and

    (b)   the consumer pays or agrees to pay the price.

(2)   A contract is a sales contract (whether or not it would be one under subsection (1)) if under the contract—

    (a)   goods are to be manufactured or produced and the trader agrees to supply them to the consumer,

    (b)   on being supplied, the goods will be owned by the consumer, and

    (c)   the consumer pays or agrees to pay the price.

(3)   A sales contract may be conditional (see section 3(5)), but in this Part 'conditional sales contract' means a sales contract under which—

    (a)   the price for the goods or part of it is payable by instalments, and

    (b)   the trader retains ownership of the goods until the conditions specified in the contract (for the payment of instalments or otherwise) are met;

and it makes no difference whether or not the consumer possesses the goods.

6.   Contracts for the hire of goods

(1)   A contract is for the hire of goods if under it the trader gives or agrees to give the consumer possession of the goods with the right to use them, subject to the terms of the contract, for a period determined in accordance with the contract.

(2)   But a contract is not for the hire of goods if it is a hire-purchase agreement.

7.   Hire-purchase agreements

(1)   A contract is a hire-purchase agreement if it meets the two conditions set out below.

(2)   The first condition is that under the contract goods are hired by the trader in return for periodical payments by the consumer (and 'hired' is to be read in accordance with section 6(1)).

(3)   The second condition is that under the contract ownership of the goods will transfer to the consumer if the terms of the contract are complied with and—

    (a)   the consumer exercises an option to buy the goods,

    (b)   any party to the contract does an act specified in it, or

    (c)   an event specified in the contract occurs.

(4)   But a contract is not a hire-purchase agreement if it is a conditional sales contract.

8.   Contracts for transfer of goods

A contract to supply goods is a contract for transfer of goods if under it the trader transfers or agrees to transfer ownership of the goods to the consumer and—

    (a)   the consumer provides or agrees to provide consideration otherwise than by paying a price, or

    (b)   the contract is, for any other reason, not a sales contract or a hire-purchase agreement.

What statutory rights are there under a goods contract?

9.   Goods to be of satisfactory quality

(1)   Every contract to supply goods is to be treated as including a term that the quality of the goods is satisfactory.

(2)   The quality of goods is satisfactory if they meet the standard that a reasonable person would consider satisfactory, taking account of—

    (a)   any description of the goods,

    (b)   the price or other consideration for the goods (if relevant), and

    (c)   all the other relevant circumstances (see subsection (5)).

(3)   The quality of goods includes their state and condition; and the following aspects (among others) are in appropriate cases aspects of the quality of goods—

    (a)   fitness for all the purposes for which goods of that kind are usually supplied;

    (b)   appearance and finish;

    (c)   freedom from minor defects;

(d)   safety;

(e)   durability.

(4)   The term mentioned in subsection (1) does not cover anything which makes the quality of the goods unsatisfactory—

    (a)   which is specifically drawn to the consumer's attention before the contract is made,

    (b)   where the consumer examines the goods before the contract is made, which that examination ought to reveal, or

    (c)   in the case of a contract to supply goods by sample, which would have been apparent on a reasonable examination of the sample.

(5)   The relevant circumstances mentioned in subsection (2)(c) include any public statement about the specific characteristics of the goods made by the trader, the producer or any representative of the trader or the producer.

(6)   That includes, in particular, any public statement made in advertising or labelling.

(7)   But a public statement is not a relevant circumstance for the purposes of subsection (2)(c) if the trader shows that—

    (a)   when the contract was made, the trader was not, and could not reasonably have been, aware of the statement,

    (b)   before the contract was made, the statement had been publicly withdrawn or, to the extent that it contained anything which was incorrect or misleading, it had been publicly corrected, or

    (c)   the consumer's decision to contract for the goods could not have been influenced by the statement.

(8)   In a contract to supply goods a term about the quality of the goods may be treated as included as a matter of custom.

(9)   See section 19 for a consumer's rights if the trader is in breach of a term that this section requires to be treated as included in a contract.

10.   Goods to be fit for particular purpose

(1)   Subsection (3) applies to a contract to supply goods if before the contract is made the consumer makes known to the trader (expressly or by implication) any particular purpose for which the consumer is contracting for the goods.

(2)   Subsection (3) also applies to a contract to supply goods if—

    (a)   the goods were previously sold by a credit-broker to the trader,

    (b)   in the case of a sales contract or contract for transfer of goods, the consideration or part of it is a sum payable by instalments, and

    (c)   before the contract is made, the consumer makes known to the credit-broker (expressly or by implication) any particular purpose for which the consumer is contracting for the goods.

(3)   The contract is to be treated as including a term that the goods are reasonably fit for that purpose, whether or not that is a purpose for which goods of that kind are usually supplied.

(4)   Subsection (3) does not apply if the circumstances show that the consumer does not rely, or it is unreasonable for the consumer to rely, on the skill or judgment of the trader or credit-broker.

(5)   In a contract to supply goods a term about the fitness of the goods for a particular purpose may be treated as included as a matter of custom.

(6)   See section 19 for a consumer's rights if the trader is in breach of a term that this section requires to be treated as included in a contract.

11.   Goods to be as described

(1)   Every contract to supply goods by description is to be treated as including a term that the goods will match the description.

(2)   If the supply is by sample as well as by description, it is not sufficient that the bulk of the goods matches the sample if the goods do not also match the description.

(3)   A supply of goods is not prevented from being a supply by description just because—

    (a)   the goods are exposed for supply, and

    (b)   they are selected by the consumer.

(4) Any information that is provided by the trader about the goods and is information mentioned in paragraph (a) of Schedule 1 or 2 to the Consumer Contracts (Information, Cancellation and Additional Charges) Regulations 2013 (SI 2013/3134) (main characteristics of goods) is to be treated as included as a term of the contract.

(5) A change to any of that information, made before entering into the contract or later, is not effective unless expressly agreed between the consumer and the trader.

(6) See section 2(5) and (6) for the application of subsections (4) and (5) where goods are sold at public auction.

(7) See section 19 for a consumer's rights if the trader is in breach of a term that this section requires to be treated as included in a contract.

12. Other pre-contract information included in contract

(1) This section applies to any contract to supply goods.

(2) Where regulation 9, 10 or 13 of the Consumer Contracts (Information, Cancellation and Additional Charges) Regulations 2013 (SI 2013/3134) required the trader to provide information to the consumer before the contract became binding, any of that information that was provided by the trader other than information about the goods and mentioned in paragraph (a) of Schedule 1 or 2 to the Regulations (main characteristics of goods) is to be treated as included as a term of the contract.

(3) A change to any of that information, made before entering into the contract or later, is not effective unless expressly agreed between the consumer and the trader.

(4) See section 2(5) and (6) for the application of this section where goods are sold at public auction.

(5) See section 19 for a consumer's rights if the trader is in breach of a term that this section requires to be treated as included in the contract.

13. Goods to match a sample

(1) This section applies to a contract to supply goods by reference to a sample of the goods that is seen or examined by the consumer before the contract is made.

(2) Every contract to which this section applies is to be treated as including a term that—

    (a) the goods will match the sample except to the extent that any differences between the sample and the goods are brought to the consumer's attention before the contract is made, and

    (b) the goods will be free from any defect that makes their quality unsatisfactory and that would not be apparent on a reasonable examination of the sample.

(3) See section 19 for a consumer's rights if the trader is in breach of a term that this section requires to be treated as included in a contract.

14. Goods to match a model seen or examined

(1) This section applies to a contract to supply goods by reference to a model of the goods that is seen or examined by the consumer before entering into the contract.

(2) Every contract to which this section applies is to be treated as including a term that the goods will match the model except to the extent that any differences between the model and the goods are brought to the consumer's attention before the consumer enters into the contract.

(3) See section 19 for a consumer's rights if the trader is in breach of a term that this section requires to be treated as included in a contract.

15. Installation as part of conformity of the goods with the contract

(1) Goods do not conform to a contract to supply goods if—

    (a) installation of the goods forms part of the contract,

    (b) the goods are installed by the trader or under the trader's responsibility, and

    (c) the goods are installed incorrectly.

(2) See section 19 for the effect of goods not conforming to the contract.

16. Goods not conforming to contract if digital content does not conform

(1) Goods (whether or not they conform otherwise to a contract to supply goods) do not conform to it if—

    (a) the goods are an item that includes digital content, and

     (b)   the digital content does not conform to the contract to supply that content (for which see section 42(1)).

  (2)   See section 19 for the effect of goods not conforming to the contract.

17. Trader to have right to supply the goods etc.

(1)   Every contract to supply goods, except one within subsection (4), is to be treated as including a term—

    (a)   in the case of a contract for the hire of goods, that at the beginning of the period of hire the trader must have the right to transfer possession of the goods by way of hire for that period,

    (b)   in any other case, that the trader must have the right to sell or transfer the goods at the time when ownership of the goods is to be transferred.

(2)   Every contract to supply goods, except a contract for the hire of goods or a contract within subsection (4), is to be treated as including a term that—

    (a)   the goods are free from any charge or encumbrance not disclosed or known to the consumer before entering into the contract,

    (b)   the goods will remain free from any such charge or encumbrance until ownership of them is to be transferred, and

    (c)   the consumer will enjoy quiet possession of the goods except so far as it may be disturbed by the owner or other person entitled to the benefit of any charge or encumbrance so disclosed or known.

(3)   Every contract for the hire of goods is to be treated as including a term that the consumer will enjoy quiet possession of the goods for the period of the hire except so far as the possession may be disturbed by the owner or other person entitled to the benefit of any charge or encumbrance disclosed or known to the consumer before entering into the contract.

(4)   This subsection applies to a contract if the contract shows, or the circumstances when they enter into the contract imply, that the trader and the consumer intend the trader to transfer only—

    (a)   whatever title the trader has, even if it is limited, or

    (b)   whatever title a third person has, even if it is limited.

(5)   Every contract within subsection (4) is to be treated as including a term that all charges or encumbrances known to the trader and not known to the consumer were disclosed to the consumer before entering into the contract.

(6)   Every contract within subsection (4) is to be treated as including a term that the consumer's quiet possession of the goods—

    (a)   will not be disturbed by the trader, and

    (b)   will not be disturbed by a person claiming through or under the trader, unless that person is claiming under a charge or encumbrance that was disclosed or known to the consumer before entering into the contract.

(7)   If subsection (4)(b) applies (transfer of title that a third person has), the contract is also to be treated as including a term that the consumer's quiet possession of the goods—

    (a)   will not be disturbed by the third person, and

    (b)   will not be disturbed by a person claiming through or under the third person, unless the claim is under a charge or encumbrance that was disclosed or known to the consumer before entering into the contract.

(8)   In the case of a contract for the hire of goods, this section does not affect the right of the trader to repossess the goods where the contract provides or is to be treated as providing for this.

(9)   See section 19 for a consumer's rights if the trader is in breach of a term that this section requires to be treated as included in a contract.

18. No other requirement to treat term about quality or fitness as included

(1)   Except as provided by sections 9, 10, 13 and 16, a contract to supply goods is not to be treated as including any term about the quality of the goods or their fitness for any particular purpose, unless the term is expressly included in the contract.

(2)   Subsection (1) is subject to provision made by any other enactment (whenever passed or made).

What remedies are there if statutory rights under a goods contract are not met?

19.   Consumer's rights to enforce terms about goods

(1)   In this section and sections 22 to 24 references to goods conforming to a contract are references to—

  (a)   the goods conforming to the terms described in sections 9, 10, 11, 13 and 14,

  (b)   the goods not failing to conform to the contract under section 15 or 16, and

  (c)   the goods conforming to requirements that are stated in the contract.

(2)   But, for the purposes of this section and sections 22 to 24, a failure to conform as mentioned in subsection (1)(a) to (c) is not a failure to conform to the contract if it has its origin in materials supplied by the consumer.

(3)   If the goods do not conform to the contract because of a breach of any of the terms described in sections 9, 10, 11, 13 and 14, or if they do not conform to the contract under section 16, the consumer's rights (and the provisions about them and when they are available) are—

  (a)   the short-term right to reject (sections 20 and 22);

  (b)   the right to repair or replacement (section 23); and

  (c)   the right to a price reduction or the final right to reject (sections 20 and 24).

(4)   If the goods do not conform to the contract under section 15 or because of a breach of requirements that are stated in the contract, the consumer's rights (and the provisions about them and when they are available) are—

  (a)   the right to repair or replacement (section 23); and

  (b)   the right to a price reduction or the final right to reject (sections 20 and 24).

(5)   If the trader is in breach of a term that section 12 requires to be treated as included in the contract, the consumer has the right to recover from the trader the amount of any costs incurred by the consumer as a result of the breach, up to the amount of the price paid or the value of other consideration given for the goods.

(6)   If the trader is in breach of the term that section 17(1) (right to supply etc.) requires to be treated as included in the contract, the consumer has a right to reject (see section 20 for provisions about that right and when it is available).

(7)   Subsections (3) to (6) are subject to section 25 and subsections (3)(a) and (6) are subject to section 26.

(8)   Section 28 makes provision about remedies for breach of a term about the time for delivery of goods.

(9)   This Chapter does not prevent the consumer seeking other remedies—

  (a)   for a breach of a term that this Chapter requires to be treated as included in the contract,

  (b)   on the grounds that, under section 15 or 16, goods do not conform to the contract, or

  (c)   for a breach of a requirement stated in the contract.

(10) Those other remedies may be ones—

  (a)   in addition to a remedy referred to in subsections (3) to (6) (but not so as to recover twice for the same loss), or

  (b)   instead of such a remedy, or

  (c)   where no such remedy is provided for.

(11) Those other remedies include any of the following that is open to the consumer in the circumstances—

  (a)   claiming damages;

  (b)   seeking specific performance;

  (c)   seeking an order for specific implement;

  (d)   relying on the breach against a claim by the trader for the price;

  (e)   for breach of an express term, exercising a right to treat the contract as at an end.

(12) It is not open to the consumer to treat the contract as at an end for breach of a term that this Chapter requires to be treated as included in the contract, or on the grounds

that, under section 15 or 16, goods do not conform to the contract, except as provided by subsections (3), (4) and (6).

(13) In this Part, treating a contract as at an end means treating it as repudiated.

(14) For the purposes of subsections (3)(b) and (c) and (4), goods which do not conform to the contract at any time within the period of six months beginning with the day on which the goods were delivered to the consumer must be taken not to have conformed to it on that day.

(15) Subsection (14) does not apply if—

    (a)   it is established that the goods did conform to the contract on that day, or

    (b)   its application is incompatible with the nature of the goods or with how they fail to conform to the contract.

20. Right to reject

(1)   The short-term right to reject is subject to section 22.

(2)   The final right to reject is subject to section 24.

(3)   The right to reject under section 19(6) is not limited by those sections.

(4)   Each of these rights entitles the consumer to reject the goods and treat the contract as at an end, subject to subsections (20) and (21).

(5)   The right is exercised if the consumer indicates to the trader that the consumer is rejecting the goods and treating the contract as at an end.

(6)   The indication may be something the consumer says or does, but it must be clear enough to be understood by the trader.

(7)   From the time when the right is exercised—

    (a)   the trader has a duty to give the consumer a refund, subject to subsection (18), and

    (b)   the consumer has a duty to make the goods available for collection by the trader or (if there is an agreement for the consumer to return rejected goods) to return them as agreed.

(8)   Whether or not the consumer has a duty to return the rejected goods, the trader must bear any reasonable costs of returning them, other than any costs incurred by the consumer in returning the goods in person to the place where the consumer took physical possession of them.

(9)   The consumer's entitlement to receive a refund works as follows.

(10) To the extent that the consumer paid money under the contract, the consumer is entitled to receive back the same amount of money.

(11) To the extent that the consumer transferred anything else under the contract, the consumer is entitled to receive back the same amount of what the consumer transferred, unless subsection (12) applies.

(12) To the extent that the consumer transferred under the contract something for which the same amount of the same thing cannot be substituted, the consumer is entitled to receive back in its original state whatever the consumer transferred.

(13) If the contract is for the hire of goods, the entitlement to a refund extends only to anything paid or otherwise transferred for a period of hire that the consumer does not get because the contract is treated as at an end.

(14) If the contract is a hire-purchase agreement or a conditional sales contract and the contract is treated as at an end before the whole of the price has been paid, the entitlement to a refund extends only to the part of the price paid.

(15) A refund under this section must be given without undue delay, and in any event within 14 days beginning with the day on which the trader agrees that the consumer is entitled to a refund.

(16) If the consumer paid money under the contract, the trader must give the refund using the same means of payment as the consumer used, unless the consumer expressly agrees otherwise.

(17) The trader must not impose any fee on the consumer in respect of the refund.

(18) There is no entitlement to receive a refund—

    (a)   if none of subsections (10) to (12) applies,

    (b)   to the extent that anything to which subsection (12) applies cannot be given back in its original state, or

(c) where subsection (13) applies, to the extent that anything the consumer transferred under the contract cannot be divided so as to give back only the amount, or part of the amount, to which the consumer is entitled.

(19) It may be open to a consumer to claim damages where there is no entitlement to receive a refund, or because of the limits of the entitlement, or instead of a refund.

(20) Subsection (21) qualifies the application in relation to England and Wales and Northern Ireland of the rights mentioned in subsections (1) to (3) where—

    (a) the contract is a severable contract,

    (b) in relation to the final right to reject, the contract is a contract for the hire of goods, a hire-purchase agreement or a contract for transfer of goods, and

    (c) section 26(3) does not apply.

(21) The consumer is entitled, depending on the terms of the contract and the circumstances of the case—

    (a) to reject the goods to which a severable obligation relates and treat that obligation as at an end (so that the entitlement to a refund relates only to what the consumer paid or transferred in relation to that obligation), or

    (b) to exercise any of the rights mentioned in subsections (1) to (3) in respect of the whole contract.

21. Partial rejection of goods

(1) If the consumer has any of the rights mentioned in section 20(1) to (3), but does not reject all of the goods and treat the contract as at an end, the consumer—

    (a) may reject some or all of the goods that do not conform to the contract, but

    (b) may not reject any goods that do conform to the contract.

(2) If the consumer is entitled to reject the goods in an instalment, but does not reject all of those goods, the consumer—

    (a) may reject some or all of the goods in the instalment that do not conform to the contract, but

    (b) may not reject any goods in the instalment that do conform to the contract.

(3) If any of the goods form a commercial unit, the consumer cannot reject some of those goods without also rejecting the rest of them.

(4) A unit is a 'commercial unit' if division of the unit would materially impair the value of the goods or the character of the unit.

(5) The consumer rejects goods under this section by indicating to the trader that the consumer is rejecting the goods.

(6) The indication may be something the consumer says or does, but it must be clear enough to be understood by the trader.

(7) From the time when a consumer rejects goods under this section—

    (a) the trader has a duty to give the consumer a refund in respect of those goods (subject to subsection (10)), and

    (b) the consumer has a duty to make those goods available for collection by the trader or (if there is an agreement for the consumer to return rejected goods) to return them as agreed.

(8) Whether or not the consumer has a duty to return the rejected goods, the trader must bear any reasonable costs of returning them, other than any costs incurred by the consumer in returning those goods in person to the place where the consumer took physical possession of them.

(9) Section 20(10) to (17) apply to a consumer's right to receive a refund under this section (and in section 20(13) and (14) references to the contract being treated as at an end are to be read as references to goods being rejected).

(10) That right does not apply—

    (a) if none of section 20(10) to (12) applies,

    (b) to the extent that anything to which section 20(12) applies cannot be given back in its original state, or

    (c) to the extent that anything the consumer transferred under the contract cannot be divided so as to give back only the amount, or part of the amount, to which the consumer is entitled.

(11) It may be open to a consumer to claim damages where there is no right to receive a refund, or because of the limits of the right, or instead of a refund.

(12) References in this section to goods conforming to a contract are to be read in accordance with section 19(1) and (2), but they also include the goods conforming to the terms described in section 17.

(13) Where section 20(21)(a) applies the reference in subsection (1) to the consumer treating the contract as at an end is to be read as a reference to the consumer treating the severable obligation as at an end.

22. Time limit for short-term right to reject

(1) A consumer who has the short-term right to reject loses it if the time limit for exercising it passes without the consumer exercising it, unless the trader and the consumer agree that it may be exercised later.

(2) An agreement under which the short-term right to reject would be lost before the time limit passes is not binding on the consumer.

(3) The time limit for exercising the short-term right to reject (unless subsection (4) applies) is the end of 30 days beginning with the first day after these have all happened—

  (a) ownership or (in the case of a contract for the hire of goods, a hire-purchase agreement or a conditional sales contract) possession of the goods has been transferred to the consumer,

  (b) the goods have been delivered, and

  (c) where the contract requires the trader to install the goods or take other action to enable the consumer to use them, the trader has notified the consumer that the action has been taken.

(4) If any of the goods are of a kind that can reasonably be expected to perish after a shorter period, the time limit for exercising the short-term right to reject in relation to those goods is the end of that shorter period (but without affecting the time limit in relation to goods that are not of that kind).

(5) Subsections (3) and (4) do not prevent the consumer exercising the short-term right to reject before something mentioned in subsection (3)(a), (b) or (c) has happened.

(6) If the consumer requests or agrees to the repair or replacement of goods, the period mentioned in subsection (3) or (4) stops running for the length of the waiting period.

(7) If goods supplied by the trader in response to that request or agreement do not conform to the contract, the time limit for exercising the short-term right to reject is then either—

  (a) 7 days after the waiting period ends, or

  (b) if later, the original time limit for exercising that right, extended by the waiting period.

(8) The waiting period—

  (a) begins with the day the consumer requests or agrees to the repair or replacement of the goods, and

  (b) ends with the day on which the consumer receives goods supplied by the trader in response to the request or agreement.

23. Right to repair or replacement

(1) This section applies if the consumer has the right to repair or replacement (see section 19(3) and (4)).

(2) If the consumer requires the trader to repair or replace the goods, the trader must—

  (a) do so within a reasonable time and without significant inconvenience to the consumer, and

  (b) bear any necessary costs incurred in doing so (including in particular the cost of any labour, materials or postage).

(3) The consumer cannot require the trader to repair or replace the goods if that remedy (the repair or the replacement)—

  (a) is impossible, or

  (b) is disproportionate compared to the other of those remedies.

(4) Either of those remedies is disproportionate compared to the other if it imposes costs on the trader which, compared to those imposed by the other, are unreasonable, taking into account—

  (a) the value which the goods would have if they conformed to the contract,

      (b)   the significance of the lack of conformity, and

      (c)   whether the other remedy could be effected without significant inconvenience to the consumer.

(5)   Any question as to what is a reasonable time or significant inconvenience is to be determined taking account of—

      (a)   the nature of the goods, and

      (b)   the purpose for which the goods were acquired.

(6)   A consumer who requires or agrees to the repair of goods cannot require the trader to replace them, or exercise the short-term right to reject, without giving the trader a reasonable time to repair them (unless giving the trader that time would cause significant inconvenience to the consumer).

(7)   A consumer who requires or agrees to the replacement of goods cannot require the trader to repair them, or exercise the short-term right to reject, without giving the trader a reasonable time to replace them (unless giving the trader that time would cause significant inconvenience to the consumer).

(8)   In this Chapter, 'repair' in relation to goods that do not conform to a contract, means making them conform.

24.   Right to price reduction or final right to reject

(1)   The right to a price reduction is the right—

      (a)   to require the trader to reduce by an appropriate amount the price the consumer is required to pay under the contract, or anything else the consumer is required to transfer under the contract, and

      (b)   to receive a refund from the trader for anything already paid or otherwise transferred by the consumer above the reduced amount.

(2)   The amount of the reduction may, where appropriate, be the full amount of the price or whatever the consumer is required to transfer.

(3)   Section 20(10) to (17) applies to a consumer's right to receive a refund under subsection (1)(b).

(4)   The right to a price reduction does not apply—

      (a)   if what the consumer is (before the reduction) required to transfer under the contract, whether or not already transferred, cannot be divided up so as to enable the trader to receive or retain only the reduced amount, or

      (b)   if anything to which section 20(12) applies cannot be given back in its original state.

(5)   A consumer who has the right to a price reduction and the final right to reject may only exercise one (not both), and may only do so in one of these situations—

      (a)   after one repair or one replacement, the goods do not conform to the contract;

      (b)   because of section 23(3) the consumer can require neither repair nor replacement of the goods; or

      (c)   the consumer has required the trader to repair or replace the goods, but the trader is in breach of the requirement of section 23(2)(a) to do so within a reasonable time and without significant inconvenience to the consumer.

(6)   There has been a repair or replacement for the purposes of subsection (5)(a) if—

      (a)   the consumer has requested or agreed to repair or replacement of the goods (whether in relation to one fault or more than one), and

      (b)   the trader has delivered goods to the consumer, or made goods available to the consumer, in response to the request or agreement.

(7)   For the purposes of subsection (6) goods that the trader arranges to repair at the consumer's premises are made available when the trader indicates that the repairs are finished.

(8)   If the consumer exercises the final right to reject, any refund to the consumer may be reduced by a deduction for use, to take account of the use the consumer has had of the goods in the period since they were delivered, but this is subject to subsections (9) and (10).

(9)   No deduction may be made to take account of use in any period when the consumer had the goods only because the trader failed to collect them at an agreed time.

(10) No deduction may be made if the final right to reject is exercised in the first 6 months (see subsection (11)), unless—

      (a)   the goods consist of a motor vehicle, or

     (b)   the goods are of a description specified by order made by the Secretary of State by statutory instrument.

(11) In subsection (10) the first 6 months means 6 months beginning with the first day after these have all happened—

     (a)   ownership or (in the case of a contract for the hire of goods, a hire-purchase agreement or a conditional sales contract) possession of the goods has been transferred to the consumer,

     (b)   the goods have been delivered, and

     (c)   where the contract requires the trader to install the goods or take other action to enable the consumer to use them, the trader has notified the consumer that the action has been taken.

(12) In subsection (10)(a) 'motor vehicle'—

     (a)   in relation to Great Britain, has the same meaning as in the Road Traffic Act 1988 (see sections 185 to 194 of that Act);

     (b)   in relation to Northern Ireland, has the same meaning as in the Road Traffic (Northern Ireland) Order 1995 (SI 1995/2994 (NI 18)) (see Parts I and V of that Order).

(13) But a vehicle is not a motor vehicle for the purposes of subsection (10)(a) if it is constructed or adapted—

     (a)   for the use of a person suffering from some physical defect or disability, and

     (b)   so that it may only be used by one such person at any one time.

(14) An order under subsection (10)(b)—

     (a)   may be made only if the Secretary of State is satisfied that it is appropriate to do so because of significant detriment caused to traders as a result of the application of subsection (10) in relation to goods of the description specified by the order;

     (b)   may contain transitional or transitory provision or savings.

(15) No order may be made under subsection (10)(b) unless a draft of the statutory instrument containing it has been laid before, and approved by a resolution of, each House of Parliament.

Other rules about remedies under goods contracts

25.   Delivery of wrong quantity

(1)   Where the trader delivers to the consumer a quantity of goods less than the trader contracted to supply, the consumer may reject them, but if the consumer accepts them the consumer must pay for them at the contract rate.

(2)   Where the trader delivers to the consumer a quantity of goods larger than the trader contracted to supply, the consumer may accept the goods included in the contract and reject the rest, or may reject all of the goods.

(3)   Where the trader delivers to the consumer a quantity of goods larger than the trader contracted to supply and the consumer accepts all of the goods delivered, the consumer must pay for them at the contract rate.

(4)   Where the consumer is entitled to reject goods under this section, any entitlement for the consumer to treat the contract as at an end depends on the terms of the contract and the circumstances of the case.

(5)   The consumer rejects goods under this section by indicating to the trader that the consumer is rejecting the goods.

(6)   The indication may be something the consumer says or does, but it must be clear enough to be understood by the trader.

(7)   Subsections (1) to (3) do not prevent the consumer claiming damages, where it is open to the consumer to do so.

(8)   This section is subject to any usage of trade, special agreement, or course of dealing between the parties.

26.   Instalment deliveries

(1)   Under a contract to supply goods, the consumer is not bound to accept delivery of the goods by instalments, unless that has been agreed between the consumer and the trader.

(2) The following provisions apply if the contract provides for the goods to be delivered by stated instalments, which are to be separately paid for.

(3) If the trader makes defective deliveries in respect of one or more instalments, the consumer, apart from any entitlement to claim damages, may be (but is not necessarily) entitled—

    (a) to exercise the short-term right to reject or the right to reject under section 19(6) (as applicable) in respect of the whole contract, or

    (b) to reject the goods in an instalment.

(4) Whether paragraph (a) or (b) of subsection (3) (or neither) applies to a consumer depends on the terms of the contract and the circumstances of the case.

(5) In subsection (3), making defective deliveries does not include failing to make a delivery in accordance with section 28.

(6) If the consumer neglects or refuses to take delivery of or pay for one or more instalments, the trader may—

    (a) be entitled to treat the whole contract as at an end, or

    (b) if it is a severable breach, have a claim for damages but not a right to treat the whole contract as at an end.

(7) Whether paragraph (a) or (b) of subsection (6) (or neither) applies to a trader depends on the terms of the contract and the circumstances of the case.

27. Consignation, or payment into court, in Scotland

(1) Subsection (2) applies where—

    (a) a consumer has not rejected goods which the consumer could have rejected for breach of a term mentioned in section 19(3) or (6),

    (b) the consumer has chosen to treat the breach as giving rise only to a claim for damages or to a right to rely on the breach against a claim by the trader for the price of the goods, and

    (c) the trader has begun proceedings in court to recover the price or has brought a counter-claim for the price.

(2) The court may require the consumer—

    (a) to consign, or pay into court, the price of the goods, or part of the price, or

    (b) to provide some other reasonable security for payment of the price.

Other rules about goods contracts

28. Delivery of goods

(1) This section applies to any sales contract.

(2) Unless the trader and the consumer have agreed otherwise, the contract is to be treated as including a term that the trader must deliver the goods to the consumer.

(3) Unless there is an agreed time or period, the contract is to be treated as including a term that the trader must deliver the goods—

    (a) without undue delay, and

    (b) in any event, not more than 30 days after the day on which the contract is entered into.

(4) In this section—

    (a) an 'agreed' time or period means a time or period agreed by the trader and the consumer for delivery of the goods;

    (b) if there is an obligation to deliver the goods at the time the contract is entered into, that time counts as the 'agreed' time.

(5) Subsections (6) and (7) apply if the trader does not deliver the goods in accordance with subsection (3) or at the agreed time or within the agreed period.

(6) If the circumstances are that—

    (a) the trader has refused to deliver the goods,

    (b) delivery of the goods at the agreed time or within the agreed period is essential taking into account all the relevant circumstances at the time the contract was entered into, or

    (c) the consumer told the trader before the contract was entered into that delivery in accordance with subsection (3), or at the agreed time or within the agreed period, was essential,

then the consumer may treat the contract as at an end.

(7)   In any other circumstances, the consumer may specify a period that is appropriate in the circumstances and require the trader to deliver the goods before the end of that period.

(8)   If the consumer specifies a period under subsection (7) but the goods are not delivered within that period, then the consumer may treat the contract as at an end.

(9)   If the consumer treats the contract as at an end under subsection (6) or (8), the trader must without undue delay reimburse all payments made under the contract.

(10)   If subsection (6) or (8) applies but the consumer does not treat the contract as at an end—

(a)   that does not prevent the consumer from cancelling the order for any of the goods or rejecting goods that have been delivered, and

(b)   the trader must without undue delay reimburse all payments made under the contract in respect of any goods for which the consumer cancels the order or which the consumer rejects.

(11)   If any of the goods form a commercial unit, the consumer cannot reject or cancel the order for some of those goods without also rejecting or cancelling the order for the rest of them.

(12)   A unit is a 'commercial unit' if division of the unit would materially impair the value of the goods or the character of the unit.

(13)   This section does not prevent the consumer seeking other remedies where it is open to the consumer to do so.

(14)   See section 2(5) and (6) for the application of this section where goods are sold at public auction.

29.   Passing of risk

(1)   A sales contract is to be treated as including the following provisions as terms.

(2)   The goods remain at the trader's risk until they come into the physical possession of—

(a)   the consumer, or

(b)   a person identified by the consumer to take possession of the goods.

(3)   Subsection (2) does not apply if the goods are delivered to a carrier who—

(a)   is commissioned by the consumer to deliver the goods, and

(b)   is not a carrier the trader named as an option for the consumer.

(4)   In that case the goods are at the consumer's risk on and after delivery to the carrier.

(5)   Subsection (4) does not affect any liability of the carrier to the consumer in respect of the goods.

(6)   See section 2(5) and (6) for the application of this section where goods are sold at public auction.

30.   Goods under guarantee

(1)   This section applies where—

(a)   there is a contract to supply goods, and

(b)   there is a guarantee in relation to the goods.

(2)   'Guarantee' here means an undertaking to the consumer given without extra charge by a person acting in the course of the person's business (the 'guarantor') that, if the goods do not meet the specifications set out in the guarantee statement or in any associated advertising—

(a)   the consumer will be reimbursed for the price paid for the goods, or

(b)   the goods will be repaired, replaced or handled in any way.

(3)   The guarantee takes effect, at the time the goods are delivered, as a contractual obligation owed by the guarantor under the conditions set out in the guarantee statement and in any associated advertising.

(4)   The guarantor must ensure that—

(a)   the guarantee sets out in plain and intelligible language the contents of the guarantee and the essential particulars for making claims under the guarantee,

(b)   the guarantee states that the consumer has statutory rights in relation to the goods and that those rights are not affected by the guarantee, and

(c)   where the goods are offered within the territory of the United Kingdom, the guarantee is written in English.

(5)   The contents of the guarantee to be set out in it include, in particular—
    (a)   the name and address of the guarantor, and
    (b)   the duration and territorial scope of the guarantee.

(6)   The guarantor and any other person who offers to supply to consumers the goods which are the subject of the guarantee must, on request by the consumer, make the guarantee available to the consumer within a reasonable time, in writing and in a form accessible to the consumer.

(7)   What is a reasonable time is a question of fact.

(8)   If a person fails to comply with a requirement of this section, the enforcement authority may apply to the court for an injunction or (in Scotland) an order of specific implement against that person requiring that person to comply.

(9)   On an application the court may grant an injunction or (in Scotland) an order of specific implement on such terms as it thinks appropriate.

(10)   In this section—
    'court' means—
    (a)   in relation to England and Wales, the High Court or the county court,
    (b)   in relation to Northern Ireland, the High Court or a county court, and
    (c)   in relation to Scotland, the Court of Session or the sheriff;
    'enforcement authority' means—
    (a)   the Competition and Markets Authority,
    (b)   a local weights and measures authority in Great Britain, and
    (c)   the Department of Enterprise, Trade and Investment in Northern Ireland.

Can a trader contract out of statutory rights and remedies under a goods contract?

31.   Liability that cannot be excluded or restricted

(1)   A term of a contract to supply goods is not binding on the consumer to the extent that it would exclude or restrict the trader's liability arising under any of these provisions—
    (a)   section 9 (goods to be of satisfactory quality);
    (b)   section 10 (goods to be fit for particular purpose);
    (c)   section 11 (goods to be as described);
    (d)   section 12 (other pre-contract information included in contract);
    (e)   section 13 (goods to match a sample);
    (f)   section 14 (goods to match a model seen or examined);
    (g)   section 15 (installation as part of conformity of the goods with the contract);
    (h)   section 16 (goods not conforming to contract if digital content does not conform);
    (i)   section 17 (trader to have right to supply the goods etc.);
    (j)   section 28 (delivery of goods);
    (k)   section 29 (passing of risk).

(2)   That also means that a term of a contract to supply goods is not binding on the consumer to the extent that it would—
    (a)   exclude or restrict a right or remedy in respect of a liability under a provision listed in subsection (1),
    (b)   make such a right or remedy or its enforcement subject to a restrictive or onerous condition,
    (c)   allow a trader to put a person at a disadvantage as a result of pursuing such a right or remedy, or
    (d)   exclude or restrict rules of evidence or procedure.

(3)   The reference in subsection (1) to excluding or restricting a liability also includes preventing an obligation or duty arising or limiting its extent.

(4)   An agreement in writing to submit present or future differences to arbitration is not to be regarded as excluding or restricting any liability for the purposes of this section.

(5)   Subsection (1)(i), and subsection (2) so far as it relates to liability under section 17, do not apply to a term of a contract for the hire of goods.

(6)   But an express term of a contract for the hire of goods is not binding on the consumer to the extent that it would exclude or restrict a term that section 17 requires to be treated as included in the contract, unless it is inconsistent with that term (and see also section 62 (requirement for terms to be fair)).

(7)   See Schedule 3 for provision about the enforcement of this section.

32.   Contracts applying law of a country other than the United Kingdom

(1)   If—
    (a)   the law of a country or territory other than the United Kingdom or any part of the United Kingdom is chosen by the parties to be applicable to a sales contract, but
    (b)   the sales contract has a close connection with the United Kingdom,
this Chapter, except the provisions in subsection (2), applies despite that choice.

(2)   The exceptions are—
    (a)   sections 11(4) and (5) and 12;
    (b)   sections 28 and 29;
    (c)   section 31(1)(d), (j) and (k).

(3)   For cases where those provisions apply, or where the law applicable has not been chosen or the law of an EEA State is chosen, see Regulation (EC) No. 593/2008 of the European Parliament and of the Council of 17 June 2008 on the law applicable to contractual obligations as that Regulation has effect as retained direct EU legislation (including that Regulation as applied by regulation 5 of the Law Applicable to Contractual Obligations (England and Wales and Northern Ireland) Regulations 2009 and regulation 4 of the Law Applicable to Contractual Obligations (Scotland) Regulations 2009), unless the case is one in respect of which Regulation (EC) No. 593/2006 has effect by virtue of Article 66 of the EU withdrawal agreement, in which case see that Regulation as it has effect by virtue of that Article.

CHAPTER 3
DIGITAL CONTENT

What digital content contracts are covered?

33.   Contracts covered by this Chapter

(1)   This Chapter applies to a contract for a trader to supply digital content to a consumer, if it is supplied or to be supplied for a price paid by the consumer.

(2)   This Chapter also applies to a contract for a trader to supply digital content to a consumer, if—
    (a)   it is supplied free with goods or services or other digital content for which the consumer pays a price, and
    (b)   it is not generally available to consumers unless they have paid a price for it or for goods or services or other digital content.

(3)   The references in subsections (1) and (2) to the consumer paying a price include references to the consumer using, by way of payment, any facility for which money has been paid.

(4)   A trader does not supply digital content to a consumer for the purposes of this Part merely because the trader supplies a service by which digital content reaches the consumer.

(5)   The Secretary of State may by order provide for this Chapter to apply to other contracts for a trader to supply digital content to a consumer, if the Secretary of State is satisfied that it is appropriate to do so because of significant detriment caused to consumers under contracts of the kind to which the order relates.

(6)   An order under subsection (5)—
    (a)   may, in particular, amend this Act;
    (b)   may contain transitional or transitory provision or savings.

(7)   A contract to which this Chapter applies is referred to in this Part as a 'contract to supply digital content'.

(8)   This section, other than subsection (4), does not limit the application of section 46.

(9)   The power to make an order under subsection (5) is exercisable by statutory instrument.

(10) No order may be made under subsection (5) unless a draft of the statutory instrument containing it has been laid before, and approved by a resolution of, each House of Parliament.

What statutory rights are there under a digital content contract?

34. Digital content to be of satisfactory quality

(1) Every contract to supply digital content is to be treated as including a term that the quality of the digital content is satisfactory.

(2) The quality of digital content is satisfactory if it meets the standard that a reasonable person would consider satisfactory, taking account of—

    (a) any description of the digital content,

    (b) the price mentioned in section 33(1) or (2)(b) (if relevant), and

    (c) all the other relevant circumstances (see subsection (5)).

(3) The quality of digital content includes its state and condition; and the following aspects (among others) are in appropriate cases aspects of the quality of digital content—

    (a) fitness for all the purposes for which digital content of that kind is usually supplied;

    (b) freedom from minor defects;

    (c) safety;

    (d) durability.

(4) The term mentioned in subsection (1) does not cover anything which makes the quality of the digital content unsatisfactory—

    (a) which is specifically drawn to the consumer's attention before the contract is made,

    (b) where the consumer examines the digital content before the contract is made, which that examination ought to reveal, or

    (c) where the consumer examines a trial version before the contract is made, which would have been apparent on a reasonable examination of the trial version.

(5) The relevant circumstances mentioned in subsection (2)(c) include any public statement about the specific characteristics of the digital content made by the trader, the producer or any representative of the trader or the producer.

(6) That includes, in particular, any public statement made in advertising or labelling.

(7) But a public statement is not a relevant circumstance for the purposes of subsection (2)(c) if the trader shows that—

    (a) when the contract was made, the trader was not, and could not reasonably have been, aware of the statement,

    (b) before the contract was made, the statement had been publicly withdrawn or, to the extent that it contained anything which was incorrect or misleading, it had been publicly corrected, or

    (c) the consumer's decision to contract for the digital content could not have been influenced by the statement.

(8) In a contract to supply digital content a term about the quality of the digital content may be treated as included as a matter of custom.

(9) See section 42 for a consumer's rights if the trader is in breach of a term that this section requires to be treated as included in a contract.

35. Digital content to be fit for particular purpose

(1) Subsection (3) applies to a contract to supply digital content if before the contract is made the consumer makes known to the trader (expressly or by implication) any particular purpose for which the consumer is contracting for the digital content.

(2) Subsection (3) also applies to a contract to supply digital content if—

    (a) the digital content was previously sold by a credit-broker to the trader,

    (b) the consideration or part of it is a sum payable by instalments, and

    (c) before the contract is made, the consumer makes known to the credit-broker (expressly or by implication) any particular purpose for which the consumer is contracting for the digital content.

(3) The contract is to be treated as including a term that the digital content is reasonably fit for that purpose, whether or not that is a purpose for which digital content of that kind is usually supplied.

(4) Subsection (3) does not apply if the circumstances show that the consumer does not rely, or it is unreasonable for the consumer to rely, on the skill or judgment of the trader or credit-broker.

(5) A contract to supply digital content may be treated as making provision about the fitness of the digital content for a particular purpose as a matter of custom.

(6) See section 42 for a consumer's rights if the trader is in breach of a term that this section requires to be treated as included in a contract.

36. Digital content to be as described

(1) Every contract to supply digital content is to be treated as including a term that the digital content will match any description of it given by the trader to the consumer.

(2) Where the consumer examines a trial version before the contract is made, it is not sufficient that the digital content matches (or is better than) the trial version if the digital content does not also match any description of it given by the trader to the consumer.

(3) Any information that is provided by the trader about the digital content that is information mentioned in paragraph (a), (j) or (k) of Schedule 1 or paragraph (a), (v) or (w) of Schedule 2 (main characteristics, functionality and compatibility) to the Consumer Contracts (Information, Cancellation and Additional Charges) Regulations 2013 (SI 2013/3134) is to be treated as included as a term of the contract.

(4) A change to any of that information, made before entering into the contract or later, is not effective unless expressly agreed between the consumer and the trader.

(5) See section 42 for a consumer's rights if the trader is in breach of a term that this section requires to be treated as included in a contract.

37. Other pre-contract information included in contract

(1) This section applies to any contract to supply digital content.

(2) Where regulation 9, 10 or 13 of the Consumer Contracts (Information, Cancellation and Additional Charges) Regulations 2013 (SI 2013/3134) required the trader to provide information to the consumer before the contract became binding, any of that information that was provided by the trader other than information about the digital content and mentioned in paragraph (a), (j) or (k) of Schedule 1 or paragraph (a), (v) or (w) of Schedule 2 to the Regulations (main characteristics, functionality and compatibility) is to be treated as included as a term of the contract.

(3) A change to any of that information, made before entering into the contract or later, is not effective unless expressly agreed between the consumer and the trader.

(4) See section 42 for a consumer's rights if the trader is in breach of a term that this section requires to be treated as included in a contract.

38. No other requirement to treat term about quality or fitness as included

(1) Except as provided by sections 34 and 35, a contract to supply digital content is not to be treated as including any term about the quality of the digital content or its fitness for any particular purpose, unless the term is expressly included in the contract.

(2) Subsection (1) is subject to provision made by any other enactment, whenever passed or made.

39. Supply by transmission and facilities for continued transmission

(1) Subsection (2) applies where there is a contract to supply digital content and the consumer's access to the content on a device requires its transmission to the device under arrangements initiated by the trader.

(2) For the purposes of this Chapter, the digital content is supplied—
   (a) when the content reaches the device, or
   (b) if earlier, when the content reaches another trader chosen by the consumer to supply, under a contract with the consumer, a service by which digital content reaches the device.

(3) Subsections (5) to (7) apply where—
   (a) there is a contract to supply digital content, and
   (b) after the trader (T) has supplied the digital content, the consumer is to have access under the contract to a processing facility under arrangements made by T.

(4) A processing facility is a facility by which T or another trader will receive digital content from the consumer and transmit digital content to the consumer (whether or not other features are to be included under the contract).

(5)   The contract is to be treated as including a term that the processing facility (with any feature that the facility is to include under the contract) must be available to the consumer for a reasonable time, unless a time is specified in the contract.

(6)   The following provisions apply to all digital content transmitted to the consumer on each occasion under the facility, while it is provided under the contract, as they apply to the digital content first supplied—
    (a)   section 34 (quality);
    (b)   section 35 (fitness for a particular purpose);
    (c)   section 36 (description).

(7)   Breach of a term treated as included under subsection (5) has the same effect as breach of a term treated as included under those sections (see section 42).

40. Quality, fitness and description of content supplied subject to modifications

(1)   Where under a contract a trader supplies digital content to a consumer subject to the right of the trader or a third party to modify the digital content, the following provisions apply in relation to the digital content as modified as they apply in relation to the digital content as supplied under the contract—
    (a)   section 34 (quality);
    (b)   section 35 (fitness for a particular purpose);
    (c)   section 36 (description).

(2)   Subsection (1)(c) does not prevent the trader from improving the features of, or adding new features to, the digital content, as long as—
    (a)   the digital content continues to match the description of it given by the trader to the consumer, and
    (b)   the digital content continues to conform to the information provided by the trader as mentioned in subsection (3) of section 36, subject to any change to that information that has been agreed in accordance with subsection (4) of that section.

(3)   A claim on the grounds that digital content does not conform to a term described in any of the sections listed in subsection (1) as applied by that subsection is to be treated as arising at the time when the digital content was supplied under the contract and not the time when it is modified.

41. Trader's right to supply digital content

(1)   Every contract to supply digital content is to be treated as including a term—
    (a)   in relation to any digital content which is supplied under the contract and which the consumer has paid for, that the trader has the right to supply that content to the consumer;
    (b)   in relation to any digital content which the trader agrees to supply under the contract and which the consumer has paid for, that the trader will have the right to supply it to the consumer at the time when it is to be supplied.

(2)   See section 42 for a consumer's rights if the trader is in breach of a term that this section requires to be treated as included in a contract.

What remedies are there if statutory rights under a digital content contract are not met?

42. Consumer's rights to enforce terms about digital content

(1)   In this section and section 43 references to digital content conforming to a contract are references to the digital content conforming to the terms described in sections 34, 35 and 36.

(2)   If the digital content does not conform to the contract, the consumer's rights (and the provisions about them and when they are available) are—
    (a)   the right to repair or replacement (see section 43);
    (b)   the right to a price reduction (see section 44).

(3)   Section 16 also applies if an item including the digital content is supplied.

(4)   If the trader is in breach of a term that section 37 requires to be treated as included in the contract, the consumer has the right to recover from the trader the amount of any costs incurred by the consumer as a result of the breach, up to the amount of the price paid for the digital content or for any facility within section 33(3) used by the consumer.

(5)   If the trader is in breach of the term that section 41(1) (right to supply the content) requires to be treated as included in the contract, the consumer has the right to a refund (see section 45 for provisions about that right and when it is available).

(6)   This Chapter does not prevent the consumer seeking other remedies for a breach of a term to which any of subsections (2), (4) or (5) applies, instead of or in addition to a remedy referred to there (but not so as to recover twice for the same loss).

(7)   Those other remedies include any of the following that is open to the consumer in the circumstances—
   (a)   claiming damages;
   (b)   seeking to recover money paid where the consideration for payment of the money has failed;
   (c)   seeking specific performance;
   (d)   seeking an order for specific implement;
   (e)   relying on the breach against a claim by the trader for the price.

(8)   It is not open to the consumer to treat the contract as at an end for breach of a term to which any of subsections (2), (4) or (5) applies.

(9)   For the purposes of subsection (2), digital content which does not conform to the contract at any time within the period of six months beginning with the day on which it was supplied must be taken not to have conformed to the contract when it was supplied.

(10) Subsection (9) does not apply if—
   (a)   it is established that the digital content did conform to the contract when it was supplied, or
   (b)   its application is incompatible with the nature of the digital content or with how it fails to conform to the contract.

43.   Right to repair or replacement

(1)   This section applies if the consumer has the right to repair or replacement.

(2)   If the consumer requires the trader to repair or replace the digital content, the trader must—
   (a)   do so within a reasonable time and without significant inconvenience to the consumer; and
   (b)   bear any necessary costs incurred in doing so (including in particular the cost of any labour, materials or postage).

(3)   The consumer cannot require the trader to repair or replace the digital content if that remedy (the repair or the replacement)—
   (a)   is impossible, or
   (b)   is disproportionate compared to the other of those remedies.

(4)   Either of those remedies is disproportionate compared to the other if it imposes costs on the trader which, compared to those imposed by the other, are unreasonable, taking into account—
   (a)   the value which the digital content would have if it conformed to the contract,
   (b)   the significance of the lack of conformity, and
   (c)   whether the other remedy could be effected without significant inconvenience to the consumer.

(5)   Any question as to what is a reasonable time or significant inconvenience is to be determined taking account of—
   (a)   the nature of the digital content, and
   (b)   the purpose for which the digital content was obtained or accessed.

(6)   A consumer who requires or agrees to the repair of digital content cannot require the trader to replace it without giving the trader a reasonable time to repair it (unless giving the trader that time would cause significant inconvenience to the consumer).

(7)   A consumer who requires or agrees to the replacement of digital content cannot require the trader to repair it without giving the trader a reasonable time to replace it (unless giving the trader that time would cause significant inconvenience to the consumer).

(8)   In this Chapter, 'repair' in relation to digital content that does not conform to a contract, means making it conform.

44.   Right to price reduction

(1)   The right to a price reduction is the right to require the trader to reduce the price to the consumer by an appropriate amount (including the right to receive a refund for anything already paid above the reduced amount).

(2)   The amount of the reduction may, where appropriate, be the full amount of the price.

(3)   A consumer who has that right may only exercise it in one of these situations—

    (a)   because of section 43(3)(a) the consumer can require neither repair nor replacement of the digital content, or

    (b)   the consumer has required the trader to repair or replace the digital content, but the trader is in breach of the requirement of section 43(2)(a) to do so within a reasonable time and without significant inconvenience to the consumer.

(4)   A refund under this section must be given without undue delay, and in any event within 14 days beginning with the day on which the trader agrees that the consumer is entitled to a refund.

(5)   The trader must give the refund using the same means of payment as the consumer used to pay for the digital content, unless the consumer expressly agrees otherwise.

(6)   The trader must not impose any fee on the consumer in respect of the refund.

45.   Right to a refund

(1)   The right to a refund gives the consumer the right to receive a refund from the trader of all money paid by the consumer for the digital content (subject to subsection (2)).

(2)   If the breach giving the consumer the right to a refund affects only some of the digital content supplied under the contract, the right to a refund does not extend to any part of the price attributable to digital content that is not affected by the breach.

(3)   A refund must be given without undue delay, and in any event within 14 days beginning with the day on which the trader agrees that the consumer is entitled to a refund.

(4)   The trader must give the refund using the same means of payment as the consumer used to pay for the digital content, unless the consumer expressly agrees otherwise.

(5)   The trader must not impose any fee on the consumer in respect of the refund.

Compensation for damage to device or to other digital content

46.   Remedy for damage to device or to other digital content

(1)   This section applies if—

    (a)   a trader supplies digital content to a consumer under a contract,

    (b)   the digital content causes damage to a device or to other digital content,

    (c)   the device or digital content that is damaged belongs to the consumer, and

    (d)   the damage is of a kind that would not have occurred if the trader had exercised reasonable care and skill.

(2)   If the consumer requires the trader to provide a remedy under this section, the trader must either—

    (a)   repair the damage in accordance with subsection (3), or

    (b)   compensate the consumer for the damage with an appropriate payment.

(3)   To repair the damage in accordance with this subsection, the trader must—

    (a)   repair the damage within a reasonable time and without significant inconvenience to the consumer, and

    (b)   bear any necessary costs incurred in repairing the damage (including in particular the cost of any labour, materials or postage).

(4)   Any question as to what is a reasonable time or significant inconvenience is to be determined taking account of—

    (a)   the nature of the device or digital content that is damaged, and

    (b)   the purpose for which it is used by the consumer.

(5)   A compensation payment under this section must be made without undue delay, and in any event within 14 days beginning with the day on which the trader agrees that the consumer is entitled to the payment.

(6)   The trader must not impose any fee on the consumer in respect of the payment.

(7)   A consumer with a right to a remedy under this section may bring a claim in civil proceedings to enforce that right.

(8)   The Limitation Act 1980 and the Limitation (Northern Ireland) Order 1989 (SI 1989/1339 (NI 11)) apply to a claim under this section as if it were an action founded on simple contract.
(9)   The Prescription and Limitation (Scotland) Act 1973 applies to a right to a remedy under this section as if it were an obligation to which section 6 of that Act applies.

Can a trader contract out of statutory rights and remedies under a digital content contract?

47.   Liability that cannot be excluded or restricted

(1)   A term of a contract to supply digital content is not binding on the consumer to the extent that it would exclude or restrict the trader's liability arising under any of these provisions—
 (a)   section 34 (digital content to be of satisfactory quality),
 (b)   section 35 (digital content to be fit for particular purpose),
 (c)   section 36 (digital content to be as described),
 (d)   section 37 (other pre-contract information included in contract), or
 (e)   section 41 (trader's right to supply digital content).
(2)   That also means that a term of a contract to supply digital content is not binding on the consumer to the extent that it would—
 (a)   exclude or restrict a right or remedy in respect of a liability under a provision listed in subsection (1),
 (b)   make such a right or remedy or its enforcement subject to a restrictive or onerous condition,
 (c)   allow a trader to put a person at a disadvantage as a result of pursuing such a right or remedy, or
 (d)   exclude or restrict rules of evidence or procedure.
(3)   The reference in subsection (1) to excluding or restricting a liability also includes preventing an obligation or duty arising or limiting its extent.
(4)   An agreement in writing to submit present or future differences to arbitration is not to be regarded as excluding or restricting any liability for the purposes of this section.
(5)   See Schedule 3 for provision about the enforcement of this section.
(6)   For provision limiting the ability of a trader under a contract within section 46 to exclude or restrict the trader's liability under that section, see section 62.

CHAPTER 4
SERVICES

What services contracts are covered?

48.   Contracts covered by this Chapter

(1)   This Chapter applies to a contract for a trader to supply a service to a consumer.
(2)   That does not include a contract of employment or apprenticeship.
(3)   In relation to Scotland, this Chapter does not apply to a gratuitous contract.
(3A) This Chapter does not apply to anything that is governed by Regulation (EU) No 181/2011 of the European Parliament and of the Council of 16 February 2011 concerning the rights of passengers in bus and coach transport and amending Regulation (EC) No 2006/2004.
(4)   A contract to which this Chapter applies is referred to in this Part as a 'contract to supply a service'.
(5)   The Secretary of State may by order made by statutory instrument provide that a provision of this Chapter does not apply in relation to a service of a description specified in the order.
(6)   The power in subsection (5) includes power to provide that a provision of this Chapter does not apply in relation to a service of a description specified in the order in the circumstances so specified.
(7)   An order under subsection (5) may contain transitional or transitory provision or savings.
(8)   No order may be made under subsection (5) unless a draft of the statutory instrument containing it has been laid before, and approved by a resolution of, each House of Parliament.

What statutory rights are there under a services contract?

49. Service to be performed with reasonable care and skill

(1) Every contract to supply a service is to be treated as including a term that the trader must perform the service with reasonable care and skill.

(2) See section 54 for a consumer's rights if the trader is in breach of a term that this section requires to be treated as included in a contract.

50. Information about the trader or service to be binding

(1) Every contract to supply a service is to be treated as including as a term of the contract anything that is said or written to the consumer, by or on behalf of the trader, about the trader or the service, if—

    (a) it is taken into account by the consumer when deciding to enter into the contract, or

    (b) it is taken into account by the consumer when making any decision about the service after entering into the contract.

(2) Anything taken into account by the consumer as mentioned in subsection (1)(a) or (b) is subject to—

    (a) anything that qualified it and was said or written to the consumer by the trader on the same occasion, and

    (b) any change to it that has been expressly agreed between the consumer and the trader (before entering into the contract or later).

(3) Without prejudice to subsection (1), any information provided by the trader in accordance with regulation 9, 10 or 13 of the Consumer Contracts (Information, Cancellation and Additional Charges) Regulations 2013 (SI 2013/3134) is to be treated as included as a term of the contract.

(4) A change to any of the information mentioned in subsection (3), made before entering into the contract or later, is not effective unless expressly agreed between the consumer and the trader.

(5) See section 54 for a consumer's rights if the trader is in breach of a term that this section requires to be treated as included in a contract.

51. Reasonable price to be paid for a service

(1) This section applies to a contract to supply a service if—

    (a) the consumer has not paid a price or other consideration for the service,

    (b) the contract does not expressly fix a price or other consideration, and does not say how it is to be fixed, and

    (c) anything that is to be treated under section 50 as included in the contract does not fix a price or other consideration either.

(2) In that case the contract is to be treated as including a term that the consumer must pay a reasonable price for the service, and no more.

(3) What is a reasonable price is a question of fact.

52. Service to be performed within a reasonable time

(1) This section applies to a contract to supply a service, if—

    (a) the contract does not expressly fix the time for the service to be performed, and does not say how it is to be fixed, and

    (b) information that is to be treated under section 50 as included in the contract does not fix the time either.

(2) In that case the contract is to be treated as including a term that the trader must perform the service within a reasonable time.

(3) What is a reasonable time is a question of fact.

(4) See section 54 for a consumer's rights if the trader is in breach of a term that this section requires to be treated as included in a contract.

53. Relation to other law on contract terms

(1) Nothing in this Chapter affects any enactment or rule of law that imposes a stricter duty on the trader.

(2) This Chapter is subject to any other enactment which defines or restricts the rights, duties or liabilities arising in connection with a service of any description.

What remedies are there if statutory rights under a services contract are not met?

54. Consumer's rights to enforce terms about services

(1) The consumer's rights under this section and sections 55 and 56 do not affect any rights that the contract provides for, if those are not inconsistent.

(2) In this section and section 55 a reference to a service conforming to a contract is a reference to—

(a) the service being performed in accordance with section 49, or

(b) the service conforming to a term that section 50 requires to be treated as included in the contract and that relates to the performance of the service.

(3) If the service does not conform to the contract, the consumer's rights (and the provisions about them and when they are available) are— (a) the right to require repeat performance (see section 55); (b) the right to a price reduction (see section 56).

(4) If the trader is in breach of a term that section 50 requires to be treated as included in the contract but that does not relate to the service, the consumer has the right to a price reduction (see section 56 for provisions about that right and when it is available).

(5) If the trader is in breach of what the contract requires under section 52 (performance within a reasonable time), the consumer has the right to a price reduction (see section 56 for provisions about that right and when it is available).

(6) This section and sections 55 and 56 do not prevent the consumer seeking other remedies for a breach of a term to which any of subsections (3) to (5) applies, instead of or in addition to a remedy referred to there (but not so as to recover twice for the same loss).

(7) Those other remedies include any of the following that is open to the consumer in the circumstances—

(a) claiming damages;

(b) seeking to recover money paid where the consideration for payment of the money has failed;

(c) seeking specific performance;

(d) seeking an order for specific implement;

(e) relying on the breach against a claim by the trader under the contract;

(f) exercising a right to treat the contract as at an end.

55. Right to repeat performance

(1) The right to require repeat performance is a right to require the trader to perform the service again, to the extent necessary to complete its performance in conformity with the contract.

(2) If the consumer requires such repeat performance, the trader—

(a) must provide it within a reasonable time and without significant inconvenience to the consumer; and

(b) must bear any necessary costs incurred in doing so (including in particular the cost of any labour or materials).

(3) The consumer cannot require repeat performance if completing performance of the service in conformity with the contract is impossible.

(4) Any question as to what is a reasonable time or significant inconvenience is to be determined taking account of—

(a) the nature of the service, and

(b) the purpose for which the service was to be performed.

56. Right to price reduction

(1) The right to a price reduction is the right to require the trader to reduce the price to the consumer by an appropriate amount (including the right to receive a refund for anything already paid above the reduced amount).

(2) The amount of the reduction may, where appropriate, be the full amount of the price.

(3) A consumer who has that right and the right to require repeat performance is only entitled to a price reduction in one of these situations—

(a) because of section 55(3) the consumer cannot require repeat performance; or

(b) the consumer has required repeat performance, but the trader is in breach of the requirement of section 55(2)(a) to do it within a reasonable time and without significant inconvenience to the consumer.

(4)   A refund under this section must be given without undue delay, and in any event within 14 days beginning with the day on which the trader agrees that the consumer is entitled to a refund.

(5)   The trader must give the refund using the same means of payment as the consumer used to pay for the service, unless the consumer expressly agrees otherwise.

(6)   The trader must not impose any fee on the consumer in respect of the refund.

Can a trader contract out of statutory rights and remedies under a services contract?

57.   Liability that cannot be excluded or restricted

(1)   A term of a contract to supply services is not binding on the consumer to the extent that it would exclude the trader's liability arising under section 49 (service to be performed with reasonable care and skill).

(2)   Subject to section 50(2), a term of a contract to supply services is not binding on the consumer to the extent that it would exclude the trader's liability arising under section 50 (information about trader or service to be binding).

(3)   A term of a contract to supply services is not binding on the consumer to the extent that it would restrict the trader's liability arising under any of sections 49 and 50 and, where they apply, sections 51 and 52 (reasonable price and reasonable time), if it would prevent the consumer in an appropriate case from recovering the price paid or the value of any other consideration. (If it would not prevent the consumer from doing so, Part 2 (unfair terms) may apply.)

(4)   That also means that a term of a contract to supply services is not binding on the consumer to the extent that it would—

   (a)   exclude or restrict a right or remedy in respect of a liability under any of sections 49 to 52,

   (b)   make such a right or remedy or its enforcement subject to a restrictive or onerous condition,

   (c)   allow a trader to put a person at a disadvantage as a result of pursuing such a right or remedy, or

   (d)   exclude or restrict rules of evidence or procedure.

(5)   The references in subsections (1) to (3) to excluding or restricting a liability also include preventing an obligation or duty arising or limiting its extent.

(6)   An agreement in writing to submit present or future differences to arbitration is not to be regarded as excluding or restricting any liability for the purposes of this section.

(7)   See Schedule 3 for provision about the enforcement of this section.

CHAPTER 5
GENERAL AND SUPPLEMENTARY PROVISIONS

58.   Powers of the court

(1)   In any proceedings in which a remedy is sought by virtue of section 19(3) or (4), 42(2) or 54(3), the court, in addition to any other power it has, may act under this section.

(2)   On the application of the consumer the court may make an order requiring specific performance or, in Scotland, specific implement by the trader of any obligation imposed on the trader by virtue of section 23, 43 or 55.

(3)   Subsection (4) applies if—

   (a)   the consumer claims to exercise a right under the relevant remedies provisions, but

   (b)   the court decides that those provisions have the effect that exercise of another right is appropriate.

(4)   The court may proceed as if the consumer had exercised that other right.

(5)   If the consumer has claimed to exercise the final right to reject, the court may order that any reimbursement to the consumer is reduced by a deduction for use, to take account of the use the consumer has had of the goods in the period since they were delivered.

(6)   Any deduction for use is limited as set out in section 24(9) and (10).

(7)   The court may make an order under this section unconditionally or on such terms and conditions as to damages, payment of the price and otherwise as it thinks just.

(8) The 'relevant remedies provisions' are—
    (a) where Chapter 2 applies, sections 23 and 24;
    (b) where Chapter 3 applies, sections 43 and 44;
    (c) where Chapter 4 applies, sections 55 and 56.

59. Interpretation

(1) These definitions apply in this Part (as well as the key definitions in section 2)—
'conditional sales contract' has the meaning given in section 5(3);
'Consumer Rights Directive' means Directive 2011/83/EU of the European Parliament and of the Council of 25 October 2011 on consumer rights, amending Council Directive 93/13/EEC and Directive 1999/44/EC of the European Parliament and of the Council and repealing Council Directive 85/577/EEC and Directive 97/7/EC of the European Parliament and of the Council;
'credit-broker' means a person acting in the course of a business of credit brokerage carried on by that person;
'credit brokerage' means—
    (a) introducing individuals who want to obtain credit to persons carrying on any business so far as it relates to the provision of credit,
    (b) introducing individuals who want to obtain goods on hire to persons carrying on a business which comprises or relates to supplying goods under a contract for the hire of goods, or
    (c) introducing individuals who want to obtain credit, or to obtain goods on hire, to other persons engaged in credit brokerage;
'delivery' means voluntary transfer of possession from one person to another;
'enactment' includes—
    (a) an enactment contained in subordinate legislation within the meaning of the Interpretation Act 1978,
    (b) an enactment contained in, or in an instrument made under, a Measure or Act of the National Assembly for Wales,
    (c) an enactment contained in, or in an instrument made under, an Act of the Scottish Parliament, and
    (d) an enactment contained in, or in an instrument made under, Northern Ireland legislation;
'producer', in relation to goods or digital content, means—
    (a) the manufacturer,
    (b) the importer into the United Kingdom, or
    (c) any person who purports to be a producer by placing the person's name, trade mark or other distinctive sign on the goods or using it in connection with the digital content.
(2) References in this Part to treating a contract as at an end are to be read in accordance with section 19(13).

60. Changes to other legislation

Schedule 1 (amendments consequential on this Part) has effect.

PART 2
UNFAIR TERMS

What contracts and notices are covered by this Part?

61. Contracts and notices covered by this Part

(1) This Part applies to a contract between a trader and a consumer.
(2) This does not include a contract of employment or apprenticeship.
(3) A contract to which this Part applies is referred to in this Part as a 'consumer contract'.
(4) This Part applies to a notice to the extent that it—
    (a) relates to rights or obligations as between a trader and a consumer, or
    (b) purports to exclude or restrict a trader's liability to a consumer.
(5) This does not include a notice relating to rights, obligations or liabilities as between an employer and an employee.

(6) It does not matter for the purposes of subsection (4) whether the notice is expressed to apply to a consumer, as long as it is reasonable to assume it is intended to be seen or heard by a consumer.

(7) A notice to which this Part applies is referred to in this Part as a 'consumer notice'.

(8) In this section 'notice' includes an announcement, whether or not in writing, and any other communication or purported communication.

What are the general rules about fairness of contract terms and notices?

62. Requirement for contract terms and notices to be fair

(1) An unfair term of a consumer contract is not binding on the consumer.

(2) An unfair consumer notice is not binding on the consumer.

(3) This does not prevent the consumer from relying on the term or notice if the consumer chooses to do so.

(4) A term is unfair if, contrary to the requirement of good faith, it causes a significant imbalance in the parties' rights and obligations under the contract to the detriment of the consumer.

(5) Whether a term is fair is to be determined—
  (a) taking into account the nature of the subject matter of the contract, and
  (b) by reference to all the circumstances existing when the term was agreed and to all of the other terms of the contract or of any other contract on which it depends.

(6) A notice is unfair if, contrary to the requirement of good faith, it causes a significant imbalance in the parties' rights and obligations to the detriment of the consumer.

(7) Whether a notice is fair is to be determined—
  (a) taking into account the nature of the subject matter of the notice, and
  (b) by reference to all the circumstances existing when the rights or obligations to which it relates arose and to the terms of any contract on which it depends.

(8) This section does not affect the operation of—
  (a) section 31 (exclusion of liability: goods contracts),
  (b) section 47 (exclusion of liability: digital content contracts),
  (c) section 57 (exclusion of liability: services contracts), or
  (d) section 65 (exclusion of negligence liability).

63. Contract terms which may or must be regarded as unfair

(1) Part 1 of Schedule 2 contains an indicative and non-exhaustive list of terms of consumer contracts that may be regarded as unfair for the purposes of this Part.

(2) Part 1 of Schedule 2 is subject to Part 2 of that Schedule; but a term listed in Part 2 of that Schedule may nevertheless be assessed for fairness under section 62 unless section 64 or 73 applies to it.

(3) The Secretary of State may by order made by statutory instrument amend Schedule 2 so as to add, modify or remove an entry in Part 1 or Part 2 of that Schedule.

(4) An order under subsection (3) may contain transitional or transitory provision or savings.

(5) No order may be made under subsection (3) unless a draft of the statutory instrument containing it has been laid before, and approved by a resolution of, each House of Parliament.

(6) A term of a consumer contract must be regarded as unfair if it has the effect that the consumer bears the burden of proof with respect to compliance by a distance supplier or an intermediary with an obligation under any enactment or rule implementing the Distance Marketing Directive.

(7) In subsection (6)—
  'the Distance Marketing Directive' means Directive 2002/65/EC of the European Parliament and of the Council of 23 September 2002 concerning the distance marketing of consumer financial services and amending Council Directive 90/619/EEC and Directives 97/7/EC and 98/27/EC;
  'distance supplier' means—
  (a) a supplier under a distance contract within the meaning of the Financial Services (Distance Marketing) Regulations 2004 (SI 2004/2095), or

(b)   a supplier of unsolicited financial services within the meaning of regulation 15 of those regulations;

'enactment' includes an enactment contained in subordinate legislation within the meaning of the Interpretation Act 1978;

'intermediary' has the same meaning as in the Financial Services (Distance Marketing) Regulations 2004;

'rule' means a rule made by the Financial Conduct Authority or the Prudential Regulation Authority under the Financial Services and Markets Act 2000 or by a designated professional body within the meaning of section 326(2) of that Act.

64.   Exclusion from assessment of fairness

(1)   A term of a consumer contract may not be assessed for fairness under section 62 to the extent that—
  (a)   it specifies the main subject matter of the contract, or
  (b)   the assessment is of the appropriateness of the price payable under the contract by comparison with the goods, digital content or services supplied under it.

(2)   Subsection (1) excludes a term from an assessment under section 62 only if it is transparent and prominent.

(3)   A term is transparent for the purposes of this Part if it is expressed in plain and intelligible language and (in the case of a written term) is legible.

(4)   A term is prominent for the purposes of this section if it is brought to the consumer's attention in such a way that an average consumer would be aware of the term.

(5)   In subsection (4) 'average consumer' means a consumer who is reasonably wellinformed, observant and circumspect.

(6)   This section does not apply to a term of a contract listed in Part 1 of Schedule 2.

65.   Bar on exclusion or restriction of negligence liability

(1)   A trader cannot by a term of a consumer contract or by a consumer notice exclude or restrict liability for death or personal injury resulting from negligence.

(2)   Where a term of a consumer contract, or a consumer notice, purports to exclude or restrict a trader's liability for negligence, a person is not to be taken to have voluntarily accepted any risk merely because the person agreed to or knew about the term or notice.

(3)   In this section 'personal injury' includes any disease and any impairment of physical or mental condition.

(4)   In this section 'negligence' means the breach of—
  (a)   any obligation to take reasonable care or exercise reasonable skill in the performance of a contract where the obligation arises from an express or implied term of the contract,
  (b)   a common law duty to take reasonable care or exercise reasonable skill,
  (c)   the common duty of care imposed by the Occupiers' Liability Act 1957 or the Occupiers' Liability Act (Northern Ireland) 1957, or
  (d)   the duty of reasonable care imposed by section 2(1) of the Occupiers' Liability (Scotland) Act 1960.

(5)   It is immaterial for the purposes of subsection (4)—
  (a)   whether a breach of duty or obligation was inadvertent or intentional, or
  (b)   whether liability for it arises directly or vicariously.

(6)   This section is subject to section 66 (which makes provision about the scope of this section).

66.   Scope of section 65

(1)   Section 65 does not apply to—
  (a)   any contract so far as it is a contract of insurance, including a contract to pay an annuity on human life, or
  (b)   any contract so far as it relates to the creation or transfer of an interest in land.

(2)   Section 65 does not affect the validity of any discharge or indemnity given by a person in consideration of the receipt by that person of compensation in settlement of any claim the person has.

(3) Section 65 does not—
  (a) apply to liability which is excluded or discharged as mentioned in section 4(2)(a) (exception to liability to pay damages to relatives) of the Damages (Scotland) Act 2011, or
  (b) affect the operation of section 5 (discharge of liability to pay damages: exception for mesothelioma) of that Act.

(4) Section 65 does not apply to the liability of an occupier of premises to a person who obtains access to the premises for recreational purposes if—
  (a) the person suffers loss or damage because of the dangerous state of the premises, and
  (b) allowing the person access for those purposes is not within the purposes of the occupier's trade, business, craft or profession.

67. Effect of an unfair term on the rest of a contract

Where a term of a consumer contract is not binding on the consumer as a result of this Part, the contract continues, so far as practicable, to have effect in every other respect.

68. Requirement for transparency

(1) A trader must ensure that a written term of a consumer contract, or a consumer notice in writing, is transparent.
(2) A consumer notice is transparent for the purposes of subsection (1) if it is expressed in plain and intelligible language and it is legible.

69. Contract terms that may have different meanings

(1) If a term in a consumer contract, or a consumer notice, could have different meanings, the meaning that is most favourable to the consumer is to prevail.
(2) Subsection (1) does not apply to the construction of a term or a notice in proceedings on an application for an injunction or interdict under paragraph 3 of Schedule 3.

How are the general rules enforced?

70. Enforcement of the law on unfair contract terms

(1) Schedule 3 confers functions on the Competition and Markets Authority and other regulators in relation to the enforcement of this Part.
(2) For provision about the investigatory powers that are available to those regulators for the purposes of that Schedule, see Schedule 5.

Supplementary provisions

71. Duty of court to consider fairness of term

(1) Subsection (2) applies to proceedings before a court which relate to a term of a consumer contract.
(2) The court must consider whether the term is fair even if none of the parties to the proceedings has raised that issue or indicated that it intends to raise it.
(3) But subsection (2) does not apply unless the court considers that it has before it sufficient legal and factual material to enable it to consider the fairness of the term.

72. Application of rules to secondary contracts

(1) This section applies if a term of a contract ('the secondary contract') reduces the rights or remedies or increases the obligations of a person under another contract ('the main contract').
(2) The term is subject to the provisions of this Part that would apply to the term if it were in the main contract.
(3) It does not matter for the purposes of this section—
  (a) whether the parties to the secondary contract are the same as the parties to the main contract, or
  (b) whether the secondary contract is a consumer contract.
(4) This section does not apply if the secondary contract is a settlement of a claim arising under the main contract.

73.   Disapplication of rules to mandatory terms and notices

(1)   This Part does not apply to a term of a contract, or to a notice, to the extent that it reflects—

(a)   mandatory statutory or regulatory provisions, or

(b)   the provisions or principles of an international convention to which the United Kingdom is a party.

(2)   In subsection (1) 'mandatory statutory or regulatory provisions' includes rules which, according to law, apply between the parties on the basis that no other arrangements have been established.

74.   Contracts applying law of a country other than the United Kingdom

(1)   If—

(a)   the law of a country or territory other than the United Kingdom or any part of the United Kingdom is chosen by the parties to be applicable to a consumer contract, but

(b)   the consumer contract has a close connection with the United Kingdom,

this Part applies despite that choice.

(2)   For cases where the law applicable has not been chosen or the law of an EEA State is chosen, see Regulation (EC) No. 593/2008 of the European Parliament and of the Council of 17 June 2008 on the law applicable to contractual obligations as that Regulation has effect as retained direct EU legislation (including that Regulation as applied by regulation 5 of the Law Applicable to Contractual Obligations (England and Wales and Northern Ireland) Regulations 2009 and regulation 4 of the Law Applicable to Contractual Obligations (Scotland) Regulations 2009), unless the case is one in respect of which Regulation (EC) No. 593/2008 has effect by virtue of Article 66 of the EU withdrawal agreement, in which case see that Regulation as it has effect by virtue of that Article.

75.   Changes to other legislation

Schedule 4 (amendments consequential on this Part) has effect.

76.   Interpretation of Part 2

(1)   In this Part—

'consumer contract' has the meaning given by section 61(3);

'consumer notice' has the meaning given by section 61(7);

'transparent' is to be construed in accordance with sections 64(3) and 68(2).

(2)   The following have the same meanings in this Part as they have in Part 1—

'trader' (see section 2(2));

'consumer' (see section 2(3));

'goods' (see section 2(8));

'digital content' (see section 2(9)).

(3)   Section 2(4) (trader who claims an individual is not a consumer must prove it) applies in relation to this Part as it applies in relation to Part 1.

Section 63   SCHEDULE 2

CONSUMER CONTRACT TERMS WHICH MAY BE REGARDED AS UNFAIR

PART 1
LIST OF TERMS

1.   A term which has the object or effect of excluding or limiting the trader's liability in the event of the death of or personal injury to the consumer resulting from an act or omission of the trader.

2.   A term which has the object or effect of inappropriately excluding or limiting the legal rights of the consumer in relation to the trader or another party in the event of total or partial non-performance or inadequate performance by the trader of any of the contractual obligations, including the option of offsetting a debt owed to the trader against any claim which the consumer may have against the trader.

3.   A term which has the object or effect of making an agreement binding on the consumer in a case where the provision of services by the trader is subject to a condition whose realisation depends on the trader's will alone.

4.   A term which has the object or effect of permitting the trader to retain sums paid by the consumer where the consumer decides not to conclude or perform the contract, without providing for the consumer to receive compensation of an equivalent amount from the trader where the trader is the party cancelling the contract.

5.   A term which has the object or effect of requiring that, where the consumer decides not to conclude or perform the contract, the consumer must pay the trader a disproportionately high sum in compensation or for services which have not been supplied.

6.   A term which has the object or effect of requiring a consumer who fails to fulfil his obligations under the contract to pay a disproportionately high sum in compensation.

7.   A term which has the object or effect of authorising the trader to dissolve the contract on a discretionary basis where the same facility is not granted to the consumer, or permitting the trader to retain the sums paid for services not yet supplied by the trader where it is the trader who dissolves the contract.

8.   A term which has the object or effect of enabling the trader to terminate a contract of indeterminate duration without reasonable notice except where there are serious grounds for doing so.

9.   A term which has the object or effect of automatically extending a contract of fixed duration where the consumer does not indicate otherwise, when the deadline fixed for the consumer to express a desire not to extend the contract is unreasonably early.

10.   A term which has the object or effect of irrevocably binding the consumer to terms with which the consumer has had no real opportunity of becoming acquainted before the conclusion of the contract.

11.   A term which has the object or effect of enabling the trader to alter the terms of the contract unilaterally without a valid reason which is specified in the contract.

12.   A term which has the object or effect of permitting the trader to determine the characteristics of the subject matter of the contract after the consumer has become bound by it.

13.   A term which has the object or effect of enabling the trader to alter unilaterally without a valid reason any characteristics of the goods, digital content or services to be provided.

14.   A term which has the object or effect of giving the trader the discretion to decide the price payable under the contract after the consumer has become bound by it, where no price or method of determining the price is agreed when the consumer becomes bound.

15.   A term which has the object or effect of permitting a trader to increase the price of goods, digital content or services without giving the consumer the right to cancel the contract if the final price is too high in relation to the price agreed when the contract was concluded.

16.   A term which has the object or effect of giving the trader the right to determine whether the goods, digital content or services supplied are in conformity with the contract, or giving the trader the exclusive right to interpret any term of the contract.

17.   A term which has the object or effect of limiting the trader's obligation to respect commitments undertaken by the trader's agents or making the trader's commitments subject to compliance with a particular formality.

18.   A term which has the object or effect of obliging the consumer to fulfil all of the consumer's obligations where the trader does not perform the trader's obligations.

19.   A term which has the object or effect of allowing the trader to transfer the trader's rights and obligations under the contract, where this may reduce the guarantees for the consumer, without the consumer's agreement.

20.   A term which has the object or effect of excluding or hindering the consumer's right to take legal action or exercise any other legal remedy, in particular by—

      (a)   requiring the consumer to take disputes exclusively to arbitration not covered by legal provisions,

      (b)   unduly restricting the evidence available to the consumer, or

      (c)   imposing on the consumer a burden of proof which, according to the applicable law, should lie with another party to the contract.

PART 2
SCOPE OF PART 1

Financial services

21.   Paragraph 8 (cancellation without reasonable notice) does not include a term by which a supplier of financial services reserves the right to terminate unilaterally a contract of indeterminate duration without notice where there is a valid reason, if the supplier is required to inform the consumer of the cancellation immediately.

22.   Paragraph 11 (variation of contract without valid reason) does not include a term by which a supplier of financial services reserves the right to alter the rate of interest payable by or due to the consumer, or the amount of other charges for financial services without notice where there is a valid reason, if—
        (a) the supplier is required to inform the consumer of the alteration at the earliest opportunity, and
        (b) the consumer is free to dissolve the contract immediately.

Contracts which last indefinitely

23.   Paragraphs 11 (variation of contract without valid reason), 12 (determination of characteristics of goods etc., after consumer bound) and 14 (determination of price after consumer bound) do not include a term under which a trader reserves the right to alter unilaterally the conditions of a contract of indeterminate duration if—
        (a) the trader is required to inform the consumer with reasonable notice, and
        (b) the consumer is free to dissolve the contract.

Sale of securities, foreign currency etc.

24.   Paragraphs 8 (cancellation without reasonable notice), 11 (variation of contract without valid reason), 14 (determination of price after consumer bound) and 15 (increase in price) do not apply to—
        (a) transactions in transferable securities, financial instruments and other products or services where the price is linked to fluctuations in a stock exchange quotation or index or a financial market rate that the trader does not control, and
        (b) contracts for the purchase or sale of foreign currency, traveller's cheques or international money orders denominated in foreign currency.

Price index clauses

25.   Paragraphs 14 (determination of price after consumer bound) and 15 (increase in price) do not include a term which is a price-indexation clause (where otherwise lawful), if the method by which prices vary is explicitly described.

Section 70   SCHEDULE 3

ENFORCEMENT OF THE LAW ON UNFAIR CONTRACT TERMS AND NOTICES

Application of Schedule

1.   This Schedule applies to—
        (a) a term of a consumer contract,
        (b) a term proposed for use in a consumer contract,
        (c) a term which a third party recommends for use in a consumer contract, or
        (d) a consumer notice.

Consideration of complaints

2.   (1) A regulator may consider a complaint about a term or notice to which this Schedule applies (a 'relevant complaint').
        (2) If a regulator other than the CMA intends to consider a relevant complaint, it must notify the CMA that it intends to do so, and must then consider the complaint.
        (3) If a regulator considers a relevant complaint, but decides not to make an application under paragraph 3 in relation to the complaint, it must give reasons for its decision to the person who made the complaint.

Application for injunction or interdict

3. (1)   A regulator may apply for an injunction or (in Scotland) an interdict against a person if the regulator thinks that—
    (a)   the person is using, or proposing or recommending the use of, a term or notice to which this Schedule applies, and
    (b)   the term or notice falls within any one or more of sub-paragraphs (2), (3) or (5).
    (2)   A term or notice falls within this sub-paragraph if it purports to exclude or restrict liability of the kind mentioned in—
    (a)   section 31 (exclusion of liability: goods contracts),
    (b)   section 47 (exclusion of liability: digital content contracts),
    (c)   section 57 (exclusion of liability: services contracts), or
    (d)   section 65(1) (business liability for death or personal injury resulting from negligence).
    (3)   A term or notice falls within this sub-paragraph if it is unfair to any extent.
    (4)   A term within paragraph 1(1)(b) or (c) (but not within paragraph 1(1)(a)) is to be treated for the purposes of section 62(4) and (5) (assessment of fairness) as if it were a term of a contract.
    (5)   A term or notice falls within this sub-paragraph if it breaches section 68 (requirement for transparency).
    (6)   A regulator may apply for an injunction or interdict under this paragraph in relation to a term or notice whether or not it has received a relevant complaint about the term or notice.

Notification of application

4. (1)   Before making an application under paragraph 3, a regulator other than the CMA must notify the CMA that it intends to do so.
    (2)   The regulator may make the application only if—
    (a)   the period of 14 days beginning with the day on which the regulator notified the CMA has ended, or
    (b)   before the end of that period, the CMA agrees to the regulator making the application.

Determination of application

5. (1)   On an application for an injunction under paragraph 3, the court may grant an injunction on such conditions, and against such of the respondents, as it thinks appropriate.
    (2)   On an application for an interdict under paragraph 3, the court may grant an interdict on such conditions, and against such of the defenders, as it thinks appropriate.
    (3)   The injunction or interdict may include provision about—
    (a)   a term or notice to which the application relates, or
    (b)   any term of a consumer contract, or any consumer notice, of a similar kind or with a similar effect.
    (4)   It is not a defence to an application under paragraph 3 to show that, because of a rule of law, a term to which the application relates is not, or could not be, an enforceable contract term.
    (5)   If a regulator other than the CMA makes the application, it must notify the CMA of—
    (a)   the outcome of the application, and
    (b)   if an injunction or interdict is granted, the conditions on which, and the persons against whom, it is granted.

Undertakings

6. (1)   A regulator may accept an undertaking from a person against whom it has applied, or thinks it is entitled to apply, for an injunction or interdict under paragraph 3.
    (4)   The undertaking may provide that the person will comply with the conditions that are agreed between the person and the regulator about the use of terms or notices, or terms or notices of a kind, specified in the undertaking.

(5) If a regulator other than the CMA accepts an undertaking, it must notify the CMA of—
    (a) the conditions on which the undertaking is accepted, and
    (b) the person who gave it.

Publication, information and advice

7. (1) The CMA must arrange the publication of details of—
    (a) any application it makes for an injunction or interdict under paragraph 3,
    (b) any injunction or interdict under this Schedule, and
    (c) any undertaking under this Schedule.

(2) The CMA must respond to a request whether a term or notice, or one of a similar kind or with a similar effect, is or has been the subject of an injunction, interdict or undertaking under this Schedule.

(3) Where the term or notice, or one of a similar kind or with a similar effect, is or has been the subject of an injunction or interdict under this Schedule, the CMA must give the person making the request a copy of the injunction or interdict.

(4) Where the term or notice, or one of a similar kind or with a similar effect, is or has been the subject of an undertaking under this Schedule, the CMA must give the person making the request—
    (a) details of the undertaking, and
    (b) if the person giving the undertaking has agreed to amend the term or notice, a copy of the amendments.

(5) The CMA may arrange the publication of advice and information about the provisions of this Part.

(6) In this paragraph—
    (a) references to an injunction or interdict under this Schedule are to an injunction or interdict granted on an application by the CMA under paragraph 3 or notified to it under paragraph 5, and
    (b) references to an undertaking are to an undertaking given to the CMA under paragraph 6 or notified to it under that paragraph.

Meaning of 'regulator'

8. (1) In this Schedule 'regulator' means—
    (a) the CMA,
    (b) the Department of Enterprise, Trade and Investment in Northern Ireland,
    (c) a local weights and measures authority in Great Britain,
    (d) the Financial Conduct Authority,
    (e) the Office of Communications,
    (f) the Information Commissioner,
    (g) the Gas and Electricity Markets Authority,
    (h) the Water Services Regulation Authority,
    (i) the Office of Rail Regulation,
    (j) the Northern Ireland Authority for Utility Regulation, or
    (k) the Consumers' Association.

(2) The Secretary of State may by order made by statutory instrument amend subparagraph (1) so as to add, modify or remove an entry.

(3) An order under sub-paragraph (2) may amend sub-paragraph (1) so as to add a body that is not a public authority only if the Secretary of State thinks that the body represents the interests of consumers (or consumers of a particular description).

(4) The Secretary of State must publish (and may from time to time vary) other criteria to be applied by the Secretary of State in deciding whether to add an entry to, or remove an entry from, sub-paragraph (1).

(5) An order under sub-paragraph (2) may make consequential amendments to this Schedule (including with the effect that any of its provisions apply differently, or do not apply, to a body added to sub-paragraph (1)).

(6) An order under sub-paragraph (2) may contain transitional or transitory provision or savings.

(7)   No order may be made under sub-paragraph (2) unless a draft of the statutory instrument containing it has been laid before, and approved by a resolution of, each House of Parliament.

(8)   In this paragraph 'public authority' has the same meaning as in section 6 of the Human Rights Act 1998.

Other definitions

9.   In this Schedule—

'the CMA' means the Competition and Markets Authority;

'injunction' includes an interim injunction;

'interdict' includes an interim interdict.

The Financial Conduct Authority

10.   The functions of the Financial Conduct Authority under this Schedule are to be treated as functions of the Authority under the Financial Services and Markets Act 2000.

STATUTORY INSTRUMENTS

COMMERCIAL AGENTS (COUNCIL DIRECTIVE) REGULATIONS 1993 (SI 1993, No. 3053)

PART I

GENERAL

1.   Citation, commencement and applicable law

(1)   These Regulations may be cited as the Commercial Agents (Council Directive) Regulations 1993 and shall come into force on 1st January 1994.

(2)   These Regulations govern the relations between commercial agents and their principals and, subject to paragraph (3), apply in relation to the activities of commercial agents in Great Britain.

(3)   A court or tribunal shall:

(a)   apply the law of the other member State concerned in place of regulations 3 to 22 where the parties have agreed that the agency contract is to be governed by the law of that member State;

(b)   (whether or not it would otherwise be required to do so) apply these Regulations where the law of another member State corresponding to these Regulations enables the parties to agree that the agency contract is to be governed by the law of a different member State and the parties have agreed that it is to be governed by the law of England and Wales or Scotland.

2.   Interpretation, application and extent

(1)   In these Regulations—

'commercial agent' means a self-employed intermediary who has continuing authority to negotiate the sale or purchase of goods on behalf of another person (the 'principal'), or to negotiate and conclude the sale or purchase of goods on behalf of and in the name of that principal; but shall be understood as not including in particular:

(i)   a person who, in his capacity as an officer of a company or association, is empowered to enter into commitments binding on that company or association;

(ii)   a partner who is lawfully authorised to enter into commitments binding on his partners;

(iii)   a person who acts as an insolvency practitioner (as that expression is defined in section 388 of the Insolvency Act 1986) or the equivalent in any other jurisdiction;

'commission' means any part of the remuneration of a commercial agent which varies with the number or value of business transactions;

'EEA Agreement' means the Agreement on the European Economic Area signed at Oporto on 2nd May 1992 as adjusted by the Protocol signed at Brussels on 17th March 1993;

'member State' includes a State which is a contracting party to the EEA Agreement;

'restraint of trade clause' means an agreement restricting the business activities of a commercial agent following termination of the agency contract.

(2)   These Regulations do not apply to—

    (a)   commercial agents whose activities are unpaid;

    (b)   commercial agents when they operate on commodity exchanges or in the commodity market;

    (c)   the Crown Agents for Overseas Governments and Administrations, as set up under the Crown Agents Act 1979, or its subsidiaries.

(3)   The provisions of the Schedule to these Regulations have effect for the purpose of determining the persons whose activities as commercial agents are to be considered secondary.

(4)   These Regulations shall not apply to the persons referred to in paragraph (3) above.

(5)   These Regulations do not extend to Northern Ireland.

PART II

RIGHTS AND OBLIGATIONS

3.   Duties of a commercial agent to his principal

(1)   In performing his activities a commercial agent must look after the interests of his principal and act dutifully and in good faith.

(2)   In particular, a commercial agent must—

    (a)   make proper efforts to negotiate and, where appropriate, conclude the transactions he is instructed to take care of;

    (b)   communicate to his principal all the necessary information available to him;

    (c)   comply with reasonable instructions given by his principal.

4.   Duties of a principal to his commercial agent

(1)   In his relations with his commercial agent a principal must act dutifully and in good faith.

(2)   In particular, a principal must—

    (a)   provide his commercial agent with the necessary documentation relating to the goods concerned;

    (b)   obtain for his commercial agent the information necessary for the performance of the agency contract, and in particular notify his commercial agent within a reasonable period once he anticipates that the volume of commercial transactions will be significantly lower than that which the commercial agent could normally have expected.

(3)   A principal shall, in addition, inform his commercial agent within a reasonable period of his acceptance or refusal of, and of any non-execution by him of, a commercial transaction which the commercial agent has procured for him.

5.   Prohibition on derogation from regulations 3 and 4 and consequence of breach

(1)   The parties may not derogate from regulations 3 and 4 above.

(2)   The law applicable to the contract shall govern the consequence of breach of the rights and obligations under regulations 3 and 4 above.

PART III
REMUNERATION

6.   Form and amount of remuneration in absence of agreement

(1)   In the absence of any agreement as to remuneration between the parties, a commercial agent shall be entitled to the remuneration that commercial agents appointed for the goods forming the subject of his agency contract are customarily allowed in the place where he carries on his activities and, if there is no such customary practice, a commercial agent shall be entitled to reasonable remuneration taking into account all the aspects of the transaction.

(2)   This regulation is without prejudice to the application of any enactment or rule of law concerning the level of remuneration.

(3)   Where a commercial agent is not remunerated (wholly or in part) by commission, regulations 7 to 12 below shall not apply.

7.   Entitlement to commission on transactions concluded during agency contract

(1)   A commercial agent shall be entitled to commission on commercial transactions concluded during the period covered by the agency contract—

(a)   where the transaction has been concluded as a result of his action; or

(b)   where the transaction is concluded with a third party whom he has previously acquired as a customer for transactions of the same kind.

(2)   A commercial agent shall also be entitled to commission on transactions concluded during the period covered by the agency contract where he has an exclusive right to a specific geographical area or to a specific group of customers and where the transaction has been entered into with a customer belonging to that area or group.

8.   Entitlement to commission on transactions concluded after agency contract has terminated

Subject to regulation 9 below, a commercial agent shall be entitled to commission on commercial transactions concluded after the agency contract has terminated if—

(a)   the transaction is mainly attributable to his efforts during the period covered by the agency contract and if the transaction was entered into within a reasonable period after that contract terminated; or

(b)   in accordance with the conditions mentioned in regulation 7 above, the order of the third party reached the principal or the commercial agent before the agency contract terminated.

9.   Apportionment of commission between new and previous commercial agents

(1)   A commercial agent shall not be entitled to the commission referred to in regulation 7 above if that commission is payable, by virtue of regulation 8 above, to the previous commercial agent, unless it is equitable because of the circumstances for the commission to be shared between the commercial agents.

(2)   The principal shall be liable for any sum due under paragraph (1) above to the person entitled to it in accordance with that paragraph, and any sum which the other commercial agent receives to which he is not entitled shall be refunded to the principal.

10.   When commission due and date for payment

(1)   Commission shall become due as soon as, and to the extent that, one of the following circumstances occurs:

(a)   the principal has executed the transaction; or

(b)   the principal should, according to his agreement with the third party, have executed the transaction; or

(c)   the third party has executed the transaction.

(2)   Commission shall become due at the latest when the third party has executed his part of the transaction or should have done so if the principal had executed his part of the transaction, as he should have.

(3) The commission shall be paid not later than on the last day of the month following the quarter in which it became due, and, for the purposes of these Regulations, unless otherwise agreed between the parties, the first quarter period shall run from the date the agency contract takes effect, and subsequent periods shall run from that date in the third month thereafter or the beginning of the fourth month, whichever is the sooner.

(4) Any agreement to derogate from paragraphs (2) and (3) above to the detriment of the commercial agent shall be void.

11. Extinction of right to commission

(1) The right to commission can be extinguished only if and to the extent that—
   (a)   it is established that the contract between the third party and the principal will not be executed; and
   (b)   that fact is due to a reason for which the principal is not to blame.

(2) Any commission which the commercial agent has already received shall be refunded if the right to it is extinguished.

(3) Any agreement to derogate from paragraph (1) above to the detriment of the commercial agent shall be void.

12. Periodic supply of information as to commission due and right of inspection of principal's books

(1) The principal shall supply his commercial agent with a statement of the commission due, not later than the last day of the month following the quarter in which the commission has become due, and such statement shall set out the main components used in calculating the amount of the commission.

(2) A commercial agent shall be entitled to demand that he be provided with all the information (and in particular an extract from the books) which is available to his principal and which he needs in order to check the amount of the commission due to him.

(3) Any agreement to derogate from paragraphs (1) and (2) above shall be void.

(4) Nothing in this regulation shall remove or restrict the effect of, or prevent reliance upon, any enactment or rule of law which recognises the right of an agent to inspect the books of a principal.

PART IV

CONCLUSION AND TERMINATION OF THE AGENCY CONTRACT

13. Right to signed written statement of terms of agency contract

(1) The commercial agent and principal shall each be entitled to receive from the other, on request, a signed written document setting out the terms of the agency contract including any terms subsequently agreed.

(2) Any purported waiver of the right referred to in paragraph (1) above shall be void.

14. Conversion of agency contract after expiry of fixed period

An agency contract for a fixed period which continues to be performed by both parties after that period has expired shall be deemed to be converted into an agency contract for an indefinite period.

15. Minimum periods of notice for termination of agency contract

(1) Where an agency contract is concluded for an indefinite period either party may terminate it by notice.

(2) The period of notice shall be—
   (a)   1 month for the first year of the contract;
   (b)   2 months for the second year commenced;
   (c)   3 months for the third year commenced and for the subsequent years; and the parties may not agree on any shorter periods of notice.

(3) If the parties agree on longer periods than those laid down in paragraph (2) above, the period of notice to be observed by the principal must not be shorter than that to be observed by the commercial agent.

(4)   Unless otherwise agreed by the parties, the end of the period of notice must coincide with the end of a calendar month.

(5)   The provisions of this regulation shall also apply to an agency contract for a fixed period where it is converted under regulation 14 above into an agency contract for an indefinite period subject to the proviso that the earlier fixed period must be taken into account in the calculation of the period of notice.

16.   Savings with regard to immediate termination

These Regulations shall not affect the application of any enactment or rule of law which provides for the immediate termination of the agency contract—

(a)   because of the failure of one party to carry out all or part of his obligations under that contract; or

(b)   where exceptional circumstances arise.

17.   Entitlement of commercial agent to indemnity or compensation on termination of agency contract

(1)   This regulation has effect for the purpose of ensuring that the commercial agent is, after termination of the agency contract, indemnified in accordance with paragraphs (3) to (5) below or compensated for damage in accordance with paragraphs (6) and (7) below.

(2)   Except where the agency contract otherwise provides, the commercial agent shall be entitled to be compensated rather than indemnified.

(3)   Subject to paragraph (9) and to regulation 18 below, the commercial agent shall be entitled to an indemnity if and to the extent that—

    (a)   he has brought the principal new customers or has significantly increased the volume of business with existing customers and the principal continues to derive substantial benefits from the business with such customers; and

    (b)   the payment of this indemnity is equitable having regard to all the circumstances and, in particular, the commission lost by the commercial agent on the business transacted with such customers.

(4)   The amount of the indemnity shall not exceed a figure equivalent to an indemnity for one year calculated from the commercial agent's average annual remuneration over the preceding five years and if the contract goes back less than five years the indemnity shall be calculated on the average for the period in question.

(5)   The grant of an indemnity as mentioned above shall not prevent the commercial agent from seeking damages.

(6)   Subject to paragraph (9) and to regulation 18 below, the commercial agent shall be entitled to compensation for the damage he suffers as a result of the termination of his relations with his principal.

(7)   For the purpose of these Regulations such damage shall be deemed to occur particularly when the termination takes place in either or both of the following circumstances, namely circumstances which—

    (a)   deprive the commercial agent of the commission which proper performance of the agency contract would have procured for him whilst providing his principal with substantial benefits linked to the activities of the commercial agent; or

    (b)   have not enabled the commercial agent to amortize the costs and expenses that he had incurred in the performance of the agency contract on the advice of his principal.

(8)   Entitlement to the indemnity or compensation for damage as provided for under paragraphs (2) to (7) above shall also arise where the agency contract is terminated as a result of the death of the commercial agent.

(9)   The commercial agent shall lose his entitlement to the indemnity or compensation for damage in the instances provided for in paragraphs (2) to (8) above if within one year following termination of his agency contract he has not notified his principal that he intends pursuing his entitlement.

18.   Grounds for excluding payment of indemnity or compensation under regulation 17

The indemnity or compensation referred to in regulation 17 above shall not be payable to the commercial agent where—

(a)   the principal has terminated the agency contract because of default attributable to the commercial agent which would justify immediate termination of the agency contract pursuant to regulation 16 above; or

(b)   the commercial agent has himself terminated the agency contract, unless such termination is justified—

  (i)   by circumstances attributable to the principal, or

  (ii)   on grounds of the age, infirmity or illness of the commercial agent in consequence of which he cannot reasonably be required to continue his activities; or

(c)   the commercial agent, with the agreement of his principal, assigns his rights and duties under the agency contract to another person.

19.   Prohibition on derogation from regulations 17 and 18

The parties may not derogate from regulations 17 and 18 to the detriment of the commercial agent before the agency contract expires.

20.   Restraint of trade clauses

(1)   A restraint of trade clause shall be valid only if and to the extent that—

  (a)   it is concluded in writing; and .

  (b)   it relates to the geographical area or the group of customers and the geographical area entrusted to the commercial agent and to the kind of goods covered by his agency under the contract.

(2)   A restraint of trade clause shall be valid for not more than two years after termination of the agency contract.

(3)   Nothing in this regulation shall affect any enactment or rule of law which imposes other restrictions on the validity or enforceability of restraint of trade clauses or which enables a court to reduce the obligations on the parties resulting from such clauses.

PART V
MISCELLANEOUS AND SUPPLEMENTAL

21.   Disclosure of information

Nothing in these Regulations shall require information to be given where such disclosure would be contrary to public policy.

22.   Service of notice etc

(1)   Any notice, statement or other document to be given or supplied to a commercial agent or to be given or supplied to the principal under these Regulations may be so given or supplied:

  (a)   by delivering it to him;

  (b)   by leaving it at his proper address addressed to him by name;

  (c)   by sending it by post to him addressed either to his registered address or to the address of his registered or principal office;

  or by any other means provided for in the agency contract.

(2)   Any such notice, statement or document may—

  (a)   in the case of a body corporate, be given or served on the secretary or clerk of that body;

  (b)   in the case of a partnership, be given to or served on any partner or on any person having the control or management of the partnership business.

23.   Transitional provisions

(1)   Notwithstanding any provision in an agency contract made before 1st January 1994, these Regulations shall apply to that contract after that date and, accordingly any provision which is inconsistent with these Regulations shall have effect subject to them.

(2) Nothing in these Regulations shall affect the rights and liabilities of a commercial agent or a principal which have accrued before 1st January 1994.

THE SCHEDULE

1. The activities of a person as a commercial agent are to be considered secondary where it may reasonably be taken that the primary purpose of the arrangement with his principal is other than as set out in paragraph 2 below.

2. An arrangement falls within this paragraph if—
   (a) the business of the principal is the sale, or as the case may be purchase, of goods of a particular kind; and
   (b) the goods concerned are such that—
      (i) transactions are normally individually negotiated and concluded on a commercial basis, and
      (ii) procuring a transaction on one occasion is likely to lead to further transactions in those goods with that customer on future occasions, or to transactions in those goods with other customers in the same geographical area or among the same group of customers, and
   that accordingly it is in the commercial interests of the principal in developing the market in those goods to appoint a representative to such customers with a view to the representative devoting effort, skill and expenditure from his own resources to that end.

3. The following are indications that an arrangement falls within paragraph 2 above, and the absence of any of them is an indication to the contrary—
   (a) the principal is the manufacturer, importer or distributor of the goods;
   (b) the goods are specifically identified with the principal in the market in question rather than, or to a greater extent than, with any other person;
   (c) the agent devotes substantially the whole of his time to representative activities (whether for one principal or for a number of principals whose interests are not conflicting);
   (d) the goods are not normally available in the market in question other than by means of the agent;
   (e) the arrangement is described as one of commercial agency.

4. The following are indications that an arrangement does not fall within paragraph 2 above—
   (a) promotional material is supplied direct to potential customers;
   (b) persons are granted agencies without reference to existing agents in a particular area or in relation to a particular group;
   (c) customers normally select the goods for themselves and merely place their orders through the agent.

5. The activities of the following categories of persons are presumed, unless the contrary is established, not to fall within paragraph 2 above—
   Mail order catalogue agents for consumer goods.
   Consumer credit agents.

LATE PAYMENT OF COMMERCIAL DEBTS REGULATIONS 2002
(SI 2002, No. 1674)

3. Proceedings restraining use of grossly unfair terms

(1) In this regulation, 'representative body' means an organisation established to represent the collective interests of any enterprise, either in general or in a particular sector or area.

(2) Paragraph (3) applies where a person acting in the course of a business enters (or intends to enter) as purchaser into a contract to which the Late Payment of Commercial Debts (Interest) Act 1998 applies.

(3) On the application of a representative body, the High Court may grant an injunction on such terms as it thinks fit restraining the person from relying on a term in the

contract, or engaging in a practice in relation to the contract, where that term or practice relates to—

(a)   the date or period for payment of a debt;

(b)   the right to interest for late payment of a debt; or

(c)   compensation arising out the late payment of a debt;

and in all the circumstances of the case that term or practice appears to the High Court to be grossly unfair.

GENERAL PRODUCT SAFETY REGULATIONS 2005
(SI 2005, No. 1803)

PART 1

GENERAL

1.   Citation, commencement and revocation

(1)   These Regulations may be cited as the General Product Safety Regulations 2005 and shall come into force on 1st October 2005 with the exception of the reference to a civil partner in regulation 43(2) which shall come into force on 5th December 2005.

(2)   The General Product Safety Regulations 1994 are hereby revoked.

2.   Interpretation

In these Regulations—

'the 1987 Act' means the Consumer Protection Act 1987;

'contravention' includes a failure to comply and cognate expressions shall be construed accordingly;

'dangerous product' means a product other than a safe product;

'distributor' means a professional in the supply chain whose activity does not affect the safety properties of a product;

'enforcement authority' means the Secretary of State, any other Minister of the Crown in charge of a government department, any such department and any authority or council mentioned in regulation 10;

'general safety requirement' means the requirement that only safe products should be placed on the market;

'magistrates' court' in relation to Northern Ireland, means a court of summary jurisdiction;

'the market' means the United Kingdom market;

'notice' means a notice in writing;

'officer', in relation to an enforcement authority, means a person authorised in writing to assist the authority in carrying out its functions under or for the purposes of the enforcement of these Regulations and safety notices, except in relation to an enforcement authority which is a government department where it means an officer of that department;

'producer' means—

(a)   the manufacturer of a product, when he is established in the United Kingdom and any other person presenting himself as the manufacturer by affixing to the product his name, trade mark or other distinctive mark, or the person who reconditions the product;

(b)   when the manufacturer is not established in the United Kingdom—

     (i)   if he has a representative established in the United Kingdom, the representative,

     (ii)   in any other case, the person established in the United Kingdom that places a product from a country outside the United Kingdom on the market;

(c)   other professionals in the supply chain, insofar as their activities may affect the safety properties of a product;

'product' means a product which is intended for consumers or likely, under reasonably foreseeable conditions, to be used by consumers even if not intended for them and which is supplied or made available, whether for consideration or not, in the course of a commercial activity and whether it is new, used or reconditioned and includes a product that is supplied or made available to consumers for their own use in the context of providing a service. 'product' does not include equipment used by service providers themselves to supply a service to consumers, in particular equipment on which consumers ride or travel which is operated by a service provider;

'recall' means any measure aimed at achieving the return of a dangerous product that has already been supplied or made available to consumers;

'recall notice' means a notice under regulation 15;

'record' includes any book or document and any record in any form;

'relevant enactment' means any retained EU law derived from an EU instrument harmonising the conditions for the marketing of products in the EU but does not include Regulation (EC) No 765/2008 of the European Parliament and the Council setting out the requirements for accreditation and market surveillance relating to the marketing of products and repealing Regulation (EEC) No 339/93;

'requirement to mark' means a notice under regulation 12;

'requirement to warn' means a notice under regulation 13;

'safe product' means a product which, under normal or reasonably foreseeable conditions of use including duration and, where applicable, putting into service, installation and maintenance requirements, does not present any risk or only the minimum risks compatible with the product's use, considered to be acceptable and consistent with a high level of protection for the safety and health of persons. In determining the foregoing, the following shall be taken into account in particular—

(a) the characteristics of the product, including its composition, packaging, instructions for assembly and, where applicable, instructions for installation and maintenance,

(b) the effect of the product on other products, where it is reasonably foreseeable that it will be used with other products,

(c) the presentation of the product, the labelling, any warnings and instructions for its use and disposal and any other indication or information regarding the product, and

(d) the categories of consumers at risk when using the product, in particular children and the elderly.

The feasibility of obtaining higher levels of safety or the availability of other products presenting a lesser degree of risk shall not constitute grounds for considering a product to be a dangerous product;

'safety notice' means a suspension notice, a requirement to mark, a requirement to warn, a withdrawal notice or a recall notice;

'serious risk' means a serious risk, including one the effects of which are not immediate, requiring rapid intervention;

'supply' in relation to a product includes making it available, in the context of providing a service, for use by consumers;

'suspension notice' means a notice under regulation 11;

'withdrawal' means any measure aimed at preventing the distribution, display or offer of a dangerous product to a consumer;

'withdrawal notice' means a notice under regulation 14.

3. Application

(1) Each provision of these Regulations applies to a product in so far as there are no specific provisions with the same objective in any relevant enactment governing the safety of the product.

(2) Where a product is subject to specific safety requirements imposed by rules of any relevant enactment, these Regulations shall apply only to the aspects and risks or category of risks not covered by those requirements. This means that:

(a) the definition of 'safe product' and 'dangerous product' in regulation 2 and regulations 5 and 6 shall not apply to such a product in so far as concerns the risks or category of risks covered by the specific provisions of the enactment, and

(b) the remainder of these Regulations shall apply except where there are specific provisions governing the aspects covered by those regulations with the same objective.

4. These Regulations do not apply to a second-hand product supplied as a product to be repaired or reconditioned prior to being used, provided the supplier clearly informs the person to whom he supplies the product to that effect.

PART 2

OBLIGATIONS OF PRODUCERS AND DISTRIBUTORS

5. General safety requirement

(1) No producer shall place a product on the market unless the product is a safe product.

(2) No producer shall offer or agree to place a product on the market or expose or possess a product for placing on the market unless the product is a safe product.

(3) No producer shall offer or agree to supply a product or expose or possess a product for supply unless the product is a safe product.

(4) No producer shall supply a product unless the product is a safe product.

6. Presumption of conformity

(1) Where, in the absence of specific provisions in any relevant enactment governing the safety of a product, the product conforms to the specific rules of any other law of part of the United Kingdom laying down the health and safety requirements which the product must satisfy in order to be marketed in the United Kingdom, the product shall be deemed safe so far as concerns the aspects covered by such rules.

(2) Where a product conforms to a voluntary national standard of the United Kingdom ('S') which meets the conditions in paragraph (2A), the product shall be presumed to be a safe product so far as concerns the risks and categories of risk covered by S.

(2A) The conditions referred to in paragraph (2) are that—

    (a) the Secretary of State considers S appropriate for the purposes of giving rise to the presumption of conformity; and

    (b) the Secretary of State has published the reference to S in a manner the Secretary of State considers appropriate.

(3) In circumstances other than those referred to in paragraphs (1) and (2), the conformity of a product to the general safety requirement shall be assessed taking into account—

    (a) ...

    (b) national standards drawn up in the United Kingdom,

    (c) recommendations of the Secretary of State setting guidelines on product safety assessment,

    (d) product safety codes of good practice in the sector concerned,

    (e) the state of the art and technology, and

    (f) reasonable consumer expectations concerning safety.

(4) Conformity of a product with the criteria designed to ensure the general safety requirement is complied with, in particular the provisions mentioned in paragraphs (1) to (3), shall not bar an enforcement authority from exercising its powers under these Regulations in relation to that product where there is evidence that, despite such conformity, it is dangerous.

7. Other obligations of producers

(1) Within the limits of his activities, a producer shall provide consumers with the relevant information to enable them—

    (a) to assess the risks inherent in a product throughout the normal or reasonably foreseeable period of its use, where such risks are not immediately obvious without adequate warnings, and

    (b) to take precautions against those risks.

(2) The presence of warnings does not exempt any person from compliance with the other requirements of these Regulations.

(3) Within the limits of his activities, a producer shall adopt measures commensurate with the characteristics of the products which he supplies to enable him to—

    (a) be informed of the risks which the products might pose, and

    (b) take appropriate action including, where necessary to avoid such risks, withdrawal, adequately and effectively warning consumers as to the risks or, as a last resort, recall.

(4) The measures referred to in paragraph (3) include—
    (a) except where it is not reasonable to do so, an indication by means of the product or its packaging of—
        (i) the name and address of the producer, and
        (ii) the product reference or where applicable the batch of products to which it belongs; and
    (b) where and to the extent that it is reasonable to do so—
        (i) sample testing of marketed products,
        (ii) investigating and if necessary keeping a register of complaints concerning the safety of the product, and
        (iii) keeping distributors informed of the results of such monitoring where a product presents a risk or may present a risk.

8. Obligations of distributors

(1) A distributor shall act with due care in order to help ensure compliance with the applicable safety requirements and in particular he—
    (a) shall not expose or possess for supply or offer or agree to supply, or supply, a product to any person which he knows or should have presumed, on the basis of the information in his possession and as a professional, is a dangerous product; and
    (b) shall, within the limits of his activities, participate in monitoring the safety of a product placed on the market, in particular by—
        (i) passing on information on the risks posed by the product,
        (ii) keeping the documentation necessary for tracing the origin of the product,
        (iii) producing the documentation necessary for tracing the origin of the product, and cooperating in action taken by a producer or an enforcement authority to avoid the risks.
(2) Within the limits of his activities, a distributor shall take measures enabling him to cooperate efficiently in the action referred to in paragraph (1)(b)(iii).

9. Obligations of producers and distributors

(1) Subject to paragraph (2), where a producer or a distributor knows that a product he has placed on the market or supplied poses risks to the consumer that are incompatible with the general safety requirement, he shall forthwith notify an enforcement authority in writing of that information and—
    (a) the action taken to prevent risk to the consumer;
    (b) ...
(2) Paragraph (1) shall not apply—
    (a) in the case of a second-hand product supplied as an antique or as a product to be repaired or reconditioned prior to being used, provided the supplier clearly informed the person to whom he supplied the product to that effect,
    (b) in conditions concerning isolated circumstances or products.
(3) In the event of a serious risk the notification under paragraph (1) shall include the following—
    (a) information enabling a precise identification of the product or batch of products in question,
    (b) a full description of the risks that the product presents,
    (c) all available information relevant for tracing the product, and
    (d) a description of the action undertaken to prevent risks to the consumer.
(4) Within the limits of his activities, a person who is a producer or a distributor shall co-operate with an enforcement authority (at the enforcement authority's request) in action taken to avoid the risks posed by a product which he supplies or has supplied. Every enforcement authority shall maintain procedures for such co-operation, including procedures for dialogue with the producers and distributors concerned on issues related to product safety.

PART 3
ENFORCEMENT

10.   Enforcement

(1)   It shall be the duty of every authority to which paragraph (4) applies to enforce within its area these Regulations and safety notices.

(2)   An authority in England or Wales to which paragraph (4) applies shall have the power to investigate and prosecute for an alleged contravention of any provision imposed by or under these Regulations which was committed outside its area in any part of England and Wales.

(3)   A district council in Northern Ireland shall have the power to investigate and prosecute for an alleged contravention of any provision imposed by or under these Regulations which was committed outside its area in any part of Northern Ireland.

(4)   The authorities to which this paragraph applies are:

   (a)   in England, a county council, district council, London Borough Council, the Common Council of the City of London in its capacity as a local authority and the Council of the Isles of Scilly,

   (b)   in Wales, a county council or a county borough council,

   (c)   in Scotland, a council constituted under section 2 of the Local Government etc. (Scotland) Act 1994,

   (d)   in Northern Ireland any district council.

(5)   An enforcement authority shall in enforcing these Regulations act in a manner proportionate to the seriousness of the risk and shall take due account of the precautionary principle. In this context, it shall encourage and promote voluntary action by producers and distributors. Notwithstanding the foregoing, an enforcement authority may take any action under these Regulations urgently and without first encouraging and promoting voluntary action if a product poses a serious risk.

11.   Suspension notices

(1)   Where an enforcement authority has reasonable grounds for suspecting that a requirement of these Regulations has been contravened in relation to a product, the authority may, for the period needed to organise appropriate safety evaluations, checks and controls, serve a notice ('a suspension notice') prohibiting the person on whom it is served from doing any of the following things without the consent of the authority, that is to say—

   (a)   placing the product on the market, offering to place it on the market, agreeing to place it on the market or exposing it for placing on the market, or

   (b)   supplying the product, offering to supply it, agreeing to supply it or exposing it for supply.

(2)   A suspension notice served by an enforcement authority in relation to a product may require the person on whom it is served to keep the authority informed of the whereabouts of any such product in which he has an interest.

(3)   A consent given by the enforcement authority for the purposes of paragraph (1) may impose such conditions on the doing of anything for which the consent is required as the authority considers appropriate.

12.   Requirements to mark

(1)   Where an enforcement authority has reasonable grounds for believing that a product is a dangerous product in that it could pose risks in certain conditions, the authority may serve a notice ('a requirement to mark') requiring the person on whom the notice is served at his own expense to undertake either or both of the following, as specified in the notice—

   (a)   to ensure that the product is marked in accordance with requirements specified in the notice with warnings as to the risks it may present,

   (b)   to make the marketing of the product subject to prior conditions as specified in the notice so as to ensure the product is a safe product.

(2)   The requirements referred to in paragraph (1)(a) shall be such as to ensure that the product is marked with a warning which is suitable, clearly worded and easily comprehensible.

13.   Requirements to warn

Where an enforcement authority has reasonable grounds for believing that a product is a dangerous product in that it could pose risks for certain persons, the authority may serve a notice ('a requirement to warn') requiring the person on whom the notice is served at his own expense to undertake one or more of the following, as specified in the notice—

(a)   where and to the extent it is practicable to do so, to ensure that any person who could be subject to such risks and who has been supplied with the product be given warning of the risks in good time and in a form specified in the notice,

(b)   to publish a warning of the risks in such form and manner as is likely to bring those risks to the attention of any such person,

(c)   to ensure that the product carries a warning of the risks in a form specified in the notice.

14.   Withdrawal notices

(1)   Where an enforcement authority has reasonable grounds for believing that a product is a dangerous product, the authority may serve a notice ('a withdrawal notice') prohibiting the person on whom it is served from doing any of the following things without the consent of the authority, that is to say—

   (a)   placing the product on the market, offering to place it on the market, agreeing to place it on the market or exposing it for placing on the market, or

   (b)   supplying the product, offering to supply it, agreeing to supply it or exposing it for supply.

(2)   A withdrawal notice may require the person on whom it is served to take action to alert consumers to the risks that the product presents.

(3)   In relation to a product that is already on the market, a withdrawal notice may only be served by an enforcement authority where the action being undertaken by the producer or the distributor concerned in fulfilment of his obligations under these Regulations is unsatisfactory or insufficient to prevent the risks concerned to the health and safety of persons.

(4)   Paragraph (3) shall not apply in the case of a product posing a serious risk requiring, in the view of the enforcement authority, urgent action.

(5)   A withdrawal notice served by an enforcement authority in relation to a product may require the person on whom it is served to keep the authority informed of the whereabouts of any such product in which he has an interest.

(6)   A consent given by the enforcement authority for the purposes of paragraph (1) may impose such conditions on the doing of anything for which the consent is required as the authority considers appropriate.

15.   Recall notices

(1)   Subject to paragraph (4), where an enforcement authority has reasonable grounds for believing that a product is a dangerous product and that it has already been supplied or made available to consumers, the authority may serve a notice ('a recall notice') requiring the person on whom it is served to use his reasonable endeavours to organise the return of the product from consumers to that person or to such other person as is specified in the notice.

(2)   A recall notice may require—

   (a)   the recall to be effected in accordance with a code of practice applicable to the product concerned, or

   (b)   the recipient of the recall notice to—

      (i)   contact consumers who have purchased the product in order to inform them of the recall, where and to the extent it is practicable to do so,

      (ii)   publish a notice in such form and such manner as is likely to bring to the attention of purchasers of the product the risk the product poses and the fact of the recall, or

      (iii) make arrangements for the collection or return of the product from consumers who have purchased it or for its disposal,

   and may impose such additional requirements on the recipient of the notice as are reasonable and practicable with a view to achieving the return of the product from consumers to the person specified in the notice or its disposal.

(3)   In determining what requirements to include in a recall notice, the enforcement authority shall take into consideration the need to encourage distributors, users and consumers to contribute to its implementation.

(4)   A recall notice may only be issued by an enforcement authority where—
    (a)   other action which it may require under these Regulations would not suffice to prevent the risks concerned to the health and safety of persons,
    (b)   the action being undertaken by the producer or the distributor concerned in fulfilment of his obligations under these Regulations is unsatisfactory or insufficient to prevent the risks concerned to the health and safety of persons, and
    (c)   the authority has given not less than 10 days' notice to the person on whom the recall notice is to be served of its intention to serve such a notice and where that person has before the expiry of that period by notice required the authority to seek the advice of such person as the Institute determines on the questions of—
        (i)   whether the product is a dangerous product,
        (ii) whether the issue of a recall notice is proportionate to the seriousness of the risk, and
    the authority has taken account of such advice.

(5)   Paragraphs (4)(b) and (c) shall not apply in the case of a product posing a serious risk requiring, in the view of the enforcement authority, urgent action.

(6)   Where a person requires an enforcement authority to seek advice as referred to in paragraph (4)(c), that person shall be responsible for the fees, costs and expenses of the Institute and of the person appointed by the Institute to advise the authority.

(7)   In paragraphs 4(c) and (6) 'the Institute' means the charitable organisation with registered number 803725 and known as the Chartered Institute of Arbitrators.

(8)   A recall notice served by an enforcement authority in relation to a product may require the person on whom it is served to keep the authority informed of the whereabouts of any such product to which the recall notice relates, so far as he is able to do so.

(9)   Where the conditions in paragraph (1) for serving a recall notice are satisfied and either the enforcement authority has been unable to identify any person on whom to serve a recall notice, or the person on whom such a notice has been served has failed to comply with it, then the authority may itself take such action as could have been required by a recall notice.

(10) Where—
    (a)   an authority has complied with the requirements of paragraph (4); and
    (b)   the authority has exercised its powers under paragraph (9) to take action following the failure of the person on whom the recall notice has been served to comply with that notice,
    then the authority may recover from the person on whom the notice was served summarily as a civil debt, any costs or expenses reasonably incurred by it in undertaking the action referred to in sub-paragraph (b).

(11) A civil debt recoverable under the preceding paragraph may be recovered—
    (a)   in England and Wales by way of complaint (as mentioned in section 58 of the Magistrates' Courts Act 1980,
    (b)   in Northern Ireland in proceedings under Article 62 of the Magistrate's Court (Northern Ireland) Order 1981.

16.   Supplementary provisions relating to safety notices

(1)   Whenever feasible, prior to serving a safety notice the authority shall give an opportunity to the person on whom the notice is to be served to submit his views to the authority. Where, due to the urgency of the situation, this is not feasible the person shall be given an opportunity to submit his views to the authority after service of the notice.

(2)   A safety notice served by an enforcement authority in respect of a product shall—
    (a)   describe the product in a manner sufficient to identify it;
    (b)   state the reasons on which the notice is based;
    (c)   indicate the rights available to the recipient of the notice under these Regulations and (where applicable) the time limits applying to their exercise; and
    (d)   in the case of a suspension notice, state the period of time for which it applies.

(3) A safety notice shall have effect throughout the United Kingdom.

(4) Where an enforcement authority serves a suspension notice in respect of a product, the authority shall be liable to pay compensation to a person having an interest in the product in respect of any loss or damage suffered by reason of the notice if—

    (a) there has been no contravention of any requirement of these Regulations in relation to the product; and

    (b) the exercise by the authority of the power to serve the suspension notice was not attributable to any neglect or default by that person.

(5) Where an enforcement authority serves a withdrawal notice in respect of a product, the authority shall be liable to pay compensation to a person having an interest in the product in respect of any loss or damage suffered by reason of the notice if—

    (a) the product was not a dangerous product; and

    (b) the exercise by the authority of the power to serve the withdrawal notice was not attributable to any neglect or default by that person.

(6) Where an enforcement authority serves a recall notice in respect of a product, the authority shall be liable to pay compensation to the person on whom the notice was served in respect of any loss or damage suffered by reason of the notice if—

    (a) the product was not a dangerous product; and

    (b) the exercise by the authority of the power to serve the recall notice was not attributable to any neglect or default by that person.

(7) An enforcement authority may vary or revoke a safety notice which it has served provided that the notice is not made more restrictive for the person on whom it is served or more onerous for that person to comply with.

(8) Wherever feasible prior to varying a safety notice the authority shall give an opportunity to the person on whom the original notice was served to submit his views to the authority.

17. Appeals against safety notices

(1) A person on whom a safety notice has been served and a person having an interest in a product in respect of which a safety notice (other than a recall notice) has been served may, before the end of the period of 21 days beginning with the day on which the notice was served, apply for an order to vary or set aside the terms of the notice.

(2) On an application under paragraph (1) the court or the sheriff, as the case may be, shall make an order setting aside the notice only if satisfied that—

    (a) in the case of a suspension notice, there has been no contravention in relation to the product of any requirement of these Regulations,

    (b) in the case of a requirement to mark or a requirement to warn, the product is not a dangerous product,

    (c) in the case of a withdrawal notice—

        (i) the product is not a dangerous product, or

        (ii) where applicable, regulation 14(3) has not been complied with by the enforcement authority concerned,

    (d) in the case of a recall notice—

        (i) the product is not a dangerous product, or

        (ii) regulation 15(4) has not been complied with,

    (e) in any case, the serving of the safety notice concerned was not proportionate to the seriousness of the risk.

(3) On an application concerning the period of time specified in a suspension notice as the period for which it applies, the court or the sheriff, as the case may be, may reduce the period to such period as it considers sufficient for organising appropriate safety evaluations, checks and controls.

(4) On an application to vary the terms of a notice, the court or the sheriff, as the case may be, may vary the requirements specified in the notice as it considers appropriate.

(5) A person on whom a recall notice has been served and who proposes to make an application under paragraph (1) in relation to the notice may, before the end of the period of seven days beginning with the day on which the notice was served, apply to the court or the sheriff for an order suspending the effect of the notice and the court or the sheriff may, in any case where it considers it appropriate to do so, make an order suspending the effect of the notice.

(6) If the court or the sheriff makes an order suspending the effect of a recall notice under paragraph (5) in the absence of the enforcement authority, the enforcement authority may apply for the revocation of such order.

(7) An order under paragraph (5) shall take effect from the time it is made until—

   (a) it is revoked under paragraph (6),

   (b) where no application is made under paragraph (1) in respect of the recall notice within the time specified in that paragraph, the expiration of that time,

   (c) where such an application is made but is withdrawn or dismissed for want of prosecution, the date of dismissal or withdrawal of the application, or

   (d) where such an application is made and is not withdrawn or dismissed for want of prosecution, the determination of the application.

(8) Subject to paragraph (6), in Scotland the sheriff's decision under paragraph (5) shall be final.

(9) An application under this regulation may be made—

   (a) by way of complaint to any magistrates' court in which proceedings have been brought in England and Wales or Northern Ireland—

      (i) in respect of a contravention in relation to the product of a requirement imposed by or under these Regulations; or

      (ii) for the forfeiture of the product under regulation 18;

   (b) where no such proceedings have been brought, by way of complaint to any magistrates' court; or

   (c) in Scotland, by summary application to the sheriff.

(10) A person aggrieved by an order made pursuant to an application under paragraph (1) by a magistrates' court in England, Wales or Northern Ireland, or by a decision of such a court not to make such an order, may appeal against that order or decision—

   (a) in England and Wales, to the Crown Court;

   (b) in Northern Ireland, to the county court.

18. Forfeiture: England and Wales and Northern Ireland

(1) An enforcement authority in England and Wales or Northern Ireland may apply for an order for the forfeiture of a product on the grounds that the product is a dangerous product.

(2) An application under paragraph (1) may be made—

   (a) where proceedings have been brought in a magistrates' court for an offence in respect of a contravention in relation to the product of a requirement imposed by or under these Regulations, to that court,

   (b) where an application with respect to the product has been made to a magistrates' court under regulation 17 (appeals against safety notices) or 25 (appeals against detention of products and records) to that court, and

   (c) otherwise, by way of complaint to a magistrates' court.

(3) An enforcement authority making an application under paragraph (1) shall serve a copy of the application on any person appearing to it to be the owner of, or otherwise to have an interest in, the product to which the application relates, together with a notice giving him the opportunity to appear at the hearing of the application to show cause why the product should not be forfeited.

(4) A person on whom notice is served under paragraph (3) and any other person claiming to be the owner of, or otherwise to have an interest in, the product to which the application relates shall be entitled to appear at the hearing of the application and show cause why the product should not be forfeited.

(5) The court shall not make an order for the forfeiture of a product—

   (a) if any person on whom notice is served under paragraph (3) does not appear, unless service of the notice on that person is proved, or

   (b) if no notice under paragraph (3) has been served, unless the court is satisfied that in the circumstances it was reasonable not to serve notice on any person.

(6) The court may make an order for the forfeiture of a product only if it is satisfied that the product is a dangerous product.

(7) Any person aggrieved by an order made by a magistrates' court for the forfeiture of a product, or by a decision of such a court not to make such an order, may appeal against that order or decision—
    (a) in England and Wales, to the Crown Court;
    (b) in Northern Ireland, to the county court.

(8) An order for the forfeiture of a product shall not take effect until the later of—
    (i) the end of the period within which an appeal under paragraph (7) may be brought or within which an application under section 111 of the Magistrates' Courts Act 1980 or article 146 of the Magistrates' Courts (Northern Ireland) Order 1981 (statement of case) may be made, or
    (ii) if an appeal or an application is so made, when the appeal or application is determined or abandoned.

(9) Subject to the following paragraph, where a product is forfeited it shall be destroyed in accordance with such directions as the court may give.

(10) On making an order for forfeiture of a product a magistrates' court may, if it considers it appropriate to do so, direct that the product shall (instead of being destroyed) be delivered up to such person as the court may specify, on condition that the person—
    (a) does not supply the product to any person otherwise than as mentioned in paragraph (11), and
    (b) on condition, if the court considers it appropriate, that he complies with any order to pay costs or expenses (including any order under regulation 28) which has been made against him in the proceedings for the order for forfeiture.

(11) The supplies which may be permitted under the preceding paragraph are—
    (a) a supply to a person who carries on a business of buying products of the same description as the product concerned and repairing or reconditioning them,
    (b) a supply to a person as scrap (that is to say, for the value of materials included in the product rather than for the value of the product itself),
    (c) a supply to any person, provided that being so supplied the product is repaired by or on behalf of the person to whom the product was delivered up by direction of the court and that following such repair it is not a dangerous product.

19. Forfeiture: Scotland

(1) In Scotland a sheriff may make an order for forfeiture of a product on the grounds that the product is a dangerous product—
    (a) on an application by a procurator-fiscal made in the manner specified in section 134 of the Criminal Procedure (Scotland) Act 1995, or
    (b) where a person is convicted of any offence in respect of a contravention in relation to the product of a requirement imposed by or under these Regulations, in addition to any other penalty which the sheriff may impose.

(2) The procurator-fiscal making an application under paragraph (1)(a) shall serve on any person appearing to him to be the owner of, or otherwise to have an interest in, the product to which the application relates a copy of the application, together with a notice giving him the opportunity to appear at the hearing of the application to show cause why the product should not be forfeited.

(3) Service under paragraph (2) shall be carried out, and such service may be proved, in the manner specified for citation of an accused in summary proceedings under the Criminal Procedure (Scotland) Act 1995.

(4) A person upon whom notice is served under paragraph (2) and any other person claiming to be the owner of, or otherwise to have an interest in, the product to which the application relates shall be entitled to appear at the hearing of the application to show cause why the product should not be forfeited.

(5) The sheriff shall not make an order following an application under paragraph (1)(a)—
    (a) if any person on whom notice is served under paragraph (2) does not appear, unless service of the notice on that person is proved; or
    (b) if no notice under paragraph (2) has been served, unless the sheriff is satisfied that in the circumstances it was reasonable not to serve notice on any person.

(6) The sheriff may make an order under this regulation only if he is satisfied that the product is a dangerous product.

(7)   Where an order for the forfeiture of a product is made following an application by the procurator-fiscal under paragraph (1)(a), any person who appeared, or was entitled to appear to show cause why the product should not be forfeited may, within twenty-one days of the making of the order, appeal to the High Court by Bill of Suspension on the ground of an alleged miscarriage of justice; and section 182(5)(a) to (e) of the Criminal Procedure (Scotland) Act 1995 shall apply to an appeal under this paragraph as it applies to a stated case under Part X of that Act.

(8)   An order following an application under paragraph (1)(a) shall not take effect—
   (a)   until the end of the period of twenty-one days beginning with the day after the day on which the order is made; or
   (b)   if an appeal is made under paragraph (7) within that period, until the appeal is determined or abandoned.

(9)   An order under paragraph (1)(b) shall not take effect—
   (a)   until the end of the period within which an appeal against the order could be brought under the Criminal Procedure (Scotland) Act 1995; or
   (b)   if an appeal is made within that period, until the appeal is determined or abandoned.

(10)   Subject to paragraph (11), a product forfeited under this regulation shall be destroyed in accordance with such directions as the sheriff may give.

(11)   If he thinks fit, the sheriff may direct that the product be released to such person as he may specify, on condition that that person does not supply the product to any other person otherwise than as mentioned in paragraph (11) of regulation 18.

20.   Offences

(1)   A person who contravenes regulations 5 or 8(1)(a) shall be guilty of an offence and liable on conviction on indictment to imprisonment for a term not exceeding 12 months or to a fine not exceeding £20,000 or to both, or on summary conviction to imprisonment for a term not exceeding three months or to a fine not exceeding the statutory maximum or to both.

(2)   A person who contravenes regulation 7(1), 7(3) (by failing to take any of the measures specified in regulation 7(4)), 8(1)(b)(i), (ii) or (iii) or 9(1) shall be guilty of an offence and liable on summary conviction to imprisonment for a term not exceeding three months or to a fine not exceeding level 5 on the standard scale or to both.

(3)   A producer or distributor who does not give notice to an enforcement authority under regulation 9(1) in respect of a product he has placed on the market or supplied commits an offence where it is proved that he ought to have known that the product poses risks to consumers that are incompatible with the general safety requirement and he shall be liable on summary conviction to imprisonment for a term not exceeding three months or to a fine not exceeding level 5 on the standard scale or to both.

(4)   A person who contravenes a safety notice shall be guilty of an offence and liable on conviction on indictment to imprisonment for a term not exceeding 12 months or to a fine not exceeding £20,000 or to both, or on summary conviction to imprisonment for a term not exceeding three months or to a fine not exceeding the statutory maximum or to both.

21.   Test purchases

(1)   An enforcement authority shall have power to organise appropriate checks on the safety properties of a product, on an adequate scale, up to the final stage of use or consumption and for that purpose may make a purchase of a product or authorise an officer of the authority to make a purchase of a product.

(2)   Where a product purchased under paragraph (1) is submitted to a test and the test leads to—
   (a)   the bringing of proceedings for an offence in respect of a contravention in relation to the product of any requirement imposed by or under these Regulations or for the forfeiture of the product under regulation 18 or 19, or
   (b)   the serving of a safety notice in respect of the product, and (c) the authority is requested to do so and it is practicable for the authority to comply with the request,

then the authority shall allow the person from whom the product was purchased, a person who is a party to the proceedings, on whom the notice was served or who has an interest in the product to which the notice relates, to have the product tested.

22. Powers of entry and search etc.

(1) An officer of an enforcement authority may at any reasonable hour and on production, if required, of his credentials exercise any of the powers conferred by the following provisions of this regulation.

(2) The officer may, for the purposes of ascertaining whether there has been a contravention of a requirement imposed by or under these Regulations, enter any premises other than premises occupied only as a person's residence and inspect any record or product.

(3) The officer may, for the purpose of ascertaining whether there has been a contravention of a requirement imposed by or under these Regulations, examine any procedure (including any arrangements for carrying out a test) connected with the production of a product.

(4) If the officer has reasonable grounds for suspecting that the product has not been placed on the market or supplied in the United Kingdom since it was manufactured or imported he may for the purpose of ascertaining whether there has been a contravention in relation to the product of a requirement imposed by or under these Regulations—

   (a) require a person carrying on a commercial activity, or employed in connection with a commercial activity, to supply all necessary information relating to the activity, including by the production of records,

   (b) require any record which is stored in an electronic form and is accessible from the premises to be produced in a form—
      (i) in which it can be taken away, and
      (ii) in which it is visible and legible.

   (c) for the purpose of ascertaining (by testing or otherwise) whether there has been any such contravention, seize and detain samples of the product,

   (d) take copies of, or of an entry in, any records produced by virtue of sub-paragraph (a).

(5) If the officer has reasonable grounds for suspecting that there has been a contravention in relation to a product of a requirement imposed by or under these Regulations, he may—

   (a) for the purpose of ascertaining whether there has been any such contravention, require a person carrying on a commercial activity, or employed in connection with a commercial activity, to supply all necessary information relating to the activity, including by the production of records,

   (b) for the purpose of ascertaining whether there has been any such contravention, require any record which is stored in an electronic form and is accessible from the premises to be produced in a form—
      (i) in which it can be taken away, and
      (ii) in which it is visible and legible,

   (c) for the purpose of ascertaining (by testing or otherwise) whether there has been any such contravention, seize and detain samples of the product,

   (d) take copies of, or of an entry in, any records produced by virtue of sub-paragraph (a).

(6) The officer may seize and detain any products or records which he has reasonable grounds for believing may be required as evidence in proceedings for an offence in respect of a contravention of any requirement imposed by or under these Regulations.

(7) If and to the extent that it is reasonably necessary to do so to prevent a contravention of any requirement imposed by or under these Regulations, the officer may, for the purpose of exercising his power under paragraphs (4) to (6) to seize products or records—

   (a) require any person having authority to do so to open any container or to open any vending machine; and

   (b) himself open or break open any such container or machine where a requirement made under sub-paragraph (a) in relation to the container or machine has not been complied with.

23. **Provisions supplemental to regulation 22 and search warrants etc.**

(1) An officer seizing any products or records shall, before he leaves the premises, provide to the person from whom they were seized a written notice—

    (a) specifying the products (including the quantity thereof) and records seized,

    (b) stating the reasons for their seizure, and

    (c) explaining the right of appeal under regulation 25.

(2) References in paragraph (1) and regulation 25 to the person from whom something has been seized, in relation to a case in which the power of seizure was exercisable by reason of the product having been found on any premises, are references to the occupier of the premises at the time of the seizure.

(3) If a justice of the peace—

    (a) is satisfied by written information on oath that there are reasonable grounds for believing either—

        (i) that any products or records which an officer has power to inspect under regulation 22 are on any premises and that their inspection is likely to disclose evidence that there has been a contravention of any requirement imposed by or under these Regulations, or

        (ii) that such a contravention has taken place, is taking place or is about to take place on any premises, and

    (b) is also satisfied by such information either—

        (i) that admission to the premises has been or is likely to be refused and that notice of the intention to apply for a warrant under this paragraph has been given to the occupier, or

        (ii) that an application for admission, or the giving of such a notice, would defeat the object of the entry or that the premises are unoccupied or that the occupier is temporarily absent and it might defeat the object of the entry to await his return.

    the justice may by warrant under his hand, which shall continue in force for a period of one month, authorise any officer of an enforcement authority to enter the premises, if need be by force.

(4) An officer entering premises by virtue of regulation 22 or a warrant under paragraph (3) may take him such other persons and equipment as may appear to him necessary.

(5) On leaving any premises which a person is authorised to enter by a warrant under paragraph (3), that person shall, if the premises are unoccupied or the occupier is temporarily absent—

    (a) leave the premises as effectively secured against trespassers as he found them,

    (b) attach a notice such as is mentioned in paragraph (1) in a prominent place at the premises.

(6) Where a product seized by an officer of an enforcement authority under regulation 22 or 23 is submitted to a test, the authority shall inform the person mentioned in paragraph (1) of the result of the test and, if—

    (a) proceedings are brought for an offence in respect of a contravention in relation to the product of any requirement imposed by or under these Regulations or for the forfeiture of the product under regulation 18 or 19; or

    (b) a safety notice is served in respect of the product; and

    (c) the authority is requested to do so and it is practicable for him to comply with the request,

    then the authority shall allow a person who is a party to the proceedings or, on whom the notice was served or who has an interest in the product to which the notice relates to have the product tested.

(7) If a person who is not an officer of an enforcement authority purports to act as such under regulation 22 or under this regulation he shall be guilty of an offence and liable on summary conviction to a fine not exceeding level 5 on the standard scale.

(8) In the application of this section to Scotland, the reference in paragraph (3) to a justice of the peace shall include a reference to a sheriff and the reference to written information on oath shall be construed as a reference to evidence on oath.

(9) In the application of this section to Northern Ireland, the reference in paragraph (3) to a justice of the peace shall include a reference to a lay magistrate and the references to an information on oath shall be construed as a reference to a complaint on oath.

24. Obstruction of officers

(1) A person who—

(a) intentionally obstructs an officer of an enforcement authority who is acting in pursuance of any provision of regulations 22 or 23; or

(b) intentionally fails to comply with a requirement made of him by an officer of an enforcement authority under any provision of those regulations; or

(c) without reasonable cause fails to give an officer of an enforcement authority who is so acting any other assistance or information which the officer may reasonably require of him for the purposes of the exercise of the officer's functions under any provision of those regulations,

shall be guilty of an offence and liable on summary conviction to a fine not exceeding level 5 on the standard scale.

(2) A person shall be guilty of an offence if, in giving any information which is required by him by virtue of paragraph (1)(c)—

(a) he makes a statement which he knows is false in a material particular; or

(b) he recklessly makes a statement which is false in a material particular.

(3) A person guilty of an offence under paragraph (2) shall be liable—

(a) on conviction on indictment, to a fine;

(b) on summary conviction, to a fine not exceeding the statutory maximum.

25. Appeals against detention of products and records

(1) A person referred to in regulation 23(1) may apply for an order requiring any product or record which is for the time being detained under regulation 22 or 23 by an enforcement authority or by an officer of such an authority to be released to him or to another person.

(2) An application under the preceding paragraph may be made—

(a) to any magistrates' court in which proceedings have been brought in England and Wales or Northern Ireland—

(i) for an offence in respect of a contravention in relation to the product of a requirement imposed by or under these Regulation, or

(ii) for the forfeiture of the product under regulation 18,

(b) where no such proceedings have been brought, by way of complaint to a magistrates' court;

(c) in Scotland, by summary application to the sheriff.

(3) On an application under paragraph (1) to a magistrates' court or to the sheriff, the court or the sheriff may make an order requiring a product or record to be released only if the court or sheriff is satisfied—

(a) that proceedings

(i) for an offence in respect of any contravention in relation to the product or, in the case of a record, the product to which the record relates, of any requirement imposed by or under these Regulations; or

(ii) for the forfeiture of the product or, in the case of a record, the product to which the record relate, under regulation 18 or 19,

have not been brought or, having been brought, have been concluded without the product being forfeited; and

(b) where no such proceedings have been brought, that more than six months have elapsed since the product or records was seized.

(4) In determining whether to make an order under this regulation requiring the release of a product or record the court or sheriff shall take all the circumstances into account including the results of any tests on the product which have been carried out by or on behalf of the enforcement authority and any statement made by the enforcement authority to the court or sheriff as to its intention to bring proceedings for an offence in respect of a contravention in relation to the product of any requirement imposed by or under these Regulations.

(5) Where—

(a) more than 12 months have elapsed since a product or records were seized and the enforcement authority has not commenced proceedings for an offence in respect of a contravention in relation to the product (or, in the case of records, the product to which the records relate) of any requirement imposed by or under these Regulations or for the forfeiture of the product under regulation 18 or 19, or

(b)   an enforcement authority has brought proceedings for an offence as mentioned in sub-paragraph (a) and the proceedings were dismissed and all rights of appeal have been exercised or the time for appealing has expired,

the authority shall be under a duty to return the product or records detained under regulation 22 or 23 to the person from whom they were seized.

(6)   Where the authority is satisfied that some other person has a better right to a product or record than the person from whom they were seized, the authority shall, instead of the duty in paragraph (5), be under a duty to return it to that other person or, as the case may be, to the person appearing to the authority to have the best right to the product or record in question.

(7)   Where different persons claim to be entitled to the return of a product or record that is required to be returned under paragraph (5), then it may be retained for as long as it reasonably necessary for the determination in accordance with paragraph (6) of the person to whom it must be returned.

(8)   A person aggrieved by an order made under this regulation by a magistrates' court in England and Wales or Northern Ireland, or by a decision of such a court not to make such an order, may appeal against that order or decision—

(a)   in England and Wales, to the Crown Court;

(b)   in Northern Ireland, to the county court;

and an order so made may contain such provision as appears to the court to be appropriate for delaying the coming into force of the order pending the making and determination of any appeal (including any application under section 111 of the Magistrates' Courts Act 1980 or article 146 of the Magistrates' Courts (Northern Ireland) Order 1981 (statement of case)).

26.   Compensation for seizure and detention

Where an officer of an enforcement authority exercises any power under regulation 22 or 23 to seize and detain a product, the enforcement authority shall be liable to pay compensation to any person having an interest in the product in respect of any loss or damage caused by reason of the exercise of the power if—

(a)   there has been no contravention in relation to the product of any requirement imposed by or under these Regulations, and

(b)   the exercise of the power is not attributable to any neglect or default by that person.

27.   Recovery of expenses of enforcement

(1)   This regulation shall apply where a court—

(a)   convicts a person of an offence in respect of a contravention in relation to a product of any requirement imposed by or under these Regulations, or

(b)   makes an order under regulation 18 or 19 for the forfeiture of a product.

(2)   The court may (in addition to any other order it may make as to costs or expenses) order the person convicted or, as the case may be, any person having an interest in the product to reimburse an enforcement authority for any expenditure which has been or may be incurred by that authority—

(a)   in connection with any seizure or detention of the product by or on behalf of the authority, or

(b)   in connection with any compliance by the authority with directions given by the court for the purposes of any order for the forfeiture of the product.

28.   Power of Secretary of State to obtain information

(1)   If the Secretary of State considers that, for the purposes of deciding whether to serve a safety notice, or to vary or revoke a safety notice which he has already served, he requires information or a sample of a product he may serve on a person a notice requiring him:

(a)   to furnish to the Secretary of State, within a period specified in the notice, such information as is specified;

(b)   to produce such records as are specified in the notice at a time and place so specified (and to produce any such records which are stored in any electronic form in a form in which they are visible and legible) and to permit a person appointed by the Secretary of State for that purpose to take copies of the records at that time and place;

    (c)   to produce such samples of a product as are specified in the notice at a time and place so specified.

(2)   A person shall be guilty of an offence if he—

    (a)   fails, without reasonable cause, to comply with a notice served on him under paragraph (1); or

    (b)   in purporting to comply with a requirement which by virtue of paragraph (1)(a) or (b) is contained in such a notice—

        (i)   furnishes information or records which he knows are false in a material particular, or

        (ii)   recklessly furnishes information or records which are false in a material particular.

(3)   A person guilty of an offence under paragraph (2) shall—

    (a)   in the case of an offence under sub-paragraph (a) of that paragraph, be liable on summary conviction to a fine not exceeding level 5 on the standard scale; and

    (b)   in the case of an offence under sub-paragraph (b) of that paragraph, be liable—

        (i)   on conviction on indictment, to a fine;

        (ii)   on summary conviction, to a fine not exceeding the statutory maximum.

29.   Defence of due diligence

(1)   Subject to the following provisions of this regulation, in proceedings against a person for an offence under these Regulations it shall be a defence for that person to show that he took all reasonable steps and exercised all due diligence to avoid committing the offence.

(2)   Where in any proceedings against any person for such an offence the defence provided by paragraph (1) involves an allegation that the commission of the offence was due—

    (a)   to the act or default of another, or

    (b)   to reliance on information given by another,

that person shall not, without the leave of the court, be entitled to rely on the defence unless, not less than seven clear days before, in England, Wales and Northern Ireland, the hearing of the proceedings or, in Scotland, the trial diet, he has served a notice under paragraph (3) on the person bringing the proceedings.

(3)   A notice under this paragraph shall give such information identifying or assisting in the identification of the person who—

    (a)   committed the act or default, or

    (b)   gave the information,

as is in the possession of the person serving the notice at the time he serves it.

(4)   A person may not rely on the defence provided by paragraph (1) by reason of his reliance on information supplied by another, unless he shows that it was reasonable in all the circumstances to have relied on the information, having regard in particular—

    (a)   to the steps which he took, and those which might reasonably have been taken, for the purpose of verifying the information; and

    (b)   to whether he had any reason to disbelieve the information.

30.   Defence in relation to antiques

(1)   This regulation shall apply in proceedings against any person for an offence under regulation 20(1) in respect of the supply, offer or agreement to supply or exposure or possession for supply of second hand products supplied as antiques.

(2)   It shall be a defence for that person to show that the terms on which he supplied the product or agreed or offered to supply the product or, in the case of a product which he exposed or possessed for supply, the terms on which he intended to supply the product, contemplated the acquisition of an interest in the product by the person supplied or to be supplied.

(3)   Paragraph (2) applies only if the producer or distributor clearly informed the person to whom he supplied the product, or offered or agreed to supply the product or, in the case of a product which he exposed or possessed for supply, he intended to so inform that person, that the product is an antique.

31.   Liability of person other than principal offender

(1)   Where the commission by a person of an offence under these Regulations is due to an act or default committed by some other person in the course of a commercial activity of his, the other person shall be guilty of the offence and may be proceeded against and punished by virtue of this paragraph whether or not proceedings are taken against the first-mentioned person.

(2)   Where a body corporate is guilty of an offence under these Regulations (including where it is so guilty by virtue of paragraph (1)) in respect of any act or default which is shown to have been committed with the consent or connivance of, or to be attributable to any neglect on the part of, any director, manager, secretary or other similar officer of the body corporate or any person who was purporting to act in any such capacity he, as well as the body corporate, shall be guilty of that offence and shall be liable to be proceeded against and punished accordingly.

(3)   Where the affairs of a body corporate are managed by its members, paragraph (2) shall apply in relation to the acts and defaults of a member in connection with his functions of management as if he were a director of the body corporate.

(4)   Where a Scottish partnership is guilty of an offence under these Regulations (including where it is so guilty by virtue of paragraph (1)) in respect of any act or default which is shown to have been committed with the consent or connivance of, or to be attributable to any neglect on the part of, a partner in the partnership, he, as well as the partnership, shall be guilty of that offence and shall be liable to be proceeded against and punished accordingly.

PART 4

MISCELLANEOUS

32.   Reports

(1)   It shall be the duty of the Secretary of State to lay before each House of Parliament a report on the exercise during the period to which the report relates of the functions which are exercisable by enforcement authorities under these Regulations.

(2)   The first such report shall relate to the period beginning on the day on which these Regulations come into force and ending on 31 March 2008 and subsequent reports shall relate to a period of not more than five years beginning on the day after the day on which the period to which the previous report relates ends.

(3)   The Secretary of State may from time to time prepare and lay before each House of Parliament such other reports on the exercise of those functions as he considers appropriate.

(4)   The Secretary of State may direct an enforcement authority to report at such intervals as he may specify in the direction on the discharge by that authority of the functions exercisable by it under these Regulations.

(5)   A report under paragraph (4) shall be in such form and shall contain such particulars as are specified in the direction of the Secretary of State.

33.   Duty to notify Secretary of State

(A1)   The Secretary of State must establish and operate a database containing information relating to market surveillance and product safety.

(B1)   The database referred to in paragraph (A1) must be designed so as to enable notifications required under paragraph (1), (2) or (4), or under Article 22 of Regulation (EC) 765/2008 of the European Parliament and of the Council setting out the requirements for accreditation and market surveillance relating to the marketing of products and repealing Regulation (EEC) No 339/93, to be made to the Secretary of State through the database.

(1)   An enforcement authority which has received a notification of a risk under regulation 9(1) shall immediately notify the Secretary of State of the risk through the database referred to in paragraph (A1).

(2)   Where an enforcement authority takes a measure which restricts the placing on the market of a product, or requires its withdrawal or recall, it shall immediately notify the Secretary of State of the action taken through the database referred to in paragraph

(A1), specifying its reasons for taking the action. It shall also immediately notify the Secretary of State of any modification or lifting of such a measure.

(3) ...

(4) Where an enforcement authority adopts or decides to adopt, recommend or agree with producers and distributors, whether on a compulsory or voluntary basis, a measure or action to prevent, restrict or impose specific conditions on the possible marketing or use of a product (other than a medicinal product) by reason of a serious risk, it shall immediately notify the Secretary of State of the measure taken through the database referred to in paragraph (A1). It shall also immediately notify the Secretary of State of any modification or withdrawal of any such measure or action through the database referred to in paragraph (A1).

(10) In this regulation—

    (a) references to a product excludes a second hand product supplied as an antique or as a product to be repaired or reconditioned prior to being used, provided the supplier clearly informs the person to whom he supplies the product to that effect;

    (b) 'medicinal product' has the meaning given to it in regulation 2 of the Human Medicines Regulations 2012.

34. Provisions supplemental to regulation 33

(1) A notification under regulation 33(2) or (4) to the Secretary of State shall provide all available details and at least the following information—

    (a) information enabling the product to be identified,

    (b) a description of the risk involved, including a summary of the results of any test or analysis and of their conclusions which are relevant to assessing the level of risk,

    (c) the nature and the duration of the measures or action taken or decided on, if applicable,

    (d) information on supply chains and distribution of the product, in particular on destination countries.

35. ...

36. Market surveillance

In order to ensure a high level of consumer health and safety protection, enforcement authorities shall within the limits of their responsibility and to the extent of their ability undertake market surveillance of products employing appropriate means and procedures and cooperating with other enforcement authorities which may include:

(a) establishment, periodical updating and implementation of sectoral surveillance programmes by categories of products or risks and the monitoring of surveillance activities, findings and results,

(b) follow-up and updating of scientific and technical knowledge concerning the safety of products,

(c) the periodical review and assessment of the functioning of the control activities and their effectiveness and, if necessary revision of the surveillance approach and organisation put in place.

37. Complaints procedures

An enforcement authority shall maintain and publish a procedure by which complaints may be submitted by any person on product safety and on surveillance and control activities, which complaints shall be followed up as appropriate.

38. Co-operation between enforcement authorities

(1) It shall be the duty of an enforcement authority to co-operate with other enforcement authorities in carrying out the functions conferred on them by these Regulations. In particular—

    (a) enforcement authorities shall share their expertise and best practices with each other;

    (b) enforcement authorities shall undertake collaborative working where they have a shared interest.

(2) ...

39.   Information

(1)   An enforcement authority shall in general make available to the public such information as is available to it on the following matters relating to the risks to consumer health and safety posed by a product—

(a)   the nature of the risk,

(b)   the product identification,

and the measures taken in respect of the risk, without prejudice to the need not to disclose information for effective monitoring and investigation activities.

(2)   Paragraph (1) shall not apply to any information obtained by an enforcement authority for the purposes of these Regulations which, by its nature, is covered by professional secrecy, unless the circumstances require such information to be made public in order to protect the health and safety of consumers.

(3)   The Enterprise Act 2002 (Part 9 Restrictions on Disclosure of Information) (Amendment and Specification) Order 2003 is amended—

(i)   by the omission of the 'General Product Safety Regulations 1994' from Schedules 3 and 4; and

(ii)   by the insertion of the 'General Product Safety Regulations 2005' at the end of Schedules 3 and 4.

40.   Service of documents

(1)   A document required or authorised by virtue of these Regulations to be served on a person may be so served—

(a)   on an individual by delivering it to him or by leaving it at his proper address or by sending it by post to him at that address;

(b)   on a body corporate other than a limited liability partnership, by serving it in accordance with sub-paragraph (a) on the secretary of the body;

(c)   on a limited liability partnership, by serving it in accordance with sub-paragraph (a) on a member of the partnership; or

(d)   on a partnership, by serving it in accordance with sub-paragraph (a) on a partner or a person having the control or management of the partnership business;

(e)   on any other person by leaving it at his proper address or by sending it by post to him at that address.

(2)   For the purposes of paragraph (1), and for the purposes of section 7 of the Interpretation Act 1978 (which relates to the service of documents by post) in its application to that paragraph, the proper address of a person on whom a document is to be served by virtue of these Regulations shall be his last known address except that—

(a)   in the case of a body corporate (other than a limited liability partnership) or its secretary, it shall be the address of the registered or principal office of the body;

(b)   in the case of a limited liability partnership or a member of the partnership, it shall be the address of the registered or principal office of the partnership;

(c)   in the case of a partnership or a partner or a person having the control or management of a partnership business, it shall be the address of the principal office of the partnership,

and for the purposes of this paragraph the principal officer of a company constituted under the law of a country or territory outside the United Kingdom or of a partnership carrying on business outside the United Kingdom is its principal office within the United Kingdom.

(3)   A document required or authorised by virtue of these Regulations to be served on a person may also be served by transmitting the request by any means of electronic communication to an electronic address (which includes a fax number and an e-mail address) being an address which the person has held out as an address at which he or it can be contacted for the purposes of receiving such documents.

(4)   A document transmitted by any means of electronic communication in accordance with the preceding paragraph is, unless the contrary is proved, deemed to be received on the business day after the notice was transmitted over a public electronic communications network.

41.   Extension of time for bringing summary proceedings

(1)   Notwithstanding section 127 of the Magistrates' Courts Act 1980 or article 19 of the Magistrates' Courts (Northern Ireland) Order 1981, in England, Wales and Northern

Ireland a magistrates' court may try an information (in the case of England and Wales) or a complaint (in the case of Northern Ireland) in respect of an offence under these Regulations if (in the case of England and Wales) the information is laid or (in the case of Northern Ireland) the complaint is made within three years from the date of the offence or within one year from the discovery of the offence by the prosecutor whichever is the earlier.

(2) Notwithstanding section 136 of the Criminal Procedure (Scotland) Act 1995, in Scotland summary proceedings for an offence under these Regulations may be commenced within three years from the date of the offence or within one year from the discovery of the offence by the prosecutor whichever is the earlier.

(3) For the purposes of paragraph (2), section 136(3) of the Criminal Procedure (Scotland) Act 1995 shall apply as it applies for the purposes of that section.

42.   Civil proceedings

These Regulations shall not be construed as conferring any right of action in civil proceedings in respect of any loss or damage suffered in consequence of a contravention of these Regulations.

43.   Privileged information

(1) Nothing in these Regulations shall be taken as requiring a person to produce any records if he would be entitled to refuse to produce those records in any proceedings in any court on the grounds that they are the subject of legal professional privilege or, in Scotland, that they contain a confidential communication made by or to an advocate or solicitor in that capacity, or as authorising a person to take possession of any records which are in the possession of a person who would be so entitled.

(2) Nothing in these Regulations shall be construed as requiring a person to answer any question or give any information if to do so would incriminate that person or that person's spouse or civil partner.

44.   Evidence in proceedings for offence relating to regulation 9(1)

(1) This regulation applies where a person has given a notification to an enforcement authority pursuant to regulation 9(1).

(2) No evidence relating to that statement may be adduced and no question relating to it may be asked by the prosecution in any criminal proceedings (other than proceedings in which that person is charged with an offence under regulation 20 for a contravention of regulation 9(1)), unless evidence relating to it is adduced, or a question relating to it is asked, in the proceedings by or on behalf of that person.

45.   Transitional provisions

Where, in relation to a product, a suspension notice (within the meaning of the 1987 Act) has (by virtue of regulation 11(b) of the General Product Safety Regulations 1994) been served under section 14 of the 1987 Act and is in force immediately prior to the coming into force of these Regulations, it shall continue in force notwithstanding the revocation of the General Product Safety Regulations 1994 by these Regulations, and those Regulations shall continue to apply accordingly.

BUSINESS PROTECTION FROM MISLEADING MARKETING REGULATIONS 2008
(SI 2008, No. 1276)

PART 1
DEFINITIONS AND PROHIBITIONS

1.   Citation and Commencement

These Regulations may be cited as the Business Protection from Misleading Marketing Regulations 2008 and shall come into force on 26th May 2008.

2. Interpretation

(1) In these Regulations—

'advertising' means any form of representation which is made in connection with a trade, business, craft or profession in order to promote the supply or transfer of a product and 'advertiser' shall be construed accordingly;

'code owner' means a trader or a body responsible for—

    (a) the formulation and revision of a code of conduct; or

    (b) monitoring compliance with the code by those who have undertaken to be bound by it;

'comparative advertising' means advertising which in any way, either explicitly or by implication, identifies a competitor or a product offered by a competitor;

'court', in relation to England and Wales and Northern Ireland, means a county court or the High Court, and, in relation to Scotland, the sheriff or the Court of Session;

'enforcement authority' means the CMA, every local weights and measures authority, DETINI and GEMA;

'GEMA' means the Gas and Electricity Markets Authority;

'goods' includes ships, aircraft, animals, things attached to land and growing crops;

'premises' includes any place and any stall, vehicle, ship or aircraft;

'product' means any goods or services and includes immovable property, rights and obligations;

'ship' includes any boat and any other description of vessel used in navigation; and

'trader' means any person who is acting for purposes relating to his trade, craft, business or profession and anyone acting in the name of or on behalf of a trader.

(2) In the application of these Regulations to Scotland for references to an 'injunction' or an 'interim injunction' there shall be substituted references to an 'interdict' or an 'interim interdict' respectively.

3. Prohibition of advertising which misleads traders

(1) Advertising which is misleading is prohibited.

(2) Advertising is misleading which—

    (a) in any way, including its presentation, deceives or is likely to deceive the traders to whom it is addressed or whom it reaches; and by reason of its deceptive nature, is likely to affect their economic behaviour; or

    (b) for those reasons, injures or is likely to injure a competitor.

(3) In determining whether advertising is misleading, account shall be taken of all its features, and in particular of any information it contains concerning—

    (a) the characteristics of the product (as defined in paragraph (4));

    (b) the price or manner in which the price is calculated;

    (c) the conditions on which the product is supplied or provided; and

    (d) the nature, attributes and rights of the advertiser (as defined in paragraph (5)).

(4) In paragraph (3)(a) the 'characteristics of the product' include—

    (a) availability of the product;

    (b) nature of the product;

    (c) execution of the product;

    (d) composition of the product;

    (e) method and date of manufacture of the product;

    (f) method and date of provision of the product;

    (g) fitness for purpose of the product;

    (h) uses of the product;

    (i) quantity of the product;

    (j) specification of the product;

    (k) geographical or commercial origin of the product;

    (l) results to be expected from use of the product; or

    (m) results and material features of tests or checks carried out on the product.

(5) In paragraph (3)(d) the 'nature, attributes and rights' of the advertiser include the advertiser's—

    (a) identity;

    (b) assets;

(c)   qualifications;
(d)   ownership of industrial, commercial or intellectual property rights; or
(e)   awards and distinctions.

4.   Comparative advertising

Comparative advertising shall, as far as the comparison is concerned, be permitted only when the following conditions are met—
(a)   it is not misleading under regulation 3;
(b)   it is not a misleading action under regulation 5 of the Consumer Protection from Unfair Trading Regulations 2008 or a misleading omission under regulation 6 of those Regulations;
(c)   it compares products meeting the same needs or intended for the same purpose;
(d)   it objectively compares one or more material, relevant, verifiable and representative features of those products, which may include price;
(e)   it does not create confusion among traders—
   (i)   between the advertiser and a competitor, or
   (ii)   between the trade marks, trade names, other distinguishing marks or products of the advertiser and those of a competitor;
(f)   it does not discredit or denigrate the trade marks, trade names, other distinguishing marks, products, activities, or circumstances of a competitor;
(g)   for products with designation of origin, it relates in each case to products with the same designation;
(h)   it does not take unfair advantage of the reputation of a trade mark, trade name or other distinguishing marks of a competitor or of the designation of origin of competing products;
(i)   it does not present products as imitations or replicas of products bearing a protected trade mark or trade name.

5.   Promotion of misleading advertising and comparative advertising which is not permitted

A code owner shall not promote in a code of conduct—
(a)   advertising which is misleading under regulation 3; or
(b)   comparative advertising which is not permitted under regulation 4.

PART 2
OFFENCES

6.   Misleading advertising

A trader is guilty of an offence if he engages in advertising which is misleading under regulation 3.

7.   Penalty for offence under regulation 6

A person guilty of an offence under regulation 6 shall be liable—
(a)   on summary conviction, to a fine not exceeding the statutory maximum; or
(b)   on conviction on indictment, to a fine or imprisonment for a term not exceeding two years or both.

8.   Offences committed by bodies of persons

(1)   Where an offence under these Regulations committed by a body corporate is proved—
   (a)   to have been committed with the consent or connivance of an officer of the body, or
   (b)   to be attributable to any neglect on his part,
   the officer as well as the body corporate is guilty of the offence and liable to be proceeded against and punished accordingly.
(2)   In paragraph (1) a reference to an officer of a body corporate includes a reference to—
   (a)   a director, manager, secretary or other similar officer; and
   (b)   a person purporting to act as a director, manager, secretary or other similar officer.

(3) Where an offence under these Regulations committed by a Scottish partnership is proved—
  (a)   to have been committed with the consent or connivance of a partner, or
  (b)   to be attributable to any neglect on his part,
  the partner as well as the partnership is guilty of the offence and liable to be proceeded against and punished accordingly.

(4) In paragraph (3) a reference to a partner includes a person purporting to act as a partner.

9.   Offence due to the default of another person

(1) This regulation applies where a person 'X' —
  (a)   commits an offence under regulation 6, or
  (b)   would have committed an offence under regulation 6 but for a defence under regulation 11 or 12,
  and the commission of the offence, or of what would have been an offence but for X being able to rely on a defence under regulations 11 or 12, is due to the act or default of some other person 'Y'.

(2) Where this regulation applies Y shall be guilty of the offence subject to regulations 11 and 12 whether or not Y is a trader and whether or not Y's act or default is advertising.

(3) Y may be charged with and convicted of the offence by virtue of paragraph (2) whether or not proceedings are taken against X.

10.   Time limit for prosecution

(1) No proceedings for an offence under these Regulations shall be commenced after—
  (a)   the end of the period of three years beginning with the date of the commission of the offence; or
  (b)   the end of the period of one year beginning with the date of discovery of the offence by the prosecutor,
  whichever is earlier.

(2) For the purposes of paragraph (1)(b) a certificate signed by or on behalf of the prosecutor and stating the date on which the offence was discovered by him shall be conclusive evidence of that fact and a certificate stating that matter and purporting to be so signed shall be treated as so signed unless the contrary is proved.

(3) Notwithstanding anything in section 127(1) of the Magistrates' Courts Act 1980, an information relating to an offence under these Regulations which is triable by a magistrates' court in England and Wales may be so tried if it is laid at any time before the end of the period of twelve months beginning with the date of the commission of the offence.

(4) Notwithstanding anything in section 136 of the Criminal Procedure (Scotland) Act 1995 summary proceedings in Scotland for an offence under these Regulations may be commenced at any time before the end of the period of twelve months beginning with the date of the commission of the offence.

(5) For the purposes of paragraph (4), section 136(3) of the Criminal Procedure (Scotland) Act 1995 shall apply as it applies for the purposes of that section.

(6) Notwithstanding anything in Article 19(1) of the Magistrates' Courts (Northern Ireland) Order 1981 a complaint charging an offence under these Regulations which is triable by a magistrates' court in Northern Ireland may be so tried if it is made at any time before the end of the period of twelve months beginning with the date of the commission of the offence.

11.   Due diligence defence

(1) In any proceedings against a person for an offence under regulation 6 it is a defence for that person to prove—
  (a)   that the commission of the offence was due to—
    (i)   a mistake;
    (ii)   reliance on information supplied to him by another person;
    (iii)   the act or default of another person;
    (iv)   an accident; or
    (v)   another cause beyond his control; and

(b)   that he took all reasonable precautions and exercised all due diligence to avoid the commission of such an offence by himself or any person under his control.

(2)   A person shall not be entitled to rely on the defence provided by paragraph (1) by reason of the matters referred to in paragraph (ii) or (iii) of paragraph (1)(a) without the leave of the court unless—

(a)   he has served on the prosecutor a notice in writing giving such information identifying or assisting in the identification of that other person as was in his possession; and

(b)   the notice is served on the prosecutor at least seven clear days before the date of the hearing.

12.   Innocent publication defence

In any proceedings against a person for an offence under regulation 6 committed by the publication of advertising it is a defence for that person to prove that—

(a)   he is a person whose business it is to publish or to arrange for the publication of advertising;

(b)   he received the advertising for publication in the ordinary course of business; and

(c)   he did not know and had no reason to suspect that its publication would amount to an offence under regulation 6.

PART 3
ENFORCEMENT

13.   Duty and power to enforce

(1)   It shall be the duty of every enforcement authority to enforce these Regulations.

(1A)   Each of the following may enforce these Regulations—

(a)   The CMA;

(b)   GEMA.

(2)   Where an enforcement authority is a local weights and measures authority the duty referred to in paragraph (1) shall apply to the enforcement of these Regulations within the authority's area.

(3)   Where the enforcement authority is the Department of Enterprise, Trade and Investment in Northern Ireland the duty referred to in paragraph (1) shall apply to the enforcement of these Regulations within Northern Ireland.

(4)   In determining how to comply with its duty of enforcement every enforcement authority shall have regard to the desirability of encouraging control of advertising which is misleading under regulation 3 and comparative advertising which is not permitted under regulation 4 by such established means as it considers appropriate having regard to all the circumstances of the particular case.

(4A)   Nothing in this Regulation shall authorise GEMA to bring proceedings for an offence.

(5)   Nothing in this regulation shall authorise any enforcement authority to bring proceedings in Scotland for an offence.

14.   Notice to CMA of intended prosecution

(1)   Where an enforcement authority is a local weights and measures authority in England and Wales it may bring proceedings for an offence under regulation 6 only if—

(a)   it has notified the CMA of its intention to bring proceedings at least fourteen days before the date on which proceedings are brought; or

(b)   the CMA consents to proceedings being brought in a shorter period.

(2)   The enforcement authority must also notify the CMA of the outcome of the proceedings after they are finally determined.

(3)   Such proceedings are not invalid by reason only of the failure to comply with this regulation.

15.   Injunctions to secure compliance with the Regulations

(1)   This regulation applies where an enforcement authority considers that there has been or is likely to be a breach of regulation 3, 4 or 5.

(2)   Where this regulation applies an enforcement authority may, subject to paragraph (3), if it thinks it appropriate to do so, bring proceedings for an injunction (in which

proceedings it may also apply for an interim injunction) against any person appearing to it to be concerned or likely to be concerned with the breach.

(3)	Where the enforcement authority is a local weights and measures authority in Great Britain or GEMA it may apply for an injunction only if—

    (a)	it has notified the CMA of its intention to apply for an injunction at least fourteen days before the date on which the application is made; or

    (b)	the CMA consents to the application for an injunction being made within a shorter period.

(4)	Proceedings referred to in paragraph (2) are not invalid by reason only of the failure to comply with paragraph (3).

## 16.	Undertakings

Where an enforcement authority considers that there has been or is likely to be a breach of regulation 3, 4 or 5 it may accept from the person concerned or likely to be concerned with the breach an undertaking that he will comply with those regulations.

## 17.	Co-ordination

(1)	If more than one enforcement authority in Great Britain is contemplating bringing proceedings under regulation 15 in any particular case, the CMA may direct which enforcement authority is to bring the proceedings or decide that only it may do so.

(2)	Where the CMA directs that only it may bring such proceedings it may take into account whether compliance with regulation 3, 4 or 5 could be achieved by other means in deciding whether to bring proceedings.

## 18.	Powers of the court

(1)	The court on an application by an enforcement authority may grant an injunction on such terms as it may think fit to secure compliance with regulation 3, 4 or 5.

(2)	Before granting an injunction the court shall have regard to all the interests involved and in particular the public interest.

(3)	An injunction may relate not only to particular advertising but to any advertising in similar terms or likely to convey a similar impression.

(4)	The court may also require any person against whom an injunction (other than an interim injunction) is granted to publish in such form and manner and to such extent as the court thinks appropriate for the purpose of eliminating any continuing effects of the advertising—

    (a)	the injunction; and

    (b)	a corrective statement.

(5)	In considering an application for an injunction the court may require the person named in the application to provide evidence as to the accuracy of any factual claim made as part of the advertising of that person if, taking into account the legitimate interests of that person and any other party to the proceedings, it appears appropriate in the circumstances.

(6)	If, having been required under paragraph (5) to provide evidence as to the accuracy of a factual claim, a person—

    (a)	fails to provide such evidence, or

    (b)	provides evidence as to the accuracy of the factual claim that the court considers inadequate,

the court may consider that the factual claim is inaccurate.

(7)	The court may grant an injunction even where there is no evidence of proof of actual loss or damage or of intention or negligence on the part of the advertiser.

## 19.	Notifications of undertakings and orders to the CMA

An enforcement authority, other than the CMA, shall notify the CMA—

(a)	of any undertaking given to it under regulation 16;

(b)	of the outcome of any application made by it under regulation 15 and the terms of any order made by the court; and

(c)	of the outcome of any application made by it to enforce a previous order of the court.

20. Publication, information and advice

(1) The CMA must arrange for the publication, in such form and manner as it considers appropriate, of —

    (a)   details of any undertaking or order notified to it under regulation 19;

    (b)   details of any undertaking given to it under regulation 16;

    (c)   details of any application made by it under regulation 15 and of the terms of any undertaking given to, or order made by, the court;

    (d)   details of any application made by it to enforce a previous order of the court.

(2) An enforcement authority may arrange for the dissemination, in such form and manner as it considers appropriate, of such information and advice concerning the operation of these Regulations as appear to it to be expedient to give to the public and to all persons likely to be affected by these Regulations.

28. Crown

(1) ...

(2) The Crown is not criminally liable as a result of any provision of these Regulations.

(3) Paragraph (2) does not affect the application of any provision of these Regulations in relation to a person in the public service of the Crown.

29. Validity of agreements

An agreement shall not be void or unenforceable by reason only of a breach of these Regulations.

CONSUMER PROTECTION FROM UNFAIR TRADING REGULATIONS 2008
(SI 2008, No. 1277)

PART 1
GENERAL

1. Citation and commencement

These Regulations may be cited as the Consumer Protection from Unfair Trading Regulations 2008 and shall come into force on 26th May 2008.

2. Interpretation

(1) In these Regulations —

'average consumer' shall be construed in accordance with paragraphs (2) to (6);

'business' includes —

    (a)   a trade, craft or profession,

    (b)   the activities of any government department or local authority;

'code of conduct' means an agreement or set of rules (which is not imposed by legal or administrative requirements), which defines the behaviour of traders who undertake to be bound by it in relation to one or more commercial practices or business sectors;

'code owner' means a trader or a body responsible for —

    (a)   the formulation and revision of a code of conduct; or

    (b)   monitoring compliance with the code by those who have undertaken to be bound by it;

'commercial practice' means any act, omission, course of conduct, representation or commercial communication (including advertising and marketing) by a trader, which is directly connected with the promotion, sale or supply of a product to or from consumers, whether occurring before, during or after a commercial transaction (if any) in relation to a product;

'consumer' means an individual acting for purposes that are wholly or mainly outside that individual's business;

'digital content' means data which are produced and supplied in digital form;

'enforcement authority' means the CMA, every local weights and measures authority in Great Britain (within the meaning of section 69 of the Weights and Measures Act 1985) and the Department of Enterprise, Trade and Investment in Northern Ireland; 'goods' means any tangible moveable items but that includes water, gas and electricity if any only if they are put up for sale in a limited volume or set quantity;

'invitation to purchase' means a commercial communication which indicates characteristics of the product and the price in a way appropriate to the means of that commercial communication and thereby enables the consumer to make a purchase;

'materially distort the economic behaviour' means in relation to an average consumer, appreciably to impair the average consumer's ability to make an informed decision thereby causing him to take a transactional decision that he would not have taken otherwise;

'premises' includes any place and any stall, vehicle, ship or aircraft;

'product' means—

(a)   goods,

(b)   a service,

(c)   digital content,

(d)   immoveable property,

(e)   rights or obligations, or

(f)   a product of the bind mentioned in paragraphs (1A) and (1B), but the application of this definition to Part 4A is subject to regulations 27C and 27D.

'professional diligence' means the standard of special skill and care which a trader may reasonably be expected to exercise towards consumers which is commensurate with either—

(a)   honest market practice in the trader's field of activity, or

(b)   the general principle of good faith in the trader's field of activity;

'ship' includes any boat and any other description of vessel used in navigation;

'trader'—

(a)   means a person acting for purposes relating to that person's business whether asking personally or through another person acting in the trader's name or on the trader's behalf, and

(b)   except in Part 4A, includes a person acting in the name of or on behalf of the trader;

'transactional decision' means any decision taken by a consumer, whether it is to act or to refrain from acting, concerning—

(a)   whether, how and on what terms to purchase, make payment in whole or in part for, retain or dispose of a product; or

(b)   whether, how and on what terms to exercise a contractual right in relation to a product (but the application of this definition to regulations 5 and 7 as they apply for the purposes of Part 4A is subject to regulation 27B(2)).

(1A) A trader ('T') who demands payment from a consumer ('C') in full or partial settlement of C's liabilities or purported liabilities to T is to be treated for the purposes of these Regulations as offering to supply a product to C.

(1B) In such a case the product that T offers to supply comprises the full or partial settlement of those liabilities or purported liabilities.

(2)   In determining the effect of a commercial practice on the average consumer where the practice reaches or is addressed to a consumer or consumers account shall be taken of the material characteristics of such an average consumer including his being reasonably well informed, reasonably observant and circumspect.

(3)   Paragraphs (4) and (5) set out the circumstances in which a reference to the average consumer shall be read as in addition referring to the average member of a particular group of consumers.

(4)   In determining the effect of a commercial practice on the average consumer where the practice is directed to a particular group of consumers, a reference to the average consumer shall be read as referring to the average member of that group.

(5)   In determining the effect of a commercial practice on the average consumer—

(a)   where a clearly identifiable group of consumers is particularly vulnerable to the practice or the underlying product because of their mental or physical infirmity, age or credulity in a way which the trader could reasonably be expected to foresee, and

(b)   where the practice is likely to materially distort the economic behaviour only of that group, a reference to the average consumer shall be read as referring to the average member of that group.

(6) Paragraph (5) is without prejudice to the common and legitimate advertising practice of making exaggerated statements which are not meant to be taken literally.

PART 2
PROHIBITIONS

3.   Prohibition of unfair commercial practices

(1) Unfair commercial practices are prohibited.

(2) Paragraphs (3) and (4) set out the circumstances when a commercial practice is unfair.

(3) A commercial practice is unfair if—
   (a)   it contravenes the requirements of professional diligence; and
   (b)   it materially distorts or is likely to materially distort the economic behaviour of the average consumer with regard to the product.

(4) A commercial practice is unfair if—
   (a)   it is a misleading action under the provisions of regulation 5;
   (b)   it is a misleading omission under the provisions of regulation 6;
   (c)   it is aggressive under the provisions of regulation 7; or
   (d)   it is listed in Schedule 1.

4.   Prohibition of the promotion of unfair commercial practices

The promotion of any unfair commercial practice by a code owner in a code of conduct is prohibited.

5.   Misleading actions

(1) A commercial practice is a misleading action if it satisfies the conditions in either paragraph (2) or paragraph (3).

(2) A commercial practice satisfies the conditions of this paragraph—
   (a)   if it contains false information and is therefore untruthful in relation to any of the matters in paragraph (4) or if it or its overall presentation in any way deceives or is likely to deceive the average consumer in relation to any of the matters in that paragraph, even if the information is factually correct; and
   (b)   it causes or is likely to cause the average consumer to take a transactional decision he would not have taken otherwise.

(3) A commercial practice satisfies the conditions of this paragraph if—
   (a)   it concerns any marketing of a product (including comparative advertising) which creates confusion with any products, trade marks, trade names or other distinguishing marks of a competitor; or
   (b)   it concerns any failure by a trader to comply with a commitment contained in a code of conduct which the trader has undertaken to comply with, if—
      (i)   the trader indicates in a commercial practice that he is bound by that code of conduct, and
      (ii)   the commitment is firm and capable of being verified and is not aspirational, and it causes or is likely to cause the average consumer to take a transactional decision he would not have taken otherwise, taking account of its factual context and of all its features and circumstances.

(4) The matters referred to in paragraph (2)(a) are—
   (a)   the existence or nature of the product;
   (b)   the main characteristics of the product (as defined in paragraph 5);
   (c)   the extent of the trader's commitments;
   (d)   the motives for the commercial practice;
   (e)   the nature of the sales process;
   (f)   any statement or symbol relating to direct or indirect sponsorship or approval of the trader or the product;
   (g)   the price or the manner in which the price is calculated;
   (h)   the existence of a specific price advantage;
   (i)   the need for a service, part, replacement or repair;
   (j)   the nature, attributes and rights of the trader (as defined in paragraph 6);
   (k)   the consumer's rights or the risks he may face.

(5) In paragraph (4)(b), the 'main characteristics of the product' include—
    (a) availability of the product;
    (b) benefits of the product;
    (c) risks of the product;
    (d) execution of the product;
    (e) composition of the product;
    (f) accessories of the product;
    (g) after-sale customer assistance concerning the product;
    (h) the handling of complaints about the product;
    (i) the method and date of manufacture of the product;
    (j) the method and date of provision of the product;
    (k) delivery of the product;
    (l) fitness for purpose of the product;
    (m) usage of the product;
    (n) quantity of the product;
    (o) specification of the product;
    (p) geographical or commercial origin of the product;
    (q) results to be expected from use of the product; and
    (r) results and material features of tests or checks carried out on the product.

(6) In paragraph (4)(j), the 'nature, attributes and rights' as far as concern the trader include the trader's—
    (a) identity;
    (b) assets;
    (c) qualifications;
    (d) status;
    (e) approval;
    (f) affiliations or connections;
    (g) ownership of industrial, commercial or intellectual property rights; and
    (h) awards and distinctions.

(7) In paragraph (4)(k) 'consumer's rights' include rights the consumer may have under Part 5A of the Sale of Goods Act 1979 or Part 1B of the Supply of Goods and Services Act 1982.

6.   Misleading omissions

(1) A commercial practice is a misleading omission if, in its factual context, taking account of the matters in paragraph (2)—
    (a) the commercial practice omits material information,
    (b) the commercial practice hides material information,
    (c) the commercial practice provides material information in a manner which is unclear, unintelligible, ambiguous or untimely, or
    (d) the commercial practice fails to identify its commercial intent, unless this is already apparent from the context,
and as a result it causes or is likely to cause the average consumer to take a transactional decision he would not have taken otherwise.

(2) The matters referred to in paragraph (1) are—
    (a) all the features and circumstances of the commercial practice;
    (b) the limitations of the medium used to communicate the commercial practice (including limitations of space or time); and
    (c) where the medium used to communicate the commercial practice imposes limitations of space or time, any measures taken by the trader to make the information available to consumers by other means.

(3) In paragraph (1) 'material information' means—
    (a) the information which the average consumer needs, according to the context, to take an informed transactional decision; and
    (b) any information requirement which applies in relation to a commercial communication as a result of a Community obligation.

(4) Where a commercial practice is an invitation to purchase, the following information will be material if not already apparent from the context in addition to any other information which is material information under paragraph (3)—

(a)   the main characteristics of the product, to the extent appropriate to the medium by which the invitation to purchase is communicated and the product;

(b)   the identity of the trader, such as his trading name, and the identity of any other trader on whose behalf the trader is acting;

(c)   the geographical address of the trader and the geographical address of any other trader on whose behalf the trader is acting;

(d)   either—
   (i)   the price, including any taxes; or
   (ii)   where the nature of the product is such that the price cannot reasonably be calculated in advance, the manner in which the price is calculated;

(e)   where appropriate, either—
   (i)   all additional freight, delivery or postal charges; or
   (ii)   where such charges cannot reasonably be calculated in advance, the fact that such charges may be payable;

(f)   the following matters where they depart from the requirements of professional diligence—
   (i)   arrangements for payment,
   (ii)   arrangements for delivery,
   (iii)   arrangements for performance,
   (iv)   complaint handling policy;

(g)   for products and transactions involving a right of withdrawal or cancellation, the existence of such a right.

7.   Aggressive commercial practices

(1)   A commercial practice is aggressive if, in its factual context, taking account of all of its features and circumstances—

(a)   it significantly impairs or is likely significantly to impair the average consumer's freedom of choice or conduct in relation to the product concerned through the use of harassment, coercion or undue influence; and

(b)   it thereby causes or is likely to cause him to take a transactional decision he would not have taken otherwise.

(2)   In determining whether a commercial practice uses harassment, coercion or undue influence account shall be taken of—

(a)   its timing, location, nature or persistence;

(b)   the use of threatening or abusive language or behaviour;

(c)   the exploitation by the trader of any specific misfortune or circumstance of such gravity as to impair the consumer's judgment, of which the trader is aware, to influence the consumer's decision with regard to the product;

(d)   any onerous or disproportionate non-contractual barrier imposed by the trader where a consumer wishes to exercise rights under the contract, including rights to terminate a contract or to switch to another product or another trader; and

(e)   any threat to take any action which cannot legally be taken.

(3)   In this regulation—

(a)   'coercion' includes the use of physical force; and

(b)   'undue influence' means exploiting a position of power in relation to the consumer so as to apply pressure, even without using or threatening to use physical force, in a way which significantly limits the consumer's ability to make an informed decision.

PART 3
OFFENCES

8.   Offences relating to unfair commercial practices

(1)   A trader is guilty of an offence if—

(a)   he knowingly or recklessly engages in a commercial practice which contravenes the requirements of professional diligence under regulation 3(3)(a); and

(b)   the practice materially distorts or is likely to materially distort the economic behaviour of the average consumer with regard to the product under regulation 3(3)(b).

(2) For the purposes of paragraph (1)(a) a trader who engages in a commercial practice without regard to whether the practice contravenes the requirements of professional diligence shall be deemed recklessly to engage in the practice, whether or not the trader has reason for believing that the practice might contravene those requirements.

9. A trader is guilty of an offence if he engages in a commercial practice which is a misleading action under regulation 5 otherwise than by reason of the commercial practice satisfying the condition in regulation 5(3)(b).

10. A trader is guilty of an offence if he engages in a commercial practice which is a misleading omission under regulation 6.

11. A trader is guilty of an offence if he engages in a commercial practice which is aggressive under regulation 7.

12. A trader is guilty of an offence if he engages in a commercial practice set out in any of paragraphs 1 to 10, 12 to 27 and 29 to 31 of Schedule 1.

13. **Penalty for offences**

A person guilty of an offence under regulation 8, 9, 10, 11 or 12 shall be liable—
(a) on summary conviction, to a fine not exceeding the statutory maximum; or
(b) on conviction on indictment, to a fine or imprisonment for a term not exceeding two years or both.

14. **Time limit for prosecution**

(1) No proceedings for an offence under these Regulations shall be commenced after—
   (a) the end of the period of three years beginning with the date of the commission of the offence, or
   (b) the end of the period of one year beginning with the date of discovery of the offence by the prosecutor,
   whichever is earlier.

(2) For the purposes of paragraph (1)(b) a certificate signed by or on behalf of the prosecutor and stating the date on which the offence was discovered by him shall be conclusive evidence of that fact and a certificate stating that matter and purporting to be so signed shall be treated as so signed unless the contrary is proved.

(3) Notwithstanding anything in section 127(1) of the Magistrates' Courts Act 1980, an information relating to an offence under these Regulations which is triable by a magistrates' court in England and Wales may be so tried if it is laid at any time before the end of the period of twelve months beginning with the date of the commission of the offence.

(4) Notwithstanding anything in section 136 of the Criminal Procedure (Scotland) Act 1995 summary proceedings in Scotland for an offence under these Regulations may be commenced at any time before the end of the period of twelve months beginning with the date of the commission of the offence.

(5) For the purposes of paragraph (4), section 136(3) of the Criminal Procedure (Scotland) Act 1995 shall apply as it applies for the purposes of that subsection.

(6) Notwithstanding anything in Article 19(1) of the Magistrates' Courts (Northern Ireland) Order 1981 a complaint charging an offence under these Regulations which is triable by a magistrates' court in Northern Ireland may be so tried if it is made at any time before the end of the period of twelve months beginning with the date of the commission of the offence.

15. **Offences committed by bodies of persons**

(1) Where an offence under these Regulations committed by a body corporate is proved—
   (a) to have been committed with the consent or connivance of an officer of the body, or
   (b) to be attributable to any neglect on his part,
   the officer as well as the body corporate is guilty of the offence and liable to be proceeded against and punished accordingly.

(2) In paragraph (1) a reference to an officer of a body corporate includes a reference to—
  (a) a director, manager, secretary or other similar officer; and
  (b) a person purporting to act as a director, manager, secretary or other similar officer.
(3) Where an offence under these Regulations committed by a Scottish partnership is proved—
  (a) to have been committed with the consent or connivance of a partner, or
  (b) to be attributable to any neglect on his part,
  the partner as well as the partnership is guilty of the offence and liable to be proceeded against and punished accordingly.
(4) In paragraph (3) a reference to a partner includes a person purporting to act as a partner.

16. Offence due to the default of another person

(1) This regulation applies where a person 'X' —
  (a) commits an offence under regulation 9, 10, 11 or 12, or
  (b) would have committed an offence under those regulations but for a defence under regulation 17 or 18,
  and the commission of the offence, or of what would have been an offence but for X being able to rely on a defence under regulation 17 or 18, is due to the act or default of some other person 'Y'.
(2) Where this regulation applies Y is guilty of the offence, subject to regulations 17 and 18, whether or not Y is a trader and whether or not Y's act or default is a commercial practice.
(3) Y may be charged with and convicted of the offence by virtue of paragraph (2) whether or not proceedings are taken against X.

17. Due diligence defence

(1) In any proceedings against a person for an offence under regulation 9, 10, 11 or 12 it is a defence for that person to prove—
  (a) that the commission of the offence was due to—
    (i) a mistake;
    (ii) reliance on information supplied to him by another person;
    (iii) the act or default of another person;
    (iv) an accident; or
  (b) another cause beyond his control; and
  (c) that he took all reasonable precautions and exercised all due diligence to avoid the commission of such an offence by himself or any person under his control.
(2) A person shall not be entitled to rely on the defence provided by paragraph (1) by reason of the matters referred to in paragraph (ii) or (iii) of paragraph (1)(a) without leave of the court unless—
  (a) he has served on the prosecutor a notice in writing giving such information identifying or assisting in the identification of that other person as was in his possession; and
  (b) the notice is served on the prosecutor at least seven clear days before the date of the hearing.

18. Innocent publication of advertisement defence

(1) In any proceedings against a person for an offence under regulation 9, 10, 11 or 12 committed by the publication of an advertisement it shall be a defence for a person to prove that—
  (a) he is a person whose business it is to publish or to arrange for the publication of advertisements;
  (b) he received the advertisement for publication in the ordinary course of business; and
  (c) he did not know and had no reason to suspect that its publication would amount to an offence under the regulation to which the proceedings relate.
(2) In paragraph (1) 'advertisement' includes a catalogue, a circular and a price list.

PART 4
ENFORCEMENT

19. Duty and power to enforce

(1) It shall be the duty of every enforcement authority to enforce these Regulations (other than Part 4A).

(2) Where the enforcement authority is a local weights and measures authority the duty referred to in paragraph (1) shall apply to the enforcement of these Regulations within the authority's area.

(3) Where the enforcement authority is the Department of Enterprise, Trade and Investment in Northern Ireland the duty referred to in paragraph (1) shall apply to the enforcement of these Regulations within Northern Ireland.

(4) In determining how to comply with its duty of enforcement every enforcement authority shall have regard to the desirability of encouraging control of unfair commercial practices by such established means as it considers appropriate having regard to all the circumstances of the particular case.

(5) Nothing in this regulation shall authorise any enforcement authority to bring proceedings in Scotland for an offence.

PART 4A
CONSUMERS' RIGHTS TO REDRESS

27A. When does a consumer have a right to redress?

(1) A consumer has a right to redress under this Part if—
　　(a) the conditions in this regulation are met, and
　　(b) the conditions (if any) in the following provisions of this Part for the availability of that right are met.

(2) The first condition is that—
　　(a) the consumer enters into a contract with a trader for the sale or supply of a product by the trader (a 'business to consumer contract'),
　　(b) the consumer enters into a contract with a trader for the sale of goods to the trader (a 'consumer to business contract'), or
　　(c) the consumer makes a payment to a trader for the supply of a product (a 'consumer payment').

(3) Paragraph (2)(b) does not apply if, under the contract, the trader supplies or agrees to supply a product to the consumer as well as paying or agreeing to pay the consumer.

(4) The second condition is that—
　　(a) the trader engages in a prohibited practice in relation to the product, or
　　(b) in a case where a consumer enters into a business to consumer contract for goods or digital content—
　　　　(i) a producer engages in a prohibited practice in relation to the goods or digital content, and
　　　　(ii) when the contract is entered into, the trader is aware of the commercial practice that constitutes the prohibited practice or could reasonably be expected to be aware of it.

(5) In paragraph (4)(b) 'producer' means—
　　(a) a manufacturer of the goods or digital content,
　　(b) an importer of the goods or digital content into the United Kingdom, or—
　　(c) a person who purports to be a producer by placing the person's name, trade mark or other distinctive sign on the goods or using it in connection with the digital content,

and includes a producer acting personally or through another person acting in the producer's name or on the producer's behalf.

(6) The third condition is that the prohibited practice is a significant factor in the consumer's decision to enter into the contract or make the payment.

27B. What does 'prohibited practice' mean in this Part?

(1)   In this Part 'prohibited practice' means a commercial practice that—

    (a)   is a misleading action under regulation 5, or

    (b)   is aggressive under regulation 7.

(2)   Regulations 5 and 7 apply for the purposes of this Part as if for the definition of 'transactional decision' in regulation 2(1) there were substituted—

"'transactional decision' means any decision taken by a consumer to enter into a contract with a trader for the sale or supply of a product by the trader, or for the sale of goods to the trader, or to make a payment to a trader for the supply of a product.".

27C. What immoveable property is covered by this Part?

(1)   In this Part 'product' does not include immoveable property other than a relevant lease.

(2)   In this regulation 'relevant lease' in relation to England and Wales means—

    (a)   an assured tenancy within the meaning of Part 1 of the Housing Act 1988, or

    (b)   a lease under which accommodation is let as holiday accommodation.

(3)   But none of the following are relevant leases for the purposes of paragraph (2)(a)—

    (a)   a lease granted by—

        (i)   a private registered provider of social housing, or

        (ii)   a registered social landlord within the meaning of Part 1 of the Housing Act 1996(**7**);

    (b)   a lease of a dwelling-house or part of a dwelling-house—

        (i)   granted on payment of a premium calculated by reference to a percentage of the value of the dwelling-house or part or of the cost of providing it, or

        (ii)   under which the lessee (or the lessee's personal representatives) will or may be entitled to a sum calculated by reference, directly or indirectly, to the value of the dwelling-house or part;

    (c)   a lease granted to a person as a result of the exercise by a local housing authority within the meaning of the Housing Act 1996 of its functions under Part 7 (homelessness) of that Act.

(4)   In this regulation 'relevant lease' in relation to Scotland means—

    (a)   an assured tenancy within the meaning of Part 2 of the Housing (Scotland) Act 1988, or

    (b)   a lease under which accommodation is let as holiday accommodation.

(5)   In this regulation 'relevant lease' in relation to Northern Ireland means—

    (a)   a private tenancy within the meaning of Article 3 of the Private Tenancies (Northern Ireland) Order 2006, or

    (b)   a lease under which accommodation is let as holiday accommodation.

(6)   But neither of the following are relevant leases for the purposes of paragraph (5)(a)—

    (a)   a lease of a dwelling-house or part of a dwelling-house—

        (i)   granted on payment of a premium calculated by reference to a percentage of the value of the dwelling-house or part or of the cost of providing it, or

        (ii)   under which the lessee (or the lessee's personal representatives) will or may be entitled to a sum calculated by reference, directly or indirectly, to the value of the dwelling-house or part;

    (b)   a private tenancy resulting from the exercise by the Northern Ireland Housing Executive of its functions under Part 2 (homelessness) of the Housing (Northern Ireland) Order 1988.

27D. What financial services are covered by this Part?

(1)   In this Part 'product' does not include a service provided in the course of carrying on a regulated activity within the meaning of section 22 of the Financial Services and Markets Act 2000, other than a service to which paragraph (2) applies.

(2)   This paragraph applies to a service consisting of the provision of credit under an agreement which is a restricted-use credit agreement within paragraph (a) or (b) of the definition of that term in article 60L(1) of the Financial Services and Markets Act 2000 (Regulated Activities) Order 2001.

(3)   But paragraph (2) does not apply to an agreement under which the obligation of the borrower to repay is secured by a legal or equitable mortgage on land (other than timeshare accommodation).

    (4)   In paragraph (3)—

          'mortgage' includes a charge and (in Scotland) a heritable security;

          'timeshare accommodation' means overnight accommodation which is the subject of a timeshare contract within the meaning of the Timeshare, Holiday Products, Resale and Exchange Contracts Regulations 2010.

    (5)   The fact that the supply of a product within regulation 2(1A) and (1B) may constitute an activity within article 39F (debt-collecting) of the Financial Services and Markets Act 2000 (Regulated Activities) Order 2001 does not prevent this Part from applying in relation to that supply.

27E. When does the right to unwind apply to a business to consumer contract?

    (1)   A consumer has the right to unwind in respect of a business to consumer contract if the consumer indicates to the trader that the consumer rejects the product, and does so—

        (a)   within the relevant period, and

        (b)   at a time when the product is capable of being rejected.

    (2)   An indication under paragraph (1) may be something that the consumer says or does, but it must be clear.

    (3)   In paragraph (1)(a) 'the relevant period' means the period of 90 days beginning with the later of—

        (a)   the day on which the consumer enters into the contract, and

        (b)   the relevant day.

    (4)   In this Part 'the relevant day' means the day on which—

        (a)   the goods are first delivered,

        (b)   the performance of the service begins,

        (c)   the digital content is first supplied,

        (d)   the lease begins, or

        (e)   the right is first exercisable,

  (as the case may be).

    (5)   But in the case of a mixed contract, 'the relevant day' means the latest of the days mentioned in paragraph (4) that is relevant to the contract.

    (6)   In this Part 'mixed contract' means a contract relating to a product which consists of any two or more of goods, a service, digital content, immoveable property or rights.

    (7)   For the purposes of this Part, where the consumer's access to digital content on a device requires its transmission to the device under arrangements initiated by the trader, the day on which the digital content is first provided is—

        (a)   the day on which it reaches the device, or

        (b)   if earlier, the day on which it reaches another trader chosen by the consumer to supply, under a contract with the consumer, a service by which digital content reaches the device.

    (8)   For the purposes of paragraph (1)(b), a product remains capable of being rejected only if—

        (a)   the goods have not been fully consumed,

        (b)   the service has not been fully performed,

        (c)   the digital content has not been fully consumed,

        (d)   the lease has not expired, or

        (e)   the right has not been fully exercised,

  (as the case may be).

    (9)   For the purposes of paragraph (8)—

        (a)   goods have been fully consumed only if nothing is left of them, and

        (b)   digital content has been fully consumed only if the digital content was available to the consumer for a fixed period and that period has expired.

   (10) A consumer does not have the right to unwind in respect of a business to consumer contract if the consumer has exercised the right to a discount in respect of that contract and the same prohibited practice.

27F. How does the right to unwind work in the case of a business to consumer contract?

(1) Where a consumer has the right to unwind in respect of a business to consumer contract—

    (a) the contract comes to an end so that the consumer and the trader are released from their obligations under it,

    (b) the trader has a duty to give the consumer a refund (subject as follows), and

    (c) if the contract was wholly or partly for the sale or supply of goods the consumer must make the goods available for collection by the trader.

(2) The consumer's entitlement to a refund works as follows.

(3) To the extent that the consumer paid money under the contract, the consumer is entitled to receive back the same amount of money (but see paragraphs (7) to (10)).

(4) To the extent that the consumer transferred anything else under the contract, the consumer is entitled to receive back the same amount of what the consumer transferred, unless paragraph (5) applies.

(5) To the extent that the consumer transferred under the contract something for which the same amount of the same thing cannot be substituted—

    (a) the consumer is entitled to receive back in its original state whatever the consumer transferred, or

    (b) if it cannot be given back in its original state, the consumer is entitled to be paid its market price as at the time when the product was rejected.

(6) There is no entitlement to a refund if none of paragraphs (3) to (5) applies.

(7) The consumer's entitlement to receive back the same amount of money as the consumer paid is qualified by paragraphs (8) to (10) if—

    (a) the contract was for the sale or supply of a product on a regular or continuous basis, and

    (b) the period beginning with the relevant day and ending with the day on which the consumer rejected the product exceeds one month.

(8) In that case the consumer is only entitled to receive back the amount (if any) found by deducting the market price, when the consumer rejected the product, of the product supplied up to that time from the amount the consumer paid for it.

(9) But paragraph (8) does not apply if it is not appropriate to apply that deduction having regard to—

    (a) the behaviour of the person who engaged in the prohibited practice, and

    (b) the impact of the practice on the consumer.

(10) Where the product supplied up to the time when the consumer rejected it consists wholly or partly of goods, their market price is only to be taken into account under paragraph (8) to the extent that they have been consumed.

27G. How does the right to unwind work in the case of a consumer to business contract?

(1) A consumer who has a right to redress in respect of a consumer to business contract has the right to unwind in respect of that contract.

(2) Where paragraph (1) applies—

    (a) the consumer has the right to treat the contract as at an end so that the trader and the consumer are released from their obligations under it, and

    (b) the consumer has the right within paragraph (5) or (6).

(3) To treat the contract as at an end, the consumer must indicate to the trader that the contract is ended.

(4) An indication under paragraph (3) may be something that the consumer says or does, but it must be clear.

(5) If the trader is able to return the goods to the consumer in the condition they were in when sold by the consumer—

    (a) the consumer has a right to the return of the goods, and

    (b) the consumer must repay to the trader the amount (if any) that the trader has paid for the goods

(6) If paragraph (5) does not apply, the consumer has a right to a payment from the trader of the amount (if any) by which the market price of the goods when the trader paid for them exceeds what the trader paid for them.

27H. How does the right to unwind work if payments are demanded which are not due?

(1) A consumer has the right to unwind in respect of a consumer payment for a product within regulation 2(1A) and (1B) if the consumer was not required to make all or part of the payment.

(2) Where paragraph (1) applies, the consumer has the right to receive back from the trader—

    (a) the same amount of money as the consumer paid to the trader, or

    (b) in a case where the consumer was required to make part of the payment, an amount equal to the part of the payment the consumer was not required to make.

27I. How does the right to a discount work?

(1) A consumer has the right to a discount in respect of a business to consumer contract if—

    (a) the consumer has made one or more payments for the product to the trader or one or more payments under the contract have not been made, and

    (b) the consumer has not exercised the right to unwind in respect of the contract.

(2) If the consumer has made one or more payments, the consumer has the right to receive back from the trader the relevant percentage of the payment or payments.

(3) If one or more payments have not been made, the consumer has the right—

    (a) to reduce by the relevant percentage as many of those payments as is appropriate having regard to the seriousness of the prohibited practice, or

    (b) in a case within paragraph (6), to reduce all of those payments by the relevant percentage.

(4) Subject to paragraph (6), the relevant percentage is as follows—

    (a) if the prohibited practice is more than minor, it is 25%,

    (b) if the prohibited practice is significant, it is 50%,

    (c) if the prohibited practice is serious, it is 75%, and

    (d) if the prohibited practice is very serious, it is 100%.

(5) The seriousness of the prohibited practice is to be assessed by reference to—

    (a) the behaviour of the person who engaged in the practice,

    (b) the impact of the practice on the consumer, and

    (c) the time that has elapsed since the prohibited practice took place.

(6) Paragraph (4) does not apply if—

    (a) the amount payable for the product under the contract exceeds £5,000,

    (b) the market price of the product, at the time that the consumer entered into the contract, is lower than the amount payable for it under the contract, and

    (c) there is clear evidence of the difference between the market price of the product and the amount payable for it under the contract.

(7) In such a case, the relevant percentage is the percentage difference between the market price of the product and the amount payable for it under the contract.

(8) The application of this regulation does not affect any of the other rights and liabilities under the contract.

27J. How does the right to damages work?

(1) Subject as follows, a consumer has the right to damages if the consumer—

    (a) has incurred financial loss which the consumer would not have incurred if the prohibited practice in question had not taken place, or

    (b) has suffered alarm, distress or physical inconvenience or discomfort which the consumer would not have suffered if the prohibited practice in question had not taken place.

(2) The right to damages is the right to be paid damages by the trader for the loss or the alarm, distress or physical inconvenience or discomfort in question.

(3) The right to be paid damages for financial loss does not include the right to be paid damages in respect of the difference between the market price of a product and the amount payable for it under a contract.

(4) The right to be paid damages under this regulation is a right to be paid only damages in respect of loss that was reasonably foreseeable at the time of the prohibited practice.

(5) A consumer does not have the right to damages if the trader proves that—

    (a) the occurrence of the prohibited practice in question was due to—

        (i) a mistake,

        (ii) reliance on information supplied to the trader by another person,

        (iii) the act or default of a person other than the trader,

        (iv) an accident, or

        (v) another cause beyond the trader's control, and

    (b) the trader took all reasonable precautions and exercised all due diligence to avoid the occurrence of the prohibited practice.

27K. How can a consumer enforce the rights to redress?

(1) A consumer with a right to redress under this Part may bring a claim in civil proceedings to enforce that right.

(2) In Scotland, proceedings to enforce the right to unwind may be brought before the sheriff or in the Court of Session.

(3) Paragraph (4) applies if in proceedings under this regulation the consumer establishes that the consumer has—

    (a) the right to unwind,

    (b) the right to a discount, or

    (c) the right to damages.

(4) The court must make an order that gives effect to—

    (a) that right, and

    (b) any associated obligations of the consumer under this Part.

(5) The Limitation Act 1980 applies to a claim under this regulation in England and Wales as if it were an action founded on simple contract.

(6) The Limitation (Northern Ireland) Order 1989 applies to a claim under this regulation in Northern Ireland as if it were an action founded on simple contract.

27L. How does this Part relate to the existing law?

(1) Nothing in this Part affects the ability of a consumer to make a claim under a rule of law or equity, or under an enactment, in respect of conduct constituting a prohibited practice.

(2) But a consumer may not—

    (a) make a claim to be compensated under a rule of law or equity, or under an enactment, in respect of such conduct if the consumer has been compensated under this Part in respect of the conduct, or

    (b) make a claim to be compensated under this Part in respect of such conduct if the consumer has been compensated under a rule of law or equity, or under an enactment, in respect of the conduct.

(3) In this regulation 'enactment' includes—

    (a) an enactment contained in subordinate legislation within the meaning of the Interpretation Act 1978,

    (b) an enactment contained in, or in an instrument made under, a Measure or Act of the National Assembly for Wales,

    (c) an enactment contained in, or in an instrument made under, an Act of the Scottish Parliament, and

    (d) an enactment contained in, or in an instrument made under, Northern Ireland legislation.

27M. Inertia selling

(1) This regulation applies where a trader engages in the unfair commercial practice described in paragraph 29 of Schedule 1 (inertia selling).

(2) The consumer is exempted from any obligation to provide consideration for the products supplied by the trader.

(3) The absence of a response from the consumer following the supply does not constitute consent to the provision of consideration for, or the return or safekeeping of, the products.

(4)   In the case of an unsolicited supply of goods, the consumer may, as between the consumer and the trader, use, deal with or dispose of the goods as if they were an unconditional gift to the consumer.

PART 5
SUPPLEMENTARY

28.   Crown

(1)   ...

(2)   The Crown is not criminally liable as a result of any provision of these Regulations.

(3)   Paragraph (2) does not affect the application of any provision of these Regulations in relation to a person in the public service of the Crown.

29.   Validity of agreements

Except as provided by Part 4A, an agreement shall not be void or unenforceable by reason only of a breach of these Regulations.

30.   Amendments, repeals and transitional and saving provisions

(1)   Schedule 2 (which contains amendments) shall have effect.

(2)   Schedule 3 (which contains transitional and saving provisions) shall have effect.

(3)   Schedule 4 (which contains repeals and revocations) shall have effect.

Regulation 3(4)(d).

SCHEDULE 1
COMMERCIAL PRACTICES WHICH ARE IN ALL CIRCUMSTANCES
CONSIDERED UNFAIR

1.   Claiming to be a signatory to a code of conduct when the trader is not.

2.   Displaying a trust mark, quality mark or equivalent without having obtained the necessary authorisation.

3.   Claiming that a code of conduct has an endorsement from a public or other body which it does not have.

4.   Claiming that a trader (including his commercial practices) or a product has been approved, endorsed or authorised by a public or private body when the trader, the commercial practices or the product have not or making such a claim without complying with the terms of the approval, endorsement or authorisation.

5.   Making an invitation to purchase products at a specified price without disclosing the existence of any reasonable grounds the trader may have for believing that he will not be able to offer for supply, or to procure another trader to supply, those products or equivalent products at that price for a period that is, and in quantities that are, reasonable having regard to the product, the scale of advertising of the product and the price offered (bait advertising).

6.   Making an invitation to purchase products at a specified price and then—

(a)   refusing to show the advertised item to consumers,

(b)   refusing to take orders for it or deliver it within a reasonable time, or

(c)   demonstrating a defective sample of it,

with the intention of promoting a different product (bait and switch).

7.   Falsely stating that a product will only be available for a very limited time, or that it will only be available on particular terms for a very limited time, in order to elicit an immediate decision and deprive consumers of sufficient opportunity or time to make an informed choice.

8.   Undertaking to provide after-sales service to consumers with whom the trader has communicated prior to a transaction in a language which is not English (in the case of a trader located in the United Kingdom or not) and then making such service available only in another language without clearly disclosing this to the consumer before the consumer is committed to the transaction.

9.   Stating or otherwise creating the impression that a product can legally be sold when it cannot.

10. Presenting rights given to consumers in law as a distinctive feature of the trader's offer.
11. Using editorial content in the media to promote a product where a trader has paid for the promotion without making that clear in the content or by images or sounds clearly identifiable by the consumer (advertorial).
12. Making a materially inaccurate claim concerning the nature and extent of the risk to the personal security of the consumer or his family if the consumer does not purchase the product.
13. Promoting a product similar to a product made by a particular manufacturer in such a manner as deliberately to mislead the consumer into believing that the product is made by that same manufacturer when it is not.
14. Establishing, operating or promoting a pyramid promotional scheme where a consumer gives consideration for the opportunity to receive compensation that is derived primarily from the introduction of other consumers into the scheme rather than from the sale or consumption of products.
15. Claiming that the trader is about to cease trading or move premises when he is not.
16. Claiming that products are able to facilitate winning in games of chance.
17. Falsely claiming that a product is able to cure illnesses, dysfunction or malformations.
18. Passing on materially inaccurate information on market conditions or on the possibility of finding the product with the intention of inducing the consumer to acquire the product at conditions less favourable than normal market conditions.
19. Claiming in a commercial practice to offer a competition or prize promotion without awarding the prizes described or a reasonable equivalent.
20. Describing a product as 'gratis', 'free', 'without charge' or similar if the consumer has to pay anything other than the unavoidable cost of responding to the commercial practice and collecting or paying for delivery of the item.
21. Including in marketing material an invoice or similar document seeking payment which gives the consumer the impression that he has already ordered the marketed product when he has not.
22. Falsely claiming or creating the impression that the trader is not acting for purposes relating to his trade, business, craft or profession, or falsely representing oneself as a consumer.
23. Creating the false impression that after-sales service in relation to a product is available in the United Kingdom (if the product is sold there) or in an EEA State other than the one in which the product is sold.
24. Creating the impression that the consumer cannot leave the premises until a contract is formed.
25. Conducting personal visits to the consumer's home ignoring the consumer's request to leave or not to return, except in circumstances and to the extent justified to enforce a contractual obligation.
26. Making persistent and unwanted solicitations by telephone, fax, e-mail or other remote media except in circumstances and to the extent justified to enforce a contractual obligation.
27. Requiring a consumer who wishes to claim on an insurance policy to produce documents which could not reasonably be considered relevant as to whether the claim was valid, or failing systematically to respond to pertinent correspondence, in order to dissuade a consumer from exercising his contractual rights.
28. Including in an advertisement a direct exhortation to children to buy advertised products or persuade their parents or other adults to buy advertised products for them.
29. Demanding immediate or deferred payment for or the return or safekeeping of products supplied by the trader, but not solicited by the consumer.
30. Explicitly informing a consumer that if he does not buy the product or service, the trader's job or livelihood will be in jeopardy.
31. Creating the false impression that the consumer has already won, will win, or will on doing a particular act win, a prize or other equivalent benefit, when in fact either—
    (a) there is no prize or other equivalent benefit, or
    (b) taking any action in relation to claiming the prize or other equivalent benefit is subject to the consumer paying money or incurring a cost.

TIMESHARE, HOLIDAY PRODUCTS, RESALE AND EXCHANGE CONTRACTS REGULATIONS 2010
(SI 2010, No. 2960)

PART 1

GENERAL

1.   Citation and Commencement

(1)   These Regulations may be cited as the Timeshare, Holiday Products, Resale and Exchange Contracts Regulations 2010.

(2)   They come into force on 23rd February 2011.

2.   Interpretation

(1)   In these Regulations—

'ancillary contract', in relation to a timeshare contract or long-term holiday product contract, has the meaning given in regulation 22(6);

'consumer' has the meaning given in regulation 11;

'enforcement authority' has the meaning given in regulation 32(1);

'exchange contract' has the meaning given in regulation 10(1);

'holiday accommodation contract' has the meaning given in regulation 4;

'key information', in relation to a regulated contract, has the meaning given in regulation 12(3);

'long-term holiday product contract' has the meaning given in regulation 8;

'regulated contract' has the meaning given in regulation 3;

'related credit agreement', in relation to a regulated contract, has the meaning given in regulation 23(4);

'resale contract' has the meaning given in regulation 9;

'standard information form' has the meaning given in regulation 13(2);

'timeshare contract' has the meaning given in regulation 7(1);

'timeshare exchange system' has the meaning given in regulation 10(2);

'trader' has the meaning given in regulation 11.

PART 2

KEY DEFINITIONS

3.   Regulated contract

A 'regulated contract' means a contract which—

    (a)   is a holiday accommodation contract (see regulation 4) to which these Regulations apply (see regulation 5), but

    (b)   is not an excluded arrangement (see regulation 6).

4.   Holiday accommodation contracts

(1)   A 'holiday accommodation contract' means—

    (a)   a timeshare contract,

    (b)   a long-term holiday product contract,

    (c)   a resale contract, or

    (d)   an exchange contract.

(2)   See regulations 7 to 10 for definitions of these types of contract.

5.   Holiday accommodation contracts to which these Regulations apply

(1)   These Regulations apply to a holiday accommodation contract which falls within any of paragraphs (2) to (4).

(2)   A holiday accommodation contract falls within this paragraph if it is to any extent governed by the law of—

    (a)   the United Kingdom, or

    (b)   a part of the United Kingdom.

(3)   A holiday accommodation contract falls within this paragraph if—

    (a)   it is to any extent governed by the law of a third country, (b)　　the relevant accommodation is in immovable property situated in the United Kingdom (if the product is sold there) or in an EEA State, and

      (c)　　the parties to the contract are to any extent subject to the jurisdiction of a court in the United Kingdom in relation to the contract.

(4)　　A holiday accommodation contract falls within this paragraph if—

      (a)　　it is to any extent governed by the law of a third country,

      (b)　　it is not directly related to immovable property,

      (c)　　the trader carries on commercial or professional activities in the United Kingdom or by any means directs such activities to the United Kingdom, and

      (d)　　the contract falls within the scope of those activities.

(5)　　In this regulation—

      (a)　　'relevant accommodation' means—

          (i)　　the accommodation which is the subject of the contract, or

          (ii)　　in a case where a pool of accommodation is the subject of the contract, some or all of the accommodation in that pool;

      (b)　　'third country' means a country other than the United Kingdom.

6.　Excluded arrangements

(1)　　An 'excluded arrangement' is an arrangement to which any of the following paragraphs apply.

(2)　　This paragraph applies to multiple reservations of accommodation to the extent that they do not imply rights and obligations beyond those arising from the separate reservations.

(3)　　This paragraph applies to a lease agreement which provides for a single continuous period of occupation.

(4)　　This paragraph applies to a loyalty scheme, operating within a group of hotels, which provides consumers with discounts on future stays at hotels within the group where—

      (a)　　no consideration is payable in respect of membership of the scheme, and

      (b)　　consideration payable by consumers for accommodation at hotels within the group is not payable primarily for the purpose of obtaining discounts or other benefits in respect of accommodation.

(5)　　This paragraph applies to a contract of insurance where the effecting or carrying out of such a contract constitutes a regulated activity for the purposes of the Financial Services and Markets Act 2000.

7.　Timeshare contracts

(1)　　A 'timeshare contract' means a contract between a trader and a consumer—

      (a)　　under which the consumer, for consideration, acquires the right to use overnight accommodation for more than one period of occupation, and

      (b)　　which has a duration of more than one year, or contains provision allowing for the contract to be renewed or extended so that it has a duration of more than one year.

(2)　　The reference to 'accommodation' in paragraph (1) includes a reference to accommodation within a pool of accommodation.

8.　Long-term holiday product contracts

A 'long-term holiday product contract' means a contract between a trader and a consumer—

      (a)　　the main effect of which is that the consumer, for consideration, acquires the right to obtain discounts or other benefits in respect of accommodation, and

      (b)　　which has a duration of more than one year, or contains provision allowing for the contract to be renewed or extended so that it has a duration of more than one year,

irrespective of whether the contract makes provision for the consumer to acquire other services.

9.　Resale contracts

A 'resale contract' means a contract between a trader and a consumer under which the trader, for consideration, assists the consumer in buying or selling rights under a timeshare contract or under a long-term holiday product contract.

10.   Exchange contracts

(1)   An 'exchange contract' means a contract between—

    (a)   a consumer who is also party to a timeshare contract, and

    (b)   a trader,

under which the consumer, for consideration, joins a timeshare exchange system.

(2)   A 'timeshare exchange system' is a system which allows a consumer access to overnight accommodation or other services in exchange for giving other persons temporary access to the benefits deriving from the consumer's timeshare contract.

11.   'Consumer' and 'trader'

(1)   In these Regulations—

'consumer' means an individual who is not acting for the purposes of a trade, business, craft or profession;

'trader' means—

    (a)   a person acting for purposes relating to that person's trade, business, craft or profession, or

    (b)   anyone acting in the name of, or on behalf of, a person falling within paragraph (a).

(2)   Any reference in these Regulations to a consumer or trader in relation to a regulated contract, means—

    (a)   in the case of a contract which has been entered into, the consumer or trader who is party to the contract, or

    (b)   in the case of a proposed contract, the consumer and trader who will be parties to the contract, once it is entered into.

PART 3
PRE-CONTRACTUAL MATTERS

12.   Key information

(1)   Before entering into a regulated contract, the trader must—

    (a)   give the consumer the key information in relation to the contract, and

    (b)   ensure that the information meets the requirements of this regulation.

(2)   The trader must comply with paragraph (1) in good time before entering into the contract.

(3)   The 'key information' in relation to a contract means—

    (a)   the information required by Part 1 of the standard information form (see regulation 13(2)),

    (b)   the information set out in Part 2 of that form, and

    (c)   any additional information required by Part 3 of that form.

(4)   The information must be—

    (a)   clear, comprehensible and accurate, and

    (b)   sufficient to enable the consumer to make an informed decision about whether or not to enter into the contract.

(5)   The information must be provided—

    (a)   in the standard information form, completed in accordance with regulation 13(1),

    (b)   in writing,

    (c)   free of charge, and

    (d)   in a manner which is easily accessible to the consumer.

(6)   The information must be provided in English and may, in addition, be provided in another language.

(7)   ...

(8)   A trader who contravenes paragraph (5) of this Regulation commits an offence.

13.   Completing the standard information form

(1)   The standard information form must be completed as follows—

    (a)   the information required by Part 1 of the form must be inserted in the appropriate places (without deleting the existing text in that Part),

    (b)   Part 2 of the form must not be amended, and

    (c)   the information required by Part 3 of the form must be inserted in the appropriate places in accordance with any applicable notes (which may then be deleted).

(2)   The 'standard information form' means the form set out in—

    (a)   Schedule 1, in the case of a timeshare contract;

    (b)   Schedule 2, in the case of a long-term holiday product contract;

    (c)   Schedule 3, in the case of a resale contract; and

    (d)   Schedule 4, in the case of an exchange contract.

14.   Marketing and sales

(1)   Any advertising related to a regulated contract must indicate how the key information in relation to the contract can be obtained.

(2)   A trader must not offer an opportunity to enter into a regulated contract to a consumer at a promotion or sales event unless—

    (a)   the invitation to the event clearly indicates the commercial purpose and nature of the event, and

    (b)   the key information in relation to the proposed regulated contract is made available to the consumer for the duration of the event.

(3)   A trader must not market or sell a proposed timeshare contract or long-term holiday product contract as an investment if the proposed contract would be a regulated contract.

(4)   The references to key information in this regulation are references to key information which meets the requirements of regulations 12(4) to (7).

(5)   A trader who contravenes paragraph (3) commits an offence.

PART 4
REGULATED CONTRACT: FORMALITIES

15.   Form of contract

(1)   A trader must not enter into a regulated contract unless the contract complies with the requirements of this regulation.

(2)   The contract must be in writing and include—

    (a)   the identity, place of residence and signature of each of the parties;

    (b)   the date and place of conclusion of the contract.

(3)   The contract must set out the key information in relation to the contract which is required under regulation 12.

(4)   That key information must be set out—

    (a)   as terms of the contract, and

    (b)   with no changes, other than permitted changes.

(5)   'Permitted changes' means changes to the key information which were communicated to the consumer in writing before the conclusion of the contract and which—

    (a)   were expressly agreed between the trader and the consumer, or

    (b)   resulted from unusual and unforeseeable circumstances beyond the trader's control, the consequences of which could not have been avoided even if all due care had been exercised.

(6)   Any permitted changes must be expressly mentioned in the contract.

(7)   The contract must include the standard withdrawal form set out in Schedule 5.

(8)   If a trader contravenes paragraph (1)—

    (a)   the trader commits an offence, and

    (b)   the contract is unenforceable against the consumer.

16.   Obligations of trader

(1)   Before entering into a regulated contract a trader must draw the attention of the consumer to the following matters—

    (a)   the right of withdrawal under the contract (see regulation 20),

    (b)   the length of the withdrawal period (see regulation 21), and

    (c)   the prohibition on advance consideration during the withdrawal period (see regulation 25).

(2)   Before entering into a regulated contract a trader must obtain the signature of the consumer in relation to each section of the contract dealing with those matters.

(3)   When a trader and consumer enter into a regulated contract, the trader must provide the consumer with a copy of the contract at the time the contract is concluded.

(4)   If a trader fails to comply with any of paragraphs (1) to (3)—

    (a)   the trader commits an offence, and

    (b)   the contract is unenforceable against the consumer.

17.   Language of the contract

(1)   A trader must not enter into a regulated contract unless it complies with the requirements of this regulation, so far as applicable.

(2)   The contract must be drawn up in English and may, in addition, be drawn up in another language.

(3)   ...

(4)   ...

(5)   If a trader fails to draw up the contract in English the contract is unenforceable against the consumer.

18.   Translation of contract

(1)   This regulation applies to a regulated contract if—

    (a)   it is a timeshare contract, and

    (b)   the subject of the contract is a single item of specific immovable property situated in an EEA State.

(2)   The trader must not enter into the contract unless the trader has provided the consumer with a certified translation of the contract in the language, or one of the languages, of that State.

(3)   The language of the translation must be an official language of an EEA State.

(4)   Paragraphs (2) and (3) do not apply if the contract is drawn up in a language in which the translation is required or permitted to be made.

(5)   A trader who contravenes paragraphs (2) or (3) of this regulation commits an offence.

(6)   A 'certified translation' means a translation which is certified to be accurate by a person authorised to make or verify translations for the purposes of court procedings.

19.   Conflict with contractual terms

A term contained in a regulated contract is void to the extent that it purports to allow the consumer to waive the rights conferred on them by these Regulations.

PART 5
TERMINATION OF REGULATED CONTRACTS

20.   Rights of withdrawal

(1)   A consumer may withdraw from a regulated contract by giving the trader written notice of withdrawal during the withdrawal period.

(2)   For the purposes of paragraph (1), written notice is to be regarded as having been given by the consumer at the time it is sent.

(3)   The consumer does not have to give any reason for the withdrawal.

(4)   The consumer may use the standard withdrawal form included in the contract under regulation 15(7) as the notice of withdrawal.

21.   The withdrawal period

(1)   The withdrawal period for a regulated contract—

    (a)   begins on the start date, and

    (b)   ends on the date which is 14 days after the start date, subject to the following provisions.

(2)   The start date is the later of—

    (a)   the date of conclusion of the contract;

    (b)   the date on which the consumer receives a copy of the contract.

(3)   Paragraph (4) applies if a standard withdrawal form is not included in the contract in accordance with regulation 15(7).

(4) The withdrawal period ends—
   (a)   on the date which is one year and 14 days after the start date, or
   (b)   in a case where the standard withdrawal form is provided to the consumer within the period of one year beginning on the start date, on the date which is 14 days after the day on which the consumer receives the form.

(5) Paragraph (6) applies if the key information in relation to the contract is not provided to the consumer in accordance with the requirements in regulation 12(4) to (7).

(6) The withdrawal period ends—
   (a)   on the date which is three months and 14 days after the start date, or
   (b)   in a case where the key information in relation to the contract is provided to the consumer within the period of three months beginning on the start date in accordance with the requirements in regulation 12(4) to (7), on the date which is 14 days after the day on which the consumer receives the information.

(7) In a case where both paragraphs (4) and (6) apply, the withdrawal period ends on the later of the dates determined by those paragraphs.

(8) Paragraph (9) applies in a case where a timeshare contract and a related exchange contract are offered to the consumer at the same time.

(9) The withdrawal period for both contracts is to be the one which would apply to the timeshare contract under this regulation.

(10) For the purposes of paragraph (8), an exchange contract is related to a timeshare contract if the exchange contract allows the consumer to give other persons access to benefits under the timeshare contract under a timeshare exchange system (see regulation 10(2)).

22.   Effect of exercising right of withdrawal

(1) This regulation applies if a consumer withdraws from a regulated contract by giving written notice of withdrawal to the trader under regulation 20.

(2) The following obligations of the parties are terminated with effect from the date the consumer sends the notice of withdrawal—
   (a)   their obligations under the regulated contract, and
   (b)   if the regulated contract is a timeshare contract or a long-term holiday product contract, their obligations under any ancillary contract.

(3) The reference to obligations in paragraph (2) includes, in the case of a long-term holiday product contract, an obligation to pay any penalty or further instalments of the payment schedule (see regulation 26).

(4) The consumer is not liable for any costs or charges—
   (a)   in respect of the regulated contract, or
   (b)   if the regulated contract is a timeshare contract or a long-term holiday product contract, in respect of any ancillary contract.

(5) The reference to costs and charges in paragraph (4) includes any costs or charges corresponding to services provided under a contract before withdrawal.

(6) 'Ancillary contract', in relation to a timeshare contract or long-term holiday product contract ('the main contract'), means a contract under which the consumer acquires services which are related to the main contract and which are provided by—
   (a)   the trader, or
   (b)   a third party on the basis of an arrangement between the third party and the trader.

(7) An exchange contract which is related to a timeshare contract (see regulation 21(10)), is an ancillary contract in relation to the timeshare contract for the purposes of paragraph (6).

23.   Automatic termination of credit agreement

(1) This regulation applies if a consumer withdraws from a regulated contract by giving written notice of withdrawal to the trader under regulation 20.

(2) Any related credit agreement is automatically terminated at no cost to the consumer.

(3) If the trader is not also the creditor under the related credit agreement, the trader must, on receipt of the notice of withdrawal, without delay inform the creditor that the notice has been received.

(4) A credit agreement is related to a regulated contract if it is an agreement under which credit which fully or partly covers any payment under the regulated contract is granted to the consumer by—
(a) the trader, or
(b) a third party on the basis of an arrangement between the third party and the trader.

24. Termination of long-term holiday product contracts

(1) A consumer who is party to a regulated contract that is a long-term holiday product contract may terminate the contract in accordance with this regulation without incurring any penalty.
(2) The consumer may terminate the contract by giving notice of termination to the trader no later than 14 days after any day on which the consumer receives a request for payment of an instalment under regulation 26(4).
(3) The right to terminate the contract under this regulation does not affect any other right available to the consumer to terminate or withdraw from the contract.
(4) The reference to 'instalment' in paragraph (2) does not include the first instalment.

PART 6
PAYMENTS

25. Advance consideration

(1) This regulation makes provision about when consideration may be accepted in relation to regulated contracts.
(2) Paragraph (3) applies in relation to a timeshare contract, long-term holiday product contract or exchange contract.
(3) No person may accept any consideration from the consumer before the end of the withdrawal period in relation to the contract (see regulation 21).
(4) Paragraph (5) applies in relation to a resale contract, the subject of which is rights under a timeshare contract or long-term holiday product contract.
(5) No person may accept any consideration from the consumer before—
(a) the sale of those rights takes place, or
(b) the contract is otherwise terminated.
(6) For the purposes of this regulation 'consideration' includes any of the following—
(a) payments,
(b) guarantees,
(c) reservations of money on account,
(d) acknowledgements of debt.
(7) A person who contravenes paragraph (3) or (5) commits an offence.

26. Payment schedule: long-term holiday product contracts

(1) A trader must not accept any payment in respect of a regulated contract that is a long-term holiday product contract unless the payment is made in accordance with a schedule which complies with the requirements of this regulation.
(2) The schedule must provide for all payments under the contract (including any membership fee) to be divided into yearly instalments of equal value, taking into account the duration of the contract.
(3) The schedule must be prepared by the trader and provided to the consumer.
(4) The trader must send a request for payment in writing to the consumer at least 14 days before a payment of an instalment becomes due under the schedule.
(5) A trader who contravenes paragraph (1) or (4) commits an offence.

PART 7
OFFENCES: PENALTIES ETC

27. Penalties for offences

A person guilty of an offence under the preceding provisions of these Regulations is liable—
(a) on summary conviction, to a fine not exceeding the statutory maximum, or
(b) on conviction on indictment, to a fine.

28.   Offences committed by bodies of persons

(1)   Paragraph (2) applies where an offence under these Regulations committed by a body corporate is proved—

    (a)   to have been committed with the consent or connivance of an officer of the body, or

    (b)   to be attributable to any neglect on the officer's part.

(2)   The officer (as well as the body corporate) is guilty of the offence and liable to be proceeded against and punished accordingly.

(3)   In paragraphs (1) and (2) each reference to an officer of the body corporate includes a reference to—

    (a)   a director, manager, secretary or other similar officer;

    (b)   a person purporting to act as a director, manager, secretary of other similar officer;

    (c)   in a case where the affairs of the body are managed by its members, a member.

(4)   Paragraph (5) applies where an offence under these Regulations committed by a Scottish partnership is proved—

    (a)   to have been committed with the consent or connivance of a partner, or

    (b)   to be attributable to any neglect on that partner's part.

(5)   The partner as well as the partnership is guilty of the offence and liable to be proceeded against and punished accordingly.

(6)   In paragraphs (4) and (5) each reference to a partner includes a reference to a person purporting to act as a partner.

29.   Offences due to the default of another person

(1)   This regulation applies where a person ('X')—

    (a)   commits an offence under the preceding provisions of these Regulations, or

    (b)   would have committed such an offence but for a defence under regulations 30 (due diligence) or 31 (innocent publication of advertisement), and the commission of the offence, or what would have been an offence but for the defence under regulations 30 or 31, is due to the act or default of another person ('Y').

(2)   Y is guilty of the offence (subject to regulations 30 and 31), whether or not Y is a trader.

(3)   Y may be charged with and convicted of the offence by virtue of paragraph (2), whether or not proceedings are taken against X.

30.   Due diligence defence

(1)   In proceedings against a person for an offence under the preceding provisions of these Regulations it is a defence for the person to show that all reasonable steps were taken and all due diligence exercised to avoid committing the offence.

(2)   This is subject to the following provisions of this regulation.

(3)   Paragraph (4) applies where, in proceedings against any person ('the defendant') for such an offence, the defence provided by paragraph (1) involves an allegation that the commission of the offence was due to—

    (a)   the act or default of another, or

    (b)   reliance on information given by another.

(4)   The defendant is not, without the leave of the court, entitled to rely on the defence unless the defendant has served a notice under paragraph (5) on the person bringing the proceedings no later than the day which is 8 days before—

    (a)   the hearing of the proceedings or,

    (b)   in Scotland, the diet of the trial.

(5)   A notice under this paragraph must give such information identifying or assisting in the identification of the person who committed the act or default, or gave the information, as is in the possession of the defendant at the time the notice is served.

(6)   A person is not entitled to rely on the defence provided by paragraph (1) by reason of reliance on information supplied by another, unless the person shows that it was reasonable, in all the circumstances to have relied on the information having regard in particular to—

    (a)   the steps which the person took, and those which might reasonably have been taken, for the purpose of verifying the information, and

    (b)   whether the person had any reason not to believe the information.

31.   Innocent publication of advertisement defence

(1)   In proceedings against a person for an offence under regulation 14(5) committed by the publication of an advertisement it shall be a defence for the person to show that—

(a)   it is the person's business to publish or to arrange for the publication of advertisements,

(b)   the person received the advertisement for publication in the ordinary course of business, and

(c)   the person did not know and had no reason to suspect that its publication would amount to an offence under regulation 14(5).

PART 8
ENFORCEMENT

32.   Enforcement authorities

(1)   'Enforcement authority' means—

(a)   a local weights and measures authority in Great Britain (within the meaning of section 69 of the Weights and Measures Act 1985);

(b)   the Department of Enterprise Trade and Investment in Northern Ireland.

(2)   An enforcement authority in Great Britain must enforce these Regulations within its area.

(3)   The enforcement authority in Northern Ireland must enforce these Regulations within Northern Ireland.

(4)   Nothing in this regulation authorises any enforcement authority to bring proceedings in Scotland for an offence under these Regulations.

33.   Powers of officers

(1)   Paragraph (2) applies if a duly authorised officer of an enforcement authority has reasonable cause to suspect that an offence under the preceding provisions of these Regulations has been committed.

(2)   The officer may, for the purpose of ascertaining whether the offence has been committed, require a trader to produce any document relating to the trader's business and take copies of it or of any entry in it.

(3)   If such an officer has reason to believe that any documents may be required as evidence in proceedings for such an offence, the officer may seize and detain them and must, if the officer does so, inform the person from whom they are seized.

(4)   The powers in paragraphs (2) and (3) may only be exercised by an officer at a reasonable hour.

(5)   In this regulation 'document' includes information recorded in any form.

(6)   The reference in paragraph (2) to the production of documents is, in the case of a document which contains information recorded otherwise than in legible form, a reference to the production of a copy of the information in legible form.

(7)   Nothing in this regulation is to be construed as requiring a person to answer any question or give any information if to do so might incriminate that person.

(8)   Nothing in this regulation gives any power to an officer of an enforcement authority to require any person to produce, or to seize from another person, a document to which paragraph (9) applies.

(9)   This paragraph applies to any document which the other person would be entitled to refuse to produce—

(a)   in proceedings in the High Court on the grounds of legal professional privilege, or

(b)   (in Scotland) in proceedings in the Court of Session on the grounds of confidentiality of communications.

(10) In paragraph (9) 'communications' means—

(a)   communications between a professional legal adviser and his or her client, or

(b)   communications made in connection with or in contemplation of legal proceedings and for the purposes of those proceedings.

34. Obstruction of authorised officers

(1) A person commits an offence if the person —

    (a) intentionally obstructs an officer of an enforcement authority acting in pursuance of these Regulations,

    (b) intentionally fails to comply with any requirement properly made of the person by such an officer under regulation 33,

    (c) without reasonable cause fails to give such an officer any other assistance or information which the officer may reasonably require of the person for the purpose of the officer's functions under these Regulations.

(2) A person guilty of an offence under paragraph (1) is liable on summary conviction to a fine not exceeding level 5 on the standard scale.

(3) A person commits an offence if the person, in giving information to an officer of an enforcement authority who is acting in pursuance of these Regulations —

    (a) makes a statement which the person knows to be false in a material particular, or

    (b) recklessly makes a statement which is false in a material particular.

(4) A person guilty of an office under paragraph (3) is liable —

    (a) on summary conviction to a fine not exceeding level 5 on the standard scale, or

    (b) on conviction on indictment, to a fine.

35. Civil proceedings

(1) The obligation to comply with regulation 12(1) is a duty owed by the trader who proposes to enter into a regulated contract to any person with whom the trader is required to provide with information under that provision.

(2) The obligation to comply with Regulations 15(1), 16(1), 17(1) and 18(2) is, in each case, a duty owed by the trader who enters into a regulated contract to the consumer.

(3) The obligation to comply with regulation 23(3) is a duty owed by the trader who enters into a regulated contract to the creditor under a related credit agreement.

(4) A contravention of any of the obligations mentioned in paragraphs (1) to (3) is to be actionable accordingly.

(5) Liability by virtue of paragraphs (1) to (3) is not to be limited or excluded by any contractual term, by any notice or by any other provision.

37 Application of the Travel Package and Linked Travel Arrangements Regulations 2018

Nothing in these Regulations affects the application of the Package Travel and Linked Travel Regulations 2018 to regulated contracts falling within the scope of those Regulations.

CONSUMER CONTRACTS (INFORMATION, CANCELLATION AND ADDITIONAL CHARGES) REGULATIONS 2013
(SI 2013, No. 3134)

PART 1
General

1. Citation and commencement

(1) These Regulations may be cited as the Consumer Contracts (Information, Cancellation and Additional Charges) Regulations 2013 and come into force on 13th June 2014.

(2) These Regulations apply in relation to contracts entered into on or after that date.

2. Regulations superseded

The following do not apply in relation to contracts entered into on or after 13th June 2014 —

(a) the Consumer Protection (Distance Selling) Regulations 2000;

(b) the Cancellation of Contracts made in a Consumer's Home or Place of Work etc., Regulations 2008.

4.   'Consumer' and 'trader'

In these Regulations—

'consumer' means an individual acting for purposes which are wholly or mainly outside that individual's trade, business, craft or profession;

'trader' means a person acting for purposes relating to that person's trade, business, craft or profession, whether acting personally or through another person acting in the trader's name or on the trader's behalf.

5.   Other definitions

In these Regulations—

'business' includes the activities of any government department or local or public authority;

'business premises' in relation to a trader means—

(a)   any immovable retail premises where the activity of the trader is carried out on a permanent basis, or

(b)   any movable retail premises where the activity of the trader is carried out on a usual basis;

'CMA' means the Competition and Markets Authority;

'commercial guarantee', in relation to a contract, means any undertaking by the trader or producer to the consumer (in addition to the trader's duty to supply goods that are in conformity with the contract) to reimburse the price paid or to replace, repair or service goods in any way if they do not meet the specifications or any other requirements not related to conformity set out in the guarantee statement or in the relevant advertising available at the time of the contract or before it is entered into;

'court'—

(a)   in relation to England and Wales, means the county court or the High Court,

(b)   in relation to Northern Ireland, means a county court or the High Court, and

(c)   in relation to Scotland means the sheriff court or the Court of Session;

'delivery' means voluntary transfer of possession from one person to another;

'digital content' means data which are produced and supplied in digital form;

'distance contract' means a contract concluded between a trader and a consumer under an organised distance sales or service-provision scheme without the simultaneous physical presence of the trader and the consumer, with the exclusive use of one or more means of distance communication up to and including the time at which the contract is concluded;

'district heating' means the supply of heat (in the form of steam or hot water or otherwise) from a central source of production through a transmission and distribution system to heat more than one building;

'durable medium' means paper or email, or any other medium that—

(a)   allows information to be addressed personally to the recipient,

(b)   enables the recipient to store the information in a way accessible for future reference for a period that is long enough for the purposes of the information, and

(c)   allows the unchanged reproduction of the information stored;

'functionality' in relation to digital content includes region coding, restrictions incorporated for the purposes of digital rights management, and other technical restrictions;

'goods' means any tangible moveable items, but that includes water, gas and electricity if and only if they are put up for sale in a limited volume or a set quantity;

'off-premises contract' means a contract between a trader and a consumer which is any of these—

(a)   a contract concluded in the simultaneous physical presence of the trader and the consumer, in a place which is not the business premises of the trader;

(b)   a contract for which an offer was made by the consumer in the simultaneous physical presence of the trader and the consumer, in a place which is not the business premises of the trader;

(c)   a contract concluded on the business premises of the trader or through any means of distance communication immediately after the consumer was personally and individually addressed in a place which is not the business premises of the trader in the simultaneous physical presence of the trader and the consumer;

(d)   a contract concluded during an excursion organised by the trader with the aim or effect of promoting and selling goods or services to the consumer;

'on-premises contract' means a contract between a trader and a consumer which is neither a distance contract nor an off-premises contract;

'public auction' means a method of sale where—

(a)   goods or services are offered by a trader to consumers through a transparent, competitive bidding procedure run by an auctioneer,

(b)   the consumers attend or are given the possibility to attend in person, and

(c)   the successful bidder is bound to purchase the goods or services;

'sales contract' means a contract under which a trader transfers or agrees to transfer the ownership of goods to a consumer and the consumer pays or agrees to pay the price, including any contract that has both goods and services as its object;

'service' includes—

(a)   the supply of water, gas or electricity if they are not put up for sale in a limited volume or a set quantity, and

(b)   the supply of district heating;

'service contract' means a contract, other than a sales contract, under which a trader supplies or agrees to supply a service to a consumer and the consumer pays or agrees to pay the price.

6.   Limits of application: general

(1)   These Regulations do not apply to a contract, to the extent that it is—

    (a)   for—

        (i)   gambling within the meaning of the Gambling Act 2005 (which includes gaming, betting and participating in a lottery);

        (ii)   in relation to Northern Ireland, for betting, gaming or participating lawfully in a lottery within the meaning of the Betting, Gaming, Lotteries and Amusements (Northern Ireland) Order 1985; or

        (iii)   participating in a lottery which forms part of the National Lottery within the meaning of the National Lottery etc. Act 1993;

    (b)   for services of a banking, credit, insurance, personal pension, investment or payment nature;

    (c)   for the creation of immovable property or of rights in immovable property;

    (d)   for rental of accommodation for residential purposes;

    (e)   for the construction of new buildings, or the construction of substantially new buildings by the conversion of existing buildings;

    (f)   for the supply of foodstuffs, beverages or other goods intended for current consumption in the household and which are supplied by a trader on frequent and regular rounds to the consumer's home, residence or workplace;

    (g)   a package travel contract, within the scope of Directive (EU) 2015/2302 of the European Parliament and of the Council on package travel and linked travel arrangements, amending Regulation (EC) No 2006/2004 and Directive 2011/83/EU of the European Parliament and of the Council and repealing Council Directive 90/314/EEC;

    (h)   within the scope of Directive 2008/122/EC of the European Parliament and of the Council on the protection of consumers in respect of certain aspects of timeshare, long-term holiday product, resale and exchange contracts.

(2)   These Regulations do not apply to contracts—

    (a)   concluded by means of automatic vending machines or automated commercial premises;

    (b)   concluded with a telecommunications operator through a public telephone for the use of the telephone;

    (c)   concluded for the use of one single connection, by telephone, internet or fax, established by a consumer;

    (d)   under which goods are sold by way of execution or otherwise by authority of law.

(3)   Paragraph (1)(b) is subject to regulations 38(4) (ancillary contracts) and 40(3) (additional payments).

PART 2
INFORMATION REQUIREMENTS

CHAPTER 1
PROVISION OF INFORMATION

7.   **Application of Part 2**

(1)   This Part applies to on-premises, off-premises and distance contracts, subject to paragraphs (2), (3) and (4) and regulation 6.

(2)   This Part does not apply to contracts to the extent that they are—

(a)   for the supply of a medicinal product by administration by a prescriber, or under a prescription or directions given by a prescriber;

(b)   for the supply of a product by a health care professional or a person included in a relevant list, under arrangements for the supply of services as part of the health service, where the product is one that, at least in some circumstances is available under such arrangements free or on prescription.

(3)   This Part, except for regulation 14(1) to (5), does not apply to contracts to the extent that they are for passenger transport services.

(4)   This Part does not apply to off-premises contracts under which the payment to be made by the consumer is not more than £42.

(5)   In paragraph (2)—

'health care professional' and 'prescriber' have the meaning given by regulation 2(1) of the National Health Service (Pharmaceutical and Local Pharmaceutical Services) Regulations 2013;

'health service' means—

(a)   the health service as defined by section 275(1) of the National Health Service Act 2006 or section 206(1) of the National Health Service (Wales) Act 2006,

(b)   the health service as defined by section 108(1) of the National Health Service (Scotland) Act 1978, or

(c)   any of the health services under section 2(1)(a) of the Health and Social Care (Reform) Act (Northern Ireland) 2009;

'medicinal product' has the meaning given by regulation 2(1) of the Human Medicines Regulations 2012;

'relevant list' means—

(d)   a relevant list for the purposes of the National Health Service (Pharmaceutical and Local Pharmaceutical Services) Regulations 2013, or

(e)   a list maintained under those Regulations.

8.   **Making information etc. available to a consumer**

For the purposes of this Part, something is made available to a consumer only if the consumer can reasonably be expected to know how to access it.

9.   **Information to be provided before making an on-premises contract**

(1)   Before the consumer is bound by an on-premises contract, the trader must give or make available to the consumer the information described in Schedule 1 in a clear and comprehensible manner, if that information is not already apparent from the context.

(2)   Paragraph (1) does not apply to a contract which involves a day-to-day transaction and is performed immediately at the time when the contract is entered into.

(3)   If the contract is for the supply of digital content other than a price paid by the consumer—

(a)   any information that the trader gives the consumer as required by this regulation is to be treated as a term of the contract, and

(b)   a change to any of that information, made before entering into the contract or later, is not effective unless expressly agreed between the consumer and the trader.

10.   **Information to be provided before making an off-premises contract**

(1)   Before the consumer is bound by an off-premises contract, the trader—

(a)   must give the consumer the information listed in Schedule 2 in a clear and comprehensible manner, and

    (b)   if a right to cancel exists, must give the consumer a cancellation form as set out in part B of Schedule 3.

(2)   The information and any cancellation form must be given on paper or, if the consumer agrees, on another durable medium and must be legible.

(3)   The information referred to in paragraphs (l), (m) and (n) of Schedule 2 may be provided by means of the model instructions on cancellation set out in part A of Schedule 3; and a trader who has supplied those instructions to the consumer, correctly filled in, is to be treated as having complied with paragraph (1) in respect of those paragraphs.

(4)   If the trader has not complied with paragraph (1) in respect of paragraph (g), (h) or (m) of Schedule 2, the consumer is not to bear the charges or costs referred to in those paragraphs.

(5)   If the contract is for the supply of digital content other than the price paid by the consumer—

    (a)   any information that the trader gives the consumer as required by this regulation is to be treated as a term of the contract, and

    (b)   a change to any of that information, made before entering into the contract or later, is not effective unless expressly agreed between the consumer and the trader.

(6)   …

(7)   This regulation is subject to regulation 11.

11. Provision of information in connection with repair or maintenance contracts

(1)   If the conditions in paragraphs (2), (3) and (4) are met, regulation 10(1) does not apply to an off-premises contract where—

    (a)   the contract is a service contract,

    (b)   the consumer has explicitly requested the trader to supply the service for the purpose of carrying out repairs or maintenance,

    (c)   the obligations of the trader and the consumer under the contract are to be performed immediately, and

    (d)   the payment to be made by the consumer is not more than £170.

(2)   The first condition is that, before the consumer is bound by the contract, the trader gives or makes available to the consumer on paper or, if the consumer expressly agrees, on another durable medium—

    (a)   the information referred to in paragraphs (b) to (d), (f) and (g) of Schedule 2,

    (b)   an estimate of the total price, where it cannot reasonably be calculated in advance, and

    (c)   where a right to cancel exists, a cancellation form as set out in part B of Schedule 3.

(3)   The second condition is that, before the consumer is bound by the contract, the trader gives or makes available to the consumer the information referred to in paragraphs (a), (l) and (o) of Schedule 2, either on paper or another durable medium or otherwise if the consumer expressly agrees.

(4)   The third condition is that the confirmation of the contract provided in accordance with regulation 12 contains the information required by regulation 10(1).

(5)   For the right to cancel where this regulation applies, see in particular—

    (a)   regulation 28(1)(e) and (2) (cases where cancellation excluded: visit requested for urgent work);

    (b)   regulation 36 (form of consumer's request, and consequences).

12. Provision of copy or confirmation of off-premises contracts

(1)   In the case of an off-premises contract, the trader must give the consumer—

    (a)   a copy of the signed contract, or

    (b)   confirmation of the contract.

(2)   The confirmation must include all the information referred to in Schedule 2 unless the trader has already provided that information to the consumer on a durable medium prior to the conclusion of the off-premises contract.

(3)   The copy or confirmation must be provided on paper or, if the consumer agrees, on another durable medium.

(4)   The copy or confirmation must be provided within a reasonable time after the conclusion of the contract, but in any event—

   (a)   not later than the time of the delivery of any goods supplied under the contract, and

   (b)   before performance begins of any service supplied under the contract.

(5)   If the contract is for the supply of digital content not on a tangible medium and the consumer has given the consent and acknowledgement referred to in regulation 37(1) (a) and (b), the copy or confirmation must include confirmation of the consent and acknowledgement.

13.   Information to be provided before making a distance contract

(1)   Before the consumer is bound by a distance contract, the trader—

   (a)   must give or make available to the consumer the information listed in Schedule 2 in a clear and comprehensible manner, and in a way appropriate to the means of distance communication used, and

   (b)   if a right to cancel exists, must give or make available to the consumer a cancellation form as set out in part B of Schedule 3.

(2)   In so far as the information is provided on a durable medium, it must be legible.

(3)   The information referred to in paragraphs (l), (m) and (n) of Schedule 2 may be provided by means of the model instructions on cancellation set out in part A of Schedule 3; and a trader who has supplied those instructions to the consumer, correctly filled in, is to be treated as having complied with paragraph (1) in respect of those paragraphs.

(4)   Where a distance contract is concluded through a means of distance communication which allows limited space or time to display the information—

   (a)   the information listed in paragraphs (a), (b), (f), (g), (h), (l) and (s) of Schedule 2 must be provided on that means of communication in accordance with paragraphs (1) and (2), but

   (b)   the other information required by paragraph (1) may be provided in another appropriate way.

(5)   If the trader has not complied with paragraph (1) in respect of paragraph (g), (h) or (m) of Schedule 2, the consumer is not to bear the charges or costs referred to in those paragraphs.

(6)   If the contract is for the supply of digital content other than the price paid by the consumer—

   (a)   any information that the trader gives the consumer as required by this regulation shall be treated as a term of the contract, and

   (b)   a change to any of that information made before entering into the contract or later, is not effective unless expressly agreed between the consumer and the trader.

14.   Requirements for distance contracts concluded by electronic means

(1)   This regulation applies where a distance contract is concluded by electronic means.

(2)   If the contract places the consumer under an obligation to pay, the trader must make the consumer aware in a clear and prominent manner, and directly before the consumer places the order, of the information listed in paragraphs (a), (f), (g), (h), (s) and (t) of Schedule 2.

(3)   The trader must ensure that the consumer, when placing the order, explicitly acknowledges that the order implies an obligation to pay.

(4)   If placing an order entails activating a button or a similar function, the trader must ensure that the button or similar function is labelled in an easily legible manner only with the words 'order with obligation to pay' or a corresponding unambiguous formulation indicating that placing the order entails an obligation to pay the trader.

(5)   If the trader has not complied with paragraphs (3) and (4), the consumer is not bound by the contract or order.

(6)   The trader must ensure that any trading website through which the contract is concluded indicates clearly and legibly, at the latest at the beginning of the ordering process, whether any delivery restrictions apply and which means of payment are accepted.

15.   Telephone calls to conclude a distance contract

If the trader makes a telephone call to the consumer with a view to concluding a distance contract, the trader must, at the beginning of the conversation with the consumer, disclose—

    (a)   the trader's identity,

    (b)   where applicable, the identity of the person on whose behalf the trader makes the call, and

    (c)   the commercial purpose of the call.

16. Confirmation of distance contracts

(1) In the case of a distance contract the trader must give the consumer confirmation of the contract on a durable medium.

(2) The confirmation must include all the information referred to in Schedule 2 unless the trader has already provided that information to the consumer on a durable medium prior to the conclusion of the distance contract.

(3) If the contract is for the supply of digital content not on a tangible medium and the consumer has given the consent and acknowledgment referred to in Regulation 37(1)(a) and (b), the confirmation must include confirmation of the consent and acknowledgement.

(4) The confirmation must be provided within a reasonable time after the conclusion of the contract, but in any event—

    (a)   not later than the time of delivery of any goods supplied under the contract, and

    (b)   before performance begins of any service supplied under the contract.

(5) For the purposes of paragraph (4), the confirmation is treated as provided as soon as the trader has sent it or done what is necessary to make it available to the consumer.

17. Burden of proof in relation to off-premises and distance contracts

(1) In case of dispute about the trader's compliance with any provision of regulations 10 to 16, it is for the trader to show that the provision was complied with.

(2) That does not apply to proceedings—

    (a)   for an offence under regulation 19, or

    (b)   relating to compliance with an injunction, interdict or order under regulation 45.

18. Effect on contract of failure to provide information

Every contract to which this Part applies is to be treated as including a term that the trader has complied with the provisions of—

(a) regulations 9 to 14, and

(b) regulation 16.

PART 3

RIGHT TO CANCEL

27. Application of Part 3

(1) This Part applies to distance and off-premises contracts between a trader and a consumer, subject to paragraphs (2) and (3) and regulations 6 and 28.

(2) This Part does not apply to contracts to the extent that they are—

    (a)   for the supply of a medicinal product by administration by a prescriber, or under a prescription or directions given by a prescriber;

    (b)   for the supply of a product by a health care professional or a person included in a relevant list, under arrangements for the supply of services as part of the health service, where the product is one that, at least in some circumstances is available under such arrangements free or on prescription;

    (c)   for passenger transport services.

(3) This Part does not apply to off-premises contracts under which the payment to be made by the consumer is not more than £42.

(4) In paragraph (2)(a) and (b), expressions defined in regulation 7(5) have the meaning given there.

28. Limits of application: circumstances excluding cancellation

(1) This Part does not apply as regards the following—

    (a)   the supply of—

        (i)   goods, or

        (ii)   services, other than supply of water, gas, electricity or district heating, for which the price is dependent on fluctuations in the financial market which cannot be controlled by the trader and which may occur within the cancellation period;

(b)   the supply of goods that are made to the consumer's specifications or are clearly personalised;

(c)   the supply of goods which are liable to deteriorate or expire rapidly;

(d)   the supply of alcoholic beverages, where—

    (i)   their price has been agreed at the time of the conclusion of the sales contract,

    (ii)   delivery of them can only take place after 30 days, and

    (iii)   their value is dependent on fluctuations in the market which cannot be controlled by the trader;

(e)   contracts where the consumer has specifically requested a visit from the trader for the purpose of carrying out urgent repairs or maintenance;

(f)   the supply of a newspaper, periodical or magazine with the exception of subscription contracts for the supply of such publications;

(g)   contracts concluded at a public auction;

(h)   the supply of accommodation, transport of goods, vehicle rental services, catering or services related to leisure activities, if the contract provides for a specific date or period of performance.

(2)   Sub-paragraph (e) of paragraph (1) does not prevent this Part applying to a contract for—

(a)   services in addition to the urgent repairs or maintenance requested, or

(b)   goods other than replacement parts necessarily used in making the repairs or carrying out the maintenance,

if the trader supplies them on the occasion of a visit such as is mentioned in that subparagraph.

(3)   The rights conferred by this Part cease to be available in the following circumstances—

(a)   in the case of a contract for the supply of sealed goods which are not suitable for return due to health protection or hygiene reasons, if they become unsealed after delivery;

(b)   in the case of a contract for the supply of sealed audio or sealed video recordings or sealed computer software, if the goods become unsealed after delivery;

(c)   in the case of any sales contract, if the goods become mixed inseparably (according to their nature) with other items after delivery.

29.   Right to cancel

(1)   The consumer may cancel a distance or off-premises contract at any time in the cancellation period without giving any reason, and without incurring any liability except under these provisions—

(a)   regulation 34(3) (where enhanced delivery chosen by consumer);

(b)   regulation 34(9) (where value of goods diminished by consumer handling);

(c)   regulation 35(5) (where goods returned by consumer);

(d)   regulation 36(4) (where consumer requests early supply of service).

(2)   The cancellation period begins when the contract is entered into and ends in accordance with regulation 30 or 31.

(3)   Paragraph (1) does not affect the consumer's right to withdraw an offer made by the consumer to enter into a distance or off-premises contract, at any time before the contract is entered into, without giving any reason and without incurring any liability.

30.   Normal cancellation period

(1)   The cancellation period ends as follows, unless regulation 31 applies.

(2)   If the contract is—

(a)   a service contract, or

(b)   a contract for the supply of digital content which is not supplied on a tangible medium,

the cancellation period ends at the end of 14 days after the day on which the contract is entered into.

(3)   If the contract is a sales contract and none of paragraphs (4) to (6) applies, the cancellation period ends at the end of 14 days after the day on which the goods come into the physical possession of—

    (a)   the consumer, or

    (b)   a person, other than the carrier, identified by the consumer to take possession of them.

(4)   If the contract is a sales contract under which multiple goods are ordered by the consumer in one order but some are delivered on different days, the cancellation period ends at the end of 14 days after the day on which the last of the goods come into the physical possession of—

    (a)   the consumer, or

    (b)   a person, other than the carrier, identified by the consumer to take possession of them.

(5)   If the contract is a sales contract under which goods consisting of multiple lots or pieces of something are delivered on different days, the cancellation period ends at the end of 14 days after the day on which the last of the lots or pieces come into the physical possession of—

    (a)   the consumer, or

    (b)   a person, other than the carrier, identified by the consumer to take possession of them.

(6)   If the contract is a sales contract for regular delivery of goods during a defined period of more than one day, the cancellation period ends at the end of 14 days after the day on which the first of the goods come into the physical possession of—

    (a)   the consumer, or

    (b)   a person, other than the carrier, identified by the consumer to take possession of them.

31.   Cancellation period extended for breach of information requirement

(1)   This regulation applies if the trader does not provide the consumer with the information on the right to cancel required by paragraph (l) of Schedule 2, in accordance with Part 2.

(2)   If the trader provides the consumer with that information in the period of 12 months beginning with the first day of the 14 days mentioned in regulation 30(2) to (6), but otherwise in accordance with Part 2, the cancellation period ends at the end of 14 days after the consumer receives the information.

(3)   Otherwise the cancellation period ends at the end of 12 months after the day on which it would have ended under regulation 30.

32.   Exercise of the right to withdraw or cancel

(1)   To withdraw an offer to enter into a distance or off-premises contract, the consumer must inform the trader of the decision to withdraw it.

(2)   To cancel a contract under regulation 29(1), the consumer must inform the trader of the decision to cancel it.

(3)   To inform the trader under paragraph (2) the consumer may either—

    (a)   use a form following the model cancellation form in part B of Schedule 3, or

    (b)   make any other clear statement setting out the decision to cancel the contract.

(4)   If the trader gives the consumer the option of filling in and submitting such a form or other statement on the trader's website—

    (a)   the consumer need not use it, but

    (b)   if the consumer does, the trader must communicate to the consumer an acknowledgement of receipt of the cancellation on a durable medium without delay.

(5)   Where the consumer informs the trader under paragraph (2) by sending a communication, the consumer is to be treated as having cancelled the contract in the cancellation period if the communication is sent before the end of the period.

(6)   In case of dispute it is for the consumer to show that the contract was cancelled in the cancellation period in accordance with this regulation.

33.   Effect of withdrawal or cancellation

(1)   If a contract is cancelled under regulation 29(1)—

    (a)   the cancellation ends the obligations of the parties to perform the contract, and

    (b)   regulations 34 to 38 apply.

(2)   Regulations 34 and 38 also apply if the consumer withdraws an offer to enter into a distance or off-premises contract.

34.   Reimbursement by trader in the event of withdrawal or cancellation

(1)   The trader must reimburse all payments, other than payments for delivery, received from the consumer, subject to paragraph (10).

(2)   The trader must reimburse any payment for delivery received from the consumer, unless the consumer expressly chose a kind of delivery costing more than the least expensive common and generally acceptable kind of delivery offered by the trader.

(3)   In that case, the trader must reimburse any payment for delivery received from the consumer up to the amount the consumer would have paid if the consumer had chosen the least expensive common and generally acceptable kind of delivery offered by the trader.

(4)   Reimbursement must be without undue delay, and in any event not later than the time specified in paragraph (5) or (6).

(5)   If the contract is a sales contract and the trader has not offered to collect the goods, the time is the end of 14 days after—

    (a)   the day on which the trader receives the goods back, or

    (b)   if earlier, the day on which the consumer supplies evidence of having sent the goods back.

(6)   Otherwise, the time is the end of 14 days after the day on which the trader is informed of the consumer's decision to withdraw the offer or cancel the contract, in accordance with regulation 32.

(7)   The trader must make the reimbursement using the same means of payment as the consumer used for the initial transaction, unless the consumer has expressly agreed otherwise.

(8)   The trader must not impose any fee on the consumer in respect of the reimbursement.

(9)   If (in the case of a sales contract) the value of the goods is diminished by any amount as a result of handling of the goods by the consumer beyond what is necessary to establish the nature, characteristics and functioning of the goods, the trader may recover that amount from the consumer, up to the contract price.

(10)   An amount that may be recovered under paragraph (9)—

    (a)   may be deducted from the amount to be reimbursed under paragraph (1);

    (b)   otherwise, must be paid by the consumer to the trader.

(11)   Paragraph (9) does not apply if the trader has failed to provide the consumer with the information on the right to cancel required by paragraph (l) of Schedule 2, in accordance with Part 2.

(12)   For the purposes of paragraph (9) handling is beyond what is necessary to establish the nature, characteristics and functioning of the goods if, in particular, it goes beyond the sort of handling that might reasonably be allowed in a shop.

(13)   Where the provisions of this regulation apply to cancellation of a contract, the contract is to be treated as including those provisions as terms.

35.   Return of goods in the event of cancellation

(1)   Where a sales contract is cancelled under regulation 29(1), it is the trader's responsibility to collect the goods if—

    (a)   the trader has offered to collect them, or

    (b)   in the case of an off-premises contract, the goods were delivered to the consumer's home when the contract was entered into and could not, by their nature, normally be returned by post.

(2)   If it is not the trader's responsibility under paragraph (1) to collect the goods, the consumer must—

    (a)   send them back, or

   (b) hand them over to the trader or to a person authorised by the trader to receive them.

 (3) The address to which goods must be sent under paragraph (2)(a) is—

   (a) any address specified by the trader for sending the goods back;

   (b) if no address is specified for that purpose, any address specified by the trader for the consumer to contact the trader;

   (c) if no address is specified for either of those purposes, any place of business of the trader.

 (4) The consumer must send off the goods under paragraph (2)(a), or hand them over under paragraph (2)(b), without undue delay and in any event not later than 14 days after the day on which the consumer informs the trader as required by regulation 32(2).

 (5) The consumer must bear the direct cost of returning goods under paragraph (2), unless—

   (a) the trader has agreed to bear those costs, or

   (b) the trader failed to provide the consumer with the information about the consumer bearing those costs, required by paragraph (m) of Schedule 2, in accordance with Part 2.

 (6) The contract is to be treated as including a term that the trader must bear the direct cost of the consumer returning goods under paragraph (2) where paragraph (5)(b) applies.

 (7) The consumer is not required to bear any other cost of returning goods under paragraph (2).

 (8) The consumer is not required to bear any cost of collecting goods under paragraph (1) unless the trader has offered to collect the goods and the consumer has agreed to beat the costs of the trader doing so.

36. Supply of service in cancellation period

 (1) The trader must not begin the supply of a service before the end of the cancellation period provided for in regulation 30(1) unless the consumer—

   (a) has made an express request, and

   (b) in the case of an off-premises contract, has made the request on a durable medium.

 (2) In the case of a service other than supply of water, gas, electricity or district heating, the consumer ceases to have the right to cancel a service contract under regulation 29(1) if the service has been fully performed, and performance of the service began—

   (a) after a request by the consumer in accordance with paragraph (1), and

   (b) with the acknowledgement that the consumer would lose that right once the contract had been fully performed by the trader.

 (3) Paragraphs (4) to (6) apply where a contract is cancelled under regulation 29(1) and a service has been supplied in the cancellation period.

 (4) Where the service is supplied in response to a request in accordance with paragraph (1), the consumer must (subject to paragraph (6)) pay to the trader an amount—

   (a) for the supply of the service for the period for which it is supplied, ending with the time when the trader is informed of the consumer's decision to cancel the contract, in accordance with regulation 32(2), and

   (b) which is in proportion to what has been supplied, in comparison with the full coverage of the contract.

 (5) The amount is to be calculated—

   (a) on the basis of the total price agreed in the contract, or

   (b) if the total price is excessive, on the basis of the market value of the service that has been supplied, calculated by comparing prices for equivalent services supplied by other traders.

 (6) The consumer bears no cost for supply of the service, in full or in part, in the cancellation period, if—

   (a) the trader has failed to provide the consumer with the information on the right to cancel required by paragraph (l) of Schedule 2, or the information on payment of that cost required by paragraph (n) of that Schedule, in accordance with Part 2, or

(b)   the service is not supplied in response to a request in accordance with paragraph (1).

37.   Supply of digital content in cancellation period

(1)   Under a contract for the supply of digital content not on a tangible medium, the trader must not begin supply of the digital content before the end of the cancellation period provided for in regulation 30(1), unless—

(a)   the consumer has given express consent, and

(b)   the consumer has acknowledged that the right to cancel the contract under regulation 29(1) will be lost.

(2)   The consumer ceases to have the right to cancel such a contract under regulation 29(1) if, before the end of the cancellation period, supply of the digital content has begun after the consumer has given the consent and acknowledgement required by paragraph (1).

(3)   Paragraph (4) applies where a contract is cancelled under regulation 29(1) and digital content has been supplied, not on a tangible medium, in the cancellation period.

(4)   The consumer bears no cost for supply of the digital content, in full or in part, in the cancellation period, if—

(a)   the consumer has not given prior express consent to the beginning of the performance of the digital content before the end of the 14-day period referred to in regulation 30,

(b)   the consumer gave that consent but did not acknowledge when giving it that the right to cancel would be lost, or

(c)   the trader failed to provide confirmation required by regulation 12(5) or 16(3).

38.   Effects of withdrawal or cancellation on ancillary contracts

(1)   If a consumer withdraws an offer to enter into a distance or off-premises contract, or cancels such a contract under regulation 29(1), any ancillary contracts are automatically terminated, without any costs for the consumer, other than any costs under these provisions—

(a)   regulation 34(3) (where enhanced delivery chosen by consumer);

(b)   regulation 34(9) (where value of goods diminished by consumer handling);

(c)   regulation 35(5) (where goods returned by consumer);

(d)   regulation 36(4) (where consumer requests early supply of service).

(2)   When a trader is informed by a consumer under regulation 32(1) or (2) of a decision to withdraw an offer or cancel a contract, the trader must inform any other trader with whom the consumer has an ancillary contract that is terminated by paragraph (1).

(3)   An 'ancillary contract', in relation to a distance or off-premises contract (the 'main contract'), means a contract by which the consumer acquires goods or services related to the main contract, where those goods or services are provided—

(a)   by the trader, or

(b)   by a third party on the basis of an arrangement between the third party and the trader.

(4)   Regulation 6(1)(b) (exclusion of financial services contracts) does not limit the contracts that are ancillary contracts for the purposes of this regulation.

PART 4
PROTECTION FROM ADDITIONAL CHARGES

40.   Additional payments under a contract

(1)   Under a contract between a trader and a consumer, no payment is payable in addition to the remuneration agreed for the trader's main obligation unless, before the consumer became bound by the contract, the trader obtained the consumer's express consent.

(2)   There is no express consent (if there would otherwise be) for the purposes of this paragraph if consent is inferred from the consumer not changing a default option (such as a pre-ticked box on a website).

(3)   This regulation does not apply if the trader's main obligation is to supply services within regulation 6(1)(b), but in any other case it applies even if an additional payment is for such services.

(4)   Where a trader receives an additional payment which, under this regulation, is not payable under a contract, the contract is to be treated as providing for the trader to reimburse the payment to the consumer.

41.   Help-line charges over basic rate

(1)   Where a trader operates a telephone line for the purpose of consumers contacting the trader by telephone in relation to contracts entered into with the trader, a consumer contacting the trader must not be bound to pay more than the basic rate.

(2)   If in those circumstances a consumer who contacts a trader in relation to a contract is bound to pay more than the basic rate, the contract is to be treated as providing for the trader to pay to the consumer any amount by which the charge paid by the consumer for the call is more than the basic rate.

SCHEDULE 1   Regulation 9(1)
INFORMATION RELATING TO ON-PREMISES CONTRACTS

The information referred to in regulation 9(1) is—

(a)   the main characteristics of the goods, services or digital content, to the extent appropriate to the medium of communication and to the goods, services or digital content;

(b)   the identity of the trader (such as the trader's trading name), the geographical address at which the trader is established and the trader's telephone number;

(c)   the total price of the goods, services or digital content inclusive of taxes, or where the nature of the goods, services or digital content is such that the price cannot reasonably be calculated in advance, the manner in which the price is to be calculated;

(d)   where applicable, all additional delivery charges or, where those charges cannot reasonably be calculated in advance, the fact that such additional charges may be payable;

(e)   where applicable, the arrangements for payment, delivery, performance, and the time by which the trader undertakes to deliver the goods to perform the service or to supply the digital content;

(f)   where applicable, the trader's complaint handling policy;

(g)   in the case of a sales contract, a reminder that the trader is under a legal duty to supply goods that are in conformity with the contract;

(h)   where applicable, the existence and the conditions of after-sales services and commercial guarantees;

(i)   the duration of the contract, where applicable, or, if the contract is of indeterminate duration or is to be extended automatically, the conditions for terminating the contract;

(j)   where applicable, the functionality, including applicable technical protection measures, of digital content;

(k)   where applicable, any relevant compatibility of digital content with hardware and software that the trader is aware of or can reasonably be expected to have been aware of.

SCHEDULE 2   Regulations 10(1) and 13(1)
INFORMATION RELATING TO DISTANCE AND OFF-PREMISES CONTRACTS

The information referred to in regulations 10(1) and 13(1) is (subject to the note at the end of this Schedule)—

(a)   the main characteristics of the goods, services or digital content, to the extent appropriate to the medium of communication and to the goods, services or digital content;

(b)   the identity of the trader (such as the trader's trading name);

(c)   the geographical address at which the trader is established and, where available, the trader's telephone number, fax number and e-mail address, to enable the consumer to contact the trader quickly and communicate efficiently;

(d)   where the trader is acting on behalf of another trader, the geographical address and identity of that other trader;

(e)   if different from the address provided in accordance with paragraph (c), the geographical address of the place of business of the trader, and, where the trader acts on behalf of another trader, the geographical address of the place of business of that other trader, where the consumer can address any complaints;

(f)   the total price of the goods, services or digital content inclusive of taxes, or where the nature of the goods, services or digital content is such that the price cannot reasonably be calculated in advance, the manner in which the price is to be calculated,

(g)   where applicable, all additional delivery charges and any other costs or, where those charges cannot reasonably be calculated in advance, the fact that such additional charges may be payable;

(h)   in the case of a contract of indeterminate duration or a contract containing a subscription, the total costs per billing period or (where such contracts are charged at a fixed rate) the total monthly costs;

(i)   the cost of using the means of distance communication for the conclusion of the contract where that cost is calculated other than at the basic rate;

(j)   the arrangements for payment, delivery, performance, and the time by which the trader undertakes to deliver the goods, to perform the services or to supply the digital content;

(k)   where applicable, the trader's complaint handling policy;

(l)   where a right to cancel exists, the conditions, time limit and procedures for exercising that right in accordance with regulations 27 to 38;

(m)   where applicable, that the consumer will have to bear the cost of returning the goods in case of cancellation and, for distance contracts, if the goods, by their nature, cannot normally be returned by post, the cost of returning the goods;

(n)   that, if the consumer exercises the right to cancel after having made a request in accordance with regulation 36(1), the consumer is to be liable to pay the trader reasonable costs in accordance with regulation 36(4);

(o)   where under regulation 28, 36 or 37 there is no right to cancel or the right to cancel may be lost, the information that the consumer will not benefit from a right to cancel, or the circumstances under which the consumer loses the right to cancel;

(p)   in the case of a sales contract, a reminder that the trader is under a legal duty to supply goods that are in conformity with the contract;

(q)   where applicable, the existence and the conditions of after-sale customer assistance, after-sales services and commercial guarantees;

(r)   the existence of relevant codes of conduct, as defined in regulation 5(3)(b) of the Consumer Protection from Unfair Trading Regulations 2008, and how copies of them can be obtained, where applicable;

(s)   the duration of the contract, where applicable, or, if the contract is of indeterminate duration or is to be extended automatically, the conditions for terminating the contract;

(t)   where applicable, the minimum duration of the consumer's obligations under the contract;

(u)   where applicable, the existence and the conditions of deposits or other financial guarantees to be paid or provided by the consumer at the request of the trader;

(v)   where applicable, the functionality, including applicable technical protection measures, of digital content;

(w)   where applicable, any relevant compatibility of digital content with hardware and software that the trader is aware of or can reasonably be expected to have been aware of;

(x)   where applicable, the possibility of having recourse to an out-of-court complaint and redress mechanism, to which the trader is subject, and the methods for having access to it.

Note: In the case of a public auction, the information listed in paragraphs (b) to (e) may be replaced with the equivalent details for the auctioneer.

PACKAGE TRAVEL AND LINKED TRAVEL ARRANGEMENTS REGULATIONS 2018
(SI 2018, NO 634)

PART 1
GENERAL

1. Citation and commencement

(1) These Regulations may be cited as the Package Travel and Linked Travel Arrangements Regulations 2018.

(2) Except as set out in paragraph (3), these Regulations come into force on 1st July 2018.

(3) Regulation 38(4) comes into force on the later of the following —

    (a) 1st July 2018;

    (b) the day on which Schedule 1 to the Wales Act 2017 (which inserts Schedule 7A into the Government of Wales Act 2006, which regulation 38(4) amends) comes into force.

2. Interpretation

(1) In these Regulations —

'commencement date' means the date on which these Regulations come into force;

'durable medium' means any instrument which —

    (a) enables the traveller or the trader to store information addressed personally to them in a way accessible for future reference for a period of time adequate for the purposes of the information; and

    (b) allows the unchanged reproduction of the information stored;

'lack of conformity' means a failure to perform, or the improper performance of, the travel services included in a package;

'minor' means a person below the age of 18;

'organiser' means —

    (a) a trader who combines and sells, or offers for sale, packages, either directly or through another trader or together with another trader; or

    (b) the trader who transmits the traveller's data to another trader in accordance with paragraph (5)(b)(v);

'package travel contract' means a contract on a package as a whole or, if the package is provided under separate contracts, all contracts covering the travel services included in the package;

'passenger rights legislation' means —

    (a) Regulation (EC) No 261/2004 of the European Parliament and of the Council establishing common rules on compensation and assistance to passengers in the event of denied boarding and of cancellation or long delay of flights, and repealing Regulation (EEC) No 295/91;

    (b) Regulation (EC) No 1371/2007 of the European Parliament and of the Council on rail passengers' rights and obligations;

    (c) Regulation (EC) No 392/2009 of the European Parliament and of the Council on the liability of carriers of passengers by sea in the event of accidents;

    (d) Regulation (EU) No 1177/2010 of the European Parliament and of the Council concerning the rights of passengers when travelling by sea and inland waterway and amending Regulation (EC) No 2006/2004; and

    (e) Regulation (EU) No 181/2011 of the European Parliament and of the Council concerning the rights of passengers in bus and coach transport and amending Regulation (EC) No 2006/2004.

'point of sale' means —

    (a) any retail premises, whether movable or immovable;

    (b) a retail website or similar online sales facility, including where retail websites or online sales facilities are presented to travellers as a single facility; or

    (c) a telephone service;

'repatriation' means the traveller's return to the place of departure or to another place the contracting parties agree upon;

'retailer' means a trader other than the organiser who sells or offers for sale packages combined by an organiser;

'start of the package' means the beginning of the performance of travel services included in the package;

'trader' means any person who is acting, including through any other person acting in their name or on their behalf, for purposes relating to their trade, business, craft or profession in relation to contracts covered by these Regulations, whether acting in the capacity of organiser, retailer, trader facilitating a linked travel arrangement or as a travel service provider;

'travel service' means—

(a)   the carriage of passengers;

(b)   the provision of accommodation which is not intrinsically part of the carriage of passengers and is not for residential purposes;

(c)   the rental of—

    (i)   cars;

    (ii)   other motor vehicles within the meaning of regulation 4(1) of the Road Vehicles (Approval) Regulations 2009; or

    (iii)   motorcycles requiring a Category A driving licence in accordance with Part 1 of Schedule 2 (categories and sub-categories of vehicle for licensing purposes) to the Motor Vehicles (Driving Licences) Regulations 1999;

(d)   any other tourist service not intrinsically part of a travel service within the meaning of paragraph (a), (b) or (c);

'traveller' means any individual who is seeking to conclude a contract, or is entitled to travel on the basis of a contract concluded, within the scope of these Regulations;

'unavoidable and extraordinary circumstances' means a situation—

(a)   beyond the control of the party who seeks to rely on such a situation for the purpose of regulation 12(7), 13(2)(b), 15(14) or (16), 16(4)(c) or 28(3)(b); and

(b)   the consequences of which could not have been avoided even if all reasonable measures had been taken;

(2)   In these Regulations, a reference to an organiser or a retailer being 'established' is to be construed according to the meaning of 'establishment' given by regulation 4 of the Provision of Services Regulations 2009.

(3)   In these Regulations, subject to paragraph (4), a 'linked travel arrangement' means at least two different types of travel service purchased for the purpose of the same trip or holiday, not constituting a package, resulting in the conclusion of separate contracts with the individual service providers, if a trader facilitates —

(a)   on the occasion of a single visit to, or contact with, a trader's point of sale, the separate selection and separate payment of each travel service by travellers; or

(b)   in a targeted manner, the procurement of at least one additional travel service from another trader where a contract with such other trader is concluded at the latest 24 hours after the confirmation of the booking of the first travel service.

(4)   Where—

(a)   not more than one travel service of the kind listed in paragraph (a), (b) or (c) of the definition of 'travel service', and

(b)   one or more tourist services of the kind listed in paragraph (d) of that definition,

are purchased, those services do not constitute a linked travel arrangement if the tourist services referred to in sub-paragraph (b) do not account for a significant proportion of the combined value of the services and are not advertised as, and do not otherwise represent, an essential feature of the trip or holiday.

(5)   In these Regulations, subject to paragraph (6), a 'package' means a combination of at least two different types of travel services for the purpose of the same trip or holiday, if—

(a)   those services are combined by one trader, including at the request of, or in accordance with, the selection of the traveller, before a single contract on all services is concluded; or

(b)   those services are—

    (i)   purchased from a single point of sale and selected before the traveller agrees to pay,

       (ii)   offered, sold or charged at an inclusive or total price,

       (iii)   advertised or sold under the term 'package' or under a similar term,

       (iv)   combined after the conclusion of a contract by which a trader entitles the traveller to choose among a selection of different types of travel services, or

       (v)   purchased from separate traders through linked online booking processes where—

           (aa)   the traveller's name, payment details and e-mail address are transmitted from the trader with whom the first contract is concluded to another trader or traders, and

           (aa)   a contract with the latter trader or traders is concluded at the latest 24 hours after the confirmation of the booking of the first travel service,

    irrespective of whether the traveller concludes separate contracts with one or more travel service providers in respect of the services.

  (6)   A combination of travel services where not more than one type of travel service of the kind listed in paragraph (a), (b) or (c) of the definition of 'travel service' is combined with one or more tourist services of the kind listed in paragraph (d) of that definition is not a package if the latter services—

       (a)   do not account for a significant proportion of the value of the combination and are not advertised as, and do not otherwise represent, an essential feature of the combination; or

       (b)   are selected and purchased after the performance of a travel service of the kind listed in paragraph (a), (b) or (c) of the definition of 'travel service' has started.

3.   Application

  (1)   These Regulations apply to—

       (a)   packages offered for sale or sold by traders to travellers, and

       (b)   linked travel arrangements,

    which are concluded on or after the commencement date.

  (2)   These Regulations do not apply to—

       (a)   packages and linked travel arrangements covering a period of less than 24 hours, unless overnight accommodation is included;

       (b)   packages offered, and linked travel arrangements facilitated, occasionally on a not-for-profit basis for a limited group of travellers;

       (c)   packages and linked travel arrangements purchased on the basis of a general agreement.

  (3)   In paragraph (2)(c), a 'general agreement' means an agreement which is concluded between a trader and another person acting for a trade, business, craft or profession, for the purpose of booking travel arrangements in connection with that trade, business, craft or profession.

PART 2

INFORMATION DUTIES AND CONTENT OF THE PACKAGE TRAVEL CONTRACT

4.   Information duties and "the relevant person"

  (1)   Where a package travel contract is sold through a retailer—

       (a)   the organiser and the retailer must ensure that the duties imposed by regulations 5, 6 and 7 ("the information duties") are performed;

       (b)   the organiser and the retailer may agree whether the information duties are to be performed by the organiser or the retailer; and

       (c)   either the organiser or the retailer must perform the information duties.

  (2)   Where a package travel contract is not sold through a retailer, the organiser must perform the information duties imposed by regulations 5, 6 and 7.

  (3)   In this Part, the person who, in accordance with this regulation, performs, or it is agreed is to perform, a duty imposed by a provision of regulation 5, 6 or 7, is "the relevant person" for the purposes of the provision of regulation 5, 6 or 7 under which the duty is performed or it is agreed is to be performed.

5.   Information to be provided by the relevant person before concluding a contract

(1)   Subject to paragraph (3), before a package travel contract is concluded, the relevant person must provide the traveller with the information specified in Schedule 1, where applicable to the package.

(2)   Subject to paragraph (3), before a package travel contract is concluded, the relevant person must also provide the traveller with—

    (a)   where the use of hyperlinks is possible, the information in Schedule 2, using the form and wording set out in that Schedule;

    (b)   where the use of hyperlinks is not possible, or the package travel contract is to be concluded by telephone, the information in Schedule 3, using the form and wording set out in that Schedule.

(3)   Before a traveller is bound by a package of the kind described in regulation 2(5)(b)(v)—

    (a)   the relevant person and the trader to whom the data are transmitted must ensure that each of them provides the information specified in Schedule 1, in so far as it is relevant for the respective travel services they offer; and

    (b)   the relevant person must provide, at the same time, the information in Schedule 4, using the form and wording set out in that Schedule.

(4)   Any information provided to the traveller under this regulation must be provided—

    (a)   in a clear, comprehensible and prominent manner; and

    (b)   where the information is provided in writing, in a legible form.

(5)   Where the relevant person fails to provide information to the traveller in accordance with this regulation, the organiser or, where the package travel contract is sold through a retailer, both the organiser and the retailer, commit an offence and are liable—

    (a)   on summary conviction, to a fine in England and Wales, or in Scotland and Northern Ireland to a fine not exceeding the statutory maximum;

    (b)   on conviction on indictment, to a fine.

6.   Binding character of information provided before the conclusion of the contract

(1)   Where the relevant person provides to the traveller the information specified in paragraphs 1 to 10, 12 to 14 and 16 of Schedule 1, that information—

    (a)   forms an integral part of the package travel contract; and

    (b)   must not be altered unless the traveller expressly agrees otherwise with the relevant person, as the case may be.

(2)   The relevant person must communicate to the traveller any change to the information provided under regulation 5, in a clear, comprehensible and prominent manner before the conclusion of the package travel contract.

(3)   Where, before the conclusion of the package travel contract, the relevant person does not provide the information which is required to be provided under paragraph (1) in respect of additional fees, charges or other costs referred to in paragraph 12 of Schedule 1 the traveller is not required to bear those fees, charges or other costs.

(4)   It is an implied condition (or, as regards Scotland, an implied term) of the package travel contract that the relevant person complies with the provisions of this regulation.

(5)   In Scotland, any breach of the condition implied by paragraph (4) is deemed to be a material breach justifying rescission of the contract.

7.   Content of the package travel contract and other documents

(1)   The relevant person must ensure that—

    (a)   the package travel contract is in plain and intelligible language; and

    (b)   where the contract, or part of the contract, is in writing, the contract or the part of the contract, is in a legible form.

(2)   The relevant person must ensure that the package travel contract sets out the full content of the package and includes—

    (a)   the information specified in Schedule 1; and

    (b)   the information specified in Schedule 5.

(3) Subject to paragraphs (4) and (5), when the package travel contract is concluded, or without undue delay after its conclusion, the relevant person must provide the traveller with a copy or confirmation of the contract on a durable medium.

(4) Where the contract is concluded in the simultaneous physical presence of the parties, the relevant person must provide to the traveller a paper copy of the package travel contract if the traveller so requests.

(5) Where an off-premises contract is concluded, the relevant person must provide a copy or confirmation of that contract to the traveller on paper or, if the traveller agrees, on another durable medium.

(6) Where a package of the kind described in regulation 2(5)(b)(v) is concluded—

    (a) the trader to whom the data are transmitted must inform the relevant person of the conclusion of the contract leading to the creation of a package; and

    (b) the trader must provide the relevant person with the information necessary to comply with their obligations as the relevant person.

(7) As soon as the organiser is informed, under paragraph (6), that a package has been created, the relevant person must provide the information in Schedule 5 to the traveller on a durable medium.

(8) The relevant person must provide the information referred to in paragraphs (2) and (7) in a clear, comprehensible and prominent manner.

(9) The relevant person must provide the traveller in good time, before the start of the package, with the necessary receipts, vouchers and tickets, information on the scheduled times of departure and, where applicable, the deadline for check-in, as well as the scheduled times for intermediate stops, transport connections and arrival.

(10) It is an implied condition (or, as regards Scotland, an implied term) of the contract that the relevant person complies with paragraphs (1), (3) to (6) and (9).

(11) In Scotland, any breach of the condition implied by paragraph (10) is deemed to be a material breach justifying rescission of the contract.

(12) Where the relevant person fails to comply with paragraph (2), (7) or (8), the organiser or, where the package travel contract is sold through a retailer, both the organiser and the retailer, commit an offence and are liable—

    (a) on summary conviction, to a fine in England and Wales, or in Scotland and Northern Ireland to a fine not exceeding the statutory maximum;

    (b) on conviction on indictment, to a fine.

(13) In paragraph (5), "off-premises contract" has the meaning given in regulation 5 of the Consumer Contracts (Information, Cancellation and Additional Charges) Regulations 2013.

8.   Burden of proof

(1) In case of dispute about the organiser or the retailer's compliance with any provision of this Part, it is for the organiser or the retailer, as appropriate, to show that the provision was complied with.

(2) Paragraph (1) does not apply to proceedings for an offence under—

    (a) regulation 5(5); or

    (b) regulation 7(12).

PART 3

CHANGES TO THE PACKAGE TRAVEL CONTRACT BEFORE THE START OF THE PACKAGE

9.   Transfer of the package travel contract to another traveller

(1) A traveller ("the transferor") may transfer the package travel contract once it is concluded to a person ("the transferee") who satisfies all the conditions applicable to that contract.

(2) The transferor must give the organiser, on a durable medium, reasonable notice of the transfer and, for those purposes, notice which is given 7 days or more before the day on which the package starts is always deemed to be reasonable.

(3)   The organiser must inform the transferor about the additional fees, charges or other costs arising from the transfer of the package travel contract ("the transfer costs") and must provide proof of those costs.

(4)   The transfer costs—
   (a)   must not be unreasonable; and
   (b)   must not exceed the cost incurred by the organiser as a result of the transfer.

(5)   The transferor and the transferee are jointly and severally liable for the transfer costs.

(6)   The provisions of paragraphs (3) and (4) are implied as a term in every package travel contract.

10.   Alteration of the price

(1)   The provisions of this regulation are implied as a term in every package travel contract.

(2)   The prices specified in a package travel contract must not be increased once the contract is concluded unless the contract—
   (a)   states expressly that such an increase may be made;
   (b)   states that price increases are to be made solely to allow for increases which are a direct consequence of changes in—
      (i)   the price of the carriage of passengers resulting from the cost of fuel or other power sources;
      (ii)   the level of taxes or fees on the travel services included in the contract imposed by third parties not directly involved in the performance of the package, including tourist taxes, landing taxes or embarkation or disembarkation fees at ports and airports; and
      (iii) the exchange rates relevant to the package;
   (c)   provides that the traveller has the right to a price reduction corresponding to any decrease in the costs referred to in sub-paragraph (b) that occurs before the start of the package once the contract is concluded; and
   (d)   provides how the revisions referred to in sub-paragraphs (a) and (b) are to be calculated.

(3)   Irrespective of its extent, a price increase may only be made if the organiser notifies the traveller clearly and comprehensibly of it with a justification for that increase and a calculation, on a durable medium, at the latest 20 days before the start of the package.

(4)   Where a price increase exceeds 8% of the total price of the package, paragraphs (4) to (11) of regulation 11 apply.

(5)   Where, under the terms of the package travel contract, the traveller has the right to a price reduction which corresponds to a decrease in the costs referred to in paragraph (2)(b), the organiser—
   (a)   may deduct administrative expenses from any refund owed to the traveller as a result of the reduction in price; and
   (b)   must, at the traveller's request, provide proof of any expenses so deducted.

11.   Alteration of other package travel contract terms

(1)   The provisions of this regulation are implied as a term in every package travel contract.

(2)   The organiser must not unilaterally change the terms of a package travel contract before the start of the package, other than the price in accordance with regulation 10, unless—
   (a)   the contract allows the organiser to make such changes;
   (b)   the change is insignificant; and
   (c)   the organiser informs the traveller of the change in a clear, comprehensible and prominent manner on a durable medium.

(3)   Paragraphs (4) to (11) apply where, before the start of the package, the organiser—
   (a)   is constrained by circumstances beyond the control of the organiser to alter significantly any of the main characteristics of the travel services specified in paragraphs 1 to 10 of Schedule 1;
   (b)   cannot fulfil the special requirements specified in paragraph 1 of Schedule 5; or
   (c)   proposes to increase the price of the package by more than 8% in accordance with regulation 10(4).

(4)   The organiser must, without undue delay, inform the traveller in a clear, comprehensible and prominent manner on a durable medium, of—

(a) the proposed changes referred to in paragraph (3) and, where appropriate, in accordance with paragraph (7), their impact on the price of the package;

(b) a reasonable period within which the traveller must inform the organiser of the decision pursuant to paragraph (5);

(c) the consequences of the traveller's failure to respond within the period referred to in sub- paragraph (b); and

(d) any substitute package, of an equivalent or higher quality, if possible, offered to the traveller and its price.

(5) The traveller may, within a reasonable period specified by the organiser—
   (a) accept the proposed changes; or
   (b) terminate the contract without paying a termination fee.

(6) Where the traveller terminates the contract pursuant to paragraph (5)(b), the traveller may accept a substitute package, where this is offered by the organiser.

(7) Where—
   (a) the changes to the package travel contract referred to in paragraph (3), or
   (b) the substitute package referred to in paragraph (6),
   result in a package of lower quality or cost, the traveller is entitled to an appropriate price reduction.

(8) Where—
   (a) the traveller terminates the contract pursuant to paragraph (5)(b), and
   (b) the traveller does not accept a substitute package,
   the organiser must refund all payments made by or on behalf of the traveller without undue delay and in any event not later than 14 days after the contract is terminated.

(9) Where paragraph (8) applies, regulation 16(2) to (10) applies.

(10) Where the traveller does not confirm, within the period specified in paragraph (5), whether the traveller wishes to—
   (a) accept the proposed change, or
   (b) terminate the contract,
   in accordance with that paragraph, the organiser must notify the traveller, a second time, of the matters in sub-paragraphs (a) to (d) of paragraph (4).

(11) If, having been notified under paragraph (10), the traveller fails to respond, the organiser may terminate the contract and refund all payments made by or on behalf of the traveller without undue delay and in any event not later than 14 days after the contract is terminated.

12.   Termination of the package travel contract by the traveller

(1) The provisions of this regulation are implied as a term in every package travel contract.

(2) A traveller may terminate the package travel contract at any time before the start of the package.

(3) Where the traveller terminates the package travel contract under paragraph (2), the traveller may be required to pay an appropriate and justifiable termination fee to the organiser.

(4) The package travel contract may specify reasonable standard termination fees based on—
   (a) the time of the termination of the contract before the start of the package; and
   (b) the expected cost savings and income from alternative deployment of the travel services.

(5) In the absence of standardised termination fees, the amount of the termination fee must correspond to the price of the package minus the cost savings and income from alternative deployment of the travel services.

(6) The organiser must provide a justification for the amount of the termination fee if the traveller so requests.

(7) Notwithstanding paragraphs (2) to (6), in the event of unavoidable and extraordinary circumstances occurring at the place of destination or its immediate vicinity and which significantly affect—
   (a) the performance of the package, or
   (b) the carriage of passengers to the destination,

the traveller may terminate the package travel contract before the start of the package without paying any termination fee.

(8)   Where the package travel contract is terminated under paragraph (7), the traveller is entitled to a full refund of any payments made for the package but is not entitled to additional compensation.

13.   Termination of the package travel contract by the organiser

(1)   The provisions of this regulation are implied as a term in every package travel contract.

(2)   Paragraph (3) applies where—

    (a)   the number of persons enrolled for the package is smaller than the minimum number stated in the contract and the organiser notifies the traveller of the termination of the contract within the period fixed in the contract but not later than—

        (i)   in the case of trips lasting more than 6 days, 20 days before the start of the package;

        (ii)   in the case of trips lasting between 2 and 6 days, 7 days before the start of the package;

        (iii)   in the case of trips lasting less than 2 days, 48 hours before the start of the package; or

    (b)   the organiser is prevented from performing the contract because of unavoidable and extraordinary circumstances and notifies the traveller of the termination of the contract without undue delay before the start of the package.

(3)   The organiser—

    (a)   may terminate the package travel contract and provide the traveller with a full refund of any payments made for the package;

    (b)   is not liable for additional compensation.

14.   Refunds in the event of termination

(1)   The provisions of this regulation are implied as a term in every package travel contract.

(2)   Following a termination under regulation 12(2), the organiser must reimburse any payments made by or on behalf of the traveller, having deducted any termination fee.

(3)   Any—

    (a)   reimbursement required under paragraph (2), or

    (b)   refund required pursuant to—

        (i)   regulation 12(8), or

        (ii)   a termination under regulation 13(3),

must be made to the traveller without undue delay and in any event not later than 14 days after the package travel contract is terminated.

PART 4
PERFORMANCE OF THE PACKAGE

15.   Responsibility for the performance of the package

(1)   The provisions of this regulation are implied as a term in every package travel contract.

(2)   The organiser is liable to the traveller for the performance of the travel services included in the package travel contract, irrespective of whether those services are to be performed by the organiser or by other travel service providers.

(3)   The traveller must inform the organiser without undue delay, taking into account the circumstances of the case, of any lack of conformity which the traveller perceives during the performance of a travel service included in the package travel contract.

(4)   If any of the travel services are not performed in accordance with the package travel contract, the organiser must remedy the lack of conformity within a reasonable period set by the traveller unless that—

    (a)   is impossible; or

    (b)   entails disproportionate costs, taking into account the extent of the lack of conformity and the value of the travel services affected.

(5)   Where the organiser does not remedy the lack of conformity within a reasonable period set by the traveller for a reason mentioned in sub-paragraph (a) or (b) of paragraph (4), regulation 16 applies.

(6)   Where the organiser refuses to remedy the lack of conformity or where immediate remedy is required, the traveller—

    (a)   may remedy the lack of conformity; and

    (b)   is entitled to reimbursement of the necessary expenses.

(7)   A traveller to whom paragraph (6)(a) applies is not required to—

    (a)   set a reasonable period pursuant to paragraph (4), and

    (b)   if such a period has been set, wait until the end of the period, before the traveller remedies the lack of conformity.

(8)   Where the organiser is unable to provide a significant proportion of the travel services as agreed in the package travel contract, the organiser must offer, at no extra cost to the traveller, suitable alternative arrangements of, where possible, equivalent or higher quality than those specified in the contract, for the continuation of the package, including where the traveller's return to the place of departure is agreed.

(9)   Where the organiser offers proposed alternative arrangements which result in a package of lower quality than that specified in the package travel contract, the organiser must grant the traveller an appropriate price reduction.

(10)   The traveller may reject the proposed alternative arrangements offered under paragraph (8) only if—

    (a)   they are not comparable to the arrangements which were agreed in the package travel contract; or

    (b)   the price reduction granted is inadequate.

(11)   Where—

    (a)   a lack of conformity substantially affects the performance of the package; and

    (b)   the organiser fails to remedy the lack of conformity within the reasonable period,

the traveller may terminate the package travel contract without paying a termination fee and, where appropriate, is entitled to a price reduction, or compensation for damages, or both, in accordance with regulation 16.

(12)   If—

    (a)   the organiser is unable to make alternative arrangements, or

    (b)   the traveller rejects the proposed alternative arrangements in accordance with paragraph (10),

the traveller is, where appropriate, entitled to a price reduction, or compensation for damages, or both, in accordance with regulation 16 without terminating the package travel contract.

(13)   If the package includes the carriage of passengers, the organiser must, in the cases referred to in paragraphs (11) and (12), also provide repatriation of the traveller with equivalent transport without undue delay and at no extra cost to the traveller.

(14)   Where the organiser is unable to ensure the traveller's return as agreed in the package travel contract because of unavoidable and extraordinary circumstances, the organiser must bear the cost of necessary accommodation, if possible of equivalent category—

    (a)   for a period not exceeding 3 nights per traveller; or

    (b)   where a different period is specified in the Union passenger rights legislation applicable to the relevant means of transport for the traveller's return, for the period specified in that legislation.

(15)   The limitation of costs referred to in paragraph (14) does not apply to persons with reduced mobility as defined in point (a) of Article 2 of Regulation (EC) No 1107/2006 of the European Parliament and of the Council, concerning the rights of disabled persons and persons with reduced mobility when travelling by air(**a**) and any person accompanying them, pregnant women and unaccompanied minors, as well as persons in need of specific medical assistance, provided that the organiser has been notified of their particular needs at least 48 hours before the start of the package.

(16)   The organiser's liability under paragraph (14) may not be limited by reason of unavoidable and extraordinary circumstances if the relevant transport provider may not rely on such circumstances under the applicable Union passenger rights legislation.

16.   Price reduction and compensation for damages

(1)   The provisions of this regulation are implied as a term in every package travel contract.

(2)   The organiser must offer the traveller an appropriate price reduction for any period during which there is a lack of conformity, unless the organiser proves that the lack of conformity is attributable to the traveller.

(3)   The organiser must offer the traveller, without undue delay, appropriate compensation for any damage which the traveller sustains as a result of any lack of conformity.

(4)   The traveller is not entitled to compensation for damages under paragraph (3) if the organiser proves that the lack of conformity is—

    (a)   attributable to the traveller;

    (b)   attributable to a third party unconnected with the provision of the travel services included in the package travel contract and is unforeseeable or unavoidable; or

    (c)   due to unavoidable and extraordinary circumstances.

(5)   In so far as the international conventions limit the extent of, or the conditions under which, compensation is to be paid by a provider carrying out a travel service which is part of a package, the same limitations are to apply to the organiser.

(6)   In other cases, the package travel contract may limit compensation to be paid by the organiser as long as that limitation—

    (a)   does not apply to personal injury or damage caused intentionally or with negligence or does not limit any liability that cannot be limited by law; and

    (b)   does not amount to less than 3 times the total price of the package.

(7)   Any right to compensation or price reduction under these Regulations does not affect the rights of travellers under—

    (a)   the Union passenger rights legislation; and

    (b)   the international conventions.

(8)   Travellers may present claims under—

    (a)   these Regulations;

    (b)   the Union passenger rights legislation; and

    (c)   the international conventions.

(9)   Where a traveller is granted compensation or a price reduction under—

    (a)   these Regulations, and

    (b)   the Union passenger rights legislation or the international conventions,

the organiser must deduct the compensation or price reductions referred to in sub-paragraph (b) from the compensation or price reduction referred to in sub-paragraph (a) to avoid overcompensation.

(10)   In this regulation, the "international conventions" means—

    (a)   the Carriage by Air Conventions, within the meaning given in section 1(5) of the Carriage by Air Act 1961;

    (b)   the Athens Convention of 1974 on the Carriage of Passengers and their Luggage by Sea;

    (c)   the Convention of 1980 concerning International Carriage by Rail (COTIF).

17.   Possibility of contacting the organiser via the retailer

(1)   The provisions of this regulation are implied as a term in every package travel contract.

(2)   The traveller may address messages, requests or complaints in relation to the performance of the package directly to the retailer through which it was purchased.

(3)   The retailer must forward those messages, requests or complaints to the organiser without undue delay.

(4)   For the purpose of compliance with time-limits or limitation periods, receipt of the messages, requests or complaints referred to in this regulation by the retailer are to be considered as receipt by the organiser.

18.   Obligation to provide assistance

(1)   The provisions of this regulation are implied as a term in every package travel contract.

(2)   Where a traveller is in difficulty, the organiser must give appropriate assistance without undue delay, including in the circumstances referred to in regulation 15(14), in particular by—

     (a)   providing appropriate information on health services, local authorities and consular assistance; and

     (b)   assisting the traveller to make distance communications and helping the traveller to find alternative travel arrangements.

(3)   The organiser may charge a fee for such assistance if the difficulty is caused intentionally by the traveller or through the traveller's negligence but that fee—

     (a)   must be reasonable; and

     (b)   must not exceed the actual costs incurred by the organiser.

PART 5
INSOLVENCY PROTECTION

19. Insolvency protection for packages

(1)   The organiser of a package who is established in the United Kingdom must provide effective security to cover, in the event of the organiser's insolvency, the reasonably foreseeable costs of—

     (a)   refunding all payments made by or on behalf of travellers for any travel service not performed as a consequence of the insolvency, taking into account the length of the period between down payments and final payments and the completion of the packages; and

     (b)   if the carriage of passengers is included in the packages, and the performance of any package is affected by the insolvency, repatriating the traveller and, if necessary, financing the traveller's accommodation prior to the repatriation.

(2)   ...

(3)   The organiser must provide the security—

     (a)   under paragraph (1)(a), without undue delay after the traveller's request;

     (b)   under paragraph (1)(b), free of charge.

(4)   The organiser of a package who—

     (a)   is not established in the United Kingdom, and

     (b)   sells or offers for sale a package in the United Kingdom, or by any means directs such activities to the United Kingdom,

must provide security in accordance with this Part.

(5)   Without prejudice to paragraphs (1) to (4), and subject to paragraphs (6) to (8), the organiser must at least ensure that arrangements as described in—

     (a)   regulation 20,

     (b)   regulation 21,

     (c)   regulation 22, or

     (d)   regulations 23 and 24,

are in force.

(6)   Paragraph (5) does not apply to a package to the extent that—

     (a)   ...

     (b)   the package is one—

        (i)   in respect of which the organiser is required to hold a licence under the Civil Aviation (Air Travel Organisers' Licensing) Regulations 2012; or

        (ii)   that is covered by the arrangements the organiser has entered into for the purposes of those Regulations.

(7)   For the purposes of regulations 20 to 24, a contract is to be treated as having been fully performed if the package or, as the case may be, the part of the package, has been completed.

(8)   For the purposes of paragraph (7), a package is to be deemed to have been completed whether or not there has been a lack of conformity.

(9)   An organiser who fails to comply with any provision of paragraphs (1) to (5) commits an offence and is liable—

     (a)   on summary conviction, to a fine in England and Wales, or in Scotland and Northern Ireland to a fine not exceeding the statutory maximum;

     (b)   on conviction on indictment, to a fine.

(10) In the event of the organiser's insolvency, travellers may agree to continue the package where—

    (a)   it is possible to do so; and

    (b)   a person, other than that organiser, agrees to carry out the responsibilities of the organiser under the package travel contract.

(11) ...

20.   Bonding

(1) Where an organiser, for the purpose of regulation 19(5), relies on the arrangements under this regulation, the organiser must ensure that a bond is entered into by an authorised institution under which the institution, in the event of the insolvency of the organiser, binds itself to pay to an approved body of which that organiser is a member—

    (a)   a sum calculated in accordance with paragraphs (3) and (4); or

    (b)   a sum calculated in accordance with paragraph (5), if the carriage of passengers is included in the packages and the performance of the packages is affected by the insolvency.

(2) Any bond entered into pursuant to paragraph (1) must not be in force for a period exceeding 18 months.

(3) The sum referred to in paragraph (1)(a) must be such sum as may reasonably be expected to enable all monies paid by or on behalf of travellers under or in contemplation of package travel contracts which have not been fully performed to be repaid and must not in any event be a sum which is less than the minimum sum calculated in accordance with paragraph (4).

(4) The minimum sum for the purposes of paragraph (3) must be a sum which represents—

    (a)   not less than 25% of all the payments which the organiser estimates that the organiser will receive under or in contemplation of package travel contracts in the 12-month period from the date of entry into force of the bond referred to in paragraph (1), or

    (b)   the maximum amount of all the payments which the organiser expects to hold at any one time, in respect of contracts which have not been fully performed,

whichever sum is the smaller.

(5) The sum referred to in paragraph (1)(b) must be no less than—

    (a)   the minimum sum calculated in accordance with paragraph (4); and

    (b)   such additional sum as the organiser may reasonably expect to be required to cover the reasonably foreseeable costs of repatriating the travellers and, if necessary, financing the travellers' accommodation prior to the repatriation.

(6) Before a bond is entered into pursuant to paragraph (1)—

    (a)   the organiser must inform the approved body of which the organiser is a member of the minimum sum which the organiser proposes for the purposes of paragraph (3) or, where relevant, paragraph (5);

    (b)   the approved body must consider whether such sum is sufficient for those purposes; and

    (c)   if the approved body does not consider that the sum is sufficient for those purposes, the approved body must—

        (i)   inform the organiser that this is the case, and

        (ii)   state the sum which, in the opinion of the approved body, is sufficient for those purposes.

(7) Where an approved body states a sum pursuant to paragraph (6)(c)(ii), the minimum sum for the purposes of paragraph (3) or, where relevant, paragraph (5), is to be that sum.

(8) In this regulation—

"approved body" means a body which is for the time being approved by the Secretary of State for the purposes of this regulation;

"authorised institution" means a person authorised under the law of the United Kingdom, the Channel Islands or the Isle of Man to carry on the business of entering into bonds of the kind required by this regulation.

21.   Bonding where approved body has reserve fund or insurance

(1)   Where an organiser, for the purpose of regulation 19(5), relies on the arrangements under this regulation, the organiser must ensure that a bond is entered into by an authorised institution, under which the institution, in the event of the organiser's insolvency, agrees to pay to an approved body of which the organiser is a member a sum calculated in accordance with —

   (a)   paragraphs (3) and (4);

   (b)   paragraph (5), if the carriage of passengers is included in the packages and the performance of the packages is affected by the insolvency.

(2)   Any bond entered into pursuant to paragraph (1) must not be in force for a period exceeding 18 months.

(3)   The sum referred to in paragraph (1)(a) must be such sum as may be specified by the approved body as representing the lesser of—

   (a)   the maximum amount of all the payments which the organiser expects to hold at any one time in respect of contracts which have not been fully performed; or

   (b)   the minimum sum calculated in accordance with paragraph (4).

(4)   The minimum sum for the purposes of paragraph (3) must be a sum which represents not less than 10% of all the payments which the organiser estimates that the organiser will receive under or in contemplation of package travel contracts in the 12-month period from the date of entry into force of the bond referred to in paragraph (1).

(5)   The sum referred to in paragraph (1)(b) must be no less than—

   (a)   the minimum sum calculated in accordance with paragraph (4); and

   (b)   such additional sum as may be specified by the approved body as representing the amount required to cover the costs of repatriating the travellers and, if necessary, financing the travellers' accommodation prior to the repatriation.

(6)   In this regulation, "approved body" means a body which is for the time being approved by the Secretary of State for the purposes of this regulation and no such approval is to be given unless the conditions mentioned in paragraph (7) are satisfied in relation to it.

(7)   A body may not be approved for the purposes of this regulation unless—

   (a)   it has a reserve fund or insurance cover with an insurer authorised in respect of such business in the United Kingdom, the Channel Islands or the Isle of Man of an amount in each case which is designed to enable—

      (i)   in the event of the insolvency of the member, the refund of all payments made by or on behalf of travellers for any travel service not fully performed as a consequence of the insolvency; and

      (ii)   the costs of repatriating the travellers and, if necessary, financing the travellers' accommodation prior to the repatriation to be covered, where the carriage of passengers is included in the packages and the performance of the packages is affected by the insolvency; and

   (b)   where it has a reserve fund, it agrees that the fund will be held by persons and in a manner approved by the Secretary of State.

(8)   In this regulation, "authorised institution" has the meaning given in regulation 20(8).

22.   Insurance

(1)   Where an organiser, for the purpose of regulation 19(5), relies on the arrangements under this regulation, the organiser must have insurance under one or more appropriate policies with an insurer authorised in respect of such business in the United Kingdom, the Channel Islands or the Isle of Man, under which the insurer agrees to indemnify travellers in the event of the insolvency of the organiser.

(2)   The organiser must ensure that travellers are insured persons under the policy required under paragraph (1) in respect of the costs referred to in paragraph (4)(b).

(3)   The organiser must ensure that it is a term of every package travel contract that the traveller acquires the benefit of a policy of a kind mentioned in paragraph (1) in the event of the organiser's insolvency.

(4)   In this regulation, "appropriate policy" means one which—

   (a)   does not contain a condition which provides (in whatever terms) that no liability arises under the policy, or that any liability so arising ceases—

      (i)   in the event of some specified thing being done or omitted to be done after the happening of the event giving rise to a claim under the policy;

        (ii)   in the event of the policy holder not making payments under or in connection with other policies; or

        (iii)   unless the policy holder keeps specified records or makes available to, or provides the insurer with, information from those records; and

   (b)   covers the costs of—

        (i)   refunding all payments made by or on behalf of travellers for any travel service not fully performed as a consequence of the insolvency, taking into account the length of the period between down payments and final payments and the completion of the packages; and

        (ii)   if the carriage of passengers is included in the package, and the performance of the package is affected by the insolvency, repatriating the traveller and, if necessary, financing the traveller's accommodation prior to the repatriation.

23.   Monies in trust

(1)   Where an organiser, for the purpose of regulation 19(5), relies on the arrangements under this regulation, the organiser must ensure that—

   (a)   all monies, or

   (b)   where regulation 24(3) applies, a lesser sum in accordance with that regulation,

paid by or on behalf of a traveller under or in contemplation of a package travel contract are held in the United Kingdom by a person as trustee for the traveller.

(2)   The monies are to be held under paragraph (1) until—

   (a)   the contract has been fully performed; or

   (b)   any sum of money paid by or on behalf of the traveller in respect of the contract—

        (i)   has been repaid to the traveller; or

        (ii)   has been forfeited on cancellation by the traveller.

(3)   The person appointed as trustee for the purposes of paragraph (1) must be independent of the organiser.

(4)   The costs of administering the trust mentioned in paragraph (1) must be paid for by the organiser.

(5)   Any interest which is earned on the monies held by the trustee pursuant to paragraph (1) must be held for the organiser and must be payable to the organiser on demand.

(6)   Where there is produced to the trustee a statement signed by the organiser to the effect that—

   (a)   a package travel contract, the price of which is specified in that statement, has been fully performed,

   (b)   the organiser has repaid to the traveller a sum of money specified in that statement which the traveller had paid in respect of a package travel contract, or

   (c)   the traveller has on cancellation forfeited a sum of money specified in that statement which the traveller had paid in respect of a package travel contract,

the trustee must release to the organiser the sum specified in the statement.

(7)   Where the trustee considers it appropriate to do so, the trustee may require the organiser to provide further information or evidence of the matters mentioned in sub-paragraph (a), (b) or (c) of paragraph (6) before the trustee releases any sum to the organiser pursuant to that paragraph.

(8)   In the event of the organiser's insolvency, the monies held in trust by the trustee pursuant to paragraph (1) of this regulation must be applied to meet the claims of travellers who are creditors of that organiser in respect of package travel contracts in respect of which the trust mentioned in paragraph (1) has been established and which have not been fully performed.

(9)   If there is a surplus after those claims have been met, it is to form part of the estate of the organiser for the purposes of insolvency law.

24.   Insurance where monies are held in trust

(1)   This regulation applies to any organiser who, for the purpose of regulation 19(5), makes arrangements under regulation 23.

(2)   Where the organiser offers packages which include the carriage of passengers, the organiser must have insurance under one or more appropriate policies with an insurer authorised in respect of such business in accordance with regulation 22(1), under which, in the event of the insolvency of the organiser, the insurer agrees to cover the costs of—

     (a)   repatriating the traveller who has purchased a relevant package; and

     (b)   if necessary, financing the traveller's accommodation prior to the repatriation.

(3)   Where paragraph (4) applies, an organiser—

     (a)   is not required, under regulation 23(1)(a), to ensure that all monies paid by a traveller under or in contemplation of a package travel contract are held in accordance with regulation 23; and

     (b)   may, instead, ensure that a part of those monies only (the "lesser sum") is held in accordance with regulation 23, as the case may be.

(4)   This paragraph applies if the organiser has insurance under one or more appropriate policies with an insurer authorised in respect of such business in accordance with regulation 22(1), under which, in the event of the insolvency of the organiser, the insurer agrees to cover the relevant amount.

(5)   Where paragraph (2) or (4) applies, the organiser must ensure that it is a term of the relevant package travel contract that the traveller acquires the benefit of a policy of a kind mentioned in paragraph (2) or (3) in the event of the organiser's insolvency.

(6)   In this regulation, an "appropriate policy" means one which does not contain a condition which provides (in whatever terms) that no liability arises under the policy, or that any liability so arising ceases—

     (a)   in the event of some specified thing being done or omitted to be done after the happening of the event giving rise to a claim under the policy;

     (b)   in the event of the policy holder not making payments under or in connection with other policies; or

     (c)   unless the policy holder keeps specified records or provides the insurer with, or makes available to, the insurer information from those records.

(7)   In paragraph (4), "the relevant amount" means such amount in excess of the lesser sum, as may be required to cover the costs of refunding the traveller for any travel service not fully performed as a consequence of the insolvency, taking into account the length of the period between down payments and final payments and the completion of the package.

25.   Offences arising from breach of regulation 23

(1)   If the organiser makes a false statement under regulation 23(6), the organiser commits an offence and is liable—

     (a)   on summary conviction, to a fine in England and Wales, or in Scotland and Northern Ireland to a fine not exceeding the statutory maximum;

     (b)   on conviction on indictment, to a fine.

26.   Insolvency protection and information requirements for linked travel arrangements

(1)   Any trader who facilitates a linked travel arrangement and is established in the United Kingdom must provide effective security to cover, in the event of the trader's insolvency, the reasonably foreseeable costs of—

     (a)   refunding all payments the trader receives from travellers for any travel service which is part of the linked arrangement and is not performed as a consequence of the trader's insolvency, taking into account the length of the period between down payments and final payments and the completion of the linked travel arrangements; and

     (b)   if the trader is the party responsible for the carriage of passengers, and the performance of the linked travel arrangement is affected by the insolvency, the traveller's repatriation and, if necessary, financing the traveller's accommodation prior to the repatriation.

(2)   ...

(3)   The trader must provide the security—

       (a)   under paragraph (1)(a), without undue delay; and

       (b)   under paragraph (1)(b), free of charge.

(4)   Any trader who—

       (a)   is not established in the United Kingdom, and

       (b)   sells or offers for sale a linked travel arrangement in the United Kingdom, or by any means directs such activities to the United Kingdom,

    must provide security in accordance with this regulation in respect of those arrangements.

(5)   Without prejudice to paragraphs (1) to (4) and subject to paragraph (6), the trader must at least ensure that arrangements as described in—

       (a)   regulation 20,

       (b)   regulation 21,

       (c)   regulation 22, or

       (d)   regulations 23 and 24,

    are in force and, for that purpose, a reference in those regulations to "organiser" is to be read as a reference to "trader", a reference to "package" or "package travel contract" is to be read as a reference to "linked travel arrangement" and a reference to regulation 19(5) is to be read as a reference to this paragraph.

(6)   Paragraph (5) does not apply to a linked travel arrangement to the extent that the linked travel arrangement—

       (a)   ...

       (b)   includes a travel service —

           (i)   in respect of which the trader is required to hold a licence under the Civil Aviation (Air Travel Organisers' Licensing) Regulations 2012; or

           (ii)   which is covered by the arrangements the trader has entered into for the purposes of those Regulations.

(7)   Before the traveller is bound by any contract leading to the creation of a linked travel arrangement, the trader facilitating linked travel arrangements, including where the trader is not established in the United Kingdom but, by any means directs such activities to the United Kingdom, must—

       (a)   state in a clear, comprehensible and prominent manner that the traveller—

           (i)   will not benefit from any of the rights applying exclusively to packages under these Regulations and that each service provider will be solely responsible for the proper contractual performance of the service;

           (ii)   will benefit from insolvency protection in accordance with paragraphs (1) to (5); and

       (b)   provide the traveller with a copy of these Regulations.

(8)   In order to comply with paragraph (7), the trader facilitating a linked travel arrangement must provide the traveller with the information referred to in that paragraph—

       (a)   using the form and wording set out in Schedule 6, where the trader facilitates an online linked travel arrangement within the meaning of regulation 2(3)(a) and the trader is a carrier selling a return ticket;

       (b)   using the form and wording set out in Schedule 7, where the trader facilitates an online linked travel arrangement within the meaning of regulation 2(3)(a) and the trader is not a carrier selling a return ticket;

       (c)   using the form and wording set out in Schedule 8, where the linked travel arrangement is an arrangement within the meaning of regulation 2(3)(a) and the contract is concluded in the simultaneous physical presence of the trader (other than a carrier selling a return ticket) and the traveller;

       (d)   using the form and wording set out in Schedule 9, where the trader facilitates an online linked travel arrangement within the meaning of regulation 2(3)(b) and the trader is a carrier selling a return ticket; and

       (e)   using the form and wording set out in Schedule 10, where the trader facilitates an online linked travel arrangement within the meaning of regulation 2(3)(b) and the trader not a carrier selling a return ticket.

(9)   Where a linked travel arrangement is not an arrangement of the kind described in sub-paragraphs (a) to (e) of paragraph (8), the trader must provide the information referred to in paragraph (7)—

(a) in any form set out in Schedule 6, 7, 8, 9 or 10 which the trader considers is most appropriate for the purposes of providing the information, taking into account the particular circumstances of the linked travel arrangement being facilitated; and

(b) if necessary, making such amendments to that form as are reasonably required to provide the information clearly.

(10) A trader who fails to comply with any provision of paragraphs (1) to (9) commits an offence and is liable—

(a) on summary conviction, to a fine in England and Wales, or in Scotland and Northern Ireland to a fine not exceeding the statutory maximum;

(b) on conviction on indictment, to a fine.

(11) Where the trader facilitating a linked travel arrangement does not comply with the requirements set out in this regulation, the rights and obligations specified in regulations 9 and 12 to 14 and in Part 4 apply in relation to the travel services included in the linked travel arrangement.

(12) Where a linked travel arrangement is the result of the conclusion of a contract between a traveller and a trader who does not facilitate the linked travel arrangement, that trader must inform the trader facilitating the linked travel arrangement of the conclusion of the relevant contract.

PART 6
GENERAL PROVISIONS

27. Specific obligations of the retailer where the organiser is established outside the United Kingdom

(1) Where—

(a) an organiser is established outside the United Kingdom, and

(b) a retailer established in the United Kingdom sells or offers for sale packages combined by that organiser,

the retailer is subject to the obligations for organisers set out in Parts 4 and 5, unless the retailer provides evidence that the organiser complies with those Parts.

28. Liability for booking errors

(1) The provisions of this regulation are implied as a term in every package travel contract.

(2) A trader is liable—

(a) for any errors due to technical defects in the booking system which are attributable to that trader; and

(b) where the trader agrees to arrange the booking of a package or of travel services which are part of linked travel arrangements, for the errors made during the booking process.

(3) A trader is not liable for booking errors which—

(a) are attributable to the traveller; or

(b) are caused by unavoidable and extraordinary circumstances.

29. Right of redress

(1) Where an organiser or, in a case under regulation 27, a retailer—

(a) pays compensation,

(b) grants a price reduction, or

(c) meets the other obligations incumbent on the organiser or the retailer under these Regulations,

the organiser or retailer may seek redress from any third parties which contributed to the event triggering compensation, a price reduction or other obligations.

30. Rights and obligations under these Regulations

(1) A declaration by an organiser of a package or a trader facilitating a linked travel arrangement that—

(a) the organiser or trader is acting exclusively as a travel service provider, as an intermediary or in any other capacity, or

    (b)   a package or a linked travel arrangement does not constitute a package or a linked travel arrangement,

does not absolve that organiser or trader from the obligations imposed upon them under these Regulations.

(2)   A traveller may not waive any right granted to the traveller by these Regulations.

(3)   Any contractual arrangement or any statement by the traveller which—

    (a)   directly or indirectly waives or restricts the rights conferred on travellers pursuant to these Regulations, or

    (b)   aims to circumvent the application of these Regulations,

is not binding on the traveller.

PART 7
ENFORCEMENT

31.   Enforcement authority

(1)   Every local weights and measures authority in Great Britain is to be an enforcement authority for the purposes of regulations 5, 7, 19, 25 and 26 ("the relevant regulations"), and it is the duty of each such authority to enforce those provisions within their area.

(2)   The Civil Aviation Authority is to be an enforcement authority for the purposes of the relevant regulations.

(3)   The Department for the Economy in Northern Ireland is to be an enforcement authority for the purposes of the relevant regulations, and it is the duty of the Department to enforce those provisions within Northern Ireland.

32.   Due diligence defence

(1)   Subject to the following provisions of this regulation, in proceedings against any person for an offence under regulation 5(5), 7(12), 19(9), 25 or 26(10), it is a defence for that person to show that the person took all reasonable steps and exercised all due diligence to avoid committing the offence.

(2)   Where in any proceedings against any person for such an offence the defence provided by paragraph (1) involves an allegation that the commission of the offence was due to—

    (a)   the act or default of another; or

    (b)   reliance on information given by another,

that person is not, without the leave of the court, entitled to rely on the defence unless, at least 7 clear days before the hearing of the proceedings, or, in Scotland, the trial diet, the person has served a notice under paragraph (3) on the person bringing the proceedings.

(3)   A notice under this paragraph must give such information identifying or assisting in the identification of the person who committed the act or default or gave the information as is in the possession of the person serving the notice at the time the person serves it.

(4)   A person is not entitled to rely on the defence provided by paragraph (1) by reason of the person's reliance on information supplied by another, unless the person shows that it was reasonable in all the circumstances for the person to have relied on the information, having regard in particular to—

    (a)   the steps which the person took, and those which might reasonably have been taken, for the purpose of verifying the information; and

    (b)   whether the person had any reason to disbelieve the information.

33.   Liability of persons other than the principal offender

(1)   Where the commission by any person of an offence under regulation 5(5), 7(12), 19(9), 25 or 26(10) is due to an act or default committed by some other person in the course of any business of that person, the other commits the offence and may be proceeded against and punished by virtue of this paragraph whether or not proceedings are taken against the first-mentioned person.

(2)   Where a body corporate commits an offence under any of the provisions mentioned in paragraph (1) (including where it is so committed by virtue of that paragraph) in respect of any act or default which is shown to have been committed with the

consent or connivance of, or to be attributable to any neglect on the part of, any director, manager, secretary or other similar officer of the body corporate or any person who was purporting to act in any such capacity, both that person and the body corporate commit that offence and are liable to be proceeded against and punished accordingly.

(3) Where the affairs of a body corporate are managed by its members, paragraph (2) applies in relation to the acts and defaults of a member in connection with that member's functions of management as if the member were a director of the body corporate.

(4) Where an offence under any of the provisions mentioned in paragraph (1) committed in Scotland by a Scottish partnership is proved to have been committed with the consent or connivance of, or to be attributable to neglect on the part of, a partner, the partner (as well as the partnership) commits the offence and liable to be proceeded against and punished accordingly.

34. Prosecution time limit

(1) No proceedings for an offence under regulation 5(5), 7(12), 19(9), 25 or 26(10) is to be commenced after—
   (a) the end of the period of 3 years beginning within the date of the commission of the offence, or
   (b) the end of the period of 1 year beginning with the date of the discovery of the offence by the prosecutor,
   whichever is the earlier.

(2) For the purposes of this regulation, a certificate signed by or on behalf of the prosecutor and stating the date on which the offence was discovered by the prosecutor is conclusive evidence of that fact; and a certificate stating that matter and purporting to be so signed is to be treated as so signed unless the contrary is proved.

(3) In relation to proceedings in Scotland, subsection (3) of section 331 of the Criminal Procedure (Scotland) Act 1975 applies for the purposes of this regulation as it applies for the purposes of that section.

35. Saving for civil consequences

No contract is void or unenforceable, and no right of action in civil proceedings in respect of any loss arises, by reason only of the commission of an offence under regulations 5(5), 7(12), 19(9), 25 or 26(10).

36. Terms implied in contract

Where it is provided in these Regulations that a term or condition is implied in the contract it is so implied irrespective of the law which governs the contract.

PART 9
REVIEW PROVISIONS

39. Review

(1) The Secretary of State must, from time to time—
   (a) carry out a review of the regulatory provision contained in these Regulations; and
   (b) publish a report setting out the conclusions of the review.

(2) The first report must be published before 1st July 2023.

(3) Subsequent reports must be published at intervals not exceeding 5 years.

(4) Section 30(3) of the Small Business, Enterprise and Employment Act 2015 requires that a review carried out under this regulation must, so far as is reasonable, have regard to how the Directive is implemented in other member States.

(5) Section 30(4) of the Small Business, Enterprise and Employment Act 2015 requires that a report published under this regulation must, in particular—
   (a) set out the objectives intended to be achieved by the regulatory provision referred to in paragraph (1)(a);
   (b) assess the extent to which those objectives are achieved;
   (c) assess whether those objectives remain appropriate; and

(d)   if those objectives remain appropriate, assess the extent to which they could be achieved in another way which involves less onerous regulatory provision.

(6)   In this regulation, "regulatory provision" has the same meaning as in sections 28 to 32 of the Small Business, Enterprise and Employment Act 2015 (see section 32 of that Act).

		Regulations 5(1)and (3)(a),
	SCHEDULE 1	6(1) and (3), 7(2)(a) and 11(3)(a)

INFORMATION TO BE PROVIDED TO THE TRAVELLER, WHERE APPLICABLE, BEFORE THE CONCLUSION OF THE PACKAGE TRAVEL CONTRACT

1.   The main characteristics of the travel services specified in paragraphs 2 to 10.
2.   The travel destination, the itinerary and periods of stay, with dates and, where accommodation is included, the number of nights included.
3.   The means, characteristics and categories of transport, the points, dates and time of departure and return, the duration and places of intermediate stops and transport connections.
4.   Where the exact time of departure and return is not yet determined, the organiser and, where applicable, the retailer, must inform the traveller of the approximate time of departure and return.
5.   The location, main features and, where applicable, tourist category of the accommodation under the rules of the country of destination.
6.   The meals which are included in the package.
7.   The visits, excursions or other services included in the total price agreed for the package.
8.   Where it is not apparent from the context, whether any of the travel services are to be provided to the traveller as part of a group and, if so, where possible, the approximate size of the group.
9.   Where the traveller's benefit from other tourist services depends on effective oral communication, the language in which those services are to be carried out.
10.   Whether the trip or holiday is generally suitable for persons with reduced mobility and, upon the traveller's request, the precise information on the suitability of the trip or holiday taking into account the traveller's needs.
11.   The trading name and geographical address of the organiser and, where applicable, of the retailer, as well as their telephone number and, where applicable, e-mail address.
12.   The total price of the package inclusive of taxes and, where applicable, of all additional fees, charges and other costs or, where those costs cannot reasonably be calculated in advance of the conclusion of the contract, an indication of the type of additional costs which the traveller may still have to bear.
13.   The arrangements for payment, including any amount or percentage of the price which is to be paid as a down payment and the timetable for payment of the balance, or financial guarantees to be paid or provided by the traveller.
14.   The minimum number of persons required for the package to take place and the time-limit, referred to in regulation 13(2)(a), before the start of the package for the possible termination of the contract if that number is not reached.
15.   General information on passport and visa requirements, including approximate periods for obtaining visas and information on health formalities, of the country of destination.
16.   Information that the traveller may terminate the contract at any time before the start of the package in return for payment of an appropriate termination fee, or, where applicable, the standardised termination fees requested by the organiser, in accordance with regulation 12(1) to (6).
17.   Information on optional or compulsory insurance to cover the cost of termination of the contract by the traveller or the cost of assistance, including repatriation, in the event of accident, illness or death.

EU LEGISLATION

TREATY ON THE FUNCTIONING OF THE EUROPEAN UNION

CONSUMER PROTECTION

Article 169

1.   In order to promote the interests of consumers and to ensure a high level of consumer protection, the Union shall contribute to protecting the health, safety and economic interests of consumers, as well as to promoting their right to information, education and to organise themselves in order to safeguard their interests.

2.   The Union shall contribute to the attainment of the objectives referred to in paragraph 1 through:

    (a)   measures adopted pursuant to Article 114 in the context of the completion of the internal market;

    (b)   measures which support, supplement and monitor the policy pursued by the Member States.

3.   The European Parliament and the Council, acting in accordance with the ordinary legislative procedure and after consulting the Economic and Social Committee, shall adopt the measures referred to in paragraph 2(b).

4.   Measures adopted pursuant to paragraph 3 shall not prevent any Member State from maintaining or introducing more stringent protective measures. Such measures must be compatible with the Treaties. The Commission shall be notified of them.

COUNCIL DIRECTIVE 85/374/EEC

on the approximation of the laws, regulations and administrative provisions of the Member States concerning liability for defective products

THE COUNCIL OF THE EUROPEAN COMMUNITIES,

Having regard to the Treaty establishing the European Economic Community, and in particular Article 100 thereof,

Having regard to the proposal from the Commission,

Having regard to the opinion of the European Parliament,

Having regard to the opinion of the Economic and Social Committee,

Whereas approximation of the laws of the Member States concerning the liability of the producer for damage caused by the defectiveness of his products is necessary because the existing divergences may distort competition and affect the movement of goods within the common market and entail a differing degree of protection of the consumer against damage caused by a defective product to his health or property;

Whereas liability without fault on the part of the producer is the sole means of adequately solving the problem, peculiar to our age of increasing technicality, of a fair apportionment of the risks inherent in modern technological production;

Whereas liability without fault should apply only to movables which have been industrially produced; whereas, as a result, it is appropriate to exclude liability for agricultural products and game, except where they have undergone a processing of an industrial nature which could cause a defect in these products; whereas the liability provided for in this Directive should also apply to movables which are used in the construction of immovables or are installed in immovables;

Whereas protection of the consumer requires that all producers involved in the production process should be made liable, in so far as their finished product, component part or any raw material supplied by them was defective; whereas, for the same reason, liability should extend to importers of products into the Community and to persons who present themselves as producers by affixing their name, trade mark or other distinguishing feature or who supply a product the producer of which cannot be identified;

Whereas, in situations where several persons are liable for the same damage, the protection of the consumer requires that the injured person should be able to claim full compensation for the damage from any one of them; whereas, to protect the physical well-being and property of the consumer, the defectiveness of the product should be determined by reference not to its fitness for use but to the lack of the safety which the public at large is entitled to expect; whereas the safety is assessed by excluding any misuse of the product not reasonable under the circumstances;

Whereas a fair apportionment of risk between the injured person and the producer implies that the producer should be able to free himself from liability if he furnishes proof as to the existence of certain exonerating circumstances;

Whereas the protection of the consumer requires that the liability of the producer remains unaffected by acts or omissions of other persons having contributed to cause the damage; whereas, however, the contributory negligence of the injured person may be taken into account to reduce or disallow such liability;

Whereas the protection of the consumer requires compensation for death and personal injury as well as compensation for damage to property; whereas the latter should nevertheless be limited to goods for private use or consumption and be subject to a deduction of a lower threshold of a fixed amount in order to avoid litigation in an excessive number of cases; whereas this Directive should not prejudice compensation for pain and suffering and other non-material damages payable, where appropriate, under the law applicable to the case; whereas a uniform period of limitation for the bringing of action for compensation is in the interests both of the injured person and of the producer;

Whereas products age in the course of time, higher safety standards are developed and the state of science and technology progresses; whereas, therefore, it would not be reasonable to make the producer liable for an unlimited period for the defectiveness of his product; whereas, therefore, liability should expire after a reasonable length of time, without prejudice to claims pending at law;

Whereas, to achieve effective protection of consumers, no contractual derogation should be permitted as regards the liability of the producer in relation to the injured person;

Whereas under the legal systems of the Member States an injured party may have a claim for damages based on grounds of contractual liability or on grounds of non-contractual liability other than that provided for in this Directive; in so far as these provisions also serve to attain the objective of effective protection of consumers, they should remain unaffected by this Directive; whereas, in so far as effective protection of consumers in the sector of pharmaceutical products is already also attained in a Member State under a special liability system, claims based on this system should similarly remain possible;

Whereas, to the extent that liability for nuclear injury or damage is already covered in all Member States by adequate special rules, it has been possible to exclude damage of this type from the scope of this Directive;

Whereas, since the exclusion of primary agricultural products and game from the scope of this Directive may be felt, in certain Member States, in view of what is expected for the protection of consumers, to restrict unduly such protection, it should be possible for a Member State to extend liability to such products;

Whereas, for similar reasons, the possibility offered to a producer to free himself from liability if he proves that the state of scientific and technical knowledge at the time when he put the product into circulation was not such as to enable the existence of a defect to be discovered may be felt in certain Member States to restrict unduly the protection of the consumer; whereas it should therefore be possible for a Member State to maintain in its legislation or to provide by new legislation that this exonerating circumstance is not admitted; whereas, in the case of new legislation, making use of this derogation should, however, be subject to a Community stand-still procedure, in order to raise, if possible, the level of protection in a uniform manner throughout the Community;

Whereas, taking into account the legal traditions in most of the Member States, it is inappropriate to set any financial ceiling on the producer's liability without fault; whereas, in so far as there are, however, differing traditions, it seems possible to admit that a Member State may derogate from the principle of unlimited liability by providing a limit for the total liability of the producer for damage resulting from a death or personal injury and caused by identical items with the same defect, provided that this limit is established at a level sufficiently high to guarantee adequate protection of the consumer and the correct functioning of the common market;

Whereas the harmonization resulting from this cannot be total at the present stage, but opens the way towards greater harmonization; whereas it is therefore necessary that the Council receive at regular intervals, reports from the Commission on the application of this Directive, accompanied, as the case may be, by appropriate proposals;

Whereas it is particularly important in this respect that a re-examination be carried out of those parts of the Directive relating to the derogations open to the Member States, at the expiry of a period of sufficient length to gather practical experience on the effects of these derogations on the protection of consumers and on the functioning of the common market,

HAS ADOPTED THIS DIRECTIVE:

Article 1

The producer shall be liable for damage caused by a defect in his product.

Article 2

For the purpose of this Directive 'product' means all movables, with the exception of primary agricultural products and game, even though incorporated into another movable or into an immovable. 'Primary agricultural products' means the products of the soil, of stock-farming and of fisheries, excluding products which have undergone initial processing. 'Product' includes electricity.

Article 3

1.   'Producer' means the manufacturer of a finished product, the producer of any raw material or the manufacturer of a component part and any person who, by putting his name, trade mark or other distinguishing feature on the product presents himself as its producer.
2.   Without prejudice to the liability of the producer, any person who imports into the Community a product for sale, hire, leasing or any form of distribution in the course of his business shall be deemed to be a producer within the meaning of this Directive and shall be responsible as a producer.
3.   Where the producer of the product cannot be identified, each supplier of the product shall be treated as its producer unless he informs the injured person, within a reasonable time, of the identity of the producer or of the person who supplied him with the product. The same shall apply, in the case of an imported product, if this product does not indicate the identity of the importer referred to in paragraph 2, even if the name of the producer is indicated.

Article 4

The injured person shall be required to prove the damage, the defect and the causal relationship between defect and damage.

Article 5

Where, as a result of the provisions of this Directive, two or more persons are liable for the same damage, they shall be liable jointly and severally, without prejudice to the provisions of national law concerning the rights of contribution or recourse.

Article 6

1.   A product is defective when it does not provide the safety which a person is entitled to expect, taking all circumstances into account, including:
        (a)   the presentation of the product;
        (b)   the use to which it could reasonably be expected that the product would be put;
        (c)   the time when the product was put into circulation.
2.   A product shall not be considered defective for the sole reason that a better product is subsequently put into circulation.

Article 7

The producer shall not be liable as a result of this Directive if he proves:
(a)   that he did not put the product into circulation; or
(b)   that, having regard to the circumstances, it is probable that the defect which caused the damage did not exist at the time when the product was put into circulation by him or that this defect came into being afterwards; or

(c)   that the product was neither manufactured by him for sale or any form of distribution for economic purpose nor manufactured or distributed by him in the course of his business; or

(d)   that the defect is due to compliance of the product with mandatory regulations issued by the public authorities; or

(e)   that the state of scientific and technical knowledge at the time when he put the product into circulation was not such as to enable the existence of the defect to be discovered; or

(f)   in the case of a manufacturer of a component, that the defect is attributable to the design of the product in which the component has been fitted or to the instructions given by the manufacturer of the product.

Article 8

1.   Without prejudice to the provisions of national law concerning the right of contribution or recourse, the liability of the producer shall not be reduced when the damage is caused both by a defect in product and by the act or omission of a third party.

2.   The liability of the producer may be reduced or disallowed when, having regard to all the circumstances, the damage is caused both by a defect in the product and by the fault of the injured person or any person for whom the injured person is responsible.

Article 9

For the purpose of Article 1, 'damage' means:

(a)   damage caused by death or by personal injuries;

(b)   damage to, or destruction of, any item of property other than the defective product itself, with a lower threshold of 500 ECU, provided that the item of property:

   (i)   is of a type ordinarily intended for private use or consumption, and

   (ii)   was used by the injured person mainly for his own private use or consumption.

This Article shall be without prejudice to national provisions relating to non-material damage.

Article 10

1.   Member States shall provide in their legislation that a limitation period of three years shall apply to proceedings for the recovery of damages as provided for in this Directive.

The limitation period shall begin to run from the day on which the plaintiff became aware, or should reasonably have become aware, of the damage, the defect and the identity of the producer.

2.   The laws of Member States regulating suspension or interruption of the limitation period shall not be affected by this Directive.

Article 11

Member States shall provide in their legislation that the rights conferred upon the injured person pursuant to this Directive shall be extinguished upon the expiry of a period of 10 years from the date on which the producer put into circulation the actual product which caused the damage, unless the injured person has in the meantime instituted proceedings against the producer.

Article 12

The liability of the producer arising from this Directive may not, in relation to the injured person, be limited or excluded by a provision limiting his liability or exempting him from liability.

Article 13

This Directive shall not affect any rights which an injured person may have according to the rules of the law of contractual or non-contractual liability or a special liability system existing at the moment when this Directive is notified.

Article 14

This Directive shall not apply to injury or damage arising from nuclear accidents and covered by international conventions ratified by the Member States.

Article 15

1.   Each Member State may:

   (a)   by way of derogation from Article 2, provide in its legislation that within the meaning of Article 1 of this Directive 'product' also means primary agricultural products and game;

(b) by way of derogation from Article 7(e), maintain or, subject to the procedure set out in paragraph 2 of this Article, provide in this legislation that the producer shall be liable even if he proves that the state of scientific and technical knowledge at the time when he put the product into circulation was not such as to enable the existence of a defect to be discovered.

2. A Member State wishing to introduce the measure specified in paragraph 1(b) shall communicate the text of the proposed measure to the Commission. The Commission shall inform the other Member States thereof.

The Member State concerned shall hold the proposed measure in abeyance for nine months after the Commission is informed and provided that in the meantime the Commission has not submitted to the Council a proposal amending this Directive on the relevant matter. However, if within three months of receiving the said information, the Commission does not advise the Member State concerned that it intends submitting such a proposal to the Council, the Member State may take the proposed measure immediately.

If the Commission does submit to the Council such a proposal amending this Directive within the aforementioned nine months, the Member State concerned shall hold the proposed measure in abeyance for a further period of 18 months from the date on which the proposal is submitted.

3. Ten years after the date of notification of this Directive, the Commission shall submit to the Council a report on the effect that rulings by the courts as to the application of Article 7(e) and of paragraph 1(b) of this Article have on consumer protection and the functioning of the common market. In the light of this report the Council, acting on a proposal from the Commission and pursuant to the terms of Article 100 of the Treaty, shall decide whether to repeal Article 7(e).

Article 16

1. Any Member State may provide that a producer's total liability for damage resulting from a death or personal injury and caused by identical items with the same defect shall be limited to an amount which may not be less than 70 million ECU.

2. Ten years after the date of notification of this Directive, the Commission shall submit to the Council a report on the effect on consumer protection and the functioning of the common market of the implementation of the financial limit on liability by those Member States which have used the option provided for in paragraph 1. In the light of this report the Council, acting on a proposal from the Commission and pursuant to the terms of Article 100 of the Treaty, shall decide whether to repeal paragraph 1.

Article 17

This Directive shall not apply to products put into circulation before the date on which the provisions referred to in Article 19 enter into force.

Article 18

1. For the purposes of this Directive, the ECU shall be that defined by Regulation (EEC) No 3180/ 78(1), as amended by Regulation (EEC) No 2626/84. The equivalent in national currency shall initially be calculated at the rate obtaining on the date of adoption of this Directive.

2. Every five years the Council, acting on a proposal from the Commission, shall examine and, if need be, revise the amounts in this Directive, in the light of economic and monetary trends in the Community.

Article 19

1. Member States shall bring into force, not later than three years from the date of notification of this Directive, the laws, regulations and administrative provisions necessary to comply with this Directive. They shall forthwith inform the Commission thereof.

2. The procedure set out in Article 15(2) shall apply from the date of notification of this Directive.

Article 20

Member States shall communicate to the Commission the texts of the main provisions of national law which they subsequently adopt in the field governed by this Directive.

Article 21

Every five years the Commission shall present a report to the Council on the application of this Directive and, if necessary, shall submit appropriate proposals to it.

Article 22

This Directive is addressed to the Member States.

Done at Brussels, 25 July 1985.

DIRECTIVE 1999/44/EC OF THE EUROPEAN PARLIAMENT AND OF THE COUNCIL OF 25 MAY 1999

on certain aspects of the sale of consumer goods and associated guarantees

THE EUROPEAN PARLIAMENT AND THE COUNCIL OF THE EUROPEAN UNION,

Having regard to the Treaty establishing the European Community, and in particular Article 95 thereof,

Having regard to the proposal from the Commission,

Having regard to the opinion of the Economic and Social Committee,

Acting in accordance with the procedure laid down in Article 251 of the Treaty in the light of the joint text approved by the Conciliation Committee on 18 May 1999,

(1) Whereas Article 153(1) and (3) of the Treaty provides that the Community should contribute to the achievement of a high level of consumer protection by the measures it adopts pursuant to Article 95 thereof;

(2) Whereas the internal market comprises an area without internal frontiers in which the free movement of goods, persons, services and capital is guaranteed; whereas free movement of goods concerns not only transactions by persons acting in the course of a business but also transactions by private individuals; whereas it implies that consumers resident in one Member State should be free to purchase goods in the territory of another Member State on the basis of a uniform minimum set of fair rules governing the sale of consumer goods;

(3) Whereas the laws of the Member States concerning the sale of consumer goods are somewhat disparate, with the result that national consumer goods markets differ from one another and that competition between sellers may be distorted;

(4) Whereas consumers who are keen to benefit from the large market by purchasing goods in Member States other than their State of residence play a fundamental role in the completion of the internal market; whereas the artificial reconstruction of frontiers and the compartmentalisation of markets should be prevented; whereas the opportunities available to consumers have been greatly broadened by new communication technologies which allow ready access to distribution systems in other Member States or in third countries; whereas, in the absence of minimum harmonisation of the rules governing the sale of consumer goods, the development of the sale of goods through the medium of new distance communication technologies risks being impeded;

(5) Whereas the creation of a common set of minimum rules of consumer law, valid no matter where goods are purchased within the Community, will strengthen consumer confidence and enable consumers to make the most of the internal market;

(6) Whereas the main difficulties encountered by consumers and the main source of disputes with sellers concern the non-conformity of goods with the contract; whereas it is therefore appropriate to approximate national legislation governing the sale of consumer goods in this respect, without however impinging on provisions and principles of national law relating to contractual and non-contractual liability;

(7) Whereas the goods must, above all, conform with the contractual specifications; whereas the principle of conformity with the contract may be considered as common to the different national legal traditions whereas in certain national legal traditions it may not be possible to rely solely on this principle to ensure a minimum level of protection for the consumer; whereas under such legal traditions, in particular, additional national provisions may be useful to ensure that the consumer is protected in cases where the parties have agreed no specific contractual terms or where the parties have concluded contractual terms or

agreements which directly or indirectly waive or restrict the rights of the consumer and which, to the extent that these rights result from this Directive, are not binding on the consumer;

(8) Whereas, in order to facilitate the application of the principle of conformity with the contract, it is useful to introduce a rebuttable presumption of conformity with the contract covering the most common situations, whereas that presumption does not restrict the principle of freedom of contract; whereas, furthermore, in the absence of specific contractual terms, as well as where the minimum protection clause is applied, the elements mentioned in this presumption may be used to determine the lack of conformity of the goods with the contract; whereas the quality and performance which consumers can reasonably expect will depend *inter alia* on whether the goods are new or second-hand; whereas the elements mentioned in the presumption are cumulative; whereas, if the circumstances of the case render any particular element manifestly inappropriate, the remaining elements of the presumption nevertheless still apply;

(9) Whereas the seller should be directly liable to the consumer for the conformity of the goods with the contract; whereas this is the traditional solution enshrined in the legal orders of the Member States whereas nevertheless the seller should be free, as provided for by national law, to pursue remedies against the producer, a previous seller in the same chain of contracts or any other intermediary, unless he has renounced that entitlement; whereas this Directive does not affect the principle of freedom of contract between the seller, the producer, a previous seller or any other intermediary; whereas the rules governing against whom and how the seller may pursue such remedies are to be determined by national law;

(10) Whereas, in the case of non-conformity of the goods with the contract, consumers should be entitled to have the goods restored to conformity with the contract free of charge, choosing either repair or replacement, or, failing this, to have the price reduced or the contract rescinded;

(11) Whereas the consumer in the first place may require the seller to repair the goods or to replace them unless those remedies are impossible or disproportionate; whereas whether a remedy is disproportionate should be determined objectively; whereas a remedy would be disproportionate if it imposed, in comparison with the other remedy, unreasonable costs; whereas, in order to determine whether the costs are unreasonable, the costs of one remedy should be significantly higher than the costs of the other remedy;

(12) Whereas in cases of a lack of conformity, the seller may always offer the consumer, by way of settlement, any available remedy; whereas it is for the consumer to decide whether to accept or reject this proposal;

(13) Whereas, in order to enable consumers to take advantage of the internal market and to buy consumer goods in another Member State, it should be recommended that, in the interests of consumers, the producers of consumer goods that are marketed in several Member States attach to the product a list with at least one contact address in every Member State where the product is marketed;

(14) Whereas the references to the time of delivery do not imply that Member States have to change their rules on the passing of the risk;

(15) Whereas Member States may provide that any reimbursement to the consumer may be reduced to take account of the use the consumer has had of the goods since they were delivered to him; whereas the detailed arrangements whereby rescission of the contract is effected may be laid down in national law;

(16) Whereas the specific nature of second-hand goods makes it generally impossible to replace them; whereas therefore the consumer's right of replacement is generally not available for these goods; whereas for such goods, Member States may enable the parties to agree a shortened period of liability;

(17) Whereas it is appropriate to limit in time the period during which the seller is liable for any lack of conformity which exists at the time of delivery of the goods; whereas Member States may also provide for a limitation on the period during which consumers can exercise their rights, provided such a period does not expire within two years from the time of delivery; whereas where, under national legislation, the time when a limitation period starts is not the time of delivery of the goods, the total duration of the limitation period provided for by national law may not be shorter than two years from the time of delivery;

(18)   Whereas Member States may provide for suspension or interruption of the period during which any lack of conformity must become apparent and of the limitation period, where applicable and in accordance with their national law, in the event of repair, replacement or negotiations between seller and consumer with a view to an amicable settlement;

(19)   Whereas Member States should be allowed to set a period within which the consumer must inform the seller of any lack of conformity; whereas Member States may ensure a higher level of protection for the consumer by not introducing such an obligation; whereas in any case consumers throughout the Community should have at least two months in which to inform the seller that a lack of conformity exists;

(20)   Whereas Member States should guard against such a period placing at a disadvantage consumers shopping across borders; whereas all Member States should inform the Commission of their use of this provision; whereas the Commission should monitor the effect of the varied application of this provision on consumers and on the internal market; whereas information on the use made of this provision by a Member State should be available to the other Member States and to consumers and consumer organisations throughout the Community; whereas a summary of the situation in all Member States should therefore be published in the *Official Journal of the European Communities;*

(21)   Whereas, for certain categories of goods, it is current practice for sellers and producers to offer guarantees on goods against any defect which becomes apparent within a certain period; whereas this practice can stimulate competition; whereas, while such guarantees are legitimate marketing tools, they should not mislead the consumer whereas, to ensure that consumers are not misled, guarantees should contain certain information, including a statement that the guarantee does not affect the consumer's legal rights;

(22)   Whereas the parties may not, by common consent, restrict or waive the rights granted to consumers, since otherwise the legal protection afforded would be thwarted; whereas this principle should apply also to clauses which imply that the consumer was aware of any lack of conformity of the consumer goods existing at the time the contract was concluded; whereas the protection granted to consumers under this Directive should not be reduced on the grounds that the law of a non-member State has been chosen as being applicable to the contract;

(23)   Whereas legislation and case-law in this area in the various Member States show that there is growing concern to ensure a high level of consumer protection; whereas, in the light of this trend and the experience acquired in implementing this Directive, it may be necessary to envisage more far-reaching harmonisation, notably by providing for the producer's direct liability for defects for which he is responsible;

(24)   Whereas Member States should be allowed to adopt or maintain in force more stringent provisions in the field covered by this Directive to ensure an even higher level of consumer protection;

(25)   Whereas, according to the Commission recommendation of 30 March 1998 on the principles applicable to the bodies responsible for out-of-court settlement of consumer disputes, Member States can create bodies that ensure impartial and efficient handling of complaints in a national and cross-border context and which consumers can use as mediators;

(26)   Whereas it is appropriate, in order to protect the collective interests of consumers, to add this Directive to the list of Directives contained in the Annex to Directive 98/27/EC of the European Parliament and of the Council of 19 May 1998 on injunctions for the protection of consumers interests,

HAVE ADOPTED THIS DIRECTIVE:

Article 1   Scope and definitions

1.   The purpose of this Directive is the approximation of the laws, regulations and administrative provisions of the Member States on certain aspects of the sale of consumer goods and associated guarantees in order to ensure a uniform minimum level of consumer protection in the context of the internal market.

2.   For the purposes of this Directive:

(a)   *consumer:* shall mean any natural person who, in the contracts covered by this Directive, is acting for purposes which are not related to his trade, business or profession:

(b)   *consumer goods:* shall mean any tangible movable item, with the exception of:

      —   goods sold by way of execution or otherwise by authority of law,
      —   water and gas where they are not put up for sale in a limited volume or set quantity,
      —   electricity;

   (c)   *seller:* shall mean any natural or legal person who, under a contract, sells consumer goods in the course of his trade, business or profession;

   (d)   *producer:* shall mean the manufacturer of consumer goods the importer of consumer goods into the territory of the Community or any person purporting to be a producer by placing his name, trade mark or other distinctive sign to the consumer goods;

   (e)   *guarantee:* shall mean any undertaking by a seller or producer to the consumer, given without extra charge to reimburse the price paid or to replace, repair or handle consumer goods in any way if they do not meet the specifications set out in the guarantee statement or in the relevant advertising;

   (f)   *repair:* shall mean, in the event of lack of conformity bringing consumer goods into conformity with the contract of sale.

3.   Member States may provide that the expression 'consumer goods' does not cover second-hand goods sold at public auction where consumers have the opportunity of attending the sale in person.

4.   Contracts for the supply of consumer goods to be manufactured or produced shall also be deemed contracts of sale for the purpose of this Directive.

Article 2   Conformity with the contract

1.   The seller must deliver goods to the consumer which are in conformity with the contract of sale.

2.   Consumer goods are presumed to be in conformity with the contract if they:

   (a)   comply with the description given by the seller and possess the qualities of the goods which the seller has held out in the consumer as a sample or model;

   (b)   are fit for any particular purpose for which the consumer requires them and which he made known to the seller as the time of conclusion of the contract and which the seller has accepted;

   (c)   are fit for the purposes for which goods of the same type are normally used;

   (d)   show the quality and performance which are normal in goods of the same type and which the consumer can reasonably expect, given the nature of the goods and taking into account any public statements on the specific characteristics of the goods made about them by the seller, the producer or his representative, particularly in advertising or on labelling.

3.   There shall be deemed not to be a lack of conformity for the purposes of this Article if, at the time the contract was concluded, the consumer was aware, or could not reasonably be unaware of, the lack of conformity, or if the lack of conformity has its origin in materials supplied by the consumer.

4.   The seller shall not be bound by public statements, as referred to in paragraph 2(d) if he:

      —   shows that he was not, and could not reasonably have been aware of the statement in question,
      —   shows that by the time of conclusion of the contract the statement had been corrected, or
      —   shows that the decision to buy the consumer goods could not have been influenced by the statement.

5.   Any lack of conformity resulting from incorrect installation of the consumer goods shall be deemed to be equivalent to lack of conformity of the goods if installation forms part of the contract of sale of the goods and the goods were installed by the seller or under his responsibility. This shall apply equally if the product, intended to be installed by the consumer, is installed by the consumer and the incorrect installation is due to a shortcoming in the installation instructions.

Article 3   Rights of the consumer

1.   The seller shall be liable to the consumer for any lack of conformity which exists at the time the goods were delivered.

2. In the case of a lack of conformity, the consumer shall be entitled to have the goods brought into conformity free of charge by repair or replacement, in accordance with paragraph 3, or to have an appropriate reduction made in the price or the contract rescinded with regard to those goods, in accordance with paragraphs 5 and 6.

3. In the first place, the consumer may require the seller to repair the goods or he may require the seller to replace them, in either case free of charge, unless this is impossible or disproportionate.

    A remedy shall be deemed to be disproportionate if it imposes costs on the seller which, in comparison with the alternative remedy, are unreasonable, taking into account:
    — the value the goods would have if there were no lack of conformity,
    — the significance of the lack of conformity, and
    — whether the alternative remedy could be completed without significant inconvenience to the consumer.

    Any repair or replacement shall be completed within a reasonable time and without any significant inconvenience to the consumer, taking account of the nature of the goods and the purpose for which the consumer required the goods.

4. The terms 'free of charge' in paragraphs 2 and 3 refer to the necessary costs incurred to bring the goods into conformity, particularly the cost of postage, labour and materials.

5. The consumer may require an appropriate reduction of the price or have the contract rescinded:
    — if the consumer is entitled to neither repair nor replacement, or
    — if the seller has not completed the remedy within a reasonable time, or
    — if the seller has not completed the remedy without significant inconvenience to the consumer.

6. The consumer is not entitled to have the contract rescinded if the lack of conformity is minor.

Article 4   Right of redress

Where the final seller is liable to the consumer because of a lack of conformity resulting from an act or omission by the producer, a previous seller in the same chain of contracts or any other intermediary, the final seller shall be entitled to pursue remedies against the person or persons liable in the contractual chain, the person or persons liable against whom the final seller may pursue remedies, together with the relevant actions and conditions of exercise, shall be determined by national law.

Article 5   Time limits

1. The seller shall be held liable under Article 3 where the lack of conformity becomes apparent within two years as from delivery of the goods. If, under national legislation, the rights laid down in Article 3(2) are subject to a limitation period, that period shall not expire within a period of two years from the time of delivery.

2. Member States may provide that, in order to benefit from his rights, the consumer must inform the seller of the lack of conformity within a period of two months from the date on which he detected such lack of conformity.

    Member States shall inform the Commission of their use of this paragraph. The Commission shall monitor the effect of the existence of this option for the Member States on consumers and on the internal market.

    Not later than 7 January 2003, the Commission shall prepare a report on the use made by Member States of this paragraph. This report shall be published in the *Official Journal of the European Communities*.

3. Unless proved otherwise, any lack of conformity which becomes apparent within six months of delivery of the goods shall be presumed to have existed at the time of delivery unless this presumption is incompatible with the nature of the goods or the nature of the lack of conformity.

Article 6   Guarantees

1. A guarantee shall be legally binding on the offerer under the conditions laid down in the guarantee statement and the associated advertising.

2. The guarantee shall:
    — state that the consumer has legal rights under applicable national legislation governing

the sale of consumer goods and make clear that those rights are not affected by the guarantee,

— set out in plain intelligible language the contents of the guarantee and the essential particulars necessary for making claims under the guarantee, notably the duration and territorial scope of the guarantee as well as the name and address of the guarantor.

3. On request by the consumer, the guarantee shall be made available in writing or feature in another durable medium available and accessible to him.

4. Within its own territory, the Member State in which the consumer goods are marketed may, in accordance with the rules of the Treaty, provide that the guarantee be drafted in one or more languages which it shall determine from among the official languages of the Community.

5. Should a guarantee infringe the requirements of paragraphs 2, 3 or 4, the validity of this guarantee shall in no way be affected, and the consumer can still rely on the guarantee and require that it be honoured.

Article 7   Binding nature

1. Any contractual terms or agreements concluded with the seller before the lack of conformity is brought to the seller's attention which directly or indirectly waive or restrict the rights resulting from this Directive shall, as provided for by national law, not be binding on the consumer.

    Member States may provide that, in the case of second-hand goods, the seller and consumer may agree contractual terms or agreements which have a shorter time period for the liability of the seller than that set down in Article 5(1). Such period may not be less than one year.

2. Member States shall take the necessary measures to ensure that consumers are not deprived of the protection afforded by this Directive as a result of opting for the law of a non-member State as the law applicable to the contract where the contract has a close connection with the territory of the Member States.

Article 8   National law and minimum protection

1. The rights resulting from this Directive shall be exercised without prejudice to other rights which the consumer may invoke under the national rules governing contractual or non-contractual liability.

2. Member States may adopt or maintain in force more stringent provisions, compatible with the Treaty in the field covered by this Directive, to ensure a higher level of consumer protection.

Article 9

Member States shall take appropriate measures to inform the consumer of the national law transposing this Directive and shall encourage, where appropriate, professional organisations to inform consumers of their rights.

Article 11   Transposition

1. Member States shall bring into force the laws, regulations and administrative provisions necessary to comply with this Directive not later than 1 January 2002. They shall forthwith inform the Commission thereof.

    When Member States adopt these measures, they shall contain a reference to this Directive, or shall be accompanied by such reference at the time of their official publication. The procedure for such reference shall be adopted by Member States.

2. Member States shall communicate to the Commission the provisions of national law which they adopt in the field covered by this Directive.

Article 12   Review

The Commission shall, not later than 7 July 2006, review the application of this Directive and submit to the European Parliament and the Council a report. The report shall examine, *inter alia*, the case for introducing the producer's direct liability and if appropriate, shall be accompanied by proposals.

DIRECTIVE 2001/95/EC OF THE EUROPEAN PARLIAMENT AND OF THE COUNCIL

on general product safety

THE EUROPEAN PARLIAMENT AND THE COUNCIL OF THE EUROPEAN UNION,

Having regard to the Treaty establishing the European Community, and in particular Article 95 thereof,

Having regard to the proposal from the Commission,

Having regard to the opinion of the Economic and Social Committee,

Acting in accordance with the procedure referred to in Article 251 of the Treaty, in the light of the joint text approved by the Conciliation Committee on 2 August 2001,

Whereas:

(1)   Under Article 16 of Council Directive 92/59/EEC of 29 June 1992 on general product safety, the Council was to decide, four years after the date set for the implementation of the said Directive, on the basis of a report of the Commission on the experience acquired, together with appropriate proposals, whether to adjust Directive 92/59/EEC. It is necessary to amend Directive 92/59/EEC in several respects, in order to complete, reinforce or clarify some of its provisions in the light of experience as well as new and relevant developments on consumer product safety, together with the changes made to the Treaty, especially in Articles 152 concerning public health and 153 concerning consumer protection, and in the light of the precautionary principle. Directive 92/59/EEC should therefore be recast in the interest of clarity. This recasting leaves the safety of services outside the scope of this Directive, since the Commission intends to identify the needs, possibilities and priorities for Community action on the safety of services and liability of service providers, with a view to presenting appropriate proposals.

(2)   It is important to adopt measures with the aim of improving the functioning of the internal market, comprising an area without internal frontiers in which the free movement of goods, persons, services and capital is assured.

(3)   In the absence of Community provisions, horizontal legislation of the Member States on product safety, imposing in particular a general obligation on economic operators to market only safe products, might differ in the level of protection afforded to consumers. Such disparities, and the absence of horizontal legislation in some Member States, would be liable to create barriers to trade and distortion of competition within the internal market.

(4)   In order to ensure a high level of consumer protection, the Community must contribute to protecting the health and safety of consumers. Horizontal Community legislation introducing a general product safety requirement, and containing provisions on the general obligations of producers and distributors, on the enforcement of Community product safety requirements and on rapid exchange of information and action at Community level in certain cases, should contribute to that aim.

(5)   It is very difficult to adopt Community legislation for every product which exists or which may be developed; there is a need for a broad-based, legislative framework of a horizontal nature to deal with such products, and also to cover lacunae, in particular pending revision of the existing specific legislation, and to complement provisions in existing or forthcoming specific legislation, in particular with a view to ensuring a high level of protection of safety and health of consumers, as required by Article 95 of the Treaty.

(6)   It is therefore necessary to establish at Community level a general safety requirement for any product placed on the market, or otherwise supplied or made available to consumers, intended for consumers, or likely to be used by consumers under reasonably foreseeable conditions even if not intended for them. In all these cases the products under consideration can pose risks for the health and safety of consumers which must be prevented. Certain second-hand goods should nevertheless be excluded by their very nature.

(7)   This Directive should apply to products irrespective of the selling techniques, including distance and electronic selling.

(8)   The safety of products should be assessed taking into account all the relevant aspects, in particular the categories of consumers which can be particularly vulnerable to the risks posed by the products under consideration, in particular children and the elderly.

(9)   This Directive does not cover services, but in order to secure the attainment of the protection objectives in question, its provisions should also apply to products that are supplied or made available to consumers in the context of service provision for use by them. The safety of the equipment used by service providers themselves to supply a service to consumers does not come within the scope of this Directive since it has to be dealt with in conjunction with the safety of the service provided. In particular, equipment on which consumers ride or travel which is operated by a service provider is excluded from the scope of this Directive.

(10)   Products which are designed exclusively for professional use but have subsequently migrated to the consumer market should be subject to the requirements of this Directive because they can pose risks to consumer health and safety when used under reasonably foreseeable conditions.

(11)   In the absence of more specific provisions, within the framework of Community legislation covering safety of the products concerned, all the provisions of this Directive should apply in order to ensure consumer health and safety.

(12)   If specific Community legislation sets out safety requirements covering only certain risks or categories of risks, with regard to the products concerned the obligations of economic operators in respect of these risks are those determined by the provisions of the specific legislation, while the general safety requirement of this Directive should apply to the other risks.

(13)   The provisions of this Directive relating to the other obligations of producers and distributors, the obligations and powers of the Member States, the exchanges of information and rapid intervention situations and dissemination of information and confidentiality apply in the case of products covered by specific rules of Community law, if those rules do not already contain such obligations.

(14)   In order to facilitate the effective and consistent application of the general safety requirement of this Directive, it is important to establish European voluntary standards covering certain products and risks in such a way that a product which conforms to a national standard transposing a European standard is to be presumed to be in compliance with the said requirement.

(15)   With regard to the aims of this Directive, European standards should be established by European standardisation bodies, under mandates set by the Commission assisted by appropriate Committees. In order to ensure that products in compliance with the standards fulfil the general safety requirement, the Commission assisted by a committee composed of representatives of the Member States, should fix the requirements that the standards must meet. These requirements should be included in the mandates to the standardisation bodies.

(16)   In the absence of specific regulations and when the European standards established under mandates set by the Commission are not available or recourse is not made to such standards, the safety of products should be assessed taking into account in particular national standards transposing any other relevant European or international standards, Commission recommendations or national standards, international standards, codes of good practice, the state of the art and the safety which consumers may reasonably expect. In this context, the Commission's recommendations may facilitate the consistent and effective application of this Directive pending the introduction of European standards or as regards the risks and/ or products for which such standards are deemed not to be possible or appropriate.

(17)   Appropriate independent certification recognised by the competent authorities may facilitate proof of compliance with the applicable product safety criteria.

(18)   It is appropriate to supplement the duty to observe the general safety requirement by other obligations on economic operators because action by such operators is necessary to prevent risks to consumers under certain circumstances.

(19)   The additional obligations on producers should include the duty to adopt measures commensurate with the characteristics of the products, enabling them to be informed of the risks that these products may present, to supply consumers with information enabling them to assess and prevent risks, to warn consumers of the risks posed by dangerous products already supplied to them, to withdraw those products from the market and, as a last resort, to recall them when necessary, which may involve, depending on the provisions applicable in the Member States, an appropriate form of compensation, for example exchange or reimbursement.

(20) Distributors should help in ensuring compliance with the applicable safety requirements. The obligations placed on distributors apply in proportion to their respective responsibilities. In particular, it may prove impossible, in the context of charitable activities, to provide the competent authorities with information and documentation on possible risks and origin of the product in the case of isolated used objects provided by private individuals.

(21) Both producers and distributors should cooperate with the competent authorities in action aimed at preventing risks and inform them when they conclude that certain products supplied are dangerous. The conditions regarding the provision of such information should be set in this Directive to facilitate its effective application, while avoiding an excessive burden for economic operators and the authorities.

(22) In order to ensure the effective enforcement of the obligations incumbent on producers and distributors, the Member States should establish or designate authorities which are responsible for monitoring product safety and have powers to take appropriate measures, including the power to impose effective, proportionate and dissuasive penalties, and ensure appropriate coordination between the various designated authorities.

(23) It is necessary in particular for the appropriate measures to include the power for Member States to order or organise, immediately and efficiently, the withdrawal of dangerous products already placed on the market and as a last resort to order, coordinate or organise the recall from consumers of dangerous products already supplied to them. Those powers should be applied when producers and distributors fail to prevent risks to consumers in accordance with their obligations. Where necessary, the appropriate powers and procedures should be available to the authorities to decide and apply any necessary measures rapidly.

(24) The safety of consumers depends to a great extent on the active enforcement of Community product safety requirements. The Member States should, therefore, establish systematic approaches to ensure the effectiveness of market surveillance and other enforcement activities and should ensure their openness to the public and interested parties.

(25) Collaboration between the enforcement authorities of the Member States is necessary in ensuring the attainment of the protection objectives of this Directive. It is, therefore, appropriate to promote the operation of a European network of the enforcement authorities of the Member States to facilitate, in a coordinated manner with other Community procedures, in particular the Community Rapid Information System (RAPEX), improved collaboration at operational level on market surveillance and other enforcement activities, in particular risk assessment, testing of products, exchange of expertise and scientific knowledge, execution of joint surveillance projects and tracing, withdrawing or recalling dangerous products.

(26) It is necessary, for the purpose of ensuring a consistent, high level of consumer health and safety protection and preserving the unity of the internal market, that the Commission be informed of any measure restricting the placing on the market of a product or requiring its withdrawal or recall from the market. Such measures should be taken in compliance with the provisions of the Treaty, and in particular Articles 28, 29 and 30 thereof.

(27) Effective supervision of product safety requires the setting-up at national and Community levels of a system of rapid exchange of information in situations of serious risk requiring rapid intervention in respect of the safety of a product. It is also appropriate in this Directive to set out detailed procedures for the operation of the system and to give the Commission, assisted by an advisory committee, power to adapt them.

(28) This Directive provides for the establishment of nonbinding guidelines aimed at indicating simple and clear criteria and practical rules which may change, in particular for the purpose of allowing efficient notification of measures restricting the placing on the market of products in the cases referred to in this Directive, whilst taking into account the range of situations dealt with by Member States and economic operators. The guidelines should in particular include criteria for the application of the definition of serious risks in order to facilitate consistent implementation of the relevant provisions in case of such risks.

(29) It is primarily for Member States, in compliance with the Treaty and in particular with Articles 28, 29 and 30 thereof, to take appropriate measures with regard to dangerous products located within their territory.

(30) However, if the Member States differ as regards the approach to dealing with the risk posed by certain products, such differences could entail unacceptable disparities in consumer protection and constitute a barrier to intra-Community trade.

(31)   It may be necessary to deal with serious product-safety problems requiring rapid intervention which affect or could affect, in the immediate future, all or a significant part of the Community and which, in view of the nature of the safety problem posed by the product, cannot be dealt with effectively in a manner commensurate with the degree of urgency, under the procedures laid down in the specific rules of Community law applicable to the products or category of products in question.

(32)   It is therefore necessary to provide for an adequate mechanism allowing, as a last resort, for the adoption of measures applicable throughout the Community, in the form of a decision addressed to the Member States, to cope with situations created by products presenting a serious risk. Such a decision should entail a ban on the export of the product in question, unless in the case in point exceptional circumstances allow a partial ban or even no ban to be decided upon, particularly when a system of prior consent is established. In addition, the banning of exports should be examined with a view to preventing risks to the health and safety of consumers. Since such a decision is not directly applicable to economic operators, Member States should take all necessary measures for its implementation. Measures adopted under such a procedure are interim measures, save when they apply to individually identified products or batches of products. In order to ensure the appropriate assessment of the need for, and the best preparation of such measures, they should be taken by the Commission, assisted by a committee, in the light of consultations with the Member States, and, if scientific questions are involved falling within the competence of a Community scientific committee, with the scientific committee competent for the risk concerned.

(33)   The measures necessary for the implementation of this Directive should be adopted in accordance with Council Decision 1999/468/EC of 28 June 1999 laying down the procedures for the exercise of implementing powers conferred on the Commission.

(34)   In order to facilitate effective and consistent application of this Directive, the various aspects of its application may need to be discussed within a committee.

(35)   Public access to the information available to the authorities on product safety should be ensured. However, professional secrecy, as referred to in Article 287 of the Treaty, must be protected in a way which is compatible with the need to ensure the effectiveness of market surveillance activities and of protection measures.

(36)   This Directive should not affect victims' rights within the meaning of Council Directive 85/374/ EEC of 25 July 1985 on the approximation of the laws, regulations and administrative provisions of the Member States concerning liability for defective products.

(37)   It is necessary for Member States to provide for appropriate means of redress before the competent courts in respect of measures taken by the competent authorities which restrict the placing on the market of a product or require its withdrawal or recall.

(38)   In addition, the adoption of measures concerning imported products, like those concerning the banning of exports, with a view to preventing risks to the safety and health of consumers must comply with the Community's international obligations.

(39)   The Commission should periodically examine the manner in which this Directive is applied and the results obtained, in particular in relation to the functioning of market surveillance systems, the rapid exchange of information and measures adopted at Community level, together with other issues relevant for consumer product safety in the Community, and submit regular reports to the European Parliament and the Council on the subject.

(40)   This Directive should not affect the obligations of Member States concerning the deadline for transposition and application of Directive 92/59/EEC,

HAVE ADOPTED THIS DIRECTIVE:

CHAPTER I
OBJECTIVE — SCOPE — DEFINITIONS

Article 1

1.   The purpose of this Directive is to ensure that products placed on the market are safe.

2.   This Directive shall apply to all the products defined in Art. 2(a). Each of its provisions shall apply in so far as there are no specific provisions with the same objective in rules of Community law governing the safety of the products concerned. Where products are subject to specific safety requirements imposed by Community legislation, this Directive

shall apply only to the aspects and risks or categories of risks not covered by those requirements. This means that:
(a)   Articles 2(b) and (c), 3 and 4 shall not apply to those products insofar as concerns the risks or categories of risks covered by the specific legislation;
(b)   Articles 5 to 18 shall apply except where there are specific provisions governing the aspects covered by the said Articles with the same objective.

Article 2

For the purposes of this Directive:
(a)   'product' shall mean any product – including in the context of providing a service – which is intended for consumers or likely, under reasonably foreseeable conditions, to be used by consumers even if not intended for them, and is supplied or made available, whether for consideration or not, in the course of a commercial activity, and whether new, used or reconditioned.
      This definition shall not apply to second-hand products supplied as antiques or as products to be repaired or reconditioned prior to being used, provided that the supplier clearly informs the person to whom he supplies the product to that effect;
(b)   'safe product' shall mean any product which, under normal or reasonably foreseeable conditions of use including duration and, where applicable, putting into service, installation and maintenance requirements, does not present any risk or only the minimum risks compatible with the product's use, considered to be acceptable and consistent with a high level of protection for the safety and health of persons, taking into account the following points in particular:
      (i)   the characteristics of the product, including its composition, packaging, instructions for assembly and, where applicable, for installation and maintenance;
      (ii)   the effect on other products, where it is reasonably foreseeable that it will be used with other products;
      (iii) the presentation of the product, the labelling, any warnings and instructions for its use and disposal and any other indication or information regarding the product;
      (iv) the categories of consumers at risk when using the product, in particular children and the elderly.
      The feasibility of obtaining higher levels of safety or the availability of other products presenting a lesser degree of risk shall not constitute grounds for considering a product to be 'dangerous';
(c)   'dangerous product' shall mean any product which does not meet the definition of 'safe product' in (b);
(d)   'serious risk' shall mean any serious risk, including those the effects of which are not immediate, requiring rapid intervention by the public authorities;
(e)   'producer' shall mean:
      (i)   the manufacturer of the product, when he is established in the Community, and any other person presenting himself as the manufacturer by affixing to the product his name, trade mark or other distinctive mark, or the person who reconditions the product;
      (ii)   the manufacturer's representative, when the manufacturer is not established in the Community or, if there is no representative established in the Community, the importer of the product;
      (iii) other professionals in the supply chain, insofar as their activities may affect the safety properties of a product;
(f)   'distributor' shall mean any professional in the supply chain whose activity does not affect the safety properties of a product;
(g)   'recall' shall mean any measure aimed at achieving the return of a dangerous product that has already been supplied or made available to consumers by the producer or distributor;
(h)   'withdrawal' shall mean any measure aimed at preventing the distribution, display and offer of a product dangerous to the consumer.

CHAPTER II
GENERAL SAFETY REQUIREMENT, CONFORMITY ASSESSMENT CRITERIA AND EUROPEAN STANDARDS

Article 3
1. Producers shall be obliged to place only safe products on the market.
2. A product shall be deemed safe, as far as the aspects covered by the relevant national legislation are concerned, when, in the absence of specific Community provisions governing the safety of the product in question, it conforms to the specific rules of national law of the Member State in whose territory the product is marketed, such rules being drawn up in conformity with the Treaty, and in particular Articles 28 and 30 thereof, and laying down the health and safety requirements which the product must satisfy in order to be marketed.

   A product shall be presumed safe as far as the risks and risk categories covered by relevant national standards are concerned when it conforms to voluntary national standards transposing European standards, the references of which have been published by the Commission in the *Official Journal of the European Communities* in accordance with Article 4. The Member States shall publish the references of such national standards.
3. In circumstances other than those referred to in paragraph 2, the conformity of a product to the general safety requirement shall be assessed by taking into account the following elements in particular, where they exist:
   (a) voluntary national standards transposing relevant European standards other than those referred to in paragraph 2;
   (b) the standards drawn up in the Member State in which the product is marketed;
   (c) Commission recommendations setting guidelines on product safety assessment;
   (d) product safety codes of good practice in force in the sector concerned;
   (e) the state of the art and technology;
   (f) reasonable consumer expectations concerning safety.
4. Conformity of a product with the criteria designed to ensure the general safety requirement, in particular the provisions mentioned in paragraphs 2 or 3, shall not bar the competent authorities of the Member States from taking appropriate measures to impose restrictions on its being placed on the market or to require its withdrawal from the market or recall where there is evidence that, despite such conformity, it is dangerous.

Article 4
1. For the purposes of this Directive, the European standards referred to in the second subparagraph of Article 3(2) shall be drawn up as follows:
   (a) the requirements intended to ensure that products which conform to these standards satisfy the general safety requirement shall be determined in accordance with the procedure laid down in Article 15(2);
   (b) on the basis of those requirements, the Commission shall, in accordance with Directive 98/34/EC of the European Parliament and of the Council of 22 June 1998 laying down a procedure for the provision of information in the field of technical standards and regulations and of rules on information society services call on the European standardisation bodies to draw up standards which satisfy these requirements;
   (c) on the basis of those mandates, the European standardisation bodies shall adopt the standards in accordance with the principles contained in the general guidelines for cooperation between the Commission and those bodies;
   (d) the Commission shall report every three years to the European Parliament and the Council, within the framework of the report referred to in Article 19(2), on its programmes for setting the requirements and the mandates for standardisation provided for in subparagraphs (a) and (b) above. This report will, in particular, include an analysis of the decisions taken regarding requirements and mandates for standardisation referred to in subparagraphs (a) and (b) and regarding the standards referred to in subparagraph (c). It will also include information on the products for which the Commission intends to set the requirements and the mandates in question, the product risks to be considered and the results of any preparatory work launched in this area.

2.   The Commission shall publish in the *Official Journal of the European Communities* the references of the European standards adopted in this way and drawn up in accordance with the requirements referred to in paragraph 1.

If a standard adopted by the European standardisation bodies before the entry into force of this Directive ensures compliance with the general safety requirement, the Commission shall decide to publish its references in the *Official Journal of the European Communities*.

If a standard does not ensure compliance with the general safety requirement, the Commission shall withdraw reference to the standard from publication in whole or in part.

In the cases referred to in the second and third subparagraphs, the Commission shall, on its own initiative or at the request of a Member State, decide in accordance with the procedure laid down in Article 15(2) whether the standard in question meets the general safety requirement. The Commission shall decide to publish or withdraw after consulting the Committee established by Article 5 of Directive 98/34/EC. The Commission shall notify the Member States of its decision.

CHAPTER III
OTHER OBLIGATIONS OF PRODUCERS AND OBLIGATIONS OF DISTRIBUTORS

Article 5

1.   Within the limits of their respective activities, producers shall provide consumers with the relevant information to enable them to assess the risks inherent in a product throughout the normal or reasonably foreseeable period of its use, where such risks are not immediately obvious without adequate warnings, and to take precautions against those risks.

The presence of warnings does not exempt any person from compliance with the other requirements laid down in this Directive.

Within the limits of their respective activities, producers shall adopt measures commensurate with the characteristics of the products which they supply, enabling them to:

(a)   be informed of risks which these products might pose;

(b)   choose to take appropriate action including, if necessary to avoid these risks, withdrawal from the market, adequately and effectively warning consumers or recall from consumers.

The measures referred to in the third subparagraph shall include, for example:

(a)   an indication, by means of the product or its packaging, of the identity and details of the producer and the product reference or, where applicable, the batch of products to which it belongs, except where not to give such indication is justified and

(b)   in all cases where appropriate, the carrying out of sample testing of marketed products, investigating and, if necessary, keeping a register of complaints and keeping distributors informed of such monitoring.

Action such as that referred to in (b) of the third subparagraph shall be undertaken on a voluntary basis or at the request of the competent authorities in accordance with Article 8(1)(f). Recall shall take place as a last resort, where other measures would not suffice to prevent the risks involved, in instances where the producers consider it necessary or where they are obliged to do so further to a measure taken by the competent authority. It may be effected within the framework of codes of good practice on the matter in the Member State concerned, where such codes exist.

2.   Distributors shall be required to act with due care to help to ensure compliance with the applicable safety requirements, in particular by not supplying products which they know or should have presumed, on the basis of the information in their possession and as professionals, do not comply with those requirements. Moreover, within the limits of their respective activities, they shall participate in monitoring the safety of products placed on the market, especially by passing on information on product risks, keeping and providing the documentation necessary for tracing the origin of products, and cooperating in the action taken by producers and competent authorities to avoid the risks. Within the limits of their respective activities they shall take measures enabling them to cooperate efficiently.

3.   Where producers and distributors know or ought to know, on the basis of the information in their possession and as professionals, that a product that they have placed on the market poses risks to the consumer that are incompatible with the general safety requirement, they shall immediately inform the competent authorities of the Member States thereof under the

conditions laid down in Annex I, giving details, in particular, of action taken to prevent risk to the consumer.

The Commission shall, in accordance with the procedure referred to in Article 15(3), adapt the specific requirements relating to the obligation to provide information laid down in Annex I.

4.   Producers and distributors shall, within the limits of their respective activities, cooperate with the competent authorities, at the request of the latter, on action taken to avoid the risks posed by products which they supply or have supplied. The procedures for such cooperation, including procedures for dialogue with the producers and distributors concerned on issues related to product safety, shall be established by the competent authorities.

CHAPTER IV
SPECIFIC OBLIGATIONS AND POWERS OF THE MEMBER STATES

Article 6
1.   Member States shall ensure that producers and distributors comply with their obligations under this Directive in such a way that products placed on the market are safe.
2.   Member States shall establish or nominate authorities competent to monitor the compliance of products with the general safety requirements and arrange for such authorities to have and use the necessary powers to take the appropriate measures incumbent upon them under this Directive.
3.   Member States shall define the tasks, powers, organisation and cooperation arrangements of the competent authorities. They shall keep the Commission informed, and the Commission shall pass on such information to the other Member States.

Article 7
Member States shall lay down the rules on penalties applicable to infringements of the national provisions adopted pursuant to this Directive and shall take all measures necessary to ensure that they are implemented. The penalties provided for shall be effective, proportionate and dissuasive. Member States shall notify those provisions to the Commission by 15 January 2004 and shall also notify it, without delay, of any amendment affecting them.

Article 8
1.   For the purposes of this Directive, and in particular of Art. 6 thereof, the competent authorities of the Member States shall be entitled to take, inter alia, the measures in (a) and in (b) to (f) below, where appropriate:
        (a)   for any product:
              (i)   to organise, even after its being placed on the market as being safe, appropriate checks on its safety properties, on an adequate scale, up to the final stage of use or consumption;
              (ii)   to require all necessary information from the parties concerned;
              (iii) to take samples of products and subject them to safety checks;
        (b)   for any product that could pose risks in certain conditions:
              (i)   to require that it be marked with suitable, clearly worded and easily comprehensible warnings, in the official languages of the Member State in which the product is marketed, on the risks it may present;
              (ii)   to make its marketing subject to prior conditions so as to make it safe;
        (c)   for any product that could pose risks for certain persons: to order that they be given warning of the risk in good time and in an appropriate form, including the publication of special warnings;
        (d)   for any product that could be dangerous: for the period needed for the various safety evaluations, checks and controls, temporarily to ban its supply, the offer to supply it or its display;
        (e)   for any dangerous product: to ban its marketing and introduce the accompanying measures required to ensure the ban is complied with;
        (f)   for any dangerous product already on the market:
              (i)   to order or organise its actual and immediate withdrawal, and alert consumers to the risks it presents;

(ii)   to order or coordinate or, if appropriate, to organise together with producers and distributors its recall from consumers and its destruction in suitable conditions.

2.   When the competent authorities of the Member States take measures such as those provided for in paragraph 1, in particular those referred to in (d) to (f), they shall act in accordance with the Treaty, and in particular Articles 28 and 30 thereof, in such a way as to implement the measures in a manner proportional to the seriousness of the risk, and taking due account of the precautionary principle.

In this context, they shall encourage and promote voluntary action by producers and distributors, in accordance with the obligations incumbent on them under this Directive, and in particular Chapter III thereof, including where applicable by the development of codes of good practice.

If necessary, they shall organise or order the measures provided for in paragraph 1(f) if the action undertaken by the producers and distributors in fulfilment of their obligations is unsatisfactory or insufficient. Recall shall take place as a last resort. It may be effected within the framework of codes of good practice on the matter in the Member State concerned, where such codes exist.

3.   In particular, the competent authorities shall have the power to take the necessary action to apply with due dispatch appropriate measures such as those mentioned in paragraph 1, (b) to (f), in the case of products posing a serious risk. These circumstances shall be determined by the Member States, assessing each individual case on its merits, taking into account the guidelines referred to in point 8 of Annex II.

4.   The measures to be taken by the competent authorities under this Article shall be addressed, as appropriate, to:
(a)   the producer;
(b)   within the limits of their respective activities, distributors and in particular the party responsible for the first stage of distribution on the national market;
(c)   any other person, where necessary, with a view to cooperation in action taken to avoid risks arising from a product.

Article 9

1.   In order to ensure effective market surveillance, aimed at guaranteeing a high level of consumer health and safety protection, which entails cooperation between their competent authorities, Member States shall ensure that approaches employing appropriate means and procedures are put in place, which may include in particular:
(a)   establishment, periodical updating and implementation of sectoral surveillance programmes by categories of products or risks and the monitoring of surveillance activities, findings and results;
(b)   follow-up and updating of scientific and technical knowledge concerning the safety of products;
(c)   periodical review and assessment of the functioning of the control activities and their effectiveness and, if necessary, revision of the surveillance approach and organisation put in place.

2.   Member States shall ensure that consumers and other interested parties are given an opportunity to submit complaints to the competent authorities on product safety and on surveillance and control activities and that these complaints are followed up as appropriate. Member States shall actively inform consumers and other interested parties of the procedures established to that end.

Article 10

1.   The Commission shall promote and take part in the operation in a European network of the authorities of the Member States competent for product safety, in particular in the form of administrative cooperation.

2.   This network operation shall develop in a coordinated manner with the other existing Community procedures, particularly RAPEX. Its objective shall be, in particular, to facilitate:
(a)   the exchange of information on risk assessment, dangerous products, test methods and results, recent scientific developments as well as other aspects relevant for control activities;
(b)   the establishment and execution of joint surveillance and testing projects;

(c) the exchange of expertise and best practices and cooperation in training activities;
(d) improved cooperation at Community level with regard to the tracing, withdrawal and recall of dangerous products.

CHAPTER V
EXCHANGES OF INFORMATION AND RAPID INTERVENTION SITUATIONS

Article 11

1. Where a Member State takes measures which restrict the placing on the market of products – or require their withdrawal or recall – such as those provided for in Article 8(1)(b) to (f), the Member State shall, to the extent that such notification is not required under Article 12 or any specific Community legislation, inform the Commission of the measures, specifying its reasons for adopting them. It shall also inform the Commission of any modification or lifting of such measures.

   If the notifying Member State considers that the effects of the risk do not or cannot go beyond its territory, it shall notify the measures concerned insofar as they involve information likely to be of interest to Member States from the product safety standpoint, and in particular if they are in response to a new risk which has not yet been reported in other notifications.

   In accordance with the procedure laid down in Article 15(3) of this Directive, the Commission shall, while ensuring the effectiveness and proper functioning of the system, adopt the guidelines referred to in point 8 of Annex II. These shall propose the content and standard form for the notifications provided for in this Article, and, in particular, shall provide precise criteria for determining the conditions for which notification is relevant for the purposes of the second subparagraph.

2. The Commission shall forward the notification to the other Member States, unless it concludes, after examination on the basis of the information contained in the notification, that the measure does not comply with Community law. In such a case, it shall immediately inform the Member State which initiated the action.

Article 12

1. Where a Member State adopts or decides to adopt, recommend or agree with producers and distributors, whether on a compulsory or voluntary basis, measures or actions to prevent, restrict or impose specific conditions on the possible marketing or use, within its own territory, of products by reason of a serious risk, it shall immediately notify the Commission thereof through RAPEX. It shall also inform the Commission without delay of modification or withdrawal of any such measure or action.

   If the notifying Member State considers that the effects of the risk do not or cannot go beyond its territory, it shall follow the procedure laid down in Article 11, taking into account the relevant criteria proposed in the guidelines referred to in point 8 of Annex II.

   Without prejudice to the first subparagraph, before deciding to adopt such measures or to take such action, Member States may pass on to the Commission any information in their possession regarding the existence of a serious risk.

   In the case of a serious risk, they shall notify the Commission of the voluntary measures laid down in Article 5 of this Directive taken by producers and distributors.

2. On receiving such notifications, the Commission shall check whether they comply with this Article and with the requirements applicable to the functioning of RAPEX, and shall forward them to the other Member States, which, in turn, shall immediately inform the Commission of any measures adopted.

3. Detailed procedures for RAPEX are set out in Annex II. They shall be adapted by the Commission in accordance with the procedure referred to in Article 15(3).

4. Access to RAPEX shall be open to applicant countries, third countries or international organisations, within the framework of agreements between the Community and those countries or international organisations, according to arrangements defined in these agreements. Any such agreements shall be based on reciprocity and include provisions on confidentiality corresponding to those applicable in the Community.

Article 13

1.   If the Commission becomes aware of a serious risk from certain products to the health and safety of consumers in various Member States, it may, after consulting the Member States, and, if scientific questions arise which fall within the competence of a Community Scientific Committee, the Scientific Committee competent to deal with the risk concerned, adopt a decision in the light of the result of those consultations, in accordance with the procedure laid down in Art. 15(2), requiring Member States to take measures from among those listed in Article 8(1)(b) to (f) if, at one and the same time:

   (a)   it emerges from prior consultations with the Member States that they differ significantly on the approach adopted or to be adopted to deal with the risk; and

   (b)   the risk cannot be dealt with, in view of the nature of the safety issue posed by the product, in a manner compatible with the degree of urgency of the case, under other procedures laid down by the specific Community legislation applicable to the products concerned; and

   (c)   the risk can be eliminated effectively only by adopting appropriate measures applicable at Community level, in order to ensure a consistent and high level of protection of the health and safety of consumers and the proper functioning of the internal market.

2.   The decisions referred to in paragraph 1 shall be valid for a period not exceeding one year and may be confirmed, under the same procedure, for additional periods none of which shall exceed one year.

   However, decisions concerning specific, individually identified products or batches of products shall be valid without a time limit.

3.   Export from the Community of dangerous products which have been the subject of a decision referred to in paragraph 1 shall be prohibited unless the decision provides otherwise.

4.   Member States shall take all necessary measures to implement the decisions referred to in paragraph 1 within less than 20 days, unless a different period is specified in those decisions.

5.   The competent authorities responsible for carrying out the measures referred to in paragraph 1 shall, within one month, give the parties concerned an opportunity to submit their views and shall inform the Commission accordingly.

CHAPTER VI
COMMITTEE PROCEDURES

Article 14

1.   The measures necessary for the implementation of this Directive relating to the matters referred to below shall be adopted in accordance with the regulatory procedure provided for in Article 15(2):

   (a)   the measures referred to in Article 4 concerning standards adopted by the European standardisation bodies;

   (b)   the decisions referred to in Article 13 requiring Member States to take measures as listed in Article 8(1)(b) to (f).

2.   The measures necessary for the implementation of this Directive in respect of all other matters shall be adopted in accordance with the advisory procedure provided for in Article 15(3).

Article 15

1.   The Commission shall be assisted by a Committee.

2.   Where reference is made to this paragraph, Articles 5 and 7 of Decision 1999/468/EC shall apply, having regard to the provisions of Article 8 thereof.

   The period laid down in Article 5(6) of Decision 1999/468/EC shall be set at 15 days.

3.   Where reference is made to this paragraph, Articles 3 and 7 of Decision 1999/468/EC shall apply, having regard to the provisions of Article 8 thereof.

4.   The Committee shall adopt its rules of procedure.

CHAPTER VII
FINAL PROVISIONS

Article 16

1.   Information available to the authorities of the Member States or the Commission relating to risks to consumer health and safety posed by products shall in general be available to the public, in accordance with the requirements of transparency and without prejudice to the restrictions required for monitoring and investigation activities. In particular the public shall have access to information on product identification, the nature of the risk and the measures taken.

However, Member States and the Commission shall take the steps necessary to ensure that their officials and agents are required not to disclose information obtained for the purposes of this Directive which, by its nature, is covered by professional secrecy in duly justified cases, except for information relating to the safety properties of products which must be made public if circumstances so require, in order to protect the health and safety of consumers.

2.   Protection of professional secrecy shall not prevent the dissemination to the competent authorities of information relevant for ensuring the effectiveness of market monitoring and surveillance activities. The authorities receiving information covered by professional secrecy shall ensure its protection.

Article 17

This Directive shall be without prejudice to the application of Directive 85/374/EEC.

Article 18

1.   Any measure adopted under this Directive and involving restrictions on the placing of a product on the market or requiring its withdrawal or recall must state the appropriate reasons on which it is based. It shall be notified as soon as possible to the party concerned and shall indicate the remedies available under the provisions in force in the Member State in question and the time limits applying to such remedies.

The parties concerned shall, whenever feasible, be given an opportunity to submit their views before the adoption of the measure. If this has not been done in advance because of the urgency of the measures to be taken, they shall be given such opportunity in due course after the measure has been implemented.

Measures requiring the withdrawal of a product or its recall shall take into consideration the need to encourage distributors, users and consumers to contribute to the implementation of such measures.

2.   Member States shall ensure that any measure taken by the competent authorities involving restrictions on the placing of a product on the market or requiring its withdrawal or recall can be challenged before the competent courts.

3.   Any decision taken by virtue of this Directive and involving restrictions on the placing of a product on the market or requiring its withdrawal or its recall shall be without prejudice to assessment of the liability of the party concerned, in the light of the national criminal law applying in the case in question.

Article 19

1.   The Commission may bring before the Committee referred to in Article 15 any matter concerning the application of this Directive and particularly those relating to market monitoring and surveillance activities.

2.   Every three years, following 15 January 2004, the Commission shall submit a report on the implementation of this Directive to the European Parliament and the Council.

The report shall in particular include information on the safety of consumer products, in particular on improved traceability of products, the functioning of market surveillance, standardisation work, the functioning of RAPEX and Community measures taken on the basis of Article 13. To this end the Commission shall conduct assessments of the relevant issues, in particular the approaches, systems and practices put in place in the Member States, in the light of the requirements of this Directive and the other Community legislation relating to product safety. The Member States shall provide the Commission with all the necessary assistance and information for carrying out the assessments and preparing the reports.

Article 20
The Commission shall identify the needs, possibilities and priorities for Community action on the safety of services and submit to the European Parliament and the Council, before 1 January 2003, a report, accompanied by proposals on the subject as appropriate.

Article 21
1.   Member States shall bring into force the laws, regulations and administrative provisions necessary in order to comply with this Directive with effect from 15 January 2004. They shall forthwith inform the Commission thereof. When Member States adopt those measures, they shall contain a reference to this Directive or be accompanied by such reference on the occasion of their official publication. The methods of making such reference shall be laid down by Member States.
2.   Member States shall communicate to the Commission the provisions of national law which they adopt in the field covered by this Directive.

Article 22
Directive 92/59/EEC is hereby repealed from 15 January 2004, without prejudice to the obligations of Member States concerning the deadlines for transposition and application of the said Directive as indicated in Annex III.

References to Directive 92/59/EEC shall be construed as references to this Directive and shall be read in accordance with the correlation table in Annex IV.

Article 23
This Directive shall enter into force on the day of its publication in the *Official Journal of the European Communities*.

Article 24
This Directive is addressed to the Member States.

Done at Brussels, 3 December 2001.

ANNEX I

REQUIREMENTS CONCERNING INFORMATION ON PRODUCTS THAT DO NOT COMPLY WITH THE GENERAL SAFETY REQUIREMENT TO BE PROVIDED TO THE COMPETENT AUTHORITIES BY PRODUCERS AND DISTRIBUTORS

1.   The information specified in Article 5(3), or where applicable by specific requirements of Community rules on the product concerned, shall be passed to the competent authorities appointed for the purpose in the Member States where the products in question are or have been marketed or otherwise supplied to consumers.
2.   The Commission, assisted by the Committee referred to in Article 15, shall define the content and draw up the standard form of the notifications provided for in this Annex, while ensuring the effectiveness and proper functioning of the system. In particular, it shall put forward, possibly in the form of a guide, simple and clear criteria for determining the special conditions, particularly those concerning isolated circumstances or products, for which notification is not relevant in relation to this Annex.
3.   In the event of serious risks, this information shall include at least the following:
   (a)   information enabling a precise identification of the product or batch of products in question;
   (b)   a full description of the risk that the products in question present;
   (c)   all available information relevant for tracing the product;
   (d)   a description of the action undertaken to prevent risks to consumers.

ANNEX II

PROCEDURES FOR THE APPLICATION OF RAPEX AND GUIDELINES FOR NOTIFICATIONS

1. RAPEX covers products as defined in Article 2(a) that pose a serious risk to the health and safety of consumers. Pharmaceuticals, which come under Directives 75/319/EEC and 81/851/EEC, are excluded from the scope of RAPEX.

2. RAPEX is essentially aimed at a rapid exchange of information in the event of a serious risk. The guidelines referred to in point 8 define specific criteria for identifying serious risks.

3. Member States notifying under Article 12 shall provide all available details. In particular, the notification shall contain the information stipulated in the guidelines referred to in point 8 and at least:

   (a) information enabling the product to be identified;
   (b) a description of the risk involved, including a summary of the results of any tests/analyses and of their conclusions which are relevant to assessing the level of risk;
   (c) the nature and the duration of the measures or action taken or decided on, if applicable;
   (d) information on supply chains and distribution of the product, in particular on destination countries.

   Such information must be transmitted using the special standard notification form and by the means stipulated in the guidelines referred to in point 8.

   When the measure notified pursuant to Article 11 or Article 12 seeks to limit the marketing or use of a chemical substance or preparation, the Member States shall provide as soon as possible either a summary or the references of the relevant data relating to the substance or preparation considered and to known and available substitutes, where such information is available. They will also communicate the anticipated effects of the measure on consumer health and safety together with the assessment of the risk carried out in accordance with the general principles for the risk evaluation of chemical substances as referred to in Article 10(4) of Regulation (EEC) No 793/93 in the case of an existing substance or in Article 3(2) of Directive 67/548/EEC in the case of a new substance. The guidelines referred to in point 8 shall define the details and procedures for the information requested in that respect.

4. When a Member State has informed the Commission, in accordance with Article 12(1), third subparagraph, of a serious risk before deciding to adopt measures, it must inform the Commission within 45 days whether it confirms or modifies this information.

5. The Commission shall, in the shortest time possible, verify the conformity with the provisions of the Directive of the information received under RAPEX and, may, when it considers it to be necessary and in order to assess product safety, carry out an investigation on its own initiative.

   In the case of such an investigation, Member States shall supply the Commission with the requested information to the best of their ability.

6. Upon receipt of a notification referred to in Article 12, the Member States are requested to inform the Commission, at the latest within the set period of time stipulated in the guidelines referred to in point 8, of the following:

   (a) whether the product has been marketed in their territory;
   (b) what measures concerning the product in question they may be adopting in the light of their own circumstances, stating the reasons, including any differing assessment of risk or any other special circumstance justifying their decision, in particular lack of action or of follow-up;
   (c) any relevant supplementary information they have obtained on the risk involved, including the results of any tests or analyses carried out.

   The guidelines referred to in point 8 shall provide precise criteria for notifying measures limited to national territory and shall specify how to deal with notifications concerning risks which are considered by the Member State not to go beyond its territory.

7. Member States shall immediately inform the Commission of any modification or lifting of the measure(s) or action(s) in question.

8. The Commission shall prepare and regularly update, in accordance with the procedure laid down in Article 15(3), guidelines concerning the management of RAPEX by the Commission and the Member States.

9.   The Commission may inform the national contact points regarding products posing serious risks, imported into or exported from the Community and the European Economic Area.
10.   Responsibility for the information provided lies with the notifying Member State.
11.   The Commission shall ensure the proper functioning of the system, in particular classifying and indexing notifications according to the degree of urgency. Detailed procedures shall be laid down by the guidelines referred to in point 8.

ANNEX III
PERIOD FOR THE TRANSPOSITION AND APPLICATION OF THE REPEALED DIRECTIVE
(REFERRED TO IN THE FIRST SUBPARAGRAPHE OF ARTICLE 22)

Directive	*Period for transposition*	*Period for bringing into application*
Directive 92/59/EEC	29 June 1994	29 June 1994

ANNEX IV
CORRELATION TABLE
(REFERRED TO IN THE SECOND SUBPARAGRAPH OF ARTICLE 22)

This Directive	*Directive 92/59/EEC*
Article 1	Article 1
Article 2	Article 2
Article 3	Article 4
Article 4	—
Article 5	Article 3
Article 6	Article 5
Article 7	Article 5(2)
Article 8	Article 6
Article 9	—
Article 10	—
Article 11	Article 7
Article 12	Article 8
Article 13	Article 9
Articles 14 and 15	Article 10
Article 16	Article 12
Article 17	Article 13
Article 18	Article 14
Article 19	Article 15
Article 20	—
Article 21	Article 17
Article 22	Article 18
Article 23	Article 19
Annex I	—
Annex II	Annex
Annex III	—
Annex IV	—

DIRECTIVE 2005/29/EC OF THE EUROPEAN PARLIAMENT AND OF THE COUNCIL OF 11 MAY 2005

concerning unfair business-to-consumer commercial practices in the internal market and amending Council Directive 84/450/EEC, Directives 97/7/EC, 98/27/EC and 2002/65/EC of the European Parliament and of the Council and Regulation (EC) No 2006/2004 of the European Parliament and of the Council ('Unfair Commercial Practices Directive')
(Text with EEA relevance)

THE EUROPEAN PARLIAMENT AND THE COUNCIL OF THE EUROPEAN UNION,

Having regard to the Treaty establishing the European Community, and in particular Article 95 thereof,

Having regard to the proposal from the Commission,

Having regard to the opinion of the European Economic and Social Committee,

Acting in accordance with the procedure laid down in Article 251 of the Treaty,

Whereas:

(1)   Article 153(1) and (3)(a) of the Treaty provides that the Community is to contribute to the attainment of a high level of consumer protection by the measures it adopts pursuant to Article 95 thereof.

(2)   In accordance with Article 14(2) of the Treaty, the internal market comprises an area without internal frontiers in which the free movement of goods and services and freedom of establishment are ensured. The development of fair commercial practices within the area without internal frontiers is vital for the promotion of the development of cross border activities.

(3)   The laws of the Member States relating to unfair commercial practices show marked differences which can generate appreciable distortions of competition and obstacles to the smooth functioning of the internal market. In the field of advertising, Council Directive 84/450/ EEC of 10 September 1984 concerning misleading and comparative advertising establishes minimum criteria for harmonising legislation on misleading advertising, but does not prevent the Member States from retaining or adopting measures which provide more extensive protection for consumers. As a result, Member States' provisions on misleading advertising diverge significantly.

(4)   These disparities cause uncertainty as to which national rules apply to unfair commercial practices harming consumers' economic interests and create many barriers affecting business and consumers. These barriers increase the cost to business of exercising internal market freedoms, in particular when businesses wish to engage in cross border marketing, advertising campaigns and sales promotions. Such barriers also make consumers uncertain of their rights and undermine their confidence in the internal market.

(5)   In the absence of uniform rules at Community level, obstacles to the free movement of services and goods across borders or the freedom of establishment could be justified in the light of the case-law of the Court of Justice of the European Communities as long as they seek to protect recognised public interest objectives and are proportionate to those objectives. In view of the Community's objectives, as set out in the provisions of the Treaty and in secondary Community law relating to freedom of movement, and in accordance with the Commission's policy on commercial communications as indicated in the Communication from the Commission entitled 'The follow-up to the Green Paper on Commercial Communications in the Internal Market', such obstacles should be eliminated. These obstacles can only be eliminated by establishing uniform rules at Community level which establish a high level of consumer protection and by clarifying certain legal concepts at Community level to the extent necessary for the proper functioning of the internal market and to meet the requirement of legal certainty.

(6)   This Directive therefore approximates the laws of the Member States on unfair commercial practices, including unfair advertising, which directly harm consumers' economic interests an thereby indirectly harm the economic interests of legitimate competitors. In line with the principle of proportionality, this Directive protects consumers from the consequences of such unfair commercial practices where they are material but recognises that in some cases the impact on consumers may be negligible. It neither covers nor affects the national laws on unfair commercial practices which harm only competitors' economic interests or which relate to a transaction between traders; taking full account of the principle of subsidiarity, Member States will continue to be able to regulate such practices, in conformity with Community law, if they choose to do so. Nor does this Directive cover or affect the provisions of Directive 84/450/EEC on advertising which misleads business but which is not misleading for consumers and on comparative advertising. Further, this Directive does not affect accepted advertising and marketing practices, such as legitimate product placement, brand differentiation or the offering of incentives which may legitimately affect consumers' perceptions of products and influence their behaviour without impairing the consumer's ability to make an informed decision.

(7)   This Directive addresses commercial practices directly related to influencing consumers' transactional decisions in relation to products. It does not address commercial practices carried out primarily for other purposes, including for example commercial communication aimed at investors, such as annual reports and corporate promotional literature. It does not address legal requirements related to taste and decency which vary widely among the Member States. Commercial practices such as, for example, commercial solicitation in the streets, may be undesirable in Member States for cultural reasons. Member States should accordingly be able to continue to ban commercial practices in their territory, in conformity with Community law, for reasons of taste and decency even where such practices do not limit consumers' freedom of choice. Full account should be taken of the context of the individual case concerned in applying this Directive, in particular the general clauses thereof.

(8)   This Directive directly protects consumer economic interests from unfair business-to-consumer commercial practices. Thereby, it also indirectly protects legitimate businesses from their competitors who do not play by the rules in this Directive and thus guarantees fair competition in fields coordinated by it. It is understood that there are other commercial practices which, although not harming consumers, may hurt competitors and business customers. The Commission should carefully examine the need for Community action in the field of unfair competition beyond the remit of this Directive and, if necessary, make a legislative proposal to cover these other aspects of unfair competition.

(9)   This Directive is without prejudice to individual actions brought by those who have been harmed by an unfair commercial practice. It is also without prejudice to Community and national rules on contract law, on intellectual property rights, on the health and safety aspects of products, on conditions of establishment and authorisation regimes, including those rules which, in conformity with Community law, relate to gambling activities, and to Community competition rules and the national provisions implementing them. The Member States will thus be able to retain or introduce restrictions and prohibitions of commercial practices on grounds of the protection of the health and safety of consumers in their territory wherever the trader is based, for example in relation to alcohol, tobacco or pharmaceuticals. Financial services and immovable property, by reason of their complexity and inherent serious risks, necessitate detailed requirements, including positive obligations on traders. For this reason, in the field of financial services and immovable property, this Directive is without prejudice to the right of Member States to go beyond its provisions to protect the economic interests of consumers. It is not appropriate to regulate here the certification and indication of the standard of fineness of articles of precious metal.

(10)   It is necessary to ensure that the relationship between this Directive and existing Community law is coherent, particularly where detailed provisions on unfair commercial practices apply to specific sectors. This Directive therefore amends Directive 84/450/EEC, Directive 97/7/EC of the European Parliament and of the Council of 20 May 1997 on the protection of consumers in respect of distance contracts, Directive 98/27/EC of the European Parliament and of the Council of 19 May 1998 on injunctions for the protection of consumers' interests and Directive 2002/65/EC of the European Parliament and of the Council of 23 September 2002 concerning the distance marketing of consumer financial services. This Directive accordingly applies only in so far as there are no specific Community law provisions regulating specific aspects of unfair commercial practices, such as information requirements and rules on the way the information is presented to the consumer. It provides protection for consumers where there is no specific sectoral legislation at Community level and prohibits traders from creating a false impression of the nature of products. This is particularly important for complex products with high levels of risk to consumers, such as certain financial services products. This Directive consequently complements the Community acquis, which is applicable to commercial practices harming consumers' economic interests.

(11)   The high level of convergence achieved by the approximation of national provisions through this Directive creates a high common level of consumer protection. This Directive establishes a single general prohibition of those unfair commercial practices distorting consumers' economic behaviour. It also sets rules on aggressive commercial practices, which are currently not regulated at Community level.

(12)   Harmonisation will considerably increase legal certainty for both consumers and business. Both consumers and business will be able to rely on a single regulatory framework based

on clearly defined legal concepts regulating all aspects of unfair commercial practices across the EU. The effect will be to eliminate the barriers stemming from the fragmentation of the rules on unfair commercial practices harming consumer economic interests and to enable the internal market to be achieved in this area.

(13)   In order to achieve the Community's objectives through the removal of internal market barriers, it is necessary to replace Member States' existing, divergent general clauses and legal principles. The single, common general prohibition established by this Directive therefore covers unfair commercial practices distorting consumers' economic behaviour. In order to support consumer confidence the general prohibition should apply equally to unfair commercial practices which occur outside any contractual relationship between a trader and a consumer or following the conclusion of a contract and during its execution. The general prohibition is elaborated by rules on the two types of commercial practices which are by far the most common, namely misleading commercial practices and aggressive commercial practices.

(14)   It is desirable that misleading commercial practices cover those practices, including misleading advertising, which by deceiving the consumer prevent him from making an informed and thus efficient choice. In conformity with the laws and practices of Member States on misleading advertising, this Directive classifies misleading practices into misleading actions and misleading omissions. In respect of omissions, this Directive sets out a limited number of key items of information which the consumer needs to make an informed transactional decision. Such information will not have to be disclosed in all advertisements, but only where the trader makes an invitation to purchase, which is a concept clearly defined in this Directive. The full harmonisation approach adopted in this Directive does not preclude the Member States from specifying in national law the main characteristics of particular products such as, for example, collectors' items or electrical goods, the omission of which would be material when an invitation to purchase is made. It is not the intention of this Directive to reduce consumer choice by prohibiting the promotion of products which look similar to other products unless this similarity confuses consumers as to the commercial origin of the product and is therefore misleading. This Directive should be without prejudice to existing Community law which expressly affords Member States the choice between several regulatory options for the protection of consumers in the field of commercial practices. In particular, this Directive should be without prejudice to Article 13(3) of Directive 2002/58/EC of the European Parliament and of the Council of 12 July 2002 concerning the processing of personal data and the protection of privacy in the electronic communications sector.

(15)   Where Community law sets out information requirements in relation to commercial communication, advertising and marketing that information is considered as material under this Directive. Member States will be able to retain or add information requirements relating to contract law and having contract law consequences where this is allowed by the minimum clauses in the existing Community law instruments. A non-exhaustive list of such information requirements in the acquis is contained in Annex II. Given the full harmonisation introduced by this Directive only the information required in Community law is considered as material for the purpose of Article 7(5) thereof. Where Member States have introduced information requirements over and above what is specified in Community law, on the basis of minimum clauses, the omission of that extra information will not constitute a misleading omission under this Directive. By contrast Member States will be able, when allowed by the minimum clauses in Community law, to maintain or introduce more stringent provisions in conformity with Community law so as to ensure a higher level of protection of consumers' individual contractual rights.

(16)   The provisions on aggressive commercial practices should cover those practices which significantly impair the consumer's freedom of choice. Those are practices using harassment, coercion, including the use of physical force, and undue influence.

(17)   It is desirable that those commercial practices which are in all circumstances unfair be identified to provide greater legal certainty. Annex I therefore contains the full list of all such practices. These are the only commercial practices which can be deemed to be unfair without a case-by-case assessment against the provisions of Articles 5 to 9. The list may only be modified by revision of the Directive.

(18)   It is appropriate to protect all consumers from unfair commercial practices; however the Court of Justice has found it necessary in adjudicating on advertising cases since the enactment of Directive 84/450/EEC to examine the effect on a notional, typical consumer. In line with the principle of proportionality, and to permit the effective application of the protections contained in it, this Directive takes as a benchmark the average consumer, who is reasonably well informed and reasonably observant and circumspect, taking into account social, cultural and linguistic factors, as interpreted by the Court of Justice, but also contains provisions aimed at preventing the exploitation of consumers whose characteristics make them particularly vulnerable to unfair commercial practices. Where a commercial practice is specifically aimed at a particular group of consumers, such as children, it is desirable that the impact of the commercial practice be assessed from the perspective of the average member of that group. It is therefore appropriate to include in the list of practices which are in all circumstances unfair a provision which, without imposing an outright ban on advertising directed at children, protects them from direct exhortations to purchase. The average consumer test is not a statistical test. National courts and authorities will have to exercise their own faculty of judgement, having regard to the case-law of the Court of Justice, to determine the typical reaction of the average consumer in a given case.

(19)   Where certain characteristics such as age, physical or mental infirmity or credulity make consumers particularly susceptible to a commercial practice or to the underlying product and the economic behaviour only of such consumers is likely to be distorted by the practice in a way that the trader can reasonably foresee, it is appropriate to ensure that they are adequately protected by assessing the practice from the perspective of the average member of that group.

(20)   It is appropriate to provide a role for codes of conduct, which enable traders to apply the principles of this Directive effectively in specific economic fields. In sectors where there are specific mandatory requirements regulating the behaviour of traders, it is appropriate that these will also provide evidence as to the requirements of professional diligence in that sector. The control exercised by code owners at national or Community level to eliminate unfair commercial practices may avoid the need for recourse to administrative or judicial action and should therefore be encouraged. With the aim of pursuing a high level of consumer protection, consumers' organisations could be informed and involved in the drafting of codes of conduct.

(21)   Persons or organisations regarded under national law as having a legitimate interest in the matter must have legal remedies for initiating proceedings against unfair commercial practices, either before a court or before an administrative authority which is competent to decide upon complaints or to initiate appropriate legal proceedings. While it is for national law to determine the burden of proof, it is appropriate to enable courts and administrative authorities to require traders to produce evidence as to the accuracy of factual claims they have made.

(22)   It is necessary that Member States lay down penalties for infringements of the provisions of this Directive and they must ensure that these are enforced. The penalties must be effective, proportionate and dissuasive.

(23)   Since the objectives of this Directive, namely to eliminate the barriers to the functioning of the internal market represented by national laws on unfair commercial practices and to provide a high common level of consumer protection, by approximating the laws, regulations and administrative provisions of the Member States on unfair commercial practices, cannot be sufficiently achieved by the Member States and can therefore be better achieved at Community level, the Community may adopt measures, in accordance with the principle of subsidiarity as set out in Art. 5 of the Treaty. In accordance with the principle of proportionality, as set out in that Article, this Directive does not go beyond what is necessary in order to eliminate the internal market barriers and achieve a high common level of consumer protection.

(24)   It is appropriate to review this Directive to ensure that barriers to the internal market have been addressed and a high level of consumer protection achieved. The review could lead to a Commission proposal to amend this Directive, which may include a limited extension to the derogation in Art. 3(5), and/or amendments to other consumer protection legislation reflecting the Commission's Consumer Policy Strategy commitment to review the existing acquis in order to achieve a high, common level of consumer protection.

(25)   This Directive respects the fundamental rights and observes the principles recognised in particular by the Charter of Fundamental Rights of the European Union,
HAVE ADOPTED THIS DIRECTIVE:

CHAPTER 1
GENERAL PROVISIONS

Article 1   Purpose

The purpose of this Directive is to contribute to the proper functioning of the internal market and achieve a high level of consumer protection by approximating the laws, regulations and administrative provisions of the Member States on unfair commercial practices harming consumers' economic interests.

Article 2   Definitions

For the purposes of this Directive:

(a)   'consumer' means any natural person who, in commercial practices covered by this Directive, is acting for purposes which are outside his trade, business, craft or profession;

(b)   'trader' means any natural or legal person who, in commercial practices covered by this Directive, is acting for purposes relating to his trade, business, craft or profession and anyone acting in the name of or on behalf of a trader;

(c)   'product' means any goods or service including immovable property, rights and obligations;

(d)   'business-to-consumer commercial practices' (hereinafter also referred to as commercial practices) means any act, omission, course of conduct or representation, commercial communication including advertising and marketing, by a trader, directly connected with the promotion, sale or supply of a product to consumers;

(e)   'to materially distort the economic behaviour of consumers' means using a commercial practice to appreciably impair the consumer's ability to make an informed decision, thereby causing the consumer to take a transactional decision that he would not have taken otherwise;

(f)   'code of conduct' means an agreement or set of rules not imposed by law, regulation or administrative provision of a Member State which defines the behaviour of traders who undertake to be bound by the code in relation to one or more particular commercial practices or business sectors;

(g)   'code owner' means any entity, including a trader or group of traders, which is responsible for the formulation and revision of a code of conduct and/or for monitoring compliance with the code by those who have undertaken to be bound by it;

(h)   'professional diligence' means the standard of special skill and care which a trader may reasonably be expected to exercise towards consumers, commensurate with honest market practice and/or the general principle of good faith in the trader's field of activity;

(i)   'invitation to purchase' means a commercial communication which indicates characteristics of the product and the price in a way appropriate to the means of the commercial communication used and thereby enables the consumer to make a purchase;

(j)   'undue influence' means exploiting a position of power in relation to the consumer so as to apply pressure, even without using or threatening to use physical force, in a way which significantly limits the consumer's ability to make an informed decision;

(k)   'transactional decision' means any decision taken by a consumer concerning whether, how and on what terms to purchase, make payment in whole or in part for, retain or dispose of a product or to exercise a contractual right in relation to the product, whether the consumer decides to act or to refrain from acting;

(l)   'regulated profession' means a professional activity or a group of professional activities, access to which or the pursuit of which, or one of the modes of pursuing which, is conditional, directly or indirectly, upon possession of specific professional qualifications, pursuant to laws, regulations or administrative provisions.

Article 3   Scope

1. This Directive shall apply to unfair business-to-consumer commercial practices, as laid down in Article 5, before, during and after a commercial transaction in relation to a product.
2. This Directive is without prejudice to contract law and, in particular, to the rules on the validity, formation or effect of a contract.
3. This Directive is without prejudice to Community or national rules relating to the health and safety aspects of products.
4. In the case of conflict between the provisions of this Directive and other Community rules regulating specific aspects of unfair commercial practices, the latter shall prevail and apply to those specific aspects.
5. For a period of six years from 12 June 2007, Member States shall be able to continue to apply national provisions within the field approximated by this Directive which are more restrictive or prescriptive than this Directive and which implement directives containing minimum harmonisation clauses. These measures must be essential to ensure that consumers are adequately protected against unfair commercial practices and must be proportionate to the attainment of this objective. The review referred to in Article 18 may, if considered appropriate, include a proposal to prolong this derogation for a further limited period.
6. Member States shall notify the Commission without delay of any national provisions applied on the basis of paragraph 5.
7. This Directive is without prejudice to the rules determining the jurisdiction of the courts.
8. This Directive is without prejudice to any conditions of establishment or of authorisation regimes, or to the deontological codes of conduct or other specific rules governing regulated professions in order to uphold high standards of integrity on the part of the professional, which Member States may, in conformity with Community law, impose on professionals.
9. In relation to 'financial services', as defined in Directive 2002/65/EC, and immovable property, Member States may impose requirements which are more restrictive or prescriptive than this Directive in the field which it approximates.
10. This Directive shall not apply to the application of the laws, regulations and administrative provisions of Member States relating to the certification and indication of the standard of fineness of articles of precious metal.

Article 4   Internal market

Member States shall neither restrict the freedom to provide services nor restrict the free movement of goods for reasons falling within the field approximated by this Directive.

CHAPTER 2
UNFAIR COMMERCIAL PRACTICES

Article 5   Prohibition of unfair commercial practices

1. Unfair commercial practices shall be prohibited.
2. A commercial practice shall be unfair if:
   (a) it is contrary to the requirements of professional diligence, and
   (b) it materially distorts or is likely to materially distort the economic behaviour with regard to the product of the average consumer whom it reaches or to whom it is addressed, or of the average member of the group when a commercial practice is directed to a particular group of consumers.
3. Commercial practices which are likely to materially distort the economic behaviour only of a clearly identifiable group of consumers who are particularly vulnerable to the practice or the underlying product because of their mental or physical infirmity, age or credulity in a way which the trader could reasonably be expected to foresee, shall be assessed from the perspective of the average member of that group. This is without prejudice to the common and legitimate advertising practice of making exaggerated statements or statements which are not meant to be taken literally.
4. In particular, commercial practices shall be unfair which:
   (a) are misleading as set out in Articles 6 and 7, or
   (b) are aggressive as set out in Articles 8 and 9.

5.   Annex I contains the list of those commercial practices which shall in all circumstances be regarded as unfair. The same single list shall apply in all Member States and may only be modified by revision of this Directive.

SECTION 1
MISLEADING COMMERCIAL PRACTICES

Article 6   Misleading actions
1.   A commercial practice shall be regarded as misleading if it contains false information and is therefore untruthful or in any way, including overall presentation, deceives or is likely to deceive the average consumer, even if the information is factually correct, in relation to one or more of the following elements, and in either case causes or is likely to cause him to take a transactional decision that he would not have taken otherwise:
   (a)   the existence or nature of the product;
   (b)   the main characteristics of the product, such as its availability, benefits, risks, execution, composition, accessories, aftersale customer assistance and complaint handling, method and date of manufacture or provision, delivery, fitness for purpose, usage, quantity, specification, geographical or commercial origin or the results to be expected from its use, or the results and material features of tests or checks carried out on the product;
   (c)   the extent of the trader's commitments, the motives for the commercial practice and the nature of the sales process, any statement or symbol in relation to direct or indirect sponsorship or approval of the trader or the product;
   (d)   the price or the manner in which the price is calculated, or the existence of a specific price advantage;
   (e)   the need for a service, part, replacement or repair;
   (f)   the nature, attributes and rights of the trader or his agent, such as his identity and assets, his qualifications, status, approval, affiliation or connection and ownership of industrial, commercial or intellectual property rights or his awards and distinctions;
   (g)   the consumer's rights, including the right to replacement or reimbursement under Directive 1999/44/EC of the European Parliament and of the Council of 25 May 1999 on certain aspects of the sale of consumer goods and associated guarantees, or the risks he may face.
2.   A commercial practice shall also be regarded as misleading if, in its factual context, taking account of all its features and circumstances, it causes or is likely to cause the average consumer to take a transactional decision that he would not have taken otherwise, and it involves:
   (a)   any marketing of a product, including comparative advertising, which creates confusion with any products, trade marks, trade names or other distinguishing marks of a competitor;
   (b)   non-compliance by the trader with commitments contained in codes of conduct by which the trader has undertaken to be bound, where:
      (i)   the commitment is not aspirational but is firm and is capable of being verified, and
      (ii)   the trader indicates in a commercial practice that he is bound by the code.

Article 7   Misleading omissions
1.   A commercial practice shall be regarded as misleading if, in its factual context, taking account of all its features and circumstances and the limitations of the communication medium, it omits material information that the average consumer needs, according to the context, to take an informed transactional decision and thereby causes or is likely to cause the average consumer to take a transactional decision that he would not have taken otherwise.
2.   It shall also be regarded as a misleading omission when, taking account of the matters described in paragraph 1, a trader hides or provides in an unclear, unintelligible, ambiguous or untimely manner such material information as referred to in that paragraph or fails to identify the commercial intent of the commercial practice if not already apparent from the context, and where, in either case, this causes or is likely to cause the average consumer to take a transactional decision that he would not have taken otherwise.

3.   Where the medium used to communicate the commercial practice imposes limitations of space or time, these limitations and any measures taken by the trader to make the information available to consumers by other means shall be taken into account in deciding whether information has been omitted.

4.   In the case of an invitation to purchase, the following information shall be regarded as material, if not already apparent from the context:

(a)   the main characteristics of the product, to an extent appropriate to the medium and the product;

(b)   the geographical address and the identity of the trader, such as his trading name and, where applicable, the geographical address and the identity of the trader on whose behalf he is acting;

(c)   the price inclusive of taxes, or where the nature of the product means that the price cannot reasonably be calculated in advance, the manner in which the price is calculated, as well as, where appropriate, all additional freight, delivery or postal charges or, where these charges cannot reasonably be calculated in advance, the fact that such additional charges may be payable;

(d)   the arrangements for payment, delivery, performance and the complaint handling policy, if they depart from the requirements of professional diligence;

(e)   for products and transactions involving a right of withdrawal or cancellation, the existence of such a right.

5.   Information requirements established by Community law in relation to commercial communication including advertising or marketing, a non-exhaustive list of which is contained in Annex II, shall be regarded as material.

SECTION 2
AGGRESSIVE COMMERCIAL PRACTICES

Article 8   Aggressive commercial practices

A commercial practice shall be regarded as aggressive if, in its factual context, taking account of all its features and circumstances, by harassment, coercion, including the use of physical force, or undue influence, it significantly impairs or is likely to significantly impair the average consumer's freedom of choice or conduct with regard to the product and thereby causes him or is likely to cause him to take a transactional decision that he would not have taken otherwise.

Article 9   Use of harassment, coercion and undue influence

In determining whether a commercial practice uses harassment, coercion, including the use of physical force, or undue influence, account shall be taken of:

(a)   its timing, location, nature or persistence;

(b)   the use of threatening or abusive language or behaviour;

(c)   the exploitation by the trader of any specific misfortune or circumstance of such gravity as to impair the consumer's judgement, of which the trader is aware, to influence the consumer's decision with regard to the product;

(d)   any onerous or disproportionate non-contractual barriers imposed by the trader where a consumer wishes to exercise rights under the contract, including rights to terminate a contract or to switch to another product or another trader;

(e)   any threat to take any action that cannot legally be taken.

CHAPTER 3
CODES OF CONDUCT

Article 10   Codes of conduct

This Directive does not exclude the control, which Member States may encourage, of unfair commercial practices by code owners and recourse to such bodies by the persons or organisations referred to in Article 11 if proceedings before such bodies are in addition to the court or administrative proceedings referred to in that Article.

Recourse to such control bodies shall never be deemed the equivalent of foregoing a means of judicial or administrative recourse as provided for in Article 11.

CHAPTER 4
FINAL PROVISIONS

Article 11   Enforcement

1. Member States shall ensure that adequate and effective means exist to combat unfair commercial practices in order to enforce compliance with the provisions of this Directive in the interest of consumers. Such means shall include legal provisions under which persons or organisations regarded under national law as having a legitimate interest in combating unfair commercial practices, including competitors, may:

    (a)   take legal action against such unfair commercial practices; and/or

    (b)   bring such unfair commercial practices before an administrative authority competent either to decide on complaints or to initiate appropriate legal proceedings.

    It shall be for each Member State to decide which of these facilities shall be available and whether to enable the courts or administrative authorities to require prior recourse to other established means of dealing with complaints, including those referred to in Art. 10. These facilities shall be available regardless of whether the consumers affected are in the territory of the Member State where the trader is located or in another Member State.

    It shall be for each Member State to decide:

    (a)   whether these legal facilities may be directed separately or jointly against a number of traders from the same economic sector; and

    (b)   whether these legal facilities may be directed against a code owner where the relevant code promotes non-compliance with legal requirements.

2. Under the legal provisions referred to in paragraph 1, Member States shall confer upon the courts or administrative authorities powers enabling them, in cases where they deem such measures to be necessary taking into account all the interests involved and in particular the public interest:

    (a)   to order the cessation of, or to institute appropriate legal proceedings for an order for the cessation of, unfair commercial practices; or

    (b)   if the unfair commercial practice has not yet been carried out but is imminent, to order the prohibition of the practice, or to institute appropriate legal proceedings for an order for the prohibition of the practice,

    even without proof of actual loss or damage or of intention or negligence on the part of the trader.

    Member States shall also make provision for the measures referred to in the first subparagraph to be taken under an accelerated procedure:

    —   either with interim effect, or

    —   with definitive effect,

    on the understanding that it is for each Member State to decide which of the two options to select.

    Furthermore, Member States may confer upon the courts or administrative authorities powers enabling them, with a view to eliminating the continuing effects of unfair commercial practices the cessation of which has been ordered by a final decision:

    (a)   to require publication of that decision in full or in part and in such form as they deem adequate;

    (b)   to require in addition the publication of a corrective statement.

3. The administrative authorities referred to in paragraph 1 must:

    (a)   be composed so as not to cast doubt on their impartiality;

    (b)   have adequate powers, where they decide on complaints, to monitor and enforce the observance of their decisions effectively;

    (c)   normally give reasons for their decisions.

    Where the powers referred to in paragraph 2 are exercised exclusively by an administrative authority, reasons for its decisions shall always be given. Furthermore, in this case, provision must be made for procedures whereby improper or unreasonable exercise of its powers by the administrative authority or improper or unreasonable failure to exercise the said powers can be the subject of judicial review.

Article 12   Courts and administrative authorities: substantiation of claims

Member States shall confer upon the courts or administrative authorities powers enabling them in the civil or administrative proceedings provided for in Article 11:

(a)   to require the trader to furnish evidence as to the accuracy of factual claims in relation to a commercial practice if, taking into account the legitimate interest of the trader and any other party to the proceedings, such a requirement appears appropriate on the basis of the circumstances of the particular case; and

(b)   to consider factual claims as inaccurate if the evidence demanded in accordance with (a) is not furnished or is deemed insufficient by the court or administrative authority.

Article 13   Penalties

Member States shall lay down penalties for infringements of national provisions adopted in application of this Directive and shall take all necessary measures to ensure that these are enforced. These penalties must be effective, proportionate and dissuasive.

Article 14   Amendments to Directive 84/450/EEC

Directive 84/450/EEC is hereby amended as follows:

1.   Article 1 shall be replaced by the following:

'*Article 1*

The purpose of this Directive is to protect traders against misleading advertising and the unfair consequences thereof and to lay down the conditions under which comparative advertising is permitted.';

2.   in Article 2:

— point 3 shall be replaced by the following:

'3.   'trader' means any natural or legal person who is acting for purposes relating to his trade, craft, business or profession and any one acting in the name of or on behalf of a trader.',

— the following point shall be added:

'4.   'code owner' means any entity, including a trader or group of traders, which is responsible for the formulation and revision of a code of conduct and/or for monitoring compliance with the code by those who have undertaken to be bound by it.';

3.   Article 3a shall be replaced by the following:

'*Article 3a*

1.   Comparative advertising shall, as far as the comparison is concerned, be permitted when the following conditions are met:

(a)   it is not misleading within the meaning of Articles 2(2), 3 and 7(1) of this Directive or Articles 6 and 7 of Directive 2005/29/EC of the European Parliament and of the Council of 11 May 2005 concerning unfair business-to-consumer commercial practices in the internal market;

(b)   it compares goods or services meeting the same needs or intended for the same purpose;

(c)   it objectively compares one or more material, relevant, verifiable and representative features of those goods and services, which may include price;

(d)   it does not discredit or denigrate the trade marks, trade names, other distinguishing marks, goods, services, activities, or circumstances of a competitor;

(e)   for products with designation of origin, it relates in each case to products with the same designation;

(f)   it does not take unfair advantage of the reputation of a trade mark, trade name or other distinguishing marks of a competitor or of the designation of origin of competing products;

(g)   it does not present goods or services as imitations or replicas of goods or services bearing a protected trade mark or trade name;

(h)   it does not create confusion among traders, between the advertiser and a competitor or between the advertiser's trade marks, trade names, other distinguishing marks, goods or services and those of a competitor.'

4.   Article 4(1) shall be replaced by the following:

'1.   Member States shall ensure that adequate and effective means exist to combat misleading advertising in order to enforce compliance with the provisions on comparative advertising in the interest of traders and competitors. Such means shall include legal provisions under which persons or organisations regarded under national

law as having a legitimate interest in combating misleading advertising or regulating comparative advertising may:
- (a) take legal action against such advertising; or
- (b) bring such advertising before an administrative authority competent either to decide on complaints or to initiate appropriate legal proceedings.'

It shall be for each Member State to decide which of these facilities shall be available and whether to enable the courts or administrative authorities to require prior recourse to other established means of dealing with complaints, including those referred to in Article 5.

It shall be for each Member State to decide:
- (a) whether these legal facilities may be directed separately or jointly against a number of traders from the same economic sector; and
- (b) whether these legal facilities may be directed against a code owner where the relevant code promotes non-compliance with legal requirements.';

5. Article 7(1) shall be replaced by the following:
'1. This Directive shall not preclude Member States from retaining or adopting provisions with a view to ensuring more extensive protection, with regard to misleading advertising, for traders and competitors.'

Article 15 Amendments to Directives 97/7/EC and 2002/65/EC

1. Article 9 of Directive 97/7/EC shall be replaced by the following:
'*Article 9*
Inertia selling
Given the prohibition of inertia selling practices laid down in Directive 2005/29/EC of 11 May 2005 of the European Parliament and of the Council concerning unfair business-to-consumer commercial practices in the internal market, Member States shall take the measures necessary to exempt the consumer from the provision of any consideration in cases of unsolicited supply, the absence of a response not constituting consent.'

2. Article 9 of Directive 2002/65/EC shall be replaced by the following:
'*Article 9*
Given the prohibition of inertia selling practices laid down in Directive 2005/29/EC of 11 May 2005 of the European Parliament and of the Council concerning unfair business-to-consumer commercial practices in the internal market and without prejudice to the provisions of Member States' legislation on the tacit renewal of distance contracts, when such rules permit tacit renewal, Member States shall take measures to exempt the consumer from any obligation in the event of unsolicited supplies, the absence of a reply not constituting consent.'

Article 16 Amendments to Directive 98/27/EC and Regulation (EC) No 2006/2004

1. In the Annex to Directive 98/27/EC, point 1 shall be replaced by the following:
'1. Directive 2005/29/EC of the European Parliament and of the Council of 11 May 2005 concerning unfair business-to-consumer commercial practices in the internal market (OJ L 149, 11.6.2005, p. 22).'

2. In the Annex to Regulation (EC) No 2006/2004 of the European Parliament and of the Council of 27 October 2004 on cooperation between national authorities responsible for the enforcement of the consumer protection law (the Regulation on consumer protection cooperation) the following point shall be added:
'16. Directive 2005/29/EC of the European Parliament and of the Council of 11 May 2005 concerning unfair business-to-consumer commercial practices in the internal market (OJ L 149, 11.6.2005, p. 22).'

Article 17 Information

Member States shall take appropriate measures to inform consumers of the national law transposing this Directive and shall, where appropriate, encourage traders and code owners to inform consumers of their codes of conduct.

Article 18 Review

1. By 12 June 2011 the Commission shall submit to the European Parliament and the Council a comprehensive report on the application of this Directive, in particular of Articles 3(9) and 4 and Annex I, on the scope for further harmonisation and simplification of Community

law relating to consumer protection, and, having regard to Article 3(5), on any measures that need to be taken at Community level to ensure that appropriate levels of consumer protection are maintained. The report shall be accompanied, if necessary, by a proposal to revise this Directive or other relevant parts of Community law.

2.   The European Parliament and the Council shall endeavour to act, in accordance with the Treaty, within two years of the presentation by the Commission of any proposal submitted under paragraph 1.

Article 19   Transposition

Member States shall adopt and publish the laws, regulations and administrative provisions necessary to comply with this Directive by 12 June 2007. They shall forthwith inform the Commission thereof and inform the Commission of any subsequent amendments without delay.

They shall apply those measures by 12 December 2007. When Member States adopt those measures, they shall contain a reference to this Directive or be accompanied by such a reference on the occasion of their official publication. Member States shall determine how such reference is to be made.

Article 20   Entry into force

This Directive shall enter into force on the day following its publication in the *Official Journal of the European Union*.

Article 21   Addressees

This Directive is addressed to the Member States.

Done at Strasbourg, 11 May 2005.

ANNEX I

COMMERCIAL PRACTICES WHICH ARE IN ALL CIRCUMSTANCES CONSIDERED UNFAIR

Misleading commercial practices
1.   Claiming to be a signatory to a code of conduct when the trader is not.
2.   Displaying a trust mark, quality mark or equivalent without having obtained the necessary authorisation.
3.   Claiming that a code of conduct has an endorsement from a public or other body which it does not have.
4.   Claiming that a trader (including his commercial practices) or a product has been approved, endorsed or authorised by a public or private body when he/it has not or making such a claim without complying with the terms of the approval, endorsement or authorisation.
5.   Making an invitation to purchase products at a specified price without disclosing the existence of any reasonable grounds the trader may have for believing that he will not be able to offer for supply or to procure another trader to supply, those products or equivalent products at that price for a period that is, and in quantities that are, reasonable having regard to the product, the scale of advertising of the product and the price offered (bait advertising).
6.   Making an invitation to purchase products at a specified price and then:
(a)   refusing to show the advertised item to consumers; or
(b)   refusing to take orders for it or deliver it within a reasonable time; or
(c)   demonstrating a defective sample of it,
with the intention of promoting a different product (bait and switch)
7.   Falsely stating that a product will only be available for a very limited time, or that it will only be available on particular terms for a very limited time, in order to elicit an immediate decision and deprive consumers of sufficient opportunity or time to make an informed choice.
8.   Undertaking to provide after-sales service to consumers with whom the trader has communicated prior to a transaction in a language which is not an official language of the Member State where the trader is located and then making such service available only in another language without clearly disclosing this to the consumer before the consumer is committed to the transaction.

9. Stating or otherwise creating the impression that a product can legally be sold when it cannot.
10. Presenting rights given to consumers in law as a distinctive feature of the trader's offer.
11. Using editorial content in the media to promote a product where a trader has paid for the promotion without making that clear in the content or by images or sounds clearly identifiable by the consumer (advertorial). This is without prejudice to Council Directive 89/552/EEC.
12. Making a materially inaccurate claim concerning the nature and extent of the risk to the personal security of the consumer or his family if the consumer does not purchase the product.
13. Promoting a product similar to a product made by a particular manufacturer in such a manner as deliberately to mislead the consumer into believing that the product is made by that same manufacturer when it is not.
14. Establishing, operating or promoting a pyramid promotional scheme where a consumer gives consideration for the opportunity to receive compensation that is derived primarily from the introduction of other consumers into the scheme rather than from the sale or consumption of products.
15. Claiming that the trader is about to cease trading or move premises when he is not.
16. Claiming that products are able to facilitate winning in games of chance.
17. Falsely claiming that a product is able to cure illnesses, dysfunction or malformations.
18. Passing on materially inaccurate information on market conditions or on the possibility of finding the product with the intention of inducing the consumer to acquire the product at conditions less favourable than normal market conditions.
19. Claiming in a commercial practice to offer a competition or prize promotion without awarding the prizes described or a reasonable equivalent.
20. Describing a product as 'gratis', 'free', 'without charge' or similar if the consumer has to pay anything other than the unavoidable cost of responding to the commercial practice and collecting or paying for delivery of the item.
21. Including in marketing material an invoice or similar document seeking payment which gives the consumer the impression that he has already ordered the marketed product when he has not.
22. Falsely claiming or creating the impression that the trader is not acting for purposes relating to his trade, business, craft or profession, or falsely representing oneself as a consumer.
23. Creating the false impression that after-sales service in relation to a product is available in a Member State other than the one in which the product is sold.

Aggressive commercial practices

24. Creating the impression that the consumer cannot leave the premises until a contract is formed.
25. Conducting personal visits to the consumer's home ignoring the consumer's request to leave or not to return except in circumstances and to the extent justified, under national law, to enforce a contractual obligation.
26. Making persistent and unwanted solicitations by telephone, fax, e-mail or other remote media except in circumstances and to the extent justified under national law to enforce a contractual obligation. This is without prejudice to Art. 10 of Directive 97/7/EC and Directives 95/46/EC and 2002/58/EC.
27. Requiring a consumer who wishes to claim on an insurance policy to produce documents which could not reasonably be considered relevant as to whether the claim was valid, or failing systematically to respond to pertinent correspondence, in order to dissuade a consumer from exercising his contractual rights.
28. Including in an advertisement a direct exhortation to children to buy advertised products or persuade their parents or other adults to buy advertised products for them. This provision is without prejudice to Article 16 of Directive 89/552/EEC on television broadcasting.
29. Demanding immediate or deferred payment for or the return or safekeeping of products supplied by the trader, but not solicited by the consumer except where the product is a substitute supplied in conformity with Article 7(3) of Directive 97/7/EC (inertia selling).
30. Explicitly informing a consumer that if he does not buy the product or service, the trader's job or livelihood will be in jeopardy.
31. Creating the false impression that the consumer has already won, will win, or will on doing a particular act win, a prize or other equivalent benefit, when in fact either:

— there is no prize or other equivalent benefit, or
— taking any action in relation to claiming the prize or other equivalent benefit is subject to the consumer paying money or incurring a cost.

ANNEX II
COMMUNITY LAW PROVISIONS SETTING OUT RULES FOR ADVERTISING AND COMMERCIAL COMMUNICATION

Articles 4 and 5 of Directive 97/7/EC

Article 3 of Council Directive 90/314/EEC of 13 June 1990 on package travel, package holidays and package tours

Article 3(3) of Directive 94/47/EC of the European Parliament and of the Council of 26 October 1994 on the protection of purchasers in respect of certain aspects of contracts relating to the purchase of a right to use immovable properties on a timeshare basis

Article 3(4) of Directive 98/6/EC of the European Parliament and of the Council of 16 February 1998 on consumer protection in the indication of the prices of products offered to consumers

Articles 86 to 100 of Directive 2001/83/EC of the European Parliament and of the Council of 6 November 2001 on the Community code relating to medicinal products for human use

Articles 5 and 6 of Directive 2000/31/EC of the European Parliament and of the Council of 8 June 2000 on certain legal aspects of information society services, in particular electronic commerce, in the Internal Market (Directive on electronic commerce)

Article 1(d) of Directive 98/7/EC of the European Parliament and of the Council of 16 February 1998 amending Council Directive 87/102/EEC for the approximation of the laws, regulations and administrative provisions of the Member States concerning consumer credit

Articles 3 and 4 of Directive 2002/65/EC

Article 1(9) of Directive 2001/107/EC of the European Parliament and of the Council of 21 January 2002 amending Council Directive 85/611/EEC on the coordination of laws, regulations and administrative provisions relating to undertakings for collective investment in transferable securities (UCITS) with a view to regulating management companies and simplified prospectuses

Articles 12 and 13 of Directive 2002/92/EC of the European Parliament and of the Council of 9 December 2002 on insurance mediation

Article 36 of Directive 2002/83/EC of the European Parliament and of the Council of 5 November 2002 concerning life assurance

Article 19 of Directive 2004/39/EC of the European Parliament and of the Council of 21 April 2004 on markets in financial instruments

Articles 31 and 43 of Council Directive 92/49/EEC of 18 June 1992 on the coordination of laws, regulations and administrative provisions relating to direct insurance other than life assurance (third non-life insurance Directive)

Articles 5, 7 and 8 of Directive 2003/71/EC of the European Parliament and of the Council of 4 November 2003 on the prospectus to be published when securities are offered to the public or admitted to trading

INTERNATIONAL RULES

UNIFORM CUSTOMS AND PRACTICE FOR DOCUMENTARY CREDITS (UCP 600)*

Article 1 Application of UCP
The Uniform Customs and Practice for Documentary Credits, 2007 Revision, ICC Publication no. 600 ('UCP') are rules that apply to any documentary credit ('credit') (including, to the extent to which they may be applicable, any standby letter of credit) when the text of the credit expressly indicates that it is subject to these rules. They are binding on all parties thereto unless expressly modified or excluded by the credit.

---

* ICC Publication N° 600 (E) – ISBN 978-92-842-1257-6 © 2006 International Chamber of Commerce (ICC), reproduced with permission

Article 2   Definitions

For the purpose of these rules:

Advising bank means the bank that advises the credit at the request of the issuing bank.

Applicant means the party on whose request the credit is issued.

Banking day means a day on which a bank is regularly open at the place at which an act subject to these rules is to be performed.

Beneficiary means the party in whose favour a credit is issued.

Complying presentation means a presentation that is in accordance with the terms and conditions of the credit, the applicable provisions of these rules and international standard banking practice.

Confirmation means a definite undertaking of the confirming bank, in addition to that of the issuing bank, to honour or negotiate a complying presentation.

Confirming bank means the bank that adds its confirmation to a credit upon the issuing bank's authorization or request.

Credit means any arrangement, however named or described, that is irrevocable and thereby constitutes a definite undertaking of the issuing bank to honour a complying presentation.

Honour means:

(a)   to pay at sight if the credit is available by sight payment.

(b)   to incur a deferred payment undertaking and pay at maturity if the credit is available by deferred payment.

(c)   to accept a bill of exchange ('draft') drawn by the beneficiary and pay at maturity if the credit is available by acceptance.

Issuing bank means the bank that issues a credit at the request of an applicant or on its own behalf.

Negotiation means the purchase by the nominated bank of drafts (drawn on a bank other than the nominated bank) and/or documents under a complying presentation, by advancing or agreeing to

advance funds to the beneficiary on or before the banking day on which reimbursement is due to the nominated bank.

Nominated bank means the bank with which the credit is available or any bank in the case of a credit available with any bank.

Presentation means either the delivery of documents under a credit to the issuing bank or nominated bank or the documents so delivered.

Presenter means a beneficiary, bank or other party that makes a presentation.

Article 3   Interpretations

For the purpose of these rules:

Where applicable, words in the singular include the plural and in the plural include the singular.

A credit is irrevocable even if there is no indication to that effect.

A document may be signed by handwriting, facsimile signature, perforated signature, stamp, symbol or any other mechanical or electronic method of authentication.

A requirement for a document to be legalized, visaed, certified or similar will be satisfied by any signature, mark, stamp or label on the document which appears to satisfy that requirement.

Branches of a bank in different countries are considered to be separate banks.

Terms such as 'first class', 'well known', 'qualified', 'independent', 'official', 'competent' or 'local' used to describe the issuer of a document allow any issuer except the beneficiary to issue that document. Unless required to be used in a document, words such as 'prompt', 'immediately' or 'as soon as possible' will be disregarded.

The expression 'on or about' or similar will be interpreted as a stipulation that an event is to occur during a period of five calendar days before until five calendar days after the specified date, both start and end dates included.

The words 'to', 'until', 'till', 'from' and 'between' when used to determine a period of shipment include the date or dates mentioned, and the words 'before' and 'after' exclude the date mentioned.

The words 'from' and 'after' when used to determine a maturity date exclude the date mentioned.

The terms 'first half' and 'second half' of a month shall be construed respectively as the 1st to the 15th and the 16th to the last day of the month, all dates inclusive.

The terms 'beginning', 'middle' and 'end' of a month shall be construed respectively as the 1st to the 10th, the 11th to the 20th and the 21st to the last day of the month, all dates inclusive.

Article 4   Credits v. Contracts

(a)   A credit by its nature is a separate transaction from the sale or other contract on which it may be based. Banks are in no way concerned with or bound by such contract, even if any reference whatsoever to it is included in the credit. Consequently, the undertaking of a bank to honour, to negotiate or to fulfil any other obligation under the credit is not subject to claims or defences by the applicant resulting from its relationships with the issuing bank or the beneficiary. A beneficiary can in no case avail itself of the contractual relationships existing between banks or between the applicant and the issuing bank.

(b)   An issuing bank should discourage any attempt by the applicant to include, as an integral part of the credit, copies of the underlying contract, proforma invoice and the like.

Article 5   Documents v. Goods, Services or Performance

Banks deal with documents and not with goods, services or performance to which the documents may relate.

Article 6   Availability, Expiry Date and Place for Presentation

(a)   A credit must state the bank with which it is available or whether it is available with any bank. A credit available with a nominated bank is also available with the issuing bank.

(b)   A credit must state whether it is available by sight payment, deferred payment, acceptance or negotiation.

(c)   A credit must not be issued available by a draft drawn on the applicant.

(d)   (i)   A credit must state an expiry date for presentation. An expiry date stated for honour or negotiation will be deemed to be an expiry date for presentation.

    (ii)   The place of the bank with which the credit is available is the place for presentation. The place for presentation under a credit available with any bank is that of any bank. A place for presentation other than that of the issuing bank is in addition to the place of the issuing bank.

(e)   Except as provided in sub-article 29(a), a presentation by or on behalf of the beneficiary must be made on or before the expiry date.

Article 7   Issuing Bank Undertaking

(a)   Provided that the stipulated documents are presented to the nominated bank or to the issuing bank and that they constitute a complying presentation, the issuing bank must honour if the credit is available by:

    (i)   sight payment, deferred payment or acceptance with the issuing bank;

    (ii)   sight payment with a nominated bank and that nominated bank does not pay;

    (iii)   deferred payment with a nominated bank and that nominated bank does not incur its deferred payment undertaking or, having incurred its deferred payment undertaking, does not pay at maturity;

    (iv)   acceptance with a nominated bank and that nominated bank does not accept a draft drawn on it or, having accepted a draft drawn on it, does not pay at maturity;

    (v)   negotiation with a nominated bank and that nominated bank does not negotiate.

(b)   An issuing bank is irrevocably bound to honour as of the time it issues the credit.

(c)   An issuing bank undertakes to reimburse a nominated bank that has honoured or negotiated a complying presentation and forwarded the documents to the issuing bank. Reimbursement for the amount of a complying presentation under a credit available by acceptance or deferred payment is due at maturity, whether or not the nominated bank prepaid or purchased before maturity. An issuing bank's undertaking to reimburse a nominated bank is independent of the issuing bank's undertaking to the beneficiary.

Article 8   Confirming Bank Undertaking

(a)   Provided that the stipulated documents are presented to the confirming bank or to any other nominated bank and that they constitute a complying presentation, the confirming bank must:

    (i)   honour, if the credit is available by

        (a)   sight payment, deferred payment or acceptance with the confirming bank;

        (b)   sight payment with another nominated bank and that nominated bank does not pay;

        (c)   deferred payment with another nominated bank and that nominated bank does not incur its deferred payment undertaking or, having incurred its deferred payment undertaking, does not pay at maturity;

(d) acceptance with another nominated bank and that nominated bank does not accept a draft drawn on it or, having accepted a draft drawn on it, does not pay at maturity;

(e) negotiation with another nominated bank and that nominated bank does not negotiate.

(ii) negotiate, without recourse, if the credit is available by negotiation with the confirming bank.

(b) A confirming bank is irrevocably bound to honour or negotiate as of the time it adds its confirmation to the credit.

(c) A confirming bank undertakes to reimburse another nominated bank that has honoured or negotiated a complying presentation and forwarded the documents to the confirming bank. Reimbursement for the amount of a complying presentation under a credit available by acceptance or deferred payment is due at maturity, whether or not another nominated bank prepaid or purchased before maturity. A confirming bank's undertaking to reimburse another nominated bank is independent of the confirming bank's undertaking to the beneficiary.

(d) If a bank is authorized or requested by the issuing bank to confirm a credit but is not prepared to do so, it must inform the issuing bank without delay and may advise the credit without confirmation.

Article 9   Advising of Credits and Amendments

(a) A credit and any amendment may be advised to a beneficiary through an advising bank. An advising bank that is not a confirming bank advises the credit and any amendment without any undertaking to honour or negotiate.

(b) By advising the credit or amendment, the advising bank signifies that it has satisfied itself as to the apparent authenticity of the credit or amendment and that the advice accurately reflects the terms and conditions of the credit or amendment received.

(c) An advising bank may utilize the services of another bank ('second advising bank') to advise the credit and any amendment to the beneficiary. By advising the credit or amendment, the second advising bank signifies that it has satisfied itself as to the apparent authenticity of the advice it has received and that the advice accurately reflects the terms and conditions of the credit or amendment received.

(d) A bank utilizing the services of an advising bank or second advising bank to advise a credit must use the same bank to advise any amendment thereto.

(e) If a bank is requested to advise a credit or amendment but elects not to do so, it must so inform, without delay, the bank from which the credit, amendment or advice has been received.

(f) If a bank is requested to advise a credit or amendment but cannot satisfy itself as to the apparent authenticity of the credit, the amendment or the advice, it must so inform, without delay, the bank from which the instructions appear to have been received. If the advising bank or second advising bank elects nonetheless to advise the credit or amendment, it must inform the beneficiary or second advising bank that it has not been able to satisfy itself as to the apparent authenticity of the credit, the amendment or the advice.

Article 10   Amendments

(a) Except as otherwise provided by article 38, a credit can neither be amended nor cancelled without the agreement of the issuing bank, the confirming bank, if any, and the beneficiary.

(b) An issuing bank is irrevocably bound by an amendment as of the time it issues the amendment. A confirming bank may extend its confirmation to an amendment and will be irrevocably bound as of the time it advises the amendment. A confirming bank may, however, choose to advise an amendment without extending its confirmation and, if so, it must inform the issuing bank without delay and inform the beneficiary in its advice.

(c) The terms and conditions of the original credit (or a credit incorporating previously accepted amendments) will remain in force for the beneficiary until the beneficiary communicates its acceptance of the amendment to the bank that advised such amendment. The beneficiary should give notification of acceptance or rejection of an amendment. If the beneficiary fails to give such notification, a presentation that complies with the credit and to any not yet accepted amendment will be deemed to be notification of acceptance by the beneficiary of such amendment. As of that moment the credit will be amended.

(d) A bank that advises an amendment should inform the bank from which it received the amendment of any notification of acceptance or rejection.

(e)   Partial acceptance of an amendment is not allowed and will be deemed to be notification of rejection of the amendment.

(f)   A provision in an amendment to the effect that the amendment shall enter into force unless rejected by the beneficiary within a certain time shall be disregarded.

Article 11   Teletransmitted and Pre-Advised Credits and Amendments

(a)   An authenticated teletransmission of a credit or amendment will be deemed to be the operative credit or amendment, and any subsequent mail confirmation shall be disregarded. If a teletransmission states 'full details to follow' (or words of similar effect), or states that the mail confirmation is to be the operative credit or amendment, then the teletransmission will not be deemed to be the operative credit or amendment. The issuing bank must then issue the operative credit or amendment without delay in terms not inconsistent with the teletransmission.

(b)   A preliminary advice of the issuance of a credit or amendment ('pre-advice') shall only be sent if the issuing bank is prepared to issue the operative credit or amendment. An issuing bank that sends a pre-advice is irrevocably committed to issue the operative credit or amendment, without delay, in terms not inconsistent with the pre-advice.

Article 12   Nomination

(a)   Unless a nominated bank is the confirming bank, an authorization to honour or negotiate does not impose any obligation on that nominated bank to honour or negotiate, except when expressly agreed to by that nominated bank and so communicated to the beneficiary.

(b)   By nominating a bank to accept a draft or incur a deferred payment undertaking, an issuing bank authorizes that nominated bank to prepay or purchase a draft accepted or a deferred payment undertaking incurred by that nominated bank.

(c)   Receipt or examination and forwarding of documents by a nominated bank that is not a confirming bank does not make that nominated bank liable to honour or negotiate, nor does it constitute honour or negotiation.

Article 13   Bank-to-Bank Reimbursement Arrangements

(a)   If a credit states that reimbursement is to be obtained by a nominated bank ('claiming bank') claiming on another party ('reimbursing bank'), the credit must state if the reimbursement is subject to the ICC rules for bank-to-bank reimbursements in effect on the date of issuance of the credit.

(b)   If a credit does not state that reimbursement is subject to the ICC rules for bank-to-bank reimbursements, the following apply:

    (i)   An issuing bank must provide a reimbursing bank with a reimbursement authorization that conforms with the availability stated in the credit. The reimbursement authorization should not be subject to an expiry date.

    (ii)   A claiming bank shall not be required to supply a reimbursing bank with a certificate of compliance with the terms and conditions of the credit.

    (iii)   An issuing bank will be responsible for any loss of interest, together with any expenses incurred, if reimbursement is not provided on first demand by a reimbursing bank in accordance with the terms and conditions of the credit.

    (iv)   A reimbursing bank's charges are for the account of the issuing bank. However, if the charges are for the account of the beneficiary, it is the responsibility of an issuing bank to so indicate in the credit and in the reimbursement authorization. If a reimbursing bank's charges are for the account of the beneficiary, they shall be deducted from the amount due to a claiming bank when reimbursement is made. If no reimbursement is made, the reimbursing bank's charges remain the obligation of the issuing bank.

(c)   An issuing bank is not relieved of any of its obligations to provide reimbursement if reimbursement is not made by a reimbursing bank on first demand.

Article 14   Standard for Examination of Documents

(a)   A nominated bank acting on its nomination, a confirming bank, if any, and the issuing bank must examine a presentation to determine, on the basis of the documents alone, whether or not the documents appear on their face to constitute a complying presentation.

(b)   A nominated bank acting on its nomination, a confirming bank, if any, and the issuing bank shall each have a maximum of five banking days following the day of presentation to determine if a presentation is complying. This period is not curtailed or otherwise affected by the occurrence on or after the date of presentation of any expiry date or last day for presentation.

(c)   A presentation including one or more original transport documents subject to articles 19, 20, 21, 22, 23, 24 or 25 must be made by or on behalf of the beneficiary not later than 21 calendar days after the date of shipment as described in these rules, but in any event not later than the expiry date of the credit.

(d)   Data in a document, when read in context with the credit, the document itself and international standard banking practice, need not be identical to, but must not conflict with, data in that document, any other stipulated document or the credit.

(e)   In documents other than the commercial invoice, the description of the goods, services or performance, if stated, may be in general terms not conflicting with their description in the credit.

(f)   If a credit requires presentation of a document other than a transport document, insurance document or commercial invoice, without stipulating by whom the document is to be issued or its data content, banks will accept the document as presented if its content appears to fulfil the function of the required document and otherwise complies with sub-article 14(d).

(g)   A document presented but not required by the credit will be disregarded and may be returned to the presenter.

(h)   If a credit contains a condition without stipulating the document to indicate compliance with the condition, banks will deem such condition as not stated and will disregard it.

(i)   A document may be dated prior to the issuance date of the credit, but must not be dated later than its date of presentation.

(j)   When the addresses of the beneficiary and the applicant appear in any stipulated document, they need not be the same as those stated in the credit or in any other stipulated document, but must be within the same country as the respective addresses mentioned in the credit. Contact details (telefax, telephone, email and the like) stated as part of the beneficiary's and the applicant's address will be disregarded. However, when the address and contact details of the applicant appear as part of the consignee or notify party details on a transport document subject to articles 19, 20, 21, 22, 23, 24 or 25, they must be as stated in the credit.

(k)   The shipper or consignor of the goods indicated on any document need not be the beneficiary of the credit.

(l)   A transport document may be issued by any party other than a carrier, owner, master or charterer provided that the transport document meets the requirements of articles 19, 20, 21, 22, 23 or 24 of these rules.

Article 15   Complying Presentation

(a)   When an issuing bank determines that a presentation is complying, it must honour.

(b)   When a confirming bank determines that a presentation is complying, it must honour or negotiate and forward the documents to the issuing bank.

(c)   When a nominated bank determines that a presentation is complying and honours or negotiates, it must forward the documents to the confirming bank or issuing bank.

Article 16   Discrepant Documents, Waiver and Notice

(a)   When a nominated bank acting on its nomination, a confirming bank, if any, or the issuing bank determines that a presentation does not comply, it may refuse to honour or negotiate.

(b)   When an issuing bank determines that a presentation does not comply, it may in its sole judgement approach the applicant for a waiver of the discrepancies. This does not, however, extend the period mentioned in sub-article 14(b).

(c)   When a nominated bank acting on its nomination, a confirming bank, if any, or the issuing bank decides to refuse to honour or negotiate, it must give a single notice to that effect to the presenter. The notice must state:

(i)   that the bank is refusing to honour or negotiate; and

(ii)   each discrepancy in respect of which the bank refuses to honour or negotiate; and

(iii) (a)   that the bank is holding the documents pending further instructions from the presenter; or

       (b)   that the issuing bank is holding the documents until it receives a waiver from the applicant and agrees to accept it, or receives further instructions from the presenter prior to agreeing to accept a waiver; or

       (c)   that the bank is returning the documents; or

(d)   that the bank is acting in accordance with instructions previously received from the presenter.

(e)   The notice required in sub-article 16(c) must be given by telecommunication or, if that is not possible, by other expeditious means no later than the close of the fifth banking day following the day of presentation.

(f)   A nominated bank acting on its nomination, a confirming bank, if any, or the issuing bank may, after providing notice required by sub-article 16(c)(iii)(a) or (b), return the documents to the presenter at any time.

(g)   If an issuing bank or a confirming bank fails to act in accordance with the provisions of this article, it shall be precluded from claiming that the documents do not constitute a complying presentation.

(h)   When an issuing bank refuses to honour or a confirming bank refuses to honour or negotiate and has given notice to that effect in accordance with this article, it shall then be entitled to claim a refund, with interest, of any reimbursement made.

Article 17   Original Documents and Copies

(a)   At least one original of each document stipulated in the credit must be presented.

(b)   A bank shall treat as an original any document bearing an apparently original signature, mark, stamp, or label of the issuer of the document, unless the document itself indicates that it is not an original.

(c)   Unless a document indicates otherwise, a bank will also accept a document as original if it:
    (i)   appears to be written, typed, perforated or stamped by the document issuer's hand; or
    (ii)   appears to be on the document issuer's original stationery; or
    (iii) states that it is original, unless the statement appears not to apply to the document presented.

(d)   If a credit requires presentation of copies of documents, presentation of either originals or copies is permitted.

(e)   If a credit requires presentation of multiple documents by using terms such as 'in duplicate', 'in two fold' or 'in two copies', this will be satisfied by the presentation of at least one original and the remaining number in copies, except when the document itself indicates otherwise.

Article 18   Commercial Invoice

(a)   A commercial invoice:
    (i)   must appear to have been issued by the beneficiary (except as provided in article 38);
    (ii)   must be made out in the name of the applicant (except as provided in sub-article 38(g));
    (iii) must be made out in the same currency as the credit; and
    (iv) need not be signed.

(b)   A nominated bank acting on its nomination, a confirming bank, if any, or the issuing bank may accept a commercial invoice issued for an amount in excess of the amount permitted by the credit, and its decision will be binding upon all parties, provided the bank in question has not honoured or negotiated for an amount in excess of that permitted by the credit.

(c)   The description of the goods, services or performance in a commercial invoice must correspond with that appearing in the credit.

Article 19   Transport Document Covering at Least Two Different Modes of Transport

(a)   A transport document covering at least two different modes of transport (multimodal or combined transport document), however named, must appear to:
    (i)   indicate the name of the carrier and be signed by:
       •   the carrier or a named agent for or on behalf of the carrier, or
       •   the master or a named agent for or on behalf of the master.
    Any signature by the carrier, master or agent must be identified as that of the carrier, master or agent.
    Any signature by an agent must indicate whether the agent has signed for or on behalf of the carrier or for or on behalf of the master.
    (ii)   indicate that the goods have been dispatched, taken in charge or shipped on board at the place stated in the credit, by:
    pre-printed wording, or

a stamp or notation indicating the date on which the goods have been dispatched, taken in charge or shipped on board.

The date of issuance of the transport document will be deemed to be the date of dispatch, taking in charge or shipped on board, and the date of shipment. However, if the transport document indicates, by stamp or notation, a date of dispatch, taking in charge or shipped on board, this date will be deemed to be the date of shipment.

    (iii)   indicate the place of dispatch, taking in charge or shipment and the place of final destination stated in the credit, even if:

        (a)   the transport document states, in addition, a different place of dispatch, taking in charge or shipment or place of final destination, or

        (b)   the transport document contains the indication 'intended' or similar qualification in relation to the vessel, port of loading or port of discharge.

    (iv)   be the sole original transport document or, if issued in more than one original, be the full set as indicated on the transport document.

    (v)   contain terms and conditions of carriage or make reference to another source containing the terms and conditions of carriage (short form or blank back transport document). Contents of terms and conditions of carriage will not be examined.

    (vi)   contain no indication that it is subject to a charter party.

(b)   For the purpose of this article, transhipment means unloading from one means of conveyance and reloading to another means of conveyance (whether or not in different modes of transport) during the carriage from the place of dispatch, taking in charge or shipment to the place of final destination stated in the credit.

(c)   (i)   A transport document may indicate that the goods will or may be transhipped provided that the entire carriage is covered by one and the same transport document.

    (ii)   A transport document indicating that transhipment will or may take place is acceptable, even if the credit prohibits transhipment.

Article 20   Bill of Lading

(a)   A bill of lading, however named, must appear to:

    (i)   indicate the name of the carrier and be signed by:
- the carrier or a named agent for or on behalf of the carrier, or
- the master or a named agent for or on behalf of the master.

Any signature by the carrier, master or agent must be identified as that of the carrier, master or agent.

Any signature by an agent must indicate whether the agent has signed for or on behalf of the carrier or for or on behalf of the master.

    (ii)   indicate that the goods have been shipped on board a named vessel at the port of loading stated in the credit by:

pre-printed wording, or

an on board notation indicating the date on which the goods have been shipped on board. The date of issuance of the bill of lading will be deemed to be the date of shipment unless the bill of lading contains an on board notation indicating the date of shipment, in which case the date stated in the on board notation will be deemed to be the date of shipment.

If the bill of lading contains the indication 'intended vessel' or similar qualification in relation to the name of the vessel, an on board notation indicating the date of shipment and the name of the actual vessel is required.

    (iii)   indicate shipment from the port of loading to the port of discharge stated in the credit.

If the bill of lading does not indicate the port of loading stated in the credit as the port of loading, or if it contains the indication 'intended' or similar qualification in relation to the port of loading, an on board notation indicating the port of loading as stated in the credit, the date of shipment and the name of the vessel is required. This provision applies even when loading on board or shipment on a named vessel is indicated by preprinted wording on the bill of lading.

    (iv)   be the sole original bill of lading or, if issued in more than one original, be the full set as indicated on the bill of lading.

(v)   contain terms and conditions of carriage or make reference to another source containing the terms and conditions of carriage (short form or blank back bill of lading). Contents of terms and conditions of carriage will not be examined.

(vi) contain no indication that it is subject to a charter party.

(b)   For the purpose of this article, transhipment means unloading from one vessel and reloading to another vessel during the carriage from the port of loading to the port of discharge stated in the credit.

(c)   (i)   A bill of lading may indicate that the goods will or may be transhipped provided that the entire carriage is covered by one and the same bill of lading.

(ii) A bill of lading indicating that transhipment will or may take place is acceptable, even if the credit prohibits transhipment, if the goods have been shipped in a container, trailer or LASH barge as evidenced by the bill of lading.

(d)   Clauses in a bill of lading stating that the carrier reserves the right to tranship will be disregarded.

Article 21   Non-Negotiable Sea Waybill

(a)   A non-negotiable sea waybill, however named, must appear to:

(i)   indicate the name of the carrier and be signed by:
- the carrier or a named agent for or on behalf of the carrier, or
- the master or a named agent for or on behalf of the master.

Any signature by the carrier, master or agent must be identified as that of the carrier, master or agent.

Any signature by an agent must indicate whether the agent has signed for or on behalf of the carrier or for or on behalf of the master.

(ii) indicate that the goods have been shipped on board a named vessel at the port of loading stated in the credit by:

pre-printed wording, or

an on board notation indicating the date on which the goods have been shipped on board. The date of issuance of the non-negotiable sea waybill will be deemed to be the date of shipment unless the non-negotiable sea waybill contains an on board notation indicating the date of shipment, in which case the date stated in the on board notation will be deemed to be the date of shipment.

If the non-negotiable sea waybill contains the indication 'intended vessel' or similar qualification in relation to the name of the vessel, an on board notation indicating the date of shipment and the name of the actual vessel is required.

(iii) indicate shipment from the port of loading to the port of discharge stated in the credit.

If the non-negotiable sea waybill does not indicate the port of loading stated in the credit as the port of loading, or if it contains the indication 'intended' or similar qualification in relation to the port of loading, an on board notation indicating the port of loading as stated in the credit, the date of shipment and the name of the vessel is required. This provision applies even when loading on board or shipment on a named vessel is indicated by pre-printed wording on the non-negotiable sea waybill.

(iv) be the sole original non-negotiable sea waybill or, if issued in more than one original, be the full set as indicated on the non-negotiable sea waybill.

(v)   contain terms and conditions of carriage or make reference to another source containing the terms and conditions of carriage (short form or blank back non-negotiable sea waybill). Contents of terms and conditions of carriage will not be examined.

(vi) contain no indication that it is subject to a charter party.

(b)   For the purpose of this article, transhipment means unloading from one vessel and reloading to another vessel during the carriage from the port of loading to the port of discharge stated in the credit.

(c)   (i)   A non-negotiable sea waybill may indicate that the goods will or may be transhipped provided that the entire carriage is covered by one and the same non-negotiable sea waybill.

(ii) A non-negotiable sea waybill indicating that transhipment will or may take place is acceptable, even if the credit prohibits transhipment, if the goods have been shipped in a container, trailer or LASH barge as evidenced by the non-negotiable sea waybill.

(d)   Clauses in a non-negotiable sea waybill stating that the carrier reserves the right to tranship will be disregarded.

Article 22   Charter Party Bill of Lading

(a)   A bill of lading, however named, containing an indication that it is subject to a charter party (charter party bill of lading), must appear to:

(i)   be signed by:

- the master or a named agent for or on behalf of the master, or
- the owner or a named agent for or on behalf of the owner, or
- the charterer or a named agent for or on behalf of the charterer.

Any signature by the master, owner, charterer or agent must be identified as that of the master, owner, charterer or agent. Any signature by an agent must indicate whether the agent has signed for or on behalf of the master, owner or charterer.

An agent signing for or on behalf of the owner or charterer must indicate the name of the owner or charterer.

(ii)   indicate that the goods have been shipped on board a named vessel at the port of loading stated in the credit by:

pre-printed wording, or

an on board notation indicating the date on which the goods have been shipped on board. The date of issuance of the charter party bill of lading will be deemed to be the date of shipment unless the charter party bill of lading contains an on board notation indicating the date of shipment, in which case the date stated in the on board notation will be deemed to be the date of shipment.

(iii) indicate shipment from the port of loading to the port of discharge stated in the credit. The port of discharge may also be shown as a range of ports or a geographical area, as stated in the credit.

(iv)   be the sole original charter party bill of lading or, if issued in more than one original, be the full set as indicated on the charter party bill of lading.

(b)   A bank will not examine charter party contracts, even if they are required to be presented by the terms of the credit.

Article 23   Air Transport Document

(a)   An air transport document, however named, must appear to:

(i)   indicate the name of the carrier and be signed by: the carrier, or

a named agent for or on behalf of the carrier.

Any signature by the carrier or agent must be identified as that of the carrier or agent. Any signature by an agent must indicate that the agent has signed for or on behalf of the carrier.

(ii)   indicate that the goods have been accepted for carriage.

(iii) indicate the date of issuance. This date will be deemed to be the date of shipment unless the air transport document contains a specific notation of the actual date of shipment, in which case the date stated in the notation will be deemed to be the date of shipment. Any other information appearing on the air transport document relative to the flight number and date will not be considered in determining the date of shipment.

(iv)   indicate the airport of departure and the airport of destination stated in the credit.

(v)   be the original for consignor or shipper, even if the credit stipulates a full set of originals.

(vi)   contain terms and conditions of carriage or make reference to another source containing the terms and conditions of carriage. Contents of terms and conditions of carriage will not be examined.

(b)   For the purpose of this article, transhipment means unloading from one aircraft and reloading to another aircraft during the carriage from the airport of departure to the airport of destination stated in the credit.

(c)   (i)   An air transport document may indicate that the goods will or may be transhipped, provided that the entire carriage is covered by one and the same air transport document.

(ii)   An air transport document indicating that transhipment will or may take place is acceptable, even if the credit prohibits transhipment.

Article 24   Road, Rail or Inland Waterway Transport Documents

(a)   A road, rail or inland waterway transport document, however named, must appear to:

(i)   indicate the name of the carrier and: be signed by the carrier or a named agent for or on behalf of the carrier, or indicate receipt of the goods by signature, stamp or notation by the carrier or a named agent for or on behalf of the carrier.

Any signature, stamp or notation of receipt of the goods by the carrier or agent must be identified as that of the carrier or agent.

Any signature, stamp or notation of receipt of the goods by the agent must indicate that the agent has signed or acted for or on behalf of the carrier.

If a rail transport document does not identify the carrier, any signature or stamp of the railway company will be accepted as evidence of the document being signed by the carrier.

(ii)   indicate the date of shipment or the date the goods have been received for shipment, dispatch or carriage at the place stated in the credit. Unless the transport document contains a dated reception stamp, an indication of the date of receipt or a date of shipment, the date of issuance of the transport document will be deemed to be the date of shipment.

(iii)   indicate the place of shipment and the place of destination stated in the credit.

(b)   (i)   A road transport document must appear to be the original for consignor or shipper or bear no marking indicating for whom the document has been prepared.

(ii)   A rail transport document marked 'duplicate' will be accepted as an original.

(iii)   A rail or inland waterway transport document will be accepted as an original whether marked as an original or not.

(c)   In the absence of an indication on the transport document as to the number of originals issued, the number presented will be deemed to constitute a full set.

(d)   For the purpose of this article, transhipment means unloading from one means of conveyance and reloading to another means of conveyance, within the same mode of transport, during the carriage from the place of shipment, dispatch or carriage to the place of destination stated in the credit.

(e)   (i)   A road, rail or inland waterway transport document may indicate that the goods will or may be transhipped provided that the entire carriage is covered by one and the same transport document.

(ii)   A road, rail or inland waterway transport document indicating that transhipment will or may take place is acceptable, even if the credit prohibits transhipment.

Article 25   Courier Receipt, Post Receipt or Certificate of Posting

(a)   A courier receipt, however named, evidencing receipt of goods for transport, must appear to:

(i)   indicate the name of the courier service and be stamped or signed by the named courier service at the place from which the credit states the goods are to be shipped; and

(ii)   indicate a date of pick-up or of receipt or wording to this effect. This date will be deemed to be the date of shipment.

(b)   A requirement that courier charges are to be paid or prepaid may be satisfied by a transport document issued by a courier service evidencing that courier charges are for the account of a party other than the consignee.

(c)   A post receipt or certificate of posting, however named, evidencing receipt of goods for transport, must appear to be stamped or signed and dated at the place from which the credit states the goods are to be shipped. This date will be deemed to be the date of shipment.

Article 26   'On Deck', 'Shipper's Load and Count', 'Said by Shipper to Contain' and Charges Additional to Freight

(a)   A transport document must not indicate that the goods are or will be loaded on deck. A clause on a transport document stating that the goods may be loaded on deck is acceptable.

(b)   A transport document bearing a clause such as 'shipper's load and count' and 'said by shipper to contain' is acceptable.

(c)   A transport document may bear a reference, by stamp or otherwise, to charges additional to the freight.

Article 27   Clean Transport Document

A bank will only accept a clean transport document. A clean transport document is one bearing no clause or notation expressly declaring a defective condition of the goods or their packaging. The word 'clean' need not appear on a transport document, even if a credit has a requirement for that transport document to be 'clean on board'.

Article 28   Insurance Document and Coverage

(a) An insurance document, such as an insurance policy, an insurance certificate or a declaration under an open cover, must appear to be issued and signed by an insurance company, an underwriter or their agents or their proxies. Any signature by an agent or proxy must indicate whether the agent or proxy has signed for or on behalf of the insurance company or underwriter.

(b) When the insurance document indicates that it has been issued in more than one original, all originals must be presented.

(c) Cover notes will not be accepted.

(d) An insurance policy is acceptable in lieu of an insurance certificate or a declaration under an open cover.

(e) The date of the insurance document must be no later than the date of shipment, unless it appears from the insurance document that the cover is effective from a date not later than the date of shipment.

(f) (i) The insurance document must indicate the amount of insurance coverage and be in the same currency as the credit.

    (ii) A requirement in the credit for insurance coverage to be for a percentage of the value of the goods, of the invoice value or similar is deemed to be the minimum amount of coverage required.

    If there is no indication in the credit of the insurance coverage required, the amount of insurance coverage must be at least 110% of the CIF or CIP value of the goods.

    When the CIF or CIP value cannot be determined from the documents, the amount of insurance coverage must be calculated on the basis of the amount for which honour or negotiation is requested or the gross value of the goods as shown on the invoice, whichever is greater.

    (iii) The insurance document must indicate that risks are covered at least between the place of taking in charge or shipment and the place of discharge or final destination as stated in the credit.

(g) A credit should state the type of insurance required and, if any, the additional risks to be covered. An insurance document will be accepted without regard to any risks that are not covered if the credit uses imprecise terms such as 'usual risks' or 'customary risks'.

(h) When a credit requires insurance against 'all risks' and an insurance document is presented containing any 'all risks' notation or clause, whether or not bearing the heading 'all risks', the insurance document will be accepted without regard to any risks stated to be excluded.

(i) An insurance document may contain reference to any exclusion clause.

(j) An insurance document may indicate that the cover is subject to a franchise or excess (deductible).

Article 29   Extension of Expiry Date or Last Day for Presentation

(a) If the expiry date of a credit or the last day for presentation falls on a day when the bank to which presentation is to be made is closed for reasons other than those referred to in article 36, the expiry date or the last day for presentation, as the case may be, will be extended to the first following banking day.

(b) If presentation is made on the first following banking day, a nominated bank must provide the issuing bank or confirming bank with a statement on its covering schedule that the presentation was made within the time limits extended in accordance with sub-article 29(a).

(c) The latest date for shipment will not be extended as a result of sub-article 29(a).

Article 30   Tolerance in Credit Amount, Quantity and Unit Prices

(a) The words 'about' or 'approximately' used in connection with the amount of the credit or the quantity or the unit price stated in the credit are to be construed as allowing a tolerance not to exceed 10% more or 10% less than the amount, the quantity or the unit price to which they refer.

(b) A tolerance not to exceed 5% more or 5% less than the quantity of the goods is allowed, provided the credit does not state the quantity in terms of a stipulated number of packing units or individual items and the total amount of the drawings does not exceed the amount of the credit.

(c) Even when partial shipments are not allowed, a tolerance not to exceed 5% less than the amount of the credit is allowed, provided that the quantity of the goods, if stated in the credit, is shipped in full and a unit price, if stated in the credit, is not reduced or that sub-article 30(b) is not applicable. This tolerance does not apply when the credit stipulates a specific tolerance or uses the expressions referred to in sub-article 30(a).

Article 31   Partial Drawings or Shipments

(a)   Partial drawings or shipments are allowed.

(b)   A presentation consisting of more than one set of transport documents evidencing shipment commencing on the same means of conveyance and for the same journey, provided they indicate the same destination, will not be regarded as covering a partial shipment, even if they indicate different dates of shipment or different ports of loading, places of taking in charge or dispatch. If the presentation consists of more than one set of transport documents, the latest date of shipment as evidenced on any of the sets of transport documents will be regarded as the date of shipment. A presentation consisting of one or more sets of transport documents evidencing shipment on more than one means of conveyance within the same mode of transport will be regarded as covering a partial shipment, even if the means of conveyance leave on the same day for the same destination.

(c)   A presentation consisting of more than one courier receipt, post receipt or certificate of posting will not be regarded as a partial shipment if the courier receipts, post receipts or certificates of posting appear to have been stamped or signed by the same courier or postal service at the same place and date and for the same destination.

Article 32   Instalment Drawings or Shipments

If a drawing or shipment by instalments within given periods is stipulated in the credit and any instalment is not drawn or shipped within the period allowed for that instalment, the credit ceases to be available for that and any subsequent instalment.

Article 33   Hours of Presentation

A bank has no obligation to accept a presentation outside of its banking hours.

Article 34   Disclaimer on Effectiveness of Documents

A bank assumes no liability or responsibility for the form, sufficiency, accuracy, genuineness, falsification or legal effect of any document, or for the general or particular conditions stipulated in a document or superimposed thereon; nor does it assume any liability or responsibility for the description, quantity, weight, quality, condition, packing, delivery, value or existence of the goods, services or other performance represented by any document, or for the good faith or acts or omissions, solvency, performance or standing of the consignor, the carrier, the forwarder, the consignee or the insurer of the goods or any other person.

Article 35   Disclaimer on Transmission and Translation

A bank assumes no liability or responsibility for the consequences arising out of delay, loss in transit, mutilation or other errors arising in the transmission of any messages or delivery of letters or documents, when such messages, letters or documents are transmitted or sent according to the requirements stated in the credit, or when the bank may have taken the initiative in the choice of the delivery service in the absence of such instructions in the credit. If a nominated bank determines that a presentation is complying and forwards the documents to the issuing bank or confirming bank, whether or not the nominated bank has honoured or negotiated, an issuing bank or confirming bank must honour or negotiate, or reimburse that nominated bank, even when the documents have been lost in transit between the nominated bank and the issuing bank or confirming bank, or between the confirming bank and the issuing bank. A bank assumes no liability or responsibility for errors in translation or interpretation of technical terms and may transmit credit terms without translating them.

Article 36   Force Majeure

A bank assumes no liability or responsibility for the consequences arising out of the interruption of its business by Acts of God, riots, civil commotions, insurrections, wars, acts of terrorism, or by any strikes or lockouts or any other causes beyond its control. A bank will not, upon resumption of its business, honour or negotiate under a credit that expired during such interruption of its business.

Article 37   Disclaimer for Acts of an Instructed Party

(a)   A bank utilizing the services of another bank for the purpose of giving effect to the instructions of the applicant does so for the account and at the risk of the applicant.

(b)   An issuing bank or advising bank assumes no liability or responsibility should the instructions it transmits to another bank not be carried out, even if it has taken the initiative in the choice of that other bank.

(c)   A bank instructing another bank to perform services is liable for any commissions, fees, costs or expenses ('charges') incurred by that bank in connection with its instructions. If a credit states that charges are for the account of the beneficiary and charges cannot be collected or deducted from proceeds, the issuing bank remains liable for payment of charges. A credit or amendment should not stipulate that the advising to a beneficiary is conditional upon the receipt by the advising bank or second advising bank of its charges.

(d)   The applicant shall be bound by and liable to indemnify a bank against all obligations and responsibilities imposed by foreign laws and usages.

Article 38   Transferable Credits

(a)   A bank is under no obligation to transfer a credit except to the extent and in the manner expressly consented to by that bank.

(b)   For the purpose of this article:

Transferable credit means a credit that specifically states it is 'transferable'. A transferable credit may be made available in whole or in part to another beneficiary ('second beneficiary') at the request of the beneficiary ('first beneficiary').

Transferring bank means a nominated bank that transfers the credit or, in a credit available with any bank, a bank that is specifically authorized by the issuing bank to transfer and that transfers the credit. An issuing bank may be a transferring bank.

Transferred credit means a credit that has been made available by the transferring bank to a second beneficiary.

(c)   Unless otherwise agreed at the time of transfer, all charges (such as commissions, fees, costs or expenses) incurred in respect of a transfer must be paid by the first beneficiary.

(d)   A credit may be transferred in part to more than one second beneficiary provided partial drawings or shipments are allowed.

A transferred credit cannot be transferred at the request of a second beneficiary to any subsequent beneficiary. The first beneficiary is not considered to be a subsequent beneficiary.

(e)   Any request for transfer must indicate if and under what conditions amendments may be advised to the second beneficiary. The transferred credit must clearly indicate those conditions.

(f)   If a credit is transferred to more than one second beneficiary, rejection of an amendment by one or more second beneficiary does not invalidate the acceptance by any other second beneficiary, with respect to which the transferred credit will be amended accordingly. For any second beneficiary that rejected the amendment, the transferred credit will remain unamended.

(g)   The transferred credit must accurately reflect the terms and conditions of the credit, including confirmation, if any, with the exception of:
  —   the amount of the credit,
  —   any unit price stated therein,
  —   the expiry date,
  —   the period for presentation, or
  —   the latest shipment date or given period for shipment,

any or all of which may be reduced or curtailed.

The percentage for which insurance cover must be effected may be increased to provide the amount of cover stipulated in the credit or these articles.

The name of the first beneficiary may be substituted for that of the applicant in the credit.

If the name of the applicant is specifically required by the credit to appear in any document other than the invoice, such requirement must be reflected in the transferred credit.

(h)   The first beneficiary has the right to substitute its own invoice and draft, if any, for those of a second beneficiary for an amount not in excess of that stipulated in the credit, and upon such substitution the first beneficiary can draw under the credit for the difference, if any, between its invoice and the invoice of a second beneficiary.

(i)   If the first beneficiary is to present its own invoice and draft, if any, but fails to do so on first demand, or if the invoices presented by the first beneficiary create discrepancies that did not exist in the presentation made by the second beneficiary and the first beneficiary fails to correct them on first demand, the transferring bank has the right to present the documents as received from the second beneficiary to the issuing bank, without further responsibility to the first beneficiary.

(j)   The first beneficiary may, in its request for transfer, indicate that honour or negotiation is to be effected to a second beneficiary at the place to which the credit has been transferred, up to and including the expiry date of the credit. This is without prejudice to the right of the first beneficiary in accordance with sub-article 38(h).

(k)   Presentation of documents by or on behalf of a second beneficiary must be made to the transferring bank.

Article 39   Assignment of Proceeds

The fact that a credit is not stated to be transferable shall not affect the right of the beneficiary to assign any proceeds to which it may be or may become entitled under the credit, in accordance with the provisions of applicable law. This article relates only to the assignment of proceeds and not to the assignment of the right to perform under the credit.

UNITED NATIONS CONVENTION ON CONTRACTS FOR THE INTERNATIONAL SALE OF GOODS*

PREAMBLE

The States Parties to this Convention,

Bearing in mind the broad objectives in the resolutions adopted by the sixth special session of the General Assembly of the United Nations on the establishment of a New International Economic Order,

Considering that the development of international trade on the basis of equality and mutual benefit is an important element in promoting friendly relations among States,

Being of the opinion that the adoption of uniform rules which govern contracts for the international sale of goods and take into account the different social, economic and legal systems would contribute to the removal of legal barriers in international trade and promote the development of international trade,

Have agreed as follows:

PART I
SPHERE OF APPLICATION AND GENERAL PROVISIONS
CHAPTER I
SPHERE OF APPLICATION

Article 1

1.   This Convention applies to contracts of sale of goods between parties whose places of business are in different States:
     (a)   when the States are Contracting States; or
     (b)   when the rules of private international law lead to the application of the law of a Contracting State.

2.   The fact that the parties have their places of business in different States is to be disregarded whenever this fact does not appear either from the contract or from any dealings between, or from information disclosed by, the parties at any time before or at the conclusion of the contract.

3.   Neither the nationality of the parties nor the civil or commercial character of the parties or of the contract is to be taken into consideration in determining the application of this Convention.

Article 2

This Convention does not apply to sales:
(a)   of goods bought for personal, family or household use, unless the seller, at any time before or at the conclusion of the contract, neither knew nor ought to have known that the goods were bought for any such use;
(b)   by auction;
(c)   on execution or otherwise by authority of law;
(d)   of stocks, shares, investment securities, negotiable instruments or money;
(e)   of ships, vessels, hovercraft or aircraft;
(f)   of electricity.

Article 3

1.   Contracts for the supply of goods to be manufactured or produced are to be considered sales unless the party who orders the goods undertakes to supply a substantial part of the materials necessary for such manufacture or production.
2.   This Convention does not apply to contracts in which the preponderant part of the obligations of the party who furnishes the goods consists in the supply of labour or other services.

Article 4

This Convention governs only the formation of the contract of sale and the rights and obligations of the seller and the buyer arising from such a contract. In particular, except as otherwise expressly provided in this Convention, it is not concerned with:
(a)   the validity of the contract or of any of its provisions or of any usage;
(b)   the effect which the contract may have on the property in the goods sold.

Article 5

This Convention does not apply to the liability of the seller for death or personal injury caused by the goods to any person.

Article 6

The parties may exclude the application of this Convention or, subject to article 12, derogate from or vary the effect of any of its provisions.

CHAPTER II
GENERAL PROVISIONS

Article 7

1.   In the interpretation of this Convention, regard is to be had to its international character and to the need to promote uniformity in its application and the observance of good faith in international trade.
2.   Questions concerning matters governed by this Convention which are not expressly settled in it are to be settled in conformity with the general principles on which it is based or, in the absence of such principles, in conformity with the law applicable by virtue of the rules of private international law.

Article 8

1.   For the purposes of this Convention statements made by and other conduct of a party are to be interpreted according to his intent where the other party knew or could not have been unaware what that intent was.
2.   If the preceding paragraph is not applicable, statements made by and other conduct of a party are to be interpreted according to the understanding that a reasonable person of the same kind as the other party would have had in the same circumstances.

3.   In determining the intent of a party or the understanding a reasonable person would have had, due consideration is to be given to all relevant circumstances of the case including the negotiations, any practices which the parties have established between themselves, usages and any subsequent conduct of the parties.

Article 9
1.   The parties are bound by any usage to which they have agreed and by any practices which they have established between themselves.
2.   The parties are considered, unless otherwise agreed, to have impliedly made applicable to their contract or its formation a usage of which the parties knew or ought to have known and which in international trade is widely known to, and regularly observed by, parties to contracts of the type involved in the particular trade concerned.

Article 10
For the purposes of this Convention:
(a)   if a party has more than one place of business, the place of business is that which has the closest relationship to the contract and its performance, having regard to the circumstances known to or contemplated by the parties at any time before or at the conclusion of the contract;
(b)   if a party does not have a place of business, reference is to be made to his habitual residence.

Article 11
A contract of sale need not be concluded in or evidenced by writing and is not subject to any other requirement as to form. It may be proved by any means, including witnesses.

Article 12
Any provision of article 11, article 29 or Part II of this Convention that allows a contract of sale or its modification or termination by agreement or any offer, acceptance or other indication of intention to be made in any form other than in writing does not apply where any party has his place of business
in a Contracting State which has made a declaration under article 96 of this Convention. The parties may not derogate from or vary the effect of this article.

Article 13
For the purposes of this Convention 'writing' includes telegram and telex.

PART II
FORMATION OF THE CONTRACT

Article 14
1.   A proposal for concluding a contract addressed to one or more specific persons constitutes an offer if it is sufficiently definite and indicates the intention of the offeror to be bound in case of acceptance. A proposal is sufficiently definite if it indicates the goods and expressly or implicitly fixes or makes provision for determining the quantity and the price.
2.   A proposal other than one addressed to one or more specific persons is to be considered merely as an invitation to make offers, unless the contrary is clearly indicated by the person making the proposal.

Article 15
1.   An offer becomes effective when it reaches the offeree.
2.   An offer, even if it is irrevocable, may be withdrawn if the withdrawal reaches the offeree before or at the same time as the offer.

Article 16
1.   Until a contract is concluded an offer may be revoked if the revocation reaches the offeree before he has dispatched an acceptance.
2.   However, an offer cannot be revoked:

(a) if it indicates, whether by stating a fixed time for acceptance or otherwise, that it is irrevocable; or

(b) if it was reasonable for the offeree to rely on the offer as being irrevocable and the offeree has acted in reliance on the offer.

Article 17

An offer, even if it is irrevocable, is terminated when a rejection reaches the offeror.

Article 18

1. A statement made by or other conduct of the offeree indicating assent to an offer is an acceptance. Silence or inactivity does not in itself amount to acceptance.

2. An acceptance of an offer becomes effective at the moment the indication of assent reaches the offeror. An acceptance is not effective if the indication of assent does not reach the offeror within the time he has fixed or, if no time is fixed, within a reasonable time, due account being taken of the circumstances of the transaction, including the rapidity of the means of communication employed by the offeror. An oral offer must be accepted immediately unless the circumstances indicate otherwise.

3. However, if, by virtue of the offer or as a result of practices which the parties have established between themselves or of usage, the offeree may indicate assent by performing an act, such as one relating to the dispatch of the goods or payment of the price, without notice to the offeror, the acceptance is effective at the moment the act is performed, provided that the act is performed within the period of time laid down in the preceding paragraph.

Article 19

1. A reply to an offer which purports to be an acceptance but contains additions, limitations or other modifications is a rejection of the offer and constitutes a counter-offer.

2. However, a reply to an offer which purports to be an acceptance but contains additional or different terms which do not materially alter the terms of the offer constitutes an acceptance, unless the offeror, without undue delay, objects orally to the discrepancy or dispatches a notice to that effect. If he does not so object, the terms of the contract are the terms of the offer with the modifications contained in the acceptance.

3. Additional or different terms relating, among other things, to the price, payment, quality and quantity of the goods, place and time of delivery, extent of one party's liability to the other or the settlement of disputes are considered to alter the terms of the offer materially.

Article 20

1. A period of time for acceptance fixed by the offeror in a telegram or a letter begins to run from the moment the telegram is handed in for dispatch or from the date shown on the letter or, if no such date is shown, from the date shown on the envelope. A period of time for acceptance fixed by the offeror by telephone, telex or other means of instantaneous communication, begins to run from the moment that the offer reaches the offeree.

2. Official holidays or non-business days occurring during the period for acceptance are included in calculating the period. However, if a notice of acceptance cannot be delivered at the address of the offeror on the last day of the period because that day falls on an official holiday or a non-business day at the place of business of the offeror, the period is extended until the first business day which follows.

Article 21

1. A late acceptance is nevertheless effective as an acceptance if without delay the offeror orally so informs the offeree or dispatches a notice to that effect.

2. If a letter or other writing containing a late acceptance shows that it has been sent in such circumstances that if its transmission had been normal it would have reached the offeror in due time, the late acceptance is effective as an acceptance unless, without delay, the offeror orally informs the offeree that he considers his offer as having lapsed or dispatches a notice to that effect.

Article 22

An acceptance may be withdrawn if the withdrawal reaches the offeror before or at the same time as the acceptance would have become effective.

Article 23

A contract is concluded at the moment when an acceptance of an offer becomes effective in accordance with the provisions of this Convention.

Article 24

For the purposes of this Part of the Convention, an offer, declaration of acceptance or any other indication of intention "reaches" the addressee

when it is made orally to him or delivered by any other means to him personally, to his place of business or mailing address or, if he does not have a place of business or mailing address, to his habitual residence.

PART III
SALE OF GOODS

CHAPTER I
GENERAL PROVISIONS

Article 25

A breach of contract committed by one of the parties is fundamental if it results in such detriment to the other party as substantially to deprive him of what he is entitled to expect under the contract, unless the party in breach did not foresee and a reasonable person of the same kind in the same circumstances would not have foreseen such a result.

Article 26

A declaration of avoidance of the contract is effective only if made by notice to the other party.

Article 27

Unless otherwise expressly provided in this Part of the Convention, if any notice, request or other communication is given or made by a party in accordance with this Part and by means appropriate in the circumstances, a delay or error in the transmission of the communication or its failure to arrive does not deprive that party of the right to rely on the communication.

Article 28

If, in accordance with the provisions of this Convention, one party is entitled to require performance of any obligation by the other party, a court is not bound to enter a judgement for specific performance unless the court would do so under its own law in respect of similar contracts of sale not governed by this Convention.

Article 29

1.   A contract may be modified or terminated by the mere agreement of the parties.
2.   A contract in writing which contains a provision requiring any modification or termination by agreement to be in writing may not be otherwise modified or terminated by agreement. However, a party may be precluded by his conduct from asserting such a provision to the extent that the other party has relied on that conduct.

CHAPTER II
OBLIGATIONS OF THE SELLER

Article 30

The seller must deliver the goods, hand over any documents relating to them and transfer the property in the goods, as required by the contract and this Convention.

SECTION I
DELIVERY OF THE GOODS AND HANDING OVER OF DOCUMENTS

Article 31

If the seller is not bound to deliver the goods at any other particular place, his obligation to deliver consists:

(a) if the contract of sale involves carriage of the goods—in handing the goods over to the first carrier for transmission to the buyer;

(b) if, in cases not within the preceding subparagraph, the contract relates to specific goods, or unidentified goods to be drawn from a specific stock or to be manufactured or produced, and at the time of the conclusion of the contract the parties knew that the goods were at, or were to be manufactured or produced at, a particular place—in placing the goods at the buyer's disposal at that place;

(c) in other cases—in placing the goods at the buyer's disposal at the place where the seller had his place of business at the time of the conclusion of the contract.

Article 32

1. If the seller, in accordance with the contract or this Convention, hands the goods over to a carrier and if the goods are not clearly identified to the contract by markings on the goods, by shipping documents or otherwise, the seller must give the buyer notice of the consignment specifying the goods.

2. If the seller is bound to arrange for carriage of the goods, he must make such contracts as are necessary for carriage to the place fixed by means of transportation appropriate in the circumstances and according to the usual terms for such transportation.

3. If the seller is not bound to effect insurance in respect of the carriage of the goods, he must, at the buyer's request, provide him with all available information necessary to enable him to effect such insurance.

Article 33

The seller must deliver the goods:

(a) if a date is fixed by or determinable from the contract, on that date;

(b) if a period of time is fixed by or determinable from the contract, at any time within that period unless circumstances indicate that the buyer is to choose a date; or

(c) in any other case, within a reasonable time after the conclusion of the contract.

Article 34

If the seller is bound to hand over documents relating to the goods, he must hand them over at the time and place and in the form required by the contract. If the seller has handed over documents before that time, he may, up to that time, cure any lack of conformity in the documents, if the exercise of this right does not cause the buyer unreasonable inconvenience or unreasonable expense. However, the buyer retains any right to claim damages as provided for in this Convention.

SECTION II
CONFORMITY OF THE GOODS AND THIRD-PARTY CLAIMS

Article 35

1. The seller must deliver goods which are of the quantity, quality and description required by the contract and which are contained or packaged in the manner required by the contract.

2. Except where the parties have agreed otherwise, the goods do not conform with the contract unless they:

(a) are fit for the purposes for which goods of the same description would ordinarily be used;

(b) are fit for any particular purpose expressly or impliedly made known to the seller at the time of the conclusion of the contract, except where the circumstances show that the buyer did not rely, or that it was unreasonable for him to rely, on the seller's skill and judgement;

(c)   possess the qualities of goods which the seller has held out to the buyer as a sample or model;

(d)   are contained or packaged in the manner usual for such goods or, where there is no such manner, in a manner adequate to preserve and protect the goods.

3.   The seller is not liable under subparagraphs *(a)* to *(d)* of the preceding paragraph for any lack of conformity of the goods if, at the time of the conclusion of the contract, the buyer knew or could not have been unaware of such lack of conformity.

Article 36

1.   The seller is liable in accordance with the contract and this Convention for any lack of conformity which exists at the time when the risk passes to the buyer, even though the lack of conformity becomes apparent only after that time.

2.   The seller is also liable for any lack of conformity which occurs after the time indicated in the preceding paragraph and which is due to a breach of any of his obligations, including a breach of any guarantee that for a period of time the goods will remain fit for their ordinary purpose or for some particular purpose or will retain specified qualities or characteristics.

Article 37

If the seller has delivered goods before the date for delivery, he may, up to that date, deliver any missing part or make up any deficiency in the quantity of the goods delivered, or deliver goods in replacement of any non-conforming goods delivered or remedy any lack of conformity in the goods delivered, provided that the exercise of this right does not cause the buyer unreasonable inconvenience or unreasonable expense. However, the buyer retains any right to claim damages as provided for in this Convention.

Article 38

1.   The buyer must examine the goods, or cause them to be examined, within as short a period as is practicable in the circumstances.

2.   If the contract involves carriage of the goods, examination may be deferred until after the goods have arrived at their destination.

3.   If the goods are redirected in transit or redispatched by the buyer without a reasonable opportunity for examination by him and at the time of the conclusion of the contract the seller knew or ought to have known of the possibility of such redirection or redispatch, examination may be deferred until after the goods have arrived at the new destination.

Article 39

1.   The buyer loses the right to rely on a lack of conformity of the goods if he does not give notice to the seller specifying the nature of the lack of conformity within a reasonable time after he has discovered it or ought to have discovered it.

2.   In any event, the buyer loses the right to rely on a lack of conformity of the goods if he does not give the seller notice thereof at the latest within a period of two years from the date on which the goods were actually handed over to the buyer, unless this time limit is inconsistent with a contractual period of guarantee.

Article 40

The seller is not entitled to rely on the provisions of articles 38 and 39 if the lack of conformity relates to facts of which he knew or could not have been unaware and which he did not disclose to the buyer.

Article 41

The seller must deliver goods which are free from any right or claim of a third party, unless the buyer agreed to take the goods subject to that right or claim. However, if such right or claim is based on industrial property or other intellectual property, the seller's obligation is governed by article 42.

Article 42

1.   The seller must deliver goods which are free from any right or claim of a third party based on industrial property or other intellectual property, of which at the time of the conclusion of the contract the seller knew or could not have been unaware, provided that the right or claim is based on industrial property or other intellectual property:

(a)   under the law of the State where the goods will be resold or otherwise used, if it was contemplated by the parties at the time of the conclusion of the contract that the goods would be resold or otherwise used in that State; or

(b)   in any other case, under the law of the State where the buyer has his place of business.

2.   The obligation of the seller under the preceding paragraph does not extend to cases where:

(a)   at the time of the conclusion of the contract the buyer knew or could not have been unaware of the right or claim; or

(b)   the right or claim results from the seller's compliance with technical drawings, designs, formulae or other such specifications furnished by the buyer.

Article 43

1.   The buyer loses the right to rely on the provisions of article 41 or article 42 if he does not give notice to the seller specifying the nature of the right or claim of the third party within a reasonable time after he has become aware or ought to have become aware of the right or claim.

2.   The seller is not entitled to rely on the provisions of the preceding paragraph if he knew of the right or claim of the third party and the nature of it.

Article 44

Notwithstanding the provisions of paragraph (1) of article 39 and paragraph (1) of article 43, the buyer may reduce the price in accordance with article 50 or claim damages, except for loss of profit, if he has a reasonable excuse for his failure to give the required notice.

SECTION III
REMEDIES FOR BREACH OF CONTRACT BY THE SELLER

Article 45

1.   If the seller fails to perform any of his obligations under the contract or this Convention, the buyer may:

(a)   exercise the rights provided in articles 46 to 52;

(b)   claim damages as provided in articles 74 to 77.

2.   The buyer is not deprived of any right he may have to claim damages by exercising his right to other remedies.

3.   No period of grace may be granted to the seller by a court or arbitral tribunal when the buyer resorts to a remedy for breach of contract.

Article 46

1.   The buyer may require performance by the seller of his obligations unless the buyer has resorted to a remedy which is inconsistent with this requirement.

2.   If the goods do not conform with the contract, the buyer may require delivery of substitute goods only if the lack of conformity constitutes a fundamental breach of contract and a request for substitute goods is made either in conjunction with notice given under article 39 or within a reasonable time thereafter.

3.   If the goods do not conform with the contract, the buyer may require the seller to remedy the lack of conformity by repair, unless this is unreasonable having regard to all the circumstances. A request for repair must be made either in conjunction with notice given under article 39 or within a reasonable time thereafter.

Article 47

1.   The buyer may fix an additional period of time of reasonable length for performance by the seller of his obligations.

2.   Unless the buyer has received notice from the seller that he will not perform within the period so fixed, the buyer may not, during that period, resort to any remedy for breach of contract. However, the buyer is not deprived thereby of any right he may have to claim damages for delay in performance.

Article 48

1. Subject to article 49, the seller may, even after the date for delivery, remedy at his own expense any failure to perform his obligations, if he can do so without unreasonable delay and without causing the buyer unreasonable inconvenience or uncertainty of reimbursement by the seller of expenses advanced by the buyer. However, the buyer retains any right to claim damages as provided for in this Convention.
2. If the seller requests the buyer to make known whether he will accept performance and the buyer does not comply with the request within a reasonable time, the seller may perform within the time indicated in his request. The buyer may not, during that period of time, resort to any remedy which is inconsistent with performance by the seller.
3. A notice by the seller that he will perform within a specified period of time is assumed to include a request, under the preceding paragraph, that the buyer make known his decision.
4. A request or notice by the seller under paragraph (2) or (3) of this article is not effective unless received by the buyer.

Article 49

1. The buyer may declare the contract avoided:
    (a) if the failure by the seller to perform any of his obligations under the contract or this Convention amounts to a fundamental breach of contract; or
    (b) in case of non-delivery, if the seller does not deliver the goods within the additional period of time fixed by the buyer in accordance with paragraph (1) of article 47 or declares that he will not deliver within the period so fixed.
2. However, in cases where the seller has delivered the goods, the buyer loses the right to declare the contract avoided unless he does so:
    (a) in respect of late delivery, within a reasonable time after he has become aware that delivery has been made;
    (b) in respect of any breach other than late delivery, within a reasonable time:
        (i) after he knew or ought to have known of the breach;
        (ii) after the expiration of any additional period of time fixed by the buyer in accordance with paragraph (1) of article 47, or after the seller has declared that he will not perform his obligations within such an additional period; or
        (iii) after the expiration of any additional period of time indicated by the seller in accordance with paragraph (2) of article 48, or after the buyer has declared that he will not accept performance.

Article 50

If the goods do not conform with the contract and whether or not the price has already been paid, the buyer may reduce the price in the same proportion as the value that the goods actually delivered had at the time of the delivery bears to the value that conforming goods would have had at that time. However, if the seller remedies any failure to perform his obligations in accordance with article 37 or article 48 or if the buyer refuses to accept performance by the seller in accordance with those articles, the buyer may not reduce the price.

Article 51

1. If the seller delivers only a part of the goods or if only a part of the goods delivered is in conformity with the contract, articles 46 to 50 apply in respect of the part which is missing or which does not conform.
2. The buyer may declare the contract avoided in its entirety only if the failure to make delivery completely or in conformity with the contract amounts to a fundamental breach of the contract.

Article 52

1. If the seller delivers the goods before the date fixed, the buyer may take delivery or refuse to take delivery.
2. If the seller delivers a quantity of goods greater than that provided for in the contract, the buyer may take delivery or refuse to take delivery of the excess quantity. If the buyer takes delivery of all or part of the excess quantity, he must pay for it at the contract rate.

CHAPTER III
OBLIGATIONS OF THE BUYER

Article 53

The buyer must pay the price for the goods and take delivery of them as required by the contract and this Convention.

SECTION I
PAYMENT OF THE PRICE

Article 54

The buyer's obligation to pay the price includes taking such steps and complying with such formalities as may be required under the contract or any laws and regulations to enable payment to be made.

Article 55

Where a contract has been validly concluded but does not expressly or implicitly fix or make provision for determining the price, the parties are considered, in the absence of any indication to the contrary, to have impliedly made reference to the price generally charged at the time of the conclusion of the contract for such goods sold under comparable circumstances in the trade concerned.

Article 56

If the price is fixed according to the weight of the goods, in case of doubt it is to be determined by the net weight.

Article 57

1.   If the buyer is not bound to pay the price at any other particular place, he must pay it to the seller:
(a)   at the seller's place of business; or
(b)   if the payment is to be made against the handing over of the goods or of documents, at the place where the handing over takes place.
2.   The seller must bear any increase in the expenses incidental to payment which is caused by a change in his place of business subsequent to the conclusion of the contract.

Article 58

1.   If the buyer is not bound to pay the price at any other specific time, he must pay it when the seller places either the goods or documents controlling their disposition at the buyer's disposal in accordance with the contract and this Convention. The seller may make such payment a condition for handing over the goods or documents.
2.   If the contract involves carriage of the goods, the seller may dispatch the goods on terms whereby the goods, or documents controlling their disposition, will not be handed over to the buyer except against payment of the price.
3.   The buyer is not bound to pay the price until he has had an opportunity to examine the goods, unless the procedures for delivery or payment agreed upon by the parties are inconsistent with his having such an opportunity.

Article 59

The buyer must pay the price on the date fixed by or determinable from the contract and this Convention without the need for any request or compliance with any formality on the part of the seller.

SECTION II
TAKING DELIVERY

Article 60

The buyer's obligation to take delivery consists:
(a)   in doing all the acts which could reasonably be expected of him in order to enable the seller to make delivery; and
(b)   in taking over the goods.

SECTION III
REMEDIES FOR BREACH OF CONTRACT BY THE BUYER

Article 61

1.   If the buyer fails to perform any of his obligations under the contract or this Convention, the seller may:
(a)   exercise the rights provided in articles 62 to 65;
(b)   claim damages as provided in articles 74 to 77.
2.   The seller is not deprived of any right he may have to claim damages by exercising his right to other remedies.
3.   No period of grace may be granted to the buyer by a court or arbitral tribunal when the seller resorts to a remedy for breach of contract.

Article 62

The seller may require the buyer to pay the price, take delivery or perform his other obligations, unless the seller has resorted to a remedy which is inconsistent with this requirement.

Article 63

1.   The seller may fix an additional period of time of reasonable length for performance by the buyer of his obligations.
2.   Unless the seller has received notice from the buyer that he will not perform within the period so fixed, the seller may not, during that period, resort to any remedy for breach of contract. However, the seller is not deprived thereby of any right he may have to claim damages for delay in performance.

Article 64

1.   The seller may declare the contract avoided:
(a)   if the failure by the buyer to perform any of his obligations under the contract or this Convention amounts to a fundamental breach of contract; or
(b)   if the buyer does not, within the additional period of time fixed by the seller in accordance with paragraph (1) of article 63, perform his obligation to pay the price or take delivery of the goods, or if he declares that he will not do so within the period so fixed.
2.   However, in cases where the buyer has paid the price, the seller loses the right to declare the contract avoided unless he does so:
(a)   in respect of late performance by the buyer, before the seller has become aware that performance has been rendered; or
(b)   in respect of any breach other than late performance by the buyer, within a reasonable time:
(i)   after the seller knew or ought to have known of the breach; or
(ii)   after the expiration of any additional period of time fixed by the seller in accordance with paragraph (1) of article 63, or after the buyer has declared that he will not perform his obligations within such an additional period.

Article 65

1.   If under the contract the buyer is to specify the form, measurement or other features of the goods and he fails to make such specification either on the date agreed upon or within a reasonable time after receipt of a request from the seller, the seller may, without prejudice

to any other rights he may have, make the specification himself in accordance with the requirements of the buyer that may be known to him.

2.   If the seller makes the specification himself, he must inform the buyer of the details thereof and must fix a reasonable time within which the buyer may make a different specification. If, after receipt of such a communication, the buyer fails to do so within the time so fixed, the specification made by the seller is binding.

CHAPTER IV
PASSING OF RISK

Article 66

Loss of or damage to the goods after the risk has passed to the buyer does not discharge him from his obligation to pay the price, unless the loss or damage is due to an act or omission of the seller.

Article 67

1.   If the contract of sale involves carriage of the goods and the seller is not bound to hand them over at a particular place, the risk passes to the buyer when the goods are handed over to the first carrier for transmission to the buyer in accordance with the contract of sale. If the seller is bound to hand the goods over to a carrier at a particular place, the risk does not pass to the buyer until the goods are handed over to the carrier at that place. The fact that the seller is authorized to retain documents controlling the disposition of the goods does not affect the passage of the risk.

2.   Nevertheless, the risk does not pass to the buyer until the goods are clearly identified to the contract, whether by markings on the goods, by shipping documents, by notice given to the buyer or otherwise.

Article 68

The risk in respect of goods sold in transit passes to the buyer from the time of the conclusion of the contract. However, if the circumstances so indicate, the risk is assumed by the buyer from the time the goods were handed over to the carrier who issued the documents embodying the contract of carriage. Nevertheless, if at the time of the conclusion of the contract of sale the seller knew or ought to have known that the goods had been lost or damaged and did not disclose this to the buyer, the loss or damage is at the risk of the seller.

Article 69

1.   In cases not within articles 67 and 68, the risk passes to the buyer when he takes over the goods or, if he does not do so in due time, from the time when the goods are placed at his disposal and he commits a breach of contract by failing to take delivery.

2.   However, if the buyer is bound to take over the goods at a place other than a place of business of the seller, the risk passes when delivery is due and the buyer is aware of the fact that the goods are placed at his disposal at that place.

3.   If the contract relates to goods not then identified, the goods are considered not to be placed at the disposal of the buyer until they are clearly identified to the contract.

Article 70

If the seller has committed a fundamental breach of contract, articles 67, 68 and 69 do not impair the remedies available to the buyer on account of the breach.

CHAPTER V
PROVISIONS COMMON TO THE OBLIGATIONS OF THE SELLER AND OF THE BUYER

SECTION I
ANTICIPATORY BREACH AND INSTALMENT CONTRACTS

Article 71
1.   A party may suspend the performance of his obligations if, after the conclusion of the contract, it becomes apparent that the other party will not perform a substantial part of his obligations as a result of:
    (a)   a serious deficiency in his ability to perform or in his credit-worthiness; or
    (b)   his conduct in preparing to perform or in performing the contract.
2.   If the seller has already dispatched the goods before the grounds described in the preceding paragraph become evident, he may prevent the handing over of the goods to the buyer even though the buyer holds a document which entitles him to obtain them. The present paragraph relates only to the rights in the goods as between the buyer and the seller.
3.   A party suspending performance, whether before or after dispatch of the goods, must immediately give notice of the suspension to the other party and must continue with performance if the other party provides adequate assurance of his performance.

Article 72
1.   If prior to the date for performance of the contract it is clear that one of the parties will commit a fundamental breach of contract, the other party may declare the contract avoided.
2.   If time allows, the party intending to declare the contract avoided must give reasonable notice to the other party in order to permit him to provide adequate assurance of his performance.
3.   The requirements of the preceding paragraph do not apply if the other party has declared that he will not perform his obligations.

Article 73
1.   In the case of a contract for delivery of goods by instalments, if the failure of one party to perform any of his obligations in respect of any instalment constitutes a fundamental breach of contract with respect to that instalment, the other party may declare the contract avoided with respect to that instalment.
2.   If one party's failure to perform any of his obligations in respect of any instalment gives the other party good grounds to conclude that a fundamental breach of contract will occur with respect to future instalments, he may declare the contract avoided for the future, provided that he does so within a reasonable time.
3.   A buyer who declares the contract avoided in respect of any delivery may, at the same time, declare it avoided in respect of deliveries already made or of future deliveries if, by reason of their interdependence, those deliveries could not be used for the purpose contemplated by the parties at the time of the conclusion of the contract.

SECTION II
DAMAGES

Article 74
Damages for breach of contract by one party consist of a sum equal to the loss, including loss of profit, suffered by the other party as a consequence of the breach. Such damages may not exceed the loss which the party in breach foresaw or ought to have foreseen at the time of the conclusion of the contract, in the light of the facts and matters of which he then knew or ought to have known, as a possible consequence of the breach of contract.

Article 75
If the contract is avoided and if, in a reasonable manner and within a reasonable time after avoidance, the buyer has bought goods in replacement or the seller has resold the goods, the party claiming damages may recover the difference between the contract price and the

price in the substitute transaction as well as any further damages recoverable under article 74.

Article 76

1.   If the contract is avoided and there is a current price for the goods, the party claiming damages may, if he has not made a purchase or resale under article 75, recover the difference between the price fixed by the contract and the current price at the time of avoidance as well as any further damages recoverable under article 74. If, however, the party claiming damages has avoided the contract after taking over the goods, the current price at the time of such taking over shall be applied instead of the current price at the time of avoidance.

2.   For the purposes of the preceding paragraph, the current price is the price prevailing at the place where delivery of the goods should have been made or, if there is no current price at that place, the price at such other place as serves as a reasonable substitute, making due allowance for differences in the cost of transporting the goods.

Article 77

A party who relies on a breach of contract must take such measures as are reasonable in the circumstances to mitigate the loss, including loss of profit, resulting from the breach. If he fails to take such measures, the party in breach may claim a reduction in the damages in the amount by which the loss should have been mitigated.

SECTION III
INTEREST

Article 78

If a party fails to pay the price or any other sum that is in arrears, the other party is entitled to interest on it, without prejudice to any claim for damages recoverable under article 74.

SECTION IV
EXEMPTIONS

Article 79

1.   A party is not liable for a failure to perform any of his obligations if he proves that the failure was due to an impediment beyond his control and that he could not reasonably be expected to have taken the impediment into account at the time of the conclusion of the contract or to have avoided or overcome it, or its consequences.

2.   If the party's failure is due to the failure by a third person whom he has engaged to perform the whole or a part of the contract, that party is exempt from liability only if:

(a)   he is exempt under the preceding paragraph; and

(b)   the person whom he has so engaged would be so exempt if the provisions of that paragraph were applied to him.

3.   The exemption provided by this article has effect for the period during which the impediment exists.

4.   The party who fails to perform must give notice to the other party of the impediment and its effect on his ability to perform. If the notice is not received by the other party within a reasonable time after the party who fails to perform knew or ought to have known of the impediment, he is liable for damages resulting from such non-receipt.

5.   Nothing in this article prevents either party from exercising any right other than to claim damages under this Convention.

Article 80

A party may not rely on a failure of the other party to perform, to the extent that such failure was caused by the first party's act or omission.

SECTION V
EFFECTS OF AVOIDANCE

Article 81
1.   Avoidance of the contract releases both parties from their obligations under it, subject to any damages which may be due. Avoidance does not affect any provision of the contract for the settlement of disputes or any other provision of the contract governing the rights and obligations of the parties consequent upon the avoidance of the contract.
2.   A party who has performed the contract either wholly or in part may claim restitution from the other party of whatever the first party has supplied or paid under the contract. If both parties are bound to make restitution, they must do so concurrently.

Article 82
1.   The buyer loses the right to declare the contract avoided or to require the seller to deliver substitute goods if it is impossible for him to make restitution of the goods substantially in the condition in which he received them.
2.   The preceding paragraph does not apply:
    (a)   if the impossibility of making restitution of the goods or of making restitution of the goods substantially in the condition in which the buyer received them is not due to his act or omission;
    (b)   if the goods or part of the goods have perished or deteriorated as a result of the examination provided for in article 38; or
    (c)   if the goods or part of the goods have been sold in the normal course of business or have been consumed or transformed by the buyer in the course of normal use before he discovered or ought to have discovered the lack of conformity.

Article 83
A buyer who has lost the right to declare the contract avoided or to require the seller to deliver substitute goods in accordance with article 82 retains all other remedies under the contract and this Convention.

Article 84
1.   If the seller is bound to refund the price, he must also pay interest on it, from the date on which the price was paid.
2.   The buyer must account to the seller for all benefits which he has derived from the goods or part of them:
    (a)   if he must make restitution of the goods or part of them; or
    (b)   if it is impossible for him to make restitution of all or part of the goods or to make restitution of all or part of the goods substantially in the condition in which he received them, but he has nevertheless declared the contract avoided or required the seller to deliver substitute goods.

SECTION VI
PRESERVATION OF THE GOODS

Article 85
If the buyer is in delay in taking delivery of the goods or, where payment of the price and delivery of the goods are to be made concurrently, if he fails to pay the price, and the seller is either in possession of the goods or otherwise able to control their disposition, the seller must take such steps as are reasonable in the circumstances to preserve them. He is entitled to retain them until he has been reimbursed his reasonable expenses by the buyer.

Article 86
1.   If the buyer has received the goods and intends to exercise any right under the contract or this Convention to reject them, he must take such steps to preserve them as are

reasonable in the circumstances. He is entitled to retain them until he has been reimbursed his reasonable expenses by the seller.

2. If goods dispatched to the buyer have been placed at his disposal at their destination and he exercises the right to reject them, he must take possession of them on behalf of the seller, provided that this can be done without payment of the price and without unreasonable inconvenience or unreasonable expense. This provision does not apply if the seller or a person authorized to take charge of the goods on his behalf is present at the destination. If the buyer takes possession of the goods under this paragraph, his rights and obligations are governed by the preceding paragraph.

Article 87

A party who is bound to take steps to preserve the goods may deposit them in a warehouse of a third person at the expense of the other party provided that the expense incurred is not unreasonable.

Article 88

1. A party who is bound to preserve the goods in accordance with article 85 or 86 may sell them by any appropriate means if there has been an unreasonable delay by the other party in taking possession of the goods or in taking them back or in paying the price or the cost of preservation, provided that reasonable notice of the intention to sell has been given to the other party.
2. If the goods are subject to rapid deterioration or their preservation would involve unreasonable expense, a party who is bound to preserve the goods in accordance with article 85 or 86 must take reasonable measures to sell them. To the extent possible he must give notice to the other party of his intention to sell.
3. A party selling the goods has the right to retain out of the proceeds of sale an amount equal to the reasonable expenses of preserving the goods and of selling them. He must account to the other party for the balance.

PART IV
FINAL PROVISIONS

Article 89

The Secretary-General of the United Nations is hereby designated as the depositary for this Convention.

Article 90

This Convention does not prevail over any international agreement which has already been or may be entered into and which contains provisions
concerning the matters governed by this Convention, provided that the parties have their places of business in States parties to such agreement.

Article 91

1. This Convention is open for signature at the concluding meeting of the United Nations Conference on Contracts for the International Sale of Goods and will remain open for signature by all States at the Headquarters of the United Nations, New York until 30 September 1981.
2. This Convention is subject to ratification, acceptance or approval by the signatory States.
3. This Convention is open for accession by all States which are not signatory States as from the date it is open for signature.
4. Instruments of ratification, acceptance, approval and accession are to be deposited with the Secretary-General of the United Nations.

Article 92

1. A Contracting State may declare at the time of signature, ratification, acceptance, approval or accession that it will not be bound by Part II of this Convention or that it will not be bound by Part III of this Convention.

2.   A Contracting State which makes a declaration in accordance with the preceding paragraph in respect of Part II or Part III of this Convention is not to be considered a Contracting State within paragraph (1) of article 1 of this Convention in respect of matters governed by the Part to which the declaration applies.

Article 93

1.   If a Contracting State has two or more territorial units in which, according to its constitution, different systems of law are applicable in relation to the matters dealt with in this Convention, it may, at the time of signature, ratification, acceptance, approval or accession, declare that this Convention is to extend to all its territorial units or only to one or more of them, and may amend its declaration by submitting another declaration at any time.
2.   These declarations are to be notified to the depositary and are to state expressly the territorial units to which the Convention extends.
3.   If, by virtue of a declaration under this article, this Convention extends to one or more but not all of the territorial units of a Contracting State, and if the place of business of a party is located in that State, this place of business, for the purposes of this Convention, is considered not to be in a Contracting State, unless it is in a territorial unit to which the Convention extends.
4.   If a Contracting State makes no declaration under paragraph (1) of this article, the Convention is to extend to all territorial units of that State.

Article 94

1.   Two or more Contracting States which have the same or closely related legal rules on matters governed by this Convention may at any time declare that the Convention is not to apply to contracts of sale or to their formation where the parties have their places of business in those States. Such declarations may be made jointly or by reciprocal unilateral declarations.
2.   A Contracting State which has the same or closely related legal rules on matters governed by this Convention as one or more non-Contracting States may at any time declare that the Convention is not to apply to contracts of sale or to their formation where the parties have their places of business in those States.
3.   If a State which is the object of a declaration under the preceding paragraph subsequently becomes a Contracting State, the declaration made will, as from the date on which the Convention enters into force in respect of the new Contracting State, have the effect of a declaration made under paragraph (1), provided that the new Contracting State joins in such declaration or makes a reciprocal unilateral declaration.

Article 95

Any State may declare at the time of the deposit of its instrument of ratification, acceptance, approval or accession that it will not be bound by subparagraph (1)*(b)* of article 1 of this Convention.

Article 96

A Contracting State whose legislation requires contracts of sale to be concluded in or evidenced by writing may at any time make a declaration in accordance with article 12 that any provision of article 11, article 29, or Part II of this Convention, that allows a contract of sale or its modification or termination by agreement or any offer, acceptance, or other indication of intention to be made in any form other than in writing, does not apply where any party has his place of business in that State.

Article 97

1.   Declarations made under this Convention at the time of signature are subject to confirmation upon ratification, acceptance or approval.
2.   Declarations and confirmations of declarations are to be in writing and be formally notified to the depositary.
3.   A declaration takes effect simultaneously with the entry into force of this Convention in respect of the State concerned. However, a declaration of which the depositary receives formal notification after such entry into force takes effect on the first day of the month following the expiration of six months after the date of its receipt by the depositary.

Reciprocal unilateral declarations under article 94 take effect on the first day of the month following the expiration of six months after the receipt of the latest declaration by the depositary.

4. Any State which makes a declaration under this Convention may withdraw it at any time by a formal notification in writing addressed to the depositary. Such withdrawal is to take effect on the first day of the month following the expiration of six months after the date of the receipt of the notification by the depositary.

5. A withdrawal of a declaration made under article 94 renders inoperative, as from the date on which the withdrawal takes effect, any reciprocal declaration made by another State under that article.

Article 98

No reservations are permitted except those expressly authorized in this Convention.

Article 99

1. This Convention enters into force, subject to the provisions of paragraph (6) of this article, on the first day of the month following the expiration of twelve months after the date of deposit of the tenth instrument of ratification, acceptance, approval or accession, including an instrument which contains a declaration made under article 92.

2. When a State ratifies, accepts, approves or accedes to this Convention after the deposit of the tenth instrument of ratification, acceptance, approval or accession, this Convention, with the exception of the Part excluded, enters into force in respect of that State, subject to the provisions of paragraph (6) of this article, on the first day of the month following the expiration of twelve months after the date of the deposit of its instrument of ratification, acceptance, approval or accession.

3. A State which ratifies, accepts, approves or accedes to this Convention and is a party to either or both the Convention relating to a Uniform Law on the Formation of Contracts for the International Sale of Goods done at The Hague on 1 July 1964 (1964 Hague Formation Convention) and the Convention relating to a Uniform Law on the International Sale of Goods done at The Hague on 1 July 1964 (1964 Hague Sales Convention) shall at the same time denounce, as the case may be, either or both the 1964 Hague Sales Convention and the 1964 Hague Formation Convention by notifying the Government of the Netherlands to that effect.

4. A State party to the 1964 Hague Sales Convention which ratifies, accepts, approves or accedes to the present Convention and declares or has declared under article 92 that it will not be bound by Part II of this Convention shall at the time of ratification, acceptance, approval or accession denounce the 1964 Hague Sales Convention by notifying the Government of the Netherlands to that effect.

5. A State party to the 1964 Hague Formation Convention which ratifies, accepts, approves or accedes to the present Convention and declares or has declared under article 92 that it will not be bound by Part III of this Convention shall at the time of ratification, acceptance, approval or accession denounce the 1964 Hague Formation Convention by notifying the Government of the Netherlands to that effect.

6. For the purpose of this article, ratifications, acceptances, approvals and accessions in respect of this Convention by States parties to the 1964 Hague Formation Convention or to the 1964 Hague Sales Convention shall not be effective until such denunciations as may be required on the part of those States in respect of the latter two Conventions have themselves become effective. The depositary of this Convention shall consult with the Government of the Netherlands, as the depositary of the 1964 Conventions, so as to ensure necessary coordination in this respect.

Article 100

1. This Convention applies to the formation of a contract only when the proposal for concluding the contract is made on or after the date when the Convention enters into force in respect of the Contracting States referred to in subparagraph (1)*(a)* or the Contracting State referred to in subparagraph (1)*(b)* of article 1.

2.   This Convention applies only to contracts concluded on or after the date when the Convention enters into force in respect of the Contracting States referred to in subparagraph (1)*(a)* or the Contracting State referred to in subparagraph (1)*(b)* of article 1.

Article 101
1.   A Contracting State may denounce this Convention, or Part II or Part III of the Convention, by a formal notification in writing addressed to the depositary.
2.   The denunciation takes effect on the first day of the month following the expiration of twelve months after the notification is received by the depositary. Where a longer period for the denunciation to take effect is specified in the notification, the denunciation takes effect upon the expiration of such longer period after the notification is received by the depositary.

INDEX

Printed in Great Britain
by Amazon

84744694R00249